PENGUIN LITERARY BIOGRAPHIES

RUDYARD KIPLING

Charles Carrington, writer and lecturer, was born in 1897 and educated in New Zealand and at Christ Church, Oxford. He served as a young soldier in the First World War and again in the Second World War as a Lieutenant-Colonel on the Staff. After several teaching posts he became one of the managers of the Cambridge University Press. From 1954 to 1962 he was Professor of Commonwealth Relations at the Royal Institute of International Affairs (Chatham House). He has organized Commonwealth Conferences, has lectured for the British Council and has contributed regularly to *The Times Literary Supplement*. His principal works, except the authorized *Life Of Kipling* are his *School History of England*, written in collaboration with his colleague J. H. Jackson, which sold a quarter of a million copies, and *The British Overseas* (1950), which twenty-five years later was said to be 'still the best short history of the Empire' by the Oxford Bibliography. He has also contributed to many learned journals. His final book is an account of the Second World War, *Soldier at Bomber Command*.

CHARLES CARRINGTON

Rudyard Kipling

His Life and Work

PENGUIN BOOKS
in association with Macmillan

Penguin Books Ltd, Harmondsworth, Middlesex, England
Viking Penguin Inc., 40 West 23rd Street, New York, New York 10010, U.S.A.
Penguin Books Australia Ltd, Ringwood, Victoria, Australia
Penguin Books Canada Limited, 2801 John Street, Markham, Ontario, Canada L3R 1B4
Penguin Books (N.Z.) Ltd, 182–190 Wairau Road, Auckland 10, New Zealand

First published by Macmillan London Ltd 1955
Published in Pelican Books 1970
Reprinted in Penguin Books 1986

Made and printed in Great Britain by
Hazell Watson & Viney Limited,
Member of the BPCC Group,
Aylesbury, Bucks
Typeset in Linotype Baskerville

*The Curse of all Art is that the devotee or disciple
is always more certain than the Priest*

RUDYARD KIPLING

Contents

Preface

My qualifications for writing this book are not unique, but are shared with thousands of my contemporaries.

I learned to read in the year when *Just So Stories* was the children's book of the season, and when I asked for more the *Jungle Books* were waiting for me. In a manner of speaking, I went to school with *Stalky & Co.* I discovered English History with 'Dan' and 'Una' and, as I remember, *Plain Tales from the Hills* was the first 'grown-up' book that I found out for myself. In 1914, as a very young soldier, I formed my notions of the grandeur and misery of army life upon the *Barrack-Room Ballads*, and knew from the story of the 'Brushwood Boy' that a hard conventional exterior might conceal a strange and sensitive inner life. It was my good fortune when young to travel a great deal about the world, always with the rhythms of *The Seven Seas* singing themselves in my ears. Every later publication of Kipling's was an event in my life, though I could not in maturity give him the uncritical support I had given in youth; and when he died I judged – rightly – that an epoch had ended.

At times I have been infuriated by some facets of Kipling's sparkling talent; but, looking back on my life, I find no other writer who has seen through the eyes of my generation with such a sharpness of observation. I owe far more to Kipling than to some of the great classic figures of literature, who inspire my reverence but do not draw me with them into their higher sphere. There is no other writer, great or small, whose work I know so well, and I have been often astonished to find how many others, of all ages, knew him as well as I did, even when the critics told us he was clean out of fashion.

I never set eyes upon the man! He shunned publicity

and begged his critics not to question other than the books he left behind; but such a desire was too much to expect of a generation which had watched the progress of his work with such attention. Even before his death Mrs Kipling had been putting some materials together for the use, as it seems, of a biographer. This was the exception she made to the rules that every in-letter was destroyed as soon as it was answered, that no unauthorized scrap of her husband's handwriting should be taken out of their house.

To draw out the elusive, retiring figure of Rudyard Kipling from behind the screen of his published works required the willing cooperation of those few who knew him well. When his surviving daughter, Mrs George Bambridge, authorized me to begin my work upon the family papers, I knew little of his personality and doubted whether a stranger could break through his rule of privacy. The frankness with which I was received soon dispersed my fears and – far more than that – Mrs Bambridge has given me so much good advice, has corrected so many errors I had fallen into, has contributed so many comments, anecdotes, side-lights, and episodes, in addition to providing me with several long descriptive passages, that her name should properly appear with mine as part-author, on the title-page. I hasten, however, to assert that the final responsibility for what appears in this book is mine, and that I must accept the blame for any errors which Mrs Bambridge has not eliminated.

At the end of our long and pleasant cooperation I can express my gratitude only by dedicating the book to the lady who is already known to thousands of readers as 'Una'.

C. E. CARRINGTON

London
March 1955

Preface to the Pelican Edition

I AM obliged to readers, especially to Mr Roger Lancelyn Green, for pointing out several minor errors in the first edition; they have now been corrected. The only substantial changes are a more accurate itinerary of Kipling's world-voyage in 1891, prepared by Mr J. B. Primrose (*Kipling Journal*, March and December 1963), and a fuller account of the background to *The Light that Failed*. Both revisions remove obscurities in his domestic affairs. I owe particular thanks to Mrs J. H. Robertson and to Dr G. Kitson Clark for reminiscences of Miss 'Flo' Garrard and Miss Mabel Price, who saw much of Kipling in 1890.

I now offer a belated apology to my friend, Mr A. F. Scott, whose name was accidentally omitted from the acknowledgements. Chapter 14 owes much to his judicious advice.

C. E. C.

August 1968

Acknowledgements

HER Majesty the Queen has graciously approved the publication of those paragraphs which describe Rudyard Kipling's relations with the Royal Family.

My obligation to Mrs George Bambridge, without whose constant help this book could not have been written, is recorded elsewhere. I next mention Miss Cecily Nicholson, Secretary, successively, to Rudyard Kipling, to Mrs Kipling, and to Mrs Bambridge. The Kipling Papers have been arranged and indexed by her with such skill and judgement that my task has been much lightened. Her transcripts are models of accuracy. I am also obliged to Miss R. D. Groom for secretarial assistance, to Mr P. G. Burbidge for making the index, and to Mr C. P. Snow for editorial advice.

It is a privilege to mention the owners or curators of the larger collections which have been thrown open to me: Mrs W. M. Carpenter, Mrs Nelson Doubleday, Mr and Mrs F. Cabot Holbrook, Mr John Connell, Mr Howard C. Rice, Jun., Mr W. A. Jackson (the Houghton Library, Harvard), Mr John Gordan (the New York Public Library), Mr Frederick R. Goff (Library of Congress, Washington), the Librarians of Rhodes House and of New College, Oxford, of the Toronto Public Library, and of the Yale Library.

For personal information about Kipling I am obliged to several of his relatives: Mrs G. L. Thirkell, Miss Florence Macdonald, Sir Hugh Poynter, Bart; and to the Viscountess Milner, Mrs H. Babcock, Mrs B. Lee-Booker, Mrs A. Ogilvie, Lord Beaverbrook, Lord Dunsany, The Rt Hon. L. S. Amery, Mr F. H. Andrews, Sir S. C. Cockerell, Dr Philip Gosse, Mr Edwin Haward, Mr E. C. Kyte, Mr E. Price, and Mr W. P. Watt. I must specially mention a group of friends in Vermont: Mr Howard Rice, Sen., Mrs H. Gale, Mrs W. S. Grey, Mrs Holbrook, Mrs Knapp, Miss Ruth Knapp, and Miss Manly.

I am obliged to the following ladies and gentlemen who have helped me on particular points: Mr E. E. Allen (of the P. & O. Company), Mr B. M. Bazley, Lady Violet Bonham Carter, Mr J. H. C. Brooking, Sir F. Brown, Lieut.-General Sir F. M. Browning, Mr T. S. Eliot, Mr T. E. Elwell, Mr R. E. Harbord, Mr I. Kaplan, Sir George Malcolm of Poltalloch, Mr E. C. Matthews, Sir Owen Morshead, Mr Carl Naumburg, Mr F. C. Pritchard (of Woodhouse Grove School),

Mr E. E. Reynolds, Mr R. H. Rogers (of Rochester, New York), and Dr T. G. P. Spear.

My general thanks are due to Mr Archibald Lyall with whom I planned the first draft of this book many years ago, to Mr and Mrs Christopher Morris for their kindly but penetrating criticism, and to my brother the Archbishop of Quebec who may usually be held responsible for any bright ideas that find their way into my work.

I have also received countless suggestions and hints from others who are too numerous to distinguish here, and I beg them to accept my general thanks.

For permission to quote copyright passages I am also indebted to the following: the *Atlantic Monthly* for extracts from articles by Edmonia Hill and C. E. Norton; the representatives of Rupert Brooke and Messrs Sidgwick & Jackson, Ltd; Mr William M. Cruikshank for extracts from letters by Theodore Roosevelt; Mr T. S. Eliot and Messrs Faber & Faber, Ltd; Messrs Victor Gollancz, Ltd, for the extract from *Schooldays with Kipling*, by G. C. Beresford; Mr Rupert Hart-Davis for the extract from his *Hugh Walpole*; the Estate of the late Henry James; Messrs MacGibbon & Kee, Ltd, for an extract from *Memories*, by Sir Desmond MacCarthy; Messrs Methuen & Co., Ltd, for quotations from their editions of Kipling's verse; Messrs John Murray, Ltd, for the extract from *The Lost Historian*, by D. Chapman-Huston; Miss Dorothy Ponton; The Times Publishing Co., Ltd; the author's Executors for the extract from *The New Machiavelli*, by H. G. Wells; and Mrs Yeats and the Clarendon Press for the extract from the Introduction to the *Oxford Book of Modern Verse*, by W. B. Yeats.

Chronology of Kipling's Life and Work

1865   R. K. born at Bombay
1871–7   At Southsea
1878–82   At the United Services College, Westward Ho!
1881   *Schoolboy Lyrics* privately printed in India
1882–7   On the Staff of the *Civil and Military Gazette*, Lahore
1886   *Departmental Ditties*
1887–9   On the staff of the *Pioneer*, Allahabad
1888   *Plain Tales from the Hills*, and stories for the Indian
              Railway Library (collected, 1890, in *Soldiers Three* and
              Wee Willie Winkie)
1889   To London via Japan and U.S.A. *From Sea to Sea*
1890   Literary success in London. *The Light that Failed*
1891   *Life's Handicap*. Voyage to South Africa, Australia, New
              Zealand. Last visit to India
1892   Marriage. *The Naulahka*. *Barrack-Room Ballads*. Voyage
              to Japan. To Brattleboro, Vermont
1893   *Many Inventions*
1894   *The Jungle Book*
1895   *The Second Jungle Book*
1896   *The Seven Seas*. Return to England. Torquay
1897   *Captains Courageous*. Removal to Rottingdean. 'Reces-
              sional'
1898   *The Day's Work*
1899   *Stalky & Co.*, 'The White Man's Burden'. Last visit to
              U.S.A. Death of R. K.'s elder daughter
1900–1908   In South Africa every year from January to March
1901   *Kim*
1902   *Just So Stories*. Removed to 'Bateman's', Burwash, Sussex
1903   *The Five Nations*
1904   *Traffics and Discoveries*
1906   *Puck of Pook's Hill*
1907   Nobel prize for literature. Voyage to Canada
1909   *Actions and Reactions*
1910   *Rewards and Fairies*
1913   Voyage to Egypt. *Letters of Travel. Songs from Books*
1915   R. K.'s son missing, believed killed, in France

A FRAGMENT

Written before Kipling's sixteenth birthday

Lo! as a little child
Looks from its window on a mighty town,
And sees the roofs as far as eye can reach,
But thinks not, knows not – nay, will not believe –
That there are Fathers, Mothers, Sisters, Homes
All like his own, a thousand homely talks,
Manners and customs – so I saw the world
With millions of my brethren. Then I wrote;
And all my verse sprang fire-new from a brain
That loved it and believed it. But the world
Coldly, in silence, passed my numbers by.
Therefore I sang in fury! When the years
Brought with them coolness, all too late I found
There were ten thousand thousand thoughts
    like mine!

Prologue

THE Queen's first Jubilee in 1887 came at the height of the Victorian achievement. For thirty years the English had enjoyed peace at home while all the other great nations had in turn been racked by war. Not Spain in the sixteenth century, nor France in the eighteenth, had so demonstrably led the world as did Victorian England with its utilitarian outlook, liberal policy, maritime power, and exuberant vitality; and now there were signs, visible at least to some shrewd observers, that the best days were over. English supremacy, unchallenged in the eighteen-sixties, the Age of Palmerston, had been asserted a little too self-consciously in the eighteen-seventies, the Age of Disraeli, and was openly challenged in the eighteen-eighties, the Age of Gladstone. The United States had surpassed Great Britain in population and was increasing its production at a higher rate of acceleration; the new German Empire had appeared as an industrial and colonial competitor; the Russians, now masters of Central Asia, seemed to threaten the North-West Frontier of India. Gladstone's second administration ended in a torrent of troubles; his mission to pacify Ireland had led to the entanglement over Home Rule; the death of Gordon had lowered British prestige in the East; the memory of defeat at Majuba rankled. Meanwhile strange stirrings in the working-class at home betokened the rise of a revolutionary movement which had been dormant since the days of the Chartists. The Trafalgar Square Riots, when the West End of London was in the hands of a mob, were a portent, something that had not happened within living memory.

'Society', which in the era of prosperous agriculture had been almost frozen into an exclusive caste by the country gentry, was cracking up, under the pressure of new money from outside and agrarian distress from within. Forty years of Free Trade had established the victory of the shippers, bankers, and merchants over the squires and farmers, by filling London with new men. A general sense that the times were changing, that the continuous progress of the Victorian age was taking some new turn, was expressed in the fashionable phrase, *fin de siècle.*

While the old Queen lingered on the stage, through the eighties and the nineties, the statesmen of her mature middle period had gone, except Gladstone, who still survived and in old age still towered over the younger men of both parties. As with the statesmen, so with the thinkers and writers to whom the Victorians looked for guidance; they were dead before the Jubilee year or, like Newman and Ruskin, they were exhausted. Thackeray and Dickens had long since departed; Browning died in 1889 and Tennyson, though he lived till 1892, had finished his work; Swinburne published nothing of note after 1889. With the deaths of George Eliot in 1880, Trollope in 1882, Charles Reade in 1884, Wilkie Collins in 1889, the great age of the Victorian novel drew to a close. Then came a pause in English literature; Thomas Hardy completed his series of Wessex romances in 1887 and did not begin to shock society with his tragedies until *Tess* was published at the end of 1891; all Meredith's best work was written before 1885; George Moore and Henry James were hesitating between their earlier and their later manner. Gissing, though much of his work appeared in this interval, attracted small attention. The novelists of the next generation, Wells, Conrad, Bennett, Galsworthy, all appeared some years later than Kipling, their precocious contemporary; nor did the revival of the theatre belong to these years; neither Wilde nor Shaw nor Barrie nor Synge had yet produced a play. Between 1887 and 1890 the only publishing 'sensation' was Mrs Humphry Ward's *Robert Elsmere* (1888), no more than a competent piece of fiction and an interesting social document.

It was Kipling who wrote the epitaph upon the 'three-deckers', the serious portly novels in three volumes which had formed the provender of the educated reader for a hundred years. After *Robert Elsmere*, no worthy successor appeared.

There were no giants in literary London in those days, not even giants of the decadence. Hitherto, the 'aesthetic movement' had been more concerned with the decorative arts than with literature, taking the form of a revolt against the prevailing ugliness of life in the new machine age, and often advocating a return to the supposed virtues of the Middle Ages. If Morris and Burne-Jones have a lesson for posterity it is respect for technical accomplishment; not Art for Art's sake but artistry for honour's sake. Their characteristic weakness was escapism, turning away their eyes lest they should behold ugliness. At the same time, in the world of letters, light romances, and tales of fantastic or comical adventure written for boys and enjoyed by adults, cut to such length that they could be read in one long evening and could even be printed in one number of a monthly magazine, were capturing the public taste. *Treasure Island* in 1883, *King Solomon's Mines* in 1885, *Three Men in a Boat* in 1889 were the new rivals to the traditional three-volume novel. To be sure, when so great a master as R. L. Stevenson told so good a yarn as *Treasure Island*, there was justice in receiving it as a masterpiece in its kind. He wrote like a gentleman, like an artist, like an angel as some would say; but he failed to find subject-matter in the working world around him.

In 1889, the year of the London Dock Strike and the Parnell Commission, the year when *The Gondoliers* filled the stalls of the Savoy, no novel remembered today was published except Stevenson's *Master of Ballantrae*, a sombre tragedy which has never been a favourite among his works. At the end of the year, a young man arrived unnoticed in London with a sheaf of ballads and stories to sell, and with two or three introductions to editors. The December

number of *Macmillan's Magazine* contained one of his ballads which set the town on fire, with words which are not
likely to be forgotten:

Oh, East is East, and West is West, and never the twain shall
    meet,
Till Earth and Sky stand presently at God's great Judgement
    Seat.

Eighteen-ninety was Rudyard Kipling's year. There had
been nothing like his sudden rise to fame and fortune since
Byron awoke one morning to find that the publication of
Childe Harold had made him famous. Whereas the public
knew nothing of Kipling, several discerning critics had
heard rumours of a new literary star arising in the East,
and were on the watch for him. He had no difficulty in disposing of his wares. Eighteen-ninety saw the publication or
re-publication in England and America of more than eighty
short stories from his pen, many ballads, and, at the end
of the year, a novel. The market was flooded with his work
in verse and prose, with his juvenile and his more mature
writing, with much that has outlasted its critics, and with
much that would have been better forgotten. A chorus of
praise, not unmixed with astonishment, was the first reaction of the reviewers, and a judicious leading article in
The Times assured Kipling's position as a star of the first
magnitude. Enthusiastic as these eulogies were, the shrewd-
est critics made some reservation. Mr Kipling was very
young and very confident, but had he staying-power? The
literary world waited agog for his novel and hastily reconsidered its verdict when the novel appeared, for *The
Light that Failed* revealed many weaknesses of taste, of
construction, and of style. It was in some respects an unpleasant book and, with its publication, the inevitable reaction set in against an author who had enjoyed, so easily
and so early in life, a literary success for which master
craftsmen had toiled half a lifetime in vain. Voices arose
decrying Kipling, sometimes for his faults of style, but more

commonly out of dislike for his subject-matter. The un-
qualified praise of his wonder-year, 1890, was succeeded by a
period of violent controversy about Kipling, in no wise mollified by the author's studied contempt for the critics. Little
was known of him but that he loved privacy, a characteristic
that always attracts publicity.

The paradox of Kipling's career is that his popularity with
the reading public grew in inverse proportion to his reputation with the critics. The cult of Art for Art's sake made
its devotees less able and less anxious to observe objectively,
or to record their impressions faithfully. They hated Kipling because he told them truths they did not wish to hear,
among others the simple fact that England's greatness lay
in her dominions overseas. Kipling used golden words to
demonstrate that words were worth little in the presence of
deeds. This literary man seemed to betray his order by
asserting that literary men were not the most important
people in the world, or not until they practised their Art
for Duty's sake. But what were the sources and the sanctions
of Duty? That, the reading public seemed to understand
rather better than the critics. The quirks and twists of
literary fashion, the loves and hates of the professional men
of letters, meant little to Kipling, as they meant little to
the mass of his fellow-countrymen. To the masses, the
writers of the decadence were a topic for sly jokes and for
no other consideration. The progress of English Society
in the nineties moved another way, towards the acceptance
of new burdens, new responsibilities, new rewards. Its prophets were not Wilde and Beardsley, but Kipling and Wells
and Shaw, and for the moment, for the year 1890 at least,
Kipling alone.

The body of poetry and prose which he issued in authorized editions in his lifetime includes four or five complete
romances, two hundred and fifty short stories, a thousand
pages of verse, and several miscellaneous volumes. The first
book produced under his own authority in London and New
York appeared in 1890; the last in 1932, by which time there

had been violent and repeated changes in literary fashion. According to the verdict of the critics, Kipling's literary credit reached its zenith in the early eighteen-nineties, declined and was almost extinguished before his death, to be revived by some connoisseurs in the nineteen-forties. By another criterion, his reputation moved through quite different phases. Not only his most approved writings but all his authorized work, year after year, and decade after decade, remained in the class that the book trade calls 'best-sellers', and were still in that class twenty years after his death, although these books were never issued in cheap editions. What other contemporary writer has enjoyed this longevity?

Successful writers, in general, fall into two classes. Either they are the sensation of a season and soon forgotten for ever, or they are raised by the critics into a higher grade and regarded as classics. Kipling, like Dickens and like Defoe, was a popular writer whose work had a 'sensational' success that did not die with the season, that did not need puffing by the reviewers. From 1890 to 1932, and even to 1955, there was no lack of buyers for this line of goods even though the publicists no longer urged the public to acquire it. When his politics were most out of fashion, he still had no lack of readers, and many an anti-imperialist of the left wing read him on the sly.

The coldness of the critics, after their first incautious enthusiasm, is not so remarkable as the downright hostility of some of the best of them. It was not perversity that made men so different as Frank Harris and Arnold Bennet, William Sharp and Max Beerbohm, Oscar Wilde and George Sampson, attack him so bitterly. To this day he makes men lose their tempers, a sure proof of his importance. The student of literature cannot neglect or ignore him. So good a critic as Mr Edmund Wilson displays most clearly a characteristic that many readers of Kipling have shown; he loves and hates, he abuses Kipling and cannot abstain from reading on. A writer of the younger generation has described himself as one of those to whom 'no single syllable of Kipling's has ever given a moment's pleasure'.* Is not this an extraordinary observation? The power and the style of Kipling, it implies, are so effective that those who dislike the matter will not allow themselves to admit any merit in the manner. No Protestant critic writes of Newman in that way; no Tory man of letters reacts like that against Bernard Shaw.

Rudyard Kipling's power lies in his ability to evoke love or hate, or love and hate together, in almost every reader; his lovers are still innumerable, and often as blinded by emotion as the haters. What was the message that struck so deeply into the hearts of those who first heard it in 1890? What sort of man was it who did so much to form the characters of all that generation which is now elderly or middle-aged? What was the secret of his strength?

The Modern Short Story, by H. E. Bates.

KIPLINGS AND MACDONALDS

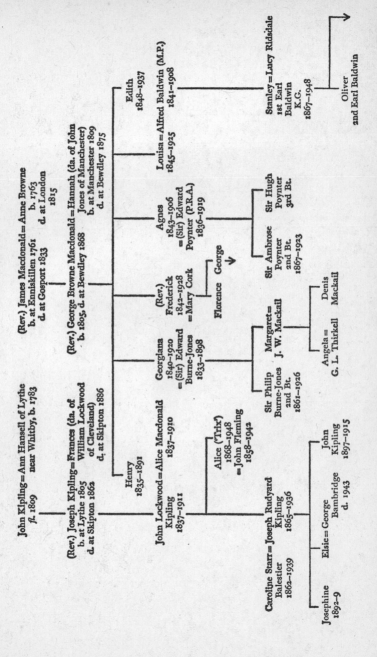

The Puzzler (1909)

The Celt in all his variants from Builth to Bally-hoo,
His mental processes are plain – one knows what he will do,
And can logically predicate his finish by his start;
But the English – ah, the English! – they are quite a race
  apart.

Their psychology is bovine, their outlook crude and raw.
They abandon vital matters to be tickled with a straw;
But the straw that they were tickled with – the chaff that
  they were fed with –
They convert into a weaver's beam to break their foeman's
  head with.

For undemocratic reasons and for motives not of State,
They arrive at their conclusions – largely inarticulate.
Being void of self-expression they confide their views to
  none;
But sometimes in a smoking-room, one learns why things
  were done.

Yes, sometimes in a smoking-room, through clouds of 'Ers'
  and 'Ums',
Obliquely and by inference, illumination comes,
On some step that they have taken, or some action they
  approve –
Embellished with the *argot* of the Upper Fourth Remove.

In telegraphic sentences, half nodded to their friends,
They hint a matter's inwardness – and there the matter ends.
And while the Celt is talking from Valencia to Kirkwall,
The English – ah, the English! – don't say anything at all.

[1]

Kiplings and Macdonalds

ON more than one occasion Rudyard Kipling described himself as a Yorkshireman, although he never lived in Yorkshire and rarely visited the North Country. Towards the end of his life he was engaged in desultory correspondence with a Mr Sunderland, a Yorkshire acquaintance who had made a hobby of investigating the origins of the Kipling family. Kipling's replies to Sunderland's observations and inquiries were courteous but cool. 'I am sorry', he wrote, 'not to be able to respond to your interest – as a matter of fact, I do not; and as I have no son to whom this information would later possibly be of interest, I cannot trouble you to proceed any further in this matter.' He had, however, supplied Sunderland with some scraps of family lore, and these may be worth preserving as Kipling's own belief about his ancestry. 'Yes, the family is certainly Yorkshire, and I believe some of it came from Snaith way and thereabouts. ... I don't think a genealogical hunt would be of much use. ... I abandoned the search long ago ... my knowledge of my family is of the sketchiest. They seem to have included small farmers, bell-founders, clock-makers, and the like, scattered all over the Ridings, and, I suppose, originally with some far-off connexion with the hamlet [Kipling] that carries their name. ... I believe the sons were christened Joseph and John in alternate generations.'* [1]

We may begin with the Rev. Joseph Kipling, son of John Kipling a farmer, a respected Methodist minister who, according to the rules of his Church, occupied a succession of

*The numbers used after some of the passages quoted in the text are intended to refer the reader to the sources given in the Notes at the end of the book.

pulpits in Yorkshire. He married Frances Lockwood,* the
daughter of an architect, and the family tradition ran that
her father thought she might have made a better match.
While the Rev. Joseph held the circuit at Pickering, his
eldest son was born on 6 July 1837,[2] and was christened
John Lockwood. Ministers' families were accustomed to frequent removals, and little John Kipling went with his
parents to Horncastle, Howden, and Bridlington. They sent
him to school at Woodhouse Grove, the well-known Methodist boarding-school near Leeds. In 1851, when no more
than thirteen years old, John went up to London by excursion train to see the Great Exhibition in Hyde Park, an experience that directed the course of his life. Ten years later,
in 1861, he was employed as a sculptor during the building
of the Victoria and Albert Museum at South Kensington,
where his portrait is to be seen in a mural for which he
stood as a model. Of his early manhood little is known except that he eked out his earnings in London by giving
French lessons until, at about the age of twenty-two, he
settled at Burslem to get practical experience of pottery-
designing in the firm of Pinder, Bourne & Co. His father
died at Skipton, in the West Riding, in 1862; his mother
lived on at Skipton until 1886, the grandparent whom young
Rudyard Kipling knew best, and his only link with his
Yorkshire forebears.†

John Lockwood Kipling at Burslem was a notable young
man, who would be better remembered today if he had not
been overshadowed by his more celebrated son. His schooling at Woodhouse Grove, where he had been unhappy, had
been thorough, and much more liberal than it was likely

* Her maternal grandfather, Mr W. Merry, was agent to Lord Mul-
grave. He appears as the seated figure in Wilkie's well-known picture,
Rent-day, and closely resembles his great-grandson, Lockwood
Kipling.

† Lockwood Kipling had a younger brother, Joseph, and two sisters,
one of whom, Rudyard's Aunt Hannah, lived to a great age. Rudyard
helped to support her in the nineteen-thirties, when she was past
ninety years old.

to have been at a Public School in those unreformed days. He was a man of wide reading and close observation. In the Arts-and-Crafts movement which derived from the Great Exhibition his was a strictly practical contribution. He had a never-failing zest for technical processes, an almost feminine sensibility to textures and tones and scents, an artisan's skill with tools and implements; above all, he was himself an artist, expressing his sense of form and colour and touch, with pen, brush, and modelling-clay. His son always admitted that the father had the surer prose style. He was a little man, remarkably solid and immovable, and always good-humoured. No one ever said a hard word about John Lockwood Kipling.

A scholar and artist, primed with the newest principles from South Kensington, must have been a rarity in Staffordshire ninety years ago, and so it was inevitable that he should fall into the company of other people in the Midlands with literary tastes and advanced views. It was through the young Methodist minister at Burslem, the Rev. Frederick Macdonald, that John Kipling found himself admitted to such a society. 'He brought intellectual and artistic qualities into our midst,' wrote Frederick Macdonald, 'as from another and different realm. Companionship with him was a continual refreshing.' Frederick Macdonald was one of a large family, two sons and five daughters, all lively, handsome, and intelligent, and his sisters occasionally came over to Burslem to visit him. According to the most reliable of several reminiscences, it was at a picnic party at Lake Rudyard, given by the Miss Pinders, the daughters of his employer, that John Kipling met his future wife in the spring of 1863. Among the guests were Frederick Macdonald and his sister Alice, whom, two years later, John Kipling married in London.[3]

The Macdonalds were a truly remarkable circle of relatives, one of those affectionate family groups that maintain an intimate sense of union when their members are physically separated, that absorb into the group the wives and husbands of their members. The Kiplings of Yorkshire parted, went their own ways, and disappear from the story; the Macdonalds clung together, generation after generation.

Their blood was exclusively Scottish, Irish, and Welsh. In the dispersion that followed the '45, a family of Macdonalds had emigrated to Ulster and there, at Enniskillen, James Macdonald was born in 1761. Brought up a loyal episcopalian, he came under the direct influence of John Wesley, who persuaded him to join the Methodists. James Macdonald educated himself, entered the ministry in 1785, and was appointed to an English circuit. He died in 1833, by which time his son, George Browne Macdonald, born in 1805, had also entered the ministry. George Macdonald had an advantage which had been denied to his father; he was given a good education at Woodhouse Grove, the school at which his future son-in-law was also to be a pupil a few years later. The simplicity of those days may be judged by the fact that James Macdonald brought up his family in comfort, and educated them, on a salary of £80 a year; George Macdonald, a generation later, on £160 a year.

The vagaries of life as a Methodist minister took the Rev. George Macdonald to Birmingham in the eighteen-fifties. There his eldest son, Henry, was one of a conspicuous group of scholars at King Edward's School, whose leader was Edward Burne-Jones. Some years later when Burne-Jones set himself up as a painter, sharing a studio in London with William Morris, Henry Macdonald was a frequent visitor. So was the younger brother Frederick and his sister Georgiana. She married Burne-Jones in 1860 and, seven years later, they settled in a large old-fashioned house, The Grange, North End Road, Fulham, which had once been the home of the novelist, Richardson. The Grange was the gathering-place of the Macdonalds and all their set for more than thirty years.

Georgiana was already married and assuming the position of head of the family when Frederick introduced their

sister Alice to John Kipling at Lake Rudyard. Since their
parents were old and ailing it was Georgiana who managed
her sister's wedding, from North End Road, and it was
Frederick who gave his sister away. John Lockwood Kipling and Alice Macdonald were married at St Mary
Abbots' Church on 18 March 1865, a bitterly cold day.
There was a lavish reception where they should have met
all the lions of literary and artistic London. Swinburne was
there, the two Rossettis were there, but not the bride or
the bridegroom, who had made the bold decision to go to
India, and whose ship unexpectedly sailed on the day of the
party. In their absence, Ford Madox Brown made merri-
ment by stumbling over the bridegroom's unusual name, referring to him as 'John Gilpin'.

Lockwood Kipling cared little for the blandishments of
society; his head was never turned by fashionable cults in
art. Serene, smiling, and indifferent, he went his own way.
His wife, a handsome, sharp-featured little woman with
auburn hair, blue eyes, and a very lively tongue, would have
been a match for any wit the Burne-Jones could have
entertained. 'My sister had the nimblest mind I have ever
known', wrote Frederick Macdonald. 'She saw things in a
moment and did not so much reason as pounce on her conclusions. Accuracy in detail was not so much her forte as
swift insight, and the kind of vision that is afforded by
flashes of lightning. Her power of speech was unsurpassed
– her chief difficulty being that she found language a slow-
moving medium of expression that failed to keep up with
her thought. She tumbled over her words, because they
could not come out fast enough.'

But the Kiplings were off, with no more than a stock of
self-confidence and self-reliance to support their marriage.
John Kipling, popular though he was with all who met
him, was socially no great match for the witty Miss Macdonald. He was lucky to have got a minor appointment as
principal of a new school of art at Bombay, supposedly
through his brother-in-law's influence. But India was far

away, an unknown land, with which neither his nor her family had any previous association, unless it was Henry Macdonald's abortive bid for a post in the Civil Service. To India they went, in spite of the anxiety of her parents, determined to stand on their own feet and make their own way.

Their first child, born at Bombay before the end of the year on 30 December 1865, was given two names, Joseph after his Kipling grandfather, and Rudyard, at the suggestion of his aunt, Louisa Macdonald, after the place where his parents had first met. At Bewdley, where the Macdonald grandparents lived in retirement, Louisa met and married the wealthy iron-master, Alfred Baldwin (who later was to be Chairman of the Great Western Railway and father of a Prime Minister). He was something better as a match than the unknown penniless art-teacher who had carried Alice off to India. Louisa's was a double wedding for, on the same day, her sister Agnes married one of Edward Burne-Jones's friends, a young artist named Poynter, who had already made a name at the Royal Academy.

Four of the five Macdonald sisters were now married, and it may be noticed that all had been wedded according to the rites of the Church of England. Macdonald Methodism had never been a narrow sectarianism. The original James Macdonald seems to have been one of those early Methodists who regarded themselves rather as a party within the national Church than a sect outside it. His son George, though a Methodist minister, was married in Manchester Cathedral. George's son Frederick, who had brought John Kipling into their circle, was a well-read, widely travelled man of the world. His sisters regarded him as the intellectual member of the family. Though he lived to become President of the Methodist Conference, he expressed deep sympathy and respect for orthodox churchmen. The drift back from 'chapel' to 'church' began with Georgiana when she married Edward Burne-Jones. Alice conformed to what was becoming the family tradition, though neither she nor

her husband became regular communicant Church members. The little Rudyard was never a Methodist; he was
baptized in Bombay Cathedral, his sponsors being John
Griffiths, his father's assistant, and his Aunt Louisa, by
proxy.

From The City of Sleep (1894)

Over the edge of the purple down,
  Ere the tender dreams begin,
Look – we may look – at the Merciful Town,
  But we may not enter in!
Outcasts all, from her guarded wall
  Back to our watch we creep:
We – pity us! ah, pity us!
  We wakeful; oh, pity us! –
We that go back with Policeman Day –
  Back from the City of Sleep!

[2]

Childhood:
Bombay and Southsea
(1865–77)

BOMBAY, when John and Alice Kipling arrived there, at the beginning of the hot weather of 1865, was a new commercial city at the crest of a wave of prosperity. The Indian Empire itself was not yet seven years old, and the memories of the Mutiny, which darkened its origins for dwellers in the old Bengal Presidency, did little to disturb the western seaboard. Under the enlightened rule of Sir Bartle Frere, Bombay, which had been a backwater, was rapidly becoming the most progressive of Asiatic cities, the most European in appearance, with its broad streets of solid masonry, behind which were hidden the slums that housed the new proletariat of workers in the cotton-mills. Even the setback, when American cotton reappeared in the market at the end of the Civil War, not long after the Kiplings' arrival, was less disastrous than at first it appeared to be. During the boom years the main railway lines had been linked into an Indian system which established Bombay as the western outlet for all Indian trade; and the opening of the Suez Canal in 1869 made Bombay, in fact, the Gateway of India. Much of the wealth and enterprise belonged to the Parsee community, then, as now, remarkable for their public spirit; and no citizen of Bombay was more rightly respected than Sir Jamsetjee Jeejeebhoy, who endowed the school of art where Lockwood* Kipling was appointed 'Professor of Architectural Sculpture'.

*His wife and family usually called him John. To the rest of his acquaintances he was known as Mr Lockwood Kipling, and by that name he will be called in this book.

It was Lockwood Kipling's task to foster the decaying arts and crafts of India, and to oppose the tendency of Indian craftsmen to copy all that was worst in Victorian commercial art. He was to induce them to adapt their own craft traditions, to the needs of the industrial age; in short, to conduct a crusade in India like that which William Morris had undertaken in England. His restless curiosity, his friendly manner, his minute observation, his manual dexterity, his skill with pen and pencil, soon made him the repository of information, on the costumes, devices, ornaments, tools, utensils, materials, and techniques of almost every trade and caste in India, an indispensable adviser to anyone who was getting up an exhibition, founding a technical school, or investigating an industrial process. He began with sculpture, an art that needed reviving, not founding, in India, and it is remembered that he carved one, at least, of the public monuments of Bombay with his own hands.

In this new bustling city with its fluctuating prosperity, Rudyard Kipling spent his infancy, ignorant both of the new wealth and the old poverty around him. His world was the garden of a bungalow in the compound of the school of art. Across a strip of watered grass, wide as a prairie to a little boy in the burning sun, was his father's studio where fascinating games were played with modelling-clay and chips of sculptor's-work. It was inhabited by his father's friends, men who wore the strangest clothes and answered to the oddest names. One of them, a Parsee named Pestonjee Bomonjee, wearing the shining cylindrical hat that was the mark of his people, lived to record sixty years afterwards that Rudyard, at five years old, never forgot a face or a name.[1]

More familiar than these persons in the studio was Meeta, the Hindu bearer, with whom Rudyard talked so constantly in the vernacular that it was necessary to remind him to speak English when he joined his parents in the drawing-room. The _ayah_, who belonged more properly to his baby sister, was a Goanese Roman Catholic, and on their early morning walks sometimes took him into the chapel of her faith; as Meeta, when he was in charge, did not scruple to take the little boy to Shiva's temple. He did not much distinguish between these alternate devotions.

A break came in this course of life when Rudyard, at no more than two years and six months old, was taken home to England by his parents, and so precocious was he in his development, so retentive of visual memories, that he was able to recall one scene, at least, of this journey, forty years later when next he passed that way again. His recollection went back to a time before the Suez Canal was cut through the Isthmus, when passengers from India went overland from Suez to Alexandria. 'There was a train across a desert, and a halt in it, and a small girl wrapped in a shawl on the seat opposite me whose face stands out still.' He was lifted down from the train because, he was told, it was on fire, a problem that did not alarm him as no doubt it alarmed his parents. 'What stuck in his sleepy mind was the absurd name of the place and his father's prophecy that when he grew up he would "come that way in a big steamer". So, all his life, the word "Zagazig" carried memories of a brick shed, the flicker of an oil-lamp's floating wick, a sky full of eyes, and an engine coughing in a desert at the world's end.'[2]

It was March 1868 when the Kiplings returned to England and the house of the Macdonald grandparents at Bewdley : 'a dark land', thought little Rudyard, 'and a darker room full of cold, in one wall of which a white woman made a naked fire'. He cried out with dread, not having seen such a thing before; nor had he ever seen a staircase. His old and ailing grandparents noted him down as a talkative inquisitive child, more forward and self-assertive than Victorian children were expected to be. The Kiplings did not stay long at Bewdley, and did not see Grandfather Macdonald again; he died that autumn murmuring on his death-bed, 'Lord, what things I lie here and remember'.

Again it was to the Burne-Joneses' house that Alice
Kipling turned for hospitality. Her second child, Alice,
always known as 'Trix', was born there on 11 June 1868,
the event for which, we may suppose, they had come to England.

For four more cool seasons and three more hot seasons,
Rudyard, his sister, and their parents lived a happy uneventful life in Bombay, broken only by visits to the hill-
station at Nassick. A land filled with wonders, and a westward sea, were crystallized in his infantine memories by
drives to the coconut groves of Mahim in the sunset. Sea-
ward, 'there were far-going Arab dhows on the pearly
waters, and gaily dressed Parsees wading out to worship the
sun'; landward, the palmgroves swaying in the sunset
breeze. 'I have always felt', wrote Kipling in old age, 'the
menacing darkness of tropical eventide, as I have loved the
voices of night-winds through palm or banana leaves, and
the song of the tree-frogs.'[3] It was in this afterglow that he
pictured the family circles of indulgent parents and kindly,
obsequious, native servants; this was the background of his
age of innocence, the heaven that lay about him in his infancy.

All Anglo-Indian* families were haunted by a spectre,
the dreaded day of separation when the children must be
sent home for their education. It came early by customary
standards to the Kipling family, when Rudyard was five
and a half years old and Trix was not yet three, perhaps because of their mother's uncertain health. Her eldest son's
birth had cost her a long and dangerous labour (relieved,
the servants said, only when one of them hastened to ran-
som the child's life by sacrificing a kid to Kali); her
daughter's birth in London had been even more difficult; a
third child was born, and died, in the hot weather of 1870.
Probably she was determined to be in England with her

---

*In this book the word 'Anglo-Indian' is used, as Kipling and his
contemporaries always used it, to signify an Englishman residing in
India.

two children before the hot weather returned again. Whatever the reason, the decision was taken and the four left Bombay on 15 April 1871 for a six-month furlough. Again a sea voyage marked an epoch in Rudyard's infant mind, or rather, the two voyages blended together in his hazy recollection to form a single image, 'a time in a ship with an immense semi-circle blocking all vision on each side of her'.

In December the parents deposited their children in lodgings at Southsea before returning to India. Perhaps unwisely, they made no effort to forewarn little Rudyard of this calamity, but slipped away without stirring the children's emotion by any passionate display of affection. Rudyard, just before his sixth birthday, was left to discover for himself the meaning of separation from his father and mother; Trix was still too young to know what was the nature of her misfortune. The two children had been left as paying guests in the house of a retired naval officer [4] whose name had been obtained from an advertisement in a newspaper. According to Anglo-Indian custom their new guardians were given honorary rank as relatives, becoming 'Uncle Harry' and 'Aunty Rosa'. Rudyard lived with them for five years and three months, from his sixth to his eleventh year; Trix remained some years longer.

Since this period of deepening misery was to leave unhealed scars upon the spirit of Rudyard Kipling, it is necessary to ask why this child of loving and intelligent parents was compelled to suffer so long, unpitied and unnoticed. Why were the children entrusted to the naval captain's wife, and not to either of their grandmothers or to one of their married aunts? Trix used to say in later life that her Kipling grandmother at Skipton ought to have been chosen as her guardian, but old Mrs Kipling's name does not appear in such few letters as survive from this period. Aunt Louie (Baldwin), Aunt Aggie (Poynter), above all Aunt Georgie (Burne-Jones) – Rudyard's beloved Aunt Georgie to whom he afterwards paid such tributes of affection – all three were making their way in the world and had young children of an age with the young Kiplings. Was it in fact necessary to board the Kiplings out with strangers? The talented Macdonald sisters met as frequently as they could, visited one another's houses, spoke in the most affectionate terms of one another, not least of Alice exiled among the unfamiliar perils of life in India. They were good-natured, they were hospitable, they were amusing; but they were not forthcoming, nor were they motherly. Even Aunt Georgie, who spent her life in managing and protecting her unworldly genius of a husband, was found a little formidable by strangers until a breach was made in the reserve with which she surrounded herself. She did not give her confidence, or open her heart, easily. Her nephew and niece adored her; they seemed well-fed and well cared for; why should she doubt that her highly competent sister Alice had done what was best for them? Alice Kipling, for her part, agreed with her husband that self-reliance was the master-virtue. She was not well off. Who can say what economies and restraints were necessary at Bombay in order to maintain the two children at Southsea; yet the Kiplings would pay their own way and not admit dependence upon relatives who in the seventies were beginning to outstrip them in worldly success. The Macdonald grandmother with two of the aunts came down to Southsea in 1872 to visit the two children, and found them thriving in apparent comfort.

Four accounts survive of Kipling's childhood at Southsea, and differ only in emphasis. He wrote his own account in *Something of Myself*, the fragment of autobiography begun, but neither completed nor revised, in his old age; before his death, Trix gave her account of the same events, and from these two versions a reliable story can be constructed. But more significant are the two imaginative versions which Kipling issued under the guise of fiction, much earlier in his life, when the events were clearer in his memory and when the emotions of childhood were more compelling. His readers could not know, when the story called 'Baa, Baa, Black Sheep' first appeared, in 1888, that it was a piece of autobiography, heightened in colour, yet following the events of his childhood in all but a few details. Nor could contemporary readers say more of the first chapter of *The Light that Failed* than that it was out of key with the rest of the book. It is another version of the same story with the material factors transposed, and, in this form, it reveals more passion, more of the unconscious working of the 'black sheep's' mind than either of his plain narratives.

At Southsea little Rudyard became the black sheep of his new family. So long as 'Uncle Harry', the old sea-captain, was alive, Rudyard got some protection. 'Uncle Harry' liked the boy, taught him old sea-songs, introduced him to *Jorrocks*, and delighted him by talking like a sailor in a book; he actually used to say, 'Shiver my timbers!'[5] But, soon, he died, leaving Rudyard to the mercies of 'Aunty Rosa' and her son. She was jealous for her own young Harry, five or six years older than Rudyard but, we may suppose, without a quarter of his vivacity and eager interest in the world. This motive of unconscious jealousy did not affect her conduct towards Trix who was a general favourite with her and with the whole family. It would be easy to dismiss 'Aunty Rosa' as a tyrant, a cruel foster-mother, and no doubt easy for her friends to defend her character. She must have been a good woman and a good housewife, or the sad story of 'Black Sheep' would have ended with exposure and disputation. It did not; even when the wretched Rudyard was at last released from her domination, there was no breach between the two families. Trix remained in her house several years longer, and Rudyard visited Trix at Southsea as a big boy without, so far as we know, any awkwardness over meeting 'Aunty Rosa' again. The wretchedness of those five years lay buried in that inaccessible hiding-place, the secret heart of a child.

'Aunty Rosa' had difficulties to contend with, Rudyard

was a restless, clumsy boy, very little used to genteel discipline. He sprawled over the sofas, he talked continually, he asked the most searching questions, he knew more than little boys were expected to know and paraded his knowledge in the company of his elders, he had Anglo-Indian notions of nursery etiquette, he was unresponsive to demonstrations of sentiment, and altogether unlike his sweet affectionate little sister. It was disgraceful, 'Aunty Rosa' must have thought, that at nearly six years old he had not yet begun to read or write; and disconcerting that, as soon as he did learn, he talked incessantly about characters from books. If he had been spoiled by indulgent parents in Bombay, 'Aunty Rosa' was determined to do her duty by him in Southsea, to correct his manners and cure him of 'showing off'.

It was an establishment run with the full vigour of the Evangelical as revealed to the Woman. I had never heard of Hell, so I was introduced to it in all its terrors – I and whatever luckless little slavey might be in the house, whom severe rationing had led to steal food. Once I saw the Woman beat such a girl who picked up the kitchen poker and threatened retaliation. Myself I was regularly beaten. The Woman had an only son of twelve or thirteen as religious as she. I was a real joy to him, for when his mother had finished with me for the day he (we slept in the same room) took me on and roasted the other side.

If you cross-examine a child of seven or eight on his day's doings (specially when he wants to go to sleep) he will contradict himself very satisfactorily. If each contradiction be set down as a lie and retailed at breakfast, life is not easy. I have known a certain amount of bullying, but this was calculated torture – religious as well as scientific. Yet it made me give attention to the lies I soon found it necessary to tell: and this, I presume, is the foundation of literary effort.

But my ignorance was my salvation. I was made to read without explanation, under the usual fear of punishment. And on a day that I remember it came to me that 'reading' was not 'the Cat lay on the Mat', but a means to everything that would make me happy. So I read all that came within my reach. As soon as my pleasure in this was known, deprivation from reading was added to my punishments. I then read by stealth and the more earnestly ...

Coming out of church once I smiled. The Devil-Boy demanded why. I said I didn't know, which was child's truth. He replied that I *must* know. People didn't laugh for nothing. Heaven knows what explanation I put forward; but it was duly reported to the Woman as a 'lie'. Result, afternoon upstairs with the Collect to learn. I learned most of the Collects that way and a great deal of the Bible. The son after three or four years went into a Bank and was generally too tired on his return to torture me, unless things had gone wrong with him. I learned to know what was coming from his step into the house.

But, for a month each year I possessed a paradise which I verily believe saved me. Each December I stayed with my Aunt Georgie, my mother's sister, wife of Sir Edward Burne-Jones, at The Grange, North End Road. At first I must have been escorted there, but later I went alone, and arriving at the house would reach up to the open-work iron bell-pull on the wonderful gate that let me into all felicity. When I had a house of my own, and The Grange was emptied of meaning, I begged for and was given that bell-pull for my entrance, in the hope that other children might also feel happy when they rang it.

*

Nor was my life an unsuitable preparation for my future, in that it demanded constant wariness, the habit of observation, and attendance on moods and tempers; the noting of discrepancies between speech and action; a certain reserve of demeanour; and automatic suspicion of sudden favours. Brother Lippo Lippi, in his own harder case, as a boy discovered:—

> 'Why, soul and sense of him grow sharp alike,
> He learns the look of things and none the less
> For admonition'.

So it was with me.

My troubles settled themselves in a few years. My eyes went wrong, and I could not well see to read. For which reason I read the more and in bad lights. My work at the terrible little day-school where I had been sent suffered in consequence, and my monthly reports showed it. The loss of 'reading-time' was the worst of my 'home' punishments for bad school-work. One report was so bad that I threw it away and said that I had never received it. But this is a hard world for the amateur liar. My web of deceit was swiftly exposed – the Son spared time after banking-hours to help in the auto-da-fé – and I was well beaten and sent to school through the streets of Southsea with the placard 'Liar' between my shoulders. In the long run these things, and many more of the like, drained me of any capacity for real, personal hate for the rest of my days. So close must any life-filling passion lie to its opposite. 'Who having known the Diamond will concern himself with glass?' [6]

Five long years of life at Southsea taught Rudyard some lessons that he never forgot, the stoic lessons that the mind must make its own happiness, that any troubles can be endured if the sufferer has resources of his own to sustain him. He learned, too, that family affection is the greatest good in life, and the absence of it the greatest evil. The loyalty of Trix, who repeatedly defended him against 'Aunty Rosa's' sharp tongue – it was all she could do – was the great comfort, and another was the glimpse of happier life at North End Road, where everyone was kind and trusting. Best of all pleasures at North End Road was to lean over the banisters on the top landing when Uncle Ned was entertaining his friends 'and listen to the loveliest sound in the world – deep-voiced men laughing together over dinner'. If it was 'Uncle Topsy', the name the children gave to William Morris, he might regale them with stories of the Vikings, but if it was a person called Browning his conversation would be for the grown-ups alone.

But on a certain day – one tried to fend off the thought of it – the delicious dream would end, and one would return to the House of Desolation, and for the next two or three mornings there cry on waking up. Hence more punishments and cross-examinations.

Often and often afterwards, the beloved Aunt would ask me why I had never told anyone how I was being treated. Children tell little more than animals, for what comes to them they accept as eternally established. Also, badly-treated children have a clear notion of what they are likely to get if they betray the secrets of a prison-house before they are clear of it.[7]

The Grange, in North End Road, offered a gleam, a vision of happiness which was not his own. Far away in the East, and half-forgotten, was his real home, linked to him only by letters from his father who sent him books to read, his chief resource, if Harry and 'Aunty Rosa' would leave him in peace to read them, if his eyes did not fail him in the dark basement nursery.

There came a time when even 'Aunty Rosa' learned that her charge was not naughty but ill. A doctor soon diagnosed the trouble as a neglected defect in Rudyard's eyesight which must be corrected by the use of glasses; and, for a time, forbade him to strain his eyesight with reading. Thus, his last weeks at Southsea were spent in a boredom that was worse than punishment. Then, suddenly, without warning, his mother arrived from India. When she first came into his room to kiss her son good-night, he flung up an arm to guard off the cuff that he had been trained to expect.

The happiest year of Rudyard's young life began with his mother's arrival, in March 1877. She took him away from Southsea to a farm near Loughton in Epping Forest, where he and Trix were allowed to run wild, and ride ponies, all the summer. Their cousin, Stan Baldwin, a year or two younger than Rudyard, came to stay, and the two boys got into healthy mischief together. Return to the House of Desolation no longer threatened, and its terrors slipped out of his consciousness like the oppression of a nightmare. The shadow lifted from his mind as the material shadow lifted from his eyesight; his mother's presence (for a boy of eleven can stand a great deal of mothering) was a cure for one, as the doctor's prescription for the other. That he must wear powerful glasses for the rest of his life was no great burden if they gave him access again to his story-books. In 1877

Rudyard had no story of his own worth telling, only the carefree life of a boy in a happy home. But not altogether, 'for when young lips have drunk deep of the bitter waters of Hate, Suspicion, and Despair, all the Love in the world will not wholly take away that knowledge.' [8]

From A School Song (1899)

Western wind and open surge
   Took us from our mothers,
Flung us on a naked shore
(Twelve bleak houses by the shore!
Seven summers by the shore!)
   'Mid two hundred brothers.

.   .   .   .

There we met with famous men
   Set in office o'er us;
And they beat on us with rods –
Faithfully with many rods –
Daily beat on us with rods,
   For the love they bore us!

.   .   .   .

Each degree of Latitude
   Strung about Creation
Seeth one or more of us
(Of one muster each of us),
Diligent in that he does,
   Keen in his vocation.

.   .   .   .

This we learned from famous men,
   Knowing not its uses,
When they showed, in daily work,
Man must finish off his work –
Right or wrong, his daily work –
   And without excuses.

.   .   .   .

Wherefore praise we famous men
   From whose bays we borrow –
They that put aside To-day –
All the joys of their To-day –
And with toil of their To-day
   Bought for us To-morrow!

Bless and praise we famous men —
Men of little showing —
For their work continueth,
And their work continueth,
Broad and deep continueth,
  Great beyond their knowing.

[3]

Public School
(1878–82)

WHEN, at twelve years old, it was time for Rudyard to resume his schooling, his parents can have had little doubt about where to send him; their dear friend Cormell Price, already well known to Rudyard as 'Uncle Crom', would be his teacher.

In the days when Price and 'Ned' Jones and Henry Macdonald had been school-fellows at Birmingham, there had been little to show which of the three would go farthest in the world. At Oxford 'Crom' had been an active, popular member of William Morris's set, and had taken a hand with 'Ned' and the others in painting the celebrated Pre-Raphaelite frescoes at the Union, but, when 'Ned' and William Morris decided to throw in their lot with Rossetti, he parted from them to try his fortune as a medical student. Rossetti, who wanted all his friends to be painters, deplored 'Crom's' defection and would not let him lapse from their group. He made fun of 'Crom's' new trade, sought out his company, and took him about the town to Bohemian parties with 'Jones' and 'Hunt 'and 'Brown', none of them yet distinguished by their more elegant second names.

But 'Crom' was still unsatisfied; he abandoned medicine and went off to Russia as English tutor in a noble family. In the anglophile period after the Crimean War there was a great demand in Russia for English tutors and governesses, a stream of well-educated young persons who brought back with them, and popularized, the taste for Russian literature – mostly in French translations. Burne-Jones and Morris often wished 'Crom' home again, and welcomed him when he returned in 1863 to organize the 'modern side' at

Haileybury, one of the new Public Schools founded in imitation of Arnold's Rugby.

Another new Public School, the United Services College, was founded in 1874 by a group of Army officers who wanted to provide their sons with a cheap education. They were fortunate in getting 'Crom' as their first headmaster, and he was able to take away with him from Haileybury a nucleus of boys who 'migrated' for the privilege of being coached for their Army Entrance Examination under 'Crom's' skilled tuition. The rise of the new schools was closely connected with the introduction of competitive examinations as the sole means of qualifying for the public services. The Indian Civil Service had been recruited from the successful candidates in an examination since 1855, Gladstone had made competitive examination the rule in the home Civil Service in 1870, and the last great stronghold of privilege fell when he abolished the purchase of officers' commissions in the Army, in 1871. The 'Army Exam' now became a challenge to the new Public Schools, a formidable obstacle at the end of the school course for many a boy of the upper middle-classes.

In later life Kipling's devotion to his headmaster, and through his headmaster to his old school, led him to make exaggerated claims for the United Services College as a 'school before its time'. That is just what it was not. It was a school that precisely satisfied a need for preparing boys for the new competitive examinations; and when the Army Exam ceased to be a troublesome obstacle the school lost ground.

The system and spirit of the United Services College were largely borrowed from Haileybury, that is to say, it was Anglo-Indian in tradition. Most of the boys were soldiers' sons, and many had been born in India. But in spite of its name and its martial origins the United Services College was as unlike a 'Military Academy' as a school could be. In the first place it was cheap, the boys lived in Spartan simplicity, and the management was conducted with parsimony. There were no parades, no uniforms, no bands or flags, no school cadet corps, no patriotic propaganda, nor would it have occurred to any master or boy that such things could be regarded as anything but gross bad form. It was a training ground for youths who were assumed to be gentlemen, and who were qualifying for entrance to the public service where they would work professionally, un-obtrusively, anonymously, for entrance to an army whose officers changed into plain clothes at the instant of coming off duty.

'Crom' Price was no militarist, he was russophile and francophile and disposed to be a liberal, as were his friends the Burne-Joneses, especially 'Aunt Georgie'. It was recorded that, though they cared little for party politics as a rule, Price and Burne-Jones had once appeared together on a public platform at a meeting of protest against Disraeli's foreign policy.

The respect in which the College differed from the general run of mid-Victorian Public Schools was its secular tone; there was no school chapel; Price was not in holy orders and was not a strong churchman. Rudyard Kipling passed through his hands quite untouched by the religious enthusiasms, either evangelical or high-church, that stirred the hearts of so many intelligent young men in the eighteen-eighties.

The strength of the school was its position at the little watering-place in Bideford Bay which had been fancifully named Westward Ho! as a tribute to Charles Kingsley's popular romance. The proprietors of the school had bought up a row of lodging-houses, 'twelve bleak houses by the shore', and had converted them into a school building, by running a corridor or covered way the whole length of the terrace. At one end they had added a large bare hall, known as the gymnasium, which served for assemblies, daily prayers, and indoor exercise. Other amenities there were none but those provided by nature; 'western wind and open surge'; miles of cliff and combe and headland running

westward to Hartland Point; Bideford Bay with the broad
estuary of the Torridge; a rough expanse of scrub and
sandhills, known as the Burrows and laid out for the newly
imported game of golf; and the Pebble Ridge where the
Atlantic surf beat on a steep rough bar of shingle.

The school was in only the fifth year of its existence when
Kipling arrived as a new boy. As yet, the traditional rules
of conduct which stabilize school life and which give a
sense of security, even if they are felt to be constricting,
had not crystallized. Discipline, both in respect of the
authorized school rules, and of the code which the boys
enforced on one another, was irregular and harsh. The
masters, like the senior boys, were a job lot, got together,
as chance had permitted, to give the place a start. It was a
rough experience and again Kipling was cut off from the
family life that alone satisfied his deepest emotion, but he
was not wretched as he had been at Southsea. He was bigger and stronger now, and he acquired a new comfort in
masculine comradeship. From the very first day he found a
friend, a sharp-featured Irish boy with a detached air and
an acidulated tongue. His name was George Beresford and
though, perhaps, he never meant as much to Kipling as
Kipling meant to him, he broke the spell of solitary home-
sickness. In later years, Kipling wrote of him under the
name of 'M'Turk'.

Beresford also wrote reminiscences of his 'Schooldays with
Kipling' and, though they sometimes seem no less imaginative than the account which Kipling put forward as fiction,
the two versions yield much authentic information when
collated.

Into the small-boys' house at Westward Ho! [wrote Beresford]
in the grey chill January days of 1878 there fluttered a cheery,
capering, podgy, little fellow, as precocious as ever he could be.
Or, rather, a broad smile appeared with a small boy behind it,
carrying it about and pointing it in all directions. ... Over the
smile there was, strangely enough, a pair of spectacles. The two
did not seem to go together, as in those days spectacles were re-

garded as a mark of extreme seriousness and crabbed age. ...
When you looked more closely at this new boy, you were
astonished to see what seemed to be a moustache right across
the smile, and so it was – an early spring moustache just out of
the ground of his upper lip. ... Kipling was rather short for his
age of just twelve years, but he took it out in extra width. He
was not noticeably muscular or sinewy, and was accordingly in-
effectual at fisticuffs, for which, in any case, his exceedingly
short sight unfitted him. He preferred to side-track physical
violence by his tact and friendliness and by not quarrelling with
any boy unless he had allies. He was always noticeable for his
caution and his habit of 'getting there' by diplomatic means.[1]

By all accounts, Kipling's appearance was most unusual.
The golden-brown hair of his childhood was now darken-
ing and, above the faint pencilling of moustache which so
surprised his contemporaries, there already protruded the
heavy black eyebrows which caricaturists enlarged upon,
in later years. The thrusting line of his profile with its pro-
truding, deeply cloven chin gave him a singularly aggressive appearance which was dispelled when he raised his
round thick glasses, resting them on the penthouse of his
eyebrows, to confront his questioner with a humorous gaze
from brilliant blue eyes. In those days he used his glasses
for long sight, and read – he was always reading – with the
naked eye, jerking his head backwards and forwards as he
pored over the page. He was the only boy in the school to
wear spectacles, from which came his school nickname of
'Gig-lamps' or 'Gigger'.

In Kipling's early years at Westward Ho!, which he spent
in daily company with Beresford, they passed through a
period of ill-treatment by a brutal assistant-master who
might have strayed out of some novel by Dickens. This was
the Rev. J. C. Campbell, the school chaplain, of whom another boy wrote, 'I can never recall his face without an expression of ferocity on it, nor his hand without a cane in
it.'[2] Modern readers will not be surprised to learn that
Campbell was an emotional preacher. When in Kipling's

second year Campbell left for another appointment he preached a farewell sermon of such unctuous eloquence that the hearts of his little victims were melted. They mutually agreed that old Campbell should be forgiven and should be offered some parting testimonial. Not so thought 'Gigger'; he brought them all to their senses by saying emphatically: 'Two years' bullying is not paid for with half an hour's blubbering in a pulpit'.

Campbell's place was taken by the Rev. C. Willes ('Gillett' in *Stalky & Co.*), a comfortable easy-going 'muscular Christian', who won the friendship if not the particular respect of Beresford and Kipling. They were prepared for confirmation under his perfunctory instruction, and were confirmed in Bideford Church by the Bishop of Exeter, an event that seems to have made no mark upon the mental development of either boy. Nothing was added to Kipling's religious training at Westward Ho!; all that he had, he owed to 'Aunty Rosa' who had drilled the Prayer-book collects and the Bible stories into him at Southsea.

As yet, in his first years at school, the real interest of his life was elsewhere. His father had again come home from India in 1878 to supervise the Indian exhibit at the Paris Exposition and, in the summer holidays, took young Rudyard, not yet thirteen, to Paris with him.

Lockwood gave his son a free pass to the Exposition, which was not yet open to the public, and a franc or two daily to buy his lunch at a cheap restaurant. Rudyard ran wild in Paris, playing at paper-chases in the Tuileries Gardens with an English friend, a Christ's Hospital boy in blue cassock and yellow stockings. Mostly they prowled in the back premises of the Exposition, talking to the workmen in schoolboy French, and exploring among curiosities and art treasures, all the more alluring when half-disengaged from their wrappings. How things were put together, and what they looked like in the workshop, interested Rudyard most of all. A strange interest for a boy was his notice of a subject-picture in Paris, an illustration of the death of

Manon Lescaut. Why it should have haunted his imagination he could not say nor, twelve years later, when the seed
bore fruit, could he yet express all that he wished to say of
it. He did not learn how much France and the French way
of life meant to him until, in middle age, these boyish
memories of his first visit gained a new significance.[3]

At thirteen years old Rudyard knew that he belonged to
a different world from the other boys at his school, or rather
that he belonged to two worlds, theirs and the world of
literary London. He had a secret bond of union with the
headmaster, who in the holidays was by courtesy his 'Uncle
Crom'; he and 'Crom' were at home among people who
wrote, people who painted, people who exhibited in Paris.
Beresford noticed that young Kipling seemed to have read
everything, all sorts of grown-up books, while the other boys
were content with 'Jack Harkaway' and 'Ned Kelly'. In ten
minutes he seemed to extract the essence of a difficult book
which anyone else might have taken a week to read.
Though he never paraded his knowledge and certainly
never alluded to his distinguished friends, he gave the impression of being the perfectly well-informed man of the
world. At one time he and Beresford studied contemporary
art together in the Bideford print-shops. It was plain that
'Gigger' knew all about the rival schools, the Academy and
the Aesthetes, though he never mentioned the fact that one
of his aunts was married to Edward Poynter, R.A., and another to Burne-Jones, a pillar of the Grosvenor Gallery.
Beresford did not know this in his schooldays.

Then came a time when Beresford and Kipling with three
other boys were allowed the privilege of sharing a large
study. They now began to cultivate an adolescent social life,
of which one manifestation was amateur theatricals. The
study produced a play, a burlesque pantomime, to the old
story of Aladdin, with topical songs which 'Gigger' could
turn out with easy fluency. This was an epoch in the school
life of the group, but was followed by what seemed a disaster. The room was required for another purpose and the

group of five friends was dispersed. 'Gigger' and Beresford looked about and found an unused closet – it was hardly more – which they got permission to convert into a study for three boys. It was then necessary to admit a worthy partner to their enterprise; they soon agreed to invite 'Stalky' Dunsterville.

Thus began in 1880 the partnership, known in the school as 'Stalky & Co.', which has given delight to hundreds of thousands of readers for more than fifty years in one of the classic tales of boyhood. Books about the life of children written from their own point of view were an original invention of the nineteenth century. Stories for children and even stories about children there had always been, and children had always told stories to one another, but the cult of childhood as a mode of life with its own values and its own standards gave a new impulse to literature. By any reckoning Kipling's *Stalky & Co.* must stand high in the list of books in this genre. It shares a peculiar quality of fantasy with another classic of childhood, published a few years earlier, Mark Twain's *Tom Sawyer*. Each of these books is 'true' in the sense that the local colour is minutely accurate and the characters drawn from life; each is a romance in the sense that the incidents are vastly exaggerated. No schoolboys ever carried out, or could have carried out, such audacious enterprises as did 'Stalky', 'M'Turk', and 'Beetle' (the name Kipling affixed to himself), or such as are ascribed to Tom Sawyer and Huck Finn. But the fantasy, in both instances, is true to the imaginative life of many a boy. This is how they behave in their daydreams, these are the witticisms, the ingenuities, the audacities they would have produced if only the world of fact resembled the world of fancy.

This is only half the account that must be given of *Stalky & Co.* To many readers the book seemed grossly offensive. So judicious a critic as George Sampson dismissed it as 'an unpleasant book about unpleasant boys in an unpleasant school'. The realism was somewhat shocking to a generation accustomed to the evangelical sobriety of earlier school stories. The best book of this kind ever written, *Tom Brown's Schooldays*, contains horrider brutalities and wilder lawlessness than anything in *Stalky & Co.*, but it is a moral tale written upon the theme of the moulding of Tom's character into the pattern of ethics approved at Dr Arnold's Rugby. In Kipling's story the violence and the heartless cruelty which, as everyone knows, occur wherever boys are gathered together, are paraded with boyish gusto, and the formation of character at Westward Ho! is less explicit. Kipling put it on record that he wrote the book as a tract, and on a closer examination it will be found that the crudities and flippancies of this book, too, conduce to a moral purpose.

School life can be a microcosm of the greater world, and Kipling's cosmology took shape at Westward Ho! From the alternating light and darkness of his childhood he had stepped out into a wider world, a masculine world, and a world of work like manhood, not a world of play like childhood. School life was ordered, progressive, and directed to an end which all approved. A willing subordination to the fundamental rules was then right and reasonable, but this did not in the least imply a pedantic adherence to all the superficial and accidental observances and prohibitions to which prigs gave an inflated importance. The school itself was a praiseworthy, a useful institution, because of its immediate relation to the processes of adult life; its whole was greater than the sum of its parts, and a respect for the whole did not imply a respect for the parts considered separately; nor did the system require toleration of those who did not understand its real nature and direction. A man should keep the rules or take the consequences; he should finish his daily work whole-heartedly, and without offering excuses for failure. Self-reliance meant not merely a willing acceptance of the Law, but much more than that, a readiness to exploit every opportunity to be found within its widest limits, a contempt for short views and niggardly interpretations of its purpose.

This we learned from famous men,
Knowing not we learned it.
Only, as the years went by —
Lonely, as the years went by —
Far from help as years went by,
Plainer we discerned it.

It may be thought difficult to reconcile this explanation
with the fact that most of the incidents in *Stalky & Co*. deal
with breaking school rules. But the three confederates set
firm limits to their irregularities, in the book; and in real
life were not such miscreants as they pretended to be.
'Stalky', like each of the others, wrote his reminiscences of
schooldays, and his account is the least imaginative of the
three. Lionel Dunsterville, though of about the same age as
his two friends, had been sent to Westward Ho! two years
before them. As the youngest boy in the school he had been
cruelly ill-treated by the undisciplined young ruffians who
made the first generation of seniors. When Beresford and
Kipling arrived, in more civilized times, they listened with
horrified fascination to his reminiscences of the heroic age.
He was an adventurous unaccountable boy, with an unhappy
home life, and a taste for solitary escapades. There was a
type of exploit in which he excelled, a feat or practical joke
achieved without leaving any trace by which the perpetrator
could be identified. This was the sort of conduct which, in
the school slang, was described as 'stalky', the quality of a
scout or stalker; and this was the meaning of Dunsterville's
nickname.[4] Beresford recorded a number of 'Stalky's' actual
feats which are of no great interest except as suggesting the
petty episodes which Kipling worked up into the epical adventures of 'Stalky & Co.'. He would sit in an examination
laboriously hiding a paper on his knee until he could provoke a master into ordering him to produce it. The paper
would then prove to be blank. He would allow himself to be
seen going a little way out of bounds and, as soon as he was
sure of being pursued, would double back and establish an
alibi. He would evade the Church Service on Sunday morn-

ing by slipping behind a buttress as the procession filed into the porch and, an hour later, would join the emerging crowd, conspicuous with 'top hat, gloves, and prayer book'.

The three boys in Number Five Study made 'Stalky' their leader in most enterprises. All three cultivated an air of detachment from the merely boyish activities of their fellows. Beresford's line was ironical superiority, 'Stalky's' was adventurous individualism, while Kipling, with his spectacles, his moustache, and his worldly knowledge, seemed years older than his age. One pedant who was exposed to the criticism of Number Five Study was their housemaster, Mr M. H. Pugh ('Prout' in *Stalky & Co.*). A suspicious, humourless, well-meaning man, who could make nothing of these three boys because they did not conform to the stock pattern of schoolboy life, he recognized no loftier conception of loyalty than observance of routine. They obeyed his petty regulations so far as was inevitable and otherwise ignored him. A more sympathetic teacher was Mr H. A. Evans ('Hartopp') to whom the boys owed a debt of gratitude for many acts of kindness and encouragement. He was that useful sort of schoolmaster who does more work out of class than in class at organizing activities and stimulating hobbies. He formed a natural history society, which Stalky & Co. frankly adopted as a justification for long rambles along the cliffs and up the lanes of rural Devon. He was an assiduous promoter of theatricals, with a talent for acting. A great event at Westward Ho! was the performance of *The Rivals,* in December 1881, with all three members of Number Five Study in the cast.

Evans was not very handsomely treated in *Stalky & Co.*, where his character is played down by contrast with that of 'Mr King', Kipling's most celebrated schoolmaster. 'King' is a composite character, chiefly built upon William Crofts who instructed Kipling in Latin and English Literature. The real Crofts is now so deeply buried beneath the fictitious 'King' that it is difficult to restore him to life. There is no doubt that their verbal duels marked a deep-seated bond of

sympathy between this enthusiastic teacher and his talented
pupil; and that the other boys were amazed at their dialec-
tical exchanges. Kipling made it his business in class to
draw out Mr Crofts, and Crofts made it his to stimulate
Kipling by irony and allusion. What would have been
cruelty to a less mature pupil, and perhaps was cruelty to
Kipling's fellows, was nourishment to Kipling's faculties. He
throve on the abuse that Crofts lavished on him, picked his
brain, looted his rich vocabulary, stored away his epigrams
for digestion at leisure, and kept his own temper under the
lash of the master's tongue, meeting the harshest strictures
with a bland smile and a vacant stare from those brilliant
blue eyes, which actually saw very little when his glasses
were perched up on his eyebrows. Of all Kipling's teachers,
Crofts taught him most, by damping down his exuberance,
by forcing him to study the classical writers, by ridiculing
his more pretentious experiments in verse. At no time in
his adult life did Kipling much care what the critics said
of him. They could hardly be ruder to him than Crofts had
been, and they could not force him to attend, as could
Crofts.

But 'King' in *Stalky & Co.* is not quite the same man.* He
owes some features to another member of the staff, F. W.
Haslam, who grounded Kipling in Latin during his first two
years at school and then departed, to become a professor of
classics in New Zealand. Haslam introduced Kipling to
Horace, which he 'loathed for two years, forgot for twenty
years, then loved with an abiding passion for the rest of his
life'. The great political odes in the third Book of Horace
made a substantial part of Kipling's education, which revealed itself ever more clearly in his mature verse style.
Westward Ho! was a modern school, in which the old-
fashioned classical training was neglected, to the great disgust of Haslam and Crofts. Apart from those Odes of

* The later 'Stalky' stories, 'Regulus', 'The United Idolators', 'The
Propagation of Knowledge', present 'Mr King' in a more favourable
light.

Horace which he was obliged to study, Kipling had small Latin and less Greek – no Greek at all beyond a few elementary lessons on the Greek Testament.

It was Crofts who guided Kipling's taste in English Literature, largely by indirect methods. 'Gigger' was already known as the school poet when Crofts referred to him as 'Gigadibs, the literary man', and hurled a copy of Browning's *Men and Women* at his head so that he could find out for himself where the quotation came from. This was the most judicious of gifts, which taught him more than whole seminars of formal instruction. He was already in a mood to imitate any new model. Poe and Swinburne began to give way to Browning, who provided him with a new wealth of matter and style. He was prepared to accept the name of 'Gigadibs' and to furnish his cabin for the voyage outward-bound into life as 'Bishop Blougram' recommended; he saw himself again as 'Fra Lippo Lippi' 'watching folk's faces'.[5]

The shapes of things; their colours, lights and shades.

Behind Crofts, as a background to the life of Number Five Study, was the serene unobtrusive figure of Cormell Price, the headmaster, a believer in the art of solving problems by judiciously leaving things alone. Not a classic, not a pietist, not a sportsman, not even a strong disciplinarian, Cormell Price was unusual among Victorian headmasters. It was Crofts, the second master, who embodied these traditional characters, and deplored that classics, cricket, and churchmanship were not taken more seriously at Westward Ho!; it was Crofts who worked to build up the United Services College as a conventional Public School. He believed, as his contemporaries mostly did, in the virtues of corporal punishment. Not so the headmaster, a mild and kindly man. Price, who is called 'Bates' in *Stalky & Co.*, is there represented as a flogging teacher in the old tradition, a character which, said Beresford, was quite inconceivable to anyone who had known him. No such episode as that described in the story called 'A Little Prep' in which 'Bates'

flogged all the senior boys, ever occurred at Westward Ho!,
though similar holocausts were known at some other
schools. As for the suggestion that Price could have flogged
Kipling, Beresford regarded it as laughable. Rudyard and
his 'Uncle Crom' conferred not only as family friends but,
said Beresford, almost as social equals. Kipling's mature
manner was such that he could not be treated as a child
during his residence in Number Five Study.

Cormell Price never preached, and rarely addressed the
assembled school. He devoted himself to managing his
mixed team of assistants by tactful adjustment, and to getting his Army Class through their examinations. He was a
brilliant teacher of English composition, and it was a
shrewd decision on his part to put Kipling through the
usual 'grind' although he was not going 'up for the Army'.
He coached Kipling especially in précis-writing, a dreaded
obstacle in the Army Examination, and a discipline that
Kipling, the born writer, would need more than any soldier. There seems never to have been any doubt that 'Gigger'
would become a literary man. His defect of sight prevented
him from playing ball-games with the other boys, and gave
Price the opportunity to nourish his talents, by special treatment, apart from them.

An attempt had been made to produce a school journal
which had lapsed after three numbers, as such attempts
often do. In 1881 Price launched it again with Kipling as
editor. The *United Services College Chronicle* does not differ much from other such journals, nor are Kipling's own
contributions much above the standard of what may be
expected from clever schoolboys. It was, however, the first
injection into his veins of the printer's ink that he never
again worked out of his system. He was delighted with his
school magazine, wrote three-quarters of it, sub-edited it,
corrected proofs, and took the deepest interest in its production at a little printing shop at Bideford.

What were the formative influences in literature that gave
direction to his thoughts, and mannerisms to his style, in

this early imitative period of youth? He had pored over
Defoe and Bunyan, Fielding and Smollett, Dickens and
Thackeray even in his Southsea days. The first unusual book
– unusual, that is to say, for a Victorian child – recorded by
him as significant was Emerson's *Poems,* which he tackled
in Epping Forest at the age of twelve. Contemporary
American writing always attracted him. Echoes of Edgar
Allan Poe recur again and again in his early verse and
prose; he rated Longfellow higher as a poet than the common estimate today; then, with the easy receptiveness of
youth, he was swept away with enthusiasm for Walt Whitman, to the disgust of Mr Crofts who ridiculed this esoteric
craze. Milton and Tennyson were enough for Mr Crofts.
The American humorists were much to the taste of Number
Five Study, and, if the young Kipling can be said to have
belonged to a 'literary school', it was to the school of Bret
Harte. He was an admirer of Mark Twain too, and when
Harris's *Uncle Remus* came out in 1880 Kipling, like all the
school and half the nation, was inflamed by it as by a fever.
Boys and girls, if they are to be readers, should be omni-
vorous, and find their own way from softer to harder morsels.
The boy who had found something attractive in Emerson
at the age of twelve was ready for solid fare at fifteen.
Beresford, like his betters in that age, was a disciple of Ruskin, and read *Fors Clavigera,* as it came out in weekly parts
in the early eighties. This, and Carlyle's *Sartor Resartus,* no
easy reading whatever else may be thought of it, were the
books that the three boys talked over in the hiding-place
they made for themselves among the furze-bushes of the
Burrows, and later in the room they hired from a cottager as
a secret retreat. Emerson, Carlyle, Ruskin, Browning account
for the mode of thought in which young Kipling began to
form his own philosophy.

A book that taught him a technique was Landor's *Imaginary Conversations,* which set him to the task of writing in
various styles and manners. Throughout life he easily composed parodies and imitations, and used them as an exercise

in his craft of writing. More than most authors he wrote verses and tales in character, as conversation pieces in which the plot is revealed by a monologue, necessarily delivered in another style than his own; and, before he had learned the mastery of this technique, his work was coloured with derivative patches of imitation, conscious or unconscious. Especially in his early verse, characteristic though it is, the reader may remark with assurance, this stanza is after Swinburne, this after Poe, this after Browning.

It was now that Cormell Price took the decisive step in Kipling's education. He gave Kipling

the run of his brown-bound, tobacco-scented library; prohibiting nothing, recommending nothing. There Beetle [Kipling] found a fat arm-chair, a silver ink-stand and unlimited pens and paper. There were scores and scores of ancient dramatists, there were Haklyut, his Voyages; French translations of Muscovite authors called Pushkin and Lermontoff; little tales of a heady and bewildering nature, interspersed with unusual songs – Peacock was that writer's name; there were Borrow's *Lavengro*; an odd theme, purporting to be a translation of something called a 'Rubaiyat', which the Head said was a poem not yet come to its own; there were hundreds of volumes of verse – Crashaw; Dryden; Alexander Smith; L.E.L.; Lydia Sigourney; Fletcher and a Purple Island; Donne; Marlowe's *Faust*; Ossian; *The Earthly Paradise*; *Atalanta in Calydon*; and Rossetti – to name only a few. Then the Head drifting in under pretence of playing censor to the paper, would read here a verse and here another of these poets, opening up avenues. And, slow-breathing, with half-shut eyes above his cigar, would he speak of great men living, and journals, long dead, founded in their riotous youth; of years when all the planets were little new-lit stars trying to find their places in the uncaring void, and he, the Head, knew them as young men know one another.[6]

In his last year at Westward Ho! Kipling was already reaching forward to the wider world. His education had become a matter of personal relation with 'the Head', his private life was concentrated in the happy family of Number Five Study. The three had made a compromise with the school organization and did not allow it to dominate their lives; Dunsterville and Beresford had their examinations to prepare for; Kipling was steeped in his reading and writing, and editing. Unknown to the school in general, unknown even to his study-mates, was the fact that Kipling was already the author of a book. Far away in India, his mother had collected, and persuaded his father to print for private circulation, a volume of *Schoolboy Lyrics* (1881), written by their talented son. Even the author did not know of this until much later. None of these verses have been reprinted in the standard collections of Kipling's poetry, and the volume is of interest today only as a collector's rarity. When the Kiplings left Lahore, twelve years later, heaps of unwanted copies of *Schoolboy Lyrics* were thrown away, as the collectors had not yet got wind of them. Cormell Price must, surely, have been in the secret of their publication, and must have corresponded with his old friend, Lockwood Kipling, now at Lahore, though the letters are not extant; it must have been with 'Crom's' connivance that young Rudyard's career was fostered. As early as December 1881, about the date when *Schoolboy Lyrics* appeared, Lockwood Kipling wrote to another friend that he proposed to 'bring Rudyard out to India next year, and get him some newspaper work. Oxford we can't afford. Ruddy thirsts for a man's life and a man's work'; and Ruddy developed so fast in the next six months that his promotion to manhood came even sooner. The little chubby laughing boy whom Beresford had befriended in 1878 was now, in 1882, a sturdy, talkative fellow of sixteen, muscular but not athletic. Swimming was the only sport permitted by his bad eyesight and swimming was his pleasure in the last year at school.

The three boys were venturesome, careless of the petty restrictions imposed by school-law, but innocent of all the grosser vices, ignorant of all the rending passions. A little poaching, a little smoking (which for some obscure reason was regulated by taboos in Victorian schools), some expeditions out of bounds, some calculated defiances of the school

authorities, were not seen as grave matters by anyone except
by Mr Pugh and his kind. It was more significant that Kipling and Beresford were the arbiters of taste in the school,
and Dunsterville learned how to profit from their reputation.
They decorated the study with a stencilled pattern of chocolate and French grey in the best style of the aesthetic movement, bought pottery in the Bideford curiosity shops, and
took pride in preserving rejected fragments of medieval
wood-carving when Bideford Church was restored. But when
their taste developed and they wearied of these acquisitions,
it was 'Stalky' who thought of selling them by auction to
their envious school-fellows. 'Stalky', always penniless, was
an adept at raising funds by selling what was superfluous,
somebody's Sunday trousers to the Bideford pawnbroker, if
the financial stringency was tight enough. Kipling, too,
could raise money in his own way, and impressed the other
two by selling an article to a London newspaper for no less
than a guinea.*

The summer term of 1882 was the last in which the partnership was maintained. Kipling was to leave for India in
the autumn while the other two were to sit for their examination in 1883. Kipling was restive, he was not sure that he
wanted to go to India even though it meant rejoining his
beloved parents. He was not to be a soldier like Stalky, nor
a civil engineer like Beresford; he intended to be – was already – a literary man, and London, not Lahore, was the
centre of the literary world. He told Beresford that he would
cable to his father: 'I have married a wife and therefore I
cannot come', a remark that Beresford regarded as a mere
joke, though it had a sharper point to it than he supposed.
For a few weeks more, Kipling could be a boy and be
amused by childish things. A lucky chance arose of scoring
a last point against Mr Crofts, when Beresford found a duplicate of the examination paper which Crofts had set, on

* We have Kipling's word for this, in *Land and Sea Tales*. The article
has not been identified, unless he refers to a poem, 'Two Lives', in the
World , 9 November 1882.

Milton's 'Lycidas'. No question of honour was involved since
Beresford was not sitting for the examination and Kipling
was taking it as a mere test of industry, which could bring
him no prize or promotion. Kipling learned the answers to
all the questions and Crofts, with the utmost reluctance, was
obliged to award him full marks. Crofts bore no malice, and
gave his best pupil a copy of *Aurora Leigh* as a parting gift.

Kipling's last numbers of the *College Chronicle* reflect the
rapid maturing of his own character. Number ten contains
the first of his early poems to display the Horatian neatness
and compression which are so typical of his later verse. Confronted with Horace's Ode, *Donec gratus eram tibi,* as a
task, which he had omitted to prepare and which he was
punished for neglecting, he reproduced it in broad Devon-
shire, a version that merits preservation.[7]

> *He* – So long as 'twuz me alone
> An' there wasn't no other chaps,
> I was praoud as a King on 'is throne –
> Happier tu, per'aps.

> *She* – So long as 'twuz only I
> An' there wasn't no other she
> Yeou cared for so much – surely
> I was glad as glad could be.

> *He* – But now I'm in lovv with Jane Pritt –
> She can play the piano, she can;
> An' if dyin' 'ud 'elp 'er a bit
> I'd die laike a man.

> *She* – Yeou'm like me. I'm in lovv with young Frye –
> Him as lives out tu Appledore Quay;
> An' if dyin' 'ud 'elp 'im I'd die –
> Twice ovver for he.

> *He* – But s'posin' I threwed up Jane
> An' niver went walkin' with she –
> An' come back to yeou again –
> How 'ud that be?

R.K. – 4

> *She* – Frye's sober. Yeou've allus done badly –
>   An' yeou shifts like cut net-floats, yeou du :
>   But – I'd throw that young Frye ovver gladly
>   An' lovv 'ee right thru !

Number eight of the *Chronicle*, March 1882, contains the poem 'Ave Imperatrix !', which Mr Eliot found worthy of a place in his selection from Kipling's Verse. It surprised Beresford, it surprised Stalky, and Beresford stated that it even surprised the author. Perhaps no critic then noticed that it was a direct imitation of a poem which Oscar Wilde had published, with the same title, a year earlier. It was a tribute, in the conventional language of patriotism and loyalty, to Queen Victoria, after her escape from death by assassination. No one then regarded 'Gigger' as a writer of 'patriotic' verse. He was a rebel and a progressive, which is to say, in 1882 – paradoxically – that he was a decadent. His friends, his teachers, were liberals, his tastes were 'aesthetic', the writers he most admired were the fashionable pessimists. One of his favourite poems was James Thomson's *City of Dreadful Night*. If he were to take the loyalist side in controversy, it could only be as another provocation to Crofts, the pacifist and liberal. The poem hardly seemed in character, but before another year was out Kipling's view of life would be revealed as something unsuspected.

There was much about Rudyard Kipling that Beresford and Dunsterville did not know. In the holidays he vanished into a world that differed profoundly from that known to the average officer's family. As he grew older and could travel alone, he paid visits to a widening circle of cousins on the Macdonald side, most of them a year or two younger than himself. His English home, in his later years at school, was with three sisters, Mrs Winnard, and the two Miss Craiks, old family friends who lived at Warwick Gardens, South Kensington. They were immersed in literary society, proud of having known Carlyle, and intimate with the admired writers of the eighties. But theirs was a little house and their habits too neat and quiet to satisfy a singularly active, curious, noisy, talkative schoolboy, always prying into things to find out how they worked, a boy who never for a moment abstained from laughing and joking. There was one year (1880) when his mother came home, in time to nurse him through a bout of quinsy at Warwick Gardens and, when Trix came to join them, the little house overflowed. Ruddy was then sent to his cousins, Fred Macdonald's children, who never forgot his visit; never had they known such larks.* Not far away were the Poynters, at that date the most eminent branch of the family, since their father was a fashionable R.A. At the Poynters' or at the Burne-Joneses', as in his father's house, all the talk was of the fine arts and in the jargon of the studio. Later in life Ruddy was to be on the closest terms of friendship with Ambrose Poynter; at this time he saw more of his Burne-Jones cousins. Perhaps his closest friend was Margaret Burne-Jones, the cousin nearest his own age, who shared with him, and Trix, a round of private jokes and secret nicknames. The earliest writings of Rudyard Kipling to see the light were in the family magazine, *The Scribbler,* which he produced with the Burne-Jones and Morris children in 1879.

Rudyard and Trix sometimes spent holidays together. She recalled one summer at Witley in Surrey, where the nightingales kept them awake, and another occasion when he came down to Southsea to bring her away from Mrs Holloway's. This was in 1880, when Rudyard was fourteen and a half years old, and when something occurred which may explain why he was more mature than Beresford or Dunsterville. He fell in love.

Another paying guest whose parents were abroad, a girl called Florence Garrard, had come to live with 'Aunty Rosa' at Southsea; she was a little older than Rudyard, a

* He came in one day tense with anger – rolled on the nursery floor in fury. 'Why, Ruddy! What's the matter?' 'The porter at the station boxed my ears.' 'But what made him box your ears?' 'Oh, I expect I cheeked him.' His manner changed; he smiled, and went towards the door with a purposeful look. 'Where are you going, Ruddy?' 'Back to the station to cheek that porter again.' [Miss F. Macdonald.]

straight slender girl with a beautiful ivory-pale face and a
cloud of dark hair, but badly brought up in continental
hotels and very ill-educated. With a shrewd sophisticated
manner, she was self-centred and elusive, lacking in sympathy and affection. Trix was devoted to her and pleased to
supervise her reading, while Rudyard fell an easy prey. Man-
like he idolized her as a Pre-Raphaelite heroine; and boylike
he noticed with malicious pleasure that she kept a pet goat
which always butted 'Aunty Rosa'. Calf-love is not to be
despised because it shows symptoms which the immune consider ludicrous. Where and how often Flo and Rudyard met
was their own secret. He was faithful to her image for five or
six years at least, and hard-hit again when he met her long
afterwards. When he was ordered off to India, he begged
her to consent to an engagement – he was then sixteen and
she seventeen or eighteen; when he sailed, he supposed himself to be engaged to her.[8] But she? Her story is lost. She
reserved herself, to make a career of her own with her drawings, which were not much admired by the Kiplings. A
sketch-book of hers which survives in America is decorated
with 'doodles' by Rudyard, on the blank pages. Her drawings are the conventional studies of Victorian art schools;
his scribbles reveal a much stronger line and clearer vision.[9]

Rudyard was to leave England in September so as to arrive in India at the end of the hot weather. His last summer
holiday he spent partly at Rottingdean where a colony of
cousins on the Macdonald side made their holiday home,
and partly at Skipton with his Kipling grandmother, 'an
old-fashioned Puritan saint, with a face like a chaste cameo'.
On 20 September 1882 he sailed from Tilbury by the P. & O.
steamer *Brindisi*, alone and seasick, in drizzling rain.

From The New Knighthood (1909)

Who lays on the sword?
'I,' said the Sun,
'Before he has done,
'I'll lay on the sword.'

.   .   .   .

Who gives him his spur?
'I,' said his Chief,
Exacting and brief,
'I'll give him the spur.'

.   .   .   .

Who'll shake his hand?
'I,' said the Fever,
'And I'm no deceiver,
'I'll shake his hand.'

.   .   .   .

Who brings him the wine?
'I,' said Quinine,
'It's a habit of mine.
'I'll come with his wine.'

.   .   .   .

Who'll put him to proof?
'I,' said All Earth.
'Whatever he's worth,
'I'll put to the proof.'

.   .   .   .

Who'll choose him for Knight?
'I,' said his Mother,
'Before any other,
'My very own Knight.'

.   .   .   .

And after this fashion, adventure to seek,
Was Sir Galahad made – as it might be last week!

[4]

Lahore and Simla
(1882–7)

To a boy who was just beginning to take an interest in
public affairs, a voyage to India in the autumn of 1882 was
indeed an adventure; it took him through the middle of a
battlefield. The year 1882 was the climax of a period of
colonial wars, which, according to your political alignment,
you might describe as the bloody consequence of Disraeli's
aggressive policy, or the confusion caused by Gladstone's
weak handling of situations bequeathed to him in hopeful
shape. The nation had muddled through the Zulu War in
1879, had accepted defeat at Majuba in 1880, had watched
without comprehension the wanton invasion and the equally
wanton evacuation of Afghanistan, uncertain whether to applaud Roberts's brilliant campaigns or to lament a costly
reverse at Maiwand. But it was Gladstone, not Disraeli, who
intervened in Egypt with operations by sea and land, which
were a model of efficiency. Egypt was bankrupt, and controlled by an international commission which was obliged
to act when the nationalist revolt of Arabi Pasha broke out.
Massacres took place in Cairo, the British Consul was attacked and, when Arabi's men mounted batteries on the
foreshore against the French and British fleets in the harbour at Alexandria, Gladstone authorized the bombardment
of the forts by the British fleet alone, a naval operation that
won great celebrity. This last appearance in action of the
old three-decker Navy occurred on 11 July 1882, during Kipling's final term at school. A few days later Sir Garnet Wol-
seley landed at Ismailia with an army that included the
Brigade of Guards. All went like clockwork and, after a
night march through the desert, Sir Garnet totally defeated

Arabi Pasha at the cost of 450 British casualties, and thus began the British occupation of Egypt.

Nine days after the battle of Tel-el-Kebir Rudyard Kipling's ship left London River for the East. The newspapers, in this golden age of the war-correspondents, were filled with telegraphed reports of the battle; the weeklies with pages of illustration worked up from sketches made by war-artists at the front. The Suez Canal was the prize of victory, the centre of attention, and it was reported that snipers had fired upon the last P. & O. mailboat as it passed through. Dunsterville, a schoolboy still at Westward Ho!, must have been consumed with envy of 'Gigger' now a man of the world, outward bound for the seat of war. On 2 October he was at Port Said, where his ship lay four days before venturing into the Canal; he reached Suez on the seventh. Not a line of direct evidence survives to show what this born journalist made of his opportunity then and there. While, fifty miles from Port Said, the battlefield lay open, strewn with unburied corpses, the exits from the town were blocked by sentries, and it is unlikely that he saw more than 'the straight line of the Canal, the blazing sands, the procession of shipping, and the white hospitals where the English soldiers lay'.[1] That he absorbed and remembered the sights and sounds of a base-camp close behind the battle, and sensed the raffish atmosphere of Port Said and Suez, is evident from the boldly imaginative sketches he inserted into *The Light that Failed*, ten years later.

More directly he was moved by the two-sidedness of his life. The two halves of it were symbolized by the contrast between Europe and Asia. 'East of Suez' he was in an old mental atmosphere as well as in another economy. In childhood the voyage to England, from light to darkness, had symbolized a transition from perfect happiness to protracted misery. But now, he was not so sure. Dark Europe had given him friendship and promised him love. What more had bright Asia to offer? Recalling this hesitation at the edge of the East, he wrote in later years:

Port Said marks a certain dreadful and exact division between East and West. Up to that point – it is a fringe of palms
against the sky – the impetus of home memories and the echo of
home interests carry the young man along very comfortably on
his first journey. But at Suez one must face things. People,
generally the most sympathetic, leave the boat there; the older
men who are going on have discovered each other and begun to
talk shop; no newspapers come aboard, only clipped Reuter
telegrams; the world seems cruelly large and self-absorbed. ...
Then one begins to wonder when one will see those palms from
the other side. Then the black hour of home-sickness, vain
regrets, foolish promises, and weak despair shuts down with the
smell of strange earth and the cadence of strange tongues.

He reached Bombay, his birthplace, on 18 October 1882,
and the bright world of Asia revealed to him a new nostalgia. This, not dark Europe, was after all his home, the
place of his happy childhood. He would warn his school-
fellows to have no regrets or fears, for each of them, Anglo-
Indians by right, would make a discovery on returning to
India.

The evening smells and the sight of the hibiscus and poin-
settias will unlock his tongue in words and sentences that he
thought he had clean forgotten, and he will go back to his ship
as a prince entering on his Kingdom.[2]

Lahore, where Lockwood and Alice Kipling had been living for seven years, was a pleasant station during the cool
season, with about seventy British residents in the civil lines.
Lockwood had come from Bombay to continue his former
work as Principal of the Mayo School of Art and Curator of
the Lahore Museum. In the first days after his arrival Rudyard helped in the Museum which his father had made a
model collection of Indian arts and archaeology, much used
by students and crowded with Indian sightseers.

The Museum stands, just as it is described in the first
chapter of *Kim,* near the Mall, the wide boulevard that runs
from the European quarter to the old walled city. Out beyond the canal was Mian Mir, the military cantonment that

housed a British Infantry Battalion and a battery of Artillery. Nearer to the city stood bungalows in large gardens, the Punjab Club, colleges and schools, and a row of shops and offices in European style behind a line of acacias. Among them, in two wooden sheds, was placed the printing office of the *Civil and Military Gazette*, the provincial newspaper of which Rudyard was to be assistant editor. In November he commenced work and on Christmas Eve, a week before his seventeenth birthday, he found himself in temporary control, because the editor, Stephen Wheeler, was in bed after a carriage accident. Stephen Wheeler was perhaps a little piqued at being confronted, and then temporarily supplanted, by this lively subordinate, none the less because the youngster was a protégé of the proprietors.

The *Civil and Military Gazette* had been founded, ten years earlier, by two remarkable men, both of them sons of British soldiers, who had taken their discharge in India, had settled, and had married in the country. Rudyard's first patron, James Walker, had started a prosperous career by organizing transport between the Plains and the summer capital at Simla; the other founder, William Rattigan, was a leading member of the Lahore Bar. Together they made a success of their journal, largely because it was carried by a well-established printing house, which held the printing contract for the provincial authorities and, accordingly, their editorial policy was presumed to be a reflection of the views of the Punjab Government. Next, they had taken the bold step of buying a controlling interest in a larger concern, six hundred miles down-country, the *Pioneer*, which George Allen had established at Allahabad, then the railway centre of India. Unlike the *Civil and Military Gazette*, the *Pioneer* became an all-India newspaper with a name for being so well-informed that its pronouncements were often taken as demi-official. Howard Hensman, the *Pioneer* representative at Simla, was reputed to know all the secrets, especially to be in the confidence of Sir Frederick Roberts, the Commander-in-Chief. ('Roberts made him,' it used to be whispered, 'and he made Roberts.') Down at Allahabad Allen was known as a brilliant organizer whose success was due to finding talented subordinates and riding them with a loose rein, a system that sometimes ran him and his paper into trouble. Allen, like Walker, was an old friend of Lockwood Kipling and his wife, both of whom wrote occasionally for the *Pioneer*. He watched over Rudyard, too, and found openings for him.

A paper in Lahore was worth while because of the key position of the Punjab in the Indian Empire. It was a new province, conquered and annexed less than thirty years before the Kiplings came to Lahore, the scene of the labours, of John Lawrence and his team of assistants, the most efficient band of administrators in Indian history. The Punjab was notable for progress in irrigation, land settlement, and afforestation, for roads and railways; it was a healthy prosperous wheat-growing province with a population of sturdy peasants, a more pleasing place to English eyes than crowded fever-stricken Bengal, the land of political unrest.

In the cool weather the civil lines at Lahore were agreeable enough, but the Mall led to something more significant, the old walled city, perhaps the most picturesque of all the cities of Islam, where two hundred thousand people of all the races of Asia lived as their forefathers had lived in the days of the Arabian Nights. Lahore was predominantly a Moslem city famous for the Mosque of Wazir Khan, for the Shalimar Gardens, and for the tomb of the Emperor Jahangir, beyond the broad shingly bed of the River Ravi. It was more recently celebrated for the short-lived and memorable Sikh kingdom of Runjeet Singh, the last lord of the grim square fortress, stained with much blood, haunted by many ghosts, which commanded the town, over against the great mosque. Many old men, still living in Lahore in 1882, could well remember the great king whose court was the last in India quite untainted by western progress. In Kipling's day a company of British infantry were encamped among the faded splendours of Runjeet's Palace, to overawe Sikh and Moslem alike. Now they, too, are gone, and the Moslems have resumed their sway over a city half in ruins that hide the bodies of uncounted Sikhs killed in the massacres of 1947.

In 1883 the re-discovery of India was a complete and absorbing occupation to young Rudyard; it was sheer delight to be treated as a man, not only at home but at work and at the Punjab Club. He had his personal servant, a Moslem and the son of his father's servant, his own quarters in his parents' bungalow, his horse – a temperamental bay pony named 'Joe' which he found difficult to manage – and a trap in which he drove down to the office. There, he was half the European staff, and sometimes more than that, because Stephen Wheeler was often ill with fever. Machines and type, which he thought he understood already, and one hundred and seventy Indian printing-hands were under his eye, but when Wheeler was on duty he was kept hard at routine. Wheeler formed the notion that young Kipling was too literary a chap; and was concerned to knock the nonsense out of him. The junior's task was to read the telegrams from the news-agencies and make up copy for the edition that went to press at midnight. To that he was restricted and for that work 'Uncle Crom's' training had prepared him. Lockwood Kipling thought that routine under an exacting chief was a useful discipline for his talented exuberant son.

Ruddy is getting on well [he wrote to friend], having mastered the details of his work in a very short time. His chief, Mr Wheeler, is very tetchy and irritable, and by dint of his exertions in patience and forbearance, the boy is training for heaven as well as for editorship. I am sure he is better here ... where there are no music-hall ditties to pick up, no young persons to philander about with, and a great many other negatives of the most wholesome description. All that makes Lahore profoundly dull makes is safe for young persons.[3]

Mrs Kipling was not so sure. Her boy was devoted to her, but his temperament caused her some little anxiety. What boy of seventeen does not arouse questionings in his mother's heart? She had regretted the reticence of his school letters, had questioned the prudence of forcing so lively a youngster on the three old ladies of Warwick Gardens, had waited avidly for his arrival, and now found him strangely moody. If Trix's story may be accepted, Ruddy sulked for three days when he found that his mother had printed his *Schoolboy Lyrics* without his permission. A man's life and a man's independence did not, at first, quite sort with domesticity. What appealed to him was a room of his own.

In June 1883, having stayed down on the Plains later than usual to see Rudyard through his first bout of Indian heat, she left her husband and her son, while setting sail for England to meet her daughter. For some weeks, when his father went on leave to the Hills, Rudyard was alone in the house with the Indian servants. Then he, too, had his thirty days at Simla, staying with James Walker, his employer. In August he was again alone at Lahore with the season at its most oppressive, much fever in the station, and the number of Europeans reduced to a dozen jaded, sickly men whose women-folk were away at the Hills. Work was more exacting in short-handed times, and must be done, fever or no fever. The *Civil and Military* must go to press. The modern reader should be reminded that this was India in the heroic age, without refrigerators, without electric fans, without D.D.T. It was hardly yet understood that cholera was a water-borne infection, not known that mosquitoes carried malaria. An English *sahib* might enjoy some rude luxuries in India, but tropical disease then struck down its victims, high- or low-caste, without social discrimination. Was it more disheartening to sit alone, sweating in a darkened bungalow, or to spend the evening in chance company at the Club where prickly heat made prickly tempers? Kipling was the youngest Englishman in the station, the

junior in a newspaper office, a post which did not rank high
among appointments in that caste-ridden society. As yet he
was only an honorary member of the Club, lucky to have
the entrée, and not a popular member. Political feeling
ran high that season over the Ilbert Bill which deprived
Anglo-Indians of the legal privilege of trial by European
judges in special courts. When the proprietors of his newspaper,* who at first had opposed the Bill, decided to withdraw from active opposition, Kipling was actually hissed in
the smoking-room of the Club, and was so green that he did
not know why.

During that hot weather of 1883, for the first time in his
life, he knew loneliness and found it unbearable. His work
was night-work, his lifelong habit to wander in the small
hours. After the paper had been put to press in the sultry
Indian midnight, he would find his way into the old walled
city, penetrating into courts and alleys where few Europeans
went, watching for the dawn which might bring a breath of
cooler air. There was a theme that ran in his head, uniting
loneliness, fever, and a sleeping city; it was James Thomson's *City of Dreadful Night.*

> The street-lamps burn amidst the baleful glooms,
>   Amidst the soundless solitudes immense
> Of rangèd mansions dark and still as tombs.
>   The silence which benumbs or strains the sense
> Fulfils with awe the soul's despair unweeping;
> Myriads of habitants are ever sleeping,
>   Or dead, or fled from nameless pestilence!

The motive of sleeplessness amid silent multitudes in the
tropical darkness recurs again and again in Kipling's early
verse and prose:

a stifling hot blast from the mouth of the Delhi Gate nearly ends
my resolution of entering the City of Dreadful Night at this

---

*In *Something of Myself*, R. K. hints that one of his proprietors
was angling for a knighthood. Actually, Allen, Walker, and Rattigan
were all knighted, but not until a much later date.

hour. It is compounded of all evil savours, animal and vegetable, that a walled city can brew in a day and a night. The temperature within the motionless groves of plantain and orange trees outside the city walls seems chilly by comparison.

Then silence follows – the silence that is full of the night noises of a great city. A stringed instrument of some kind is just, and only just, audible. High overhead some one throws open a window, and the rattle of the woodwork echoes down the empty street. On one of the roofs a hookah is in full blast: and the men are talking softly as the pipe gutters. ... It is close upon midnight and the heat seems to be increasing. The moonlight stripes the Mosque's high front of coloured enamel work in broad diagonal bands, and each separate dreaming pigeon in the niches and corners of the masonry throws a squat little shadow. Sheeted ghosts rise up wearily from their pallets, and flit into the dark depths of the building ... [4]

'Doré might have drawn it! Zola could describe it' – so young Kipling commented on the scene, and so, by night and alone, he formulated his own version of it. In the morning, having bathed and breakfasted and taken 'Joe' for a canter, from which horse and rider sometimes returned separately, he could put all that morbidity aside, and keep a stiff upper lip before Stephen Wheeler or the fellows at the Club. He wrote long letters to Margaret Burne-Jones, and to his Aunt Edie, the youngest of the Macdonald sisters and the only one to remain unmarried. She was at this time his confidante and, as boys do, he showed off his manliness to her.

Rudyard Kipling to Miss Edith Macdonald

Lahore, August 14th, 1883

Dearest Auntie,

Your 'expansive' note greeting me on my return from Simla where I had been spending a month with one of the proprietors to my own exceeding delight. Privilege leave, as I may have told you before, gives you the pleasant duty of enjoying yourself in a cool climate for thirty days and being paid £20 for that duty. The month was a round of picnics, dances, theatricals and so on

– and I flirted with the bottled up energy of a year on my lips.
Don't be horrified for there were about half a dozen of 'em and
I took back the lacerated fragments of my heart as I distributed
my P.P.C. cards and returned the whole intact, to Flo Garrard's
keeping as per usual. I was nearly eight hours a day in the saddle
and at the end of the month found out that I could actually ride
anywhere without turning giddy. Simla is built round the sides
of a mountain 8,400 feet high and the roads are just ledges. At
first they turned my head a good deal but in a little I was enabled to canter anyhow and anywhere. Now of course Lahore is
as level as a billiard table and Joe had had no work for a fortnight when I came back so you can imagine what a time we had.
There are 9 men and 2 ladies in the station and most of these
are going away. Practically I am living at the Club. I dine there
every night and go home to the big house to sleep. The dullness
is something hideous after all the bustle of Simla.[5]

At last the rains broke, the cool weather came, and life at
Lahore was again endurable without sleepless vigils, but
1883 ended in solitary discomfort for young Kipling. Again
he was left alone for two months in the bungalow while his
father went down to Bengal to prepare a display for the Calcutta Exhibition. He had no resource as yet, but to write
contributions for the *United Services College Chronicle*
which he despatched to 'Stalky'. He started a friendly correspondence with Mr Crofts, sending him copies of all the
verses he wrote in India, and telling him of his dull routine.
Crofts preserved these letters with care and made a collection, probably the most complete collection, of Kipling's
early work.* Then in the New Year came the beginning of
a new life, when his mother arrived from England with his
sister, Trix, not yet sixteen but as advanced for her years as
Rudyard for his. It was unusual to bring out so young an
English girl to India.

The next four years (January 1884 to November 1887)
made a rounded, complete, and satisfying period in Rudyard Kipling's life; they formed his mental habits. At seven-

* William Crofts died in 1911. His collections were sold in America
and dispersed.

teen he was a clever, precocious boy, high-spirited and asser-
tive but untidy and untrained. Only those who knew him
intimately, his mother and his 'Uncle Crom', distinguished
him in quality from other clever boys. At twenty-one he
was astonishingly mature, already the Rudyard Kipling
whose name and features and point of view were to be
world-famous. It was not the glamour of the East, nor the
splendour of the British *Raj*, nor the knowledge of cities and
men, that formed his character; he was observant enough to
have found 'copy' anywhere; it was – to use a favourite expression of his mother's – the Family Square. He surveyed
the Indian scene, which happened to be his field of action,
from the secure base of a family life that was not only
happy but four-square and, it seemed, impregnable. Father,
mother, son, and daughter, all were talented, all different in
their talents, all appreciative of each other's qualities, all
devoted to one another and to the family group. The father
– solid, practical, genial, with a hard core of north-country
granite in his composition; the mother quick, intuitive, sympathetic, witty, and sharp-tongued; the daughter slight and
graceful, poetic, intellectual; the son – as yet the least pre-
possessing member of the family but abnormally receptive.
His father's wide range of knowledge, wise simplicity, and
manual dexterity held his respect; his mother's easy skill
at managing men, her natural ascendancy in any company,
compelled his wonder; his sister's young charm — he spoke
of her as 'the Maiden' or 'the Ice-maiden' – delighted him.
At home he could be candid and happy; and at home the
other three, whom he so deeply admired, who made his life
so pleasant, whose criticism was welcome because kind, fostered his genius which they had not failed to recognize. The
family square made the only audience he cared to please.
Let the world outside approve or disapprove. The family
square could resist any external pressure.

They knew he had another love and it is hard to say how
deeply the separation from Flo Garrard wounded him. A
favourite theme of his early stories is the fading out of a

romantic attachment between a young man in India and a girl at home. In these stories he not infrequently caricatures himself in a sentence or two.

Next to a requited attachment, one of the most convenient things that a young man can carry about with him at the beginning of his career, is an unrequited attachment. It makes him feel important and business-like, and *blasé*, and cynical; and whenever he has a touch of liver, or suffers from want of exercise, he can mourn over his lost love, and be very happy in a tender, twilight fashion.[6]

Eighteen months after his departure from London, about July 1884, Flo Garrard wrote to put an end to the engagement. Perhaps the association had been wearing thin, perhaps the breach when it came was not unwelcome, even though he remained enslaved to her memory. His comment was a set of verses written before the end of the year.

> One brought Her Fire from a distant place,
> And She – what should She know of it? . . .
>
> .   .   .   .   .
>
> Sudden She crushed the embers 'neath Her heel, –
> And all light went with Her.[7]

Rudyard Kipling had no other passionate love affair in India. His work, which was always based upon his experience, reveals some study of feminine psychology, some interest in the variations of the sexual pattern, even at one time a strong attraction towards illicit unions between European men and Asiatic women, but no shred of evidence survives of any amorous experience more moving than a drawing-room flirtation, while there is much evidence that he shrank from intimacy with women, other than the two who fixed the base of the family square.

Throughout the cooler half of the year, from November to April, the four lived happily together, in a square brick-built bungalow at Lahore. It differed from twenty others only in standing isolated in a dusty compound, because the

Kiplings had progressive notions that insects brought disease, and that shrubberies too near a house brought insects. The neighbours called the bungalow 'Bikanir House' because its surroundings reminded them of the Great Indian Desert. Here 'the Pater' had his workroom filled with the tools and patterns and materials of his many arts. Mrs Kipling was an expert housekeeper, and noted for inducing her native servants to keep a standard of cleanliness rare in India in those days.

Rudyard's room was devoted to literature and, after Trix's arrival, to the joint study of English poetry. The two were continually reading and rhyming, with some sharp but helpful criticism from their mother who had an ear for a false rhythm or a false sentiment. She pruned Rudyard's verses as effectively as she eliminated Trix's schoolgirl clumsiness; he was trained into terseness of style, and she into elegance of figure. In the evenings, if he could find an hour, she taught him to dance; and in the mornings the two young people went riding – Rudyard taught Trix to ride. Poor as was his eyesight, he took pains with his riding and even played a little polo, in spite of his parents' prohibition, when time permitted.

Soon his directors began to send him off as a special reporter on public events. In March 1884 he went to Patiala State, in the train of Lord Ripon the Viceroy, and wrote home with gusto about the splendours of princely hospitality. Even a journalist, at such a time, had horses and a carriage, then actually an elephant, placed at his disposal. As a newspaperman it pleased him that he forestalled his rivals in getting off a despatch by riding thirty miles at night, across country, on a borrowed horse. This starlit ride was to provide him with an incident for *The Naulahka*.

It gratified his sense of responsibility, on this expedition, to be offered – and of course to refuse – more than one bribe from agents of Indian princes. One such affair he described, with gusto, and perhaps with some heightening of colour, in a letter to his Aunt Edie. He was invited into the room of an

Afghan *sirdar* at Lahore and was, he said, baldly invited to help himself to a bundle of bank-notes as an inducement to use the influence of his newspaper on the *sirdar*'s behalf. When he indignantly replied that he was not a *bunnia* but an English *sahib*, the *sirdar* changed his ground.

Finally he blurted out that the English were fools and didn't know the value of money but that 'all *sahibs* knew how to value women and horses'. Whereupon he sent a small boy into an inner chamber and, to my intense amusement, there came out a Cashmiri girl that Moore might have raved over. She was very handsome and beautifully dressed but I didn't quite see how she was to be introduced into an English household like ours. I rather lost my temper and abused the Khan pretty freely for this last piece of impudence and told him to go to a half-caste native newspaper-walla for what he wanted.

The third temptation was that Rudyard should take his pick of a string of horses, such beauties that, he admitted, his resolution began to waver. However, he concluded: 'I explained very gravely that I wasn't going to help him a bit and he ought to have known better than to "blacken an Englishman's face" in the way he had done'. The interview ended amicably over a cup of coffee which, he was pleased to find, contained no poison after all.[8]

In May the family moved to the Hills, leaving him to face the dismal, feverish, hot weather again. For six months there would be nothing to relish but the dwindling company at the Club. At best, he and his father would sustain one another at Bikanir House; and worse would be the long weeks when he was alone with fever, sleeplessness, and nightmares. Eighty-four was worse than eighty-three; it was a cholera year at Lahore. 'Professional nurses had not been invented, the men sat up with the men and the women with the women. The station had eleven cases in a white community of seventy, and thought it lucky that only four died.'[9] Later in the season Rudyard was laid low with gastric pains and was saved from collapse by his bearer, who dosed him with drugs compounded of opium, drugs that cured his stomach and troubled his dreams. This hot season was worse than the last because he felt his separation from the family square. The other three were at Dalhousie, a cheaper hill-station than Simla, and better suited to their slender purse. For one month he joined them, and returned to the Plains with the manuscript of *Echoes*, a volume of imitations and parodies in verse, written by himself and Trix. Most were humorous mock-heroic trifles, but one or two (among them the poem called 'Failure' which has already been quoted) were serious exercises in the style of contemporary writers. The book was printed at the *Civil and Military* office in November, and received some kindly notices from reviewers. When the first issue, a very small one, was sold out, there was even an inquiry from a Calcutta publisher about a new edition. The parodies, especially those of Robert Browning, are remarkably facile and show a neat sense of varieties in rhythm, but none of them has been thought worth preserving in the popular collections of Kipling's work. *Echoes* and the articles he wrote for his newspapers were beginning to attract a little notice in India, among the well-informed. Most of his work was still anonymous journalism, and he used several pen-names for the articles he was beginning to contribute to down-country journals.

Rudyard Kipling to Miss Edith Macdonald

Lahore, Nov. 21st, 1884

Dearest Auntie,

The beginning of your last letter cut me to the core of my somewhat leathery conscience; for, as a matter of fact, I haven't sent you a line since you acknowledged the receipt of *Echoes* and so wildly mistook the dedication thereof. No dear I did *not* write those verses for Flo, and if I had should certainly not have sent you a duplicate. Pope was the only man who ever did that and he came to a bad end. I must confess that at first I was a good deal hurt at the mistake but accidents will occur in the best regulated families and I suppose your error was one of 'em. By the way that book has been most favourably noticed all round India and the whole edition is sold out. *The World* too was good enough to give me a nice little notice and I'm proportionately pleased. There was only one paper – The *Indian Review* that cut 'em up savagely and by way of showing that I bore no malice I cut out the slashingest parts and put 'em into the adver- tisement – the consequence was all the world and his wife when they heard that the poems were vicious sent in orders for the book and we scored hugely.

Like you I've been writing a story in my leisure. It has only taken me three months and is only six pages long but I've never fallen in love with any tale of my own fashioning so much – not that it has any merit. I'm trying to work it off on some alien paper to get myself pice thereby. Now that I'm allowed to write to any rag I please I find that I can always get a few odd pounds a month for myself apart from my screw and incidentally can get myself a little bit known in our small world out here. This is an empty headed sort of letter I'm afraid but there's really nothing to write about except the weather and crops – and they won't interest you. My Love to Aunt Louie and Uncle Alfred Baldwin – It's curious to think, how little I've ever seen of the two – and my salaams to Stanley. I'd give something to be in the Sixth at Harrow as he is, with a University Education to follow.[10]

At the end of 1884 a new Viceroy, Lord Dufferin, arrived in India, an event which proved to be of personal interest to the Kiplings. Obscure hitherto, and not ranking high in the Anglo-Indian hierarchy, they soon found themselves exalted into viceregal society. The first event of Lord Duf- ferin's term of office was his ceremonial reception of the Amir Abdurrahman in March 1885 at Rawalpindi, where Rudyard was special correspondent for his paper. The Fron- tier had been remarkably quiet since the close of the Second Afghan War in 1881 and the new Amir, a formidable auto- crat, had proved a staunch ally to the British. Nevertheless it was a diplomatic triumph to persuade him to pay a state

visit to the Viceroy, who made preparations for his entertainment on a splendid scale. A city of marquees was
erected and lavishly furnished for the Viceroy's camp, and a
long programme of ceremonies, reviews, and festivities was
arranged. All went well except the weather, which was
abominable, a constant downpour of drenching rain; and all
was described at length by Rudyard for the *Pioneer* and the
Civil and Military. Kipling was among those who went on
to Peshawar and nine miles farther to Fort Jumrood at the
mouth of the Khyber Pass, to attend the formal reception
of the Amir at the frontier post. While waiting some days
at Jumrood, Kipling wandered into the Pass, turning back
only when a tribesman 'took a pot-shot' at him. This was his
first and last experience of the North-West Frontier.[11]

He was by no means ignorant of the Central Asian problem, because for months past Wheeler had kept him grinding away at translating Russian newspaper reports. (In those
days many Russian newspapers were issued in French.) Rudyard's articles on Afghanistan and its neighbours attracted
notice and he remarked, with mixed pride and annoyance,
that the London *Times* appropriated one of these articles
without acknowledgement.*

At the height of the festivities at Rawalpindi all Asia was
thrown into panic by the news that the Russians had made
a calculated aggression against Afghanistan, invading the
Amir's territory at Penjdeh in his absence. But the Amir
and Lord Dufferin faced the crisis with equanimity, and it
was considered an achievement for Dufferin that he concluded the proceedings at Rawalpindi with assurances from
the Amir of a firm front against Russian penetration. The
tension was relaxed, Dufferin returned in triumph, and even
young Rudyard won some credit as a useful, well-informed
journalist.

Though he had completed his task, he suffered for it; the

---

* To readers of Kipling's collected works, the Rawalpindi Durbar
is best remembered for the final story in the *Jungle Book* ('Soldiers
of the Queen').

hard work and the bad weather wore him out. His eyes were giving him trouble and he slept badly, with nightmares of endless columns marching in the rain. The rhythm of 'Boots, boots, boots, boots, moving up and down again', to the tune of 'John Brown's Body', drummed itself into his memory and lay dormant there for years. He got his needed holiday in May when the chance came of an adventurous trip from Simla up the Himalaya-Tibet road that loops and twists across the screes and the fertile valleys, through forest-belts of deodar, to the high mountain ranges that command the gorges of the Sutlej. The party consisted of young Kipling, a man in the Public Works Department named De Brath with his newly wedded wife, their servants from down-country, and relays of hill-coolies to carry baggage. They rode on ponies and spent the night at the wayside dâk-bungalows – mere huts – provided by the Government at the regular stages. Kipling found himself odd man out in what was almost a honeymoon party and was envious of his companions' happiness. On the journey the wife coyly admitted that she was in the family way, a felicitous event that Kipling remembered to use in *The Story of the Gadsbys*.

The two men were sadly out of condition for mountain marching. 'I feel,' wrote Kipling in his diary, 'as if hot irons were stuck down my marrow bones.' On 1 May they reached Mahasu, lay on the grass watching the eagles fly in the valley below them, and felt the strength flowing back into their limbs in the mountain air, where idleness was a blessed luxury. On the fourth day's march they climbed from the Mutiani Pass * to Narkunda with its long view of the high ranges, then dropped three thousand feet from the forests of deodar to the poppy-fields about Kotgarh, a solitary mission-station, forty miles from the nearest relief, and here they rested two days while De Brath took photographs and Kipling studied the ways of the missionary, 'the queerest little devil you ever saw'. The chief compensation Kipling could

* Now usually spelt Mathiana. Kipling spells the name Kotgarh four different ways in a few pages of diary.

find for such a secluded life was the beauty of the strong, unveiled hill-women, always loaded with ornaments of uncut turquoise. 'I should like to be padre in these parts,' he wrote.

After a further march of two days and a gruelling climb to Baghi (9,000 feet), Kipling rather reluctantly turned back towards Simla, the only *sahib* now in his little caravan. Near Narkunda, going on alone he was a little disconcerted to meet a family party of bears, the bad-tempered black bears of the Himalaya, 'all talking at the tops of their voices'. He 'thought of Elisha the Tishbite and bolted like blazes. Hadn't seen a bear loose before.'[12]

On this day [he wrote] my servant embroiled himself with a new quartette of coolies and managed to cut the eye of one of them. I was a few score miles from the nearest white man, and did not wish to be hauled before any little Hill Rajah, knowing as I did that the coolies would unitedly swear that I had directed the outrage. I therefore paid blood-money, and strategically withdrew – on foot for the most part because 'Dolly Bobs' [his grey pony] objected to every sight and most of the smells of the landscape. I had to keep the coolies who, like the politicians, would not stay put, in front of me on the six-foot-wide track, and, as is ever the case when one is in difficulties, it set in to rain. My urgent business was to make my first three days' march in one – a matter of thirty odd miles. My coolies wanted to shy off to their village and spend their ill-gotten silver. On me devolved the heart-breaking job of shepherding a retreat. It did me great good, and enabled me to put away bottles of strong Army beer at the wet evening's end in the resthouse. On our last day, a thunderstorm, which had been at work a few thousand feet below us, rose to the level of the ridge we were crossing and exploded in our midst. We were all flung on our faces, and when I was able to see again I observed the half of a well-grown pine, as neatly split lengthwise as a match by a pen-knife, in the act of hirpling down the steep hillside by itself. The thunder drowned everything, so that it seemed to be posturing in dumb show, and when it began to hop – horrible vertical hops – the effect was of pure D.T.[13]

Simla was again the hill-station chosen by the Kiplings

for the hot season of 1885. They could afford it, since Mrs
Kipling had been earning money with her pen, and Rudyard joined them for a long visit, as special correspondent
for his paper, at a respectable salary. It was his duty to describe the annual spectacle of an Empire ruled from a remote
and almost inaccessible village, seven thousand feet above
the Indian Plains.

As a hill-station, the history of Simla went back to the
eighteen-twenties. In the middle of the town was a building
like a Swiss chalet which had been occupied by an early
Governor-General, and had long since been converted by a
viceregal chef into Peliti's Grand Hotel. There had been no
carriage-road to Simla until the eighteen-fifties when Lord
Dalhousie projected the Himalaya-Tibet Road as one of his
far-reaching lines of communication. Till then there were
no wheeled vehicles in Simla, but only *jampans*, or litters for
the ladies, carried by relays of coolies. In Lord Lytton's time
a stretch of level road, the Ladies' Mile, was constructed
round the foot of the hill called Jakko which commands the
town and, thereafter, 'rickshaws' began to replace the more
cumbrous *jampans*. Still, the steepness of the slopes restricted road-making and building.

The Viceroy's palace was a cramped, inconvenient,
shooting-lodge named 'Peterhoff', where the English ladies'-
maids complained at being obliged to share bedrooms,
where the secretaries and A.D.C.s were parked out in neighbouring cottages, and where an extension for a ballroom
meant that visitors stepped out from front-door and side-
door alike on to the edge of a precipice. All the houses of
the town were in imminent danger of slipping away down
the *khud* in the landslides that occurred every wet season,
when thirty or forty inches of rain might be expected. Yet it
was the wet season, July and August, that filled Simla with
refugees from heat and fever in the Plains. Lucky were they
who could spend six or seven months in the Hills, from
April which was bright and cold until October when Simla
had the finest climate in the world.

The Government of India, inheriting the tradition of those martial rulers, the Great Moguls, was a marching camp. The Viceroy was accustomed to carry with him his Sirdar and his Divan of Councillors, to make progresses of his realm, to receive and to answer petitions wherever he might be. In the vast spaces of India Simla was no more remote than Calcutta. A mobile administration, not yet swathed in red tape, nor hampered by parliamentary controls, was as efficient in one place as in another. Efficient or not, it was from Simla that the Indian Government was administered, in days of strong personal rule, for six or seven months in the year. There the Viceroy exercised his mighty authority, shouldered his crushing responsibility, met his daily council, received envoys, summoned his vassals the provincial governors and ruling princes to audience, and managed all through a civil and a military secretary, a dozen A.D.C.s and a corps of messengers, the red-uniformed *chaprassies*, who were believed, by Indian gossips, to wield untold influence. The Commander-in-Chief too had his establishment, a rival military court, with its secretaries, A.D.C.s, and *chaprassies*, at 'Snowdon' on a rather distant hillside. Humbler, but by no means unimportant, was the summer establishment of the Lieutenant-Governor of the Punjab, in a converted villa which had been decorated by Lockwood Kipling and his pupils.

From a very early time there was a legend of fast life in Simla. Perhaps it was at the end of the Mutiny, when the revolt had ebbed far away into Central India and the hill-stations were full of wounded officers enjoying their convalescence, that the town won its reputation for gaiety. Other hill-stations were just as blest with climate and scenery, but they were dull, while Simla had the glamour of a court. Even more, it was described by prudish Victorians as a haunt of gilded luxury, a 'Capua in the Hills', and quite unjustly. But the presence of the Viceroy with his circle of young aides, he a nobleman of high rank and they often sprigs of the peerage, gave it some social importance, while for quite other reasons it abounded with place-hunters and fortune-hunters. It was an old joke in India, long before the Kiplings' day, that grass-widows flocked to Simla, not altogether heartbroken at the prospect of staying there six months while their husbands must be content with thirty or sixty days' leave from the Plains. 'Simla is full of pretty girls', wrote Lockwood Kipling, 'and has a strong light-brigade of sportive matrons of all ages. I never go near a dance, but I hear the nicest possible girls sit out in rows.'

The interest of life in Simla was its dual character, as a political headquarters and a pleasure resort. Very hard slogging work was done there, especially if there was a stiff Viceroy; the gay life flourished when there was a society leader in the Viceroy's seat.

The second season that Rudyard spent at Simla, 1885, was the first year of Lord Dufferin's rule. The newcomer was a wealthy, sophisticated *grand seigneur*, equally compounded of Irish charm and worldly wisdom. A traveller, a scholar, a wit, he had governed Canada, led an embassy to the Sultan of Turkey, given Egypt a constitution, done everything, met everyone, been everywhere; and his wife, celebrated in verse by three poets, was that rarity, a Governor's wife who strengthened her husband's hand. Nevertheless, she was a little taken aback at Simla. 'Peterhoff', she said, was the smallest house that she had ever lived in. She and her husband were too genuine and too courteous to stand on ceremony or to let their lives be regulated by the rules of precedence to which middle-class officials give such weight, but they had to distribute their favours. Lady Dufferin calculated that she entertained 640 guests to dinner in a season, in twelve large parties and twenty-five small parties; she invited 250 guests to each of her six evening receptions. To the large parties she must invite by seniority; at her small parties she could choose for herself, and need not be bored by high-ranking mediocrities. She soon discovered that the art-teacher and his family from Lahore were worth cultivating. One connexion was Lockwood's sketching-class,

which Lady Helen, the Viceroy's daughter, attended. The
Viceroy would drop in to talk art and letters with Lockwood, and would stay to enjoy Mrs Kipling's conversation.
'Dullness and Mrs Kipling cannot exist in the same room,'
he used to say. Furthermore, Trix, in her second season, was
an acknowledged beauty, a breaker of hearts, and an expert
dancer. She had talent for writing both verse and prose, and
was an accomplished amateur actress. When she also took
the fancy of Lord Clandeboye, the Viceroy's son and
A.D.C., it was rather more than the Dufferins approved. One
day the Viceroy called on Mrs Kipling to discuss this dangerous development. 'Don't you think, Mrs Kipling, your
daughter should be taken to another hill-station?' 'Don't
you think, your Excellency, that your son should be sent
home?' It was Clandeboye who went, and Trix who remained. The Viceroy, though defeated, was no less friendly.
One day he dropped in, unheralded, at 'The Tendrils', the
Kiplings' Simla lodging, and was turned away by the servants because the family was out, a rebuff that this autocrat
accepted meekly enough.[14]

The Kiplings had now been brought into the inner ring
of Simla society, to the disgust, no doubt, of many social
climbers with better official qualifications. Mrs Kipling's wit,
Mr Kipling's range of knowledge, Miss Kipling's charm and
lightness of foot, were the factors that brought about this
social triumph. Young Rudyard as yet had less to offer to the
social feast. It embarrassed him a little that he was at Simla
on business, hired to write up the social functions he attended; pleased, though, to earn a good salary and to spend
all July and August in the Hills. 'The boy has taken enthusiastically, all at once, to dancing,' wrote Lockwood Kipling to a friend, 'and being determined to do it well, bids
fair to be a very good dancer. His proprietors told him, as he
is going to Simla to represent his paper, that he must waltz
well; so what we at home couldn't persuade him to like became a duty (an odd, but really very necessary sort of duty)
and he has gone in for it heartily.'[15]

R.K.—6

What a wealth of social life there was in Simla! There was Christ Church, where Lady Dufferin played the organ and trained the choir. But the Kiplings were no great churchgoers, though Lockwood was so obliging as to design frescoes for the walls. There was the amateur dramatic club; Simla was always renowned for theatricals organized for many years by Lord William Beresford, the Military Secretary.* This was a field where talents would not lie hidden, and soon it was discovered that the boy from the *Civil and Military* could dash off the wittiest of prologues in verse which his sister would recite to perfection.

There was the Club: there was the public assembly-room at Benmore; there was polo at Annandale, the only flat green space in Simla; there was Peliti's, almost a continental café; there was the *tonga*-office in the Mall, with its bustling commerce of jaded faces coming up from the Plains, and fresh full-blooded faces returning to their duty. There were rides on sure-footed hill-ponies, every cavalier attending a lady's rickshaw; and for Rudyard there was tea in the cool dusk, beside a roaring log-fire, in the company of the other three.

Rudyard Kipling to Miss Edith Macdonald

North Bank, Simla. July 30th, 1885

I'm here at Simla with the Mother and Trix as Special Correspondent for the Civil and Military Gazette. I told you that for my work at the Durbar they raised my screw to £420 English or £35 a month. For that sum I try to give my paper as near to £40 a month of editorial notes; reviews; articles and social Simla letters. That in itself is fairly lively work and – tho' this may sound strange to you – entails as much riding, waltzing, dining out and concerts in a week as I should get at home in a lifetime. Then I have been working on Indian stories for other papers – notably the *Pioneer* which has professed its willingness to take anything I might choose to send. I've sent them a mixed assort-

---

*Lockwood Kipling hinted in a letter that Beresford was the original of 'John Wonder' in 'A Germ-destroyer'.

ment of verses; and some prose stuff. All of which have taken
the public's somewhat dense soul and been largely quoted. Also
the *Calcutta Review* has written very sweetly about a poem of
mine – in blank verse – which appears in the August number,
and is going to put in a long ghost story of a wholly novel type.
Like the Quarterlies the C.R. isn't much read but it gives one a
certain amount of prestige to have a foot in it.

Further I have really embarked to the tune of 237 foolscap
pages on my novel – Mother Maturin – an Anglo-Indian
episode. Like Topsy 'it growed' while I wrote and I find myself
now committed to a two volume business at least. It's not one
bit nice or proper but it carries a grim sort of a moral with it
and tries to deal with the unutterable horrors of lower class
Eurasian and native life as they exist outside reports and reports
and reports. I haven't got the Pater's verdict on what I've done.
He comes up in a couple of days and will then sit in judgement.
Trixie says its awfully horrid; Mother says its nasty but powerful and I know it to be in large measure true. It is an unfailing
delight to me and I'm just in that pleasant stage where the
characters are living with me always. The Parents say 'publish
it at home and let it have a chance'. I hold that India would be
the better place and have already received one offer for the book
from an Indian Paper. A few years ago one Proprietor offered
My Mother Rs 1,000 for an Anglo-Indian story. If he renews
the offer to the son I close at once and Mother Maturin,
whatever her after fate, shall appear in weekly parts. Then
maybe, I might be able to struggle home for six weeks with
what I've got already. Fancy six whole weeks at home.[16]

In 1885, as in 1883, the Kiplings spent part of the season
staying at North Bank with James Walker who made his
home in Simla. Another friend who often entertained them
was the head of the agricultural department, Edward Buck,
a member of the Viceroy's council and therefore a powerful
ally. Buck was a Simla resident of long standing and a repository of Simla lore. He had bought from Allan Hume,
the founder of the Indian National Congress, the house in
which Madame Blavatsky produced the manifestations that
made her world-famous. It was in 1879, three years before
Rudyard came to India, that Buck had exposed her methods

and ridiculed her new cult with its miraculous messages that dropped from the ceilings written on palm-leaves, and its tea-cups materialized under bushes in the garden. Lockwood Kipling had attended these seances, and quietly observed that Madame Blavatsky was 'one of the most interesting and unscrupulous impostors' he had ever met.'[9] Many Anglo-Indians were more credulous about the 'teacup creed', among them A. P. Sinnett, the editor of the *Pioneer*, who introduced more theosophist propaganda into its columns than his colleagues approved.

Simla always abounded in eccentrics: mystics and psychopaths and nymphomaniacs. The most celebrated courtesan of the century, Lola Montez, began her career at Simla. The older residences had their ghosts, especially the house called Alice's Bower (which also belonged to Buck), the traditional scene of the episode described in Kipling's 'Lispeth'. Even more spooky was the jeweller's shop kept by A. M. Jacob, the 'healer of sick pearls'. No one knew who he was or where he came from. Some said he was a Russian spy, but, spy or no, he was a conjurer and hypnotist, who bought and sold jewels with an air of mystery that enabled him to outwit most customers. There was much buying and selling in Simla, especially of house property. Another Simla landlord was Major Goad, whose son, Horace Goad, was well known in the Kiplings' day as the smartest police officer in the Punjab. He was 'supposed to have the gift of invisibility and executive control over many Devils'. His reputation with the natives provided Rudyard with 'copy' for several stories.

There were thirty or forty thousand Indian natives at Simla in the season, half of them plainsmen who had come up with their masters because the hillmen were reputed bad servants. The Simla bazaars were rookeries of wooden chalets, piled high on the steepest slopes, teeming with sojourners from all the races in India, alive with intrigue and rumour. As Kipling wrote, some years later, in *Kim*, a man who knows his way there can defy all the police of India's summer capital; so cunningly does verandah communicate with verandah, alley-way with alley-way, and bolt-hole with bolt-hole. Here live those who minister to the wants of the glad city – jhampanis who pull the pretty ladies' rickshaws by night and gamble till the dawn; grocers, oil-sellers, curio-vendors, fire-wood dealers, priests, pickpockets, and native employees of the Government: here are discussed by courtesans the things which are supposed to be profoundest secrets of the India Council; and here gather all the sub-sub-agents of half the native states.[17]

The season that the four Kiplings spent together led to the production of a family magazine called *Quartette*, which they persuaded their friends of the *Civil and Military Gazette* to issue as a Christmas Annual, at the end of the year. It contained the first two stories by Rudyard which he thought worthy of preserving in the collected editions of his later life, 'The Phantom Rickshaw' and 'The Strange Ride of Morrowbie Jukes', both of them tales of horror written markedly in the manner of Edgar Allan Poe. 'The Phantom Rickshaw' has some claim to consideration as a study of hallucination, the first and not the weakest of the many tales of psychopathic states which he was to publish. His later comment on it was: 'Some of it was weak, much was bad and out of key; but it was my first serious attempt to think in another man's skin'. It is well worth reading today. 'Morrowbie Jukes' was a grotesque, an expedition into the half-world of Indian life, far away from 'Levées and Government House Lists, past Trades' Balls – far beyond everything and everybody you ever knew in your respectable life'. In September 1884, a whole year before the publication of *Quartette*, he had written one sketch of life in an opium den, 'The Gate of the Hundred Sorrows', which showed amazing precocity. Since then he had immensely widened his range of knowledge and interest. On 7 March 1885 he noted in his diary that the notion first dawned on him of the book that he meant to be his masterpiece. For years he worked at it, accumulating material, but the book never crystallized. It remained in solution in his notebooks, an unwritten masterpiece. All Kipling's friends waited anxiously for *Mother Maturin* which was the hobby of his remaining years in India.

One of the channels by which he penetrated the underworld was Freemasonry, a system which gratified both his craving for a world-religion and his devotion to the secret bond that unites the 'Sons of Martha', the men who bear the burden of the world's work. Since first he came to India, the land of caste, in which the English *sahibs* had followed Indian custom by forming themselves into a caste as restricted as any other, he had been fascinated by the limbo that lay between and beneath caste-rules. Freemasonry was a cult for adult responsible males, a cult that transcended all castes and sects. In 1885, when still below the proper age, Kipling was admitted to the Lodge, 'Hope and Perseverance, No. 782 E.C.', at Lahore, because they wanted a secretary; and, he said, they got a bad one. In caste-ridden India Freemasonry was the only ground on which adherents of different religions could meet 'on the level'. 'I was entered,' wrote Kipling, 'by a member of the Brahmo Somaj (Hindu), passed by a Mohammedan, and raised by an Englishman. Our tyler was an Indian Jew.'[18]

Rudyard Kipling to Miss Margaret Burne-Jones

[It was an old nursery joke between them that each addressed the other by the name of 'Wop'.]

Sunday. Lahore, Sept. 26th, 1885

Dear Wop,

Now how am I to tackle your letter properly : throwing in the 'dear me how interesting' at the proper time. I will e'en turn it upside down and work backwards. Para. two from the butt end asks me if I know *The City of Dreadful Night. Do* I know it? Oh Wop! Wop! What a question.

Furthermore, did I not, one month ago, spend one weary weary night on the great minar of the Mosque of Wazir Khan, looking down upon the heat tortured city of Lahore and seventy

thousand men and women sleeping in the moonlight: and did
I not write a description of my night's vigil and christen it 'The
City of Dreadful Night'. Go to – go to Uncle Crom and ask
him for a copy of that article ...

Lahore. Friday, December 18th, 1885, 10 in the morning.

Still working by lamplight with a general impression that I've
been doing nothing else for the past thirty six hours. ... 'This
morning' was *Quartette* cleared away at five before the dawn
had broken and when the rain was coming down hard ... In my
bedroom I remember Chalmers the Scotch foreman and his
forty thieves and wondered what the end would be – wondered
so much that I left the house secretly and plashed over to the
press. As I thought, the men were on the verge of mutiny – saying they wouldn't work any more and C. was tearing his hair
over the advertisements. Ram Dass said he was cold and hungry
and eyed the brandy bottle. Now a man – any man except an
assistant editor – when he works overtime is paid for his labour
but there is no law which enforces his working all night – and
that was just what I meant my friends to do.

And what a mad night it was – Something went wrong with
the two colour title page. The type in 'Civil and Military Gazette'
was worn out and wouldn't come up properly. With gum and
bits of paper and paste and brown paper I 'packed the lay' with
these lily fingers. Stuck bits of paper behind the piece of paper
that is pressed against the type in order to bulge out the paper
into the face of the worn letters. I don't know whether that's
clear enough to your mind. It was a long and dirty job and I got
foully mired with the droppings of candle ends and paste.
Chalmers was correcting proofs of advertisements, standing over
the men to see they did it – and I assure you that by the inadequate candlelight and under the hands of asinine Punjabis
proofs were uncommon queer. As soon as I got the title page
moderately decent – it looks pretty well but a practised eye
could tell I'd been 'faking it' I placed myself under Chalmers'
orders for the rest of the time. So when I wasn't correcting proofs
of superior saddles and watches and medicines – not the out-
pourings of my mighty genius – I was going round from shift to
shift and keeping 'em in a good temper and chaffing the men
who were smoking and patting the children – for that's all they

are in their tempers – on the back and telling 'em how such work was never before produced in India and now the Calcutta printers would think shame of themselves when they heard that Punjabis worked all night like elephants. Never have I seen Ram Dass toil as he did in the early hours of this morn and never did he handle his men so neatly.

We felt mighty proud and sleepy. I got to bed at 5.30 a.m. and was exceeding late for breakfast. 'My boy,' said the Pater, eyeing my weary eyes and dishevelled locks, 'if you would only get up in the mornings and do your work you'd be ever so much better.'

And now at the end of this awful pile of M.S. to ask you a favour, and a big one. In the course of your wanderings do you ever come to know anything about the Slade Art School and the students there – the female ones I mean of course. Circumstances over which I have not the smallest control prevent my going home and seeing the school itself. There is or was a maiden there of the name of Garrard – Flo Garrard and I want to know, *how* she is and what she is doing. So far as I know youre the only person who's likely to be able to find this out for me and if possible I want you as quietly and as unobtrusively as possible to learn all you can about the girl. It's a cool sort of request to make isn't it? And I shouldn't ha' done it, but that I am at my wits end for news in this particular instance. If I said that for *any* information you gave me you should have anything in my power to give 'even unto the half of my Kingdom' you would naturally be offended so I appeal humbly to the Wop of Albion to help me for old sakes sake. I only want to know if the girl looks well and – so far as your eyes can judge – happy. Thereafter if I can serve you in any way you know who to go to.

Yours expectantly,

The Wop of Asia.[19]

His curiosity to know what had become of Flo Garrard did not prevent Rudyard from forming other attachments. About the same time when he was writing this long letter, it happened that his father also wrote, and to the same address:

We have been immensely amused by his falling in love recently, a most wholesome sign that he is growing to his proper boyhood – which sounds more topsy-turvy than it really is. The Rev. Duke is an awful military chaplain at Mian Mir, who, I am told, preaches impossible sermons but who has a lovely daughter – like the pictures of Lady Hamilton says Ruddy.

These people do not join Lahore society in dances, garden parties etc., so the boy for 2 Sundays has driven five miles to attend Mian Mir church! None of us, by the way, ever go to church.

But for the storm that has raged all day Trixie was to have gone with him, for she wishes to see the paragon.

I have not seen her, but she ought to be nice to be worth a chill drive of 5 miles, an absurd sermon and a cold church with a company of rifle-clanking soldiers and about half a dozen other people for congregation. He is vastly funny about it and I cannot make out whether there is anything in it.[20]

Among the friends Kipling made in the world of free-lance journalism was Kay Robinson, a young man not much older than himself, who had recently come out from Fleet Street to be assistant editor of the *Pioneer*. Early in 1885 Robinson wrote some dog-Latin verses for his paper, sign-ing them 'K. R.', which many people assumed to be an anagram for 'R. K.', since at that time Kipling was produc-ing ephemeral verse and prose for many Indian journals. The bibliographers have identified between twenty and thirty pseudonyms which Kipling used in early life for his miscellaneous work; he wrote under the names of 'Nickson', 'Yussuf', 'Esau Mull', 'E. M.', as well as 'K.' and 'R. K.', but he did not use the anagram 'K. R.', and wrote to Robinson to apologize for the misapplication. A friendship sprang up, by correspondence, between the two young journalists. At the end of the year Kipling was asked to write a Christmas poem for the *Pioneer*, and produced the well-known 'Christ-mas in India', a doleful exile's lament. It aroused the deri-sion of Robinson who revelled in the Indian sunshine and even enjoyed the hot weather. Rather maliciously, and in some trepidation lest he should offend his ally at Lahore, Robinson wrote a parody, 'Christmas in England', and the two sets of verses appeared in the *Pioneer*, side by side,

signed respectively 'K. R.' and 'R. K.' Kipling was delighted,
and asked Robinson to visit him on his next short leave.

In the spring of 1886 Robinson spent some weeks with
the Kiplings at Lahore and preserved an account of his impressions which is the clearest description we possess of the
family square. The two women made the most mark on him,
Mrs Kipling for her lively wit and Trix for her statuesque
beauty. It was Trix who astonished him by her knowledge of
English poetry, while Rudyard revealed himself as still a
boy with a bad social manner, abrupt in his ways and so
untidy that, at the end of the day's work, his tropical suit
was spotted all over with ink-stains 'like a dalmatian dog'.[21]

As well as Kay Robinson, a friend of his schooldays re-
entered Kipling's life in 1886.

Rudyard Kipling to Lionel ['Stalky'] Dunsterville

Lahore, Jan. 30th, 1886

Dear Old Man –
        (On second thoughts – you unmitigated old Blackguard.)

I saw your name in the trooper list, but never a hint as to
your destination and I've been cursing you fluently ever since.
Of course if you had rheumatic fever I don't mind forgiving you
but the next time you drop into India in this casual manner just
you let me know, or the consequences will be serious.

So you're at Nassik are you. Hum! There's a big house on
the top of a hill there, where Proctor Sims the Engineer lives or
used to live – close to the river. Make a reverent pilgrimage
thither O my Son and reflect that in those walls did the Saintly
Gigger spend the fourth and fifth years of his life – many ages
ago. If you know P. Sims he'll tell you. A lovely spot is Nassik.
You know the rhyme of course –

> There was a young lady of Nassik
> Whose attire was graceful and classic
> For all that she wore
> Both behind and before
> Was a wreath of the roses of Nassik.

Sorry to find you haven't even a medal for your manly breast.
Do you know I believe, if in a weak moment Government gave

you such an article, you'd go and pop it somewhere – that is to say if you haven't outgrown our old instincts in the little study. Loss of *batta* is more serious. However you may get your chance of something festive up here. The Bonerwals have killed a man – a Colonel Hutchinson – and I fancy they will be expeditioned. *Nota Bene.* Never close with an Afghan. Plug at him from a distance. There's no glory if he sticks you and precious little if you pot him. I had an experience at Jumrood which brought this home to me. I stood afar off and heaved rocks at mine adversary like David did and providentially smote him on the mouth insomuch that he lost interest in me and departed. He had a knife and seemed to object to my going on foot towards the Khaiber. Narrow-minded sort of cuss who couldn't appreciate the responsibilities of journalism. That's been all the active service I've ever seen, and I didn't like it. I tried to go to Burma for the paper but I couldn't be spared. By the way did you see that poor Durey was killed by those swine? There's £1800 worth of education gone to smash and a good fellow with it.

Thine ever

Gigger.

P.S. Your handwriting is damnable. Take a lesson by mine.
P.S. Ain't Quartette thrilling – There's a 'Jenny say qwai' about that Phantom Rickshaw that positively haunts me. I have built up a reputation in the Punjab as a chartered libertine on the strength of it.[22]

'Stalky' Dunsterville had passed through Sandhurst into a line regiment with which he served in Malta and Egypt. He had seen much gaiety and sport, and had commanded men in the desert behind Suakin, though he had not fought in any of the fiercer battles in the Sudan campaign. But 'Stalky' could no longer lord it over 'Gigger' in the old style of Number Five Study, because 'Gigger' was an old hand while 'Stalky' was a newcomer in India. They were soon parted, when 'Stalky' was posted away to his regiment, the 20th Punjabis, at Amritsar.

Kipling, too, was sent away to Jammu, to report the installation of a new Maharajah of Kashmir. His most graphic columns dealt with the wild-beast fights staged for the public amusement, between pairs of buffaloes, fighting rams, and elephants.[23] Some squeamish critics have found these descriptions disgusting, though Kipling was chiefly concerned to point out how much sound and fury was released and how little damage was done, except when a buffalo charged the spectators. After this expedition, he returned to Lahore for the worst of the hot weather.

Rudyard Kipling to Miss Margaret Burne-Jones

Lahore, June 17th 1886

Do you know what hemicrania means? A half headache. I've been having it for a few days and it is a lovely thing. One half of my head in a mathematical line from the top of my skull to the cleft of my jaw, throbs and hammers and sizzles and bangs and swears while the other half – calm and collected – takes note of the agonies next door. My disgusting doctor says it's over work again and I'm equally certain that it rose from my suddenly and violently discarding tobacco for three days. Anyhow it hurts awfully – feels like petrifaction in sections and makes one write abject drivel.

I slept right round the clock on Tuesday night from 9.30 to 9.30 and was so delighted at having my rest I forgot to bother about the heat which is seasonable – too seasonable. Three soldiers died in Cantonments last night of heat apoplexy and they've been having a funeral nearly every day for a fortnight. But Tommy *is* so careless. He drinks heavy beer, and sleeps at once after a full flesh meal and dies naturally. Did I tell you a rather grim story of what I saw the other night when I went round the guards in Fort Lahore with the subaltern of the day. I'd been round often before but never on a night like this. It was pitchy black, choking hot with a blinding dust storm out. Fort Lahore is wickedly hot always as I've learnt to my cost before now. I went into the main guard at midnight (it marked 97° in the guardroom verandah) and I saw by the lamp light every man jack of the guard stripped as near as might be *sitting up*. They daren't lie down for the lives of 'em in heat like that. It meant apoplexy. However none of my men – the gunners are the ones I know most of have collapsed so far. Personally I'm in the lap of luxury. My bedroom even at midnight which I consider the hottest time of the twenty four hours never goes beyond 86° but that means six men are working night and day in relays to keep it cool. They are queer fellows my coolies. They talk to me in the evening and tell me about their crops and families. Half the year they cultivate and the other half they come into the cities and hire out as Punkah coolies. It's worth while petting the men who keep you cool. They have a child's weakness for sweets (serves 'em instead of flesh meat) and 3½d give them all oceans of sticky sweet cakes.[24]

It was not until August 1886 that he joined the family, at Simla. This was the season when Lord Clandeboye paid attention to Trix, and Rudyard moved in the same circle. Untidy he may have been, but the Viceroy now took notice of him, wondering – as everyone wondered – how he came to know so much, as if he had 'photographed the inmost councils of state'. Among his friends that season were two of the A.D.C.s, Lord Herbrand Russell, the Duke of Bedford's heir, and Captain Ian Hamilton of the Gordons, a rising young soldier. In his memoirs written in extreme old age Sir Ian Hamilton related that he sent one of Kipling's early stories home to some literary friends who tried it on William Sharp, the critic and poet. According to Hamilton Sharp shrank from it in horror. Old men's memories of youth are not always to be trusted, and Ian Hamilton's memory may have deceived him as to the date, but he goes on to say that when he went home, a year later in 1887, to stay with the Balfours at Whittinghame he found everyone in that intellectual stratosphere talking of the new prodigy from India. If so, they were two years ahead of the market.

It was in the cool weather of 1886–7 that Kipling, aged just twenty-one, began to produce the stories and verses that made him famous. He returned from Simla to find with delight that Stephen Wheeler was going home, exhausted by fever and the climate. Wheeler had kept his assistant's nose pretty well to the grindstone for the best part of four years, filling his time with routine work and discouraging his imaginative writing, but Kipling was thankful to his exacting chief and never regretted having earned his living the hard way. Wheeler taught him, he said,

that an order was to be obeyed at a run, not a walk, and that any notions of the fitness or unfitness of any particular kind of work for the young had better be held over till the last page was locked up for press.

In later years he and Wheeler were to meet again, and each was to do the other a service. For the present Kipling was relieved to see the last of him, and was delighted when Kay Robinson was sent up from Allahabad to be the new editor of the *Civil and Military*. Under Wheeler the paper had been dull, and Robinson was commissioned to 'put some sparkle into it'. He and his sparkling assistant drank a bottle of champagne together to inaugurate the livelier age. It was now August, the hottest of the hot weather, and they sat at work in singlet and cotton trousers, smoking perpetually, each with a fox-terrier at his feet – Kipling's 'Vic' as full of sparkle as his master. Robinson had worked for the London *Globe*, an evening paper with the special feature of a short middle-page article every day on some popular theme, that occupied the right-hand column and 'turned over' to finish on the following page. 'Turnovers' on the model of the *Globe* were to be the field for Kipling's talents in the new reign of Kay Robinson at Lahore. They must be topical, arresting, and short, restricted to 2,000 words, just the discipline in letters that Kipling needed. The best of them are still in print as *Plain Tales from the Hills*.

Kay was delighted with his new assistant, astonished at his abounding energy and wit. 'He had the buoyancy of a cork, he was bubbling over with poetry,' said Kay. 'If you want to find a man who will cheerfully do the work of three men, you must catch a young genius.' For a year they worked together at Lahore with happy enthusiasm and, knowing his man better, Kay discovered that he was not the hobbledehoy he seemed to be. When the cold weather came, and

'society' returned to Lahore, Kipling grew careful and correct
in his costume and showed a liking for feminine society. He
neither played whist (bridge was not yet invented) nor tennis, and now rarely took horse-exercise, but he was regular
at the dances. Strange to say, he avoided the Club, said Kay.
His conversation was so brilliant that he did not care to
show it off. There was a senior member at the Club who
disapproved of Kipling and persistently tried to snub him.
Though Kipling's power of repartee was so striking that he
always had the best of his exchanges with this curmudgeon
he disliked the atmosphere of ill-will, yet he was no shirker.
Kay was surprised at the chances and risks he encountered
to get 'copy' in the lowest quarters of the town in the midst
of communal riots; and, one night when some gay young
sparks invaded Kipling's room with the intention of ragging
him, Kipling leapt from his bed to confront them with a
revolver. The most remarkable thing about him, as Lord
Dufferin had noticed, was his mysterious faculty for assimilating local colour without apparent effort. He knew more
about the low life of Lahore than the police, more about the
tone of the regiments at Mian Mir than the chaplain. Kay
particularly remembered one of his confidants, a Pathan
called Mahbub Ali, 'indescribably filthy but with magnificent mien and features', who used to visit Kipling whenever he came to Lahore, with news of the unruly almost
unknown world of Central Asia beyond the Khyber Pass.
The cavalry subalterns were astonished at Kipling's knowledge of horses and steeple-chasing. 'Where does the youngster pick it all up?' asked the Veterinary Officer of Kay
Robinson in the Club.[25] Part of the answer is to be found in
his natural faculty, part in the fact that he was his father's
son. Few Englishmen knew India better, and few were more
generally loved and trusted than Lockwood Kipling, whose
name opened many doors.

The time had come for Kipling to launch a volume of
collected verse in a style which was popular, even traditional,
in Anglo-India.

There is always an under-current of song, a little bitter for the most part, running through the Indian papers. Sometimes a man in Bangalore would be moved to song, and a man on the Bombay side would answer him, and a man in Bengal would echo back, till at last we would all be crowing together like cocks before daybreak.[26]

So Kipling described the literary background of his first acknowledged book. The verses appeared in his newspapers, some under the heading of 'Bungalow Ballads', and then were reissued with the better title of *Departmental Ditties*. The book did not look like a book; it was part of the joke that he printed and bound it in the style and shape of a Government office file, tied up with a bow of the pink tape that is called 'red tape'. The first edition was immensely popular in India, soon sold out, and is now a rarity. Though issued without an author's name, there was little doubt who, in the small world of Anglo-India, had written these verses. Before the end of the year, a second edition, more conventional in form, and bearing the name of Rudyard Kipling, was issued by the firm of Thacker & Spink at Calcutta, who bought them outright from the author for five hundred rupees. Though some copies were offered for sale in London they attracted little attention outside India, as yet. These verses were topical in character and local in their appeal. Kipling himself had no illusions about *Departmental Ditties* which he regarded as frivolity.

They were made to ease off the perpetual strife between the manager extending his advertisements and my chief fighting for his reading-matter. They were born to be sacrificed. Rukh Din the foreman would say: 'Your potery very good, sir; just coming proper length to-day. One third column, just proper.'[27]

The author was sufficiently gratified when the critics compared them with Bret Harte's poems, which was not rating them high as poetry. Like Bret Harte's verses, the *Ditties* are largely echoes from other writers; some are imitations of W. M. Praed, W. S. Gilbert, or J. E. Fitzgerald; some are no more than family jokes. One light piece describing the

envy of a young girl for an older woman's popularity has
given pleasure to many readers:

> The young men come, the young men go,
>   Each pink and white and neat,
> She's older than their mothers, but
>   They grovel at Her feet.
> They walk beside Her *rickshaw*-wheels —
>   None ever walk by mine;
> And that's because I'm seventeen
> And She is forty-nine.

It can hardly be a coincidence that this verse was written
when Kipling's shy sister was seventeen, and his brilliant
talkative mother forty-nine years old. The book made its
name for the cynical comments on patronage and promotion
in the Anglo-Indian hierarchy. It was the talk of Simla in
the season of 1886 since everyone understood the allusions
and recognized the caricatures. Lockwood Kipling had the
satisfaction of hearing all sorts of complimentary things
about his son. 'Lord Dufferin, who frequently comes into our
sketching-room, professed to be greatly struck by the uncommon combination of satire with grace and delicacy, also
with what he calls the boy's infallible ear for rhythm and
cadence.' Another grandee, Sir Auckland Colvin, who was
himself a victim of the poet's satire, wrote him a 'most enthusiastic note'. And the Walkers, his employers, now
treated young Kipling as 'a spoilt child of the house' when
he came up to stay with them in Simla.

Towards the end of the year he made his first dent in the
protective crust of the London literary circle. Kay Robinson
had sent home eight review copies to friends in the Trade
and one attracted the attention of Andrew Lang, the writer
of a monthly article of literary gossip for *Longman's Magazine.* He gave *Departmental Ditties* a kind but condescending column of notice beginning with regret that the modest
author did not reveal his name. The book, he said, was a

quaint and amusing example of the variety of literature known
as Anglo-Indian verse. ... On the whole these are melancholy
ditties. Jobs and posts and pensions, and the wives of their neighbours, appear to be much coveted by Her Majesty's Civil Servants in India.

With relief, Andrew Lang turned away to Kipling's pretty
verses on 'Springtime in India' with their nostalgia for
springtime in England. This was what he found most admirable in *Departmental Ditties.* The first effect of Kipling's
work, here and in general, was shocking; he was regarded
as a cynical young man who laid bare the seamy side of
Indian life; but the first edition did not include the pieces
which have best stood the test of popular approval.*

The approval of the Viceroy and the grave councillors at
Simla was not a negligible start for a young man, though
satire is a dangerous weapon to flourish under an autocratic
Government. It is unjustified to suppose that Anglo-India
was a philistinish community with low literary standards,
since every prominent person in Simla had qualified for his
post by examination, and the best appointments were reserved for men with high academic honours. Yet, to versify
at Simla, even with a court jester's licence, was not a sufficient career.

Kay could not understand why Kipling was content to
stay in India, where his talents were hidden. Why did he
not go to London? Kipling's reply was that he thought it his
duty to serve seven years with the newspaper that had given
him his chance and had taught him his trade. He was
happy at heart and willing to suffer the misery of the hot
weather, even to take a sort of pride in his endurance of it,
for the sake of his work. The family square still made a
secure background to his life; the office – since Kay Robinson had come – was a place of joyful activity not of grinding routine. At Simla he felt himself to have penetrated the
arcana and to have his finger on the pulse of empire; at

* 'The Galley-Slaves', his valediction to India, appeared only in the
third edition, published in London in 1890.

Lahore he was absorbed in his study of the Indian underworld. His verses had won him a little modest fame; his
'turnover' articles for the *Civil and Military* were extending his powers, and in his own room at Bikanir House was
the mounting pile of sheets that were to make the *Book of
Mother Maturin*. Some day, he knew, he must leave home
and return to the literary world. A novel he read in the
autumn of 1886, *All in a Garden Fair*, by Sir Walter Besant,
proved unsettling and pointed out his next step though he
was not yet ready to take it.

This forgotten Victorian favourite had an obvious relation to the life of Rudyard Kipling. It is a pleasant tale of
three young rivals, who compete for the love of a girl they
have all known since a childhood spent in Epping Forest
(where Rudyard too had spent his happiest hours). The
young men grow up and separate. One of them goes into
the City where he quickly makes, and loses, a great fortune
by shady finance, thus sacrificing to Mammon his chance
of winning the prize of love. The second is a poet who first
starves in a London garret, then compounds with the world
by working as a journalist. Although preyed upon and
fleeced by unscrupulous editors, he wins a sufficient reputation to support his Art, and to this Art he dedicates his life.
The third lover goes to Shanghai on business, remains faithful to his love, and returns, at the end of the book, to win
her.

Just what lesson Kipling deduced from this simple story is
not at once apparent, beyond the obvious lesson that,
whether he wanted easy money, or literary fame, or his
first love, he must look for them in London not Lahore.
He was certainly not averse from money-making, and his
conduct when he did return to London suggests that his
notions of editors and publishers in Fleet Street were derived from the sharks who preyed upon the poet in Besant's
novel. Beyond that, some of the novelist's remarks about
the East sowed a seed of doubt about the utility of life in
India.

I have seen a great quantity of most interesting things [says 'Will' in the novel, as Rudyard might have said in real life]. I am living among a most remarkable people, whose ways are not our ways. ... Besides dancing, I have learned to ride, to talk without arguing, to smoke cigarettes, and to play whist. ... As for adventures, there are none as yet; as for work, it is as monotonous here as in England. I am like a knight who put on all his armour and went out in search of adventures and found none. I might as well have looked for them in the Chigwell Road.

Upon this revolutionary report, that life overseas might be as commonplace as life at home, Besant had a further comment to make in his novel, and made it with a mannerism that later critics have supposed peculiar to Kipling.

Which things are an allegory [wrote Besant]. There is a thing concerning colonial life which is little comprehended. It is that ideas change slowly out there. The things which change ideas are the new discoveries, the new theories, the new men which are continually turning up at home. We who stay at home are borne along, whether we like it or no, by the current; we change our thoughts, our faiths, our standpoint, with the change that goes on around us. What is wild Radicalism one day is mild Liberalism the next. But in the colonies it is not so. One takes out a stock of ideas and comes home again with them practically the same, and it is not till returning home again that one finds how great is the gulf which a few years have made.

We have Kipling's word for it in his autobiography, amply supported from his family letters, that this popular novel by a writer of the second rank was 'a revelation, a hope and strength' to him, about the time of his twenty-first birthday. He read and re-read it, and learned from it what he might achieve. Many a young man has got a first-rate idea out of a second-rate book. This idea was working at the back of Kipling's mind while he was writing weekly 'turnovers' for Kay Robinson at Lahore, and finding arguments for maintaining his corner of the family square a year or two longer. While the West began to pull at his heart-strings, at the string of ambition, he saw the Indian Empire in a clearer light: the gigantic bulk of native India, so complex, so rich with humanity, so remote from western understanding, so lovable, so helpless, was organized, modernized, protected, and cautiously moved forward into the path of progress by a corps of young English officials who gave to it their youth and health with no expectation of any reward beyond a bare livelihood. If India was being wickedly exploited, certainly they were not the exploiters. It could not be denied, by anyone who took the trouble to inquire, that they were giving India internal security, communications, precautions against famine, irrigation, afforestation, even the rudiment of an educational system, on a scale that no other country in continental Asia or Africa could approach. These young Englishmen had much to be proud of, and it was a matter of pride with Kipling to serve for seven years in this unselfish army.

Everyone who lent a hand to keep the machine running was a comrade. Idlers, critics, and reformers who wanted to tamper with the works, were treated with contempt. At Lahore in the hot weather one could see the engines running with the cowling stripped off; at Simla in the season one could divert oneself with satirical comment about the passengers on the top deck of the Ship of State. But these passengers could not hinder the relentless progress of the machine which was sustained by the labour of an anonymous, unthanked multitude of working officials, inspired by the public-school tradition which Kipling expressed in the phrase:

> The game is more than the player of the game,
> And the ship is more than the crew! [28]

So, he thought, it might drive on its course down the centuries. Nevertheless, as a connoisseur of personalities, it gave him pleasure to see at the head of affairs the slightly bored, slightly cynical figure of Lord Dufferin, who was so brightly aware that 'ideas changed slowly' at Simla, so convinced of the necessity to make the best of the second-rate. This was the background to *Plain Tales from the Hills*.

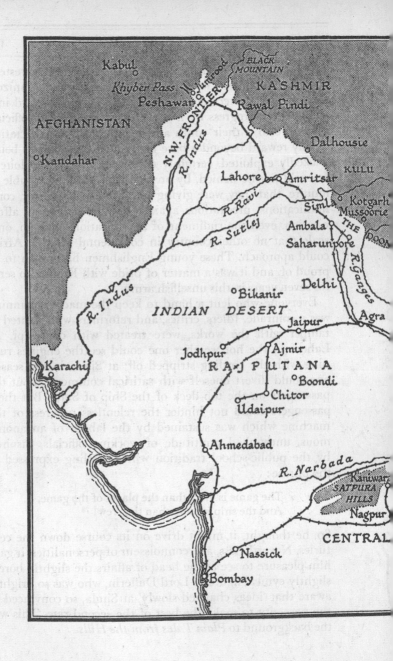

Kabul
Khyber Pass
Peshawar
N.W. FRONTIER
R. Indus
BLACK
MOUNTAIN
KASHMIR
Rawal Pindi
Jumrood
AFGHANISTAN
Kandahar
Dalhousie
KULU
Lahore Amritsar
R. Ravi
Simla Kotgarh
Mussoorie
R. Sutlej
Ambala
Saharunpore
THE DOON
R. Ganges
R. Indus
INDIAN DESERT
Delhi
Bikanir
Agra
Jaipur
Jodhpur Ajmir
RAJPUTANA
Karachi
Boondi
Chitor
Udaipur
Ahmedabad
R. Narbada
Kaniware
SATPURA
HILLS
Nagpur
CENTRAL
Nassick
Bombay

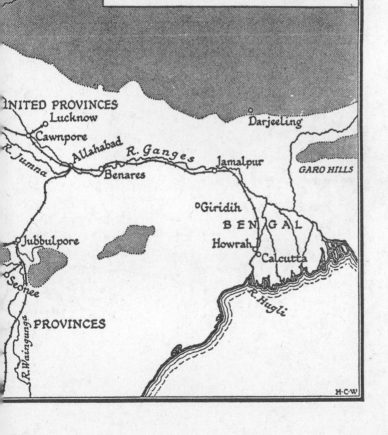

KIPLING'S INDIA

The Grand Trunk Road follows the line of the railway, approximately, from Allahabad to Peshawar.

Scale of Miles

0   100   200   300

Land above 1500 feet is shaded

UNITED PROVINCES

Lucknow

Cawnpore

R. Jumna

Allahabad

R. Ganges

Benares

Jamalpur

Darjeeling

GARO HILLS

Giridih

BENGAL

Howrah

Jubbulpore

Calcutta

Seonee

R. Hugli

R. Wainganga

PROVINCES

H·C·W

From Jobson's Amen (1914)

'Blessèd be the English and all that they profess.
Cursèd be the Savages that prance in nakedness!'
'Amen,' quo' Jobson, 'but where I used to lie
Was neither shirt nor pantaloons to catch my brethren by:

'But a well-wheel slowly creaking, going round, going round,
By a water-channel leaking over drowned, warm ground —
Parrots very busy in the trellised pepper-vine —
And a high sun over Asia shouting: "Rise and shine!"'

·   ·   ·   ·

'Blessèd be the English and all they make or do.
Cursèd be the Hereticks who doubt that this is true!'
'Amen,' quo' Jobson, 'but where I mean to die
Is neither rule nor calliper to judge the matter by:

'But Himalaya heavenward-heading, sheer and vast, sheer
    and vast,
In a million summits bedding on the last world's past —
A certain sacred mountain where the scented cedars climb,
And — the feet of my Belovèd hurrying back through Time!'

Simla and Allahabad
(1887–9)

EIGHTEEN EIGHTY-SEVEN was the year of *Plain Tales from the Hills*. Throughout the early months of the year Rudyard was working with Kay Robinson at Lahore. In the summer he again spent his month's leave with the family at Simla and, on returning to the Plains, began a new way of life. George Allen made the decision on a point which had often been discussed before, to bring his fledgeling genius to the more important office of the *Pioneer*, at Allahabad in the region now called the United Provinces, a change from Moslem to Hindu India. It was also a break with the family square, but that was not so formidable an event as it would have been three years earlier. Rudyard was twenty-two years old, and in appearance remarkably mature for his age. He was not now disposed to be desperately lonely and he prided himself on being a salted Anglo-Indian, nor was he without friends in Allahabad. His Simla patron, Sir Edward Buck, could introduce him to Professor S. A. Hill, a meteorologist in Government service, who had recently been appointed to Allahabad as professor of science at the Muir College. Aleck Hill was a quiet, burly man with a bushy dark beard. Except that he was a devoted amateur photographer (in that heroic age of dark-rooms, tripod-mountings, and patent developers) we can find little to record of him. His wife, Edmonia Hill (known as 'Ted'), was to play a principal part in Rudyard Kipling's life. She was a lively young American lady from Beaver, Pennsylvania, aged about thirty, with a broad plump face, a pretty snub nose, and a shock of dark curls coming down in a widow's peak on her brow.[1]

Towards the end of the year Mrs Hill met Rudyard, at the Allens' house, and wrote to her young sister who was still in Pennsylvania:

When we were seated at table and conversation was in full swing, my partner called my attention to a short dark-haired man of uncertain age, with a heavy moustache and wearing very thick glasses, who sat opposite, saying: 'That is Rudyard Kipling, who has just come from Lahore to be on the staff of the *Pi*. He is writing those charming sketches of the native states, *Letters of Marque*, which the *Pi*. is publishing.'

Mr Kipling looks about forty, as he is beginning to be bald, but he is in reality just twenty-two. He was animation itself, telling his stories admirably, so that those about him were kept in gales of laughter. He fairly scintillated, but when more sober topics were discussed he was posted along all lines. After dinner, when the men joined the ladies in the drawing-room, evidently the retiring young author had marked me for an American, and, seeking copy perhaps, he came to the fireplace where I was standing and began questioning me about my homeland. I am surprised at his knowledge of people and places. He is certainly worth knowing, and we shall ask him to dinner soon.[2]

The acquaintance quickly ripened but it was not until the following June that a close and daily association grew up between Rudyard and his new friend. During the cool weather of 1887–8 he was living a bachelor life at the Allahabad Club with his own horse and trap, and his Moslem servant, Kadir Baksh. There was a much larger European resident population at Allahabad than at Lahore and a less interesting native city. No longer 'a full half' of the managing staff of a country newspaper, he was a special reporter employed by the large organization of the *Pioneer*. Since one of his tasks was to edit its magazine supplement, the *Week's News*, he immediately offered to supply fiction from his own pen, at a cheap rate, in order to save the expense of buying the serial rights of established and costly authors. What he wanted was a wider spread of canvas for his teeming compositions and, modestly, he omitted to secure his copyright in the material he now turned out in profusion.

The 'turnovers' for the *Civil and Military* were discontinued, and the best of them were published as *Plain Tales from the Hills*, a few weeks after his meeting with Mrs Hill. He sent her a copy with a dedicatory verse: [3]

> Would they were worthier. That's too late –
> Framed pictures stand no further stippling.
> Forgive the faults.
>
> March '88
>
> To Mrs Hill
>
> From Rudyard Kipling.

Thirty-two of the *Plain Tales* had been printed in the *Civil and Military*; the remaining eight made their first appearance when the book was published, in January 1888. This time, there was no question of private distribution, and the book was released through the ordinary channels of the Trade by Thacker Spink & Co. of Calcutta. The Indian allotment was sold out rapidly, while the thousand copies despatched to London for the English market long remained on the publishers' shelves unnoticed. These stories, however, were so competent that they were bound to find their place; they were laconic, brilliant, versatile, knowing, cocksure, provoking, and sometimes scandalous. Above all, they were startling and that was a great merit in the decline of the Victorian age. Later, they were allowed by Kipling's admirers in England to fall into the second rank of popularity, but not so abroad. They translated well into French (as *Simples Contes des Collines*), perhaps because they are loaded with gallicisms, and in France they have always been rated high. They are essential to an understanding of Kipling's place in literature.

Written in haste and written to order, the stories are of uniform length, 2,000 to 2,500 words, that is to say, very short. The limitation of space to a column and a half in his newspaper obliged the author to compress his effects and to eliminate superfluous words. The style, to put it baldly, is that of the gossip-column. In good popular journalism today this conversational style is common, but what other popular journalism than Kipling's has never been allowed to run out of print for sixty years? Not only did he display a talent for finding 'copy' in unexpected places, he devised a way of working up the merest trifles, the tritest anecdotes, into stories, *contes*, that reminded well-read reviewers of Maupassant. Sometimes it was a court case at Lahore, sometimes a confidence whispered by his partner at a Simla Ball; a scrap of gossip from the Punjab Club; a yarn told by a tipsy soldier to impress a civilian; a beggar's hard-luck story; or, if nothing else was to hand, an anecdote from some old-fashioned book served up *réchauffé*. The tone was always that of smoking-room conversation, beginning and breaking off abruptly, interleaved with asides and cynical comments. These diversions, having served their purpose of focusing some point, were chopped off short with the catch-phrase, 'But that is another story', a phrase which caught on like an epidemic in the nineties. From Emerson, Kipling borrowed the device of heading every tale with a relevant scrap of original verse, and these poetical fragments reveal, even more clearly than the prose stories, his facility at getting the strongest effect from slight material.

The earliest in date of the *Plain Tales*, and one of the most powerful, is 'The Gate of the Hundred Sorrows', written before the author's nineteenth birthday. It has no plot, no climax, but conveys by word-painting the drugged, drowsy atmosphere of an opium-den. 'My friend, Gabriel Misquitta the half-caste, spoke it all, between moonset and morning, six weeks before he died.' It is one of six stories that deal with Indian low life, in the Eurasian borderland where loss of caste brings unavoidable penalties. Two more stories, of Indian domesticity within caste-rules, are told with deeper sympathy. Twenty-four stories, more than half the book, relate events in Anglo-Indian society, many of them in the viceregal circle at Simla. Four turn on the character of 'Mrs Hauksbee', a married woman living apart from her husband and able to manipulate affairs of state by social pressure. 'She was a little, brown, thin, almost skinny woman, with big, rolling violet-blue eyes, and the sweetest manners in the world.' [4] In two other stories the hero is the police-officer, 'Strickland', who 'held the extraordinary theory that a policeman in India should try to know as much about the native as the natives themselves. But this has done him no good in the eyes of the Indian Government.' [5] Nine of the stories are about army life, and in four of them there appear the group of three common soldiers, 'Mulvaney, Learoyd, and Ortheris', who were to become Kipling's most celebrated characters. As yet they were but lightly sketched and none of these early soldiers' tales ranks high in popularity, unless perhaps 'The Madness of Private Ortheris' (1888) with its cockney litany of home-sickness for London. 'I'm sick to go 'Ome – go 'Ome – go 'Ome. ... I'm sick for London again; sick for the sounds of 'er, an' the sights of 'er, and the stinks of 'er; orange-peel and has-phalte an' gas comin' in over Vaux'all Bridge.' Five or six of the stories have an uncanny twist, reminiscent of Edgar Allan Poe, and one, 'By Word of Mouth', is a convincing ghost-story. Four or five are farcical, with intimations of Kipling's taste for rather cruel practical jokes. Two of the stories deal with child-life and one of them, 'The Story of Muhammad Din', revealed that love and understanding of little children was already a dominant in Rudyard Kipling's character.

As an example of the technique that distinguishes *Plain Tales* from other contemporary short stories, I propose to examine the tale called 'False Dawn', which first appeared in the published book. It is an anecdote about a man who accidentally proposed to the wrong woman during the darkness and confusion of an Indian dust-storm. The misunderstandings of a night are relieved only by the coming of the dawn.

No man [the tale begins] will ever know the exact truth of this story; though women may sometimes whisper it to one another after a dance, when they are putting up their hair for the night

and comparing lists of victims. A man, of course, cannot assist
at these functions. So the tale must be told from the outside – in
the dark – all wrong.

Darkness is the prevailing tone and 'dark' the keyword of
the tale. After a sentence or two about jealousy between
sisters, Kipling begins to talk about a man called Saumarez
– never clearly described – and about his attachment to the
two Miss Copleighs.

> The Station wherein all these things happened was, though
> not a little one, off the line of rail, and suffered through want of
> attention. There were no gardens, or bands or amusements
> worth speaking of, and … people were grateful for small things
> to interest them.

It was at the beginning of the hot weather when most
people were moving away to the Hills, that 'we' – that is
Kipling the narrator, and some undifferentiated others –
arranged a moonlight riding picnic, 'the great Pop Picnic',
in order to provide Saumarez with a decent opportunity to
pop the question to the eldest sister, Maud Copleigh.

> We met at the parade-ground at ten: the night was fearfully
> hot. The horses sweated even at walking-pace, but anything was
> better than sitting still in our own dark houses. When we moved
> off under the full moon we were four couples, one triplet, and
> Me. Saumarez rode with the Copleigh girls, and I loitered at the
> tail of the procession wondering with whom Saumarez would
> ride home. Every one was happy and contented; but we all felt
> that things were going to happen.

The tempo of the story rises as the lovers lose themselves
in the darkness and Kipling remarks upon the coming of a
storm.

> I had felt that the air was growing hotter and hotter; but
> nobody seemed to notice it until the moon went out and a burn-
> ing hot wind began lashing the orange-trees with a sound like the
> noise of the sea. Before we knew where we were the dust-storm
> was on us, and everything was roaring, whirling darkness.

At the height of the storm 'with the thunder clattering overhead, and the lightning spurting like water from a sluice', the younger sister, Edith Copleigh, came stumbling against Kipling, calling for her horse and to be taken home.

I felt her brush past me and go away. It was too dark to say where. Then the whole sky was split open with one tremendous flash as if the end of the world were coming, and all the women shrieked. Almost directly after this I felt a man's hand on my shoulder, and heard Saumarez bellowing in my ear. Through the rattling of the trees and howling of the wind, I did not catch his words at once, but at last I heard him say, 'I've proposed to the wrong one. What shall I do?'

Against this background of violence and noise, the vulgar conventions and the sly cynicism of the opening paragraphs take on a new complexion. The storm has broken down the reticence of the lovers, and gradually breaks down the mis-understanding of the narrator. In the darkness Saumarez has chosen the wrong woman to whisper to, and the in-tently prurient spectators have also deceived themselves. He has fulfilled their expectations by proposing to the elder Miss Copleigh although the younger has been his intended quarry.

Kipling now rides away in the confusion to find the right Miss Copleigh, while Saumarez is left to make the best of his explanations to the wrong one, 'to wipe the happy look out of Maud Copleigh's face'. 'I had a perfectly unnecessary notion that everything must be done decently and in order.' The storm had died away, and in the deceptive pallor that precedes the dawn the party reassembled.

As Miss Copleigh and I limped up, Saumarez came forward to meet us, and when he helped her down from her saddle, he kissed her before all the picnic. It was like a scene in a theatre, and the likeness was heightened by all the dust-white, ghostly-looking men and women under the orange-trees clapping their hands – as if they were watching a play.

The story ends with the request that Kipling should ride home with the rejected elder sister. '"Nothing would give me greater pleasure," I said. So we formed up, six couples in all, and went back two by two. Maud Copleigh did not talk to me at any length.'

A vulgar, improbable tale, revealed, as Oscar Wilde put it, by lurid flashes, but strangely moving. The desultory talk, the suburban morality, the salacious prying into this very private affair, form the monochrome background against which the lightning reveals the naked will of the lovers in reckless realism. When daylight comes the other jaded picnickers look as unreal as actors bowing before the curtain. 'I never saw anything so un-English in my life,' says the knowing narrator.

This was the method that Kipling was to elaborate in his maturer works; he would construct a frame about his picture and contrast the picture with the frame. He would intensify his effects by placing them under a spotlight at the back of the stage, as a play within the play. At one remove from the audience, the Player-king can put across melodrama that would be tearing a passion to tatters if delivered directly over the footlights by the Prince of Denmark.

Sometimes the dramatic quality is that of a tableau or set-piece. The scenery is built up, the characters are grouped, and, by the whole context, a situation is revealed with awful clarity. Kipling rarely used the device of the 'twist' by which Maupassant, for example, releases in the last few sentences the hidden key that suddenly enables the reader to see the matter in a new light. Nor is there much narrative, as a rule, in the best Kipling stories. He shows us characters in action by suggesting rather than describing their deeds. What a man does, that he is! The nearest parallel in English literature to these short, intense, concentrated dramas is to be found in verse not prose – in Browning's *Dramatic Lyrics* which so strongly influenced Kipling as a schoolboy. The *Plain Tales* are constructed on the same plan as 'My Last Duchess' or 'The Bishop Orders his Tomb'.

The immediate and astonishing success of the *Plain Tales* in India was inevitable, since the characters were recognized as typical and were often identified. Kay Robinson said that everyone in the Punjab knew who 'Mrs Hauksbee' was, but Mrs Hill, who lived far away from Simla and frequented another hill-station in the hot weather, was not so sure. She thought she knew, and Rudyard rallied her playfully about her guesses. Some of the other characters were plain enough, and are revealed under their true names in his letters, but 'Mrs Hauksbee' * was disguised, as were most of Kipling's story-characters.

Rudyard Kipling at Allahabad to Mrs Hill at Mussoorie

May 1st, 1888

You ask what did Mrs Kipling say to it – the Sermon. She didn't say much but she wrote a good deal. Here's an extract from her letter. 'It's clever and subtle and all that and *I* see the morality in it but, O my boy, how do *you* know it? Don't tell me about "guessing in the dark". It's an insult to your old Mother's intelligence. If Mrs Hauksbee enlightened you I'm not sorry that she has gone home.' Mrs H's departure to other and better climes was postponed from the 13th to the 27th and now that I have read the passenger list of the steamer of that date I see why. Well, she was very kind to me in her curiously cynical way and I owe her thanks for half a hundred ideas and some stories. A hasty pencil note from Bombay gives me her farewell and her opinions. She says: – 'Goodbye and cultivate humility. Your last is not bad – very bad – but it lacks depth and you have made a mistake in not marking the change between the moods, towards the end. They should slide into one another, whatever they may do in real life. You have painted them without transition and the effect is streaky. Otherwise it is passable. I leave you to make my peace with the infuriated amateurs who will have read "All these men and women merely players". My barque is on the strand and my ship is on the shore and, please God, I shall not return.'

May 2nd, 1888

I dined with him [Straight] on Monday and the talk turned on the everlasting battle between the Law and the criminal. For

* The original of 'Mrs Hauksbee' has been identified as Mrs F. C. Burton. See *Kipling Journal*, June 1958.

one hour and a half from the coffee to the second cheroot Straight unburdened himself of anecdote after anecdote – each one more grisly than the last. He has been concerned in most of the more distinguished murder trials of the past twenty years and 'what he don't know aint hardly worth the knowin' '. I learnt how the Condemned receive their death sentences and how they stood at the last moment; how one hair and an overlooked blood spot supplied a chain of evidence strong enough to draw a man to the gallows – and a score of other equally fascinating and equally horrible things till, at last, as Hawthorne says, 'Me seemed that I should never draw a breath of pure air again.' I am not much in love with my own mind – its a scrubby grubby sort o' thing but my faith! 'tis cream laid, wire wove, triple glazed, ivory bank post note paper compared to the mental condition of one who has sat in judgement professionally upon his fellow men.[6]

Rudyard's new duties at Allahabad required him to travel to various parts of northern India. In November 1887 he visited the Rajput states of the Indian Desert, a memorable journey which filled his notebooks with 'copy'. He used it then for the series of articles entitled *Letters of Marque* (afterwards reissued in the volume, *From Sea to Sea*), and drew on this journey extensively for local colour in *The Light that Failed, The Naulahka*, and many short stories. His visit to the abandoned city of Amber was a memorable experience which he turned to much advantage, above all in the *Jungle Books* where it reappeared as the 'Cold Lairs'. A rather foolhardy walk, by night and alone, in the ruins of Chitor gave him further material to be worked into these pictures.

But when he began to write fiction for the *Week's News*, his new liberty allowed him to extend his scope, perhaps a little imprudently. Henceforth no mere Plain Tales 'jammed into rigid frames, but three- or five-thousand-word cartoons once a week. So did young Lippo Lippi, whose child I was, look on the blank walls of his monastery when he was bidden decorate them.'

'"Twas ask and have, Choose for more's ready.'[7] His

work appeared, far too copiously, in the *Week's News* and the *Pioneer Mail* throughout the whole of 1888. Of all his life-work this is the most various in quality, since no writer could maintain his standards when writing so fast and publishing so quickly. Mrs Hill was a kinder critic than Stephen Wheeler, kinder, too, than Kipling's sharp-tongued mother, and at this time there was no one to discourage him from printing whatever he liked for a hungry market. First issued in the *Pioneer* supplements, his stories were quickly published in groups as paperbacked books. The firm of A. H. Wheeler & Co. held the contract for Indian railway bookstalls and their Mr E. E. Moreau hit upon the admirable plan of issuing cheap reprints, at one rupee each, for reading in the train. Six volumes of Kipling's new short stories were issued as the first six numbers of the Indian Railway Library before the end of the year 1888. These little books in grey paper covers created the first Kipling boom; they were carried by travellers and tourists, all over Asia and all over the world, getting the notice in London and New York that *Departmental Ditties* and *Plain Tales* at first failed to get. These were the stories that gave the public, outside India, its first impression of Rudyard Kipling, and the £200 he received on account of royalties gave him, for the first time, a balance in the bank.

To modern readers this section of Kipling's work is known from the two larger volumes (*Soldiers Three* and *Wee Willie Winkie*), into which the Railway books were afterwards collected. The most ambitious was *The Story of the Gadsbys*, a short sentimental novel, consisting of eight episodes told in dialogue. Sentimental though it is, *The Story of the Gadsbys* was considered 'daring' in 1888, because of its satirical reflections on *mariage à la mode*. Captain Gadsby of the Pink Hussars is represented as spoiling his career by making a love-match, and the ironical comment of his friend, Captain Mafflin, that 'a good man married is a good man marred', is presented by the author as his final word on the subject. If *The Story of the Gadsbys*

had been written by an elderly *roué* in 1912 it would have
been nothing much; written in 1888 by a young bachelor
aged twenty-two, it was astonishing. Kipling thought it
had some merit, and even his father admitted that 'it
wasn't all so damned bad'. It is one of those derivative pieces
of Kipling's earlier years, which we can trace back to its
several tributary sources. The notion was taken from a
fashionable French novel of the period, Gyp's *Autour du
Mariage*. The plot, which is developed with a great parade
of feminine observation and not without some revealing
naïvetés, describes the courtship and early married life of a
man of the world and an innocent girl.

A study of Kipling's letters reveals the whole background
of the tale. The original 'Gadsby' was a Captain Beames of
the 19th Bengal Lancers who used to visit Kipling in his
quarters late at night, to unburden himself about a love-
affair with a girl of seventeen. Kipling quite openly exploited him as 'copy', and reported the progress of the affair
in his letters to Mrs Hill, whom he consulted about feminine
niceties in the first instalment. 'The man was a fiction, was
he? I've had him under the lens since 8.15 this evening.'

The fifth volume in the Railway Series includes 'The
Man who would be King' which several good critics have
selected as Kipling's masterpiece. The method of picture-
and-frame is nowhere more effectively developed. The tale
begins with a night journey in an 'intermediate' railway carriage in company of a whisky-sodden ne'er-do-well who
ingratiates himself by exchanging masonic signs with Kipling, and persuades him to carry a confidential message. So
far, the story is an actual experience in Kipling's life. The
loafer reappears one hot night with a companion when Kipling is sitting up late at the newspaper office, feverish and
exhausted, but tense with anxiety for some scrap of news
from the West which must be inserted before the morning
edition can go to press. This again was his frequent and
actual experience. Against the frame of observed fact, the
author placed his contrasting fiction, in which the two vaga-

bonds, regarding him as their accomplice, unfolded their crazy scheme for carving out a kingdom in Central Asia, a news item that would have eclipsed the expected telegram from Europe, if one could believe in it. To Kipling's surprise they equipped themselves with disguises, camels, and arms, and vanished over the Frontier. 'I would have prayed for them,' he wrote, 'but, that night, a real king died in Europe, and demanded an obituary notice.'

Two years passed, and again Kipling was waiting at night to send the newspaper to press.

At three o'clock I cried 'Print off', and turned to go, when there crept to my chair what was left of a man. He was bent into a circle, his head was sunk between his shoulders, and he moved his feet one over the other like a bear. I could hardly see whether he walked or crawled – this rag-wrapped, whining cripple who addressed me by name, crying that he was come back ... 'I've come back,' he repeated; 'and I was the King of Kafiristan – me and Dravot – crowned kings we was! In this office we settled it – you setting there ... and you've been setting here ever since – O Lord!'

Then follows the long recital, patiently drawn from this crazy, broken creature in fragmentary phrases, of the kingdom won and lost by the two adventurers, alone, beyond the Pamirs. It runs to 7,000 words out of the 12,000 required for the whole story, and the emphasis is skilfully reversed. Hitherto all the force and drama of the tale have been concentrated upon the routine of the newspaper office which has ears only for rumour from the Western World. Now tragedy on an epic scale has started up at the door, a tale of horror like one of those decadent Jacobean dramas that Kipling studied so closely all his life long. The two vagabonds, who had formerly seemed impertinent intruders on the stage, steal the limelight, one dying and the other dead, having played out his part. As the cripple ended his tale

he fumbled in the mass of rags round his bent waist; brought out a black horsehair bag embroidered with silver thread, and shook therefrom on my table – the dried, withered head of Daniel Dravot. The morning sun that had long been paling the lamps struck the red beard and blind sunken eyes; struck, too, a heavy circlet of gold studded with raw turquoises ... on the battered temples.

'The Man who would be King' is a long story, but not a word too long. Such high praise cannot be given to some others of Kipling's stories written at this period. Even 'The Drums of the Fore and Aft', though generally ranked among Kipling's successes, drags a little. It starts too slowly and too captiously, with 1,500 words of rather petulant talk about army reform. Then Kipling turns to the barrack-life of the 'Fore and Aft', a regiment that has not been under fire in a generation. Their self-confidence and their innocent delight when ordered on active service, their childlike pretence of being soldiers is exemplified in the character of the two naughty drummer-boys, Lew and Jakin, whose indiscipline defies control by the bandmaster, the sergeant-major, and even by that remote demi-god, the Colonel. Drummer-boys in mid-Victorian fiction were wont to be child-heroes, and not seldom child-saints. It was with gusto that Kipling developed the theme of precocious depravity in the drums of the Fore and Aft.

Jakin was a stunted child of fourteen and Lew was about the same age. When not looked after, they smoked and drank. They swore habitually after the manner of the barrack-room, which is cold-swearing and comes from between clenched teeth; and they fought religiously once a week. Jakin had sprung from some London gutter and may or may not have passed through Dr Barnardo's hands ere he arrived at the dignity of drummer-boy. Lew could remember nothing but the regiment and the delight of listening to the Band from his earliest years ... he was most mistakenly furnished with the head of a cherub: insomuch that beautiful ladies who watched the Regiment in church were wont to speak of him as a 'darling'. They never heard his vitriolic comments on their manners and morals, as he walked back to barracks with the Band.

After this long introduction (another 4,000 words) the tale moved swiftly to its climax – a rout. The regiment breaks, in panic flight, before a charge of Afghan fanatics. Such things have happened to many regiments, in many battles, and this episode is based upon no one disaster.* But in this instance the situation is retrieved by the two boys who rally the fugitives, with fife and drum, not moved to this action by a desire for glory but because they were a little tipsy with rum from a soldier's bottle. While pricking the bubble of mock-heroism and sham-romance, Kipling does not shirk the admission that the spark of real heroism was there too, beneath the surface. Whether brought into play by rum, necessity, or hysteria, it was indeed used, and valued.

'The Drums of the Fore and Aft' is not a nursery tale. The same volume, *Wee Willie Winkie*, contains three other stories which established Kipling's reputation as a writer on child-life. Two of them, the story which gives its title to the volume and 'His Majesty the King', are conventional tales in a genre which delighted our grandparents. The heroes of these two stories are angel-children whose innocent pranks reconcile quarrelling lovers and unite broken families. They are studio-pieces not much unlike Mrs Burnett's *Little Lord Fauntleroy* (1886), the masterpiece among sentimental juveniles. Insincerity in the subject-matter produced a corresponding insincerity in the style, with the result that these stories provide the crudest examples of the young Kipling's characteristic faults.

The fourth story, 'Baa, Baa, Black Sheep' (1888), falls into a very different category. Though many incidents in Kipling's books are founded upon incidents in his life, his works

---

* The episode of the two drummer-boys is taken from *Military Transactions of the British Nation in Indostan*, vol. iii, p. 486, by R. Orme (1763). But the battle is based upon the action of Ahmed Khel, 19 April 1880, in which the 59th Regiment made a good recovery after a momentary panic. The 59th, Mulvaney's 'Ould Regiment', was amalgamated with the 30th and renamed the East Lancashires. They were stationed at Mian Mir, 1880–85.

include only this one fragment of candid autobiography. Kipling's unhappy childhood at Southsea is a well-attested period of his life. But candid revelations of childhood were not so popular in 1888 as they became a generation later, and at least one serious reviewer expressed a preference for angel children. He explained at length in the *Athenaeum* for December 1890 that all the tales in *Wee Willie Winkie* were commendable except 'Baa, Baa, Black Sheep' which was 'not true to life'.

One more of the stories in the Railway Library deserves mention, 'A Wayside Comedy' which appeared in the volume *Under the Deodars*. At the end of his life, Kipling selected this story as one of the half-dozen in which his 'daemon', the intuitive sense of fitness, did not play him false. He worked hard for 'economy of implication', and struck the keynote for his tale, a rather unpleasant picture of adultery and deception in an isolated group of friends, with a single phrase, the 'burdensome geniality' of the unobservant husband who, alone, did not know what all the others knew. It was the kind of story that, in those days, was described as a shade too 'French', and in France it has always been much admired.

One whole volume, the first, was devoted to stories about the 'Soldiers Three', Mulvaney, Learoyd, and Ortheris, and the other volumes also included stories of military life. What, in fact, did Kipling know of the Army in 1888?

Throughout the seven years that Kipling spent in India, the whole Indian Empire was prosperous and internally peaceful. After the conclusion of the Second Afghan War, in 1881, there was no heavy fighting on the North-West Frontier for many years though, as ever in the days of the British *Raj*, a large army was deployed on the frontier, mobilized for active service.

While never quite at peace, the tribes of the debatable area across the border did not provoke another large expedition until October 1888, a few weeks before Kipling's departure from India. Then it was necessary to march a whole division of troops into a region never before penetrated by the British, the Black Mountain at the northern extremity of the North-West Frontier. It was an arduous but not a costly campaign, and was concluded after a few skirmishes, with a loss of twenty-five British soldiers.

Kipling's early stories of frontier fighting must therefore have been derived from books, or from soldiers' yarns about their experience in earlier wars before he came to the East. His later stories, written after his return to the West, contain several clear references to the Black Mountain campaign. But, during the eighties, the Indian Army was twice employed in foreign wars: in the Egyptian War of 1884–5 and in the Conquest of Burma, 1885–7. Kipling's sole experience of Egypt was his passage through the Suez Canal in 1882. We know that he had an informant in the person of 'Stalky' whose stories he would readily accept, and who came to Lahore from Egypt. Of Burma Kipling knew nothing at first-hand, until he called in a sea-going liner at Rangoon and Moulmein for a few days in 1889. Accordingly, we find his Burmese pieces somewhat remote and romantic. Two that give graphic accounts of incidents in the war ('The Ballad of Boh da Thone', August 1888; 'A Conference of the Powers', May 1890) are carefully disposed to focus attention on the circumstances in which the tale is told afterwards, not on the local colour of the Burmese jungle. It is of the North-West Frontier that he writes with a sort of authority and again we know that he spent only a few days there, in 1885. What, then, are the sources of his information?

Critics of Kipling's work have tended to underestimate his debt to books. As he could glance at a scene, and pin-point and recall the touch of colour that he needed, so he could glance through a book, select an incident, and make it his own. The files and the works of reference in the *Civil and Military* office, his father's library, and his father's encyclopedic knowledge of India, gave him many an anecdote or queer scrap of information which he did not hesitate to use where it would fit.

No one need be surprised to learn that 'Cupid's Arrows' is based upon an incident in *Daniel Deronda*, that 'The Killing of Hatim Tai' is taken from Hone's *Everyday Book*, that the story of the two drummer-boys who saved the army is to be found in Orme's *Military Transactions*, that 'Snarleyow' is an episode from Sergeant Bancroft's history of the Bengal Horse Artillery, that 'The Ballad of East and West' is a romantic version of a tale that was in print long before Kipling's day, that 'Gunga Din' was the name he gave to Juma, the heroic water-carrier of the guides at the siege of Delhi.

Some of the stories were historic before Kipling gave them his distinctive mark, some were the current coin of the barrack-room, the tall stories told by the old soldiers to the recruits. 'The Lost Legion' was a tradition of 1857 arising out of John Nicholson's punishment of the mutinous 55th Native Infantry. 'The Jacket' was an exploit ascribed to Captain Dalbiac, a gunner-officer in the Egyptian war. 'The Big Drunk Draf' (not an unfamiliar episode to those who remember the old army) was claimed by Lieutenant A. A. Howell of the Northumberland Fusiliers as his own. 'The Taking of Lungtungpen' by a raiding-party of naked soldiers was reported in the *Civil and Military* as an actual achievement of the 2nd Queen's Regiment, a few weeks before Kipling wrote it up as fiction. 'Namgay Doola' was an incident of the Black Mountain campaign.[8]

Without doubt there are many other military episodes and characters that might be identified from Kipling's soldier stories. He never pretended to invent; it was his pride to record the traditional army legends, and he took the liberty of a Walter Scott or a Robert Burns in remodelling them for a new audience. Where he differed from other writers of battle-pieces was in his extraordinary talent for getting under the skin of his characters and seeing what their eyes must have seen.

An' now the hugly bullets come peckin' through the dust,
An' no one wants to face 'em, but every beggar must;
So, like a man in irons, which isn't glad to go,
They moves 'em off by companies uncommon stiff an' slow.[9]

Let that be compared with any other account that has ever been written of soldiers going into battle! How did he know that they looked like that?

English literature had long been rich in songs and stories about the navy. Both in romantic and in realistic writing, the Jolly Tars had for centuries enjoyed the favour and the understanding of the reading public. The English tradition, rightly or wrongly, associated the sailor with the fight for freedom, with defence against foreign tyrants; while the soldier, however courageous, was the hireling of usurpers, the instrument of unpopular aggressive war-makers, and so was despised, disliked, and ignored. In literature, the attention he got was confined to the professional heroics of the military historians, while amateur opinion was mostly based on Wellington's cynical remark that his army was recruited from the scum of the earth. Socially, the private soldiers were in fact drawn from the unemployed or unemployable, so that 'going for a soldier' was, in the respectable working-class, regarded as the last degradation, analogous with 'going to the bad'. Once enlisted and marked out by a uniform, the soldiery formed a caste apart and a caste of untouchables, living under conditions in barracks that were not even healthy. Particularly, the incidence of venereal disease was appalling.

Between officers and men there was a social barrier that could rarely be surmounted. The officers, above all, were gentlemen, and it was only by showing aristocratic qualities that a ranker might, in some rare instances, qualify for an officer's commission. Among the gentry, commissioned rank was regarded as a social guarantee; but among the great mass of the Victorian English, the evangelical middle-classes, an army officer commanded scant respect. Yet, underlying the surface flow of anti-militarism there remained a hidden current of admiration, not rational and not articulate, for the redcoats, with their strange insignia and pomp, whose life seemed so far removed from the workaday world of England in the nineteenth century. Who were they then, these smart neat young officers, this rough and hearty rank and file who led a double life: appearing sometimes in the police-court news as drunken, diseased reprobates; sometimes as the heroes of quite fabulous adventures in far distant lands, the thin red line of Balaclava, the storming-columns of Delhi, the defenders of Rorke's Drift, the men who advanced across the desert by night to Tel-el-Kebir, who marched through the mountain-passes in tropical heat from Kabul to Kandahar?

Search English literature and you will find no treatment of the English soldier on any adequate scale between Shakespeare and Kipling. He who wishes to know how British soldiers fight, how officers and men regard one another, how they talk the night before the battle, will seek the information in *King Henry V*, or in *Barrack-Room Ballads*, for it is to be found almost nowhere else in our English classics. Cromwell's and Marlborough's and Wolfe's and Wellington's soldiers are vanished as though they had never been: they have their panegyrics but not their living records.

It does not appear that Kipling paid much attention to the army during his first two or three years in India. He tells us that he dined with the British regiment at Mian Mir (presumably the 30th East Lancashires) a few weeks after his arrival. A boy of seventeen, and a civilian, he was too shy to speak. Although he met some subalterns on leave at Simla there is no record of his striking up any close friendships with them. From the visit to Rawalpindi and the frontier in 1885 we may safely derive his first original composition on a military subject with a smack about it of that penetrating realism which marked his best work.

> The flying bullet down the Pass,
> That whistles clear: 'All flesh is grass.'

These lines give the key to the poem, 'Arithmetic on the Frontier' which appeared in the first edition of *Departmental Ditties* (June 1886).

> A scrimmage in a Border Station –
> A canter down some dark defile –
> Two thousand pounds of education
> Drops to a ten-rupee *jezail* –
> The Crammer's boast, the Squadron's pride,
> Shot like a rabbit in a ride!

The two earliest of the *Plain Tales* to deal with military subjects are 'The Arrest of Lieutenant Golightly', November 1886, and 'His Wedded Wife', February 1887. 'Lieutenant Golightly', a slight anecdote, is given the local colour of Kipling's own retreat from Narkunda to Simla in the previous summer. 'His Wedded Wife' is a clever story, with a smack of 'Stalky' about it, describing a practical joke played in an officers' mess. Everything Kipling wrote about the army before 1887 deals with the officers and the life of the officers' mess. When he began to investigate the canteen and the barrack-rooms with his unobtrusive observation we do not know, but Kay Robinson said that he knew the 'tone' of the regiments at Mian Mir better than the Chaplain.

The first story in which Mulvaney, Ortheris, and Learoyd * appear is 'The Three Musketeers', March 1887, not in its own right an important story. Kipling describes it as told to him, by the three in chorus, in the refreshment room at Umballa Station, where he used to change trains for Simla. Though the characters of the soldiers, the Irishman, the Cockney, and the dalesman from the West Riding, are clearly distinguished, the author did not claim to know them well. 'Young mon, what's the notebook for?' asked Learoyd pointedly at the end of the anecdote. But since the three proved useful as a medium for 'turnover' articles, he

* Kipling liked to give his characters unusual names. In 1886 there were a Surgeon Mulvaney and a Lieutenant Learoyd at Mian Mir. The names of the characters in 'The Man who would be King' were suggested by Mrs Hill.

reproduced them three times again before the year was out.
The fourth of these stories, 'The Madness of Private Ortheris', October 1887, is by general consent important. Here
it will be sufficient to say that by the time we reach it, the
three soldiers have been provided with personal histories
from which it should be possible to identify them, if indeed
they are founded on fact.

Before investigating Kipling's soldier friends in India it
may be well to recall the first two soldiers whom he ever
knew well, Sergeant Kearney and Sergeant-major Schofield, the two veterans employed successively at Westward
Ho! as 'school sergeants', that is as janitors, drill-instruc-
tors, and general assistants with the school discipline. When
Kipling went to school as a little boy it was in the time of
Sergeant Kearney, a huge, drunken old Irishman who delighted in talking about the Sikh Wars of the eighteen-
forties. Kearney retired in 1879, giving place to Schofield, a
smart brisk little cockney whose character is indicated by
his school nickname of 'Weasel'.* It seems unlikely that
these two, who gave Kipling his first impressions of the soldier's character, should not have contributed some features
to the characters of Mulvaney and Ortheris.

We are told of the three musketeers in the four early
stories that they had seen service at the battle of Ahmed
Khel in the second Afghan War, and that when these
stories were told, they had recently returned from the war
in Burma. In a later story it is expressly stated that they
fought in these two wars and in another on the northern
frontier, which must be the Black Mountain campaign of
1888. No line regiment in the British Army actually served
in all three of these wars. We are therefore forced to assume
that Kipling took liberties with his substratum of fact (as
he usually did) when writing his soldier tales. They are not
to be regarded as told, like *Stalky & Co.*, within a framework of actuality. No evidence has come to light that he did

* 'Foxy' in *Stalky & Co.* He disliked the character Kipling gave
him (*Kipling Journal*, No. 23).

in fact maintain a three-year friendship with any three soldiers, and the disposition of troops in India with their frequent changes of station makes it unlikely. It may be that a chance meeting with three soldiers at Umballa gave him a peg on which to hang all his succeeding stories of barrack-life, whatever their origin.

He grew tired of writing about them. He tried an alternative line with stories about 'Gunner Barnabas' who never became a favourite with the public.* Then, in March 1888, he discharged Mulvaney from the Army and wrote a story ('The Big Drunk Draf'') about him as a civilian on the Indian Railways. By July all three had been discharged, and 'Private Learoyd's Story' was written in a reminiscent vein about past happenings. In September he boldly wrote a sketch called 'The Last of the Stories', in which he called up these and others of his characters to bid them farewell. It was no good; he could no more kill them than Conan Doyle, a year or two later, could kill Sherlock Holmes. Mulvaney would crop up time after time with an Irish accent that was ever more outrageous.

After his return to England, Kipling again revived the 'Three Musketeers', and then wrote the stories about them which have been most noticed by modern critics, 'The Courting of Dinah Shadd', 'On Greenhow Hill', and 'Love o' Women'. They made a deep impression on the public and won extravagant praise from some critics, bitter hostility from others. Liked or disliked, they could not be ignored.

Kipling's view of army life in India is gloomy on the whole, a life with few pleasures, no glamour, and no luxury for the rank and file.† The heat and the fever, the recurrent epidemics of cholera, the boredom that leads to hysterical

---

*A powerful story that does not use the 'Three Musketeers' is 'In the Matter of a Private' (*Soldiers Three*).

† 'We aren't no thin red 'eroes, nor we aren't no blackguards too,
But single men in barricks, most remarkable like you;
An' if sometimes our conduck isn't all your fancy paints,
Why, single men in barricks don't grow into plaster saints.'

(*Tommy*)

outbreaks of insubordination and violence, the jealous rages that flare into fighting madness among men who have loaded weapons always to hand; such features as these compose the picture. 'Hot-weather shooting cases' were part of the routine of the law-courts, to be reported by the sweating feverish assistant editor of the *Civil and Military*, as his letters testify from 1884 onwards. Murders, courts martial, executions bulked big in his picture of a soldier's life. The relief of tension came with the recurring campaigns on the frontier, to which the soldiers looked forward with excited pleasure, though the wars offered small prospect of plunder or promotion.

' 'Tain't so much the bloomin' fightin', though there's enough o' that. It's the bloomin' food and the bloomin' climate. Frost all night except when it hails, and bilin' sun all day, and the water stinks fit to knock you down. 'Tain't no bloomin' picnic in those parts, I can tell you.'[10]

Nor were the campaigns uniformly victorious. His most successful battle-picture is of a failure in morale, the breaking of the 'Fore and Aft' under fire.

The regiment of the line that Kipling knew best was the 5th Northumberland Fusiliers, who were stationed at Mian Mir from 1886 to 1888; he calls them the 'Tyneside Tailtwisters'. They had fought in the Afghan War, though not in any action which can be identified in a Kipling story; and they fought again in the Black Mountain in 1888; they did not serve in Burma. Kipling knew the officers rather than the men, and it was of this regiment that he wrote the story, 'Only a Subaltern', which contains 'Bobby Wicks', the very young officer, whose devotion is given absolutely to the regiment, and whose virtues are circumscribed by the limits of his profession. Later, when he has made good as an officer, there will be time to explore the higher octaves of life. He has the goodness of simplicity, and his crowning merit is unflinching moral and physical courage, for which there should be a testing time, the day when he must lead his men to face fire; but for 'Bobby Wicks' the time never comes. His tragedy is that he dies young and untried, in the minor heroism of a cholera epidemic, not in the crucial test of battle to which he has devoted himself as a willing victim.

'Bobby Wicks' is the finest specimen of a type which recurs in Kipling's stories, the only typical series in the whole of his cast of characters. They have the public-school virtues of loyalty and common sense, and their absolute standard of honesty is taken for granted. If they drink a little, the habit never interferes with their duty; if they wench, the weakness is kept decently out of sight. They are the young Anglo-Indians for whom and about whom much of his early work was written.

You might suppose 'Bobby Wicks' crude, a philistine or a prig, but you would be wrong. His inarticulate unexpressiveness is a mask put up against the world to hide an emotional life which may be as strange as that of the 'Brushwood Boy', as rich as that of Holden, who married 'without benefit of clergy'. These two are revealed, in their private lives, as individuals of rare distinction, though, in their public lives, they are English types, flattened and smoothed by a conventional education.

The other characters are seen as if through the eyes of these young men. None of his women in the earlier stories quite stands alone, they are as they would appear to a very observant dancing-partner. His private soldiers (excepting the later Mulvaney) are seen as the pride or the exasperation of their company officers, not as men on their own. His colonels and headmasters and viceroys are regarded from below with a satiric touch that reveals the underlying hero-worship. Every elderly man has a smack of his wise father, every competent middle-aged woman a hint of his mother. 'Bobby Wicks' is, as yet, the only kind of man he has fully understood, and it is through the eyes of 'Bobby Wicks' that he sometimes sees with a flash of intuitive genius into the soul of some drunken soldier, or unfortunate half-caste, or neglected child.

With 'Bobby Wicks' he was so sure, the portraiture so firm, the observation so true, the diagnosis so apposite, that he moulded a whole generation of young Englishmen into that type. They rose up in their thousands in 1914, and sacrificed themselves in the image that Kipling had created.

Early in 1888 he made a trip down-country for the *Pioneer*, visiting Benares where, characteristically, he was more interested in the reactions of the other tourists than in the sights shown to them. Then at the Great Eastern Hotel in Calcutta he smelt the unforgettable sewage-smell of the Hugli and saw the dull correct commercial society of the British-Indian capital. He wrote at large on municipal politics, on harbour-control, and on the pilot-service that so cheaply, safely, and quietly, mastered the shifting sand-banks of the Ganges Delta. Night in the sleeping city as ever fascinated him, drawing him on to go the rounds with the vice-squad of the Calcutta police. On its own account dissipation in that world had no charm for him.

When Rudyard came back to Allahabad in April, it was as a guest of Professor and Mrs Hill in a ramshackle bunga-low called 'Belvedere', which became his home for his last year in India. It stood in

a large garden, only half-cultivated, with bushes as big as sum-mer-houses of Marshall Niel roses, lime and orange trees, clumps of bamboos, and thickets of high grass.

where Darzee the tailor-bird stitched his nest of leaves and Nag the cobra hatched out eggs in the heaps of garden refuse – one of the best-known gardens in the world.[11] Soon his hosts went off to Mussoorie which was their hill-station, and then Rudyard was suddenly recalled up-country to La-hore, as deputy for Kay Robinson who was going on leave. For the last time, since he had made up his mind to quit India soon, he spent the hot season in the Punjab plains, grinding away at the routine of the *Civil and Military*.

His compensation now was to write long gossiping letters,

in the form of a running journal kept almost every day, to Mrs Hill at Mussoorie. One topic he wrote about at length was Captain Beames's confidences, which he was regurgitating as 'Captain Gadsby's'; another was a love-affair of his own. But who was the unknown 'My Lady' to whom he declared an undying though unrequited affection in his letters to Mrs Hill? It was not, he assured her, Tillie Venner with whom he promenaded to the bandstand in the jaded dusty public garden at Lahore. It was not Ethel Edge, the Chief Justice's daughter, though he admitted his name had been coupled with Ethel's; nor was it Miss Parry-Lambert, though everyone supposed Rudyard was engaged to her since he had written that story, 'Venus Annodomini', about her mother. In letter after letter 'My Lady' appears but not in any materialized form. The reader begins to suppose her a figment of the young writer's fancy, a projection, perhaps, of Mrs Hill herself, to whom he must not declare his devotion.

The heat in Lahore became intolerable. He suffered from heart palpitations, and hardly held out till mid-June when, at last, he was released to join his friends at Mussoorie, for a short visit. Then driving through the Sewalik Hills and the Doon Country, he made his way to join the family. From 22 June to 15 July 1888 was his last Simla season, when, with the added delight of writing every day to Mrs Hill, he was happier than ever before.

Rudyard Kipling at Simla to Mrs Hill at Allahabad

At 'Craigsville': Simla. 22.6.88

It was a pleasant home coming but what touched me more than all was the folly of my small terrier – parted with and forgotten seven months ago. She heard my step, this fat white waddler, and was the first to come to me with ecstatic wriggles and jumps and bounds and fawnings such as dogs use to fill in their lack of speech. Then she promptly foreswore her allegiance to both mother and maid who had petted her and fed her as no dog has been fed I am sure, and for the rest of the evening would have nothing of any one but me whom she nuzzled and whimpered over, thrusting her nose into my hand and demanding imperiously that I should notice her. None of us thought that she would remember and I own that I had quite forgotten; but she belied us all – dear little beast. In a moment of expansiveness I said egotistically: – 'I shall think better of myself henceforward.' 'Hear him!' said the Mother. 'Anyone but a man would have said that he would think better of the dog.' Whereby I knew in verity that I had come back to the old life and the ways thereof.

But not wholly, for it is owned that I am no longer ownable and only a visitor in the land. The Mother says that is so and the Sister too and their eyes see far – 'You belong to yourself,' says the Mother, and the Maiden says: – 'You don't belong to us at any rate,' and even in the making of this confession we come together after the wreck of the old home on a new and pleasant platform.[12]

His mother was pleased that he had made up his mind to live with his new friends at 'Belvedere', if only he would control his temper, and watch his surly moods. 'Living alone has made you so old and uninterested,' she said. 'You'll have to be civil, Ruddy.'

Meanwhile Simla abounded as ever with pretty unattached girls. There was no escaping from Miss Parry-Lambert, until his mother produced a counter-irritant in 'Gussie' Tweddell whom he was expected to like because she, too, wrote poetry, but Trix and Ruddy only thought her verses as funny as her name. Though a carefree time for Ruddy, it was not so for Trix who was in and out of a love-affair that would not come to a crisis. Another sign of change in his little world was the end of his old easy correspondence with Margaret Burne-Jones. She was to be married to a classical Don, named Mackail, a liberal in politics of whom Ruddy could not much approve. He could hardly address her again as 'Dearest Wop'.

Part of this holiday was spent by the Kiplings with a rather distinguished house-party at the 'Retreat', Sir Edward Buck's villa a few miles away. The letters to Mussoorie, now, were full of talk about Mrs Napier, a gossiping, over-dressed lady who believed herself to be in the Viceroy's confidence. That season, the Kiplings moved rather in the military than in the civil set.* There were amateur theatricals at the Commander-in-Chief's where Rudyard played 'Brisemouche', in *A Scrap of Paper*, to the satisfaction of the company. To have won the confidence of England's greatest soldier was an achievement for a young press reporter. Rudyard said the proudest moment of his life was when he rode up Simla Mall, on 'Dolly Bobs' his grey catlike pony, beside Sir Frederick Roberts, a little red-faced man on a huge fiery chestnut, who consulted him, Mr Kipling, about what the men in barracks were really saying.

There are tales of Rudyard's last year in India implying, not improbably, that this very young man who had suddenly achieved a little fame was sometimes too forward in the company of his seniors, too ready to assert his views. He celebrated the conclusion of Lord Dufferin's reign in India with a set of verses which their subject received with something less than good humour, an experiment in the style of Browning's 'Bishop Blougram' called 'One Viceroy to Another'. A few weeks later he got the *Pioneer* into difficulties by a satirical ballad that accused Roberts, his hero, rather too pointedly, of favouritism in his military appointments. This episode was followed by a more serious error when the Indian National Congress, then a new young institution which Rudyard was not at all disposed to admire, held its annual convention at Allahabad. A remark about a sympathizer with the Congress, in Rudyard's report, provoked a personal assault upon the editor of the *Pioneer*; and an undignified exchange of lawsuits followed. So characteristic a writer as Rudyard had become could no longer be held to the task of routine reporting.

But now he was looking forward to his next move, since

*His colleague, Howard Hensman of the *Pioneer*, who could tell him more than any man about frontier fighting, was with him at Simla that season.

the conditions of his home life, as well as of his work, were changing. His father was in England that summer, on professional business, and Trix at last announced her engagement to John Fleming, a soldier seconded to the Survey Department. Both Rudyard and his mother had suffered much from the heat, and he was advised by his doctor not to spend another hot-weather on the Indian Plains. He had begun to save a little money, and the £200 advance which he had received for his Railway books would buy him a steamer passage to England. London, the theatres, springtime in the English Home Counties called him; he made up his mind to go.

After returning to Allahabad, he had one more journey to make for the *Pioneer*, to the railway workshops and coal-fields of industrial Bengal, before settling down happily in his own room at 'Belvedere' to write his soldier stories. For some weeks he had the house to himself while the Hills went off to Jubbulpore. Almost every day he wrote to Mrs Hill, and her replies included the professor's photographs of Central India, a district which he knew by hearsay from Sterndale's books on sport and natural history. The marble cliffs of the Nerbudda Gorge, thronged with wild bees, the bald harsh outcrops of rock on the stony plains, the line of the Satpura Hills, and the jungles and grazing-grounds along the Waingunga River, were fixed in his inward vision, though he never saw them outwardly.

For company in October he was thrown back upon the Club, where, as a rule, he was a shy and silent member. He struck up a communal friendship with the British regiment in the fort, the 31st East Surreys, a lively corps of cockneys. Captain Bayless of the East Surreys was just then his closest companion. It was a time for renewing his army connexion because the frontier was stood to arms. Rudyard lost a friend, killed in action with the force that marched into the Black Mountain that month, and anxiously awaited news of the Northumberland Fusiliers, who were there.

When the cool weather came, the happiness that he

hoped for at Allahabad was marred by the serious illness of Mrs Hill. Her life was in danger from meningitis and, when she recovered, she decided to spend her convalescence at home in America. A new plan formed in his mind, he would travel east-about to England and would visit her at her home in Pennsylvania. As he so often felt at the crises of his life, fate dealt the cards. George Allen encouraged him to go by asking him to write a set of travel-sketches for the *Pioneer*. Introductions to new friends in America showered on him: Captain Bayless of the East Surreys had relatives in Montana; his mother recalled that she had an elder brother in New York whom she had not seen for near thirty years; she could recommend him, too, to the painter Edwin Abbey, who was almost an American Pre-Raphael-ite. Through masonic friends Rudyard got other names, and best of all was his father's letter to an old friend, Lockwood de Forest (not a relative in spite of the coincidence of their rare Christian names). Rudyard decided to leave India at once, without waiting even for Trix's wedding. Eventually he managed to book a passage with Professor and Mrs Hill on S.S. *Madura* of the British India line, bound from Cal-cutta to Rangoon. His weekly letters to the *Pioneer* would bring in something, but neither he nor his editor bothered about the further rights in these travel sketches which were regarded by both as ephemeral journalism, a negligence that was to cause trouble to Rudyard for many years.[13]

In February 1889 he went up to Lahore to say farewell to the family. Lockwood was in India again, more busy, and more variously interested than ever. Had Ruddy never flown kites in Indian fashion? Well! they must go to the bazaar, now, buy some kites, and plunge into the crowd of Punjabi boys and men, who flew kites every evening beside the River Ravi. Everything was laid aside until they'd ex-hausted that game. Lahore in February has the pleasantest climate in the world. In the month of roses it was a paradise for 'globe-trotters', that class of alien intruders which Ruddy had so despised, which he was now to join.

Rudyard Kipling at Lahore to Mrs Hill at Allahabad
                                                 February 23rd, 1889

The quietness of our life here is extreme. I've looked all
through T's negatives. I've teased Vixen, smoked baccy, written
a turn-over for the C. & M., driven Trixie nearly wild with rude
remarks about her cooking – she is doing something with
lemon, white of egg and sugar on a stove and she says its cheese-
cake; gone over to the School of Art and played havoc with
everything I could find there, twisted the turnstile of the
Museum until it registered more people than ever come in one
day, and generally made myself a surpassing nuisance. There
isn't anything more to do except eat, and try to imitate a new
salad dressing that the Mother is proud of. I have filled the
Mother's heart with envy by describing your short pastry – the
stuff that crumbles into white flakes. 'But what's the good of
you if you can only *gorge* it, and then know nothing of how it's
made,' says Trixie who is prancing round the house with a
spoon in one hand and a cookery book in the other. They are
an awful busy couple, those two. Always sewing something or
cooking something. One of the first questions the Mother asked
when I told her of your illness was: '*Does* she worry herself
about the servants?' So you see you have deep and genuine
sympathizers up here in the Black North.

                                                         Sunday

Gott in himmel! An incursion of Austrian maniacs has just
swept through the house, gutted the studio and fled, carrying
the Pater with 'em to the Museum. There were two of 'em – one a
Count something or other – simply wild about India and all
that is therein. They had been consigned to us from Bombay
and we were first aware of their presence by shrill shrieks from
the drive for 'Meestare Kipleen'. Then they pranced in, one a
red bearded tornado with a cracked voice, and t'other a dried up
walnut looking sort o' man who couldn't speak English. They
wanted to go to Peshawur. They wanted to see Graeco-Buddhist
sculptures – they wanted to encamp on the Attock; they wanted
to embrace the whole blazing East and they wriggled with impatience as they explained their needs. Pater took the wildest
and I tackled t'other in a wild polyglot of French and vernacular. I guess that was a fair enough approximation to Austrian.

They tore through the Pater's portfolios; they seemed ready to tear down the pictures from the walls and the big one, backing the Pater into a corner, stood over him while he shouted: 'Tell me now about Alexandare. I am in him mooch interest. *Did* he now come to this place, and where is Taxila.' All this as though Alexandare was a brother globe-trotter who had just gone through. It takes a good deal to put the Pater out of countenance (He's my father you know) but he collapsed when he was called upon to give a résumé of Indian archaeology and I chuckled. The other man had got hold of T's photo-studies of men and animals taken to help the Pater's drawings and between gasps of Austrian admiration was wildly appealing to me for duplicates. 'I am artist you know,' was his explanation and he spoke as who should say: – I am the Almighty.[14]

Lockwood was always being saddled with such visitors. Not long before it had been two mysterious Frenchmen who had arrived at Simla across the passes from the north, no one knew when or how. No less a man than F. H. Cook (manager of Thomas Cook & Son) had visited Lockwood at Lahore, and the personal attention of the world's leading travel-agency was given to Ruddy's globe-trotting. He set off for Calcutta with enthusiasm, like a schoolboy released for a holiday; he had liberty, money in his pocket, and a sense of pride in his seven years' apprenticeship.

From The Song of the Banjo (1893)

By the bitter road the Younger Son must tread,
  Ere he win to hearth and saddle of his own, –
'Mid the riot of the shearers at the shed,
  In the silence of the herder's hut alone –
In the twilight, on a bucket upside down,
  Hear me babble what the weakest won't confess –
I am Memory and Torment – I am Town!
  I am all that ever went with evening dress!

    With my '*Tunka-tunka-tunka-tunka-tunk*!'
      So the lights – the London Lights – grow near and
        plain!
    So I rowel 'em afresh towards the Devil and the Flesh,
      Till I bring my broken rankers home again.

In desire of many marvels over sea,
  Where the new-raised tropic city sweats and roars,
I have sailed with Young Ulysses from the quay
  Till the anchor rumbled down on stranger shores.
He is blooded to the open and the sky,
  He is taken in a snare that shall not fail,
He shall hear me singing strongly, till he die,
  Like the shouting of a backstay in a gale.

    .   .   .   .

And the tunes that mean so much to you alone –
  Common tunes that make you choke and blow your nose –
Vulgar tunes that bring the laugh that brings the groan –
  I can rip your very heartstrings out with those;
With the feasting, and the folly, and the fun –
  And the lying, and the lusting, and the drink,
And the merry play that drops you, when you're done,
  To the thoughts that burn like irons if you think.

A Return to London
(March–October 1889)

KIPLING the globe-trotter left Calcutta on 9 March 1889.
On the fourteenth he was at Rangoon, on the twenty-fourth
at Singapore, on 1 April at Hong-Kong, on 15 April at
Nagasaki; on 11 May he left Yokohama for San Francisco:
a month for renascent Japan and a month for the rest of
the Far East. It is hardly to be expected that his comments
on the politics and economics of farther Asia will have the
weight of his comments on the Punjab where he lived and
worked so long. The articles he wrote light-heartedly for the
Pioneer were never meant to be perpetuated. He was on
holiday, on S.S. *Madura* with 'Ted' and 'Aleck' Hill (he
sometimes now ventured to use short names), as happy as a
child, and with a child's enthusiasm he explored the new
world of commerce and seafaring. The routine of shipboard
life, so dull for a lonely traveller, so entertaining in a congenial party of friends, presented him with a range of technical topics which occupied his mind for the next ten years.

This was the moment in history when the steamship and
the submarine cable had removed the uncertainty of sea
travel, when voyages were still long but had become sure,
so that the life of a ship's passenger had become a new
social mode – safe, select, and utterly isolated from the
world. For a few years only, not more than two generations,
did this phase endure, until space-divisions were eliminated
by the radio techniques, and time-periods minimized by
swift air travel. The liner life that Kipling knew is as extinct as the stagecoach life that Dickens knew, and Kipling
is the poet of the steamship as Dickens is the novelist of the
stagecoach. It is Kipling's discovery of ships and harbours

and seafaring men that is noteworthy from this voyage; he was quickly fascinated by the yarns that are told in liners' smoking-rooms. More than once he used his graphic, vulgar little phrase about 'men in pajamas sitting abaft the funnel and swapping lies of the purple seas'. There was the man's world of the smoking-room and the deck on the tropical night, and there was the woman's world of the saloon, where every gentleman scrupulously dressed for dinner – a world of rippling talk and laughter with 'Ted' and 'Aleck', of paper-games and rhymes scribbled on menu-cards which Ruddy threw off lightly, and which she preserved as the precious workshop chips of her young genius.

At Rangoon they went ashore together to the Shwe Dagon Pagoda where Rudyard was intoxicated with the colour. 'Give me lilac, pink, vermilion, lapis lazuli, and blistering blood-red under fierce sunlight that mellows and modifies all.' He confessed himself overcome with mixed emotion while he derided himself for being a mere tourist. But Rangoon meant more to him as the base-camp of the Burmese campaign; its streets were thronged with his beloved British 'Tommies', on the best of terms with the population here, whatever might be their relation to the dacoits in the jungle.

The three friends transferred themselves into a smaller ship which took them eastward across the Bay to Moulmein where, on a day that Rudyard never forgot, 'Aleck' set up his tripod and photographed first the elephants at work, and then a view of the sea from the terrace beside an old pagoda hung with bronze bells that the worshippers smote with stag-horns. 'I should better remember what the pagoda was like,' wrote Rudyard, 'had I not fallen deeply and irrevocably in love with a Burmese girl at the foot of the first flight of steps.'

When he reached Malaya, it had hardly yet begun to move into that current of progress which made it so prosperous twenty years later. At Penang and Singapore he first found himself face to face with the Chinese race, to whom he took an unaccountable dislike. He tasted the night-life of Hong-Kong with another young globe-trotter, and hated it. Canton he described as 'a big blue sink of a city full of tunnels, all dark and inhabited by yellow devils', which, said Professor Hill, 'was an intemperate libel on a hard-working nation'. Rudyard and the Professor wrangled about China.

Neither at Penang, Singapur, nor this place have I seen a single Chinaman asleep while daylight lasted. Nor have I seen twenty men who were obviously loafing ...
It grieves me that I cannot account for the ideas of a few hundred million men in a few hours. This much, however, seems certain. If we had control over as many Chinamen as we have natives of India, and had given them one tithe of the cosseting, the painful pushing forward, and studious, even nervous, regard of their interests and aspirations that we have given India, we should long ago have been expelled from, or have reaped the reward of, the richest land on the face of the earth.

They crossed to Japan in a P. & O. liner, which Rudyard found to be as hidebound in its regulations and as deficient of comforts as any P. & O. liner west of Suez; he was also seasick. Then came a month's idleness in old Japan, in a country hardly yet touched by western influence and touched – or so he thought – entirely for the worse. The brand-new tailor-made western clothes of the bureaucrats and soldiers were as ugly and ill-fitting as the tailor-made western political constitution. A man who was learning to think poorly of votes and resolutions and caucuses in the West could not be expected to admire them when imposed, corruptly, upon an indifferent people in the East. A parlia-mentary system, as he supposed, was unlikely to do much good, anywhere; industrialism was not to be commended in the only country in the world where arts and crafts, as Wil-liam Morris commended them, were universally practised and respected; the westernized army did not impress him very favourably; he considered the cavalry poor and the in-

fantry perhaps inferior to the British Gurkha regiments. No
one thought differently in 1889.

The Japan of romance – cherry-blossom, geishas, traditional courtesy, family devotion, all set against the landscape that was so fashionable in London studios – it was
here indeed; and on this score he agreed with the Professor.

All the pretty maidens put on their loveliest crêpe sashes –
fawn colour, pink, blue, orange, and lilac, – all the little children
picked up a baby each, and went out to be happy. In a temple
garden full of blossom I performed the miracle of Deucalion
with two cents' worth of sweets. The babies swarmed on the
instant, till, for fear of raising all the mothers too, I forbore to
give them any more. They smiled, and nodded prettily, and
trotted after me, forty strong.
Japan is a great people. Her masons play with stone,
her carpenters with wood, her smiths with iron, and her artists
with life, death, and all the eye can take in. Mercifully she
has been denied the last touch of firmness in her character
which would enable her to play with the whole round world.
We possess that – We, the nation of the glass flower-shade,
the pink worsted mat, the red and green china puppy-
dog, and the poisonous Brussels carpet. It is our compensation.

Having come to these conclusions they set sail in an American ship, the *City of Peking*, for a twenty days' voyage
across the stormy North Pacific. If, from Rudyard's loose,
slight, and gay impressions for the readers of the *Pioneer*,
we are to deduce anything about his considered opinion of
Asia, it is a sense of distaste for lazy, dirty Hindustan where
the college-trained Bengali does not 'sink his money in railway companies, or sit down and provide for the proper sani-
tation of his own city, or of his own motion cultivate the
graces of life'. There was hope for Japan, where craftsmanship and cleanliness were still practised, if only western political corruption could be held off. Japanese imperialism
never entered his mind, and it was with satisfaction that he
revised his first impressions of the army; on a second inspec-

tion they fared much better, and much, he thought, might be done with them under European command.

Seaborne trade, financial organization, naval power were the Englishman's prerogative, solely because he alone could operate them in 1889, and for many years afterwards. Kipling began to see that British India was not the centre of the system, not the normal pattern of British expansion. The sailor and the merchant, not the soldier and the Indian civilian, were the common types of British overseas. India had one solid asset – an army, and there was no other worth a moment's alarm in the Far East, as yet. He threw a careful glance at the fortifications wherever he went and speculated on the range of the British China Squadron. As far as the China Coast, British sea-power was unchallenged. In Japan he felt himself to be in the American sphere, and approached the coast of California with his critical faculties sharpened.[1]

California, sixty-five years ago, was still the 'Wild West', 'where the blindest bluffs hold good and the wildest dreams come true'. Perhaps Kipling, fresh from the gravity of the Indian Administration, was a little too ready to accept the tales told him by bar-loafers who knew nothing of the English talent for understatement. Perhaps his love of prying into unsavoury byways of foreign towns misled him, since in a fortnight at San Francisco he encountered two crimes of violence. It was the lawlessness, the custom of carrying a pistol in the pocket, the contempt for legal niceties that impressed him most.

He was a young tourist and a young politician. With a singular lack of discretion, which he bitterly lamented and never repeated, he delivered himself into the hands of the newspaper reporters who met the ship. What he said, except that he criticized a dozen cherished institutions before he had been three days in the country, will never be known. What the reporters credited him with saying was served up hot and dished up cold again and again. He never lived down his first comments on America; he 'blazed away at us', said the *New York World,* 'with a ferocity that throws Dickens and Mrs Trollope into the shade'. The letters he wrote to the *Pioneer* were damning enough and, since they were not secured by copyright, they were reprinted with horrified gusto in America. His very first comment on San Francisco harbour was somewhat tactless:

When the *City of Peking* steamed through the Golden Gate I saw with great joy that the blockhouse which guarded the mouth of the 'finest harbour in the world, Sir', could be silenced by two gunboats from Hong Kong with safety, comfort, and despatch.

'Joy' was a hard word to digest in that context, though he meant no more than that his estimate was right. A week later, he applauded with real sincerity an appeal for a stronger American Navy made by Lieutenant Carlin, the hero of the Samoa Hurricane. What he condemned in American policy was their aggressive talk and actual impotence. If they would take part in the white man's task of pacifying the world he would be the first to encourage them. While Lieutenant Carlin spoke modestly of the need for more warships he was supported by a 'coruscating Niagara of blather-skite'. 'How in the world can a white man, a Sahib of Our blood, stand up and plaster praise on his own country?'

His introduction to 'the American Eagle screaming for all it was worth' sickened him with American politics – not a difficult matter since all politics sickened him.[1]

Scores of men have told me [he said in his first week] that they would as soon concern themselves with the public affairs of the city or State as rake muck. Turn now to the august spectacle of a Government of the people, by the people, for the people. ... This mass of persons who vote is divided into two parties – Republican and Democrat. ... The Democrat as a party drinks more than the Republican, and when drunk may be heard to talk about a thing called the Tariff, which he does not understand, but which he conceives to be the bulwark of the country or else the surest power for its destruction. Sometimes he says one thing and sometimes another, in order to contradict the Republican, who is always contradicting himself.

These were unfortunate words for launching the career of a man of letters in America, and it was little help to know that he could write as intemperately of liberals in England.

He delivered himself of many other shallow comments:

When the hotel clerk ... stoops to attend to your wants, he does so whistling or humming, or picking his teeth, or pauses to converse with someone he knows. These performances, I gather, are to impress upon you that he is a free man and your equal.

Most of the men wore frock-coats and top-hats – but they all spat. They spat on principle.

They delude themselves into the belief that they talk English – and I have already been pitied for speaking with 'an English accent'. The man who pitied me spoke, so far as I was concerned, the language of thieves.

There was wealth – unlimited wealth – in the streets, but not an accent that would not be dear at fifty cents. ... These persons are harmless in the earlier stages; that is to say, a man worth three or four million dollars may be a good talker, clever, amusing, and of the world; a man with twice that amount is to be avoided; and a twenty-million man is – just twenty millions.

The American does not drink at meals as a sensible man should. Indeed he has no meals. He stuffs for ten minutes thrice a day. ... He pours his vanity into himself at unholy hours, and indeed he can hardly help it. You have no notion of what 'treating' means on the Western slope. It is more than an institution; it is a religion.

From these angry and ill-judged comments, the reader might suppose that Rudyard hated America and the Americans, but he did not. He was amused and fascinated, made many friends, and enjoyed himself immensely in San Francisco, even though the Hills had gone off by train, leaving him there alone. He was befriended by a Mrs Carr, a friend of his mother, who took him about in wealthy society. Best of all he liked a picnic on the beach with her children whom he 'filled up with ice-cream soda and peanuts'. It was pleasant to talk with Mrs Carr about old days in North End Road. The other half of his life was spent with professional friends, journalists, who twice interviewed him for the San Francisco *Examiner*.* Many accounts of other adventures in California were afterwards put out, but all seem equally fictitious. He was pleased by his reception as a distinguished guest from overseas, as his hosts were astonished at this 'little dark man with a perfectly villainous briar-pipe', but he made no great mark. 'I never knew a foreigner who asked so many questions, and such strange ones,' said one journalist.

After a few days in 'Frisco he went up the coast to Portland, Oregon, and again made friends with local newspapermen. 'We spent most of the night,' wrote one of them, 'in side-splitting laughter over a line of barrack-stories in a vernacular almost unintelligible to a New Englander.' Rudyard had come to Portland for a fishing-trip up the Columbia River, when he caught his first salmon, a twelve-pounder. Fishing was the one outdoor sport at which Rudyard was not too near-sighted to excel, and it is also on record that in his fishing-kit the natives described him as the very caricature of a travelling Englishman; they called him 'Johnny Bull'.

From Portland he went to Tacoma, then in the crisis of a land-boom which he described, with great vivacity, in *Letters of Travel*; and, forewarned against speculation, he risked no investment there. It was a different matter when he crossed the border to law-abiding British Columbia and, proud to become a landowner under the British flag, he treated himself to a town lot in Vancouver City. It must be admitted that his confidence was misplaced; they out-smarted him in Vancouver, B.C., just as they would have out-smarted him in Tacoma.

Early in July he moved across the ranges into Montana, to a cow-town where the cowboys were gathering to celebrate

*If Mrs Hill may be believed, he wrote a signed article for the paper, though it seems to have escaped the notice of the collectors.

the 'Fourth'; then spent a week in the Yellowstone Park. He did not omit to report the wonders of nature faithfully for his paper, but was more interested in making friends with a detachment of the American army. They were slovenly, they were undrilled, they were despised even more heartily by the civilians than British soldiers were despised, but they could shoot and they could ride; and their officers were serious students of their profession. Perhaps it was the discovery that many of the troopers were time-expired men from the British service that made Kipling take them seriously. He thought there was something in their mounted-infantry tactics which even Captain Gadsby of the Pink Hussars might study with advantage.[2]

Kipling's accounts of Salt Lake City, or of the stockyards at Chicago, do not differ from those of other tourists, except in sharpness of observation. It was when he reached the eastern States that he became something more than a globe-trotter. For nearly two months he made his home at Beaver, a little country town on the Monongahela, in the house of Mrs Hill's parents, leaving them occasionally to visit places of interest in the east. Mrs Hill was living with her father, Professor R. T. Taylor, the president of a small college, and with them was her young sister, Caroline Taylor, a cheerful, plump, young girl. 'Ted' had often written to Caroline about her friendship with Rudyard, and we may imagine the mixed emotions with which she presented him. 'Ted' must have been occasionally embarrassed by her devoted admirer, though no grain of evidence survives to suggest that Rudyard ever spoke to her as a lover. Almost any happily married woman in her position would have discreetly diverted his attention to her younger sister, unattached and near to Rudyard's age. By 11 August we find him somewhat coyly asking after 'Miss Carrie' when writing his usual narrative letter to Mrs Hill. He had gone off to Buffalo, in company with her cousin, Edgar Hill, to see the Falls, but what he most enjoyed on that journey was watching a grain-elevator at work. He made a trip to Washington, where some keen soldiers from the War Department found him out, and cross-questioned him about the North-West Frontier. At Philadelphia, too, it pleased him best to yarn with the deep-sea sailors along the waterfront.

In a hotel he had a refreshing experience:

'There are three gentlemen from India here, natives of your country,' quoth the clerk. 'Amen,' said I, and turned up the register to find the names of Allbless, Rustomjee, and Bryamjee, all Parsees – and Allbless, at least, of a family I krew something about. When I went in to supper I found 'em seated at a table and stealing behind 'em spake in the sweetest of vernaculars.

At Boston the historic associations caught his fancy – and more so at Lexington and Concord than at any other place he had visited. He had, also, a pilgrimage to make to a literary shrine, not to one of the New England sanctuaries, but to the house of Mark Twain, at Elmira, New York. Rudyard, who so resented intrusion on his own privacy, seems not to have noticed that his visit to Mark Twain was equally impertinent. Mark Twain received him with courtesy and gave him 'copy' for an interview which was reprinted in uncounted American papers.

Imagine a rolling, wooded, English landscape, under the softest of blue skies, dotted at three-mile intervals with fat little, quiet little villages, or aggressive manufacturing towns that the trees and the folds of the hills mercifully prevented from betraying their presence. The golden-rod blazed in the pastures against the green of the mulleins, and the cows picked their way home through the twisted paths, between the blackberry bushes.

This sightseeing was irrelevant to his real study of American life at Beaver.

Here were Americans and no aliens – men ruling themselves by themselves and for themselves and their wives and their children – in peace, order, and decency ... they were Methody folk for the most part – ay, Methody as ever trod a Yorkshire

Moor, or drove on a Sunday to some chapel of the Faith in the Dales. The old Methody talk was there, with the discipline whereby the souls of the Just are, sometimes to their intense vexation, made perfect on this earth in order that they may 'take out their letters and live and die in good standing'.

This unusual throw-back to the Methodist morale of his father's family did not distract Rudyard's eye from present humanity. He liked

The absolutely fresh, wholesome, sweet life that paid due reverence to the things of the next world, but took good care to get enough tennis in the cool of the evening; that concerned itself as honestly and thoroughly with the daily round, the trivial task as with the salvation of the soul. I had the honour of meeting in the flesh, even as Miss Louisa Alcott drew them, Meg and Joe and Beth and Amy, whom you ought to know.

He was now in love with America and with the American girl in general, rather than with the specimen that Mrs Hill had laid before him in particular, and through the American girl he came to a better understanding of the American man.

Pick an American of the second generation anywhere you please – from the cab-rank, the porters' room, or the plough-tail, – especially the plough-tail, – and the man will make you understand in five minutes that he understands what manner of thing his Republic is. He might laugh at a law that didn't suit his convenience, draw your eye-teeth into the bargain, and applaud 'cuteness on the outer verge of swindling, but you should hear him stand up and sing:
                    'My country, 'tis of thee...'

He rhapsodized, a little recklessly, about the supposed Anglo-Saxon race.

There must be born a poet who shall ... compose the greatest song of all – The Saga of the Anglo-Saxon all round the earth – a paean that shall combine the terrible slow swing of the *Battle Hymn of the Republic* with *Britannia needs no Bulwarks*, the skirl of the *British Grenadiers* with that perfect quickstep,

Marching through Georgia, and at the end the wail of the *Dead March*. Will any one take the contract? [3]

When he had cooled down a little, it was to be his own.

His holiday over and his money spent, he went to New York in September and seriously set himself to work. A cheerful sign was the sudden appearance of a whole crop of reviews of his Indian 'Railway' stories in the English magazines, while an American publisher had already paid him the compliment of issuing a pirated version of the *Plain Tales*.

No more promising work has recently appeared in the English tongue [said the *St James's Gazette*] than the Anglo-Indian stories of Mr Kipling.

A more readable or amusing book we have seldom come across [said *Vanity Fair*].

Mr Kipling does not write with rose-water [said the *World*]. The story called 'His Majesty the King' is moreover somewhat maudlin at the best and 'Baa, Baa, Black Sheep' is too grim and unlovely to be associated with the playfulness of childhood. But 'The Drums of the Fore and Aft' is a fine tale, full of rough life and spirit and touched with just the right proportion of pathos to redeem its coarseness.

The worst of recommending these publications [said a writer in the *Saturday Review*], which we do very heartily, is that apparently they are difficult to procure. They appear in paper-covered little vols., but these vols. are not found on English railway bookstalls. Very little that is so new and so good can be discovered on these shrines of fugitive literature. Mr K. is a new writer, new to the English as distinct from the Anglo-Indian public. He is so clever, so fresh, and so cynical, that he must be young.

The first analytical essay by a writer who knew Kipling's background, and knew India, was an article in *The Academy* by Sir William Hunter, a member of Lord Dufferin's Council, who had himself been satirized in *Departmental Ditties*.

Some day a writer will arise [he wrote] – perhaps this young
poet is the destined man – who will make that nobler Anglo-
Indian world known as it really is. It will then be seen by what a
hard discipline of endurance our countrymen and country-
women in India are trained to do England's greatest work on the
earth ... of this realistic side of Anglo-Indian life Mr Kipling
... gives glimpses. His serious poems seem to me the ones most
full of promise. Taken as a whole his book gives hope of a new
literary star of no mean magnitude rising in the east.[4]

Though Kipling had published little or nothing in
America he was thus not quite an unknown man when he
arrived in New York. His first call was on his father's friend,
De Forest, who gave him an introduction to Henry Harper,
the head of the New York publishing profession, and this
introduction was backed by Edwin Abbey the painter. He
called at the office of Harper Brothers on 10 September and
met with such a reception that he never forgave them. They
dimissed him with a letter 'just one and a half lines long'.
Tradition gives the words spoken to him as: 'Young man,
this house is devoted to the production of literature.'[5] Whatever were the words, they did not damp his ardour; he was off
next day in the best of spirits, with a fund of lively messages
for Caroline Taylor. He never had to ask a favour of an
American publisher again.

His last fortnight in the United States was given to the
De Forests on Long Island, and to his uncle Henry Macdonald in New York City.

My uncle reminds me pathetically from time to time that I
am the only one of his blood-kin who has come to him for thirty
years; speaks of me as 'my boy' and yarns away about literature.
The Aunt, who does not care for books, is different, but I am
making good headway there. This evening I spent in their company and she out-thawed much. ... Some day we will put it in a
book, and laugh at it all to ourselves.[6]

It was to Mrs Hill that he wrote these words. She was
still his confidante, and again he was to have the happiness
of travelling in her friendly company. Mrs Hill was return-

ing to India by way of Europe, and was taking Caroline
Taylor with her; Edgar Taylor, their cousin, squared off the
party. They arrived at Liverpool by the S.S. *City of Berlin* on
5 October 1889, and all four went on to London.

What were Rudyard's first impressions of England after
seven years' absence? No record has survived. He had gone
away a boy, certainly a precocious boy but not yet seventeen
years old; he returned a man nearing his twenty-fourth
birthday and conscious of a fund of experience that marked
him out among conventional Londoners. World travel was
rarer then than it is today, and the raw physical danger of
life in tropical Asia seemed far removed from the security of
Victorian Kensington. Young Rudyard felt himself to have
an advantage over his London acquaintances in knowing
two worlds, East and West, while they knew only one. If
they regarded him as an outlandish provincial, he returned
their condescension with amused contempt, not unmixed
with a tinge of unconscious envy.

It appears that he resumed his connexion with his childhood friends, with the 'Three Old Ladies', now very old, and
with the Burne-Joneses. While looking for a lodging, he
stayed at North End Road and after a short holiday in Paris
found an eyrie from which to survey London, in two rooms
and a landing on the third floor of a tall house called
Embankment Chambers at the foot of Villiers Street, with a
view southwards across the river, and only a few doors away
from the London office of the *Pioneer*. Mrs Hill and Miss
Taylor were there to see him established, to arrange his
sitting-room with the Bokhariot rugs and Japanese knick-
knacks he had collected on his travels, to provide company
and conversation in a chilly autumnal world.

At Lahore his mother complained that she had little news
of her son. The only intimate picture of Kipling's life in
London is revealed in the series of letters which he wrote to
his two friends after their departure for India on 25 October.
This new world in which he now felt quite alone was as

strange to him as a desert island; and its inhabitants offered him no comfort. Though they took notice of him, it was as a rarity, as a curiosity from overseas, not as a comrade.

Many persons of distinction, after his fame was assured, claimed to have launched Kipling in the literary world and, indeed, the rumour of his Indian reputation had preceded him. He had not been more than a few days in London before he was taken by Andrew Lang to the Savile Club, the acknowledged meeting-place of critics, editors, and novelists. Andrew Lang, 'detached as a cloud but never kinder in your behalf than when he seemed least concerned with you', was among other things reader for the publishing firm of Sampson Low, and had already advised them to take over the English rights of the six volumes in the *Indian Railway Library*. Arrangements were made for their reissue in London by Kipling in person, the only occasion in his life, as he said rather defiantly, when he negotiated directly with a London publisher. He visited Sampson Low's office, at St Dunstan's House near the bottom of Fetter Lane, in November, and struck some sort of bargain, but not a good one for himself. The first volume, *Soldiers Three*, in an edition of 7,000 copies for the English market, was published early in 1890, and it was not until then that Kipling's stories first became known to the general reading public in England.[7]

Meanwhile he had to live; the £200 with which he had set out from India did not carry him far; he had sold little or nothing in America, and money for his articles in the *Pioneer* was slow to arrive. Though half the editors in London, and two or three publishers were anxious to make his acquaintance, he was too proud to ask them for money in advance.

People who ask for money, however justifiably, have it remembered against them. The beloved Aunt, or any one of the Three Old Ladies, would have given to me without question; but that seemed too like confessing failure at the outset. My rent was paid; I had my dress suit; I had nothing to pawn save a collection of unmarked shirts picked up in all the ports, so I made shift to manage on what small cash I had in pocket. My rooms were above an establishment of Harris the Sausage King, who, for tuppence, gave as much sausage and mash as would carry one from breakfast to dinner when one dined with nice people who did not eat sausage for a living. Another tuppence found me a filling supper. The excellent tobacco of those days was, unless you sank to threepenny 'shag' or soared to sixpenny 'Turkish', tuppence the half-ounce: and fourpence, which included a pewter of beer or porter, was the price of admission to Gatti's Music hall.[8]

Kipling's earliest introductions in London were through two journalists to whom he was already indebted in India. One was Mowbray Morris, the editor of *Macmillan's Magazine*, who had once been art editor of the *Pioneer*; the other was his old senior, Stephen Wheeler, a friend in need. Wheeler was on the staff of the *St James's Gazette*, a literary evening paper of a kind long since defunct, and introduced Kipling to the editor, Sidney Low, who thus described their meeting:

I spent an afternoon reading *Soldiers Three* and when I went out to a dinner-party that evening I could talk of nothing but this marvellous youth who had dawned upon the eastern horizon. My host, a well-known journalist and critic of those days, laughed at my enthusiasm which he said would hardly be justified by the appearance of another Dickens. 'It may be,' I answered hotly, 'that a greater than Dickens is here.'

I got Wheeler to put me in touch with Kipling on his arrival in London, and one morning there walked into my office a short, dark, young man with a bowler hat, a rather shabby tweed overcoat, an emphatic voice, a charming smile, and behind his spectacles a pair of the brightest eyes I had ever seen. He told me that he had to make his way in English literature, and intended to do it, though at the time he was young, very poor, and (in this country) quite unknown. I suggested that he might help to keep his pot boiling by writing sketches and short stories for the *St James's*, which suggestion he willingly accepted. He also accepted my proposal to come out and lunch with me.

We sat down in the grill-room of Sweeting's Restaurant in Fleet Street. I wanted to 'draw' Kipling, and I drew him to some purpose by getting him to tell me about places he had seen in India and elsewhere. He was in no wise reluctant, being exceedingly frank and communicative, and overflowing with ideas and memories which had to find vent; and he talked in those days with the same abandon and energy as he wrote.

One after another of the lunchers laid down knife and fork to listen to him, and presently he had half the room for his audience. He was quite unconscious of the attention he evoked. ... A day or two later he sent me a contribution, which I received with delight and promptly printed. This, as far as I know, was the first piece from Kipling's pen published in England.* 9

In the same month, November 1889, the first of two long ballads was accepted by Mowbray Morris. It was typical of Kipling that his first step in starting a new career, in a new country, should be under a new name; he would not derive adventitious support from a reputation earned elsewhere. Accordingly, the poems appeared in *Macmillan's*, under the pseudonym, 'Yussuf'. The first of these two, 'The Ballad of the King's Mercy', has never been regarded as one of his major works; the second of them, 'The Ballad of East and West', which followed in the December issue, at once raised its author into the first rank of contemporary writers. No one ever seems to have doubted that it was written by Kipling. George Saintsbury selected it as one of two examples of contemporary verse worth mentioning by name in his *History of English Prosody*; and down at Farringford the aged Tennyson growled to a friend that young Kipling was 'the only one of them with the divine fire'.

* It has not positively been identified. Kipling himself disowned 'The Comet of the Season' (*St James's Gazette*, 21 November 1889), which is ascribed to him in Livingston: *Bibliography*, p. 72. Internal evidence of style and subject make it pretty clear that it could have been written by no one else. He could have had no imitators at that date.

Oh, East is East, and West is West, and never the twain shall
    meet,
Till Earth and Sky stand presently at God's great Judgement
    Seat;
But there is neither East nor West, Border, nor Breed, nor
    Birth,
When two strong men stand face to face, though they come
    from the ends of the earth!

No lines of Kipling's have been more freely quoted, and
more often misquoted in exactly the opposite sense to that
which Kipling gave them. The first couplet is an echo from
the Psalms where the figure of speech is used to express the
universality of the divine law in spite of estranging seas; the
second couplet is Kipling's commentary, with the same
theme as the psalmist. The divine spark in human nature
also transcends all earthly distinctions. This was the lifelong
message that Kipling preached, acceptance of 'the Law',
revealed to strong men who recognize one another's valour.

The strength of the Ballad lies in its galloping rhythm
which suggested to Saintsbury that Kipling had a 'soul for
the anapaest'. Its rapid and varying pace, exactly suited to
the development of the theme, showed an extraordinary ease
and mastery of words. Even Swinburne could not show such
vigour and flexibility. The subject, though painted with the
local colour of northern India and painted with brilliant
realism, was a human drama which is likely to attract
readers as long as men admire courage and love a good
horse. It is founded upon the true story of Dilawur Khan
and Colonel Lumsden of the 'Guides', an episode of the
Indian frontier in 1848; it might as well have been told in
the idiom of the Scottish Border, or of the Mexican Border,
for its theme is not that East and West differ but that men
of all races are alike at heart.[10]

As formerly at Lahore, so in London during his first
English winter, Rudyard's letters to Mrs Hill are in the form
of an intermittent journal. It reveals that in spite of his

immediate success with editors and publishers he was lonely in London and sick at heart. He longed for sunshine and for the feminine company that had given him happiness for two years past. At that time, when the critics were astonished at Rudyard's precocity, asserting that he seemed to have learned all about Life before his twenty-fourth birthday, his personal letters display an engagingly boyish side to his character, and nowhere more so than in his relation to the two women upon whom he had set his affections. The letters to the younger sister, Caroline Taylor, whom he had known only for a few weeks, are beyond question love-letters. Whether, in the formal society of the eighteen-nineties, the understanding between these two young people amounted to an engagement is not now clear, but the endearments he used, and the prospects of marriage which he discussed with Miss Taylor, were the language of conventional love-making. They reveal, too, that however 'knowing' he had been about Mrs Hauksbee and Captain Gadsby, he had not plumbed the depths of his own heart.

Rudyard wrote to Caroline Taylor with the mixture of dog-like devotion and bland condescension that is perhaps characteristic of the very young lover. These letters are not in themselves interesting, they are the common form of calf-love and may for the most part be left in the oblivion where their writer would wish them to lie. 'Heart o' mine, you, as well as I, must have discovered by this time that the writing of love-letters is no easy thing. I own that I laughed, disrespectfully, at the delicious one you sent off by the pilot – happy man was he.' No more of this! There is, however, one letter to Miss Taylor, dated 9 December 1889, from Embankment Chambers, which should perhaps be recorded in spite of the writer's disgust at any intrusion on privacy; it is his confession of faith.

Miss Taylor's father was a clergyman, of stricter puritan views even than Rudyard's Methodist grandparents, and she seems to have shared her father's orthodoxy. In a world where *Robert Elsmere*, the novel of the day, turned upon a partial loss of faith, Rudyard's laxity in his religion was no small consideration. Something Professor Hill had said gave her the impression that Rudyard was in danger of conversion to Rome. A story which he published a few months later, 'On Greenhow Hill', gives in the stage-Irish of Mulvaney a comment on the Churches which may reveal its author's tendency in 1890. His enthusiasm for the Methodist ways of Pennsylvania had been short-lived.

'I misdoubt you were built for the Primitive Methodians,' says Private Mulvaney to Private Learoyd. 'They're a new corps, anyways. I hold by the Ould Church, for she's the Mother of them all – ay, and the father, too. I like her, bekaze she's most remarkable regimental in her fittings. I may die in Honolulu, Nova Zambra or Cape Cayenne, but wherever I die, I go under the same orders an' the same words an' the same unction as tho' the Pope himself come down from the roof at St Peter's to see me off. There's neither high nor low, nor broad nor deep, nor betwixt nor between wid her, an' that's what I like.'

Though some such tribute to the Roman Church may have escaped Rudyard's lips, he responded gamely to the Professor's challenge.

No. Aleck was a little wrong. Your slave was baptised in Bombay Cathedral into the Church of England, which you call Episcopalian, was brought up as you have read in that church, and confirmed by the Bishop of Exeter in Bideford Church, in '80 or '81. Does that satisfy that I am not a veiled adherent of the Church of Rome? You have got from me what no living soul has ever done before [he went on]. I believe in the existence of a personal God to whom we are personally responsible for wrongdoing – that it is our duty to follow and our peril to disobey the ten ethical laws laid down for us by Him and His prophets. I disbelieve directly in eternal punishment, for reasons that would take too long to put down on paper. On the same grounds I disbelieve in an eternal reward. As regards the mystery of the Trinity and the Doctrine of Redemption, I regard them most reverently but I cannot give them implicit belief.

The letter concludes with an affirmation which the young man seems to drag out of himself with an effort:

I believe in God the Father Almighty, maker of Heaven and Earth and in One filled with His spirit Who did voluntarily die in the belief that the human race would be spiritually bettered thereby.

It would not be proper to deduce the theological position which Rudyard eventually reached, from this emotional outburst addressed by a very young man to a very young woman. It was not, we may suppose, enough to satisfy Miss Taylor, or her father; it is likely that Rudyard's unorthodoxy was the reason why the affair came to nothing. Perhaps it is relevant that in his next letter, addressed to Mrs Hill the elder sister, he remarks, lightly, as something unusual, that he has 'been to church – St Clement Danes'.

Rudyard Kipling's extraordinary facility for keeping his interests in distinct compartments of his mind was never more marked than in his London period.

> I would go without shirt or shoe,
> Friend, tobacco or bread,
> Sooner than lose for a minute the two
> Separate sides of my head! [11]

So he wrote, on some later occasion, and so he always seemed to organize his thought. Those who knew him best remarked upon the intensity of his interest; in conversation with friends he threw himself so absolutely into the subject under discussion that, for the time, nothing else seemed to exist for him. He opened his mind to the persons he spoke with so fully, so candidly as to penetrate their interests, see with their eyes, and enter into their emotions. 'His mind,' said one who knew him well, 'was like the leaves of a book, which could be quickly turned to suit the company he was in.' When with the Hills he was all alertness to their concerns, all sympathy for their feelings; but when they were gone, his mind was too active to rest in disconsolate loneliness.

Within twenty-four hours of the departure of his friends, he had been composing light verse for the amusement of another entirely masculine circle of acquaintance. He had been taken to the Savile Club by Andrew Lang and for his new friends there he wrote a letter in verse, a spirited parody of Bret Harte's 'Truthful James', with critical allusions to the new romance, *Cleopatra*, just published by Rider Haggard. It does not read like the work of a man with a newly broken heart. A year later, when his name came up for election to the Savile, the page in the candidates' book looked like a roll of English men of letters. He was supported by Walter Besant, James Bryce, Edward Clodd, John Collier, Sidney Colvin, Austin Dobson, Edmund Gosse, Rider Haggard, Thomas Hardy, W. E. Henley, Henry James, J. H. McCarthy, J. W. Mackail, Walter Pollock, George Saintsbury, and by others who were hardly less eminent.[12]

Very soon after Kipling's arrival in London, Edmund Gosse, with the intention of finding a friend for the newcomer, introduced him to a young American literary man named Wolcott Balestier who strongly desired his acquaintance. It did not, however, ripen into friendship until some months later. In the literary world his earliest friends were Lang, Haggard, and 'Anstey' (T. A. Guthrie, author of *Vice Versa*) and, even among these light-weights, he felt himself to be out of his element.

London is a vile place, and Anstey and Haggard and Lang and Co. are pressing on me the wisdom of identifying myself with some set, while the long-haired literati of the Savile Club are swearing that I 'invented' my soldier talk in *Soldiers Three*. Seeing that not one of these critters has been within earshot of a barrack, I am naturally wrath. But this is only the beginning of the lark. You'll see some savage criticism of my work before spring. That's what I am playing for.

Perhaps this defiance need not be taken at quite its face value, for he could be receptive of good advice. On Lord Mayor's day he fought his way through the crowds to Macmillan's office, delighted that he had finished 'The Ballad of East and West' to his satisfaction, and amenable to criticism of his other work. He even allowed Mowbray Morris to censor thirty lines of his first story written in London, the extravaganza called 'The Incarnation of Krishna Mulvaney', which was 'a little too drunken' for English middle-class taste.

Next, calling on his relatives, the Poynters, at Knightsbridge, he was in his element. There were his Aunt Aggie (Poynter), his Aunt Edie (Macdonald); his cousin Margaret, no longer his 'Dear Wop' but Mrs J. W. Mackail, and a new young cousin in the nursery, Hugh Poynter aged eight, his favourite among them all. But the party was spoiled by the presence of a literary lion, Sidney Colvin, who wrote the Life of Keats.

The same is an all-fired prig of immense water and suffers from all the nervo-hysterical diseases of the nineteenth century. Went home with him as far as Charing Cross in a 3rd smoking (which made him sick). He recounted all his symptoms and made me sick. A queer beast with match-stick fingers and a dry unwholesome skin.

Another day it was lunch with Pollock, the editor of the *Saturday Review,*

in grisly grey chambers in the Albany met Saintsbury and Jebb [he wrote]. A vile lunch. No talk. Pollock half asleep and the forks dirty. Dined at 6 (ungodly hour) with Hooper of the *Spectator.* Met a wild socialist who told me that the working man was a god. 'Then kill him,' said I and levanted.

Worst of all was a visit to George Meredith at Box Hill, an expedition which most young men of letters would have made in a different frame of mind.

Show me no more celebrities for they disillusion me sadly. Imagine an old withered little man very deaf in one ear who, as did Dagonet in the *Morte d'Arthur*,

'Skips like a withered leaf upon the floor.'

He is full to a painful overflowing of elaborated epigrammatic speech which on the first fizz strikes one as deuced good. Five minutes later one cannot remember what on earth it was all about. And neither time, tide, Heaven nor Hell, nor the sanctities of five-o'-clock tea seem to be able to stop that flow of talk. The raucous voice continues; the little old man balances himself on his toes like a Shanghai rooster to command attention, and that attention *must* be given or he sulks like a child.*

So homesick was Kipling for India that he clung to anyone who could remind him of it. When opening an account at the West End branch of his bank, the Oriental Banking Corporation, he found pleasure in being received by the manager as an Anglo-Indian customer, and greater pleasure in meeting an Anglo-Indian acquaintance in the street outside. It was Logan of the Bombay Cavalry, no doubt as lonely in London as was Kipling, and they 'danced on the pavement'. The letters to Mrs Hill recount many such incidents; a man who lives at Charing Cross and does much prowling about the streets is sure to meet his travelling acquaintance. His story 'A Conference of the Powers', no very profound matter, is taken from the common form of these entries in his journal.

Not many weeks after his arrival, he sent a set of verses in the style of Lewis Carroll to the *Civil and Military Gazette*.

> The sky, a greasy soup-tureen,
>   Shuts down atop my brow.
> Yes, I have sighed for London Town

---

* S. S. McClure, afterwards R. K.'s friend and publisher, gives the other side of these conversations in his *Autobiography*. Colvin recommended R. K. to McClure as the 'coming man'. McClure consulted Meredith, who said emphatically: 'The coming man is James Matthew Barrie.'

And I have got it now:
And half of it is fog and filth,
And half is fog and row.

But I consort with long-haired things
In velvet collar-rolls,
Who talk about the Aims of Art,
And 'theories' and 'goals',
And moo and coo with womenfolk
About their blessed souls.

But what they call 'psychology'
Is lack of liver-pill,
And all that blights their tender souls
Is eating till they're ill,
And their chief way of winning goals
Consists of sitting still.

It's Oh to meet an Army man,
Set up, and trimmed and taut,
Who does not spot hashed libraries
Or think the next man's thought,
And walks as though he owned himself,
And hogs his bristles short.[13]

The P. & O. steamers disgorged no such companion, no
subaltern or junior civilian, to share his life in London. His
two most regular callers were his cousins, Ambrose Poynter
and Philip Burne-Jones, both mightily impressed by his
man-of-the-world airs. 'Ambo' Poynter was the nearest
thing Kipling possessed to a confidant; he would come into
Embankment Chambers and lay bare his soul, hour after
hour, until he was turned out at one or two in the morning.
His trouble, apart from mere green-sickness, was the common misfortune of a successful man's son; he had inherited
his father's nervous temperament without his father's talent.
What he had to exhibit was a five-act tragedy in verse, full
of allusions which Kipling, with his meagre classical knowledge, found formidable. 'Ambo', of course, was grateful for
advice and eager for help, but unwilling to be told the truth

about his work. It was to Mrs Hill that Rudyard wrote a candid opinion.

> He estimates his poems not by the thing actually put down in black and white but by all the glorious inchoate fancies that flashed through his brain while his pen was in his hand.

Though 'Ambo' Poynter had his own career, as an architect, his poetical aspirations had their consequence in providing 'copy' for Kipling, who throughout life was haunted by the notion that buried and even inherited memories reveal themselves in dreams. Long before the Viennese scientists formulated the new psychology of the unconscious, the writers of the nineties focused attention on these problems, thus creating the mental climate in which the new psychology was born. The conflict between 'Ambo' Poynter's unrealized visions and inadequate expression suggested to Rudyard the plot of a story which, again, showed an advance in human sympathy and understanding. 'The Finest Story in the World', his tale of a London clerk who almost, but not quite, recalls memories inherited from a remote past, owes much to 'Ambo' Poynter.

The Poynters were 'society' people and Edward Poynter a fashionable painter of historical tableaux on the largest scale. His *Solomon and the Queen of Sheba*, which was to be his masterpiece, moved Rudyard to ribaldry in the style of Uncle Remus.

> It's old Brer Solomon coming down the steps of his throne to welcome Sis Sheby as she comes along with apes and peacocks and all that truck. I never saw such a blaze of colour or jumble of notions in my life. 'I thought it was oriental,' said Poynter, 'and no one knows any better here.' It's mighty curious to see behind an R.A.'s piccy and note the bits of things it is made up of. In my usual genial way I proffered advice and suggestions – two of which were accepted and as I ran out of the studio (it's one of a great range) I stepped into or onto the tray containing Hamo Thornycroft's modest lunch. He does his sculpture on milk and rusks. He was not pleased but they should not leave his lunch at the door.

Mrs Poynter (Aunt Aggie) took Rudyard into Society, to a dance in Rutland Gate and to a reception in Mayfair where he was made much of. 'Lady Wentworth, Lords Pembroke and Grosvenor backed me into a corner', he wrote to Caroline, 'and stood over me pouring out melted compliments into my throat, one after the other. And through it all I kept thinking to myself, "Unless it happened that I was the fashion for the moment, you'd let me die of want on your doorstep". And so they would.'

On the whole, the Burne-Joneses were nearer to him, less fashionable and less academic. Uncle Ned, that shy genius, was a 'mine of wisdom', the best of talkers if only he could be persuaded 'to uncork himself'; and Aunt Georgie was as dear to Rudyard Kipling the man as she had been to the boy – but she was down at Rottingdean that winter. Their son Phil was a painter, making some progress in his father's profession; though not so communicative as 'Ambo' Poynter, he, too, had troubles to confide to his cousin from the wide world. He had sold an autobiographical article to a disreputable publishing syndicate, and regretted it. Rudyard had to go down to Fleet Street to get Phil out of their clutches, an episode which he worked up into a chapter for *The Light that Failed.*

On Christmas Day he looked out to find London shrouded in fog, 'the streets nearly empty and those who were in the streets nearly full'. Never had he felt more solitary. Only Uncle Ned and Phil were at call since they too were spending a bachelor Christmas. The three went out to dine together at Solferino's, the little foreign restaurant in Rupert Street that Rudyard favoured, to find themselves the only customers, and the proprietor sitting down with the staff to a Christmas dinner, in which the three joined. Though that was a mildly pleasant experience, Rudyard went home to write at midnight to his friends in India :

there are five million people in London this night and, saving those who starve, I don't think there is one more heartsick or thoroughly wretched than that rising young author known to you as – Ruddy.

One of his observations upon London life, which recurs again and again in his writing at the period, is his disgust at the hordes of prostitutes who infested the streets about Charing Cross; he had seen nothing like it in oriental cities.[14]

> And when I take my nightly prowl,
>   'Tis passing good to meet
> The pious Briton lugging home
>   His wife and daughter sweet,
> Through four packed miles of seething vice,
>   Thrust out upon the street.

It exceeded the 'City of Dreadful Night' in horror, and offered no allurement to him.

He did not eschew humble company; there was a barber's and bird-shop in Drury Lane where he sometimes went to be shaved; there was a fishing-tackle shop which gave a meeting-place to a coarse-fishing club; there were the police of E Division who dealt with the rows of 'real ladies' outside Gatti's music-hall, and fetched the ambulance when a man cut his throat under the windows of Embankment Chambers; there was the clerk who came up to Rudyard's rooms to tell the life-history which, combined with 'Ambo' Poynter's, became the framework for 'The Finest Story in the World'; there was the comic man from Gatti's who kept on 'knocking 'em', but commented that 'life's all a blooming kick-up'; there was the elderly but upright barmaid who told Rudyard a story which he made into the poem called 'Mary, pity Women!'; there was a lascar from the Docks whom he thought of employing as a 'bearer' and who vanished after giving him the notion that became 'The Limitations of Pambé Serang'; and there was the incident of Aunt Georgie's housemaid which made a whole sub-plot in *The Light that Failed.*

My spirits were most awful low and I was beginning to weep audibly when a knock arrived at the door, and Aunt Georgie's housemaid – the cross-eyed one not the pretty one – arrived with a packet of letters from India. Then I whooped. It struck me as queer that the girl should have come across London to give the letters into my hand when she could have posted 'em. So I made enquiries. 'Where's Aunt Georgie?' 'Oh, she's gone to Rottingdean,' said the artless Anne who, I dare say, desired amusement and sought it in my chambers. So I treated her with immense distinction – the buttons are beginning to drop off my shirt-collar you must understand – and then I gravely gave her tea, and she discussed housekeeping details – coal, wrist bands, darning stockings *etc*. In the end, emboldened by much tea, which made her glisten like a newly buttered muffin, she said that it would be fit and proper for me to settle down and marry a nice steady young woman because I 'kept my things dreadful'. With a large smirk she left me to digest the advice.

There was no lack of 'copy' in London, and no lack of gratuitous advice; there were, he wrote, 'proposals from "certain people of importance", insistent and unscrupulous as horse-copers, telling me "how the ball was at my feet" and that I had only to kick it – by repeating the notes I had already struck and trailing characters I had already "created" through impossible scenes – to achieve all sorts of desirable things.' Among the advisers there was one whom Rudyard followed, Walter Besant, who would

sit behind his big frosty beard and twinkling spectacles, and deal me out wisdom concerning this new incomprehensible world. He advised me to 'keep out of the dog-fight'. He said that if I were 'in with one lot' I would have to be out with another; and that, at last, 'things would get like a girls' school where they stick out their tongues at each other when they pass'. One heard very good talk at the Savile.

Besant was one of the founders of the Authors' Society and an active worker for an agreed system of international copyright. He introduced Rudyard to A. P. Watt & Son, the literary agents, and in a few weeks they had got his affairs in order. On 5 March 1890 he was able to thank them for doubling his income in three months, and, forty years later, declared that he could not 'recall any difference that three minutes' talk could not clear up'. But the year 1890 was to reveal some knotty problems for them to solve.[15]

On 7 February Rudyard wrote to Caroline Taylor:

I am just now being chased by several publishers. I reply with great sweetness that my engagements are *complet* and that they had better go and take a walk. Publishers are not used to being treated in this manner and they return to the charge like Jew hawkers with proffers of ready money down. See'st thou the drift of this? It is to make the new man write as swiftly and as largely as possible on the novel subject. Then when he is squeezed dry they heave him away and call the newspapers to witness that there is no originality in the present writers.

Wherefore I have refused in a brief poem of five stanzas the *St James's Gazette* offer of a permanent engagement. Catch me putting my head into that old noose again – and me hardly recovered from the constant surprises of seven years' journalism.

The situation stands thus, I hold work on *Macmillan's Magazine* up to £300 a year. The Lahore paper stands me for £100 (and that's four hundred). On those two alone therefore, without turning my attention to the *St James's*, the *Spectator*, *Longman's*, and *Punch* (who all want me), I could devote myself to building up the American connection and going on straight with the books and poetry.

It will be recognized that his success was still on a modest scale, and his reputation still dependent on his earlier work. He wrote post-haste to his parents for the manuscript of *Mother Maturin* which he had left in India; perhaps it would work up into something for Longman's; but new poems just then were singing themselves most urgently in his head, ballads about soldiering set to the rhythms of the London music-hall.

On his old record, he was suddenly swept into fame by *The Times* which gave, on 25 March 1890, the signal honour of a full leading article to the whole range of his work in the Calcutta editions:

India has given us an abundance of soldiers and administrators, but she has seldom given us a writer. There is no question, however, that she has done this in the person of the author of the numerous short stories and verses of which we give the titles below. Mr Rudyard Kipling has the merit of having tapped a new vein, and of having worked it out with real originality. He is even now a very young man, in spite of his seven or eight small volumes; in fact, we believe he is not yet twenty-five.

Mr Kipling found himself famous in Indian society as the writer of sketches which were generally accepted as representing, with a fair amount of truth and a great amount of pungency, scenes of a very diverse kind. ... He is at home at Simla, and in the life of 'the station'. He deals also with that unfortunate result of our settlement in India, the Eurasian, and some of the most brilliant of his tales have this seldom successful growth for their topic. ... He may be almost called the discoverer, as far as India is concerned, of 'Tommy Atkins' as a hero of realistic romance. ... Some of the best and most penetrating of the *Plain Tales* deal with various aspects of native life, and in this department Mr Kipling's curious and seemingly almost instinctive knowledge is not less evident than in his stories of European life. ... That very grim story 'In the House of Suddhoo', the tragedy called 'Beyond the Pale', and one or two of the 'Black and White' series seem to be almost the best of Mr Kipling's writings, perhaps because they appear to lift the veil from a state of society so immeasurably different from our own ...

In nothing is Mr Kipling more successful than in his truly lurid descriptions and indications of what Indian heat can be, and what its effect on the minds and bodies of the Europeans who have to suffer it ...

Plain Tales from the Hills is the longest of the volumes, and, as its title implies, it deals mostly with Simla life. The picture that Mr Kipling gives is not altogether a pleasant one; but then he does not pretend to be an optimist or to represent society as all varnish and veneer. ... If it fails of being a first-rate picture, it is because Mr Kipling, though an admirably direct writer, is comparatively wanting in style. People have compared him with Guy de Maupassant, not, let it be observed, that he shows any disposition to emulate the French writer in his choice of subjects (which would be, indeed, even now, an impossibility for an

Englishman) but because of his incisive power of drawing
vignette portraits and of representing in half a dozen pages a
complete action. ... Guy de Maupassant is, however, a stylist
of the first order, and this Mr Kipling is not, yet, whatever he
may come to be. ... He may go very much further than he has
yet gone. Many of the stories which he has lately published in
the English magazines ... show a distinct advance in artistic
power ... and the volume called *Departmental Ditties* is in no
respect on the same level with certain verses which have
appeared with and without his name during the present year ...
    But, as yet, he has not attempted the 'long-distance race', and
the question in which the rapidly-growing number of his
readers are now most interested is whether he possesses staying
power. ... It is to be hoped he will not write himself out.
Modern magazines and their eager editors are a dangerous
snare in the way of a bright, clever, and versatile writer, who
knows that he has caught the public taste.

Which of his kindly elderly patrons at the Savile Club
was responsible for this good-natured admonition and qualified praise we do not know. His own letters prove that he
had not been spoiled by flattery but responded somewhat
ungraciously to professions of esteem. The fear that he
might over-write or, at least, over-publish seemed justified,
for the reissue of his early work went on apace, far more
actively in America than in England, and the weeks that
followed *The Times'* review saw a new Kipling boom, in the
literary circle of Henley and the *Scots Observer*.

From In the Neolithic Age (1893)

In the Neolithic Age savage warfare did I wage
  For food and fame and woolly horses' pelt.
I was singer to my clan in that dim, red Dawn of Man,
  And I sang of all we fought and feared and felt.

.   .   .   .   .

Then the silence closed upon me till They put new clothing
    on me
  Of whiter, weaker flesh and bone more frail;
And I stepped beneath Time's finger, once again a tribal
    singer,
  And a minor poet certified by Traill!

.   .   .   .   .

Still a cultured Christian age sees us scuffle, squeak, and
    rage,
  Still we pinch and slap and jabber, scratch and dirk;
Still we let our business slide – as we dropped the half-
    dressed hide –
  To show a fellow-savage how to work.

Still the world is wondrous large, – seven seas from marge
    to marge –
  And it holds a vast of various kinds of man;
And the wildest dreams of Kew are the facts of
    Khatmandhu,
  And the crimes of Clapham chaste in Martaban.

Here's my wisdom for your use, as I learned it when the
    moose
  And the reindeer roamed where Paris roars to-night:–
'There are nine and sixty ways of constructing tribal lays,.
  'And – every – single – one – of – them – is – right!'

[7]

Kipling in London
(1890–91)

WILLIAM ERNEST HENLEY, a lifelong invalid, is best remembered today as the author of one poem, a defiant
assertion of will, from what seemed likely to be a death-
bed:

> In the fell clutch of circumstance
> I have not winced nor cried aloud,
> Under the bludgeonings of chance
> My head is bloody but unbowed:

lines which were read and stored away for reference by
young Kipling in Lahore.

Some of Henley's associates in Edinburgh set him up as
editor of a weekly magazine which they intended as a
contribution to the Scottish literary revival, but Henley
made it much more than that. The *Scots Observer* first came
out in August 1889, when Kipling was on his way to London,
and within a few months it captivated the taste of the
younger literary set. Henley knew everyone from Oscar
Wilde to the young musical critic Bernard Shaw, and everyone liked him. He sedulously hunted for coming young men,
and Yeats and Barrie, as well as Kipling, were among his
early discoveries; in later years he produced Wells and Conrad. The *Scots Observer* was new in style and presentation,
a landmark in typography as well as in literature, but it did
not pay. The circulation never reached 7,000 and was
usually under 2,000, in spite of the good names of the
contributors, the brilliant editing, and the elegant lay-out. It
remained one of those literary ventures that arise in every
generation, to provide a platform for young men of talent,
and to influence public opinion only at second hand.

Rudyard Kipling could hardly be said to have graduated in the world of letters, in 1889 and 1890, without coming into Henley's orbit, and Henley was one of those who awaited Kipling's return from India with attention. The first approach seems to have been made from Kipling's side. On 1 February 1890 the *Scots Observer* published a slight piece from Kipling's pen, a lyric in the style of Lyly:

> Love and Death once ceased their strife
> At the Tavern of Man's Life.
> Called for wine, and threw – alas! –
> Each his quiver on the grass.

of which we may say that it might have been written by almost any one of Henley's young men. It gave an introduction, and Henley's patron, F. Bell, was taken by Herbert Stephen, one of Kipling's Savile Club friends, to visit the new poet at Embankment Chambers.

The subject of conversation with Bell was the provision of a series of verses which Kipling called *Barrack-Room Ballads*. The first of these, 'Danny Deever', appeared in the *Scots Observer* on 22 February and astonished the critics. According to the legend, it made Henley stand up and dance on his wooden leg, while Professor Masson, the grave commentator on Milton, waved the paper before his delighted students, crying: 'Here's Literature! Here's Literature at last!'

Bell and Stephen asked Kipling at Embankment Chambers whether he had anything else on hand, whereupon he reluctantly fished out of the waste-paper basket some political verses which, he supposed, had missed their market and were out-of-date. They were seventy lines of bitter invective against the Liberal Party, denouncing its association with the Irish Nationalists, as revealed by the Parnell Commission, the sensation of the month. A panel of judges had acquitted the Irish leaders of complicity in political murders in Ireland, not so much because they repudiated the policy of violence as because the evidence in a particular instance was shown to be a malicious forgery. The weight of Kipling's attack fell, not upon Irish Nationalists but upon English Liberals, especially upon Gladstone who relied on Irish support in parliament.

Hold up those hands of innocence – go, scare your sheep
    together,
The blundering, tripping tups that bleat behind the old bell-
    wether;
My soul! I'd sooner lie in jail for murder plain and straight,
Pure crime I'd done with my own hand for money, lust, or hate
Than take a seat in Parliament by fellow-felons cheered,
While one of those 'not provens' proved me cleared as you are
    cleared.

All that the Parnell Commission had demonstrated was summed up in the last line of his satire:

We are not ruled by murderers, but only – by their friends.

Kipling's account of the publication of this explosive piece is that *The Times* considered and rejected it. They had burned their fingers so badly over the forgeries that they were unlikely to take risks again, though after a discreet interval they quoted the verses in full without permission. Next Kipling had offered it to Frank Harris, the editor of the *Fortnightly*, who had just published 'One View of the Question', his virulent prose satire on the state of London as seen by an Indian Moslem visitor. Frank Harris's account of his dealings with Kipling does not quite square with Kipling's, but at least he declined to take the verses. Kipling's comment was that Frank Harris was the one human being that he 'could on no terms get on with'. After two rebuffs, Kipling preferred to put his verses in the waste-paper basket, where they would have remained but for the visitors from the *Scots Observer*. Henley published them on 8 March.

Broad-minded though he was in his literary taste, Henley was a partisan in politics, a Tory of the new imperialist school, and his London representative, Charles Whibley, was still further to the right. In the successive reorganizations by which they endeavoured to keep their literary venture afloat, Henley and Whibley tended to move from *belles-lettres* to politics, from Scottish to Imperial affairs; and the attachment of Kipling to their group was a step in this direction. Yet they were too intellectual, too fastidious, to catch the ear of the mob. The decade of the nineties saw the beginning of 'yellow' journalism in England, and it was Harmsworth, not Henley, who was to provide the masses with imperialist propaganda in a form they could appreciate and at a price they could pay. Henley's only appeal to a wider public was by printing *Barrack-Room Ballads*, and even these did not reach that wider public until the author reissued them in book form. It was the literary world that succumbed to the spell of 'Danny Deever'. Week by week, the ballads burst upon their shocked but delighted readers; 'Tommy' on 1 March; 'Fuzzy-Wuzzy' on 15 March; 'Loot' on 29 March; 'The Widow at Windsor' on 26 April; 'Gunga Din' on 7 June; 'Mandalay', perhaps the favourite of all, on 22 June.

Henley, too, was delighted with his new discovery, and more delighted still when he came south, in March, to meet the man. It was his custom during his visits to London to give bachelor dinner-parties to his literary friends at Sherry's in Regent Street, and for a few months Kipling was the lion among his guests. The flavour and wit of these young men's meetings – for Henley was forty and most of his guests much younger – have vanished and are lost, unless some hint of them can be discovered in the bachelor parties described in *The Light that Failed*. Whibley, a scholarly *bon-viveur* with a well-earned liver complaint, convened the dinners, and students of Kipling will notice with relish that his private address was in Brook Green, Hammersmith. Almost did this new friend occupy the place in Henley's affections left vacant since his celebrated quarrel with R. L. Stevenson a year earlier.

Kipling was more cool, though later he defended Henley vigorously against detractors.

Henley's demerits were, of course, explained to the world by loving friends after his death. I had the fortune to know him only as kind, generous, and a jewel of an editor, with the gift of fetching the very best out of his cattle, with words that would astonish oxen.

His first letter to Henley, written from Embankment Chambers, early in 1890 shows a side to Kipling's character that is not widely known; it is largely about sea-fishing:

Since we be only islands shouting misunderstandings to each other across seas of speech or writing I am going to say nothing about Henley's *Hospital Sketches*. I take off my hat and drop my sword-point. You have been where I have yet to go so I dare not ask you why you are so tired. When you get my stuff you will see how far I've walked, and where.

Yes, men tell me I am young in this country but I have put seven years of India behind me and they do not make a man younger or more cheerful. Also, luckily, they don't lead him to believe the protestations of the disinterested publisher or the blandishments of the people to whom a new writer-man is as a new purple monkey on a yellow stick. I live very largely alone and my wants are limited to a new fly-rod and some flies. *But*, you can do me immense service by sending in a memo. of reminder if it seems to you that I am spinning out my guts too swiftly, at any time.

To a young man the temptation is strong and it is to nobody's interest to tell him to go slow. Rather they want all he has at once and then he can go to the deuce, being squeezed dry. I've treated men in the same way when I was an editor. I see now [that] I was unkind.

I am off for a month's idleness now 'cause of my head. ... If it is written, I come to Edinburgh ere long and then I shall see you and – this is business – if you think it worth while you shall give me my riding-orders by word of mouth and we will elaborate a line of work.

At present I am divided between the broken top-joint of my rod and a reel that won't 'croon' properly. Literature is a weariness to the flesh – all books are wicked and the only real thing in the world is a four pound bass coming up with the tide at the mouth of the Torridge, my hook in the right-hand top angle of his mouth.[1]

While he gave Henley his entire confidence in literary concerns Rudyard kept his private life quite separate. His sister Trix, now Mrs Fleming, arrived in England with her husband, on 11 February, and turned her steps at once to Embankment Chambers. It was a shock to her to find her brother, in spite of his prosperity, in deep depression of spirits and a low state of health, not altogether due to the influenza which raged like a pestilence that winter. When she spoke to him of the kindness shown to her by Mrs Hill, at Allahabad, 'his face began to work', and, in a tangle of words, he admitted that his affection for Caroline Taylor had been mistaken. Even this was not all; something had happened in London, which struck a deeper chord in his nature, revealing a harmony that he had almost forgotten. He had met his old sweetheart, Flo Garrard, by chance in the street, and had realized in a moment that she still retained her power over him.[2]

Rudyard's prolonged ill-health and unhappiness in 1890 were the consequence of this mental conflict which, according to his custom, he shut up in his own heart, leaving no scrap of direct evidence to mark the progress of his love-affairs. He plunged himself in work with reckless energy, producing in the spring of 1890 the greater part of the *Barrack-Room Ballads*, and half a dozen long stories.

As his estrangement from Caroline Taylor widened, he resumed his attentions to Flo but without arousing her emotions. She was, as Trix said, 'naturally cold, and she wanted to live her own life and paint her very ineffective little pictures'. Rudyard had still one resource; his parents were coming home on leave to reunite the family square in London. In a mood of optimism, earlier in the year, he had telegraphed to them, proposing a holiday in England, sending them merely a reference to Genesis xlv. 9.

Haste ye, and go up to my father, and say unto him, Thus
saith thy son Joseph, God hath made me lord of all Egypt:
come down unto me; tarry not.

In May they arrived, protesting that they would be independent of his bounty, and settled for some months in Kensington, first at 29 Wynnstay Gardens and later at 101 Earl's
Court Road. Rudyard retained his foothold in Embankment
Chambers, but with renewed happiness since his father
would spend the days there working with him. Father and
son went down to Westward Ho! in June to visit Cormell
Price. Averse as he was from publicity, Rudyard's one concession to flattery was to appear at his old school as a
celebrity on whose account the boys were given a half-
holiday.

Then came more work at Embankment Chambers and
Earl's Court Road. In spite of his resolution not to write himself out, the bulk of his new work in the summer of 1890 was
prodigious, and was accompanied by volume after volume of
reissued Indian stories. Some time in August Lockwood
Kipling wrote to a friend to say that 'each new boom is
more portentous than the last'. Meanwhile Rudyard had
made himself ill with overwork, since he went at his tasks
'with a sort of fury and a bad cold'. Lockwood admitted that
he collaborated in a political article that Rudyard published
that month in the *Contemporary Review*, with the title of
'The Enlightenments of Pagett, M.P.' Though much quoted
by the reviewers and discussed by the politically minded,
this piece was, wisely, never reprinted in the standard
edition of his works; it was an attack upon the Indian
National Congress in the form of a series of imaginary
conversations between Pagett, a globe-trotting M.P., and
various characters from earlier stories.

In the same letter Lockwood mentioned another piece,
just finished, in which we may also detect signs of his helping hand; this is the Yorkshire tale, 'On Greenhow Hill'.

Against a background of fighting on the North-West Frontier, Private Learoyd the Yorkshireman tells of his youth near Skipton (where Rudyard as a boy had gone to visit his Kipling grandmother). It is his only Yorkshire story, the only one of the soldier yarns in which Learoyd comes to life, for elsewhere he is no more than a foil to Mulvaney and Ortheris. More than that, it is a work of great emotional power, almost worthy of Emily Brontë. The inner drama of Learoyd's hopeless passion for the dying daughter of the Methodist preacher is much heightened in effect by the contrasted picture of the godless, bloodthirsty, campaigning scene in which Learoyd tells his tale. Its climax is Learoyd's failure to satisfy his sweetheart's father as to his Methodist orthodoxy, and his consequent flight from Methodism, with the approval of Mulvaney the papist and Ortheris the infidel. The influence of Lockwood Kipling, who knew Yorkshire and Methodism so much better than his son, is an obvious factor but Rudyard, too, had something to say from the depths of his own heart. The story can hardly be considered in any other light than Rudyard's farewell to Caroline Taylor or, at least, that is how she and her family must have taken it. Her father, Dr Taylor, had been in England, in August, when Rudyard had shown him some courtesies. But when 'On Greenhow Hill' was published, the effect upon the old minister and his daughter must have been final. Yet a few weeks later his association with her family took a new turn, when Professor Hill died suddenly in India. Their friends must have wondered whether his young and handsome widow, to whom Rudyard had been devoted, long before he met her less attractive sister, would not resume her sway over her admirer. She did not do so. In December 1890 Mrs Hill and Miss Taylor passed through London on their way back to America. Though they exchanged calls with Mrs Kipling, no more came of it than the continuance of a cool and distant acquaintance.[3]

Never before had Rudyard handled the tones of a composition with so sure a touch as in the bright hard foreground and the deftly suggested background of 'On Greenhow Hill', a demonstration of the progress he had made in his art during the previous year of enriched experience. The early months of 1890 had seen the production of *Barrack-Room Ballads*, a new genre in poetry, and of a series of stories which far surpassed the overloaded pieces of his Allahabad period, in delicacy and insight. 'The Head of the District' had appeared in January, 'Dinah Shadd' in March, 'The Man who Was' in April, 'Without Benefit of Clergy' in June, 'On Greenhow Hill' in September, and in the summer months two stories of horror and gloom which reflected his own mood of nervous exhaustion, 'The Mark of the Beast' and 'At the End of the Passage'. Some of these stories were the working-over of old material, but the *Ballads* were brand-new, and there is still more to be considered. According to his father's account, *The Light that Failed* was completed by August 1890, and it was this that wore him out. The novel was not a version of *Mother Maturin,* but a quite new realistic piece, based upon his own life in Embankment Chambers.

When the book was finished Rudyard was at last ready to go for a long sea-voyage, on his doctor's advice. He had called upon Lord Dufferin, now appointed Ambassador at Rome, characteristically announcing himself to the servant as 'Mr Lockwood Kipling's son'. Dufferin, who of course remembered him well enough, invited him to pay a visit to his villa at Sorrento, and Rudyard booked his passage to Naples in a P. & O. steamer. Several newspapers, in announcing the forthcoming appearance of *The Light that Failed*, the event of the publishing season, announced also that the author was going abroad to recruit his health.

Most of the month of October he spent at sea or in Italy. At Dufferin's villa he learned, for the first time as he admitted, how the administrative machinery of government is handled from above. Previously he had seen it only 'from beneath, all stripped and overheated'. Lord Dufferin talked

– 'sliding into a reverie – of his work in India, Canada, and
the world at large'. And the sentence that Rudyard
treasured in his memory was, 'so, you see, there can be no
room' (or was it allowance) 'for good intentions in one's
work'. Nothing mattered in a career but to do one's best,
merely 'to do the work for which you draw the wage'.[4]

    Two days after he sailed for Italy a storm broke in Lon-
don over American piracies. One of the first endeavours
made on Kipling's behalf by A. P. Watt had been the sale
to Harper Brothers in January 1890 of 'The Courting of
Dinah Shadd', the first of five of his stories which they
issued in their *Weekly*. In September Harper's reissued them
in a paper-bound cheap edition with a preface by Kipling's
friend and patron, Andrew Lang. Perhaps, so far, they were
within their rights, and acting legitimately, if not generous-
ly. They put themselves quite out of court with Kipling,
however, by making up their book to the required length
with 'Krishna Mulvaney', a sixth piece to which they had
no right at all; and annoyed the author still more by offering him £10 as a solatium, which he indignantly rejected.
    This new annoyance threw him into a fury of indignation
against the American 'pirate' publishers who were making
free with his work. Great as the Kipling Boom was in
England, it was far greater in America and, there, nothing
prevented any printer from producing unauthorized editions
unless the copyright had been secured by the production in
America of an authorized American edition. Even before
Kipling left India, a pirated edition of *Departmental Ditties* had appeared in the United States and in the years of
his fame there was a scramble to collect and reissue any of
his works that were unprotected. For many years it was a
principal task of A. P. Watt to forestall the pirates in respect
of new work, and to outwit them in respect of the earlier
work for which there was an uncertain degree of protection
at law. Since most of Kipling's early work was journalism
written to order for the *Civil and Military* or the *Pioneer*,

there was genuine uncertainty as to the ownership of copyrights. The 'pirates' took full advantage of this uncertainty, and Kipling, in order to protect himself, reissued some of his early work in authorized editions, including some pieces which he would have preferred to let die – if only the 'pirates' would let them die, too. This is the reason why his books of the early nineties contain some slight and trivial pieces, which his maturer judgement would have treated as ephemeral. The copyright struggle was at its height in the summer of 1890 and raged for several years. A. P. Watt lost a round when an enterprising American bought up the files from the London office of the *Pioneer*, for £1,500, and carried them off, to search them at leisure for real and fancied Kiplingiana.

All this was bad enough, but Kipling found it intolerable when a respectable firm, Harper Brothers of New York, helped themselves to one of his recent stories, thus adding injury to insult, since they had ignominiously snubbed him a year previously when he offered to write for them; and insult to insult because *Harper's Monthly*, at just the same time, included a condescending allusion by W. D. Howells, the New England novelist, to 'Mr Kipling's jaunty hat-cocked-on-one-side, wink-tipping sketches'.

His frayed nerves and exhausted health can be detected in the stabbing pen-strokes with which he wrote to Henley, before leaving for Italy.

Dear Henley,

I am in trouble and furious. You know that I have written within the past few months some tales for MacM. Mag. and others. Harper & Co. bought the serial rights for America and paid me. The series in MacM. I intended to be one of twelve stories into which I purposed to put as good stuff as I could do : revise extensively and eventually republish with a preface. To-day I receive a note from Harpers (leading publishers) announcing that they have reprinted in book form *The Courting of Dinah Shadd, The Incarnation of Krishna Mulvaney, The man who was*, and all the others. They will give it their own title. (They have given it their own title). They have not had the

decency to apprize me of their intention, and to complete the
insult they fling a £10 note (the wages of one New York road
scavenger for one month) at my head. They call it an *honora-
rium*. Now I may turn out work too quickly. They are at perfect
liberty to steal when I have done my work but the grotesque
Yahoodom of nipping pieces off a half-presented foetus and
slamming it into the market makes me jump. It isn't literature,
it isn't honour. It is simply a piece of cowardly and huckstering
sharp-practice to exploit a name that, for the time being, sells.
Rather less than 12 months ago that firm in a letter one line
and seven words long told me that they would not republish
Soldiers three, the Gadsbys, and all the rest.

. What do you recommend me to do? I have of course returned
the money and told them that I cannot authorize the thing
which they call an 'Edition'. This month's Harpers magazine
brings in an elaborate patronization of me in the Editors Receiving Shop. Look at it. It completes the circle. I don't know
who the man is but the whole notion of the article is intensely
funny. The American he says, lives in a 'nimbler atmosphere'
or something of the kind. When the man was writing that, his
blasted owners were stealing my work. The critic himself was
criticizing stolen work with adjectives stolen from England. I am
much too wroth just now to write to the papers disclaiming the
edition, but I must blow off somehow so I go to you, who can
see the insult of the burglary, the savage indecency and the
utter disregard of anything except the dollars on the part of the
leading publishing firm in America.

Send me your notions on the matter. As a journalist, two
years ago I should have lifted the scalp of Harpers and the
amiable critic who 'deplores' for me, and my vulgarity. It isn't
the critics fault that he lives, as every man must live, under the
laws of his own life and environment, when he calls my stuff
lacking in appreciation of the subtler values. The thing that
makes it like a Gilbert-Sullivan opera is the raw, rank theft that
runs through the 'business' of his firm. When a burglar sits
down on the front door steps to quarrel with the pattern of the
silver-ware that he hath stolen he may be an authority on silver
but he is first of all a thief and secondly he lacks a sense of
humour. I suppose I shall be able to laugh at the business in a
little time but at present I'm too savage to do more than swear.

                                                      Ruddy.[5]

He returned from Naples to find a first-class quarrel raging in literary London over the proper reward for his labours. Norman McColl, the editor of the *Athenaeum* had taken up his case in a leading article, and a statement from Harper Brothers had appeared in the *Athenaeum*, making the situation rather worse. Harper's admitted that they had rejected his early work and had accepted his later, and better, work with deliberation. In offering him £10 for the odd story, they had followed the custom of the trade. Kipling replied in person with a long and angry letter, relating the history of his agents' correspondence with Harper Brothers, and denouncing them as simple pirates, pirates 'like Paul Jones'. Beyond that there seemed little that he could do; there was no redress at law.

Three weeks later, 22 November 1890, there came an intervention from an unexpected quarter. A letter appeared in the *Athenaeum* over the three signatures of Sir Walter Besant, Thomas Hardy, and William Black, perhaps the three most respected novelists of the day. While regretting the unsatisfactory state of the American copyright law, they championed Harper Brothers, not precisely in respect of their dealings with Kipling, but in respect of their general conduct. Harper's, they said, were honest folk who endeavoured to treat their English authors fairly. It was an error of tactics, and perhaps of taste, they implied, to accuse Harper's of piracy when an English author could only protect himself against disreputable publishers in America by relying upon well-meaning firms such as this one.

This appeasing pronouncement, intended, no doubt, to further the progress of negotiations for an international copyright agreement, exploded Kipling's wrath. In the *Athanaeum* of 6 December he published a satirical ballad, a puzzle to many a reader who has found it, out of context, in the Collected Verse. It begins abruptly with a complaint to 'The Three Captains' by the skipper of a trading brig.

'I had no fear but the seas were clear as far as a sail might fare
'Till I met with a lime-washed Yankee brig that rode off
    Finisterre.
'There were canvas blinds to his bow-gun ports to screen the
    weight he bore,
'And the signals ran for a merchantman from Sandy Hook to the
    Nore.
'He would not fly the Rovers' flag – the bloody or the black,
'But now he floated the Gridiron and now he flaunted the Jack.
'He spoke of the Law as he crimped my crew – he swore it was
    only a loan;
'But when I would ask for my own again, he swore it was none
    of my own.'

The ballad goes on with fifty lines of ferocious invective
that has tingled in the ears of countless readers who may
not have understood the allegory (of which the key is given
in the punning words 'the bezant is hard – aye – and black').
But to the complaint of ill-treatment and the threat of re-
prisal that the skipper would have liked to inflict, the Three
Captains reply with fair words:

'Good Sir, we ha' dealt with that merchantman or ever your teeth
    were cut.
'Your words be words of a lawless race, and the Law it standeth
    thus:
'He comes of a race that have never a Law, and he never has
    boarded us.
'We ha' sold him canvas and rope and spar – we know that this
    price is fair,
'And we know that he weeps for the lack of a Law as he rides off
    Finisterre.'...

The skipper called to the tall taffrail: –'And what is that to me?
'Did ever you hear of a Yankee brig that rifled a Seventy-three?
'Do I loom so large from your quarter-deck that I lift like a ship
    o' the Line?
'He has learned to run from a shotted gun and harry such craft
    as mine.

'It's mainsail haul, my bully boys all – we'll out to the seas again –

'Ere they set us to paint their pirate saint, or scrub at his grap-
nel-chain.
'It's fore-sheet-free, with her head to the sea, and the swing of
the unbought brine –
'We'll make no sport in an English court till we come as a ship
o' the Line.'

This is a spirited ballad and, though rather long drawn-
out, it is effective satire. There was little more worth saying
on either side. Before they had an opportunity to read 'The
Rhyme of the Three Captains', Harper Brothers wrote
again from New York in reply to Kipling's earlier letter.
They 'regretted that Mr Kipling should assume such an un-
gracious attitude', protested again that they were strictly
within their rights, and pointed out that he would have received much worse treatment from one of the frankly
piratical firms. This was the truth, evident to Kipling, who
had in fact been robbed right and left, but it was a poor
line of defence which Kipling had already pierced in the
ballad:

'Does he steal with tears when he buccaneers? 'Fore Gad, then,
why does he steal?'

The correspondence in the *Athenaeum* merely came to an
end. Harper Brothers continued to sell the disputed edition,
and Kipling could assert his rights only by arranging for the
publication of a rival but authorized edition of the stories
with an introduction by his friend Henry James. It was published by J. W. Lovell & Co. under the title *Mine Own
People.*
The episode is of importance in the development of Rudyard's character. It deepened his mistrust for publishers; it
shook him free of dependence upon the literary grandees
like Besant and Andrew Lang who had given him less than
no help in the struggle. 'Good intentions' counted for nothing. A man must stand upon his own feet, make his own
way in the world, be responsible to his own conscience for
the value of his work. Very well, he would launch another

venture, bring home another cargo, and watch the higgling of the market more closely next time.

Eighteen ninety-one was to be a year of new effort and of independence. The voyage, to the seas again, 'on the outward tack', might be an actual withdrawal from London – as the doctors recommended – or a symbolical voyage into new regions of endeavour. Just what did his ambition to return 'as a ship o' the Line' imply? Not only material but moral success, so great a degree of self-reliance and self-sufficiency as to be indifferent to the annoyance of Yankee pirates and the condescension of the Three Captains.

He had already taken one step forward in this new career. *The Light that Failed*, in its first form, had been published by J. W. Lovell in America on 27 November, that is a few days before the appearance in London of 'The Rhyme of the Three Captains'. The first English appearance of the novel was in *Lippincott's Monthly Magazine* for January 1891.*

Light fiction in the late Victorian age was purveyed principally in the monthlies which enterprising publishers used for launching new authors and testing new lines of appeal to the public taste. A widening public of readers demanded something brisker and livelier than the decorous three-volume novels which the circulating libraries had distributed to a genteel public in the previous generation. Lippincott, the American publisher, interested himself in this market by issuing a monthly magazine simultaneously in New York and London with a complete new novelette by a reputed author in every number. Its length, therefore, could be no more than 50,000 or 60,000 words, whereas *Robert Elsmere*, the best-seller of the previous season, had run to 300,000. Eighteen-ninety was a good year for *Lippincott's*; it began with Conan Doyle's *Sign of Four*, went on with

---

*McClure in his *Autobiography* says that Lippincott paid R. K. $800, a modest sum compared with his earnings three or four years later.

Oscar Wilde's *Dorian Gray*, and finished with the number containing *The Light that Failed*, which was five times reprinted in January 1891. J. W. Lovell published the Lippincott version as a book in New York, dating his edition a few days before the release of the monthly magazine; and Lovell's London agent, Wolcott Balestier, secured English copyright by issuing a few copies in London bound up in book form. These contrivances defeated the 'pirates' in both countries, while providing bibliographers with some puzzles for the future about priority of editions, but this was only a beginning of the mystery that shrouds *The Light that Failed*. The author allowed Lippincott's a good run with the magazine version before releasing the book in normal form to the English trade. In the magazine version the book had been a comfortable tale in which the hero and heroine decently got engaged to be married on the last page. When in March 1891 Macmillan's published *The Light that Failed* as a bound volume in London, it was found to be a quite different book, one-third longer, and with a tragic ending that threw the whole of the plot and the characterization into a new light. The author added to the mystery by his preface which stated baldly: 'This is the story of *The Light that Failed* as it was originally conceived by the writer.' Why, then, had so furiously independent an author allowed his book to appear in the form in which he had not conceived it? The reviewers were astonished. The magazine edition had been 'announced' with a blaze of publicity; the public had waited eagerly for the event of the season, a novel by this prodigy among authors; the critics had received it with many columns of judicious comment – for it was by no means all that had been expected: and their pens were hardly dry before they were called upon to review it again, converted from a pleasant piece into a bleak tragedy with four new chapters of that sort of realism which the author's detractors called brutality.

One feature of the book that contemporaries could not observe was its autobiographical quality; the incidents in the life of its hero, 'Dick Heldar', were the incidents of Rudyard's life superficially transformed. The story begins with two neglected children brought up together at the seaside by a tyrannical housekeeper. In life they had been brother and sister, in the book they are unrelated so that the author can portray their childhood friendship maturing into calf-love, until in adolescence they separate for years. 'Maisie' the heroine, like Rudyard's former sweetheart Flo Garrard, sets her heart upon a career and goes to an art-school; Dick disappears into the East for seven years of hardship and struggle, in circumstances which the stay-at-home English descry but dimly. Then the scene shifts to Egypt where Dick is a war-artist. Writer to painter is a transformation that presented Rudyard with no great difficulty. He had been brought up among painters and knew the jargon of the studios; but he had never been in the African desert, never seen a battlefield, and it was his realistic accounts of fighting in the Sudan that impressed the critics, that still impress and perhaps shock the modern reader. His uncanny skill in picking the brains of his acquaintance and making a convincing picture, replete with accurate detail, from a few hints picked up in conversation was never more evident. The critics supposed him to be writing from personal knowledge, while he had no more than soldiers' hearsay to go upon.

When the campaign was over, so the tale ran on, Dick Heldar appeared in London and took rooms in a tall building overlooking the Thames near Charing Cross. Here, at first, he was lonely and poor, though too proud to admit as much to the agents who pestered him for orders. Fame won overseas caught him up quickly, and after fame came money which he hugely appreciated. But he disliked London, found intellectual society distasteful, defied and despised the critics, treated the salesmen who handled his pictures as mere robbers. In the book Dick Heldar triumphed over a rapacious art-dealer by threatening him with physical assault, a dream-picture of what Kipling would have liked to do to the Yankee pirate. But most surprising of all, Dick

Heldar's contempt for public opinion went so far that he painted a picture in two versions, one in the 'realistic' style that his artistic conscience imposed on him, the other in a pretty Christmas annual style that would fetch the public.

After these disjointed episodes, in which Rudyard's earlier life is presented in heightened colours, the action of the novel begins to develop. 'Dick' meets his former sweetheart, a struggling art-student, as Rudyard had met Flo Garrard, and realizes that success means nothing to him without her love, while she cares only for the worldly recognition that he has won and she has not. 'Maisie' in the novel, like Flo in real life, leaves London with a girl friend. The novel then ceases to be autobiographical. 'Dick' is defrauded by his model, a worthless woman, who destroys his master-piece and leaves him alone to face the growing awareness that he is losing his sight from the effects of an old wound. Curiously, no critic noticed that the title, and the central episode of the book, are drawn from Mrs Browning's verse-novel, *Aurora Leigh*, a best-seller of those days, which had been given as a present to young Rudyard when he left school. The lover who despises his easy triumph, the woman of the streets who ruins his life-work, the ardent feminist who cares only for her art, the calamity of blindness with the same clinical details, and the dilemma forced upon both heroines, are identical.

Whatever was Rudyard's 'original' intention, and it may have been to write a variation on the theme of *Aurora Leigh*, it cannot have taken shape before February 1890, when he met Flo Garrard in the street, and neither version is likely to have been committed to paper before May, when he accepted her decision not to sacrifice her career for marriage. Early in that month he paid a short visit to Paris, where she and Mabel Price, the original of the 'red-haired girl', were sharing a studio. May was the crucial date, and the climax of *The Light that Failed* must have been written between May and August. It came off his pen red-hot; he lived it as he wrote it and, in great distress, he came to know that he had been blind in his judgement. That was the end of Flo Garrard in Rudyard's view of the matter.

Long afterwards he described *The Light that Failed* as his 'transmogrified' version of *Manon Lescaut*, a tale that had fascinated him from boyhood. Like the Chevalier des Grieux in *Manon*, Dick is drawn back, like a moth to a candle, again and again, whatever may be the defects of his sweetheart; like Manon, Maisie retains a certain aloofness, whatever may be the concessions she makes to her lover. Beyond that it is hard to find any resemblance between the French novel and the English. In *The Light that Failed* we are not confronted with the destroying passion that burns up the lovers in the French book. *Manon*, for all its bareness and austerity, is written with the firmest realism; thus do human beings behave. By comparison *The Light that Failed* is a romantic piece. Dick faces his fate with the illusions of a Byronic hero, and, rough as he is in his dealings with men, he is prim – Tennysonian – in the war of sex, too genteel to come to grips with Maisie, too self-centred in prosperity and in adversity to make any surrender to her, too bemused to love her or leave her. He is, at once, brutal and sentimental, a singularly unpleasant hero.

The critics have always been puzzled by Kipling's motive in writing this book. J. M. Barrie, who was Kipling's contemporary and friend, wrote a well-meaning column of warning in the *Contemporary Review*.

His chief defect is ignorance of life. This seems a startling charge to bring against one whose so-called knowledge of life has frightened the timid. But it is true. 'Dick Heldar's' views are Kipling's views. ... He believes that because he has knocked about the world in shady company, he has no more to learn.'

To writers of the other school, words could hardly be found for condemning the book; Richard Le Gallienne described the final paragraphs as 'squeals of homicidal mania'.[6] More damaging was Max Beerbohm's mockery of *The*

Light that Failed written some years later when a dramatized version appeared.*

Should the name of Rudyard Kipling [he asked] be put between inverted commas? Is it the veil of feminine identity? If
of Mr Kipling we knew nothing except this work, we should
assuredly make that conjecture. ... Dick Heldar doted on the
military ... strange that these heroes with their self-conscious
blurting of oaths and slang, their cheap cynicism about the
female sex, were not fondly created out of the inner consciousness of a female novelist.[7]

In spite of such voices as these, the book has been much
read and admired, especially in France, and the author himself admitted that he preferred the French version to the
English. A study of Kipling's earlier work reveals *The Light
that Failed* as a *pastiche* of extracts from his notebooks,
strung together with an autobiographical motive which,
here and there, is emphasized so strongly that the actual
reminiscences intrude upon the feigned story. Kipling confessed in a letter to Mrs Humphry Ward that he was not
satisfied with the composition of his book.

It will always be one of the darkest mysteries to me that any
human being can make a beginning, end and middle to a really
truly long story. I can think them by scores but I have not the
hand to work out the full frieze. It's just the difference between
the deep-sea steamer with twelve hundred people aboard, beside
the poor beggars sweating and scorching in the stokehold, and
the coastwise boat with a mixed cargo of notions.[8]

The strangest feature of the book is a strain of ill-nature
that runs through it; the cargo includes some very angry
notions, especially in those places where the book is mostly
plainly autobiographical. Kipling works off his rages against

* *The Light that Failed* was dramatized at least once, and filmed at
least three times. Forbes-Robertson's production (1903) was the only
one of R. K.'s works to succeed on the stage. At one time Sarah Bern-
hardt wrote to R. K. offering to produce a version. But whether she
was to take the part of Dick or of Maisie, wrote R. K. to his agent,
she did not say.

precious critics and greedy publishers through the mouth of
Dick Heldar, who seems to be the author in his most awkward frame of mind. By contrast Maisie is an unrealized
phantom figure, not half so actual as the two minor female
characters, Bessie the sluttish model, who is founded upon
Aunt Georgie's parlour-maid, and the 'red-haired girl' who
is not even given a name. These two are depicted in a few
strokes with such superb economy and strength as gives
them more vitality than any of the major characters. Maisie
may be a composite character, but the 'red-haired girl' is
surely drawn direct from the life.

Can it be doubted that such a book, written at such a time
in Kipling's career, composed of elements which can largely
be traced to identifiable scenes from his own past, does not
reflect, consciously or unconsciously, the emotions of his
own love-affair? No clue remains to the puzzle, and the
author's contempt for the prying eye of the commentator is
as pungent as Dick Heldar's – no other clue, save the dedication. Dick Heldar would have no women about him at the
end. Like Captain Mafflin of the Pink Hussars he still clung
to the subaltern's slogan that 'a young man married is a
young man marred'. His letters to Henley in 1890 repeated this hostility to the married state. The 'family
square' was still sufficient, and the complete version of *The
Light that Failed* was dedicated to his mother, the only
woman Kipling had yet learned to love.

From The Miracles (1891)

I sent a message to my dear –
    A thousand leagues and more to Her –
The dumb sea-levels thrilled to hear,
    And Lost Atlantis bore to Her!

Behind my message hard I came,
    And nigh had found a grave for me;
But that I launched of steel and flame
    Did war against the wave for me.

Uprose the deep, in gale on gale,
    To bid me change my mind again –
He broke his teeth along my rail,
    And, roaring, swung behind again.

. . . .

Earth sold her chosen men of strength
    (They lived and strove and died for me)
To drive my road a nation's length,
    And toss the miles aside for me.

. . . .

I sent the Lightnings forth to see
    Where hour by hour She waited me.
Among ten million one was She,
    And surely all men hated me!

Dawn ran to meet me at my goal –
    Ah, day no tongue shall tell again!
And little folk of little soul
    Rose up to buy and sell again!

[8]

Kipling and the Balestiers
(1891–2)

So large a part did the Balestiers of Beechwood, Vermont, play in Rudyard's life that a digression into their history will be apposite. It will be remembered that, soon after his arrival in London, he had been introduced to a young American named Wolcott Balestier, in Mrs Humphry Ward's drawing-room.

During the eighteenth century a Huguenot family named Balestier had emigrated from France to America where one of them married a daughter of Paul Revere, the Huguenot patriot of Boston. They were a roving breed with interests in the East and West Indies, and it was in Martinique that Wolcott's grandfather, Joseph Balestier, was born. He went out west in the eighteen-thirties, made money as a real-estate lawyer in the first Chicago land-boom, and, at Chicago, in its wild heroic age, he met and married Caroline Starr Wolcott, a notable woman who lived till 1901. Both sides of her family, Starrs and Wolcotts, were New Englanders of five or six generations, the best blood of Connecticut. The Wolcott family had given three Governors to the State, and one of Caroline's forebears had signed the Declaration of Independence. This intelligent and well-born couple, Joseph and Caroline Balestier, settled in New York, where he prospered at the law.

In 1868 the Balestiers bought a handsome old farmhouse (to which they gave the name of Beechwood) as a summer resort near Brattleboro, a small country town in Vermont, and there they lived in somewhat grander style than was customary in rural America, dressing for dinner and drinking French wines, two practices which provided Brattleboro with gossip. Otherwise they were as American as their neighbours, who pronounced their name 'Ballis-teèr'. Joseph Balestier died in 1888, worth more than $600,000.

His widow still spent her summers at Beechwood, as the head of a large family of children and grandchildren. A very determined, handsome, opinionated old lady, she gave much time to the affairs of the Unitarian Church in Brattleboro, where she is still remembered as 'Madam Balestier'. Her children and grandchildren were as strong-minded as she was, united by a strong family feeling and yet rather disposed to disagreement over their social responsibilities and the disposition of the family fortunes. One of the sons, Henry, married Anna Smith, an episcopalian, who drew his branch of the family into that church, and so caused a division of interests in Brattleboro. It was noticed that family parties at Beechwood were strictly selective since brothers- and sisters-in-law did not always mingle easily. Henry's wife Anna usually stayed at Mrs Kirkland's boarding-house in the town when she visited her husband's family. She was a pleasant, sensible woman, the daughter of Judge Peshine Smith, an international lawyer of world-wide repute, and she, too, was left a widow with a young family. Her four children lived with their mother at Rochester in New York State but often visited their grandmother at Brattleboro; all had a part to play in the life of Rudyard Kipling.

The eldest child, Wolcott, was the hope of the family, slight and dapper in appearance, gay and lively in manner, the idol of his class-mates at Cornell and their leader in college pranks, but delicate in health. His sisters, who had unbounded confidence in his career, adored him. Wolcott had some success as a journalist in the Western States and in New York, and was regarded as a rising man when at the end of 1888 he established himself in London, as agent for a New York publisher.

Next came Caroline, who was to be Rudyard Kipling's wife, a little active clever woman, much like her grandmother in feature and strength of character. Josephine, the younger daughter, was considered the beauty of the family; and last came Beatty, the scapegrace, the spoiled darling of his stern old grandmother. Beatty (they always called him 'Baty' at Brattleboro) had the vitality and intelligence of his sisters, and all the ease and frankness that they lacked. A sportsman and a good fellow, he was strong and handsome, free with his money when he happened to have any, and a careless borrower when he ran short. His language was rich with picturesque profanity, and he drank a great deal more than was thought proper in 'dry' Vermont. 'Baty's' exploits with horses and dogs shocked and delighted Brattleboro, where the schoolchildren were warned to climb the bank if they heard his sleigh-bells, jingling 'as loud as cow-bells' down the narrow snow-bound roads. Uphill and downhill he always drove at a gallop. His reputation as a wild guy was his particular pride.*

When Wolcott Balestier went to London, the family and all the *élite* of Brattleboro watched with admiration. He was to make his fortune by persuading authors to entrust their books to his firm; he was to solve the problem of international copyright (that Anglo-American dispute which so infuriated Rudyard); and then – he was to astonish the world as a writer. In the first stage of this programme his success was instantaneous. He set up an office in Dean's Yard beside Westminster Abbey; imported a young friend from Brattleboro as his assistant; and worked habitually till past midnight, though not without finding time to attend literary parties where he made the contacts for which he had crossed the ocean.[1]

Edmund Gosse, who brought Rudyard and Wolcott Balestier together, rightly surmised that there were grounds for a close friendship between them, though this friendship

---

* Alexander Woollcott, who knew Beatty well, collected some materials for a memoir but never completed it. Beatty, he said, was a 'violent, warm-hearted, disorderly creature . . . a charming, contentious rattlepate'. (A. Woollcott: Letters, typescript in Library of Congress.)

seems not to have matured for several months. There was
much also about Balestier against which Rudyard might
have been expected to react with disgust. He had invaded
Europe as the representative of an American publisher,
J. W. Lovell, to arrange for cheap reprints of any popular
books that might come his way, the sort of publisher that
Rudyard most detested. Like Rudyard Balestier was a journalist by training, but unlike him in having a flair for im-
posing himself upon celebrities. Within a few months he
had collected Mrs Humphry Ward, the season's best-seller;
he had Henry James on a string; he was on close friendly
terms with Whistler; and Kipling was to be his next capture.
When Balestier heard about the newcomer from India, he
was all afire with interest: 'Rudyard Kipling? What is it? Is
it a real name? A man or a woman?' By one account, he
followed up the first meeting with a call at Embankment
Chambers where finding Rudyard out at seven o'clock he
resolutely waited till midnight for his return and then
plunged into a business discussion. He had made up his
mind; he wanted Rudyard to collaborate with him in writing a novel.

The progress of their friendship and the steps by which
Rudyard, who distrusted publishers and was wary with intruders, was talked into this agreement are not now recover-
able, but on 12 July 1890 Balestier wrote to William Dean
Howells, the novelist: 'lately I have been seeing even more
of Kipling with whom I am writing a story in collaboration.
The scene is to be partly far Western American (W. B.) and
partly Indian (R. K.).' The news reached Howells about the
time he wrote the article in *Harper's Monthly* which so infuriated Kipling; and a service that Balestier was able to do
was to bring his two friends into harmony. He assured Howells that Kipling had 'not a single grain of vanity or self-
love' and conveyed some message from Howells which
Kipling instantly accepted 'with a shout of delight'. Thereafter Kipling maintained his vendetta only against Harper
Brothers and regarded Howells as a friend. In general Kip-

ling was slow to forget an injury, and this conciliation was
a triumph for Balestier. No other man ever exercised so
dominating an influence over Rudyard Kipling as did Wolcott Balestier during the eighteen months of their intimacy.
It must be deduced from his behaviour, not from his words,
for he liked to keep his friendships in different compartments, and there is no single allusion to his new friend in
his letters to Mrs Hill, nor more than a phrase or two in his
letters to Henley. The compact with Balestier was made and
during the autumn, in spite of Rudyard's exhaustion and illness, some progress was made with the book they were to
write together. By the end of the year 1890 Rudyard was
taking Wolcott's advice on business questions, rather to the
disgust of A. P. Watt, the literary agent, who was at last
getting his affairs in order. Watt wrote rather plaintively
that he could have made a better bargain for the American
rights of *The Light that Failed* than Rudyard had got for
himself through his new friend. It is significant that Balestier's firm, J. W. Lovell & Co., published the edition with the
happy ending; and a plausible explanation of the two versions is that Wolcott Balestier persuaded him to play for the
big sales in the American market at the cost of replanning
his novel. Who else in Rudyard's whole life could have persuaded him to do it?

He was not alone in being fascinated by Wolcott Balestier. This American charmed literary London, as the
memoirs of the day bear witness; but charm is volatile and
when he died young, having accomplished very little, it
evaporated, leaving nothing but allusions in old books. Jus-
tin McCarthy, Edmund Gosse, Arthur Waugh, Henry James
concur in describing him as a man of quite extraordinary
merit and talent. Henry James, in particular, framed and
reframed his eulogies in letter after letter, though perhaps it
will be fair to admit that he was disposed to think all his
ducklings were swans. Wolcott Balestier's short-lived celebrity has vanished; few of his letters, and only one or two
faded photographs of him, are extant; the two novels he

left behind are insipid; the international publishing house he founded perished with him. Yet his conquest of literary London is undoubted and his personal conquest of Rudyard Kipling was an event in the history of literature.

All the Balestier family flocked to share Wolcott's success in London, even Beatty, who was allowed to savour the delights of the West End for a short time, until the pace he went was too hot for the family reputation, whereupon he was hurried home to Vermont by his elder brother. When Wolcott's mother came with her two daughters, she was a little discomfited to find that his literary connexion did not supply them with an entry into 'Society', though they regularly met the literary lions at Edmund Gosse's Sunday evening parties. Life in London was dull until Caroline, the elder daughter, took Wolcott's domestic affairs in hand. She kept house for him with devotion and tireless industry; she ran the country cottage in the Isle of Wight where he spent his holidays. According to the family tradition, she first met Rudyard Kipling at Wolcott's office in Dean's Yard, where she had gone to consult him, with the housekeeping books under her arm. She was three years older than Rudyard.[2]

Marriage was far from Rudyard's thoughts in 1890. Flo Garrard had failed him and his first novel had resolved itself – in its more perfect form – as an anti-feminist tract. The abortive affair with Caroline Taylor had done nothing to alter Rudyard's views; but it must be remembered that he was still a very young man and, in spite of his reputation, not widely experienced in the ways of women. The family square which had been so happily reformed in London, was his social ideal, and the happy Christmas party of the four at Earl's Court Road just before Rudyard's twenty-fifth birthday was the last, perhaps the gayest, of their family festivals.

Rudyard's mother was much in his thoughts that winter. He was at work upon a more ambitious poem than he had yet attempted, as well as upon his novel, a poem which was to point out to the English people their destiny overseas, and the sacrifice demanded from them by that destiny. Hitherto he had been regarded as a hostile critic of Indian policy and administration. This was the first work of Rudyard Kipling which might have been described (if the hideous modern jargon had been then current) as imperialist propaganda. The poem would not frame itself in words; he fumbled for a phrase until his mother intervened with, 'Surely this is what you are trying to say ...' And the opening lines of 'The English Flag' took shape.[3]

> Winds of the World, give answer! They are whimpering to
> and fro –
> And what should they know of England who only England
> know? –

For the second time he had astonished the world with a phrase. The poem appeared in the *St James's Gazette* on 4 April 1891, and within a week Henley had decided to give it the place of honour in the new anthology of English Verse, *Lyra Heroica*, which he was just about to publish. For many years *Lyra Heroica* was the most popular collection of verse for boys and girls and, through this book, 'The English Flag' became, for a generation, one of the best-known of all English ballads. It contains, like so many of Kipling's writings, a line or two of contemptuous denunciation, but no arrogance about the Flag as a symbol; it asserts no moral or material superiority for Englishmen or the English way of life; it is a call to service and to sacrifice in every land and sea.

> Never the lotos closes, never the wild-fowl wake,
> But a soul goes out on the East Wind that died for England's
> sake –
> Man or woman or suckling, mother or bride or maid –
> Because on the bones of the English the English Flag is
> stayed.

The sentiment is now a little out-moded, but it was new in Victorian England, when the 'street-bred' English were

hardly yet aware that they had responsibilities away from
home. The poem was the first of a series in which Kipling
revealed these responsibilities in word-pictures of the British
territories overseas.

Meanwhile, Wolcott Balestier had been at work upon the
novel. He wrote to Howells, 18 February 1891: 'Kipling and
I have been wading deep into our story lately, and have
written rather more than two thirds of it. It begins in the
West where I have a free hand for several chapters. Then we
lock arms and march upon India. The process of collaboration is much easier than one could have supposed. We hit it
off together most smoothly. ... [Henry] James has been
reading the first part of it, and professes himself delighted
with the Western atmosphere.' *

The title of the book was to be *The Naulahka, a Novel of
East and West.* 'Naulakha', as the word should properly be
spelt, was the Hindu word for nine 'lakhs' of rupees (one
lakh=100,000), and the name was applied in India to a
fabulous jewel. The plot of the story, mere melodrama, is
concerned with an attempt by an American engineer to get
possession of the jewel, as an act of bravado with which to
impress a woman in his native town, a boom-town in Western America. The contrast between life in the Far West,
and life in the Indian principality where the 'naulakha' lies
hidden, is revealed successively, and appropriately, to the
American engineer and to the missionary lady with whom
he is in love. The American scenes bear a resemblance to
one of Balestier's earlier stories where the same place-names
occur; the Indian scenes are plainly derived from the same
source as Kipling's *Letters of Marque.* It seems likely that
they were written up by Balestier from Kipling's notes.

* The following account, probably by Will Cabot, appeared in the
Vermont Phœnix, 13 November 1891: '... the work was done by the
two friends – Balestier, who is an accomplished typewriter, sitting at
the machine and dashing off the sentences and chapters while Kipling
paced the room, each composing, suggesting, or criticizing in turn, and
the mind of each stimulating the other to its best work.'

The characterization owes an evident debt to Kipling. The two principal persons are developed from the characters in *The Light that Failed*. Nicholas Tarvin, the American engineer, seems to be Dick Heldar with an American accent, and Kate Sheriff, the missionary, a more submissive, more alluring Maisie. Again the crux of the story is the heroine's dilemma, whether to renounce her career for marriage and, in *The Naulahka*, as in the American version of *The Light that Failed*, the book ends with a conventional decision to marry.

> 'I left 'em all in couples akissing on the decks.
> I left the lovers loving and the parents signing cheques.'⁴

So Kipling wrote in rather ribald mood of similar conventional endings by other novelists.

The Naulahka is readable – anything in which Kipling had a hand is readable; here and there it is enlivened by piercing observations and forcible expressions such as no one but Kipling could have penned, but it added little to his reputation as a novelist, and not much to Wolcott Balestier's. If the book is loved, it is for the sake of the Indian palace scenes, and for the pathetic picture of the Hindu child-prince. Kipling's sympathy with the child, caught up in a world of intrigue he could not understand, and his own understanding of that oriental world, were faultless. In Kipling's own mental development we can detect some progress since *The Light that Failed*; he is not so crudely opposed to marriage as a way of life.

Before *The Naulahka* began to appear in print, there was an understanding between Rudyard and Wolcott's sister, Caroline. The family square was again broken and Rudyard was disposing himself to devise a new formula. Mrs Kipling, it is credibly recorded, no sooner set eyes on Carrie Balestier than she said: 'That woman is going to marry our Ruddy', and showed little enthusiasm for the prospect. Lockwood Kipling, always genial and accommodating, merely remarked upon her universal competence: 'Carrie Balestier,' he said, 'was a good man spoiled.' The progress of the love-affair, as its two principals would have wished, remained their own secret, and has died with them. It did not run smoothly.[5]

Rudyard's health remained extremely bad throughout his second English winter, with continual recurrence of the malarial bouts and the dysentery that he had brought from India, aggravated by mental exhaustion after his prodigious output in 1890. His parents and his doctor repeatedly urged him to take a long sea-voyage, and it may have been more than a coincidence that Edmund Gosse, his friend and Wolcott's, gave him the same advice in a long and generous, but candid, criticism of his work which appeared in the *Century Magazine*, in May 1891. 'Go east, Mr Kipling, go back to the Far East. Disappear! another Waring. Come back in ten years' time with another precious and admirable budget of loot out of wonderland.' For the present, Gosse warned him, he was publishing too much.

He did not quite take Gosse's advice, but slipped off to America, on a short voyage with his Uncle Fred Macdonald, the Methodist minister. By this time his celebrity was so great that he was much persecuted by press reporters for interviews. When first he came to England he had not spurned publicity and had even allowed an elaborate account of his life, conduct, appearance, possession, and surroundings at Embankment Chambers to be released for publication in the *World*.[6] As his fame grew, he learned to hate the symptoms of it, and to shun intruders upon his privacy. This man whom everyone wanted to see found it difficult to remain unnoticed. His moustaches, eyebrows, spectacles were recognized, wherever he went. Not only were all his movements recorded in the press, but there was also a steady stream of quite unfounded rumours about him. Very early in his day of fame, piratical publishers got hold of the articles about America which he had contributed to the *Pioneer*, and reproduced them in many unauthorized editions. The pirates outsailed him, in spite of A. P. Watt's efforts, launching version after version of his travel-sketches. Some American critics, never noticeably thick-skinned about foreign criticism of America, denounced him with fury. The Kipling boom in 1890 was vastly inflated in America by piratical publications, by the copyright struggle with Harper's, and by continual controversy in the Press about his intentions. Had he not insulted America? There was no doubt that another visit to New York would involve broadsides of publicity from friends and foes and it was, perhaps, unwise of Rudyard to attempt a visit incognito. He let it be known that ill-health obliged him to go to Italy again, and so the New York *Herald* reported, on the word of 'a friend from Beaver (Pa.)', on 13 June 1891. A week later, the *Herald* found out its mistake and published a short account of an interview with Rudyard Kipling in a New York hotel.

Fred Macdonald had set out for America to visit his brother Henry, and Rudyard accompanied him on the ship, having registered under the name of 'J. Macdonald'. It was a German ship, the food was abominable and the sea 'loppy and choppy', but the two tourists enjoyed the voyage. Someone else was so entranced by the conversation of 'J. Macdonald', and so observant of his moustache and eyebrows, as to tip the wink to the *Herald* when they reached New York. The guileless Fred Macdonald told the truth to the first reporter who came for news, merely protecting his nephew by saying that he was unwell. This, too, was news, and the reporter, whether he actually spoke to Rudyard or not, described him as almost speechless with a diseased throat – a diplomatic dumbness, perhaps. Meanwhile the two travellers found that a tragedy had made their voyage pointless, since Henry Macdonald had died while they were at sea. Fred Macdonald remained to administer his dead brother's affairs, while Rudyard, piqued at having been unmasked, at once returned to England. This rather absurd episode added to the mystery.[7]

In July he evaded the reporters. Wolcott Balestier was ill
that month and the two friends were together in the Isle of
Wight with Wolcott's mother and sisters. The visit provided Rudyard with his story of the lighthouse-keeper ('A
Disturber of Traffic'), but, whether with an eye to his health
or to his peace of mind, he was restive. As the dull English
summer drew to a close with the days turning sick and cold,
he set off on a voyage round the world. In August 1891 S.S.
Mexican of the Union line left London Docks for Madeira
and the Cape, carrying him on his first voyage into the
southern hemisphere.

He was alone. On this ship there was no friendly Mrs Hill
to share his jokes and applaud his rhymes and sketches. It
was a second start in life like his voyage to India in 1882,
but was it the means of felicity which he had supposed? The
adventure and an unrealized yearning shaped themselves in
verses which by the complexity of their rhythm and the
depth of their feeling showed themselves the work of a
maturer man. This, among Kipling's longer poems, was
thought worthy of a place in the *Oxford Book of English
Verse*.

See the shaking funnels roar, with the Peter at the fore,
    And the fenders grind and heave,
And the derricks clack and grate, as the tackle hooks the crate,
    And the fall-rope whines through the sheave;
        It's 'Gang-plank up and in,' dear lass,
        It's 'Hawsers warp her through!'
        And it's 'All clear aft' on the old trail, our own trail, the out
          trail,
        We're backing down on the Long Trail – the trail that is
        always new.

O the mutter overside, when the port-fog holds us tied,
    And the sirens hoot their dread,
When foot by foot we creep o'er the hueless viewless deep
    To the sob of the questing lead!
        It's down by the Lower Hope, dear lass,
        With the Gunfleet Sands in view,

Till the Mouse swings green on the old trail, our own trail,
    the out trail,
And the Gull Light lifts on the Long Trail – the trail that
    is always new.

Then home, get her home, where the drunken rollers comb,
  And the shouting seas drive by,
And the engines stamp and ring, and the wet bows reel and
    swing,
  And the Southern Cross rides high!
    Yes, the old lost stars wheel back, dear lass,
    That blaze in the velvet blue.
    They're all old friends on the old trail, our own trail, the
      out trail,
    They're God's own guide on the Long Trail – the trail that
      is always new.

The poem is very much more than an exulting paean of delight in a sea-voyage to the Cape; it looks forward to a goal, twenty thousand symbolic miles away, where felicity is to be shared, not savoured alone.

For two or three weeks of September Rudyard was content to linger in Cape Town, then a sleepy, dusty, little dorp where teams of oxen dawdled down Adderley Street, and where Boer and Briton still lived amicably together. In a city club he found himself one day at a lunch-party with Cecil Rhodes whose new colony of Rhodesia had just come into being, but Kipling was unobtrusive and Rhodes, as ever, inarticulate, and they made no mark on one another. More to his fancy at the time was the British naval station at Simonstown where he struck up a friendship with Captain Bayly, getting from him an invitation to go for a cruise. It was his first contact with the Royal Navy, and sailors were new types of men whom he now began to study with his penetrating eye. 'Judson and the Empire',* his first naval

*It was based upon a conversation overheard in the naval mess at Simonstown. Lieutenant S. de Horsey, R.N., then commanding H.M. gunboat *Gryper*, was the original of 'Judson'. (Letter, S. de Horsey to B. M. Bazley, 23 July 1933.)

story, about a tiff with the Portuguese on the East African coast, was a by-product of this new range of interests.[8]

Among friends he made at Cape Town was Olive Schreiner the novelist, who had the hardihood to ask him about the background to *The Light that Failed*. This was his reply:

> If all the girls in the world sat quiet and still, at the right moment, by all the men in the world, when those were in trouble, we should all be perfectly happy instead of being hurt and worried. I'll show you about this time next year why Maisie was made as she was.[9]

The reader may interpret this letter as he will.

Two days after writing this letter, on 25 September 1891, Rudyard left Cape Town for the long lonely voyage to Hobart and Wellington in the Shaw Savill liner S.S. *Doric*. She followed the great circle far to the southward to get the advantage of the westerly winds in the roaring forties, the run that has been made familiar by 'M'Andrew's Hymn':

> We'll tak' one stretch – three weeks an' odd by ony road ye steer –
> Fra' Cape Town east to Wellington – ye need an engineer.
> Fail there – ye've time to weld your shaft – ay, eat it, ere ye're spoke;
> Or make Kerguelen under sail – three jiggers burned wi' smoke!
> An' home again – the Rio run: it's no child's play to go
> Steamin' to bell for fourteen days o' snow an' floe an' blow.
> The bergs like kelpies overside that girn an' turn an' shift
> Whaur, grindin' like the Mills o' God, goes by the big South drift.
> (Hail, Snow and Ice that praise the Lord. I've met them at their work,
> An' wished we had anither route or they anither kirk.)

While he studied the sea and the men who made their living by it, a slow uncertain correspondence was passing by infrequent mail steamers between two men who had interested themselves in his affairs: Henry James in London and Robert Louis Stevenson in Samoa.

James to Stevenson, 21 March 1890

We'll tell you about Rudyard Kipling – your nascent rival. He has killed one immortal – Rider Haggard; the star of the hour, aged 24 and author of remarkable anglo-indian and extraordinarily observed barrack life – Tommy Atkins tales.

Stevenson to James, August 1890

Kipling is too clever to live.

Stevenson to James, 29 December 1890

Kipling is by far the most promising young man who has appeared since – ahem – I appeared. He amazes me by his precocity and various endowments. But he alarms me by his copiousness and haste.

James to Stevenson, 12 January 1891

The only news in literature here – such is the virtuous vacancy of our consciousness – continues to be the infant monster of a Kipling.

Stevenson to James, 28 September 1891

R K is planning to visit us.

James to Stevenson, 30 October 1891

That little black demon of a Kipling will perhaps have leaped upon your silver strand by the time this reaches you. He publicly left England to embrace you many weeks ago – carrying literary genius out of the country with him in his pocket.[10]

On 18 October Rudyard landed in New Zealand at Wellington, where he submitted gracefully to a newspaper interview, and left for the north four days later to travel by horse-and-buggy through the central plains to the 'thermal district' of Rotorua where even in 1891 some provision was made for tourists. At Auckland his fancy was so far taken that he contributed an essay to the *New Zealand Herald* –

it has never been reprinted; and to Auckland he paid the
tribute in his 'Song of the Cities' that there one might

> Wonder 'mid our fern why men depart
> To seek the Happy Isles!

It must have been at Auckland that Kipling visited the
aged statesman, Sir George Grey, whose knowledge of the
Empire was unrivalled, whose memory of fifty years' service
in Australia, Africa, and New Zealand was ripened by
scholarship and by acquaintance with all the sharpest in-
tellects of the age. Of this meeting no record has survived
except a wildly inaccurate sentence in *Something of Myself*, Kipling's fragment of autobiography which, on the
events of this voyage, is quite unreliable.

When he arrived in New Zealand it was his intention to
extend his tour for another three months in order to visit
Stevenson in Samoa, but something in London called him
home, and he was unwilling to stay too long in the Anti-
podes. In Wellington he had been ill and frustrated, and the
Shipping Office persuaded him that Samoa, with no regular
sailings, could not be fitted into his itinerary. Perhaps with
relief, he abandoned the side-trip.

On 30 October Rudyard took ship again at Auckland and
travelled down the coast of New Zealand to Wellington, to
Lyttelton the port of Christchurch, to Dunedin, and to the
Bluff, the most southerly settlement of the English-speaking
peoples in the world. At Christchurch he met an old friend,
Professor Haslam who had excoriated him with sarcasms
for his errors in elementary Latin at Westward Ho!, whose
tongue was so sharp that even Mr Crofts' had been a pleasant relief. Haslam admitted that his pupils now had the
best of him: he lectured to mixed classes and when he re-
proved the girls for false quantities they made eyes at him.
Nothing else survives of Rudyard's visit to New Zealand except a memory of a boating picnic in Wellington harbour,
and a phrase he heard spoken at Christchurch, which years
afterwards he made the starting-point of a story called 'Mrs

Bathurst'.[11] Early in November he left the Bluff for Melbourne, travelling in company with 'General' Booth of the Salvation Army, who was making an apostolic tour of the world. An odd friendship sprang up between these two dissimilar characters, the old evangelist and the young writer, a friendship which may throw a gleam of light on both.

Rudyard's visit to Australia was briefer even than his visit to New Zealand. He spent a few days at the Melbourne Club, where the newspaper-men took him up, chaffed him because *Plain Tales* had just been banned by the public library for its impropriety, and begged him to 'report' the Melbourne Cup, the greatest horse-race in the world, for one of the papers. He would not; he wrote no revelation of Australia except – ten years later – the vivid poem called 'Lichtenberg', and that was based upon no more than a train journey to Sydney and back.[12]

After three weeks in Australia he left Adelaide in S.S. *Valetta* for Colombo, again in the company of 'General' Booth. At Colombo he left his ocean-liner, crossed to Tuticorin, and took the train through southern and central India to Lahore. For four days and nights he travelled through

an India more strange to him than to the untravelled Englishman – the flat red India of palm-tree, palmyra-palm, and rice, the India of the picture-books, of *Little Henry and His Bearer* – all dead and dry in the baking heat.

A week before Christmas he reached Lahore. The 'station' was disposed to make an honoured guest of this young man who had won so much fame since he had left them thirty months previously. He appeared at the fancy bazaar organized by the Lieutenant-Governor's lady and made no objection when his portrait appeared 'among those present' in the *Civil and Military*. The proprietors, down at Allahabad, were anxious to detain him for business discussions, but he could not be held.

Some message from Carrie Balestier may have influenced his decision to turn back. Tidings of Wolcott's illness, even by cable, cannot have reached him earlier than 10 December, when he landed at Colombo. Not till he was with his parents at Lahore did he receive the decisive blow, a cable from Carrie sent from Germany summoning him because Wolcott was dead. Without waiting even over Christmas Day Rudyard left Lahore for Bombay, where he stopped only to visit the _ayah_ who had nursed him as a baby. This was his last view of India. Travelling to Trieste and taking the overland route, he reached London in fourteen days,[13] a remarkably rapid journey.

The story of Wolcott's last days is to be read in the correspondence of Henry James. Wolcott had formed a new partnership with William Heinemann to produce an international library of cheap reprints, in competition with the _Tauchnitz_ editions. Late in November, after sending the first instalment of _The Naulahka_ to press, Wolcott went over to Dresden on the affairs of his new venture, and there he was taken ill with typhoid fever. It happened that Mrs Heinemann, his partner's wife, was visiting Dresden, and she sent for Wolcott's mother, who arrived in Dresden with her two daughters to find Wolcott dying. Mrs Balestier and her younger daughter, Josephine, were reduced to dismay and impotence, and it was Carrie, the elder daughter, who took charge of everything. She sent for Henry James, their family friend.

Henry James to William James, 13 December 1891

Europäischer Hof, Dresden.

I came off hastily to this place a week ago on a miserably sad errand – a sense of obligation created by the death here, 8 days since, in a private hospital, of a most malignant and hideous typhoid (brought from London) of poor dear Wolcott Balestier, whom you saw three or four times while you were with me. He had left England ill, three weeks previously, and I thought the change of climate and forsaking of high pressure business would work an improvement. But poison was in him and he has gone

– to my very serious loss and sorrow and that of many other people as well. I was greatly attached to him – with reason – for he had rendered me admirable services and was destined to render still more and greater. .... He had a great spirit and great ideas, and his writing (which was his real ambition) ... will give those who didn't know him but little idea of what those who *did* know him (and I think I did so better than anyone) found in him.

Henry James to Mrs M. Sands, 12 December 1891

I am working through my dreary errand ... as smoothly as three stricken women – a mother and two sisters – permit. They are, however, very temperate and discreet – and one of the sisters a little person of extraordinary capacity – who will float them all successfully home. Wolcott Balestier, the young American friend beside whose grave I stood with but three or four others here on Thursday, was a very remarkable creature ... and I was exceedingly attached to him. And now, at 30, he dies – in a week – in a far away German hospital – his mother and sisters were in Paris – of a damnable vicious typhoid, contracted in his London office, the 'picturesqueness' of which he loved, as it was in Dean's Yard, Westminster, just under the Abbey Towers.

Henry James to Edmund Gosse, 10 December 1891

The English chaplain read the service. The three ladies came insistently to the grave. .... By far the most interesting is poor little concentrated Carrie, with whom I came back from the cemetery alone in one of the big black and silver coaches, with its black and silver footmen perched up behind. (She wanted to talk to me) and ... is remarkable in her force, acuteness, capacity and courage – and in the intense – almost manly nature of her emotion. She is a worthy sister of poor dear big-spirited, only-by-death-quenched Wolcott. .... She can do and face ... for all three of them, anything and everything that they will have to meet now. They are going home (to the U.S.) as soon as they can, and they are going to London first. I suppose about a week hence.[14]

The news of Wolcott's death reached Brattleboro on 7 December. Beatty, the younger brother, was established there with a pretty young wife, on a farm called 'Maple-wood', which his doting grandmother had given him. With proper feeling, Beatty was proposing to return to England to take charge of his brother's affairs, until another cable assured him that this would not be necessary. It was, in fact, Carrie who disposed of the house in the Isle of Wight and made business arrangements with Wolcott's partner, William Heinemann; but Beatty and his friends in Brattleboro rightly surmised that the three women in London were not unsupported. It was not known in Brattleboro until 28 December that the man who had been collaborating with Wolcott was to marry Wolcott's sister. Beatty then understood why his presence in London was not required, though for several days he did not know which sister; and the same doubt was current among their friends in London. It was Carrie the dominating, clever sister, not Josephine the pretty one. In letter after letter Henry James expressed his doubts about the wisdom of the match.

Rudyard arrived in London on 10 January 1892. It was bitterly cold and the whole town seemed to be down with influenza. Without regard to any social niceties, Rudyard and Carrie arranged to be married by special licence within eight days. There were no festivities, and only a few close friends were notified by letters from the bride and bride-groom. Even of these friends very few came to the church; the Burne-Joneses had influenza, the Poynters had influenza, Mrs Balestier and Josephine had influenza. The wedding was at All Soul's, Langham Place, on 18 January, in the presence of a congregation of five. 'Ambo' Poynter, as best man, was the only representative of Rudyard's family; Henry James gave away the bride; Edmund Gosse, with his wife and son,* and William Heinemann made up the congregation. Even with this haste and privacy the news

* Dr Philip Gosse, who attended the wedding as a child, has described it to the present writer. The bride, a little woman with tiny hands and feet, was wearing a brown woollen dress with buttons all down the front.

leaked out and, as they emerged, the bridegroom was disgusted to see in the porch a newspaper poster announcing his wedding. At the church door the bridal couple parted (since Carrie was obliged to nurse her mother) to meet again at Brown's Hotel, where two days later 'Ambo' Poynter and Stan Baldwin came to lunch, the only entertainment that accompanied the marriage.[15]

Henry James to William James, 6 February 1892

I saw the Rudyard Kiplings off by the *Teutonic* the other day. ... She was poor Wolcott Balestier's sister and is a hard devoted capable little person whom I don't in the least understand his marrying. It's a union of which I don't forecast the future though I gave her away at the altar in a dreary little wedding with an attendance simply of four men – her mother and sister prostrate with influenza. Kipling strikes me personally as the most complete man of genius (as distinct from fine intelligence) that I have ever known.

The reason why Rudyard hurried half-way round the world to marry Wolcott's sister is bound up with his devotion to Wolcott. There is little doubt that Wolcott fostered the match, that Wolcott on his death-bed commended the care of his family to his friend Rudyard, that Wolcott's wishes were accepted by Rudyard as obligations, yet this does not imply that Wolcott's sister was hurried into a match. She had been engaged, or almost engaged, to Rudyard many months earlier;[16] and their parting then had been signalled by the verses which have already been quoted:

Ha' done with the Tents of Shem, dear lass,
We've seen the seasons through,
And it's time to turn on the old trail, our own trail, the out
    trail. ...

This had been the burden of his song when he left his two friends, the brother and sister, in August 1891. But what were the 'Tents of Shem', and, if the 'dear lass' was not

Carrie Balestier, who was she? The obscurity is deepened
by an early draft of the poem, now in an American library,
where the line runs: 'Have done with the Tents of Shem,
dear lad!' Was it originally an appeal to Wolcott? Even if
this theorizing be rejected and the 'Long Trail' taken as
fictitious writing with no subjective undertone, the fact remains that Wolcott's death marked a crisis in Rudyard's
life. During the previous year he had written cynically about
the reaction of civilized Europeans at the approach of death.
In London, he said, there was a pompous display of grief
when an old man slipped comfortably away in a bed surrounded by loving relatives. How different it had been in
India where active young men lived in expectation of being
struck down by disease in the pride of their youth, and of
being buried, replaced by a substitute, and forgotten, in
twenty-four hours. Though he had seen men die swiftly of
cholera at Lahore, no death had actually intruded into the
family square, or into the circle of his friends during his
seven years in the East. It was in tame, civilized Europe,
after all, that a bereavement first struck him to the heart.
He never forgot the blow though, characteristically, he
rarely referred to it. On one occasion he forced himself to
say a few words to a close friend of Wolcott whom he had
long wanted to meet: 'He died so suddenly and so far away;
we had so much to say to each other, and now I have got to
wait so long before I can say it.'[17]

Devotion to Wolcott's memory was a habit of mind that
Carrie shared with Rudyard. She had bent all the energy of
her untiring mind to the service of her family, that is to the
forwarding of Wolcott's career. By his wish – as a trust from
him – she renewed and redoubled her devotion to her lover.
Until Rudyard's death, forty-four years later, the two were
inseparable and her services to him were indispensable.
She now had a genius to care for, not only a man whose
friends thought that he ought to prove himself a genius.
Emotionally, Rudyard was satisfied with a marriage that

provided him with a clear field for exploiting his talents, nor did he ever again miss the comfortable stability of the family square, which he had often missed in his London year. Carrie was the mother of his three children; she provided him with his creature comforts, shielded him from intruders, watched his health, kept his accounts, took charge of all his affairs – sometimes with an irksome particularity. The marriage, perhaps, was more satisfactory on his side than on hers. 'Poor concentrated Carrie', as Henry James described her, gave Rudyard her life's endeavour and grudged him, perhaps, his faculty for withdrawing into a world of the imagination where she could not follow him.

From the day of their marriage, Carrie Kipling began to keep a diary. After 18 January 1892 there is rarely any doubt where Rudyard was or whom he met. They had agreed to set off together on the Long Trail, a honeymoon that would take them round the world. Rudyard had about £2,000 in his bank account, and as many contracts as he cared to sign with publishers; Carrie had expectations from her mother and her grandmother, both of them widows with comfortable fortunes. Though their own affairs seemed promising enough, there was much business to be concluded in the fortnight after the marriage. On his wedding-day Rudyard found time to write to Henley, about some verses which he had brought back to England with him, a ballad called 'Tomlinson', which Henley thought 'infernal strong'. Rudyard's letter about it concluded:

I have married Miss Balestier, the sister of the man with whom I wrote the yarn in the *Century* [the *Naulahka*]. I don't as a rule let men into any part of life outside working sections, but in this case methinks you are entitled to know.

Henley took the news sadly; R. L. Stevenson's marriage to a strong-minded American had been the end of his first literary partnership, and he much feared that Rudyard Kipling's marriage would have the same effect upon his second. 'Tomlinson' was some compensation, especially as Rudyard allowed him to correct it for the press, and sent with the proof a handsome tribute to Henley's 'Song of the Sword'. Rudyard never allowed himself to be swallowed up into the group that was called the 'Henley Regatta', and when he had another poem to sell, about a tramp steamer, he let it go elsewhere. 'The Ballad of the Bolivar' had been singing itself in his head for months and he was able to sit down in the office of the *St James's Gazette* with Sidney Low and strike off the fair copy, for payment on the nail, the modest sum of fifteen guineas.[18]

While it was Carrie's affair to wind up Wolcott's business with his partners, Heinemann in London and Lovell in New York, it was Rudyard's to complete *The Naulahka*, of which two monthly instalments had already appeared in the *Century*, and of which the last instalment had not been written when Wolcott died. The third was now published, the fourth in the press, and four or five more were to be got into print. The book had been announced with immense publicity, on both sides of the Atlantic. It went with Kipling on his honeymoon, and the last few pages were written on S.S. *Teutonic*.*

In addition to *The Naulahka*, Kipling had another book ready for publication. Now he released the volume of *Barrack-Room Ballads*, for which the trade was clamouring. Indeed, an American firm had already paid him the indirect compliment of issuing a piratical edition. With the original ballads from the *Scots Observer* he included 'The Ballad of East and West', 'The English Flag', 'Tomlinson', the 'Bolivar', and 'The Long Trail', a collection of such richness, variety, and gusto, if we claim no other merit for it, as to inflate the Kipling boom seven times larger. The

*The misspelling of the title *The Naulahka* remains a puzzle. Balestier may have been responsible for the error while Kipling was abroad, but Kipling never corrected the title, though when he named his Vermont house after the book he spelt it correctly, 'Naulakha'. What would he have said if any other publisher than Balestier had been responsible for such an error?

authorized English edition was published by Methuen in April; it was reprinted three times in 1892, and fifty times in the next thirty years, much the most popular book of verse in the world for more than a generation.

Not even Rudyard's most ardent admirers have found much to say in favour of the dedication, a rhetorical Swinburnian poem to the memory of Wolcott Balestier.

> Beyond the loom of the last lone star, through open darkness hurled,
> Further than rebel comet dared or hiving star-swarm swirled,
> Sits he with those that praise our God for that they served His world.

The oddest feature of this dedication is that it was not original. Several verses of it had already appeared in the *National Observer,* in another context. What it shows defiantly is his extraordinary admiration for the lost friend in whose honour he adapted these wildly adulatory verses.

From The Fires (1912)

Men make them fires on the hearth
Each under his roof-tree,
And the Four Winds that rule the earth
They blow the smoke to me.

. . . .

Until the tears are in my eyes
And my heart is wellnigh broke
For thinking on old memories
That gather in the smoke.

With every shift of every wind
The homesick memories come,
From every quarter of mankind
Where I have made me a home.

Four times afire against the cold
And a roof against the rain –
Sorrow fourfold and joy fourfold
The Four Winds bring again!

How can I answer which is best
Of all the fires that burn?
I have been too often host or guest
At every fire in turn.

. . . .

Oh, you Four Winds that blow so strong
And know that this is true,
Stoop for a little and carry my song
To all the men I knew!

. . . .

[9]

A Home in Vermont
(1892–6)

When the Kiplings, a new-married couple, crossed the Atlantic in February 1892, they had for travelling-companion
an observant critic of Anglo-American relations, who
relished their society. *The Education of Henry Adams* contains the following, unexpected, comment:

> Fate was kind on that voyage. Rudyard Kipling ... thanks to
> the mediation of Henry James, dashed over the passenger his
> exuberant fountain of gaiety and wit – as though playing a
> garden hose on a thirsty and faded begonia. Kipling could hardly
> ever know what peace of mind he gave, for he could hardly ever
> need it himself so much; and yet, in full delight of his endless
> fun and variety, one felt the old conundrum repeat itself. Some-
> how, somewhere, Kipling and the American were not one, but
> two, and could not be glued together. ...

The 'old conundrum' did not force itself upon Rudyard's
notice during the wedding-trip. On 17 February, with a sigh
of relief at leaving New York behind them – 'New York
with her roar and rattle, her complex smells, her triply
overheated rooms, and much too energetic inhabitants' –
the Kiplings arrived at Brattleboro.

They stepped from the train to find Beatty Balestier waiting with a sleigh.

> Thirty below freezing! It was inconceivable till one stepped
> into it at midnight, and the first shock of that clear, still air took
> away the breath as does a plunge into sea-water. A walrus sitting
> on a woolpack was our host in his sleigh, and he wrapped us in
> hairy goatskin coats, caps that came down over the ears, buffalo
> robes and blankets, and yet more buffalo-robes till we, too,

looked like walruses and moved almost as gracefully. ... But for
the jingle of sleigh-bells the ride might have taken place in a
dream, for there was no sound of hoofs upon the snow, the
runners sighed a little now and again as they glided over an inequality, and all the sheeted hills round about were as dumb as
death. Only the Connecticut River kept up its heart and a lane of
black water through the packed ice; we could hear the stream
worrying round the heels of its small bergs. Elsewhere there was
nothing but snow under the moon – snow drifted to the level of
the stone fences or curling over their tops in a lip of frosted
silver; snow banked high on either side of the road, or lying
heavy on the pines and hemlocks in the woods, where the air
seemed, by comparison, as warm as a conservatory.[1]

The crisp New England winter, such wintry weather as
Rudyard, brought up in southern England and matured in
India, had never seen before, began to work in him a current of new life and vision. It was stimulating to stand on
ground, now hard with frozen snow, ground in which he
felt his wife's family to be rooted deep. They left the Main
Street of Brattleboro where the road ran northward over a
covered bridge, and drove two miles along the river-flats to
the corner by Waite's Farm. A winding steep road led off
among the elms and maples, up a hill to 'Beechwood', the
family house where old Madam Balestier, the matriarch,
lived with her termagant Irish housekeeper. A mile farther
the road came out across a sloping pasture with a wooded
hillside on the left, and on the right a broad view over the
valley towards a distant semicircle of pine-covered hills.
Here stood 'Maplewood', Beatty's new home on his seventy-
acre farm, and here the Kiplings stayed three days with
Beatty and his pretty young wife. The favourite in the party
was Marjorie, their new baby – a delight to Rudyard.

On the second day they climbed the hill to admire the
view and saw the cone of Mount Monadnock rising above
the foothills thirty miles away to the east, 'like a giant
thumbnail'. If Rudyard knew himself at home among his
wife's people, he had a longer association there, for Monad-

nock was Emerson's favourite mountain, familiar to Rudyard from his earliest reading:

> High over the river intervals,
> Above the ploughman's highest line,
> Over the owners' farthest walls!
> Up where the airy citadel
> O'erlooks the surging landscape's swell!
> Youth, for a moment free as they,
> Teach thy feet to feel the ground,
> Ere yet arrives the wintry day
> When Time thy feet has bound.
> Taste the bounty of thy birth,
> Taste the lordship of the earth.[2]

There was no doubt of it from that day; Rudyard and Carrie must stake out a claim on the family property, and by Rudyard's choice it must be high up the hillside, in sight of Mount Monadnock. Beatty, with his easy liberality, would have given him a plot of ground as a wedding-present; Carrie, with her business-like notions, was for negotiating a deal. She offered to take over the whole farm and to finance Beatty, who was always short of cash. They all went down to New York to consult the lawyers about the Balestier reversions, and the end of the matter was that Beatty conveyed about ten acres of land to the Kiplings for a nominal consideration, reserving to himself the use of the pasture and some other rights. It was a friendly agreement between two young newly married couples, conceived in generosity and good humour. The Kiplings spent another day or two at Brattleboro, then, having concluded their business and paid many calls in New York, they resumed their honeymoon.

It will not be necessary to retrace Rudyard's steps throughout his wedding tour, much of it following the path he had taken with his friends the Hills, in 1889. At one stage of the journey, however, he broke new ground, turning north from Chicago to St Paul, and so to Winnipeg and across the Canadian prairie to the Rocky Mountains and

Vancouver. The C.P.R., then the only trans-continental line
in North America, made a noble impression on him as did
the effective administration of law in Canada, signified by
the scarlet tunics of the Mounted Police. 'Her Majesty the
Queen of England and Empress of India has us in her keeping', he wrote, with a new awareness that Canada differed
from the United States. Again, he paid his way by writing
travel-sketches, innocent this time of the indiscretions that
marred his first juvenile essays in the field, and much more
lucrative. They appeared in the *Civil and Military Gazette*,
for what that was worth – and simultaneously in the New
York *Sun* and the London *Times*.[3] Kipling was famous.
No longer did he fill in his dull evenings by chumming up
with newspaper men who were then free to mis-report his
words; they came, hat in hand, and were firmly kept at bay,
by Carrie, his business manager.

On a second visit, even to Japan in spring, a man need
not repeat the tourist's round, but might merely luxuriate in
form and colour. Much of his honeymoon he spent at Yokohama where a Mrs Hunt acted as host to him and Carrie.
Each of them had friends in Japan, where the name of her
grandfather, Judge Peshine Smith, was well-remembered as
legal adviser to the Mikado who broke down the barriers
that had closed Japan against the world. Rudyard enjoyed
his visits to the Yokohama Club where he could listen to
the yarns of shipping magnates, particularly about the lawless skippers who poached seal-skins in waters which the
Russians claimed as their own, though

there's never a law of God or man runs north of Fifty-Three.[4]

Into these northern seas he never penetrated, even if he
wrote of them with understanding. In Yokohama, he recalled:

an earthquake (prophetic as it turned out) overtook us one hot
break of dawn, and we fled into the garden, where a tall crypto-
meria waggled its insane head back and forth with an 'I told
you so' expression; though not a breath was stirring. A little

later I went to the Yokohama branch of my bank on a wet fore-
noon to draw some of my solid wealth. Said the Manager to me:
'Why not take more? It will be just as easy.' I answered that I did
not care to have too much cash at one time in my careless keeping, but that when I had looked over my accounts I might come
again in the afternoon. I did so, but in that little space, my
Bank, the notice on its shut door explained, had suspended
payment. ... I returned with my news to my bride of three
months and a child to be born.[5]

The sum he had drawn was the exchange value of ten
pounds sterling; his loss when the Oriental Banking Company failed, on 9 June 1892, was nearly £2,000; his immediate resources were a return ticket to Vancouver by the
Empress of China, and $100 in a New York bank. They
had intended to cruise in the Pacific as far as Samoa at least,
but all plans for a longer honeymoon were cancelled and
again the prospect of a visit to R. L. Stevenson was abandoned. Thomas Cook handsomely refunded them the value
of their cancelled reservations and they faced the world
with equanimity, even with gaiety. During their last three
weeks in Japan they danced at a ball given by Mrs Hunt,
and went about as though nothing had happened. Rudyard
attended a meeting of creditors and it was he who proposed
that they should make a composition with the insolvent
bank for preference shares to the value of 25 per cent of
their lost deposits. The value of these shares was eventually
paid off at even better terms, though not until the Kiplings
had become too prosperous to depend upon so modest a
sum.[6] On 27 June 1892 he left Yokohama.

Already he was sending his travel-sketches to *The Times*
and the other papers, and he had begun to work on verse
and prose fiction. He was busy with 'The Rhyme of the
Three Sealers' and with 'Judson and the Empire'. Lack of
ready cash was no great obstacle to a man who could always
sell his wares and always command hospitality, and on the
voyage, with unusual geniality, he gave readings of his work
at ship's concerts. He crossed Canada as the guest of Wil-

liam Van Horne, the Chairman of the C.P.R. In July 1892
he bade farewell – finally – to Asia.

Never again did he take ship east of Suez.

At Montreal the Kiplings had a telegram from Carrie's
mother offering them the chance of a home at Brattleboro
for $10 a month. It was the hired-man's house on the Bliss
Farm, quite near to 'Beechwood'. On 26 July they reached
Brattleboro, billeted themselves on Beatty and 'resumed the
worship of Marjorie', his little daughter. After a family
council with 'Madam' Balestier, the offer of the 'Bliss Cottage' was accepted, not quite the homecoming they had
foreseen. For a year they lived in the simplest style, at first
with one Swedish maid at $18 a month, which Carrie
thought excessive. The neighbours, who were accustomed
to regard the Balestiers as swell folks with style and money,
were inclined to look askance at the penniless Englishman
whom Miss Carrie had brought into the family, but not for
long. *The Naulahka* and *Barrack-Room Ballads*, published
while they were away, had begun to bring in royalties – a
modest $150 in September, $260 in October, and a cheque
for no less than $3,888 in November from A. P. Watt; and
these were but foretastes of what was coming.

Their happiness, in the 'Bliss Cottage', is plain in Rudyard's reminiscences:

> We took it. We furnished it with a simplicity that fore-ran the
> hire-purchase system. We bought, second or third hand, a huge,
> hot-air stove which we installed in the cellar. We cut generous
> holes in our thin floors for its eight-inch tin pipes (why we were
> not burned in our beds each week of the winter I never can
> understand) and we were extraordinarily and self-centredly con-
> tent.

> As the New England summer flamed into autumn I piled cut
> spruce boughs all round the draughty cottage sill, and helped to
> put up a tiny roofless verandah along one side of it for future
> needs. When winter shut down and sleigh-bells rang all over the
> white world that tucked us in, we counted ourselves secure.
> Sometimes we had a servant. Sometimes she would find the

solitude too much for her and flee without warning, one even leaving her trunk. This troubled us not at all.

When our lead pipe froze, we could slip on our coonskin coats and thaw it out with a lighted candle. There was no space in the attic bedroom for a cradle, so we decided that a trunk-tray would be just as good. We envied no one.

My first child and daughter was born in three foot of snow on the night of December 29th 1892. Her Mother's being the 31st and mine the 30th of the same month, we congratulated her on her sense of the fitness of things, and she throve in her trunk-tray in the sunshine on the little plank verandah. Her birth brought me into contact with the best friend I made in New England – Dr Conland.[7]

Rudyard did not produce much written work in his honey-moon year. He finished off two or three belated soldier stories from his Indian period – notably 'Love o' Women' which he described to Carrie as a 'doleful tale', and worked a little at verses inspired by his travels. Mostly, he was occupied with making a home for Carrie and the baby, whom they called Josephine, after Carrie's sister.

Rudyard and Carrie had never swerved from their decision to build a house of their own. Even in their penniless days they were negotiating with an old friend named H. R. Marshall, a New York architect, for a house to be built to a novel design, on the plot of land they had acquired from Beatty, and as soon as the snow melted, they contracted to bring in labourers.

The house was named 'Naulakha' in memory of Wolcott, and the contracts for building it were handled by Beatty. The drive ran up the pasture from the road, near 'Maple-wood', to a porch on the west side between the house and the hill. All the living-rooms were on the outer slope with wide windows to south and east. Rudyard used to say it lay on the long slope like a ship mounting an ocean swell, and like a ship, it was long and narrow. At one end was the kit-chen, then came the dining-room, then a lounge into which you came from the entrance hall, then Carrie's boudoir where she sat at her desk facing the door and guarding the

last room in the line, Rudyard's library at the south end.
To this room there was no admission except past her chair;
and no tradesman or artisan, no business caller, journalist, or
busybody got through her guard to intrude upon the Master.
It was a house of modest size with no room more than
twenty feet in length, and no accommodation for more
than a few guests.

Beatty acted as general agent for all their concerns and
made at first a pretty good thing of them. It was Beatty
who bought a team of oxen, hired labourers, got contracts
for drainage, supplied farm horses, and took the hay off the
meadow. Like many Vermont farmers he was always sag-
ging along behind his liabilities, living on a mortgage, in
farming country that steadily deteriorated. But Beatty and
his pretty young wife, Mai, were alive, amusing, witty, hospitable. They gave memorable parties in which the Kiplings
took the greatest pleasure. With cakes on a plank table,
jugs of home-brewed cider, a fiddler from the town; with
all the neighbours in, they would dance in the barn till past
midnight – ungodly hours for Brattleboro. All the family
assembled at Beatty's house for their Thanksgiving Dinner
and when Conan Doyle came to stay with the Kiplings
Beatty swept him into the party. 'No one', he said, 'would
want to keep Thanksgiving in an Englishman's house.' In
the afternoons Rud and Beatty would drive off to town while
Mai sent her little Marjorie to spend the day at 'Naulakha'. Carrie had a good nursemaid now, Susan Bishop, who
could look after the little girls together. When Rud came
home he always had stories for the children, animal stories
about camels and whales and the cat that walked in the
wet wild woods up the road from Beatty's house.

Beatty was not a man to worry overmuch, and his worst
trouble was that his elder sister would treat him as a boy.
Whatever the nature of their contract, she regarded it as a
means of controlling his extravagance. Two or three times
a week, she had him up to 'Naulakha' to talk business,
handing him out his commission in irregular doles of petty

cash; five dollars one day, two dollars twenty-five another day, then fifteen dollars cash and a cheque for a larger sum with it, two dollars just before the Christmas party at 'Maplewood', and five dollars more, two days later. Sometimes there was a large settlement to make, scrupulously noted in her diary, as much as $257 at a single payment when the building of 'Naulakha' was finished, but the following month she slipped back into her routine of small sums. In aggregate the amount paid to Beatty was considerable wealth in the values of those days, over four thousand dollars in three years, but when the works about the house and garden, the stable and drive, the well, the avenue and tennis-court were finished, the flow of dollars dried up.

Before the house was quite ready, Rudyard and Carrie had the supreme pleasure — as welcome to her as to him — of a visit from Lockwood Kipling, who had at last retired, with a decoration, the C.I.E., as his reward for thirty years' service in India. Rudyard had used his influence with the new Viceroy, through their old friend Lord Dufferin, to get him a pension. Lockwood had before him twenty years of comfortable old age which he filled with literary, artistic, and archaeological activity, and with travel. Far more than his son, he was addicted to voyaging in remote countries. It was Lockwood rather than Rudyard who refreshed his tired soul from time to time with the 'bucking beam-sea roll of a black Bilbao tramp'. The Brattleboro people soon learned to recognize this very English figure tramping the roads with stick and pipe; and he soon fired Rudyard with the wanderlust. They went off together on a trip into Canada, just when the new house was ready. Carrie had to see to the removal from the 'Bliss Cottage', with the added trouble that both her maids gave notice on moving-day, the waitress merely because the cook was going, the cook because she disliked the caps that Carrie desired her to wear.

In August, when the two men came back, 'Naulakha' was ready for occupation. Lockwood approved of everything,

especially of Rudyard's library with its spacious outlook
for the day's work and its open fireplace for the evening's
comfort. He inscribed a text on the massive chimney-
piece: 'The Night cometh when No Man can Work', and
so the title of Rudyard's next volume of stories was determined.

Lockwood, also, had been venturing into authorship. In
1891 he had published his *Beast and Man in India.* The
book was dedicated to 'the other three' of the family square,
and Rudyard loyally declared it to be superior to all his
own works. It is a miscellany gathered from wide observation and wider reading, packed with legend, folk-lore, anecdotes from the Indian classics, descriptions of contrivances,
utensils and costumes, and sketches by the author in pen-
and-ink. The whimsical and the technical, the learned and
the popular, the theoretical and the practical are heaped
together on every page.

The book is a standing record of the mutual stimulus
exerted between Lockwood and his son. The father quotes
many of his son's verses, 'collected' and 'uncollected'. In
countless instances the father's anecdotes and allusions reveal the son's debt to his father's omniscience. Here you
may find Chil the kite and Tabaqui the jackal, the method
of catching crows by a decoy, the nursery song about the
wild plums in the jungle, the behaviour of snake and mon-
goose around the house, the habits of battery-mules, the
legend of a place where the elephants dance, the story of
Moti Guj, mutineer, the story of Ganesa and the money-
lender, the customs of the *bandar-log.* The range and scope
and fullness of Lockwood's collections reveal a mellower,
more tolerant, view of life than Rudyard's. The whole work
is a comment on Indian ethics, which he regards with gentle
scepticism and with no hint of western condescension. 'If
we did not daily see by how slack a hold the faith of the
West controls its life, we might marvel at the indifference
of the East to the sufferings of animals whose bodies are
believed to be tenanted by human souls.' Not cruelty but

carelessness, indifference to suffering, apathy, are the tendencies he observes, predominantly, of Man towards Beast
in India.

Lockwood's appearance in Vermont was fortunate for
Rudyard, who was again at work upon stories which called
for his father's advice. 'The Bridge-Builders' [8]* was written
that autumn, and Rudyard was also busy with an experiment in a new field; in November 1892 at the 'Bliss Cottage' he had written 'a wolf-story called "Mowgli's Brothers"'. We have his word for it, supported by Rider
Haggard's,[9] that the impulse was derived from a scene in
Haggard's Zulu romance, *Nada the Lily*, where in a riot of
supernatural fantasy, Umslopogaas is presented as running
with a pack of wolves (though there are no true wolves in
Zululand). This was but the beginning of a train of thought,
and much more is necessary to account for the origins of
the new, powerful, and lasting myth which Rudyard was to
elaborate in the first and second *Jungle Books*, the best-
sellers among his works. The fable of the man-child who
became master of the jungle, but who could not resolve the
dilemma of his ambivalent life, the apparatus of Indian
animal lore, the strange ethical concept called the Law of
the Jungle, are Rudyard's own and have no counterpart in
Rider Haggard's work.

It would be a shallow criticism of the *Jungle Books* to call
them animal stories for children, though that is the mode
in which they first enthral readers. Like their great original,
Aesop's Fables, or like the *Jataka* tales which the Kiplings
knew so well, they impress themselves on the mind at more
than one level. The fables illustrate truths which – for such
is the nature of successful fable – are not made more explicit by being interpreted at second hand. Every reader

*In India Rudyard had written accounts for the *C.M.G.* of new
bridges over the Sutlej on the Lahore-Ferozepore line, and over the
Jhelum at Chak Nizam, both in 1887. Sir A. Geddes in his *Founding
of a Family* claims that his father was the original of Findlayson in
'The Bridge-Builders'.

may find out for himself who is Mowgli, that strong, beautiful youth belonging neither to the village nor to the jungle; what allegory is expressed by his two kindly mentors, Bagheera the panther and Baloo the bear, by Shere Khan the bully whose great strength and ferocity fail him at every test, by the *Bandar-log*, those gentry of the tree-tops whose only ambition is to be noticed, who suppose a thing has been done if it has been cleverly talked about, and what is the nature of 'the Law' which binds the Jungle world into an integrated whole while allowing and even enjoining ruthless individual action within admitted bounds – the Law which especially constitutes Mowgli's brothers as the 'Free People'.*

As the creeper that girdles the tree-trunk the Law runneth forward and back –
For the strength of the Pack is the Wolf, and the strength of the Wolf is the Pack.
The Jackal may follow the Tiger, but, Cub, when thy whiskers are grown,
Remember the Wolf is a hunter – go forth and get food of thine own.
Keep peace with the Lords of the Jungle – the Tiger, the Panther, the Bear;
And trouble not Hathi the Silent, and mock not the Boar in his lair.

*As for the topography, the local colour which has given two whole generations of men an understanding of the Indian jungle, he got it mostly at second hand. The adult story, 'In the Rukh', published before 'Mowgli's Brothers' though written after it, is located in the forests of the Doon which Kipling knew pretty well. All the other Mowgli stories are precisely placed in a part of Central India which he never visited, the banks of the Waingunga river in the Seonee district. He knew this best through the description given by his friends the Hills who were there in ,1888, and brought back photographs which may be seen in the Carpenter Collection at Washington. Jungle-lore and the ways of wild animals, if he did not learn of them from his father, he drew from a well-thumbed copy of Sterndale's *Mammalia of India*, which still exists. Stories of the nursing of abandoned infants by she-wolves Sterndale regards as 'not improbable'.

Now these are the Laws of the Jungle, and many and mighty are
    they;
But the head and the hoof of the Law and the haunch and the
    hump is – Obey!

Soon after his father's return to England, there came an
evening when Rudyard confided to his wife that he had received an access of power, the 'return of a feeling of great
strength, such as he had when he first came to London and
met the men he was pitted against'.[10] Then, in 1890, he had
been inspired but unhappy, and the fruit of his labour had
been the *Barrack-Room Ballads*, *The Light that Failed*, and
a set of powerful but gloomy stories. The new flow of genius
produced the verses collected in *The Seven Seas*, the two
Jungle Books, and the diverse set of stories in the volume
called *The Day's Work*. At the time when he admitted
Carrie to this secret, he was engaged upon 'M'Andrew's
Hymn', the most elaborate and perhaps the most effective
of his dramatic lyrics. It launched upon the world the new
concept of the romance of machinery, a notion which he
expressed succinctly a few weeks later in the lines:

Confound Romance! ... And all unseen
Romance brought up the nine-fifteen.

The stories which developed the same theme, a sort of
pantheism that felt the world-soul throbbing with life, even
in railway engines and steamships, were written a little later
('The Ship that Found Herself' in 1895, '.007' in 1896).

The two volumes of jungle stories were polished off, pretty
regularly, the first in November 1892 and the last in March
1895, when 'The Spring Running' brought the series to a
conclusion, and the impulse to write more was switched off
as water is turned off at a tap.* The poems mostly lay on

---

* 'That ends up Mowgli and there is not going to be any more of
him. After that, I expect to try my hand at a series of engineers' tales
– about marine engines and such like'. From a letter dated 3 November 1895 quoted in the *Kipling Journal*, April 1946. It was written
to an unknown admirer of his work.

his hands much longer. When a boy in India, he had scribbled his light verse to pay his way while he gave sustained attention to prose composition. Now he sold stories for a living and so bought leisure for working at his poems.

Among the pieces published in *The Seven Seas* (October 1896), 'A Song of the English', a long sequence of lyrics in various moods and styles, was conceived at least as early as 1889. The greater part of it, especially the 'Song of the Cities', reflected – not always discreetly – his impressions of the seaports visited during his voyages in 1891 and 1892; the final draft was ready for the printers in March 1893. Rather earlier were 'The Gipsy Trail', Rudyard's prothalamium, and 'The Last Chantey', a variant on a theme which always fascinated him, the survival of simple earthy individuals in an ideal eternal world. 'The Last Chantey' was written before Rudyard's return to Vermont. His first winter in the 'Bliss Cottage' produced, as well as the satire, 'In the Neolithic Age', a new group of Indian Army ballads, 'Gentlemen-Rankers', 'Shillin'-a-day', 'The Lost Legion', 'The Widow's Party', 'Bobs', and 'Back to the Army again', all slight and casual pieces, which neither got much notice nor brought in much money. Rudyard was still sending occasional contributions to the *National Observer* which kept its head just above water. Henley, however, could not afford to pay more than fifteen guineas for 'The Dove of Dacca' in April 1893. Not many months earlier Rudyard had been glad to accept that sum for the 'Bolivar'; it now seemed a poor return for an author who already commanded $100 per thousand words for his prose and was likely to double that sum shortly. Scribners gave him $500 for 'M'Andrew's Hymn', a record price for a poem in America.

Rudyard did what he could for Henley and corresponded with him gaily:

Rudyard Kipling to W. E. Henley (Autumn 1893?)

After many wanderings your book has come in and it is a Book. What impresses me most is naturally the *Voluntaries* which

are high water mark. Over and above everything else I love the
way in which the music gives back the dull boom, pause, mutter
and boom again of the London Traffic as you hear it from the
centre of the Parks.

My poem Song of the Sword, dedicated to Kipling please you
will write it over again with rhymed endings. Swords sing, O
Henley *sahib*! And yet the way in which your blade comes out
of the scabbard inch by inch till it drives back again with a clang
on the last line is Good Enough. . . .

My time is divided among many things – stables and sewers
and furniture and the settling down of a house. Its great fun and
it keeps the mind off dwelling too much on words and their
texture and composition . . .

I've brought back a deck-load of notions from beyond sea and
I'm busy putting 'em in order against the time that I can write
'em out. Mostly it's a bloody flux of verse which I'm curious to
see developed. The sun and the air and the light are good in
this place and have made me healthy as I never was in my life.
I wish you could see the place. It's three miles from anywhere
and wondrous self-contained. No one can get at you and if you
don't choose to call for your mail you don't get it . . .[11]

The 'Anchor Song', finished in January 1893, was the first
to take shape of his more substantial notions in the new
manner; it was followed in March by 'The Song of the
Banjo', a more important piece than its title suggests, and in
May by 'The Merchantmen'. Later in the year Rudyard was
busy with the verses for the *Jungle Books*, and in December
Carrie reported him as humming and strumming all over
the house with rhythmical experiments. The hymn-tune,
'The Church's One Foundation', gave him a set of rhythms
which he used, in part at least, for 'M'Andrew's Hymn'; he
went on to 'The King' ('Farewell, Romance'). Then came
the second set of *Barrack-Room Ballads* which range over a
wider field of emotion than the first. No author in any
literature has composed, in verse or prose, so full and varied
and so relentlessly realistic a view of the soldier's life, with
its alternations of boredom and terror, its deadening
routine, its characteristic vices and corruptions, its rare

glories and its irrational fascination, as Rudyard Kipling in the series of verses he produced in the next two years: 'The Sergeant's Wedding' and 'For to Admire' in February 1894, 'Follow me 'Ome' in April, 'Cholera Camp' in October, 'The 'Eathen' in February 1895, 'That Day', 'The Men that Fought at Minden' and the 'Birds of Prey March' before April 1895, 'Soldier and Sailor Too' in November, 'The Ladies' and 'The Shut-eye Sentry' early in 1896. If he had written nothing else, this group of ballads, from which many lines have become familiar quotations, would preserve his name as long as soldiering remains the unavoidable lot of half-willing young men.

Other compositions of this period are not less noteworthy. Early in 1894 he completed the strange ballad called 'The Last Rhyme of True Thomas', to which I shall refer again; and during his summer visit to England he concluded several half-finished pieces which had lain on his hands, among them 'The Miracles'. His amusing comment on the decline of the three-volume novel, 'The Three-Decker', was written on that holiday, as was his harsher comment on the New World as revealed in the Chicago railway-strike, the Emersonian *pastiche* called 'An American'. After his return to Vermont, he wrote 'The "Mary Gloster"', a companion piece to 'M'Andrew's Hymn', the one, as Mr Eliot has said, exposing the failure of success, while the other exalts the success of failure. These were his boldest experiments in the genre of Browning's *Men and Women*. Among his minor verses may be mentioned 'The Mother-Lodge', a flashlight on his attitude to racial problems, which he wrote in a single morning of November while Conan Doyle was in his house as a guest.

Then came a pause; he was silenced by bad news, the death in Samoa of Robert Louis Stevenson, whom he greatly admired but had never met though they corresponded as friends. Rudyard was so deeply moved that he wrote nothing for a month.

In the following year a new range of interests provoked a

new series of prose stories while the flow of dramatic lyrics was resumed: 'The Explorer' begun in January, 'Pan in Vermont' in February,* 'The Native-Born' in September, 'The Bell Buoy' and 'The Flowers' begun in November.

Eighteen ninety-four had been a year of great content and prosperity for the Kiplings. They allowed themselves a long holiday, first an ocean cruise, and afterwards a visit to Rudyard's parents in England. On the voyage to Bermuda they struck up an acquaintance with a New York family, Mrs Catlin and her two daughters, who became their lifelong friends. In Prospero's magic isle Rudyard found a key to Shakespeare's art which he often pondered over in later years. Seeing with his own eyes that the set of the beach was congruent with the scenery of *The Tempest*, he conceived the notion of a shipwrecked sailor spinning a yarn from which Shakespeare visualized the island.

> For a bite and sup, and a bed of clean straw
> We'll tell you such marvels as man never saw,
> On a Magical Island which no one did spy
> Save this Master, that Swabber, yon Bo'sun, and I.[12]

This was certainly the method by which Rudyard picked up his own notions.

In Bermuda, though he stayed in a hotel with Carrie and the Catlins, he was much invited out by the Governor, the Admiral, and the officers of the garrison. It was a pleasure to dine in the officers' mess of the Royal Berkshire Regiment and to smell again the smell of the barracks, but best of all was the friendship of a sergeant with whom he got into casual conversation. After a time they exchanged names. 'Mr Kipling. What! the celebrated Rudyard!' and the sergeant carried him off in triumph to the sergeants'

---

* It's forty in the shade to-day, the spouting eaves declare;
The boulders nose above the drift, the southern slopes are bare;
Hug-deep in slush Apollo's car swings north along the Zodiac. Good lack, the Spring is back, and Pan is on the road!

mess. He and Carrie took tea with the sergeant's wife in the married lines, and not long afterwards appeared a ballad called 'That Day', which has impressed one young soldier, at least, as the masterpiece among Rudyard's soldier-songs. It is the account of a disaster:

> It got beyond all orders an' it got beyond all 'ope;
>   It got to shammin' wounded an' retirin' from the 'alt.
> 'Ole companies was lookin' for the nearest road to slope;
>   It were just a bloomin' knock-out – an' our fault!
>
> *Now there ain't no chorus 'ere to give,*
>   *Nor there ain't no band to play;*
> *An' I wish I was dead 'fore I done what I did,*
>   *Or seen what I seed that day!*

Fourteen years had passed since the Royal Berkshire Regiment had made its heroic last stand at Maiwand in Afghanistan, where one wing of the regiment had fought and died beside the colonel and the regimental colour, while the other wing had made a fighting retreat to Kandahar in a broken, routed army. Whoever survived from this affair, and was still serving in Bermuda in 1894, had a sorry tale to tell, but such a tale as every soldier knows to be true to the realities of war.

After three weeks in Bermuda the Kiplings went back to New York and Brattleboro. It was a little disconcerting to find that Beatty, who had been left in charge of the household at 'Naulakha' including Josephine and her nurse, had run into debt, so that accounts had to be settled before they could leave for the second part of their holiday. On 10 April they reached Southampton and went at once to Tisbury, a lonely village in the Wiltshire Downs, where Rudyard's parents had made their home after their return from India. His mother found another house which Rudyard and Carrie could rent for the summer, and all four lived for three months at Tisbury. Lockwood was busier than ever at drawing, carving, modelling, in a workshop behind their cottage.

The most delicate passages in the *Jungle Books,* notably
'The Miracle of Purun Bhagat', were written at Tisbury
under the fastidious eye of Lockwood Kipling, always his
son's severest critic.

Not far away were three great country houses where old
English hospitality was practised on the most lavish scale.
The Arundells at Wardour Castle, the Wyndhams at
'Clouds', and the Morrisons at 'Fonthill' had taken up Lockwood Kipling, as the Dufferins had taken him up at Simla,
and the unchanging life of feudal Wiltshire in this social
circle spurred Rudyard to write of the contrast between
American and English country ways. The astonishing farce,
'My Sunday at Home',* with its richly tinted pictures of an
English summer evening, was re-cast and completed at Tisbury; and the tartly unkind story of an anglicized American, which he called 'An Error in the Fourth Dimension',
was also written that summer. So much were Rudyard and
Carrie taken with the English countryside that they began
to talk of employing his cousin, 'Ambo' Poynter, to build
them an English holiday cottage, by the sea; but Carrie
thought better of it. There were several family reasons, she
thought, why they must live in America.

Rudyard often went up to London by train, sometimes
taking Carrie with him, to Brown's Hotel. He saw something of Henley and Whibley, as in his bachelor days in
London; and struck up an acquaintance with Aubrey
Beardsley, the new boy-genius who had just burst upon the
town. If Rudyard had not been a writer, he might have
been a black-and-white artist. He had a singularly clean
flowing line and, writing all his books – as he did – with a
fine pen and the best Indian ink, he was inclined to decorate the margins of his manuscripts, while pausing for

*R. K. to E. L. White, 17 August 1894: 'Heaven was kind to me
in England, where I was safely delivered of several poems, four new
Jungle Stories and a piece of broad farce, viler than "Brugglesmith",
which made me laugh for three days. . . . I wonder if people get a tithe
of the fun out of my tales than I get in doing 'em.'

thought, with arabesques and grotesques in what is now
called the Beardsley manner. It was not imitative, however,
but due to sympathy of another sort, for the habit was most
pronounced in his earlier days when Beardsley had not yet
drawn a line.

In the London season of 1894 Rudyard allowed himself
to be lionized. His portrait appeared as one of the weekly
cartoons in *Vanity Fair*; he went about with 'Ambo'
Poynter to social functions; he was present at the 'private
view' and at the Royal Academy banquet. Nothing, perhaps, was more socially eminent than a dinner given by
Lord George Hamilton for him and Lord Roberts who now
appeared almost as equals.

A distinction which he valued more highly was a visit to
his old school as the guest of honour on a solemn occasion.
'Uncle Crom' was retiring from the headmastership and was
to be given a testimonial, to which Rudyard contributed
twenty pounds. On 25 July 1894 Rudyard made one of his
rare appearances on a public platform, at 'Uncle Crom's'
farewell to the past and present pupils of the United Services College. He even made a short speech on behalf of the
'Old Boys', congratulating Cormell Price on having created
'the best school in England'. It was Price's day of triumph,
not Rudyard's, but Price made it clear that his pride as a
teacher lay in having educated the literary man who had
sprung up among his military pupils.

'You, my dear Kipling,' he said, in his reply, 'are the mouthpiece of a body dear to me beyond expression. You have rightly
dwelt upon the spirit of comradeship that prevails among our Old
Boys. ... You are the arch-apostle of comradeship, and you
practise what you preach, and you preach it as no other living
man has done or can do.'[13]

Cormell Price lived for fifteen years in retirement, resum-
ing his old association with the friends of his youth, the
Burne-Joneses and the Lockwood Kiplings. When in England, Rudyard too was drawn into this circle with the con-

sequence that he renewed an interest in his schooldays
which had been overlaid by the experiences of his young
manhood. His defiant assertion that 'Uncle Crom' was a
great headmaster, and the United Services College a great
school, reflected his own sense of loyalty rather than a considered view of contemporary education, since the school
was in fact declining. Deprived of Price's leadership it lan-
guished, and, after some misadventures, was removed from
Westward Ho! to another part of England. 'Crom' Price,
though he retained the respect and affection of all his
friends, lingered pathetically on the scene as an old man
who had not fulfilled the promise of his youth; and
Rudyard, who now began to think of a book about his
schooldays, was to write the epitaph of the school and its
creator.

Rudyard Kipling to Robert Barr (*Editor of* The Idler)

Arundell House, Tisbury. July 28, '94

A regular weather-breeder of a day today – real warmth at
last, and it waked in me a lively desire to be back in Main Street,
Brattleboro', Vt, USA, and hear the sody-water fizzing in the
drug-store and discuss the outlook for the episcopalian church
with the clerk; and get a bottle of lager in the basement of the
Brooks House, and hear the doctor tell fish-yarns, and have the
iron-headed old farmers loaf up and jerk out: 'Bin in Yurope
haint yer?' and then go home, an easy gait, through the deep
white dust with locust trees just stinking to heaven, and the
fireflies playing up and down the Swamp Road, and the Katy-
dids giving oratorios, free gratis and for nothing, to the whip-
poorwill, and everybody sitting out in the verandah after dinner,
smoking Durham tobacco in a cob pipe, with our feet on the
verandah railings, and the moon coming up behind Wantastiquet. There's one Britisher at least homesick for a section of
your depraved old land, and he's going, Please Allah! the first
week in August, by the *Kaiser Wilhelm*, and won't New York
be hot – just! There's a smell of horse-piss, Italian fruit-vendor,
nickel cigars, sour lager, and warm car-conductor drifting down
Carmine Street at this minute from Sixth Avenue, which I can
smell with the naked eye as I sit here. I shall go to Long Island,

to a friend's, and eat new corn, and I wish you were coming, too.[14]

After the vacation in England, Rudyard and Carrie returned with renewed vigour to 'Naulakha' and to little Josephine. 'My daughter is growing into a beauty,' he wrote to a friend, and he was right. She had the fair colouring of her Yorkshire forebears, with very beautiful, large, blue eyes. Even as a tiny child she had a remarkable and endearing personality, with a charm and quickness of mind far in advance of her years. Rudyard was entirely devoted to her and spent much time every day playing with her and telling her stories. When a friend wrote to ask Rudyard what was the proper tune for 'Danny Deever', he replied that he couldn't say. His small daughter divided his tunes into the 'howly-growly' ones and the 'tinkley-tinkey' ones. Which was it? Perhaps both! [15] He used to regale her in the evenings with Hindu rhymes and folk-tales which she repeated word-perfect to her dolly the next morning. At two years old she was the equal of her cousin, Beatty's daughter Marjorie, who was twice her age; and Josephine was much better brought up, for down at 'Maplewood' the Balestiers lived a harum-scarum life, while at 'Naulakha' all the English proprieties were observed. There were two maids at 'Naulakha' as well as Miss Josephine's 'nanny', and after the return from England in 1894, an English coachman whose livery and style and indubitable cockney accent caused no little stir in Brattleboro.

The Kiplings had advertised in New York for a man and wife, without encumbrances, and had been pleased to engage the services of Matthew Howard, formerly coachman to an English peer. A little, smart man, he was just the same size as Rudyard – five feet six inches tall – but made his first mark by refusing to wear a suit of Rudyard's old clothes for rough work. He wore top-boots and cord breeches even when cleaning out the stable. Howard was a good horse-master and, before he had been many weeks at 'Naulakha', he endeared himself to the Kiplings by handling a carriage accident most skifully. When he was driving Carrie behind their pair of horses, 'Rod' got his leg over the trace, 'Ric' bolted, the carriage overturned, 'Rod' was lamed, and Carrie was severely shaken. The general view was that Howard had been the hero of the day.

Not long afterwards, when Carrie wanted a housemaid, Howard offered to produce a likely girl, who was appointed, and then admitted that she was his daughter. Presently there was another vacancy, for which Howard promptly produced another daughter. He was now living in a comfortable cottage, halfway down the drive, and he smuggled into it child after half-grown child. Having got himself the post as a childless man, he revealed himself the father of six bonny children, all of whom settled in the neighbourhood. He was by then so useful to the Kiplings that his philoprogenitiveness was forgiven. The more he found to do, the less there was for Beatty to do about the place, and the smaller were Beatty's chances of earning the commission on which he lived. Everyone liked Howard, except Beatty, and Howard was the one person at 'Naulakha' who was never impressed by Beatty's blarney.[16]

'Rod and 'Ric', the carriage-horses, continued to give trouble, and the climax of equestrian life at 'Naulakha' was Rudyard's gift of a new pair of thoroughbreds, 'Nip and Tuck', to Carrie after her illness in 1895. He had bought them for $650 from Beatty, a windfall which kept Beatty solvent a few months longer. This concern with horses found its way into Rudyard's work, in the allegory of American life, 'A Walking Delegate', his first task after the return from England in 1894. Though told as a horse-story, it is more remarkable for the skilful use and contrasting of several American dialects, than for horse-lore. It led to another experiment in that vein, a few months later, a story far more deeply felt and wrought out from the heart, 'The Maltese Cat', a throwback to his own attempts at polo-playing, in India ten years earlier, and to the recollection of his own grey pony 'Dolly Bobs'.

Two years had passed since Carrie Balestier had first brought her penniless English husband to Brattleboro. A quiet, unassuming young man dressed in old country clothes, he had then seemed no great addition to the town's society. 'The Kiplings were nice people to work for', said a carpenter whom they employed, 'but you could never get real close to them, not like you and I chatting together now.' They did not mix much in the social life of the place which centred on the church meetings. They rarely attended the Episcopalian church and, though Rudyard was on friendly terms with the Rev. C. O. Day, the Congregational preacher, he did not attend his Sunday services, but met him so that they could practise golf-strokes together in the horse-pasture. A strange rumour that Rudyard spent his Sunday mornings at home 'writing hymns' made his ethical status not much clearer. The one place in Brattleboro where he was a willing visitor was the village school, and the one party the Kiplings always gave was their Christmas party to the school children, with a tree and carol-singing by the choirboys from the Episcopalian church. If he had been a good guy like Beatty, whom everyone knew and made allowances for, the town would have taken his measure, but he was incalculable by Brattleboro standards, and more so when he began to make big money.

In his letters to his English friends Rudyard harped upon the solitude of his life as its chief merit. 'It's three miles from anywhere', he wrote to Henley; 'I have time, light and quiet, three things hard to come by in London', he wrote to William Heinemann.

There were, however, a few families to whom the Kiplings gave their friendship, notably some farming families back in the hills. There were also Doctor Conland their physician, old 'Governor' Holbrook who had been State Governor of Vermont through the Civil War, there were Will and Mary Cabot who had been friends of Wolcott Balestier. Mary Cabot was one of the few women with whom Rudyard made a close friendship after his marriage.

She was admitted to confidences about his work, and she used to say she once heard him improvise seventy lines of rhymed verse without a pause. Several young men in Brattleboro long remembered his conversation and his encouragement. John Bliss, with whom he walked or drove about the countryside, and Merton Robbins, whom he advised on starting a career in publishing, spoke of him with affection, and a tribute of another kind came from Dave Carey, the baggage-master at the railway station. 'Kipling had the darndest mind', he used to say. 'He wanted to know everything about everything, and he never forgot what you told him. He would sit and listen and never stir.'

The Brattleboro gossips would have been more than human if they had not shown some signs of petty jealousy when Carrie Balestier's husband, after beginning his married life in so small a way, became in eighteen months one of the richest men in town. It was his custom at the end of the year to write a note of thanks in Carrie's personal diary, and when, in December 1894, he recorded for the third time his gratitude for a fortunate year, he noted that he had earned $25,000 (£5,000), a great sum in the values of those days.

As his fame grew, the pressure of sightseers hoping for a glimpse of the new celebrity, and of newspapermen in search of gossip, grew more intense, with the consequence that the Kiplings withdrew into a stricter privacy. It was the ill-mannered summer-boarders, not the self-respecting townsfolk, who annoyed him, and especially, he was so plagued by autograph-hunters that Carrie organized a scheme for selling his autographs at $2.50 each for the Fresh Air Fund, sponsored by the *New York Herald*. To her chagrin this was regarded as a publicity device and brought in several abusive letters.

Among their friends in New England, none were dearer to them than Charles Eliot Norton of Harvard, and his daughters. Many years before he became a Harvard professor, Norton had made a business trip to India, which

placed him in sympathy with the Kiplings. In middle life
he had been one of the Pre-Raphaelite circle in London,
and Rudyard had played with Sallie Norton in childhood
at North End Road. When Lockwood renewed the connexion, in New England an instant bond was formed between the Kiplings and the Nortons. Visits were exchanged
between 'Naulakha' and the Nortons' home at Ashfield in
Massachusetts, where Rudyard found himself free of Boston
society, and of the most austere circle of the transcenden-
talists. Since Henry James was a family friend of the
Balestiers, his brother William, the pragmatist philosopher,
received them into the intellectual society of Harvard.

They were Brahmins of Brahmins, living delightfully, but
Norton himself, full of forebodings as to the future of his land's
soul, felt the established earth sliding under him, as horses feel
coming earth-tremours.[17]

So Kipling interpreted the decline of New England trans-
cendentalism at the zenith of the 'Gilded Age'. His own
comment on the American tendency was to deplore the
'apparent waste and ineffectiveness, in the face of the
foreign inrush, of all the indigenous effort of the past generation'. Too many real Americans had been killed off in the
Civil War and too many unassimilable foreigners were
drifting in.

> His easy unswept hearth he lends
> From Labrador to Guadeloupe;
> Till, elbowed out by sloven friends,
> He camps, at sufferance, on the stoop.[18]

Meanwhile the tension of a nation expanding too fast,
growing rich too easily, losing its traditions, and feeling no
need of self restraint, expressed itself in jangling nerves.
The New England tradition, as he found it in the company of the Nortons, was the foundation on which he had
planned his household in Vermont, and it was vanishing
before his eyes, as America, under President Cleveland,
moved into another phase and mood.

Rudyard Kipling to C. E. Norton

Feb. 1895

There were two days of knife-edged cold, and a cloudless sky, a sun grinning like a skull, and a wind that ripped the bones off you. Today is only blizzard and tho' I do not see when we shall be able to use the roads we are warm and of good heart. But our house has been singing like a ship brought up in the wind's eye and the old maple has been creaking and there are five or six feet of snow generally about the place and at least ten in the air.

Beatty has achieved a magnificent cold which after skirmishing all over his body has blossomed into a sharp touch of rheumatism, and he now lies in his bed too stiff and sore to do justice to the situation. ... Did you know that Carrie burned her face opening the furnace door, about three weeks ago. It was more in the nature of a scorch than a burn but it naturally upset her very much and since then we have been living small and going softly together seeing no company. ... We talk of going to Washington to play for a month.

The baby (glory be) keeps her rude health and becomes to us daily more charming. We are sending the Pater (he is getting fat in Florence and sends me the most contemptible stories of contessas and contadinas and all the draggly out-at-elbows messy polyglot society that camps on the continent) a small pastel study of Josephine, her head, reading a book. But what can we do with a small impudence who stops the coachman and enquires magisterially after the health of each horse by name. ... We love her apropos.

Work has been going easily. I have a yearning upon me to tell tales of extended impropriety – not sexual or within hailing distance of it – but hard-bottomed unseemly yarns. One can't be serious always.[19]

The year 1895 began with Carrie's impetuous mishap in throwing open the furnace door. For a fortnight she lay ill and then, when recovery seemed near, a painful inflammation of the eyelids appeared, to the alarm of Dr Conland, who ordered her away for a long rest in a milder climate. Rud and Carrie went to Washington for six weeks and lived in rooms, which they found very expensive and not very

comfortable. She complained at paying no less than fifteen
dollars a day for their board, and it was long before she felt
well enough to enjoy her holiday. As she slowly recovered,
her soft brown hair turned grey and in a few years was
white.

They saw much society in the capital that season. John
Hay from the State Department, Lady Pauncefote, and Mr
Spring Rice from the British Legation, Professor Langley
from the Smithsonian, Mr Bliss Carman 'a so-called poet',
Mr Theo. Roosevelt, Lady Aberdeen, and Miss Leiter the
heiress who was engaged to the Hon. G. Curzon, are noted
among their callers in Carrie's diary. After the Smithsonian,
the Zoo was Rudyard's favourite resort; he frequented the
beaver enclosure and gave serious thought to re-establishing
a colony of beavers in the Connecticut river, where they
were long extinct. A friend made at this time who told him
much of American wild life, of Indians and Eskimos, was
W. Hallett Phillips, a Washington lawyer.

Rudyard made some progress with his work in Washington. The last of his Mowgli stories, 'The Spring Running',
was no sooner finished, in March 1895, than his mind turned
to a new task that again marked an extended range of observation. It was a story about "a new sort of woman', wrote
Carrie, and 'she turned out stunningly'. The subject of this
story, to which he gave the rather inappropriate title of
'William the Conqueror', is the effort made by a group of
administrators from the Punjab, when drafted south to
deal with a famine. According to his custom, he painted in
the backcloth with a Pre-Raphaelite brilliance of colour and
accuracy of detail. The scene was southern India, as he had
observed it on his last visit in December 1891, and the
climax of the story – as of that Indian visit – was a Christmas party at Lahore. But the feature which has made some
readers select this story as a masterpiece is the character of
the heroine, a 'new sort of woman', a practical, lively,
boyish woman with a man's nickname, a woman with a
crop of dark curls growing low on her forehead in a widow's

peak. In several of these respects she seems to be based upon the figure of Mrs 'Ted' Hill, whom Carrie Kipling never met. She is presented in the round, as no earlier of Kipling's heroines had been, and the story, in some phases, is told from her point of view. The episode that no one forgets is her gleam of vision, when she sees her lover not as a commonplace civil servant organizing the distribution of goats' milk to starving children, but as a demi-god:

an accident of the sunset ordered it that, when he had taken off his helmet to get the evening breeze, the low light should fall across his forehead, and he could not see what was before him; while one waiting at the tent door beheld, with new eyes, a young man beautiful as Paris, a god in a halo of golden dust, walking slowly at the head of his flocks, while at his knee ran small naked Cupids.

In April, just before the end of the holiday in Washington, Kipling was taken by Secretary Lamont to call on the President at the White House, and came home disgusted with the company he met there. To Carrie he confided that it was 'awful; inexpressible; incredible; a colossal agglomeration of reeking bounders; it made him very sorrowful'. No one is likely to assert that President Cleveland's circle of associates represented American public life at its highest, and the impact of this group upon a man with a lifelong distrust for politicians of any kind was shattering. He found in the White House all that he most disliked, a readiness to compromise with violence and dishonesty, a habit of talking loudly and acting meanly. These men might remind him of the *bandar-log* who 'sit in circles on the hall of the King's council chamber, and scratch for fleas and pretend to be men'.

The same day, the corrective was applied. He dined that evening at a man's party with Theodore Roosevelt who, as head of the Civil Service Commission, was engaged in introducing sounder standards into the public service. Roosevelt was not much older than his guest and, like him, had made a name before his thirtieth birthday as an uncompromising champion of manliness and efficiency, as an enemy of all pretentious shams.

I liked him from the first [said Rudyard] and largely believed in him. He would come to our hotel, and thank God in a loud voice that he had not one drop of British blood ['English' he should have said] in him; his ancestry being Dutch, and his creed conforming-Dopper, I think it is called. Naturally I told him nice tales about his Uncles and Aunts in South Africa who esteemed themselves the sole lawful Dutch under the canopy and dismissed Roosevelt's stock for 'Verdomder Hollanders'. Then he became really eloquent, and we would go off to the Zoo together, where he talked about grizzlies that he had met. It was laid on him at that time, to furnish his land with an adequate Navy; the existing collection of unrelated types and casual purchases being worn out. I asked him how he proposed to get it, for the American people did not love taxation. 'Out of *you*,' was the disarming reply. And so – to some extent – it was. The obedient and instructed Press explained how England – treacherous and jealous as ever – only waited round the corner to descend on the unprotected coasts of liberty, etc, etc. ... The trick worked.

But those were great and spacious and friendly days in Washington which – politics apart – Allah had not altogether deprived of a sense of humour; and the food was a thing to dream of.[20]

There was a natural sympathy between Rudyard Kipling the Englishman and Theodore Roosevelt, the American of the old stock. His doctrine of the Strenuous Life was directly drawn from Emerson's essay on Self-reliance, and, consciously or unconsciously, the two young men followed the same master. During Rudyard's last few days at Washington they saw much of one another and, though they rarely met again, they corresponded intermittently as friends, a cross-fertilization that was to have a notable effect both upon Kipling's philosophy and upon Roosevelt's political career. The spring was well forward in Vermont when Rudyard and Carrie returned to 'Naulakha'. Each year they watched for the blood-root beside the stone wall at the foot of the home pasture. Rudyard used to say whimsically that he could not bear to see it picked, as he expected the frail plant to cry out like a mandrake when its fibres were torn.

When Mr and Mrs William James from Harvard came to stay at 'Naulakha' in June, Beatty's tennis-court was finished to admiration, but the contract displeased Carrie. She paid Beatty seventy dollars, then disagreed with him about the hay-crop, and about his further contract for draining the pasture. He had overdrawn the account for his own use, and before the end of the month all the neighbours knew that brother and sister had quarrelled. What was distress and annoyance for her was ruin for Beatty, who was deep in debt, and without resources, since he had even exhausted the patience of his stern old grandmother down at 'Beechwood'. The worse his position the more he drank, and the Kiplings, who hated drunkenness, began to regret that under his agreement he had the run of the estate. 'Naulakha' was no longer a happy place when the Balestiers were at loggerheads with one another. After an unsatisfactory settlement with Beatty, on 1 July 1895, the Kiplings set off for their usual summer tour. Luckily it was no longer necessary to leave him in charge, since there was Matthew Howard, entirely trustworthy, and much more careful with the horses. They crossed the Atlantic in a German ship, which gave Rudyard a notion for a story, 'Bread upon the Waters', and spent a month in England between Tisbury and Brown's Hotel.

It was good to be home again at 'Naulakha' at the end of August, and to find that Howard had everything in perfect order. Rudyard had come back from England with a notion about a boy who lived a dream-life. Absorbing himself in it, he completed it in a fortnight, and sold it to the *Century Magazine* for $170 per thousand words. All through September and October he was busy 'singing at his Brushwood Boy poem' and polishing off the new set of Barrack-

Room Ballads, while Carrie was week by week more deeply embroiled in the unfortunate affair with Beatty, lending him money now and backing his bills.

It was peculiarly annoying that the pump was out of order again, the one domestic convenience at 'Naulakha' that never worked right. Just at the hottest season of the year, the water-supply ran out so that they were dependent on water from 'Maplewood', at a time when the two families were no longer on speaking terms, and conducted their affairs by exchange of notes. In such times the Kiplings could no longer expect Beatty, who drove into town every day, to collect their mail, and it was no pleasure to them to go where they would be stared at by sightseers and gossips. It was a comfort when, by the influence of Hallett Phillips with the President, a new branch Post Office for their own use was opened at Waite's Corner.

November brought some unexpected consolations. Kay Robinson wrote from the Middle West to say he was visiting America with his brother. They came to stay, to Rudyard's great delight – he was busy that week with 'The Flowers'; and Kay commemorated his visit by writing a long account of Kipling for *McClure's Magazine*, on the whole, the best account of Kipling's life at Lahore. A few days after Kay's visit there arrived unexpectedly from New York a huge, cheerful, fair-haired young man named Frank N. Doubleday, whom they received coldly at first since he came on business from a publisher, but who soon broke down Carrie's defences. His business was to open negotiations for a complete edition of Rudyard's works to be published by his firm, Scribners. 'Frank', F. N. D.', 'Beloved Effendi' as he soon became, achieved what no other publisher in England or America could achieve, by putting his business on a personal footing, and so became the lifelong intimate friend of Rudyard and Carrie.

Rudyard's dislike of President Cleveland's administration

was fanned into a flame in July 1895, when a long-standing dispute flared up between England and America, about the frontier between Venezuela and British Guiana. For some reason or other, President Cleveland thought the time ripe to twist the lion's tail and, on 20 July, his Secretary of State made a highly offensive reply to the British offer, roundly accusing the British of violating the Monroe Doctrine. Just then there was a change of Government in England with the consequence that the British attitude stiffened.

President Cleveland succumbed to the temptation of rallying the American people by a jingo outburst. In his message to Congress, 17 December, the last before the presidential election year, he denounced the British as aggressors against Venezuela, and asserted the right of the United States to restrain them. During the next six months, while the party organizations were preparing their election campaign, the crisis between England and America was still acute. War, on this unworthy pretext, seemed threatening, and Rudyard Kipling was not alone in thinking it inevitable. In May and June 1896, just when the party conventions were meeting in America, the Secretary of State again endeavoured to whip up the anti-British fury, while Lord Salisbury, the new Prime Minister, kept his temper. The arbitrators decided, most positively, that the British were in the right, and President Cleveland who had nothing more to gain by violence, withdrew, in his last message to Congress, from the position he had taken up a year earlier. The Venezuelan incident was closed, and Cleveland's device for winning the election was unsuccessful.

This was the series of events which Rudyard Kipling found so distressing that he decided to leave America. He was convinced that there would be a purposeless and disastrous war, and the Nortons at Harvard were disposed to agree with him.[21]

At the height of the Venezuelan crisis, in January 1896, another threat of war appeared in another quarter of the globe. Dr Jameson's attempt to filibuster the Transvaal Re-

public into the British Empire was defeated by the Boers,
and this setback to the imperialists was exploited by the
German Kaiser, who sent a telegram of congratulation to
the Transvaal Government, in terms as provocative to Britain as had been President Cleveland's message to Congress.
It inspired Rudyard to send a solemn poem to *The Times*
with the title, 'Hymn before Action'. Though not a
favourite with Kipling's readers it was at least more dignified than the absurd verses in praise of Dr Jameson, put out
by Alfred Austin the new Poet Laureate.

Rudyard Kipling to C. E. Norton

8th Jan, 1896

I seem to be between two barrels like a pheasant. If the
American mine is sprung it means dirt and slush and ultimately
death either across the Canada border or in some disembowelled
gunboat off Cape Hatteras. If the German dynamite is exploded
equally it means slaughter and most probably on the high seas.
In both cases I am armed with nothing more efficient than a
notebook, a stylographic pen, and a pair of opera-glasses. Whether
or no, anyway and inevitably, C. will be confined within the
next three or five weeks and till that time I am tied here by the
leg.

I have arranged things so that C. ought not to starve; and she
has the house and all my copyrights to boot. You see it is obviously absurd for me to sit still and go on singing from a safe
place while the men I know are on the crown of it; and it may
be that when I am closer to the scene of action I may be able
to help with a little song or two in the intervals of special correspondence. But it is borne in upon me by the inner eye that if
trouble comes I shan't live to see it out: unless I bolt and hide
myself in the wilds of Patagonia or the Pole. Even in that resort I
should be dead or worse than dead.

All these things fill me with a deep love for Mr Cleveland who
is responsible for the letting in of the waters. I permit myself
however to cherish a hope that the row or rows may be delayed
till May when I can hope to pick up C. and the children (D.V.)
and take 'em to England. I shan't mind so much then; but

whether it be peace or war this folly puts an end to my good wholesome life here; and to me that is the saddest part of it. We must begin again from the beginning and pretend that we are only anxious to let the house for a year or two. It's hard enough, God knows, but I should be a fool if, after full warning, I risked my own people's happiness and comfort in a hostile country.

As to the German situation I don't care a continental. It will wake up the colonies, I believe, and teach us to keep our powder dry. But the American thing makes me sick and sore and sorry to my heart's core. People can say what they please. There was a much more genuine absence of hostility on the English side than there was on the American. And I do sincerely believe that the American interior press is responsible for the cherishing of that hostile feeling.

Looking at it in other lights it seems to me that it will help the Empire enormously, will definitely shut out all notion of Canada's absorption into the States, except by force, and will teach us the beauties of an inter-colonial tariff – may even send us to ally with France and Russia to rearrange the rest of the world, but these are long long looks ahead, and I can only say that whatever comes I and mine are always affectionately yours.

P.S. But why Alfred Austin?* Pater told me he was living in Salisbury's pocket ever since Tennyson died; but I never expected he'd get it.[22]

Carrie's mother stayed with the Kiplings for Christmas 1895, without effecting a reconciliation between her son and daughter. Yet, with a certain bravado, Rudyard wrote in Carrie's diary on New Year's eve, 'So ends our fourth and best year.' When the snow came, Rudyard experimented with the Norwegian skis that Conan Doyle had sent him, probably the first pair of skis in Vermont. Another new sport was golf on the frozen snow, with golf-balls painted scarlet, not altogether a success because there were no limits to a drive; the ball might skid two miles down the long slope to the Connecticut river. Indoors he worked at 'The

*On 1 January 1896 Alfred Austin, a Conservative journalist, was appointed to the office of Poet Laureate which had been vacant since the death of Tennyson in October 1892.

Tomb of his Ancestors',* the last of the great series of longer Anglo-Indian stories which he had begun, seven years back, with 'A Wayside Comedy'. Then he turned to his oft-considered plan for a picaresque novel of the Indian underworld. The manuscript of *Mother Maturin* was still among his papers, and not altogether abandoned. Three times at 'Naulakha' he put his hand to the old notes which he now thought of using as the raw material of a quite new book. The notion of *Kim* was stirring in his mind, but would not take shape; 'it must be revised by the Pater', he said.

Carrie, who had spent a wretched autumn over Beatty's affairs, was now expecting her second child. Another daughter, Elsie, was born on the morning of 2 February 1896. When Dr Conland paid his regular visits to Carrie, he found time for conversation with Rudyard. Conland had been to sea as a young man, and had many yarns to spin of the fishermen on the Grand Banks. On 9 February, when all was pronounced well with mother and child, and Josephine was introduced to her new little sister, a spark was struck between Rudyard and the doctor. Rudyard would lay aside *Kim* to write a tale of the Grand Banks; for which he found the title, *Captains Courageous*, in one of his favourite old ballads, 'Mary Ambree'. 'It grows under my hand,' he said a few days later.

No other of Rudyard's romances absorbed his energies so completely as *Captains Courageous*, which took his mind off threatening politics and family quarrels. It is the only one of his stories in which all the characters are typical Americans in an American setting, and its merits are due largely to the easy comradeship with Conland which he found so stimulating and satisfying.

My part was the writing; his the details. This book took us (he rejoicing to escape from the dread respectability of our little town) to the shore-front, and the old T-wharf of Boston Harbour,

* 'John Chinn' the elder, in this story, is based upon James Outram, 'the Bayard of India'. Philip Woodruff (*The Guardians*) has more to say on its origin.

and to queer meals in sailors' eating-houses, where he renewed his youth among ex-shipmates or their kin. We assisted hospitable tug-masters to help haul three- and four-stick schooners all round the harbour; we boarded every craft that looked as if she might be useful, and we delighted ourselves to the limit of delight. Charts we got – old and new – and the crude implements of navigation such as they used off the Banks, and a battered boat-compass, still a treasure with me. (Also, by pure luck, I had sight of the first sickening uprush and vomit of iridescent coal-dusted water into the hold of a ship, a crippled iron hulk, sinking at her moorings). And Conland took large cod and the appropriate knives with which they are prepared for the hold, and demonstrated anatomically and surgically so that I could make no mistake about treating them in print. Old tales, too, he dug up, and the lists of dead and gone schooners whom he had loved, and I revelled in profligate abundance of detail – not necessarily for publication but for the joy of it. And he sent me – may he be forgiven! – out on a pollock-fisher, which is ten times fouler than any cod-schooner, and I was immortally sick, even though they tried to revive me with a fragment of unfresh pollock.[23]

The book is rich in technicalities, which are the more remarkable because Kipling's chances of studying deep-sea fishermen had been so scanty. He paid three visits to Gloucester, Mass., and one to Boston Harbour, the period of all four together being no more than fourteen days; and all that critics have been able to urge against his local colour is that it represents rather the fishing-fleet as it had been thirty years earlier when Conland was young, than the fleet as it was in 1896. A favourite with its author, *Captains Courageous* has been more admired by American than by English readers. It is an enlarged short story, not a novel, exploring a situation rather than tracing the development of character. The conversion of Harvey Cheyne from a spoilt boy into a serviceable young man is achieved too suddenly to be convincing, and too early in the book to provide a lasting theme. The reader is left with seascapes, at which Kipling excelled, and with studies of American types, caught and reproduced with photographic accuracy. As types, the fishing-skipper, the mate, the ship's boy, the Nova Scotia negro, the railway magnate,* and the rest, tell us what sort of men Kipling admired, while Harvey's mother, and her part in the story, provide a comment on the corrupt Americanism of the 'Gilded Age' that was driving him away. *Captains Courageous* began to appear serially, in *McClure's Magazine*, soon after the number which contained Kay Robinson's account of Kipling in India. Sam McClure was an American business man who won Kipling's heart. He had been everything from a pedlar to a tintype photographer along the highways, and had held intact his genius and simplicity. 'I liked and admired him', wrote Kipling, 'more than a little, for he was one of the few with whom three and a half words serve for a sentence, and as clear and straight as spring water.' The best of Kipling's earlier work in America had been sold to Richard Gilder for the *Century Magazine*, and Gilder offered $10,000 for the serial rights of *Captains Courageous*. Kipling preferred to let it go to Sam McClure for the same price.[24]

The quarrel with the Beatty Balestiers took a worse turn in 1896.

It is all most dolefully true [wrote Rudyard to Sallie Norton in January] and, having said that one feels as if there ought to be some way out of it – the consequences, I mean. I'm going to hope for the best very hard. C. is wonderfully well, considering all things, and I'm proud of her.

She had hardly recovered from the birth of Elsie when a new crisis brought the publicity they so much dreaded. On 6 March, Beatty filed a petition in bankruptcy. Opinion in Brattleboro, where everyone was now aware of the Balestier feud, was critical of both parties. Those who knew them best blamed Carrie for her tactless hectoring of her brother; it

---

*F. N. Finney, a real railway magnate, supplied the railway technicalities. He then beat the record claimed in the book for a transcontinental journey by running a train over the route.

was easy to make allowances for a generous good fellow like Beatty, even if his generosity was at his sister's expense; easy to abuse Carrie who was rich and economical and anglicized. With her strong sense of family responsibility, but with singular lack of tact, Carrie made some sort of proposal to the Balestiers that if Beatty would leave 'Maplewood' and take regular work, she would finance him and bring up his daughter, Marjorie.

The prying eyes of Brattleboro were, perhaps, the greatest annoyance of the whole affair to Rudyard. It was noticed that Carrie consulted none of her Balestier relatives, that Rudyard no longer went down the road to 'Beechwood' to read his verses to her old grandmother. Though 'Madam' Balestier was growing very old and crotchety, and was unable or unwilling to arbitrate between Beatty and Carrie, it was yet thought strange that Carrie, who drove past 'Beechwood' whenever she went to town, was never seen to bring her new baby on a visit to the old lady. Newspaper reporters scented 'copy', and were repulsed from 'Naulakha' more brusquely than ever.

I decline to be interviewed [Rudyard is reported as saying to one of them]. American reviewing is brutal and immoral. It is an outrage to be insulted on the public highways and asked to give the details of one's private life. . . . Your copyright laws have swindled me out of considerable money. Is it not enough to steal my books without intruding on my private life? When I have anything to say, I write it down and sell it. My brains are my own.

Whatever the annoyance, Rudyard and Carrie were determined to live their own lives and maintain the routine unchanged at 'Naulakha', until they could conveniently return to England. Visitors came and went, among them Owen Wister, Sam McClure, Mrs Pen Browning, the Catlin girls from New York, and Sallie Norton. New works were planned to improve the property and there was one summer day when Rudyard was so deeply interested in the erection of a pair of ornamental gate-posts that he abandoned a day's writing to watch it. In April he and Carrie, both of them rather low in health and spirits, took a few days' holiday at New York, where he met Stephen Crane and other friends. Rudyard took lessons in a New York school at the fashionable sport of bicycling, and was pretty competent when they returned to 'Naulakha'.

The spring had come and Rudyard was content to sit in the sunshine through the first days of May, amusing himself with a set of verses for a society of college boys at Yale. He had nothing much else on hand, except a scheme, never carried out, for a children's 'fairy book' about the natural history of New England.

On the afternoon of 6 May Rudyard set off alone for a spin on his wheel, along the winding, steep, and rough road that led down from 'Beechwood' to Waite's Corner. At the foot of the slope he had a spill and was ruefully picking himself up when Beatty, in a furious temper, came driving down at his usual galloping pace. 'See here! I want to talk with you!' he shouted, brandishing his whip. 'If you have anything to say, you can say it to my lawyer,' said Rudyard. Beatty broke into a torrent of oaths and accusations: Rudyard had been talking about him behind his back, had been abusing him in Brattleboro. Would he retract? Would he apologize? There was no answer. 'If you won't retract the lies you have been telling about me within a week, I'll blow out our goddamn brains!' shouted Beatty, to which Rudyard quietly replied: 'If I don't do certain things, you'll kill me?' 'By Jesus, I will,' said Beatty. 'Then,' said Rudyard, 'remember you will only have yourself to blame for the consequences!' 'Do you dare to threaten me, you little bastard?' shouted Beatty, and drove off.

These were the first words exchanged between the two brothers-in-law in six months or more, and why Beatty burst out in this way and at this time is not evident. A friend of both families has recorded that, immediately after this ludicrous scene, Beatty drove to her house in great concern, sorry that he had made an exhibition of himself. Those who knew the two men best supposed that they would have laughed off the quarrel if their wives had allowed them.

On the same authority it is said that Mai Balestier was the most vindictive of the four. It was she who resented Carrie's patronage and was deeply hurt by Carrie's proposal to bring up her child. Rudyard's action, whatever else, was remarkably imprudent; he went down to Brattleboro next morning and laid an information against his brother-in-law for threatening to murder him, and from the moment that the officers of the law took hold, his cause was lost. Publicity was what Rudyard most dreaded and, by appearing in court, he exposed himself to the full glare of the yellow press; while Beatty's point of view was just the opposite, since publicity was meat and drink to him, and might even help him to pay his debts.

On Saturday, 9 May, Beatty was arrested, and Carrie recorded in her diary that it was the most wretched and unhappy day in her life. He was arraigned before William S. Newton, Justice of the Peace, in Brattleboro for 'assault with force and arms, for using opprobrious and indecent names, and for threatening to kill' his brother-in-law. After a formal statement the proceedings were adjourned until the twelfth, that is over the week-end, and the prisoner was released on bail. As if he had not made blunders enough, Rudyard, the plaintiff, now appeared and quixotically offered to go bail for Beatty the defendant. A man as quick-witted as Beatty did not fail to see that the game was going his way. Indignantly repudiating Rudyard's offer, he found bail elsewhere and rushed to the telegraph office – this was before the day of long-distance telephones – to sell his story to the press. During the week-end, more than forty reporters from metropolitan newspapers assembled in Brattleboro where such publicity was never known before or since. Beatty met them at the railway station and Rudyard had the mortification of seeing him whirl carriage-load after carriage-load of the hated tribe, in sight of his windows, to 'Maplewood', where they were entertained with Beatty's whisky and the company of his pretty wife.

The hearing was resumed on Tuesday, 12 May, in the Town Hall of Brattleboro. The number of spectators who crowded into Justice Newton's office made it necessary to transfer the proceedings to the larger assembly hall where town meetings customarily took place. It was a field-day for the lawyers, who played up to the press by forcing Kipling to answer the questions he had often refused to answer, thus making an end of his boasted privacy. The proceedings began with the cross-examination of Kipling, the one witness, who was kept on the stand all day. The quarrel with Beatty in the lane was told in Kipling's words and displayed in its most ludicrous aspect. Was Kipling afraid? Had he run away? Had he any reason to suppose that Beatty was armed? 'He was crazy,' said Kipling, 'not in his right senses.' Would Rudyard retract his words? 'I would not retract a word under threat of death from any living man.'

Then the dealings of the brothers-in-law over the last four years were relentlessly dragged into the light. Was it not true that Kipling had made large sums of money in America? Was it not true that he had spoken certain words to Colonel Goodhue in the Brooks' House at Brattleboro? Had he said something about 'holding Beatty up by the slack of his pants'? It was true, said Rudyard, that he had said it, and that he had done it, since Beatty's dead brother, Wolcott, had asked him to look after Beatty. Rudyard had settled in America, he said, largely so that he could help him, whereupon Beatty laughed out loud in court.

Why had they quarrelled? It was Beatty who had dropped him, a year ago, said Rudyard, and since then there had been nothing to discuss between them. Rudyard had employed Beatty in the past but found him unreliable; he began his undertakings well and then tailed off. But did he actually owe the Kiplings money? No! Rudyard was forced to admit that Beatty had paid back the cash that he had

borrowed. 'You had him arrested without making any effort
to correct the false impression you had given of his dependence on you?' That was a shrewd blow. Rudyard made it
clear that he had done his best for Beatty to the end. He
had made an offer – which was rejected – to take charge of
Beatty's family, if Beatty would stop drinking, but nothing
had come of his offer.

Nothing but publicity came of the proceedings. Upon
motion of the States Attorney, Beatty was bound over for
trial 'under the familiar statute of disturbing the peace'. Justice Newton placed him under bond of $400 to keep the peace
and an additional bond of $400 for appearance at the
next appointed session of the County Court.* Beatty left the
hearing in triumph to sell his story. Rudyard, too, had something to say; with unusual frankness, he admitted to a reporter – or so the reporter said – 'that he intended to leave
that part of the country as soon as possible'.

Opinion in Brattleboro was sharply divided: there was
some animosity against Rudyard in the town, and the vulgar press crowed over him in triumph. At the following
week-end the Sunday papers splashed the story, the most
offensive among them being a Boston journal which printed
a not very clever parody of 'Danny Deever':

   'Who's that a-loping down the lane?' said the copper-ready-
      made.
     'It's Rudyard running for his life,' the First Select-man said.
     'Who's pawing up the dust behind?' said the copper-ready-
      made.
       'It's Beatty seeking brother-in-law,' the First Select-man
      said.

The serious press, though not neglectful of the publicity
value of the story, reported it fairly enough, the New York
Times and the *Tribune* with approval of Kipling's conduct, the *Herald* with a reasoned defence of Beatty Balestier. The best-informed and the most judicious comment

*Since the Kiplings left the country before the next session, the
case never came to trial.

was that of the local paper, the *Vermont Phoenix*. After deriding the travesties published in Boston, 'the descriptions that did not describe and illustrations that did not illustrate', the leader-writer of the *Phoenix* wrote a paragraph in praise of Kipling's genius with an expression of hope that he would continue to reside in Brattleboro. Then, in terms of courteous reproach, he deplored that Kipling 'had undertaken no social responsibilities, and made few personal friends' in the town. Kipling, said the writer of the article, had 'won a reputation for brusqueness by what seems to us his unfortunate way of meeting the well-meant advances of newspaper men'.[25]

On the other hand, a group of leading citizens, including Governor Holbrook and the Episcopalian and Congregational ministers, let it be known that they were on Rudyard's side, and Carrie, too, was backed by her own family.

Mrs Anna Balestier to Rudyard Kipling

May 15, 1896

Dear Rud,

I have your letter of 14. Thank you for writing but I am in no wise competent to formulate any ideas as to the future concerning Beatty ...

Whatever Beatty has done or may do, I must ever continue to keep an affectionate interest in him, being his mother, with the continual hope that it may have some spark of influence, however faint – but it will not be in the wrong direction, I promise you.

He is his own worst enemy and always has been, but he has *some* good impulses, if he would allow them to come to the surface. He has always been an enigma to me which has increased with time. ... I do not wonder that *your* patience was exhausted, but mine must hold out – always, however tried, and I shall always be,

Your loving, Mother.[26]

Meanwhile the Kiplings had withdrawn into their seclusion, consulting nobody but their lawyer, Dr Conland, and an uncle of Carrie on her father's side. What Brattleboro was saying and what the rest of the Balestier family were doing passed them by. 'These are dark days for us,' wrote Carrie, 'Rud is dull, listless, and weary', but within a week he had returned with interest to his work. On 16 May he was weighing the rival offers of the *Century* and *McClure's Magazine* for the serial rights in *Captains Courageous*; and on the nineteenth he went down to Gloucester with Conland for one last look at the fishing-fleet. This was not enough, as Carrie wrote to a friend, to restore the 'nerve and strength which was frittered away in so unworthy a cause' and, as in other times of trouble, he turned to Lockwood de Forest, his oldest friend in America. They spent a fortnight on the Gaspé coast, salmon-fishing, and it was at this time that he wrote his spirited ballad, 'The Feet of the Young Men':

Do you know the blackened timber – do you know that racing
    stream
    With the raw, right-angled log-jam at the end;
And the bar of sun-warmed shingle where a man may bask and
    dream
    To the click of shod canoe-poles round the bend?
It is there that we are going with our rods and reels and traces,
    To a silent, smoky Indian that we know –
To a couch of new-pulled hemlock, with the starlight on our
    faces,
    For the Red Gods call us out and we must go!

When he returned it was to resume the normal life at 'Naulakha', busy with his own work and interested in plans for the estate. His correspondence gave no hint of any interruption in his plans, other than telling his friends that he would be going to England in September for a long visit. Only in one letter to W. D. Howells did he make an admission:

4th June 1896

I don't think quite of quitting the land permanently. It is hard to go from where one has raised one's kids, and builded a wall and digged a well and planted a tree.

I do remember that once in your general capacity you said

something about a work of Mr Kipling which was salutary and chastening to that young man. But, as Boswell once remarked to Dr Johnson in the stately phrase of the eighteenth century:– 'It would need a hell of a lot that I took unkindly from you, Sir.' [27]

The last two months at 'Naulakha' slipped away, as the Kiplings maintained their way of life, unchanged. One day in July Rudyard sat down and completed, in a few hours, a composition in one of the most rigorous of all verse-forms. He called it 'Sestina of the Tramp-royal'.

> Therefore, from job to job I've moved along.
> Pay couldn't 'old me when my time was done,
> For something in my 'ead upset it all,
> Till I 'ad dropped whatever 'twas for good,
> An', out at sea, be'eld the dock-lights die,
> An' met my mate – the wind that tramps the world!

It was resolute, still forward-looking, but without that youthful spirit with which he had written 'The Long Trail' in 1891. Taking stock of his life, the four happy years in Vermont and the memories of India which Vermont had allowed him to recall, he found his gaze settling most clearly upon remote childhood. *The Seven Seas* was coming into proof, and he now prefaced to it a dedication addressed to the City of Bombay, his birthplace. On 28 August, his last day at 'Naulakha', Mrs Halbrook and Mary Cabot came to call, rather to the dismay of Carrie who was overwhelmed with her packing. They found Rudyard walking up and down the terrace. 'There are only two places in the world,' he said, 'where I want to live – Bombay and Brattleboro. And I can't live at either.'

Early on 29 August their neighbour John Bliss, from whom the Kiplings had once rented a cottage, drove them to the station. Only Conland was there to see them go and he discreetly slipped away without formally saying good-bye.

From The Second Voyage (1903)

We've sent our little Cupids all ashore –
  They were frightened, they were tired, they were cold.
Our sails of silk and purple go to store,
  And we've cut away our mast of beaten gold.
                    (Foul weather!)
Oh, 'tis hemp and singing pine for to stand against the brine,
  But Love he is our master as of old!

The sea has shorn our galleries away,
  The salt has soiled our gilding past remede;
Our paint is flaked and blistered by the spray,
  Our sides are half a fathom furred in weed.
                    (Foul weather!)
And the Doves of Venus fled and the petrels came instead,
  But Love he was our master at our need!

'Was Youth would keep no vigil at the bow,
  'Was Pleasure at the helm too drunk to steer –
We've shipped three able quartermasters now.
  Men call them Custom, Reverence, and Fear.
                    (Foul weather!)
They are old and scarred and plain, but we'll run no risk
again
  From any Port o' Paphos mutineer!

．　　．　　．　　．

[10]

At Torquay
(1896–7)

NEVER again was Rudyard so happy, never so sure of himself, as in the honeymoon years at 'Naulakha'. Since his wretched childhood the cards had been dealt to him by the Lords of Life – the Emersonian phrase he sometimes used – just so that he could play them to the best advantage. His understanding and mastery of his world had been adequate for his purpose.

> Ah, but a man's reach should exceed his grasp,
> Or what's a heaven for?

At the end of his rustication in Vermont his grasp had fallen short, but it was the whole world, not Beatty Balestier, that scored a point off him. The world was moving into a political crisis, the crisis of imperialism, and the decision would not be made in rural Vermont. Small-town life in a country where politics were nourished on anti-British hysteria was not a life for Rudyard Kipling, a man whose message could not be delivered from that platform. Rudyard loved Vermont, and in his letters to American friends would often reveal his hankering for the pleasant life of 'Naulakha'. Not even to himself would he admit that he was leaving Vermont for ever and, though he never spoke of it, his letters tell how often it was in his thoughts.

The summer was ending when they reached England. From Southampton the Kiplings went straight to a house they had arranged to rent at Maidencombe near Torquay, a house in which they never felt at home. Long afterwards, Rudyard made his irrational dislike for a place that should

have been likeable, the subject of a psycho-analytical story
('The House Surgeon'), rather in the manner of Henry
James. But the reason of his dislike for 'Rock House' at
Maidencombe never came to light and when he revisited it,
thirty years later, the place still cast its oppressive spell over
him.

Rudyard Kipling to Dr J. Conland

October 1, '96

Now imagine to yourself a big stone and stucco Naulakha,
long, low with two stories, stuck on the side of a steep hill falling
away almost as sharply as the lower slopes of Wantastiquet to a
hundred-foot cliff of pure red soil. Below that is the sea, about
two hundred yards from the window. ... I look straight from
my work table on to the decks of the fishing craft who come in
to look after their lobster-pots.

They settled in amid storms of wind and rain.

The glass dropped about an inch and then began pumping up
and down. The wind took about a day to get up and when it
really took hold, it licked the Channel into lather. A big poplar
on our lawn was the first to go. The wind lifted the top out of
it. Then our back-gate was sent flying, and then a huge elm
came over by the roots and nearly assassinated a hired yellow
cow we keep in the meadow. About the beginning of the storm
I saw a trawler blown out to sea – just a rag of brown sail in the
smother; and once I heard the whistle of a steamer. But though
it was clear overhead, the scud was thick over the sea; and from
a sheltered angle of the kitchen garden we looked down on a
bath of lather. Then it rained and then it blew some more, and
then the glass went crazy.[1]

How unlike was 'Rock House' to the warm wood-scented
'Naulakha' with its familiar trappings, the Bokhara rugs he
had brought from India, the tiger-skin which he used as a
carriage-rug to the astonishment of gossips in Brattleboro,

the big water-colour of the camel-corps in the desert, the military sketches given him by Détaille, the carved figures of *Jungle Book* animals given him by Joel Chandler Harris, the beam carrying his father's inscription over the mantel-shelf, and the photograph of Emerson beside his desk. Best of all had been the broad view from the library window, of woodland and meadow sloping down to the Connecticut river, the amphitheatre of hills from Sky Rocket on the left to Wantastiquet on the right, with the remote blue dome of Mount Monadnock dominating the far sky-line.

Landscapes in England were praised because they reminded him of the view from 'Naulakha'. Little Josephine often asked when they were going home and clung, as children will, to her first memories of it. Rudyard described her to a friend as altogether a little American.

Carrie Kipling to Mary Cabot

1 December, 1896

As Mr Kipling never talks of Brattleboro or reads a letter from America or does anything which remotely reminds him of that last year of calamity and sorrow, I have not told him the piece of family news. But I have put your letter away against the time when he returns to these things, and know he will enjoy it as I did. He seems now better and stronger and I hope he may turn to his work again after a little. But all the events of the last year with the leaving of 'Naulakha' as we did have made us sore and bruised, and it takes us longer than the rest to forget. Which shows me we are wrong to feel so keenly. ... I hope very much Mr Kipling will want to return, and see no reason, under certain changed conditions, why he should not.[2]

Rudyard Kipling to Dr J. Conland

October 1, 1896

Josephine, after considering things in her little head, has pronounced that 'this England is stuffy', but the moist climate agrees with her. Elsie eats and sleeps, and sleeps and eats. ... I think the wife's health is considerably better, but, as you know, she wants to take hold of all the earth and shake it. As we have a conservatory, and a gardener and his wife and a garden, and an orchard and about forty-five acres of outhouses to look after, you can guess she has a large field to exercise her talents.

I spend my time doing nothing very hard – chiefly on a wheel. There are times when I'd give a good deal for the keen sniffs of an autumn morning up on the hillside, when the first frost has wilted things in the garden and the leaves are dropping of themselves. They tell me our new barn at 'Naulakha' is rather a success. Have you seen it?

I've arranged all my stories for the Scribner edition – getting 'em into groups according to their subjects, while my father is making pictures for them. The book of verses is all but finished and I've revised the proofs for *Captains Courageous*.[3]

A few miles down the railway was Dartmouth where the old three-decker *Britannia* was still used as a training ship for naval cadets. The officers lost no time in attracting Rudyard into their society and during October he spent several days visiting them. His letters to Conland are full of nautical observations, and, with his usual facility, he now began to master naval techniques. *The Seven Seas* was published at the beginning of November, with a subscribed figure of 22,000 copies sold before publication, no small success for a book of verse. It was reviewed at once, and enthusiastically, in all the principal daily papers, and the author of 'M'Andrew's Hymn' became a welcome figure in any company of seamen. The poet of the barrack-room had enlarged his repertory and had become the poet of the engine-room. Having changed his allegiance to the Royal Navy he renewed an acquaintance with Captain E. H. Bayly, R.N., whom he had met at the Cape in 1891, and joyfully accepted an invitation to take a cruise with the Channel Fleet.

Rudyard Kipling to Dr J. Conland

March 23–29

I have at last found a Captain of our Navy, an old friend of mine, who offers me a berth aboard of a new 20-knot cruiser for the Naval Manoeuvres. Can you imagine me in oilskins chasing up and down the English Channel, playing at being a sailor? I rather look forward to the fun which begins about the middle of June.

For the last two months we – and incidentally all Europe – have been living on the edge of a volcano and even now the betting is about level as to whether the damn thing will blow up after all. I've got my billet in event of a big shindy; but it wasn't worth while going down to the Mediterranean and hanging about on a lee shore (Crete has a *vile* coast) to see Turks and Cretans fighting. One good result of the mess has been to show the continent that England has rather more of a navy than the rest of 'em put together.[4]

A succession of relatives and old friends came to visit the Kiplings at 'Rock House'. The first was 'Ambo' Poynter, and after him came his schoolboy brother, Hugh Poynter, to whom Rudyard gave a gun, and with whom he went out after the rabbits. The 'Pater' came from Tisbury to set up his studio in the coach-house with a whole kit of tools and apparatus. Soon he and Rudyard were elbow-deep in modelling-clay and absorbed in plans for illustrating the complete edition of Rudyard's works with photographs of figures in low relief. This involved technical discussion with Scribner's office in New York. Frank Doubleday, their correspondent at Scribner's, had now become a dear friend of the family and, very cautiously, he consulted Rudyard about another plan – to set up publishing on his own. He could raise only $50,000 capital, and Rudyard advised him not to do it unless he could find five times as much. Early in 1897 Frank paid a short visit to England and, not long after, he and Sam McClure made their venture with the firm of Doubleday and McClure, which published all Kipling's new books in America, for the rest of his life.

Rudyard Kipling to Dr J. Conland

March 23–29, '97

I've done a yarn about a locomotive for Scribners. ['.007'.] It
may make you laugh when you see it. Doubleday, of Scribners,
and his wife dropped in here to tea the other day and stayed to
dinner, and we heard a whole lot of news. It was very pleasant
to listen to the energetic New York accent once more, and to
learn who had been doing what and why, since we left. They
said that Fifth Ave is being laid down in asphalte. I'll believe
that when I see it. Also I had a note from Teddy Roosevelt who,
in the intervals of scrapping with the rest of the police board,
finds time to remember me.[5]

Rudyard Kipling to C. E. Norton

October 30, '96

Mother and Father have been staying with us down here in
our stone barrack of a house overlooking the sea. Our weather
is and has been – British. 'Bloody British' is the only word for
it; and I have been studying my fellow-countrymen from the
outside. Those four years in America will be blessed unto me
for all my life. We are a rummy breed – and O Lord the ponderous wealthy society. Torquay is such a place as I do desire to
upset by dancing through it with nothing on but my spectacles.
Villas, clipped hedges and shaven lawns; fat old ladies with
respirators and obese landaus. The Almighty is a discursive and
frivolous trifler compared with some of 'em.

But the land is undeniably lovely and I am making friends
with the farmers.

They are in deep sorrow at the 'Grange' over Morris's death
which seems to have been unexpected to the last. Uncle Ned
[Burne-Jones] is naturally very broken up. He felt Millais'
going more than anyone thought, the father told me. Of course
he won't leave London but we have hopes of getting Aunt
Georgie down here. Aunt Aggie [Poynter] is coming for Christmas and we are in treaty with Henry James for a visit. But he
is an evasive man, and won't leave London either. By the same
token, he's seconded me for the Athenaeum and I hope to be a
bishop before I die.

Carrie Kipling to C. E. Norton
December 31st, 1896

'Uncle Crom' Price, Rud's old headmaster and the beloved of the 'Grange' folk, has been with us for a few days. He brings better news of Aunt Georgie, who has not been strong recently.

We are thoughtful over your admonition as to further verse-making, but it's not easy to make Rud take what you are pleased to call his genius seriously. He does not believe in it, in the very least. However we have set ourselves a more serious standard and have thrown several delightful things into the scrap-basket. At present there is a story being done, and that and the *Bell-buoy* are all the work done since we came over. Rud seems happier and better than for the past year, and feels there is a lot of work in the back of his brain.

Rudyard Kipling to C. E. Norton
December 31st, 1896. C's birthday.

We are both of us awed, and if the truth be told a little scared at your article [on Kipling's poems] in the *Atlantic Monthly*. . . .* True it is, most sadly true that I have not been true to my duties but I did not know that I had been so untrue. As you know I love the fun and the riot of writing (I am daily and nightly perplexed with my own private responsibilities before God) and there are times when it is just a comfort and a delight to let out with the pen and ink – as long as it doesn't do any one any moral harm. I don't believe very much in my genius. My own notion being rather that I am set to do Fergusson for some like-to-come-along Burns whose little finger will be thicker than my loins. At least I have shown him his lead.

Then there is the danger, it seems, of a man running off into William Watson's kind of wordy rot if he, at a comparatively tender age, considers himself a poet.

But – you are the only man except my father and Uncle Ned whose disapproval or advice slays me; and I will say just as one says to one's father, when one is little, 'I'll try to think and be better next time.' But, even now, the notion that *you* should have reviewed me rather makes me gasp.

I get very little American news except a line or two from

*See below, Chapter 14.

Brattleboro. But among my letters I note with pa n, as they say,
a cutting from the *Evening Post* in which Mr E. L. Godkin is
pleased to turn up his nose at my babel of Americanisms in
Captains Courageous. Now I would be loath to destroy and
abolish Godkin for that he is a friend of yours and a man who
washes his literary hands, to boot, but if he continues in this
form of sin, he will presently be annihilated by an avalanche
from quarters that he would least suspect. I did not embark
upon the dialect of *Captains Courageous* to be scoffed at by a
New York mugwump.[6]

To those who watched world politics with an eye to the
map of the world, 1897 was an anxious year. Though the
Venezuela crisis had passed away, there was a stir throughout Islam from the Sudan to Malaya. A war in the Balkans
was damped down by the greater powers before the blaze got
out of control, and Kipling did not find it necessary to serve
as a war correspondent off the Cretan coast. On the Indian
frontier, which Kipling watched with understanding, a
series of tiresome campaigns had been touched off by the
outbreak in Chitral in 1895, and the Indian Army was more
heavily engaged in 1896 and 1897 than it had been in any
of the years that he had spent in India. It was his stories
that had made the people at home aware of the problem of
the Frontier where, decade after decade, a force of seventy
thousand men was always on active service; and it was his
verses that had provided the British public with a new hero
in 'Bobs', Lord Roberts of Kandahar. But Kipling was no
blind hero-worshipper and at Simla he had been known as a
sharp critic of 'Bobs's' administrative weakness. In January
1897 'Bobs' published his memoirs, *Forty-one Years in India*,
which was to be the year's best-seller. He sent Kipling a
copy which provoked the comment that it was most remarkable for what it left out.[7]

As a rule he did not affect an admiration for the grandees
of government; his interest lay in the administrators and
technicians who took the personal risks. Young Frederick
Roberts who won the V.C. in the Mutiny was his hero,

rather than the bemedalled Commander-in-Chief at Simla, forty-one years later. And, while the English people lionized Lord Roberts, Rudyard entertained at Torquay the hero of the Siege of Chitral, Sir George Robertson, who told him tales of the heathen of those parts that made his hair stand on end.[8] Rudyard had been turning his mind to a series of stories about his schooldays, and was then writing the two episodes which he called 'Slaves of the Lamp', the first describing 'Stalky's' life at school, and the second his application – not far from Chitral – of the lessons he had learned at school.

The next visitor at 'Rock House' was Rudyard's cousin, Florence Macdonald, who was allowed to sit in the room where he was working at his 'Stalky' stories. He would write and write; then lay down his pen and roar with laughter; then read a passage aloud to her till she would roar with laughter. 'Come on, Florence,' he would say. 'What shall we make them do now?'[9]

Philip Burne-Jones, another cousin who re-entered the Kiplings' circle, had attained some success as a painter in a conventional style very different from his father's. Phil's picture for the year 1897 made a sensation, not least because Rudyard wrote a set of illustrative verses which were printed in the catalogue. Since Rudyard made a present of them to his cousin they were never copyrighted, with the result that unauthorized versions of the picture and the poem appeared in all sorts of shapes, all over the world. On the whole, they did Rudyard's reputation little good. He was then winning a name as a serious, even a solemn, writer, a position that was recognized by his admission to the Athenaeum Club, under Rule Two which provides for the election of a small number of persons eminent in public life. Not yet thirty-two, Rudyard was by far the youngest member of the Club, and gratified by his election. On the day of his admission he dined with Alfred Milner, Cecil Rhodes, and the editor of *The Times*. A fortnight later, on 17 April, his verses for Phil's picture appeared in the *Daily Mail* and, on the twenty-fourth, the picture itself was shown at the New Gallery.

It was a specimen of an art-form which has since been superseded by the techniques of cinematography – the 'problem picture'. Slickly and competently painted in contrasted tones of dark green, white, and crimson, with a high finish, it was the kind of picture that told a story, or rather gave a hint to the spectator of a story he was expected to find out for himself, a dramatic puzzle. The scene was a bedroom: against dark curtains stood a bed and on it lay a figure of a young man, dead or swooning, while over him towered with a triumphant sneer on her lips, a tall full-blooded woman in white. The picture was called *The Vampire*; and the only explanation offered was Kipling's set of verses:

> A fool there was and he made his prayer
> (Even as you and I!)
> To a rag and a bone and a hank of hair
> (We called her the woman who did not care)
> But the fool he called her his lady fair –
> (Even as you and I!)
>
> *Oh, the years we waste and the tears we waste*
> *And the work of our head and hand*
> *Belong to the woman who did not know*
> *(And now we know that she never could know)*
> *And did not understand!*

'A rag and a bone and a hank of hair' – this was strong stuff. It brought Rudyard's reputation back to its earliest phase; it was a piece by the author of *Plain Tales from the Hills* grown ten years older; and though no one rated it high as poetry, no one who had once heard it was likely to forget it. Prick it, and the blood would spurt. Yet Rudyard seems not to have taken it seriously and never admitted it among his 'collected' works until the inclusive edition of 1919. It was an occasional piece, a compliment to cousin Phil – no more – and critics who tried to read into it Rudyard's philo-

sophy of sex failed to recognize his faculty for putting himself into the skin of a fictitious character. Only those who
knew them well commented on the fact that Phil Burne-
Jones was making a fool of himself over Mrs Patrick Campbell.[10]

When the spring came in 1897 Rudyard and Carrie took
rooms in a London hotel, where Carrie rested – she was expecting another child – while Rudyard made house-hunting
expeditions in Kent and Sussex.

Rudyard Kipling to Dr J. Conland

June 1, '97

We've been living a chaotic and disorganized life for the last
few weeks. You see we gave up the house in Devon – a lovely
place but eight months damp, rain, sea fog and mildew were
rather more than we would stand. Then we decided to take a
holiday from housekeeping while we hunted for a new house;
and to London (London in Jubilee year!) we came three weeks
ago and have been living in a hotel overlooking the Park: both
children with us. The wife is hugely enjoying the rest from
housekeeping and the demoralizing comfort of not having to
think about meals. Meantime a kindly relative has placed her
house near Brighton at our disposal for as long as we want; and
we go down on Wednesday next; to resume the dreary game of
house-hunting. I feel like a houseless gipsy; and would almost
be thankful for a tent and that – and the damnable? grind of
society in London – is my excuse for silence.

Life has been pretty mixed – not to say exciting for me lately.
I went to the big banquet of the Royal Academy to begin
with: sat next to Irving and the Poet Laureate [Alfred Austin].
Incidentally I met Hamo Thorneycroft the sculptor – brother to
the Thorneycroft who builds the torpedo-boats. Sez he to me
'Would you like to attend the steam-trials of a new thirty-knot
destroyer?' 'Rather!' sez I; and about three days later I got a
telegram advising me to come down to Chatham dockyard. So
down I went and on the way picked up the Thorneycroft crowd
who represented the contractors' interests at the trial (she had

to do her 30 knots an hour for three consecutive hours before the government would take her) and a most fascinating old navy engineer who represented the Admiralty.

We pulled out of the Medway into the mouth of the Thames at an easy twelve knots to get down to our course – from the Mouse Light to the Lower Hope reach – a lumpy sea and a thirty knot breeze.

They wrapped my neck up in a comforter, gave me heavy oilskins; and tied a souwester over my ears. The wind was pretty keen and now and then the top of a sea came aboard. She was steered from the bridge forward and we all huddled under the protection of the turtleback – practically the break of the foc'sle. Then we struck a twenty-two knot gait – and very nice it was. They began to rig up the indicators, to know how many revolutions we were doing and I went down into the engine room. Two engines of 3,000 h.p. apiece were making about 230 to the minute – maybe a trifle less.

It was like a nightmare. The vibration shook not only your body but your intestines and finally seemed to settle on your heart. The breeze along the deck made it difficult to walk. I staggered aft above the twin-screws and there saw a blue-jacket, vomiting like a girl; and in the ward-room which is right in the stern of her, I felt my false teeth shaking in my head! The pace was too good for her to roll. All we could do was to get under the lee of the conning tower while this devil's darning needle tore up and down the coast. We passed 17-knot passenger boats, flew ten miles past 'em, turned and came back and overtook them. By the way when she turned she slung you to one side like a bicycle.

The wake ran out behind us like white hot iron; the engine room was one lather of oil and water; the engines were running 400 to the minute; the gauges, the main-steam pipes and everything that wasn't actually built into her were quivering and jumping; there was half an inch of oil and water on the floors and – you couldn't see the cranks in the crank pit. It was more like Hell on a ten foot scale than anything you ever dreamed of and through the infernal din of it George Brown shouted in my ear 'Isn't she a darling!' Well, I climbed out of the engine-room rather thankfully and went up on the bridge by the Captain. You never saw a boat steer as she did. One grey headed old quarter-master held her at the wheel; and her two heavy drop-rudders

swung her over the face of the waters. We shaved a brig coming
up the Thames just to show how near we could go; and our wash
threw her up and down as though we had been a liner. We
skimmed past buoys with about five yards to spare, running all
along the edge of the Maplin Sands. We faced into that thirty
knot gale and for the honour of the thing I *had* to stay up on
the bridge. At last those awful three hours came to an end: but
not before the speaking-tubes to the Captain's bridge had been
smashed off by the vibration. Then we drew breath: and every
one said Thank God! She'd done ninety knots in those three
hours: but if it had been straightaway in deep sea, we'd have
done 31. Everything was quite cool and nothing had smashed up
and they all said I was the Mascotte. Every engineer aboard
knew *M'Andrew's Hymn* by the way and enjoyed it. Well, then
we jogged back to Sheerness at 20 knots an hour. We were all as
black as sweeps; and utterly played out. It took me two days to
get the 'jumps' out of my legs. But I wouldn't have missed the
trip for anything.

Three days later I went down to Oxford among the four
hundred year old universities and dined with the tutors and so
on at Balliol College. The boys cheered me so that the Master
couldn't say grace and altogether I had a most wonderful time.
Since then I've been flourishing about in a frock-coat and top-
hat when I wasn't dining out. Can you imagine me as a dude!
But the wife and I thought we might as well play the game now
that we were in for it. We went to the Lyceum the other night:
Irving put a private box at our disposal; and after the play we
went round and saw him and Miss Terry in their war-paint on
the stage. He's rather keen that I should write a play for him;
and I should rather like it. But actors are rummy folk. Then
Henry James came to dine with us and then I went out to a
man's party of generals and military ... where I met George
Curzon – him that married old Leiter's daughter: and is now a
flourishing political person. Also we lunched with Hay who has a
lovely house here – overlooking the line of the Jubilee procession.
He has all his work cut out for him to manage his share of the
Jubilee. London is simply packed and double packed. There are
stands and seats everywhere: and like the embassies the police
are praying for the day to be over without accidents. Estimates
say between 8 and 10,000,000 people will attend. There are
80,000 *extra* Americans in town; and Cook the tourist man has

practically chartered all the suburb of Richmond for their accommodation.

We are going down to Brighton to be out of it all. There we have a house lent us by my aunt, Lady Burne Jones; and from there we hope to find a house for ourselves . . .[11]

From A Song of the English (1893)

We were dreamers, dreaming greatly, in the man-stifled
    town;
We yearned beyond the sky-line where the strange roads go
    down.
Came the Whisper, came the Vision, came the Power with
    the Need,
Till the Soul that is not man's soul was lent us to lead.
As the deer breaks – as the steer breaks – from the herd
    where they graze,
In the faith of little children we went on our ways.
Then the wood failed – then the food failed – then the last
    water dried –
In the faith of little children we lay down and died.
On the sand-drift – on the veldt-side – in the fern-scrub we
    lay,
That our sons might follow after by the bones on the way.
Follow after – follow after! We have watered the root,
And the bud has come to blossom that ripens for fruit!
Follow after – we are waiting, by the trails that we lost,
For the sounds of many footsteps, for the tread of a host.
Follow after – follow after – for the harvest is sown:
By the bones about the wayside ye shall come to your own!

[11]

The White Man's Burden
(1897–8)

IT was Derby Day in Queen Victoria's Diamond Jubilee year, 2 June 1897, when the Kiplings moved to Rottingdean which was to be their home for five years. A lonely seaside village, off the railway, and therefore out of reach of trippers from Brighton, four miles away, it had the special merit of being a family resort, where Mr Bleyber, the landlord of the 'Plough', could remember Rudyard as a plump schoolboy.[1]

Around the village green, a mile inland from the sea, stood several houses, of which one was the summer home of the Burne-Joneses and appropriately called 'North End House'. Across the green was the large house of the Ridsdales who were members of the family, since Stan Baldwin had married the daughter of the house. Other aunts and cousins came and went, and Rudyard found himself at the centre of a large and varying group of intimate friends, all allied by marriages: Burne-Joneses, Mackails, Baldwins, Ridsdales, Poynters, Macdonalds, and Kiplings. There were many young children down for the summer to be deposited on the beach or sent off in wagonettes to picnic in the Downs under convoy of aunts and governesses; there were men of Rudyard's own age to sit up late in 'North End House' engrossed in that shop-talk which Rudyard thought the best of all social pleasures. At Rottingdean in 1897 Rudyard first formed a close friendship with Stan Baldwin – each of their wives was expecting a child; and there would often be Phil Burne-Jones, 'Ambo', and Hugh Poynter; or Jack Mackail – but Rudyard found him too donnish and radical for intimacy.

'North End House' was large and rambling, furnished by

William Morris with an eye more to the principles of craftsmanship than comfort. However, the Kiplings were comfortable enough for the summer season. Aunt Georgie willingly let the Kiplings use her seaside house, persuaded them to stay so that their child could be born there, and encouraged them to rent the house called 'The Elms' which stood like an island in the village green.

Rudyard was quietly busy at 'North End House' in June working at some verses on 'Destroyers' and was beginning to put together some nursery stories about animals, with which he had amused the children at Brattleboro three or four years back. Much as he disliked publicity, he could not ignore the Jubilee celebrations. The 'colonies', as they were still called, were much in the public notice, and the author of *The Seven Seas* was expected to be on his mettle. He attended a luncheon to the Colonial Premiers in London, on 11 June, and met the High Commissioner for Canada, a few days after the verses, 'Our Lady of the Snows', had appeared in *The Times*. Rudyard's mind was turned to colonial affairs, as Carrie noted in her diary, making what is perhaps the first use of a celebrated phrase. On 15 June, she wrote, he was at work upon a poem called 'The White Man's Burden', which he did not complete until eighteen months later. Not this poem but another, a poem which at first he rejected, was to contain his Jubilee message, effacing the bad impression he had made with 'The Vampire', and instantly raising him in public esteem to the place left vacant at the death of Tennyson.

For several years Rudyard had been in a special relation with the London *Times*. When he left England in 1892 Moberly Bell had told him that *The Times* would publish anything that he cared to submit, an offer that he interpreted in two ways. He had begun by sending Bell a series of travel-sketches in the ordinary way of journalism, and later he used *The Times* as a platform for the major poems which he designed to carry a message to his generation.

On 14 October 1895 *The Times* had published Rudyard's poem, 'The Native-Born'.

> *Manager of* The Times (*Moberly Bell*)
> *to Rudyard Kipling*
>
> October 14th, 1895
>
> My Dear Kipling,
>
> Let me thank you very heartily on my own behalf and on behalf of the proprietors of *The Times* for the really beautiful poem you have allowed us to publish in *The Times* this morning. It is, I think, the first time we have ever published a poem not written in relation to any one definite event and this caused us (as a good old conservative institution) to hesitate, but as we read and re-read your poem our scruples disappeared.[2]

'Here's richness for me,' wrote Kipling to Norton, 'and I should never have thought of trying the austere old *Times* but for you.'

'The Native-Born', an appeal from the colonial born overseas for a little understanding on the part of his English brother, was the first of these public poems. During the next forty years about twenty more of them were given to *The Times* including 'Our Lady of the Snows', 'Recessional', 'The White Man's Burden', 'The Islanders', 'The Dead King', and 'For all we have and are'. 'Given to *The Times*,' said Kipling, 'because for this kind of work I did not take payment'; and accordingly they involved him in difficulties over copyright.

It was by these rare and solemn verses that Kipling came to be accepted as the people's laureate. Since much legend has grown up about his relation with the Court, it may be useful to recall the following points. The ancient office of Poet Laureate, which had been honoured by the tenure of such men as Ben Jonson and Dryden, fell into contempt in the eighteenth century when its small emolument was used to provide a pension for some courtier with literary tastes, who was expected to produce neat complimentary odes for

royal anniversaries. During the nineteenth century there
was a change in policy, and the emolument had been conferred, successively, on three professional poets, Southey,
Wordsworth, and Tennyson. Each had been something of a
rebel in youth and each was reproached by his younger contemporaries for accepting a pension from Government in
middle age.

When Tennyson died in October 1892 he had held the
office for forty years, through the whole Victorian summer
and autumn. His influence had contributed largely to the
revival of attachment to the monarchy and to the old
Queen, and several of the state poems he had written for
royal occasions had genuine poetic merit. He was one of the
makers of the Victorian age and, except for the Queen herself and Mr Gladstone, he was one of the last to survive
among those makers. In August 1892 Gladstone had become
Prime Minister for the fourth time and, looking around for
a successor to Tennyson, could find no one. There was, indeed, one other major poet in England – Swinburne. But
Swinburne's verses had appealed to the younger generation
in the sixties, not least because of their defiance of the Victorian code of morals. Though he had abandoned his pag-
anism and republicanism, it was at the cost of his poetic
inspiration. The only other comparable poet was William
Morris, who was regarded as a dangerous revolutionary. Setting aside Swinburne and Morris, no candidates were to be
seen but minor poets who were mostly 'decadents or detri-
mentals'. There seemed to be no one qualified for the post
of Poet Laureate, either in the eighteenth- or the nineteenth-century manner.

In March 1892, just before Tennyson's death, a well-
known critic and historian, H. D. Traill, wrote an article
for the *Nineteenth Century* on this very theme. He enu-
merated fifty contemporary writers in whose work he found
some merit, but not one who could rank with the aged Tennyson. Then, in a postscript, he apologized for having overlooked the muse of the new young man, Rudyard Kipling.

For the sake of 'The Ballad of East and West', he awarded
Kipling the fifty-first place on his list, and thus Kipling became 'a minor poet certified by Traill'. The first collected
edition of *Barrack-Room Ballads* was published in the following month, and it was only then that the public (and the
politicians) could judge his adult work in bulk. But the early
Barrack-Room Ballads were rather shocking, and some of the
accompanying poems were worse. If the volume included
'The English Flag', the first of Kipling's national odes, it
also included 'Cleared' which was his contemptuous attack
launched against the Liberal Party and Gladstone. 'Go,
scare your sheep together,' Kipling adjured him, 'the blundering, tripping tups that bleat behind the old bell-wether.'
Since the old bell-wether now had the appointment of a
Poet Laureate within his patronage, he was not likely to appoint Rudyard Kipling.

If there had been any likelihood – and there was none –
Kipling's claim for consideration would have been much
strengthened after the publication of 'A Song of the English', which appeared in a popular illustrated monthly in
March 1893. In mere extent it is the longest of his poems;
in content it is the most rich and varied; its composition
most elaborate, its harmonies most surely integrated. Although the author of this work was without question a
mature and responsible interpreter of the nation's mood, he
hastened to counter any suggestion that he should be given
official status, by a purer poem with a simpler theme, 'The
Last Rhyme of True Thomas', which, by chance, was published a few days after Lord Rosebery succeeded Gladstone
as Prime Minister. Kipling had been at work upon it for
several months before Gladstone's retirement.

'The Last Rhyme' is a direct imitation of a Border ballad,
written in dialect. It describes, in an allegory too plain to
need interpretation, how a king offers to ennoble a poet and
how the poet demonstrates his superior power to enchant
the king.

> The King has called for priest and cup,
>   The King has taken spur and blade
> To dub True Thomas a belted knight,
>   And all for the sake of the songs he made.

>   .   .   .

> 'And what should I make wi' blazon and belt,
>   'Wi' keep and tail and seizin and fee,
> 'And what should I do wi' page and squire
>   'That am a king in my own countrie?

>   .   .   .

> 'For I make Honour wi' muckle mouth,
>   'As I make Shame wi' mincing feet,
> 'To sing wi' the priests at the market-cross,
>   'Or run wi' the dogs in the naked street.

>   .   .   .

> 'I ha' harpit ye up to the Throne o' God,
>   'I ha' harpit your midmost soul in three.
> 'I ha' harpit ye down to the Hinges o' Hell,
>   'And – ye – would – make – a Knight o' me!'

The ballad is of great length and contains many descriptive passages in the tradition of the Border. If Lord Rosebery's advisers read it through, they could be in no doubt about the author's view of official poetry. Apparently it was unnecessary, since Rosebery had already let slip the opinion that he would as soon appoint a court jester as a Poet Laureate.

A year passed and in August 1895 the Conservatives regained office. Lord Salisbury now became Prime Minister, and we have it on the authority of one of his private secretaries, Sir Ian Malcolm, that the appointment of a Poet Laureate was discussed with interest. The Prime Minister's nephew, Arthur Balfour, pressed for the appointment of Kipling (who was in America throughout the time of discussion).* A discreet inquiry quickly revealed his antipathy

* 'That ass Austin was made P.L. in 1896 – after much hesitation and no reflexion. I was a bottle-washer at Hatfield then. Lord S. certainly thought of Kipling for the job "though he blows his own

to any official recognition. Balfour's proposal was dropped and on 1 January 1896 Lord Salisbury appointed a Tory journalist named Alfred Austin who had written some patriotic jingles, and only ten days later Austin made an ass of himself by a laughable set of verses on the Jameson Raid. The appointment was so derisory, and was greeted with such contempt in literary society, that it was generally regarded as mere cynicism on the part of the Prime Minister. Alfred Austin did not neglect his duties, and his official utterances are still occasionally quoted as examples of unconscious humour. Meanwhile Kipling's deeper notes were being heard, and the publication of *The Seven Seas* in November 1896 revealed his full powers. As a national poet he was everything that Austin was not, and the great occasion of the Queen's second Jubilee in 1897 called his powers into play.

A persistent rumour appeared at an early date that Kipling's candidature had been vetoed by Queen Victoria, who took offence at his ballad on 'The Widow at Windsor'. No evidence has been adduced for this story except a letter (which, judged by internal evidence, cannot be authentic) in an American library.* The only connexion that can be established between the Kiplings and the Court is through Lockwood Kipling, who was well known at Windsor. He had struck up a friendship in India with the Duke of Connaught who engaged him to decorate a room in his house at Bagshot, in Indian style. This proved so pleasing that the old Queen herself desired him to arrange a suite of Indian rooms at Osborne. Lockwood installed a Hindu craftsman

---

trumpet rather loud sometimes". A. J. B. more than thought of him and wanted him to take it. So he was sounded and the answer was just as you said and as might have been expected.' (Sir Ian Malcolm to Lord Baldwin, 15 July 1943.) [3]

*   'Ave you 'eard o' the Widow at Windsor
      With a hairy gold crown on 'er 'ead?
    She 'as ships on the foam — she 'as millions at 'ome,
      An' she pays us poor beggars in red.

and supervised the work, which was watched with interest and approval by the Royal Family. The Widow at Windsor certainly had no antipathy for the elder Kipling, and she certainly shared the common contempt for Alfred Austin.

Suggestions were made to Rudyard from several quarters that he should write a Jubilee ode and to these he reacted, as might be expected, negatively. It was never his practice or intention to write to order. According to an account which seems reliable, though published long afterwards, Rudyard was persuaded by the editor of *The Times* to attempt something but made no progress. '*The Times* began sending telegrams so I shut myself in a room. . . . I found just one line I liked – 'Lest we forget' – and wrote the poem round that, arranging it to the tune of the hymn, "Eternal Father, strong to save".'[4]

Kipling was not Poet Laureate, and there was little in his early record to suggest that he would write a ceremonial ode. His comment on the Queen's first Jubilee, in 1887, had been anything but enthusiastic:

> And the Ploughman settled the share
> More deep in the sun-dried clod : –
> 'Mogul, Mahratta, and *Mlech* from the North,
> 'And White Queen over the Seas –
> 'God raiseth them up and driveth them forth
> 'As the dust of the ploughshare flies in the breeze:
> 'But the wheat and the cattle are all my care,
> 'And the rest is the will of God.'[5]

During the six months before the Diamond Jubilee *The Seven Seas* had passed through three large editions which had introduced the reading public to a new note in Kipling's repertory. The sense of climax which stirred the whole Empire in June 1897 called for an expression of faith, and no one who had read 'A Song of the English' with attention could doubt that, if Kipling spoke on such an occasion, it would be with solemnity.

On Jubilee Day, 22 June, he set aside his other tasks, his draft for a set of nursery stories, and his draft for a set of verses on the White Man's Burden, in order to return to the set piece which was to carry the refrain 'Lest we forget'. After a day that was overcast and dull in Sussex, the evening brightened as he and Carrie walked out to hear the church-bells chiming, and to watch the chain of bonfires rise and sink 'on dune and headland' along the South Coast. A poem of seven stanzas began to take shape in his mind, but he was dissatisfied with it and laid it aside. The next day he went off at a tangent; he busied himself with a political dialogue for the *St James's Gazette*, and with finishing a dramatic lyric, 'The Explorer':

> Till a voice, as bad as Conscience, rang interminable changes
> On one everlasting Whisper day and night repeated – so:
> 'Something hidden. Go and find it. Go and look behind the
> Ranges –
> 'Something lost behind the Ranges. Lost and waiting for
> you. Go!'

Again the thread was broken by a message from Captain Bayly which drew Rud and 'the Pater' off to Portsmouth on a visit to H.M.S. *Pelorus* for the Naval Review and manoeuvres. They were away for a fortnight and when the fleets had sailed, far-called to their tasks at the world's end, he returned to Rottingdean where Sallie Norton, on a visit from America, had been making company for Carrie. Aunt Georgie had also come down from London, as a guest of the Kiplings in her own house.

On the morning of the 16th July, hosts and guests were sitting together in one of the rooms of the house, Kipling at his desk, where he was running through some papers and from time to time flinging one of them into a waste-paper basket close to where Miss Norton sat. Her attention attracted, she asked if she might look at the contents of the basket. Leave was given and she picked out a sheet of paper on which was written a poem on the Diamond Jubilee, headed 'After'. She was at once struck by

its quality and protested at the idea of destroying it. It ought,
she declared, to be published.

Kipling demurred at this idea, but finally he yielded so far as
to say that he would refer the matter to the decision of 'Aunt
Georgie'. .... Lady Burne-Jones fully agreed with Miss Norton's
verdict. The poem must be published; and published it was.
Kipling sat down to revise it, reducing its length from seven to
five stanzas. Miss Norton suggested the repetition of the last
couplet of the first stanza,

> 'Lord God of Hosts, be with us yet,
> Lest we forget – lest we forget!'

as a refrain in the second and fourth, and this suggestion Kip-
long adopted, borrowing her pen for the purpose and writing
opposite the first insertion 'written with Sallie's pen – R. K.'
Then, still using Sallie's pen, he altered he last line to

> 'Thy mercy and forgiveness, Lord!'

(a change subsequently abandoned in favour of the original
version), added an 'Amen' and his signature, and then wrote
beneath:–

> 'done in council at North End House, July 16
>
>   Aunt Georgie
>   Sallie
>   Carrie and me.'[6]

A fresh copy was made, taken up to London by Aunt
Georgie whose visit to Rottingdean had come to an end, and
was despatched to *The Times* office that evening by special
messenger. She wrote next day to her niece and nephew
('very dear, both of you') to tell them with what contentment she thought of his 'splendid hymn speeding over the
world'. It appeared, 17 July, on the middle page of *The
Times* under a new title 'Recessional' and with a studied
paragraph of approval in the leading article. Again Kipling
astonished the nation by revealing its heartfelt but unrealized emotion. Humility not pride, awe not arrogance, a
sense of transience not a sense of permanence were to be
the keynotes of the imperial festival. Again Kipling con-

founded the critics by revealing an aspect of his genius which many of them grudged him.

But the poem, to which the symbolic name, 'Recessional', had been given, had certain flaws which the anti-imperialists were quick to work upon. The first verse – plain hymnology – with its echoes of the psalms and its phrase borrowed from Emerson's 'Woodnotes' – was unexceptionable, a prayer for the pervading presence of God in our consciousness so that we should never lose our sense of obligation to His Law; for the sober and temperate sense of duty that justifies the will to power.

> If, drunk with sight of power, we loose
>   Wild tongues that have not Thee in awe,
> Such boastings as the Gentiles use,
>   Or lesser breeds without the Law –
> Lord God of Hosts, be with us yet, ...

'Such boastings as the Gentiles use', the couplet gave much offence, especially among those who were sufficiently instructed in politics to appreciate that the cap fitted them. But the distinction between those who are 'within' and 'without the Law' is a distinction between the men of any class or creed who are humble because they submit to the Law and those who are arrogant because they override it. By their words and deeds you might know them, not by their accents or the colour of their skins.

The poem is open to criticism on another count; it is not so neatly phrased as some others of Kipling's verses. Like many of them it has its involved and obscure lines, its complicated metonymies in the Horatian mode, and once, at least, the syntax fails from over-compression. When, in the third stanza, he varies the refrain with the phrase:

> Judge of the Nations, spare us yet,

he fails to notice a contradiction. If he says, 'be with us ... lest we forget', he should say, 'spare us ... even though we forget'.

Admit that this celebrated poem contains a contemptuous phrase which may be counted an error in taste, admit that it contains a solecism which may be counted a fault in style, and then admire its solemnity, its vision, its permanence. This was the word given at Britain's proudest moment by the great imperialist, a call to humility and a warning that the proudest empire is ephemeral as a day's pageant.

The Kiplings admitted the special value of 'Recessional' by keeping a few of the many letters of praise that Rudyard received; it even moved his literary agent to unusual eloquence.

A. S. Watt to Rudyard Kipling

Allow me to offer you congratulations on the appearance in today's *Times* of your magnificent poem. It strikes the right note with regard to the Jubilee Celebration and will recall the nation to the source of its real strength. You are the only rightful heir to the mantles of Shakespeare, Milton, and Tennyson, and the laureate *de facto*! I tried to read 'God of our fathers' aloud this morning at home but I broke down.

S. S. McClure to Rudyard Kipling

You and the Queen made the *Times* for last Saturday the greatest newspaper ever published.

John Hay (American Minister in London) to Rudyard Kipling

I thank you for the high pleasure we all had in reading your noble 'Recessional'. It has struck everybody – not merely the critical people – as the one utterance of the year worth while.

Sir Walter Besant to Rudyard Kipling

It was far away the finest thing in the whole Jubilee literature. If the poor old Queen – or any of them – had the least feeling for letters they would – what would they do? Write and thank you at least . . .

You caught the exact feeling – what all decent people with the Puritanic touch in us wanted to have said and couldn't say. That is genius.

The Rev. F. W. Macdonald to Rudyard Kipling

My Dear Rudyard, – I am, as you know, the sole survival of Methodism in our family and line. I should like, then, to tell you how deeply your 'Recessional' has touched our whole community. You will not resent the fact that our people claim a certain interest in you, and that the thought occurred to many that the grandfathers had spoken in you, to which I would add that your verse would 'find' multitudes who would fly their sermons.

You have added a quotation to the common store, and a phrase to the language.

J. W. Mackail to Rudyard Kipling

Dear Ruddy, – In our household at least your poem in the *Times* of this morning was read with tumult of acclaim. I cannot tell you how glad I am of it, or forebear writing to say so. There are all the signs of England saving up for the most tremendous smash ever recorded in history if she does not look to her goings.

This letter from the pacifist intellectual who had married his cousin Margaret roused Rudyard to reply in terms that showed the other side of his nature, that revealed, too, some irritation at Mackail's patronage. While preaching humility and moderation to his fellow-countrymen, Rudyard did not forget that they were surrounded by armed and (in 1897) mostly hostile nations. There was a proper answer to 'such boastings as the Gentiles use'.[7]

Rudyard Kipling to J. W. Mackail

Dear Jack, – Thank you very much: but all the same, seeing what manner of armed barbarians we are surrounded with, we're about the only power with a glimmer of civilization in us. I've been round with the Channel Fleet for a fortnight and any other breed of white man, with such a weapon to their hand, would have been exploiting the round Earth in their own interests long ago. This is no ideal world but a nest of burglars, alas; and we must protect ourselves against being burgled. All

the same, we have no need to shout and yell and ramp about
our strength because that is waste of power, and because other
nations can do the advertising better than we can.

The big smash is coming one of these days, sure enough but
I think we shall pull through not without credit. It will be
common people – the 3rd class carriages – that'll save us.

Ever yours,

Ruddy.

The chorus of applause which greeted 'Recessional' far
surpassed his earlier triumphs, and this public tribute was
accompanied by an event in Rudyard's private life which
meant a thousand times more to him. Very early in the
morning of 17 August 1897 a son was born to Carrie at
'North End House'. In accordance with the family tradition
he was given his grandfather's name of John.

Rudyard Kipling to W. J. Harding

Ref: t.b.d. trials. My attention is at present taken up by one
small craft recently launched from my own works – weight
(approx.) 8·957 lbs: h.p. (indicated) 2·0464, consumption of fuel
unrecorded but fresh supplies needed every 2½ hrs. The vessel at
present needs at least 15 yrs for full completion but at the end
of that time may be an efficient addition to the Navy, for which
service it is intended. Date of launch Aug. 17th, 1.50 a.m. No
casualties. Christened John. You will understand that the new
craft requires a certain amount of attention – but I trust ere
long to be able to attend a t.b.d. trial.[8]

In September, when Carrie was fit to be moved, they
transferred themselves across the green from 'North End
House' to 'The Elms' which they rented for three guineas a
week. Even this was not their ideal house and Rudyard
spent much of the autumn house-hunting again, east into
Kent and west as far as Dorset. On 11 September he went
to Dorchester, where Thomas Hardy carried him off to inspect a lonely house occupied by an elderly lady. While Kipling examined the premises high and low, Hardy was left

making conversation in the parlour. 'I think you would like to know, Madam, that the gentleman I have brought to your house is no other than Mr Rudyard Kipling.' The remark fell flat; she had never heard of Rudyard Kipling. A few minutes later, Rudyard found himself alone with the lady and, not knowing what had passed, made the complementary remark, 'My sponsor is Thomas Hardy himself.' It was no use, she had never heard of Thomas Hardy; and the two celebrities admitted their insignificance to one another on the way home.[9]

Rudyard did not find the house he wanted, and decided to stay on at 'The Elms', but to spend the winter in a warmer climate. The whole family, and the 'Pater', prepared to leave for South Africa in the New Year. Meanwhile at Rottingdean they were never idle or lonely. Rudyard had much correspondence: with Beerbohm Tree who wanted him to write a play, with Arthur Sullivan who wanted to set 'Recessional' to music, with several influential persons who were working to get a civil list pension for W. E. Henley, now so crippled that when he came to stay at 'The Elms' his only outings were in a bath-chair. 'Uncle Ned' came down to 'North End House' in October, bringing with him 'Crom' Price and a friend J. M. Barrie, with whom Rudyard went for mighty walks across the Downs. He was working steadily at his schoolboy stories, and there was a day when he read some of them aloud to Price and 'Uncle Ned' and their young friend Sydney Cockerell. 'Do you remember that, sir?' he would say to 'Crom' Price, after each uproarious incident, and 'Crom' would reply, 'Yes, I remember that.' They enjoyed the stories and there was no ill-will in the remark that 'Crom' made afterwards to Cockerell. 'Yes, I remember many other things, too, that he might not wish me to remember.'[10]

Christmas at Rottingdean, with his own family around him, his mother as a guest, and a circle of relatives and friends, was happy indeed. On the last day of the year he wrote, as usual, a coda to Carrie's diary. 'The sixth year of

our life together. In all ways the richest to us two personally.
"She shall do him good and not evil all the days of her
life."'

On 8 January 1898 the Kiplings embarked at Southampton for Madeira, Cape Town, and the sunshine, in S.S.
Dunvegan Castle. Rudyard's earlier voyage in 1891 had
given him some acquaintance with Cape Colony but, as yet,
he had no connexion in South Africa and wrote around
to friends for advice about housekeeping at the Cape. They
settled, uncomfortably, in a boarding-house at Newlands on
the slope of Table Mountain, and stayed three months.
South Africa was to provide the fourth corner-stone in the
edifice of his materal life. India, New England, Sussex,
South Africa, east and west, north and south, were the four
lands in which this world-observer struck root.

The climate – for the southern tip of Africa can be very
hot in February – restored memories of his childhood.

'We shall go back by the boltless doors,
To the life unaltered our childhood knew –
To the naked feet on the cool, dark floors,
And the high-ceiled rooms that the Trade blows through:

'To the trumpet-flowers and the moon beyond,
And the tree-toads' chorus drowning all –
And the lisp of the split banana-frond
That talked us to sleep when we were small.

'The wayside magic, the threshold spells,
Shall soon undo what the North has done –
Because of the sights and the sounds and the smells
That ran with our youth in the eye of the sun.' [11]

There were in Cape Town in 1898 two others of the most
eminent personalities in the English-speaking world. Within a few days of their landing, the Kiplings were invited into
two social circles, that of Sir Alfred Milner and that of
Cecil Rhodes. Milner had recently arrived as the Queen's

High Commissioner, bearing instructions from Joseph Chamberlain, the Colonial Secretary, to bring the two Boer Republics to a settlement with the British Empire. Still a young man, and still unknown to the world, Milner was nevertheless a statesman to whom Kipling could give his approval. He was entirely straightforward and devoted to efficiency, almost unaware of emotional considerations in politics, patient, hard-working, and distrustful of rhetoric. He could never quite bring himself to believe that sensible men were swayed by sentiment. He was enlightened; and was convinced that enlightenment as understood in the most progressive circles of European society must convince even the Boers of the Transvaal back-veldt where their true interest lay. He did not much like the Boers, nor did they like him.

The other statesman at the Cape was Cecil Rhodes, also an Oxford man, but as different from Milner in character, temperament, and upbringing as he could be. A comfortable, practical, easy-going man, Rhodes loved the land and the people. Milner was a man of great competence and force, a man of many talents, but what was Rhodes? While no one doubted his greatness, its secret was and is elusive. A self-made millionaire, he seemed careless of money and the toys that money can buy; a silent man, he said something memorable whenever he opened his mouth; a man's man, he was bored by sport, unmoved by women; a money-spinning man of affairs, he lived in a fantastic world of dreams.

> I'd not give way for an Emperor,
> I'd hold my road for a King –
> To the Triple Crown I would not bow down –
> But this is a different thing.
> I'll not fight with the Powers of Air,
> Sentry, pass him through!
> Drawbridge let fall, 'tis the Lord of us all,
> The Dreamer whose dreams come true! [12]

Rhodes had a habit [wrote Rudyard] of jerking out sudden

questions as disconcerting as those of a child – or the Roman
Emperor he so much resembled. He said to me apropos of nothing in particular: 'What's your dream?' I answered that he was
part of it, and I think I told him that I had come down to look
at things. He showed me some of his newly established fruit-
farms in the peninsula, wonderful old Dutch houses, stalled in
deep peace, and lamented the difficulty of getting sound wood
for packing-cases and the shortcomings of native labour. But it
was his wish and his will that there should be a fruit-growing
industry in the Colony, and his chosen lieutenants made it
presently come to pass.

My use to him was mainly as a purveyor of words; for he was
largely inarticulate. After the idea had been presented – and
one had to know his code for it – he would say: 'What am I
trying to express? Say it, *say* it.' So I would say it, and if the
phrase suited not, he would work it over, chin a little down, till
it satisfied him.[13]

In March 1898 Rhodes sent Rudyard up-country to visit
his province of Rhodesia newly pacified after the Second
Matabele War and now made accessible by railway. His
route was 'from Kimberley to Khama's Country and from
Khama's Country east by north until he came to the great
grey-green greasy Limpopo River all set about with fever-
trees'.[14] Bulawayo, when Rudyard reached it, was a township
of shacks scattered hopefully along the broad streets that
Rhodes' visionary eye had planned for the future, where,
only five years earlier, Lobengula, with the smoke-reddened
eyes, had kept his savage court. So rapidly had the work of
progress gone that the fashionable sport of bicycling had
reached Bulawayo and in March 1898 the proprietor of the
town's cycle-shop was surprised at the appearance of a face,
instantly recognizable, even in Central Africa, by the spectacles, moustache, and eyebrows. It was with a hired bicycle
that Rudyard explored Bulawayo, and visited the Matoppo
Hills, in the company of Sir Charles Metcalfe. At the end
of the month he returned by way of Johannesburg with a
bagful of Matabele curiosities for Carrie and the children,
and in April they returned to England.[15]

In September Rudyard fulfilled one of his wishes, by going for a summer cruise with the Channel Squadron. They made a rendezvous in Bantry Bay where Rudyard went ashore, his first landing in Ireland. Students of Kipling's style might do well to study his original journal of the voyage (now in the New York Public Library); it is two or three times as long as the version which appeared in print as *A Fleet in Being,* and shows how he got his effects, by skilful cutting.

For Rudyard himself, as the author of 'M'Andrew's Hymn', the visit to the fleet was a personal triumph ending with a party in the wardroom of the flagship, where he recited some of the *Barrack-Room Ballads* and was carried round the room shoulder-high. Rudyard was as much at ease among the ratings on the lower deck, where, on 14 September, he was talking to a seaman when the news came round the ship that Kitchener had defeated the Khalifa at Omdurman, so that Gordon's death was at last avenged. 'Well,' said the seaman, 'we've waited about long enough, 'aven't we?' and then, 'This ought to make the French a bit sickish.'

The Battle of Omdurman was followed by a clash with the French on the Upper Nile – the Fashoda Incident – which ended with a French withdrawal in Africa and renewed negotiations in Europe. By then Kitchener had made his plans for reorganizing the Sudan, his first concern being to appeal for funds with which to found a college at Khartoum. This called forth an immediate tribute from Kipling:

For Allah created the English mad – the maddest of all
    mankind!
They do not consider the Meaning of Things; they consult not
    creed nor clan.
Behold, they clap the slave on the back, and behold, he ariseth a
    man!
They terribly carpet the earth with dead, and before their can-
    non cool,
They walk unarmed by twos and threes to call the living to
    school.

Lord Kitchener to Rudyard Kipling

December 14, 1898

Dear Mr Rudyard Kipling,

I wish to express my thanks to you for the poem on the Memorial College at Khartoum. I feel that you have greatly assisted me in the object I have in view and am very grateful. I feel sure the College will do a great deal of good throughout Northern Africa.

Yours truly,

Kitchener of Khartoum.[16]

The first crisis of imperialism became acute in 1898. 'One had a sense of "a sound of a going in the tops of the mulberry trees – of things moving into position as troops move".'[17] It was in South Africa that Rudyard felt this stir, and the personality of Rhodes revealed to him the spirit of the age.

No man had done more than Kipling to stimulate interest in the opening-up of the new worlds in the east and south. He never doubted the validity of western civilization, never lapsed into sentiment over the supposed virtues of savages; but it was the spread of law, literacy, communications, useful arts that he applauded, not the enlargement of frontiers. The Flag of England stood for service and sacrifice, not for racial superiority. The true sanction of Dominion (the phrase recalls John Wycliffe) was not national pride but 'a humble and a contrite heart'. Civilizing the world was a worth-while task, and though likely to be thankless, a task in which all might join if they would accept the Law. Rhodes, in his chastened mood after the failure of the Jameson Raid, was fully occupied with agricultural reform at the Cape, with railway construction in Rhodesia, with land-settlement, with the Cape-to-Cairo telegraph which was to be a pilot-line for the Cape-to-Cairo Railway. Rhodes, immersed in plans for material progress rather than in politics, was the leader Kipling adhered to.

The breaking-point was not in the Sudan, nor in the Transvaal, but in Cuba where, on 15 February 1898, the

U.S. battleship *Maine* was destroyed by an explosion. Whoever was responsible, the Spaniards were blamed, and the Spanish–American War ensued. Spanish rule in Cuba and the Philippines seemed to the Americans, as Boer rule in the Transvaal seemed to the British, unjustified because antiprogressive and, as in the case of the Transvaal so in the case of Cuba, the sentimental popular appeal was thought, by liberal critics, to mask the schemes of the commercial men. At least the hysteric fit of imperialism produced the same phenomena in America in 1898, and in England a year later. Kipling's prayer, though unheeded, was never more apposite:

> If, drunk with sight of power, we loose
> Wild tongues that have not Thee in awe,
> Such boastings as the Gentiles use, ...

The Kiplings had landed in England to learn that Spain and the United States were at war, and it is significant that, on the night of their arrival in London, John Hay the American Minister came to visit them at their hotel. Three days later Hay and Kipling dined at the Savoy with Rhodes who had come to England a few weeks earlier. The Spanish War drew England and America closer together and there was even talk of an alliance.

But at the same time Germany declared her policy of naval rivalry with Britain by the new Navy Law, and in Kipling's eyes it was sea-power that counted most. He had satirized the Kaiser in an early ballad ('An Imperial Rescript', 1890), and continued to regard his political vagaries with contempt. At this time Rudyard mistrusted the continental states. The well-intentioned moves of the Czar towards a general treaty of arbitration and disarmament, a few months later, provoked the fierce satire:

'Make ye no truce with Adam-zad – the Bear that walks like a Man!' [18]

And there is evidence that even the French, for whom Rudyard cultivated such strong sentiments of affection, were out of favour with him in 1898 and 1899. He would have preferred to leave the war-lords alone.

'Keep peace with the Lords of the Jungle – the Tiger, the Panther, the Bear;
And trouble not Hathi the Silent, and mock not the Boar in his lair.'

Sea-power and the White Man's Burden were the two subjects that held Kipling's attention in 1898, and both subjects led him to Anglo-American cooperation.

What did Kipling mean by the White Man's Burden? In answering this question, we must recall that, at that time, he habitually wrote verses in contemporary colloquial language, the language of the streets. In the eighteen-nineties the phrase, 'a white man', did not only mean a man with an unpigmented skin; it had a secondary symbolic meaning: a man with the moral standards of the civilized world. Of all Kipling's ballads the most familiar, the most quoted, the most often parodied was 'Gunga Din', a ballad so hackneyed that it is difficult to regard it now with an unprejudiced eye. It presented a cockney soldier's comment on a dark-skinned hero, 'the finest man I knew', and what the soldier says is:

> An' for all 'is dirty 'ide
> 'E was white, clear white, inside.

These words were not pretty, and were not physiologically informative, nor were they meant to be; but they were perfectly intelligible as the language of the people. The image of the 'white man' and his code of conduct appears repeatedly in Kipling's verse and prose, and always with a secondary as well as a primary connotation.

No one will assert that Rhodes and Kipling and Theodore Roosevelt believed in the political equality of all men, regardless of their social status, as it is asserted today; they would have contemptuously rejected any such notion. It is equally unjust to suppose that they believed in the absolute superiority of certain racial types. They lived in a world in which the British and the Americans were immeasurably the most progressive of nations; in which their standards of conduct prevailed wherever civilization spread; in which they were in fact spreading those standards all over the world. The partition of Africa, of South-East Asia, and of the Pacific, the revelation by explorers of the last secrets on the earth's surface, the linking of all the world's seaports by telegraph cables and steamship routes, the crossing of all continents by railways, the bridge-building, the engineering, and the commerce: these astonishing achievements made a revolution in history unlike anything that had ever happened before, and Kipling's genius had revealed to his generation what it was that they had done.

It had been substantially a British achievement. British rule in India which Kipling, as a young man, had lightheartedly explained and exposed to the understanding of the world was the training-school where the 'white men' had learned the nature of their mission. The moment had come in 1898 to call in the New World; the other half of the English-speaking race – 'white men' too – should join in the task.

The word that Kipling spoke in this crisis was again composed to the rhythm of a hymn-tune, and the language was again biblical. The theme was Empire and, with characteristic recklessness, he inserted a phrase or two that shocked the strait-laced:

> Take up the White man's burden –
> Send forth the best ye breed –
> God bind your sons to exile
> To serve your captives' need.

It was the first appearance in print of the famous phrase which was to echo round the world for fifty years, released in an appeal to the American people to join in the world-

wide task of extending 'the Law' and all it implied to the
remoter regions of the earth.

Their short campaign against Spain, undertaken – rightly
or wrongly – in a crusading mood, to free the Spanish
colonies from misgovernment, had ended after a few weeks'
fighting, with the consequence that America found herself a
naval and colonial power. What were the conquerors to do
with Cuba and the Philippines which had fallen so suddenly
into their hands? Just like the other colonial powers,
the Americans found that – willy-nilly – they must face the
problems of empire; they could not disengage. In the
Philippine Islands (as on a huger scale in British India) there
were peoples at every stage of culture, from Filipinos who
had been good Catholics for ten generations to jungle tribes
still in the Stone Age, and it was true enough, though tactless, of Kipling to point out that the Americans must

> ... wait in heavy harness
>   On fluttered folk and wild –
> Your new-caught, sullen peoples,
>   Half devil and half child.

These phrases, perhaps the best-remembered lines in the
poem, need the corrective of what he displayed as the prize
of imperialism; it is a task to be done without material reward, without thanks, without even a confident hope of
success.

> Take up the White man's burden –
>   And reap his old reward :
> The blame of those ye better,
>   The hate of those ye guard ...

> And when your goal is nearest
>   The end for others sought,
> Watch Sloth and heathen Folly
>   Bring all your hope to nought.

Nor are those who take up the burden to suppose that imperial rule is anything but drudgery – 'no tawdry rule of

kings'. The inducement lies only in the sense of duty; the burden comes 'to search your manhood'; and the justification will be

> Cold-edged with dear-bought wisdom,
> The judgment of your peers!

By 22 November 'The White Man's Burden' was at last finished to Rudyard's satisfaction, and his first use of it was to send a copy to Theodore Roosevelt who had just been elected Governor of New York State.

T. Roosevelt to H. Cabot Lodge

January 12, 1899

I send you an advance copy of a poem by Kipling which is rather poor poetry, but good sense from the expansionist standpoint.

H. Cabot Lodge to T. Roosevelt

January 14, 1899

Thanks for the advance copy of Kipling's poem. I like it. I think it is better poetry than you say, apart from the sense of the verses.[19]

The poem appeared in the London *Times* on 4 February and on the following day in the New York *Sun* and *Tribune*. On the sixth the American Senate voted by a sufficient majority to take over the administration of the Philippines; and not too soon, because in the same week a revolt broke out in Luzon against the American military occupation.

It was Rudyard's usual practice to run some verse and prose work side by side. While he was polishing 'The White Man's Burden' in November, he also had in hand two more 'Stalky' stories. One of them which he intended as an introduction to the series, explaining how 'Stalky' won his nickname, did not satisfy the author and was rejected from the volume called *Stalky & Co.* The other story, 'The Flag of his

Country', reflected, in the medium of a tale for boys, the topics that just then ruled the author's emotions; it describes a schoolboy's reactions to patriotic propaganda. No liberal pacifist has ever scarified the wordy exponents of lip-service to loyalty more ferociously than 'Stalky' and his friends; and, in this story, there is no doubt when the author is speaking with his own voice. No character in Kipling's portrait gallery is more cruelly satirized or more heartily condemned than the 'impeccable Conservative M.P.', whom 'Stalky' described as a 'jelly-bellied flag-flapper', when he addressed the College on the subject of patriotism.

> With a large and healthy hand he tore down ... veils, and trampled them under the well-intentioned feet of eloquence. In a raucous voice he cried aloud little matters, like the hope of Honour and the dream of Glory, that boys do not discuss even with their most intimate equals. ... He pointed them to shining goals, with fingers which smudged out all radiance on all horizons. He profaned the most secret places of their souls with outcries and gesticulations.[20]

Strange that Kipling, who so consistently and so powerfully derided and condemned these goings-on, should often be accused of promoting them! That, in fact, was his comment on the jingoism of 1898. Five years passed before Rudyard could estimate the effect of his words upon American policy. At the end of Roosevelt's first term as President, he wrote to Rudyard about his attempt to take up the White Man's Burden; it was on this record that he stood, and was elected, for a second term.

Theodore Roosevelt to Rudyard Kipling

1 November 1904

I have done a good many things in the past three years. ... It is natural that some people should have been alienated by each thing I did, and the aggregate of all that have been alienated may be more than sufficient to overthrow me. Thus, in dealing with the Philippines I have first the jack-fools who seriously think that any group of pirates and head-hunters needs nothing but independence in order that it may be turned into a dark-hued New England town-meeting, and then the entirely practical creatures who join with these extremists because I do not intend that the islands shall be exploited for corrupt purposes.

I have accomplished certain definite things. I would consider myself a hundred times over repaid if I had nothing more to my credit than Panama and the coaling-stations in Cuba. So that you see my frame of mind is a good deal like that of your old Viceroy when he addressed the new Viceroy.[21]

From MERROW DOWN (1902)

I

There runs a road by Merrow Down –
   A grassy track to-day it is –
An hour out of Guildford town,
   Above the river Wey it is.

Here, when they heard the horse-bells ring,
   The ancient Britons dressed and rode
To watch the dark Phoenicians bring
   Their goods along the Western Road.

     .   .   .   .

But long and long before that time
   (When bison used to roam on it)
Did Taffy and her Daddy climb
   That Down, and had their home on it.

     .   .   .   .

The Wey, that Taffy called Wagai,
   Was more than six times bigger then;
And all the Tribe of Tegumai
   They cut a noble figure then!

II

Of all the Tribe of Tegumai
   Who cut that figure, none remain, –
On Merrow Down the cuckoos cry –
   The silence and the sun remain.

But as the faithful years return
   And hearts unwounded sing again,
Comes Taffy dancing through the fern
   To lead the Surrey spring again.

Her brows are bound with bracken-fronds,
   And golden elf-locks fly above;
Her eyes are bright as diamonds
   And bluer than the sky above.

In moccasins and deer-skin cloak,
  Unfearing, free and fair she flits,
And lights her little damp-wood smoke
  To show her Daddy where she flits.

For far – oh, very far behind,
  So far she cannot call to him,
Comes Tegumai alone to find
  The daughter that was all to him!

[12]

Last Visit to the
United States
(1898–9)

THE summer of 1898 was marred for Rudyard by a
domestic blow. Sir Edward Burne-Jones, his dear 'Uncle
Ned', died suddenly in London on 17 June, and his ashes
were buried in the little church at Rottingdean a few yards
across the green from 'The Elms'. In his last years Burne-
Jones had achieved great fame and success, recognized by a
baronetcy, but had remained the same shy domestic man, so
difficult to draw out in conversation, so well worth drawing
out. His occasional letters, 'wild, nonsensical "lark" letters',
revealed a side to his character that the public never supposed to exist in this grave Pre-Raphaelite. All the family
assembled at Rottingdean, and Rudyard, Stan, 'Uncle
Crom', and the others in turn watched the dead man's ashes
through the night before the funeral. Rudyard wrote in great
unhappiness to C. E. Norton about his loss. Uncle Ned had
been, he said, 'more to me than any other man. He changed
my life by his visits down here.' That was now over, and
Aunt Georgie, living alone at 'North End House', drew even
closer to the Kiplings whom she consulted about writing her
husband's life. Her little granddaughter, Angela Mackail,
came several times to stay with her relatives that autumn,
and from Angela's childish memories we can derive a picture of the Kiplings at a new angle.

The three Kipling children, Josephine, Elsie, and John were
about the same age as our nursery three. Josephine very fair-
haired and blue-eyed, was my bosom friend, and though we
both adored her father, the stronger bond of patriotism drew
us yet more firmly together as Cavaliers against Cousin

Ruddy's whole-hearted impersonation of a Roundhead. ...
The war between Cavaliers and Roundheads raged furiously as
long as the Kiplings were at Rottingdean, Josephine and I
leading forlorn hopes against the Regicide and being perpetually discomfited by his superior guile.

During those long warm summers Cousin Ruddy used to try
out the *Just So Stories* on a nursery audience. Sometimes
Josephine and I would be invited into his study, a pleasant
bow-windowed room, where Cousin Ruddy sat at his work-table
looking exactly like the profile portrait of him that Uncle Phil
painted.

The *Just So Stories* are a poor thing in print compared with
the fun of hearing them told in Cousin Ruddy's deep un-
hesitating voice. There was a ritual about them, each phrase
having its special intonation which had to be exactly the same
each time and without which the stories are dried husks.
There was an inimitable cadence, an emphasis of certain
words, an exaggeration of certain phrases, a kind of intoning
here and there which made his telling unforgettable.[1]

Whenever there were young children within call, Rudyard
cultivated their society and told them stories. That was his
pleasure, which did not check the regular work he had on
hand. The volume called *The Day's Work*, containing his
short stories written in Vermont, was passed for press and
published in 1898. A dramatized version of *The Light that
Failed* was also approved, and produced a little later by
Forbes-Robertson. Rudyard completed a batch of 'Stalky'
stories and sent them off to his agent for publication in
monthly magazines. On the very next day he turned again
to *Kim*, his fourth attempt to knock that picaresque
romance into printable shape. He paid a visit to Tisbury to
consult the 'Pater' about it, and spent some days with the
Baldwins in Worcestershire. Back at Rottingdean, his evenings were spent with Aunt Georgie, or at the Boys' Social
Club he had founded in the village.

The year ended in gloom with bad news from Rudyard's
parents. Trix and her husband had come home from India,

after many years during which she had been at the hub of Simla society, as gracious as her mother and far more beautiful. A person of extreme sensibility – imaginative and nervous – she was, in the expression of those days, 'psychic', so unworldly that she seemed sometimes to move in a land of phantoms. In December her mind gave way, and it became necessary to place her under her mother's care at Tisbury; the happiness of the family square was shattered.

At rather short notice the Kiplings decided not to winter in the south that year but to pay a visit to the United States. Carrie wished to see her mother, and Rudyard had business to attend to, as a tiresome dispute over copyrights had arisen with a New York publisher.

But to take a family of young children across the North Atlantic in midwinter gave Rudyard some qualms of anxiety. His mother advised against it and was overruled by Carrie.

> When the darkened Fifties dip to the North,
>   And frost and the fog divide the air,
>   And the day is dead at his breaking-forth,
>   Sirs, it is bitter beneath the Bear![2]

In frost and fog they left Liverpool for their roughest passage, meeting a full gale in mid-Atlantic. All three children and their nurse were very sick, and the two little girls developed colds which weakened them distressingly. On 2 February when the family landed at New York they were detained for two hours at a draughty custom-house, pestered by reporters to whom they would say nothing, so that, by the time they reached the Hotel Grenoble in West 56th Street, Carrie was seriously concerned for the children. Luckily the faithful De Forests had met them at the dock; and, at the hotel, Carrie found her mother and her sister Josephine who had recently married Theo Dunham, a rising doctor. The children grew worse; their cases were now diagnosed as whooping-cough with complications, not easy complaints to care for in a city hotel, while outside in the streets there were blizzards of snow. Rudyard hardly had time to notice that the newspapers were full of quotation and comment that week, inspired or provoked by 'The White Man's Burden'. By 8 February Rudyard and Carrie were in 'great anxiety' and on that day Carrie, too, fell ill, with a high temperature. Dr Dunham was always at hand and Rudyard was comforted when Conland arrived to stand by his friends. The news he brought from Brattleboro was less encouraging. Beatty Balestier had announced to the press that he was coming to New York to sue his brother-in-law for $50,000, on a charge of malicious prosecution three years since.[3]

Carrie's illness did not last long, or she mastered it for the sake of the children. By the twelfth she was up and about, and during the following week she and Rudyard were able to attend to the social and business matters which had brought them to New York, travelling, with delighted astonishment, in an 'electric cab'. On the twentieth, as the weather was milder, they even took the children for an outing in Central Park, and visited the office of Doubleday & McClure.

There was much business to be done. There was the house, 'Naulakha', to be disposed of – or reoccupied; family affairs to be settled, and a new and very serious campaign to be fought over Rudyard's American copyrights. A. P. Watt had at last succeeded in securing the rights in Rudyard's old articles written for the Allahabad *Pioneer*, and all that he was willing to keep in print was reissued in the volume *From Sea to Sea*, fully protected by copyright at last. At the same time friendly discussions persisted between Rudyard and the American publishing house of Scribner's, who were making slow progress with the complete edition of his works. Frank Doubleday, the moving spirit in this scheme, had issued twelve volumes of the *Outward Bound* edition in 1897. He had tried to make it inclusive, while Rudyard, as usual, had done his best to suppress his juvenile trifles. Frank had urged him to revise the early work and Rudyard had preferred to leave his past alone. Frank had pushed on, while Lockwood Kipling, the true craftsman, had taken his time, ever striving for perfection in the production of his illustrations.

When Frank left Scribner's in order to set up his own publishing house of Doubleday & McClure, the *Outward Bound* edition hung fire. Again as in 1890 Kipling was outsmarted by one of the classical American publishers, who kept within the rules of trade practice while doing what Kipling thought plain piracy. No less a firm than Putnam's planned to put upon the market a rival to the *Outward Bound* edition which seemed to be at a stop. There were all sorts of Kipling pieces not covered by American copyright, and all sorts of ways of acquiring a limited right, within the letter of the law, to print the rest, in a limited edition. They accordingly set to work, quite openly, to issue the *Brush-wood Boy* edition, in competition with Scribner's. The commencement of long legal proceedings against Putnam's was the major part of Kipling's business in America in 1899, so far as the state of his domestic affairs allowed.*

When Rudyard came back to his hotel from the Century Club on 20 February, Carrie noticed that he was dull and feverish. Next day, when he was seriously ill, Theo Dunham diagnosed the case as 'inflammation in one lung'; called in a specialist, Dr Janeway; and engaged a night-nurse.

> An anxious night and more anxious day [wrote Carrie in her diary on the twenty-second]. Rud so good and patient – sleeps much – good friends and helping hands, and I feel how everyone Rud has ever spoken to has loved him, and is glad and happy to help do for him.

On the twenty-second he was conscious and quiet, while little Josephine was in a fever, with a high temperature. Carrie decided to take her away from the hotel to the De

---

*The legal proceedings were not completed until 1901, when the United States Court of Appeal gave judgement, with costs, for the defendant. The case, which cost Kipling over £1,000, hardened his prejudice against the publishing trade, even though Putnam's decided not to proceed with the *Brushwood* edition.[4]

Forests' house on Long Island, a parting which was 'a moment of conscious agony'.

From 23 February until 17 April there are but two short entries in Carrie Kipling's diary, the longest intermission since her marriage. There she was, in an uptown New York hotel, weakened after her own bout of fever, in charge of two children – one aged three years, the other aged eighteen months – both with the whooping-cough, torn with anxiety for her darling elder daughter, her doors besieged by press reporters, her irresponsible brother Beatty threatening her with an action, her husband's affairs deeply involved in legal complications, and her husband fighting for his life – delirious for many days.

Carrie Kipling to C. E. Norton
February 22, 1899

Rud is rather ill. I trust the papers will not exaggerate it. ... His simple life and decent habits, they say, will count in his favour, but his lifelong tendency to fever makes him rather a difficult patient. I have arranged to give the papers a daily bulletin which is all I know.

All who were near her commented on the iron resolution with which she took charge of everything. In addition to the day- and night-nurses who attended Rudyard, she engaged a third nurse for Elsie who showed signs of following her sister into pneumonia. But Elsie recovered quickly, and it was almost a relief to add to this news that Baby John had *only* a slight bronchitis. Two doctors, Dunham and Janeway, were giving almost their whole time to Rudyard while Conland took over the case of little Josephine. Business affairs fell to Frank Doubleday, a devoted friend, who neglected his own profession to become secretary and manager to Carrie. After the twenty-first, when the news leaked out, there were always fifteen or twenty reporters in the hotel lobbies clamouring for news. Frank took them in hand, protecting Carrie from interference and feeding them every few hours, with news-bulletins which were flashed all over the world. He had a vast correspondence to deal with – inquiries, congratulations, and – at last – condolences.

Now began a demonstration of affection and sympathy for Kipling such as no other writer, perhaps, has ever experienced. It was headline news in all the papers of the world that the inflammation had spread from Rudyard's right lung to the left, and from the lower to the upper lobes. On Friday, the twenty-fourth, the doctors admitted that his condition was 'serious'. On Saturday respiration was 'alarmingly difficult', and the bulletin admitted the 'greatest apprehension for the outcome' of his illness. Throughout the weekend Rudyard was delirious, with his mind wandering on frustrated journeys in search of R. L. Stevenson, or endless voyages with Conland in a wooden ship, or riding with armies across the steppes of Central Asia, or he was protesting against his treatment by New York crowds when put on trial with no bail allowed. On Monday, the twenty-seventh, the doctors could say no more than that they were 'not without hope'. The crisis came next day. After midnight on the twenty-eighth his temperature fell and he lapsed into a natural sleep for a few hours; on Wednesday the doctors admitted improvement; and by Saturday 4 March he was out of danger though desperately weak.

The faithful Frank Doubleday sent the good news to Rudyard's relatives in England, and then indeed the letters and telegrams poured in like a flood – too soon. While the progress of little Josephine's illness followed the pattern of her father's, a day or two behind him, she had not his reserve of strength. Always hampered in health by a delicate digestion, she was unable during this time of weakness to retain nourishment. They dared not tell her father that something like dysentery had set in, and as he passed out of the shadow, she passed into it. Carrie left Rudyard's bedside for one day to visit her child at the De Forests' house.

Sunday, March 5th.

I saw Josephine 3 times today – morning, afternoon, and at 10 p.m. for the last time. She was conscious for a moment and sent her love to 'Daddy and all'.

Monday, March 6th.

Josephine left us at 6.30 this morning.

The doctors forbade that Rudyard in his weakness should be told of this calamity, but it could not be long withheld. An appeal was made to the reporters not to publicize the child's death and, though it could not be kept out of the daily papers, it had little news-value beside the state of health of the world's most popular author. When Carrie went from the funeral straight to his bedside, remembering in time that she was dressed in black, she snatched up a scarlet shawl as she entered the room and threw it round her shoulders so that he would ask no question. How and when she broke the news to him was their own secret. Months passed before he recovered from his illness; from the shock of his daughter's death he never recovered; nor did Carrie. Reserved and self-contained as their family life had always been, it now became more exclusive.

Nevertheless the whole world had offered its sympathy, with demonstrations of a kind which, as a rule, only royalty knows. While Rudyard lay in delirium, unconscious of the tribute paid to him, hushed crowds gathered outside the Hotel Grenoble blocking the traffic in Seventh Avenue. Prayers were offered in the New York churches, and people were seen kneeling in prayer before the hotel door. It happened that no political crisis, no massacre or earthquake occurred in those days to divert the world's attention from the door behind which a poet lay at the point of death, no other news of moment except the illness of Pope Leo XIII. The *Pall Mall Gazette* splashed the two news-items across its posters, 'KIPLING AND POPE'.

Among the hundreds of letters and telegrams that came when he was reported past his crisis, the most valued were from the family, and on these we need not linger. To posterity interest lies in the uncounted messages from casual acquaintances and unknown admirers: from George Meredith and John Ruskin, from G. F. Watts and Holman Hunt, from Henry Irving and Beerbohm Tree, from Lord Dufferin and Lord Curzon, from Theodore Roosevelt and John Hay, from Conan Doyle and Rider Haggard, from Mark Twain and Marie Corelli, from Cecil Rhodes and the Editor of *The Times* and the German Kaiser.

Rudyard would have been more pleased, perhaps, by the letters from lesser folk: from Kay Robinson, from Stanley de Brath with whom he had once tramped the Himalaya Road, from the crew of H.M.S. *Pelorus*, and from the Sergeants of the Suffolk Regiment, from the Soldiers' Institute at Allahabad, from the Council of his old school at Westward Ho!, or from the boys of St Edmund's, Canterbury – there were dozens of such messages – but they came when he was too ill to see them, and were not shown him until his bereavement had made them a mockery. His nearer friends had hastened to write condolences displacing their congratulations. What could they say?

Henry James was more than usually emotional and illegible:

Henry James to Rudyard Kipling

My dear Daemonic Indestructible Youth,

You are a good one, and your wife is, if possible, a better, and your two doctors between them are the best ones of all. ... You have been magnificent and have made us all live with our hearts in our mouth. I fold you both in my arms. You have visited the mountains of the moon and come back on a tense wire, in the cold light of that satellite and with every operaglass on earth fixed on you – with no balancing-pole but your own inimitable genius. What you must have got out of it! ...

Believe me, my dear boy, your very constant and jubilant old friend.

Henry James to Carrie Kipling

March 8, 1899

I wrote last night to Rudyard – but my letter will have had the effect of a jubilation so mistimed that I now wish I could recall it. . . . Dear little delightful vanished Josephine, dear little surrendered, sacrificed soul! Forgive this incoherent expression – I am only thinking of her being worsted in the battle, and of the so happy form in which I saw her last winter at Rottingdean. But how can I even seem to allude to what you feel. . . . I believe in you [both] up to the hilt.

The consolations of religion could give little help to this free-thinking family. Even the 'Pater', writing very tenderly, could not find it in his heart to say more than: 'I can't help fancying all this weight of love may count for some thing', but one minister of religion ventured to write to Carrie as a pastor:

The Rev. C. O. Day to Carrie Kipling

Brattleboro, March 8, 1899

I know too well the profound faith of Mr Kipling and his unfaltering courage, to doubt as to his power to accept the bereavement. He will feel that a new world is his by possession; one of his own has claimed it for him and flies his flag there. A new wonder will arise in his soul, and new sweetness and depth in his poetry. He will reveal some new, clear, indubitable vision upon which many mourners for children will look and be comforted.

It was a long and dreary convalescence, cheered only by many signs of friendship. At Easter Rudyard was able to authorize a reply to the world-wide expression of sympathy in an open letter which was issued by Reuter's to unnumbered newspapers.

Will you allow me through your columns to attempt some acknowledgment of the wonderful sympathy, affection, and kindness shown towards me in my recent illness, as well as of the unfailing courtesy that controlled its expression? I am not strong enough to answer letters in detail, so must take this means of thanking, as humbly as sincerely, the countless people of goodwill throughout the world, who have put me under a debt I can never hope to repay.[5]

The Kiplings then withdrew from the public notice for many months, so far, that is to say, as the tiresome lawsuit with Putnam's permitted. A. P. Watt came over from London, as did Lockwood Kipling, to confer with lawyers and to give what comfort they could to Rudyard, who was still under the care of nurses by night and day. On 17 April Frank Doubleday carried him off to a private hotel at Lakewood, 'standing the journey better than we hoped'. The Hotel Grenoble, which had endured much, took the opportunity to give the rest of the family notice, since two children with the whooping-cough had exhausted their patience. By 6 May Dr Conland was able to report that Rudyard's lung was healed, but ordered him six months' rest; he also categorically forbade Rudyard to spend any more winters in England. When in June the whole family were fit to return home, their rendezvous was Frank's house, at Cold Springs, and on their last evening Rudyard was even well enough to attend a farewell dinner in a New York restaurant with Conland, Sam McClure, De Forest, Frank, and the 'Pater'. Rudyard was 'a little more cheerful', wrote the 'Pater' to Mrs Norton. 'I find his dim time brighter than the best of many men I know.'

With that the Kiplings said their last farewells to the United States. 'Never was such kindness shown,' wrote Carrie, and on Frank Doubleday's part it was not yet over. He accompanied them across the Atlantic with his wife, and did not return to his own affairs until he had seen them settled at Rottingdean, still protecting Rudyard from the hated glare of publicity. 'Many friends came to see us off,' wrote Carrie, 'but reporters do not get a look at him.' It was different on the ship where 'folks with no manners' were a great trouble to her, snapshotting with the hand-cameras which were coming into use. By 24 June they were back at 'The Elms', listlessly taking up the threads of life.

An admirer, Andrew Carnegie the steel magnate, had expressed his sympathy to Rudyard by offering him the use of a small house in the Highlands, and in accepting his invitation Carrie prudently improved the occasion by touching Carnegie for a subscription towards the boys' club at Rottingdean.[6]

In Scotland Rudyard regained physical well-being and slowly turned again to his work. At Creich he wrote the dedicatory verses to *Stalky & Co.*: 'Let us now praise famous men. . . .'

> Wherefore praise we famous men
> From whose bays we borrow —
> They that put aside To-day —
> All the joys of their To-day —
> And with toil of their To-day
> Bought for us To-morrow!

The routine of life, when the Kiplings returned to Rottingdean, was changed in the one important respect that there was now a private secretary, Sara Anderson, who became the mainstay of the household. Her story, which she never told, would have been worth reading, for she had first been secretary to John Ruskin, then to Lady Ritchie, and then had worked for Burne-Jones; the model of discretion, she destroyed all her papers, saving nothing for posterity.

However weakened, however saddened, Rudyard did not slacken in his interests. That autumn, after Frank Doubleday had gone, Phil Burne-Jones was working at the portrait now in the National Portrait Gallery and, as soon as he had done with Rudyard, he began the portrait of Carrie which now hangs at 'Bateman's'. Rudyard was delighted with his picture and wrote to Norton: 'Phil's portrait of me is a Regular Stunner and shows specially well in the reproduction. I resent the sleek baldness of my head, but the intellectual air and the tummy are beyond dispute.' When not engaged on the portrait Phil and Rudyard amused themselves with a hand printing-press which they had installed at 'The Elms', and it was at this time, too, that Rudyard made his first experiments with a hired motor-car, at a very early date in motoring history.

The publication of *Stalky & Co.* on 6 October 1899 brought Rudyard back into the headlines six months after the crisis of his illness. Though all the morning papers gave it space, the reception was mixed, and perhaps no other Kipling book has been more variously estimated. There was no doubt that schoolboys swallowed it with gusto, and continued to do so for generations, while their elders often found it distasteful, even nauseating. 'A more odious picture of school life can seldom have been drawn,' wrote Somerset Maugham. But Aunt Georgie liked it, and Cousin Florence liked it, and 'Uncle Crom' Price, the hero of the tale, liked it, and with them were some hundreds of thousands of other adults with strong digestions.

It added much to the Kipling cult because, alone among his works of fiction, it was plainly founded upon fact. Since the characters, if not the events, were real, the book led to an immediate investigation for origins. The souvenir-hunters located 'Uncle Crom', in retirement; 'Old Boys' of the College proudly identified themselves with this or that character in the book; interviewers called upon Sergeant-major Schofield and found him a little pained at the figure he was made to cut as 'Foxy'; someone found out that 'Stalky' was Captain Dunsterville of the Sikhs, serving at that very time in the expedition to Pekin. 'M'Turk' came to light as Beresford, and gave an interview about 'Stalky' to a Cambridge newspaper, with a consequence that was no fault of Beresford: the editor was sued for damages, soon after, on a charge of fabricating news-items, and one question asked in court was whether the 'Stalky' stories were fact

or fiction. The Judge ruled them fiction, whereupon that
part of the charge collapsed, except in the sense that it
stimulated publicity.[7]

Kipling had now reached the height of his fame, with the
inevitable consequences that his daily letter-bag was loaded
down, and his path beset by sightseers. Social invitations,
most of which he declined, came showering in when he was
in England. There was a day in the Season of 1900 when
Carrie refused two dinner-invitations for the same evening,
from Mrs Humphry Ward and the Duchess of Sutherland.
No one could fly higher than that in the literary and
fashionable worlds. Much more tiresome were the trippers
from Brighton who had now discovered the colony of celebrities at Rottingdean. There were times when Carrie had to
force her way through crowds of gaping tourists before she
could get at her own garden-gate. Rottingdean, so full of
happy memories of the three carefree years before the
calamitous visit to New York, had lost its charm.

From The Settler (1903)

Here, where my fresh-turned furrows run,
    And the deep soil glistens red,
I will repair the wrong that was done
    To the living and the dead.
Here, where the senseless bullet fell,
    And the barren shrapnel burst,
I will plant a tree, I will dig a well,
    Against the heat and the thirst.

Here, in a large and a sunlit land,
    Where no wrong bites to the bone,
I will lay my hand in my neighbour's hand,
    And together we will atone
For the set folly and the red breach
    And the black waste of it all;
Giving and taking counsel each
    Over the cattle-kraal.

             .   .   .   .

Earth, where we rode to slay or be slain,
    Our love shall redeem unto life.
We will gather and lead to her lips again
    The waters of ancient strife,
From the far and the fiercely guarded streams
    And the pools where we lay in wait,
Till the corn cover our evil dreams
    And the young corn our hate.

             .   .   .   .

Here, in the waves and the troughs of the plains,
    Where the healing stillness lies,
And the vast, benignant sky restrains
    And the long days make wise –
Bless to our use the rain and the sun
    And the blind seed in its bed,
That we may repair the wrong that was done
    To the living and the dead!

[13]

The South African War
(1899–1902)

THE year 1899, which had been so disastrous for the Kiplings, ended gloomily. It was rather a doleful Christmas, with influenza running through the family, bad news from Tisbury of Trix's health, annoyance from New York at the state of the Putnam lawsuit. Rudyard was ill again and, as soon as legal business allowed it, he prepared to leave the country. All he could find to say as a closing note to his wife's diary for the year was: 'I owe my life to Carrie'.

During his long illness the situation had taken a turn for the worse in South Africa, and before the year's end the expected war had broken out. Actually, it was Kruger who on 9 October sent an ultimatum to Lord Salisbury demanding that the Queen should ship no more troops to her African Dominions. This was followed on 11 October by the British declaration of war and the despatch of an Army Corps of 47,000 men to the Cape, under command of Sir Redvers Buller. Meanwhile the Boers made a brisk offensive against the supposedly overbearing Empire, and on every front the British garrisons were thrown on their guard. Mafeking in the far north, and Kimberley on the western frontier, were invested, and the largest concentration of British troops was soon besieged at Ladysmith in the northern salient angle of Natal. This was the decisive point of the first campaign and it was towards Ladysmith that General Buller directed the concentration of his Army Corps from England.

The first counter-moves were made by the British early in December with conspicuous lack of success. Every new war produces its own surprises, and no army before 1899 had marched into the face of well-aimed fire from magazine rifles using smokeless powder; no one could foresee its effect. Boer tactics proved to be as effective as Boer strategy was futile and in one week three British armies were soundly defeated at three widely separated points on the vast front, the most alarming being General Buller's defeat at Colenso. These were staggering blows, far more violent than the battle of Majuba twenty years before, which had been followed by a British withdrawal; but times had changed and there was now no suggestion of submission. The Army Reserve was called out in England and Lord Roberts, England's greatest soldier, was despatched to the Cape as Commander-in-Chief.

Was Kruger fighting for liberty? Or for domination? In his own Transvaal, his own *burghers* were a minority of the white population, while the *uitlanders*, mostly of British origin, created three-quarters of the State's wealth, paid three-quarters of the taxes, and were allowed no more political rights than the Kaffir labourers whose interest no politician of those days put forward. Milner claimed for the *uitlanders*, in form, only the same political rights as Afrikaners enjoyed in British Natal. In principle, and he made no secret of it, he took a longer view. Emancipation for *uitlanders* meant progressive government, efficient administration, the federation of all South Africa under the British flag. This was a political objective, and it was fair to regard the struggle between Milner and Kruger as a combat for control of all South Africa.

There was another factor in the sum, a factor that Milner and Rhodes each interpreted in his own way; it was the world-wide up-surging of the generation for whom Kipling in the previous decade had found a voice. The bridge-builders, the engineers, the road-makers, the miners, the prospectors, the ranchers – the men of the new age were led by a new star:

The gull shall whistle in his wake, the blind wave break in fire.
He shall fulfil God's utmost will, unknowing his desire.

And he shall see old planets change and alien stars arise,
And give the gale his seaworn sail in shadow of new skies.
Strong lust of gear shall drive him forth and hunger arm his hand,
To win his food from the desert rude, his pittance from the
    sand.
His neighbours' smoke shall vex his eyes, their voices break his
    rest.
He shall go forth till south is north, sullen and dispossessed.
He shall desire loneliness and his desire shall bring,
Hard on his heels, a thousand wheels, a People and a King.
He shall come back on his own track, and by his scarce-cooled
    camp
There shall he meet the roaring street, the derrick and the
    stamp:
There he shall blaze a nation's ways with hatchet and with
    brand,
Till on his last-won wilderness an Empire's outposts stand! [1]

'Strong lust of gear shall drive him forth and hunger arm his hand' – indeed the motive force that peopled all the temperate regions of the world with emigrants from Great Britain and Ireland was set to work by economic pressures, but not by economic pressures simply. Rhodes was the greatest of money-spinners but love of money was a minor element, if an element at all, in his make-up. With great energy and longer views he typified his generation:

We were dreamers, dreaming greatly, in the man-stifled town;
We yearned beyond the sky-line where the strange roads go
    down.

When the Americans and the British embarked upon those two campaigns, the Cuban War and the Boer War, which to the observer today seem so curiously out of key, they fought with an enthusiasm that is not easily explained away by economic catch-words. The petty corrupt tyrannies of the Spaniards in Cuba and of the Boers in the Transvaal were felt by enlightened men like Roosevelt and Milner to be unworthy obstacles in the way of progress. By

sweeping such cobwebby anachronisms away, they conceived themselves to be releasing the life-giving processes
that would make the twentieth century and, in America as
in Britain, the people supported them. With a cry of dismay, in both countries, the intellectuals of the left wing
denounced this technocratic enthusiasm, these aggressive
wars against weaker nations, fought, as they supposed, for
the benefit of industrialists and exploiters. The Mackails at
London and the Nortons at Harvard alike deplored the woe-
ful events that their friend Rudyard celebrated with such
gusto, but their voices were lost in the outcry of the
imperialists.

The presidential election which gave McKinley his second
term, and the British General Election which retained Lord
Salisbury in office – a vote of confidence for Joseph Chamberlain – demonstrated that the intellectuals were out of
touch with public opinion in 1900. A far more significant
symptom of real popular support for the two wars was that,
in both countries, great numbers of volunteers from all
classes of society offered themselves to serve overseas in
campaigns that would certainly be painful and profitless for
the fighting troops. Nothing like that had ever happened in
either England or America before.

In his letter to C. E. Norton during the Venezuela crisis
Kipling had taken some small comfort from the observation
that a foreign war would serve to draw Britain and her
colonies closer together. An outsider might have supposed
that the undisciplined, democratic colonials would resent
the British pressure on the two small states in South Africa,
but Kipling was right. The two most advanced social democ-
racies in the world, the colonies of New Zealand and
Queensland, were the first to send 'contingents' of volunteers to fight for the Empire against the Transvaal. Australian sheep-farmers and gold-diggers certainly had no interest in the finances of Rhodes's Chartered Company. They
fought for the *uitlanders*, who were 'white men' deprived of
political rights by Kruger's oligarchy, and 'white men' whose

manifest destiny was to unite South Africa as a free and progressive country.

In September 1899, just before the breaking-point, Rudyard was at work upon one of those pronouncements in verse which the public now expected from him, on national occasions. It was published in *The Times*, on the twenty-ninth, under the title of 'The Old Issue'. To a modern reader, steeped in the propaganda of the anti-imperialists, this poem has become almost unintelligible. A war against Kruger, Rudyard suggested, was a war for liberty, which should rally the English to their old traditions of resistance against tyranny.

> Cruel in the shadow, crafty in the sun,
> Far beyond his borders shall his teachings run.
>
> Sloven, sullen, savage, secret, uncontrolled,
> Laying on a new land evil of the old –
>
> Long-forgotten bondage, dwarfing heart and brain –
> All our fathers died to loose he shall bind again.

A few days later the storm broke and Rudyard immediately set himself to two tasks of war work: one was to form a volunteer company in the village at Rottingdean; the other was to raise money for the Soldiers' Families' Fund.

Henry James came over from Rye to lunch with the Kiplings at Rottingdean on 17 October, and Carrie noticed in her diary – 'nice man, much beloved'. He must have been astonished at the vitality of his 'indestructible', 'daemonic' friend, because Rudyard, that day, was hard at work on the most robust, full-blooded, verses he ever wrote.* These verses, Rudyard admitted, 'had some elements of direct appeal but lacked poetry'. He called them 'The Absent-minded Beggar' and published them in the *Daily Mail* on 31 October.

Sir Arthur Sullivan wedded the words to a tune guaranteed to pull teeth out of barrel-organs. Anybody could do what they chose with the result, recite, sing, intone or reprint, etc., on

*He was also that week writing 'The Elephant's Child'.

condition that they turned in all fees and profits to the main account – 'The Absent-minded Beggar Fund' which closed at about a quarter of a million [pounds sterling]. Some of this [he wrote modestly] was spent on tobacco.[2]

Having thus served their purpose, these verses were allowed to drop from sight, and for many years were not admitted by the author into a 'collected' volume. Their pace and force justify their survival. It may be noted that they sound no aggressive or imperialistic note, contain no swagger or defiance, but appeal to those who stay at home to do something better than 'killing Kruger with your mouth'.

A hundred years earlier the original 'Tommy Atkins' had marched to Brighton Camp, when Napoleon's Grand Army lay at Boulogne, singing to a delicate old air the ballad of 'The Girl I Left behind Me'. Some soldiers even then were absent-minded beggars (the phrase is a barrack-room euphemism), and hence the theme of the new song, written to a tune that was anything but delicate.

There are girls he married secret, asking no permission to,
    For he knew he wouldn't get it if he did.
There is gas and coals and vittles, and the house-rent falling due,
    And it's more than rather likely there's a kid.
There are girls he walked with casual. They'll be sorry now he's gone,
    For an absent-minded beggar they will find him,

But it ain't the time for sermons with the winter coming on.
    We must help the girl that Tommy's left behind him!
Cook's son – Duke's son – son of a belted Earl –
    Son of a Lambeth publican – it's all the same to-day!
Each of 'em doing his country's work
    (and who's to look after the girl?)
Pass the hat for your credit's sake,
              and pay – pay – pay!

The public paid; and wondered what next Rudyard Kipling would produce. 'The Vampire', 'Recessional', 'The White Man's Burden', and 'The Absent-minded Beggar' made a

series that dumbfounded the critics. The politicians, however, took their cue. On 14 December Lord Salisbury sent his
private secretary to Rottingdean to ask whether Rudyard
would accept a knighthood. Carrie noted in her diary that
he declined, 'feeling he can do his work better without it.
We are much pleased to be offered it however.'

Harmsworth of the *Daily Mail* (afterwards Lord North-
cliffe) struck up an acquaintance with the Kiplings over 'The
Absent-minded Beggar'. Naturally he wanted to give Kipling's name the utmost publicity in his campaign to raise
funds, but even in this cause Kipling shrank from it. 'I
should prefer my name being kept out,' he wrote. 'The
verses are fetching money in a wonderful way – thanks to
your management – but don't make so much of their
author.'³

On 20 January 1900 the Kiplings left England for South
Africa, and on 5 February reached Cape Town to learn
that the British forces in Natal had suffered another defeat,
at Spion Kop.

The Mount Nelson Hotel, a huge red-brick caravanserai
on the slope of Table Mountain, was crammed with war-
reporters, sightseers, adventurers, contractors, officers' wives,
and hordes of the non-combatants who crowd upon the
heels of an army. All the world passed through it on the
way to the Front; and there Rudyard met a group of journalists who were to become his friends: young Mr L. S.
Amery who had represented *The Times* at Kruger's capital,
Perceval Landon, correspondent for *The Times* with
Roberts's army, Bennet Burleigh of the *Daily Telegraph*,
H. T. Gwynne, of Reuter's, and Julian Ralph, an American
who was in Africa for the London *Daily Mail*. It was one
of Lord Roberts's distinctions that he was perhaps the first
general to appreciate the importance of the press in warfare and to take the journalists into his confidence. He sent
for Rudyard and spent with him his last evening before
leaving to take command of the army in the field.

During the next fortnight Rudyard occupied his time visiting the military hospitals, where he was doubly welcome, first as the soldiers' poet who could occasionally be persuaded to recite his ballads at a smoking-concert, secondly as the purveyor of all the comforts provided by the Absentminded Beggar Fund. He went about loaded with the plug tobacco that the soldiers loved, and this was not all that he had to give away. As must occur at the beginning of a war, when crowds of wounded suddenly appear at the Base, shortages of all kinds were revealed in the improvised hospitals.

My note-of-hand [he said] was good for as much as I cared to take about with me. The rest followed. My telegrams were given priority by sweating R.T. sergeants from all sorts of congested depots. My seat in the train was kept for me* by British Bayonets in their shirt-sleeves. My small baggage was fought for and servilely carried by Colonial details, who are not normally meek, and I was *persona gratissima* at certain Wynberg Hospitals where the nurses found I was good for pyjamas.[4]

The first good news, after Roberts had taken hold of the campaign, reached Cape Town on 16 February. The siege of Kimberley was raised, which meant the release of Cecil Rhodes, who was in the besieged town. Rudyard was one of the first to greet him, and together they set off to visit Rhodes's estates in the Western Province. When pent up in Kimberley, Rhodes had pondered over many new constructive plans, great and small, among them his plan for building a house on the 'Groote Schuur' estate which he could put at the disposal of artists or men of letters. In the first instance he would offer it to the Kiplings for as long as they cared to stay. Carrie took up this scheme with enthusiasm; on 7 March she went with Herbert Baker, the young architect to whom Rhodes gave his patronage, to select a site for the house, to be built in the Dutch Colonial style which Baker was reviving and developing. He too became a lifelong friend of the Kiplings.

Meanwhile, at the Front, Roberts followed up this success

at Kimberley by striking eastwards towards Bloemfontein and, on the day after relieving Kimberley, his leading troops engaged General Cronje, the most formidable of the Boer leaders, in the long hard-fought action of Paardeberg, the decisive battle of the war – or so it seemed. Before Cronje could be forced to surrender (27 February 1900) more than 1,500 British soldiers had been killed or wounded in front of his entrenchments, and a stream of wounded was passing down the railway line to Cape Town. In the middle of the battle Rudyard went up with an ambulance train to the rail-head at Modder River, the scene of heavy fighting a few weeks earlier, and returned with a train-load of wounded, his first experience of the realities of war. On 24 February, while on the train, he wrote a home-letter to the dictation of a wounded soldier who had lost his right arm at Paardeberg. This letter was sold for war charities, was reproduced in facsimile and was widely advertised, a form of publicity that did not please Rudyard and that he did not allow to recur.

On 12 March Lord Roberts entered Bloemfontein, the capital of the Orange Free State, and a pause was necessary before he could invade the Transvaal. During a halt of six weeks his army was ravaged by typhoid and enteric fevers, against which, in those days, there was no adequate protection.

On the day after his entry, among a hundred administrative duties, Roberts found time to arrange for the establishment of an army newspaper, perhaps the first of its species in military history. It was set on foot by his Press Censor, who commandeered the plant of a little local sheet, *The Friend* of Bloemfontein, sent for four war correspondents, and told them to begin. They were Julian Ralph, Perceval Landon, H. A. Gwynne, and F. W. Buxton (of the Johannesburg *Star*). Landon had the foresight to telegraph to Kipling for a contribution, and got by return some verses about the heroism of the Irish troops, in time for publication on St Patrick's Day. That was not all, for on the same day,

17 March, Lord Roberts wired to Kipling, asking him to join the staff of *The Friend*.

Rudyard spent his last day before going up the line walking with Milner on the slopes of Table Mountain discussing policy at the Cape. On the twenty-first he joined his friends at Bloemfontein, and was thus described by Julian Ralph who was now thrown into daily intimate contact with him:

a man of such broad build and short neck that you do not realise him to be of the average stature, wearing a broad-brimmed, flat brown hat of Boer pattern, and below that a brown short coat and very full trousers to match; a vigorous figure, quick in movement as a panther, quicker still in speech; a swinging and rolling figure with head up and hat well back, out of the way of his sight which is ever thrown upward as if he searched the sky while he walked. His face is quite a match for his body, being round and broad as well as wide-eyed and alert. His eyes are its most notable features, for they are very large and open, and each one is arched by the bushiest black eyebrows. They are habitually reflective and sober eyes, but, like a flash, they kindle with fun, and can equally quickly turn dull and stony when good occasion arises.

Thriving in the dry warm air, Rudyard renewed his youth; he flung himself into the work of the office, correcting proofs, sub-editing, and writing 'copy' with the others. 'Never again,' he said, 'will there be such a paper. Never again such a staff. Never such fine larks.'

For a fortnight he played the sub-editor with delight and energy among congenial comrades. So pleasant was their comradeship that Rudyard founded a dining-club, the 'Friendlies', with a badge and a masonic ritual which they maintained for some years, until Julian Ralph's early death. Their status was demi-official, since Lord Roberts used *The Friend* as a propaganda sheet in which to make announcements to the people of the conquered Republic. The first page was taken up with official notices; the inner pages contained campaigning news, local gossip, a few cables from overseas, and a great deal of light reading for the troops. Rudyard contributed a number of satirical pieces – 'Kopje-Book Maxims', 'Fables for the Staff', and so on, and two poems which he thought worth a place in his collected works: 'A Song of the White Men' – a still stronger version of 'The White Man's Burden' – and the generous tribute written on the death of General Joubert, the enemy's Commander-in-Chief. His hardest work was reading and editing the numerous contributions offered by soldiers, all of which he examined with care and many of which he printed. One of his best contributors was A. B. Paterson of the *Sydney Herald*, the Australian ballad-writer, whose verses, written in Kipling's own earlier manner, were as popular as Kipling's. But Rudyard had moved into a new phase and his mind was turned to something stronger than satirical light verse.

He had already made up his mind to return to England and to throw himself into the support of Milner's policy, at home. He was held in Bloemfontein a few days longer, by the duty of nursing one of his friends who had gone down with the typhoid that raged through the army. It was Julian Ralph's son and 'until we could get him into hospital,' wrote Ralph, 'Mr Kipling nursed him with consummate skill and the gentleness of a woman.' [5] But, in the last week, Rudyard allowed himself a day's holiday, to watch a battle.

Just as in Afghanistan twenty years earlier Lord Roberts attempted to pacify the country by detaching columns of troops to 'show the flag' in outlying districts. A small engagement ensued, the action of Karee Siding, which cost the British 180 casualties. Rudyard had long been known as the soldiers' poet, the author of realistic battle-pieces, and it would have surprised many of his readers to know that this was the first time he had seen troops under fire.

Karee Siding was an inconclusive, unsatisfactory affair like many in the South African War. The general's intention was to engage the Boers frontally with a holding attack by the infantry, while mounted troops worked round both flanks to cut off their retreat. The flogged-out, ill-fed cavalry could not or would not move fast enough, and when the leading infantry – they were the East Lancashires, Mulvaney's 'Ould Regiment' – charged with fixed bayonets, they found the enemy positions abandoned and empty. The Boers had slipped away on their ponies before the trap could close behind them.

Rudyard set off with Bennet Burleigh of the *Daily Telegraph*,[6] in a Cape cart loaded with food and drink for the party from *The Friend*. Burleigh described for his paper how he and Kipling walked forward among the extended lines of riflemen, halting now and then for Kipling to distribute plugs of tobacco among the nearest soldiers. Rudyard told his own story of their approach characteristically:

The enormous pale landscape swallowed up seven thousand troops without a sign, along a front of seven miles. ... At last we came to a lone farm-house in a vale adorned with no less than five white flags. Beyond the ridge was a sputter of musketry and now and then the whoop of a field-piece. 'Here,' said my guide and guardian, 'we get out and walk.' ...

The farm-house (you will see in a little why I am so detailed) held two men and, I think, two women, who received us disinterestedly. We went on into a vacant world full of sunshine and distances, where now and again a single bullet sang to himself. What I most objected to was the sensation of being under aimed fire – being, as it were, required as a head. 'What are they doing this for?' I asked my friend. 'Because they think we are the Something Light Horse. They ought to be just under this slope.' I prayed that the particularly Something Light Horse would go elsewhere, which they presently did, for the aimed fire slackened and a wandering Colonial, bored to extinction, turned up with news from a far flank. 'No; nothing doing and no one to see.' Then more cracklings and a most cautious move forward to the lip of a large hollow where sheep were grazing. Some of them began to drop and kick. 'That's both sides trying sighting-shots,' said my companion. 'What range do you make it?' I asked. 'Eight hundred, at the nearest. That's close quarters nowadays. You'll never see anything closer than this. Modern rifles make it impossible. We're hung up till something cracks somewhere.' There was a decent lull for meals on both sides, interrupted now and again by sputters. Then one indubitable shell – ridiculously like a pip-squeak in that vastness but throwing up much dirt. ... Every twenty minutes or so, one judgmatic shell pitched on our slope. We waited, seeing nothing in the emptiness, and hearing only a faint murmur as of wind along gas-jets, running in and out of the unconcerned hills.

Then pom-poms opened. These were nasty little one-pounders, ten in a belt (which usually jammed about the sixth round). On soft ground they merely thudded. On rock-face the shell breaks up and yowls like a cat. My friend for the first time seemed interested. 'If these are their pom-poms, it's Pretoria for us,' was his diagnosis. I looked behind me – the whole length of South Africa down to Cape Town – and it seemed very far. I felt that I could have covered it in five minutes under fair conditions, but – *not* with those aimed shots up my back. The pom-poms opened again at a bare rock-reef that gave the shells full value. For about two minutes a file of racing ponies, their tails and their riders' heads well down, showed and vanished northward. 'Our pom-poms,' said the correspondent. ... Then to the left, almost under us, a small piece of hanging woodland filled and fumed with our shrapnel much as a man's moustache fills with cigarette-smoke. It was most impressive and lasted for quite twenty minutes. Then silence; then a movement of men and horses from our side up the slope, and the sangar our guns had been hammering spat steady fire at them. More Boer ponies on more skylines; a last flurry of pom-poms on the right and a little frieze of far-off meek-tailed ponies, already out of rifle range.

'*Maffeesh*,' said the correspondent, and fell to writing on his knee. 'We've shifted 'em.'

Leaving our infantry to follow men on pony-back towards the Equator, we returned to the farm-house.[7]

They jogged back to Bloemfontein happily with Rudyard composing ballads in the cart: 'he was making a humming over new verses, like Robert Burns,' wrote Bennet Burleigh.

The visit to the Boer farm had a sequel. Nine months later the producers of anti-British propaganda put out a story in French Switzerland which they ascribed to Rudyard himself. He was alleged to have taken part in the murder of a civilian at the farm and to have described it with gusto.[8] The continental press just then was flooded with lies about the British, and this tale was not more absurd than many others which were taken as true. It infuriated Rudyard, who commented with asperity that what the propagandist saw was the 'reflection of his own face as he spied at our back-windows'. It gave him a notion for his own powerful but vindictive tale, 'A Sahibs' War', a hint of what the British imperialists might have done if they had behaved as they were expected to.

Throughout the war Rudyard showed admiration and even tenderness for the fighting 'burghers' on the veldt, but bitter, unrelenting hatred for the fawning non-combatants who betrayed each side in turn, for the few colonials of British origin who favoured the republican cause, for the many Afrikaners in Cape Colony who claimed protection as British subjects while openly expressing their sympathy with the rebellion which they dared not join. The point of view was common among British regular soldiers, who could hardly fail to respect the military virtues of their enemies in the field; it was quite beyond the comprehension of the average Englishman at home.

Two days after the action at Karee Siding another British force was sharply defeated in a battle which was to alter the character of the war. Roberts had sent a column to the eastward to secure the pumping station which supplied Bloemfontein with water and, on the return march, two batteries of artillery marched into an ambush at Sanna's Post. A confused, irregular battle flared up around the water-works and left a general impression of heroism on the part of the junior officers, but of indecision and inactivity on the part of the higher command. The British lost six guns and five hundred men.

Early on the morning of 31 March fugitives from the

battle found their way back to Blomfontein with alarming stories.

In an interval of our editorial labours [wrote Rudyard] I went out of the town and presently met the 'solitary horseman' of the novels. He was a Conductor – Commissariat Sergeant – who reported that the 'flower of the British Army' had been ambushed and cut up at a place called 'Sanna's Post', and passed on obviously discomposed. I had imagined the flower of that Army to be busied behind me reading our paper; but, a short while after, I met an officer who, in the old Indian days, was nicknamed 'the Sardine'. He was calm, but rather fuzzy as to the outlines of his uniform, which was frayed and ripped by bullets. Yes, there had been trouble where he came from, but he was fuller for the moment of professional admiration. . . . 'Expert job they made of it.' . . . And with many compliments to the foe, he too passed on . . .

After he'd told his tale I said to him : 'What are we going to do about it?' He said : 'Oh, I don't know. Thank Heaven we have within the land five hundred as good as they.' [9]

To restore the immediate situation at the water-works was no very difficult task, whereas the moral effect of the defeat at Sanna's Post, a classic incident in the annals of guerrilla warfare, was lasting. In Bloemfontein the civilians expected the return of the Boers, and, while the water-works were out of British control, the typhoid cases in the hospitals multiplied day by day. But Rudyard could stay no longer; as soon as the panic subsided and the town was secure, he left for the south and was back in Cape Town on 3 April.

Carrie in Cape Town had been ill and anxious, heartened only by visits from an old friend, Mary Kingsley, who had just arrived from England. Like all the world, Rudyard had been captivated by the tale of her West African travels; he used to describe her as the bravest woman he ever knew, and his admiration was increased by her unselfish desire to be useful at the Base Camp of the army. 'Being human, she must have been afraid of something,' he said, 'but one never found out what it was.'[10] She offered herself for any employment, however uncongenial. Would she nurse Boer prisoners-of-war at Simonstown in a fever hospital? She would, and with enthusiasm. Before starting work she dined with the Kiplings – 'a delightful woman', wrote Carrie in her diary – and, when they returned to England, the first call Rudyard paid was on his 'old ladies' in West Kensington, at whose house he had first met Mary Kingsley. He reached London on 28 April, and six weeks later news came that she had died of fever at Simonstown.

The pleasant way of life at Rottingdean, with its round of visits from aunts and cousins, was resumed, not without some changes. Rudyard was now drawn deeply into local and national politics. He twice dined with Joseph Chamberlain at his club, and he released several articles and stories with a strong political flavour. 'The Sin of Witchcraft', a fierce attack on disloyal elements in Cape Colony, appeared in *The Times* in April, and in May he wrote 'A Burgher of the Free State', a story with angry comments on the facing-both-ways citizens of Bloemfontein. It was his custom to read his new work aloud to Aunt Georgie at Rottingdean until for the first time he found her an unsympathetic listener. The 'Burgher' was 'not received well'. On politics, aunt and nephew could not agree and the rift which divided the nation could be perceived even in this devoted family circle.

When Rudyard came back from Bloemfontein, Carrie noted in her diary that he 'feels he has joined up all his ideas with the others of many years ago'. He had seen young England at war and, though no one questioned the courage and endurance of the soldiers, no one could fail to see their lack of training, their physical unfitness, their slow reaction when initiative and intelligence were needed. On the last page of *Stalky & Co.*, published just before the outbreak of war, he had written rather flippantly:

India's full of Stalkies – Cheltenham and Haileybury and Marlborough chaps – that we don't know anything about, and the surprises will begin when there's really a big row on. Who will be surprised? The other chaps! The gentlemen who go to the front in first-class carriages. Just imagine Stalky let loose on the south side of Europe with a sufficiency of Sikhs and a reasonable prospect of loot. Consider it quietly.

There were no Sikhs and no loot worth taking at Sanna's Post or Karee Siding, but there was also a conspicuous lack of those qualities which 'Stalky' was supposed to possess. Were all the best of the British overseas, in Australia, or in the Indian Army which was not allowed to fight in the Boer War? Or was the public-school product less admirable than he had supposed?

Perhaps the English nation needed reorganizing even more than did the Empire, a task to which he applied himself and, in the first instance, locally as a citizen. He had built a drill-hall in the village, had formed a volunteer company, and a branch of the Navy League, and was chairman of all their managing committees. One of the lessons from South Africa seemed to be that half the art of war was accurate long-range rifle-shooting. All over England, rifle clubs sprang up; at Rottingdean, Rudyard spent many hours on the range, many evenings at committee meetings in the village.

Meanwhile the summer of 1900 saw the completion of his last word on India, the story called *Kim*, at which he had been working intermittently for more than seven years. It called for many discussions with the 'Pater' at Tisbury, and even for reference to the old manuscript of *Mother Maturin* which he had started at Lahore in 1885. There came a day in August 1900 when the first draft was pronounced finished, after 'great conferences' with the 'Pater' and Sallie Norton. Even then there was much work to be done over the illustrations, and on one of his visits to Tisbury Rudyard spoke at an election meeting, on behalf of Arthur Morrison, the Conservative candidate.

Rudyard Kipling to Dr James Conland

July 24, 1900

Dear old man,

I haven't had a word out of you for goodness only knows how long – and except a little news now and again from Mrs Balestier you might just as well be in another planet.

As you know we went down to South Africa (Cape Town) for the winter and there happened to be a bit of a war on, and I had the time of my life. Carrie and the children stayed at Cape Town and I sort of drifted up country looking at hospitals and wounded men and guns and generals and wondering as I have never wondered before at the huge size of the country, but it was all deeply interesting – specially when I met the people who had been through the Siege of Kimberley. You could always tell 'em by the way they looked round for a place to hide in whenever they heard the *whizz-boom* of a Cape Town trolley car. It reminded 'em of the noise of an approaching shell. I was mean enough to laugh at 'em first – but I don't do so any more since I got under shell-fire myself and heard the cussed things booming over the small of my back.

War is a rummy job – it's a cross between poker and Sunday-school. Sometimes poker comes out on top and sometimes Sunday-school – but most often poker. The Boers hit us just as hard and just as often as they knew how; and we advanced against 'em as if they were street-rioters that we didn't want to hurt. They spied on us at their leisure, and when they wanted a rest they handed up any old gun and said they'd be loyal subjects. Then they went to their homes and rested for a week or two; and then they went on the warpath again with a new coat and a full stomach.

Then I've been down fishing with the Father and looking at old houses in Wiltshire but my *real* work this summer has been connected with the new rifle-range. I think I told you about it. We've started a rifle-club in the village of some 50 members and at last after months of waiting, we've got a 1,000 yards range among the downs; not ten minutes walk from the village. Now we are putting up a tin drill-shed where they can drill and practise Morris-tube shooting in the winter. An American workman would have run it up in a week. I've had to wait five – for non-delivery of materials and their slack laziness. The contractor who supplies the ironwork invited me to look around his forge the other day. Says I: 'Yes it would be all right if we lived in Queen Elizabeth's time. It's only three hundred years out of date – all your machinery.' Somehow or other he wasn't one little bit pleased.[11]

The Kiplings arrived in South Africa again on Christmas Day 1900. Rudyard spent the voyage working at a long story which was to give the keynote for his next book. It was to be called 'The Army of a Dream', a vision of England trained and prepared for war by freely offered service. It was a dream, from which he rudely awakened his readers on the last page by reminding them that the men who might have made it a reality had thrown away their lives in such holocausts as the ambush at Sanna's Post.

Confidence and readiness were not the keynotes of the situation in South Africa. Far from being finished, the war was breaking out anew. Lord Roberts had wiped the memory of early defeats off the slate, and had solved the gigantic problems of supply and transport which were the real obstacles to the conquest of the two republics. At political warfare he had failed, since he never realized the strength of the resistance movement which sprang up wherever the main Boer armies were defeated and dispersed. It was with the agreement of the Boer Generals that he collected women and children from the disaffected districts into concentration camps – an ill-omened name. Since the armies had not learned to master the epidemic of camp-fevers, what could be expected of the undisciplined civilians in the camps? They died in thousands, the true tragedy of the Boer War, which has never been forgotten in South Africa, though it is often forgotten that at the Peace Conference the Boer Generals thanked the British for organizing the camps.

Roberts had no sooner gone home than the Boer leaders had opened their new guerrilla campaign, which meant that his successor Kitchener had to fight a new war and to raise a new army of mounted infantry at the same time. When

Rudyard called on Milner, a few days after his arrival, it was to hear a tale of woe.

During this visit Rudyard did not again go up-country. On their arrival at the Docks, Rhodes sent a carriage to meet them with a message that their new cottage was ready and furnished. It was a low white house surrounded by a shady *stoep* and built in a modification of the Dutch Colonial style, standing low on the mountain-slope, and separated from Rhodes's 'Groote Schuur' only by woods and gardens. The 'Woolsack' * was Carrie's ideal house, her 'dear Woolsack' which, every year from 1901 to 1908, she occupied with joy and left with regret.

There Rudyard worked in peace, avoiding the English winters, and there Elsie and John spent their doubled summers within reach of the snow-white beaches of Muizenberg. It gave the Kiplings the social setting they required, at once private and yet frequented by the friends they wished to see. In 1901 almost daily visits were exchanged with Rhodes, who kept open house for all who had work to do in making South Africa. Rudyard also met Baden-Powell, now commanding a unit at the Cape, Dr Jameson, Gwynne of Reuter's, and many officers from Australia and New Zealand.

Rudyard Kipling to Dr J. Conland

20 Feb. 1901

We came out here, as usual, to avoid the English winter and have settled down in a Dutch-model house in a garden of figs and loquats and grapes *and* oranges.

Meantime, the war goes on – over a front of something like two thousand miles and a depth of a thousand roughly. The Boers are doing it very well. They keep in small parties looting and riding away and except where the carelessness of our infantry gives them a chance they take care not to attack. They can't take prisoners; they haven't any bases and they are very

---

* The nickname 'Woolsack' was a play upon the name of a previous owner of the land on which it stood – Mr Wools-Sampson.

like Apaches in their movements. But they are having the time of their lives – stealing from friends & foes alike and living on the fat of the land. I never saw such a comic war in all my born days. Cape Town is full of rebels and is the only place where martial law is not proclaimed. A man gets as much as 12 months imprisonment sometimes for assisting the enemy, and six months for helping to blow up a railway culvert. And then we wonder why the war doesn't end. They make no secret of their intentions. They want to sweep the English into the sea, to lick their own nigger and to govern South Africa with a gun instead of a ballot box. It is only the little Englanders in London who say that the Transvaal is merely fighting for its independence; but out here both sides realize it is a question of which race is to run the country.[12]

The last year of Rhodes's short life had come; his heart was failing, and he knew now that he would never live to see his vision realized of a united British Africa from the Cape to the Zambesi, with open communications through to Cairo. He, too, was content to wait for the end of the useless campaign at 'Groote Schuur' where, sooner or later, all who counted in Africa came to visit him.

Rhodes's dream, that ideal world which had sustained him through so many vicissitudes, had changed its character again, as dreams change, and had resolved itself into its final form. No longer a conspiracy of rich men to enforce peace, nor an Anglo-Saxon world-empire, the dream now shaped itself as the education of a new ruling class. The men with moral strength should rejuvenate the academies of the old world, while the learning of the academies should stimulate arts and sciences in the new frontier lands. Once he had thought that money was the source of power, but now he knew that knowledge was power. To link Oxford with his own Rhodesia was the last task he would set himself and, having spent money lavishly on material projects, he saved and economized at the end of his life to increase the endowment for his scholarships. The plans were laid in February 1901 and long were the discussions in the warm summer evenings at 'Groote Schuur'. Rhodes was not a ladies' man, but clever women, if they had something to say, were welcomed at his hospitable table, none more so than Carrie Kipling. It was she who persuaded him to increase the amount of the Rhodes Scholarships from £250 to £300 a year, which she knew was necessary for the support of a young man from overseas with no home in England.

She approved his schemes of building and planting, his encouragement of South African arts and architecture, his love of landscape and trees and animals. Wild beasts in their natural surroundings in a park enclosure pleased him deeply, and no little thing pleased him more than Carrie's decision to bring up a neglected lion-cub by hand.

When Rhodes was obliged to leave for England – his last voyage – Rudyard wrote:

Life in your cottage has been as perfect in its peace and quiet as anything in this world could offer. It has filled me full of notions – over and above the work that I have managed to get through – so that it will take me all my time to get them in order. I've done one or two things that I'm rather pleased with but it has been horribly lonely since you left. Rather like living in a landscape with half the horizon knocked out.[13]

Their summer visit to England in 1901 was uneventful. The Catlins came over from America and bore off Carrie and Rudyard on a visit to Paris, which they had not seen for many years. She had been ill that summer and Rudyard had written tenderly to her mother in America:

You have no notion what a sweet and winning little woman your Carrie has grown into. Her face gets more beautiful year by year, and her character deepens and broadens with every demand upon it. She is near an angel, but her Puritan conscience which she has inherited from her New England forbears still makes her take life too blame seriously.[14]

Just before he sailed again for Africa he made a pronouncement in *The Times* which provoked violent discussion, giving offence to many who had been his fervent admirers. It was a long poem called 'The Islanders', an appeal to the English to take national service as seriously as they took their organized games. An early result was a letter from Lord Roberts to Kipling on the subject of a campaign for compulsory military training.

The complaint of the critics about 'The Islanders' was that Rudyard did not so much warn the English of their peril as scold them for their inadequacy.

No doubt but ye are the People – your throne is above the King's.
Whoso speaks in your presence must say acceptable things:
Bowing the head in worship, bending the knee in fear –
Bringing the word well smoothen – such as a King should hear.

He began by repeating his old assertion that the craft of soldiering was held in contempt in England:

Ye hindered and hampered and crippled; ye thrust out of sight and away
Those that would serve you for honour and those that served you for pay.
Then were the judgements loosened; then was your shame revealed,
At the hands of a little people, few but apt in the field.
Yet ye were saved by a remnant (and your land's long-suffering star),
When your strong men cheered in their millions while your striplings went to the war.

*

And ye vaunted your fathomless power, and ye flaunted your iron pride,
Ere – ye fawned on the Younger Nations for the men who could shoot and ride!
Then ye returned to your trinkets; then ye contented your souls
With the flannelled fools at the wicket or the muddied oafs at the goals.

This was indeed a shock to a generation that gave such moral consequence to cricket, and many a paterfamilias wrote to one or other of the more solemn organs of the Press, in dismay that Rudyard Kipling, the Bard of Empire, should blaspheme the national idols, with his talk of 'flannelled fools' and 'muddied oafs'. Rudyard enlarged upon this theme. Their inherited way of life could be maintained only if the English would learn how to fight for it.

Ancient, effortless, ordered, cycle on cycle set,
Life so long untroubled, that ye who inherit forget
It was not made with the mountains, it is not one with the deep.
Men, not gods, devised it. Men, not gods, must keep.
Men, not children, servants, or kinsfolk called from afar,
But each man born in the Island broke to the matter of war.

He scorned his critics and derided their alternatives. What would they do in the event of war?

Will ye pitch some white pavilion, and lustily even the odds,
With nets and hoops and mallets, with rackets and bats and rods?
Will the rabbit war with your foemen – the red deer horn them for hire?
Your kept cock-pheasant keep you? – he is master of many a shire.

*

Will ye pray them or preach them, or print them, or ballot them back from your shore?
Will your workmen issue a mandate to bid them strike no more?

No earlier pronouncement of Rudyard's had touched so many victims on the raw. It flicked the old conservatives on a tender spot, hurting them more than it hurt the hostile hide-bound radicals who cared little for criticism from this quarter. The intellectuals were the last people he thought of influencing; they were 'incurious', a damning epithet which he applied to them in a single sweeping line. They were

Arid, aloof, incurious, unthinking, unthanking, gelt.

and he wasted no more words on them. So much for Jack

Mackail and his friends. 'England is a stuffy little place, mentally, morally, and physically', he wrote to Rhodes.[15]

The Kiplings did not reach the 'Woolsack' again until 7 January 1902. It was to find a deputation of newspaper reporters urgent for 'copy' about 'The Islanders'. Among them was a young man named Edgar Wallace who had come out to the Cape as a private soldier and, having graduated into war-reporting, now held Julian Ralph's old place as correspondent of the London *Daily Mail*. Rudyard advised him upon starting a career which was to win him wealth and fame as a writer of thrillers, but the profession of literature, as he warned Wallace, was 'a good mistress but a bad wife'.[16] Rudyard's own work in January was in a lighter vein. The nursery fables which he had devised for children in past years were ready for publication. He ended the series with 'The Cat that Walked by Himself' and 'The Butterfly that Stamped', both completed at the 'Woolsack' early in 1902. The 'Cat' was perhaps inspired by the gift of a handsome Persian which Carrie had just received from her Wolcott cousins.

Thereafter Rudyard had to turn to graver matters. On 6 February he heard that Rhodes was mortally ill and, until his death, called almost every day either at 'Groote Schuur' or at the Muizenberg cottage where the invalid was taken in that torrid season for sea air. Fifty years ago, when there was no air-conditioning, even the money of a multi-millionaire could not command coolness in summer heat.

On 18 March Rhodes was reported unconscious and on the evening of the 26th, word came to the 'Woolsack' that he had died murmuring 'So little done – so much to do.' Next day his body was brought to lie in state at 'Groote Schuur', and Rudyard was called into council by Dr Jameson, one of the executors, to advise about the funeral ceremonies and about putting the will into effect. At a short private service held at 'Groote Schuur' on 2 April Rudyard recited the obituary verses, of which some lines were afterwards engraved on Rhodes's memorial:

> Dreamer devout, by vision led
>   Beyond our guess or reach,
> The travail of his spirit bred
>   Cities in place of speech.
> So huge the all-mastering thought that drove –
>   So brief the term allowed –
> Nations, not words, he linked to prove
>   His faith before the crowd.
>
> .   .   .   .
>
> The immense and brooding Spirit still
>   Shall quicken and control.
> Living he was the land, and dead,
>   His soul shall be her soul!

On the following day, after a public ceremony, which the
Kiplings attended, in the Cathedral at Cape Town, Rhodes's
body was carried in procession to the railway station and
thence to Bulawayo. The executors had begged Rudyard to
go with them to Rhodes's North, and when he would not, in
his last days before leaving Africa, Jameson and Frank
Rhodes sent him special messages from Rhodesia describing
the reading of his verses over the grave in the Matoppos.[17]
It seemed hardly relevant to notice that the funeral train
had passed for a thousand miles through the war-zone
which was still harassed by Boer guerrillas. As late as 7
March the Boer General Delarey had overrun a British garrison and captured a British General, the last Boer exploit in
a campaign on the point of collapse.

The concentration camps were now under efficient control
and the absurd situation of fighting the men while feeding
their dependants could not be indefinitely maintained. 'At
long last,' wrote Rudyard, 'we were left apologizing to a
deeply indignant people, whom we had been nursing and
doctoring for a year or two.' Formal negotiations for peace
were opened on 9 April, a week before the Kiplings left for
England. It was a joyous voyage because the 'Pater' and Dr
Jameson were in the same ship with them. They came home
to a summer of rejoicing; there was peace, and there was to

be a Coronation; and best of all, Rudyard's mother came
to stay at Rottingdean with Trix, now restored to health.

Whit Sunday, 1 June 1902, brought the news that peace
was signed in South Africa: in an announcement that was a
'scoop' for the *Daily Mail*, managed by that enterprising
young journalist, Edgar Wallace. The next day a public
holiday was kept with more sober celebration than the relief of Mafeking, two years before. Public opinion had
changed about the war and there were many who could not
share Rudyard's complacency about the treatment of the
Afrikaner nation, among them Aunt Georgie, a woman of
inflexible puritan morality. Since to her the day of the Boer
capitulation – and that was what the Treaty of Vereeniging
amounted to – was a day of mourning, she took the remarkable step of hanging a black banner from the window of
'North End House' with a notice in large letters:

<blockquote>We have killed and also taken possession.</blockquote>

In quiet Rottingdean on a summer holiday no one at first
was in a mood for polemics; but when the evening came
and the young men of the village were in a noisy mood, a
crowd gathered around 'North End House' to protest. Some
attempt was made to pull the black flag down, even, according to one account, to set fire to the hedge over which
it hung. This demonstration brought Rudyard hurrying
across the green from 'The Elms' to the rescue of his dear
Aunt Georgie. There could be no doubt of Rudyard Kipling's loyalty and, after a speech which was much interrupted, he persuaded the demonstrators to go away, a
strange role for Rudyard to play, and one which could not
be kept out of the newspapers.[18]

A few months earlier he had been writing, in Africa, the
verses on 'Sussex' which seemed to root him there for ever.

<blockquote>God gives all men all earth to love,
But since man's heart is small,
Ordains for each one spot shall prove
Belovèd over all.</blockquote>

*

> Each to his choice, and I rejoice
> The lot has fallen to me
> In a fair ground – in a fair ground –
> Yea, Sussex by the sea!

In fact, Rottingdean, with its painful memories, was becoming unbearable to him and Carrie, all the more because the character of the place had changed. They hated the trippers from Brighton; there were radicals in the village – a group of them with whom Rudyard used sometimes to argue in the 'Plough Inn'; and now even the local patriots had set his teeth on edge, so that in chagrin Rudyard closed temporarily the hall he had built for the rifle club. Luckily they had at last found a suitable house; on 10 June Rudyard's solicitor cousin, George Macdonald, negotiated the purchase of the house called 'Bateman's' at Burwash, with thirty-three acres of land, for the sum of £9,300.

Carrie had been pleased to receive invitations to seats in the Abbey for the Coronation of King Edward VII. When on 24 June news came of the King's sudden illness which caused the postponement of the ceremony, Rudyard was deeply moved. So far, in his life, he had felt no more than a formal respect for the Monarchy. The 'Widow at Windsor' had retained his loyal submission without winning that passionate, fervent, devotion which she inspired in so many of her subjects. His great Jubilee poem contained no reference to Queen Victoria. During the last weeks of her life he had paid her a graceful tribute in his verses on the Commonwealth of Australia ('The Young Queen'), and that was all. Her death in January 1901 produced no contemporary comment, in Rudyard's published works or in Carrie's private diary. The month of June 1902, when he was thinking and feeling so deeply, with such mixed emotions, about the state of the nation, turned his mind, perhaps for the first time its full force, to the meaning of the English Monarchy. 'Rud greatly shocked,' wrote Carrie on the day of the King's illness, 'and more interested than ever before in the King as a man.' His verses, 'The King's Task', followed not long after. But when the deferred Coronation at last took place on 9 August, it did not suit them to go to London, and they spent the day quietly at Rottingdean.

During the war the verses and stories that Rudyard had published had been largely political; his literary achievement had been the completion of *Kim*, which harked back to an earlier period of his life. The political pieces, from 'The Absent-minded Beggar' to 'The Islanders', were not of a kind to make a direct appeal to posterity. Those who remember the mental climate of the turn of the century are now past middle age and, for the most part, it is students of social history who will turn to 'The Old Issue', 'A Song of the White Men', or 'The Reformers'. The tone of his comment on the war, as it affected his own countrymen, is best preserved in the facetious verses called 'The Lesson', which appeared in *The Times* on 29 July 1901.

Let us admit it fairly, as a business people should,
    We have had no end of a lesson : it will do us no end of good.

*

It was our fault, and our very great fault – and now we must turn
    it to use.
We have forty million reasons for failure, but not a single excuse.
So the more we work and the less we talk the better results we
    shall get –
We have had an Imperial lesson; it may make us an Empire yet!

As for the aftermath of the war, in South Africa, his programme was what Rhodes would have commended if he had lived to see it – magnanimity – to wipe out and to forget the cruel past, to face the future in a creative, co-operative spirit. The verses printed at the head of this chapter were his epilogue to the war.

> Here in a large and sunlit land,
>   Where no wrong bites to the bone,
> I will lay my hand in my neighbour's hand,

And together we will atone
For the set folly and the red breach
And the black waste of it all;
Giving and taking counsel each
Over the cattle-kraal.

His vision of the war, which he shared with Rhodes and
Milner, was always cast forward to a future when settlement
of new white men on the land would prove the key to recovered prosperity. That note recurs often in his stories and
songs of the war. The popular soldier-ballads, 'Chant-
Pagan', 'Stellenbosch', 'M.I.', 'Boots', 'Lichtenberg', 'Piet',
mostly written in 1901, were not published until 1903 when
he issued a new volume of collected verse, *The Five Nations*.
Though the sales of this book were gigantic compared with
those of any other contemporary poetry, they never
achieved the universal popularity of *Barrack-Room Ballads*
and *The Seven Seas*. This was a matter of timing, as they
appeared in that season of doldrums after a war when no
one but the old soldiers wants to hear it mentioned. Most
are topical verses, and only in one or two instances do they
approach the level of pure poetry, even as ballads. Perhaps
the most remarkable of these pieces is 'Lichtenberg', a poem
suggested by the casual remark of an Australian soldier. 'I
smelt wattle at Lichtenberg, riding in, in the rain.' The
rhythmical phrase was enough to set Rudyard's imagination at work and to produce a composition shot with light
from two contrary angles, a web of two colours varying as
the light catches warp or woof. The scene is magically like
war in Africa, and the response is wholly Australian, told in
the simplest terms, with no bright colours or startling dis-
closures. Even the sing-song Australian accent comes
through in the rhythm without need for a word of dialect.

There was some silly fire on the flank
And the small wet drizzling down –
There were sold-out shops and the bank
And the wet, wide-open town;

> *And* we were doing escort-duty
> To somebody's baggage-train,
> And I smelt wattle by Lichtenberg –
> Riding in, in the rain.
>
> It was all Australia to me –
> All I had found or missed:
> Every face I was crazy to see,
> And every woman I'd kissed . . .

In the collected works there are three full-length stories about the Boer War, all dealing with unusual aspects of it. 'The Comprehension of Private Copper' is a dialogue between a private soldier and a renegade British colonial fighting on the Boer side. 'A Sahibs' War', based upon Rudyard's visit to the farm near Karee Siding, is a version of the war as seen by a Sikh soldier who has found his way there by accident, Rudyard's notion of how the war might have been fought if the Indian Army had been employed. 'The Captive', of which we may suppose that the motive was suggested by an episode at Cape Town,* is one of Rudyard's most sophisticated, most thoroughly elaborate, stories packed with allusion and technicality, and making no concession to the casual reader. To throw yourself into it is like listening to another man's 'shop'. Rudyard described 'The Captive' as one of the stories which came to him subconsciously or, as he preferred to say, was offered to him by his 'daemon', and which therefore might have merit if laboriously polished.

I could not get my lighting into key with the tone of the monologue. The background insisted too much. My Daemon said at last: 'Paint the background first once for all, as hard as a public-house sign, and leave it alone.' This done, the rest fell into place with the American accent and outlook of the teller.

*R. K.'s letters to Conland reveal (1) that Rudyard himself imported an experimental machine-gun for trial in the field, and (2) that he made friends at Cape Town with an American soldier of fortune, a sergeant 'who had been at San Juan, and was a Democrat – a grey, grizzled tough old bird'. This American, unlike the 'captive', had volunteered to fight on the British side.

Here is the frame, in which the tale within the tale is presented, and in which Rudyard presents his version of the topsy-turvy political situation in the last year of the war.

The guard-boat lay across the mouth of the bathing-pool, her crew idly spanking the water with the flat of their oars. A red-coated militiaman, rifle in hand, sat at the bows, and a petty officer at the stern. Between the snow-white cutter and the flat-topped honey-coloured rocks on the beach the green water was troubled with shrimp-pink prisoners-of-war bathing. Behind their orderly tin camp and the electric-light poles rose those stone-dotted spurs that throw heat on Simonstown. Beneath them the little *Barracouta* nodded to the big *Gibraltar*, and the old *Penelope*, that in ten years has been bachelors' club, natural history museum, kindergarten, and prison, rooted and dug at her fixed moorings. Far out, a three-funnelled Atlantic transport with turtle bow and stern waddled in from the deep sea.

Through the mouth of his Yankee adventurer, a prisoner of the British, Rudyard speaks of two men, with the love that an author extends to his favourite characters, the Boer Commandant and the English General. In the story, all the British regular officers admit themselves 'pro-Boers' in politics; while the Boer fighting-men show much more animosity against the half-hearted Cape rebels than against the British. The Boer Commandant, Van Zyl, who does not want to fight, fights well; the British General, who respects the Boers, almost dreads the end of the war for professional reasons. He wants time to put more young troops through the mill in this 'dress-parade for Armageddon'.

The General wanted to train soldiers; Van Zyl could not see how the war would ever be finished. 'If you hold an ox by the horn and hit him by the bottom he runs round and round.' The American thought he was beginning to understand the British and had evolved his own plan for South Africa. 'If you want to realize your assets, you should lease the whole proposition to America for ninety-nine years.' But it didn't work out that way.

'When 'Omer smote 'is bloomin' lyre,
 He'd 'eard men sing by land an' sea;
An' what he thought 'e might require,
 'E went an' took – the same as me!

'The market-girls an' fishermen,
 The shepherds an' the sailors, too,
They 'eard old songs turn up again,
 But kep' it quiet – same as you!

'They knew 'e stole; 'e knew they knowed.
 They didn't tell, nor make a fuss,
But winked at 'Omer down the road,
 An' 'e winked back – the same as us!'

[14]

(1) Kipling and his
Contemporaries

WHEN the Kiplings made their home at 'Bateman's', Rudyard had been in the public eye for twelve or thirteen years
and was yet no more than thirty-six years old. He was rich
and famous, by far the most quoted of contemporary
writers, the most talked-about, the most sought-after by
snobs and sightseers. It was exasperating to critics that a man
whose work could not be fitted into any of the approved
categories should enjoy such sustained and growing popularity. In 1890 it had been suggested that he lacked staying-
power; in 1902, whatever he was, he could not be called the
'comet of a season'.

Kipling's first success had been among persons of discrimination. When Hunter had spoken of a new star rising
in the East, when Low had regarded Kipling as 'possibly
greater than Dickens', when *The Times* leader-writer had
compared him with Maupassant, these were tributes paid to
the writer of cynical tales about the governing class in India.
It was an accident of his career that the Simla stories were
not the first to catch the attention of a wider public in London and New York. The soldier songs and stories of his
second phase captured the market in 1890 and grew in popularity through the decade, sweeping his reputation away into
a wider world where the pronouncements of the professional
critics counted for little. All that generation of young men
who volunteered to fight in the Spanish-American and
Anglo-Boer wars derived their notion of colonial warfare
and of the soldier's life largely from Kipling, particularly
from his cockney ballads. He was the first writer of eminence to compose serious verses in the cockney dialect, used

hitherto for comical treatment only; and perhaps his addiction to cockney, in that phase, lowered him in the estimation of men of letters. Grotesque misspellings in such solemn verses as 'Follow me 'Ome', or 'Sestina of the Tramp-Royal', discouraged some readers and dissuaded others from regarding these works as literature. Year after year, however, he produced his cockney verses, to the delight of the unacademic.

Meanwhile, in 1893 and 1894, he had embarked upon the new experiment of the *Jungle Books*, an even greater success than the *Barrack-Room Ballads*, and still after sixty years the most popular of Kipling's works. It is in the *Jungle Books* that we must search for the principle called 'the Law' which dominated Kipling's philosophy of life. It is not new; it had been expressed a generation earlier with force and eloquence in Emerson's essay on 'Self-reliance', which, significantly, had been prefaced with the gnomic rhyme:

> Cast the Bantling on the rocks.
> Suckle him with the she-wolf's teat;
> Wintered with the hawk and fox,
> Power and speed be hands and feet.

The message given by Emerson to his child cast into the world-jungle had been: 'accept the place the divine providence has found for you, the society of your contemporaries, the connexion of events'. How, then, to reconcile a fearless independence in action with an acquiescence in the universal plan?

'Your genuine action will explain itself, and will explain all your other actions. Your conformity explains nothing. Act singly, and what you have done singly will justify you now. Power is in nature the essential measure of right. Nature suffers nothing to remain in its Kingdom which cannot help itself.'

It was Kipling's corollary to the philosophy of self-reliance to expound the relation of the man to the machine in the new industrial age. The engineer, more than most men, is a master because, in Emerson's awkward phrase, he is 'plastic and permeable to principles'.

From coupler-flange to spindle-guide I see Thy hand, O God –
Predestination in the stride o' yon connectin'-rod.
John Calvin might ha' forged the same – enormous, certain, slow –
Ay, wrought it in the furnace-flame – *my* 'Institutio'.

So speaks M'Andrew, the Scottish engineer, of his machine, the engine of which he is at once master and servant, which conforms to the law of nature and yet is altogether dependent on his skill and courage.

Fra' skylight-lift to furnace-bars, backed, bolted, braced an' stayed,
An' singin' like the Mornin' Stars for joy that they are made;
While, out o' touch o' vanity, the sweatin' thrust-block says:
'Not unto us the praise, or man – not unto us the praise!'
Now, a' together, hear them lift their lesson – theirs an' mine:
'Law, Orrder, Duty an' Restraint, Obedience, Discipline!'
Mill, forge an' try-pit taught them that when roarin' they arose,
An' whiles I wonder if a soul was gied them wi' the blows.
Oh for a man to weld it then, in one trip-hammer strain,
Till even first-class passengers could tell the meanin' plain!

Kipling was a modest man about his own achievement – too modest, as he wrote to Charles Eliot Norton, to claim that he himself was the new Robert Burns, sent to 'sing the song of steam'. No other has appeared and no one could have done it better.[1]

From 1889 until 1908 there was no year in which he did not take a long sea voyage, and his love of sailors as types of self-reliant men of action came to surpass even his earlier love of soldiers. The relation of the seaman to his ship gave him a version of modern life more consonant with the widening world of the eighteen-nineties than his earlier image of the wolf-child in the jungle. 'The game is more than the player of the game, and the ship is more than the crew': there were times when he felt this as a sort of

animism. Had the engine a soul, the ship a life of its own?
There is a letter to Henley in which he allowed his fancy
to run free with this conceit:

> The way collisions at sea come about is this . . . the iron in the
> mine and under the hammer, and in the plates and engine room,
> has a sort of blind lust beaten into it, for to meet and I suppose
> nautically to copulate with other iron and steel being linked into
> the frame of another ship. All the seven seas over, the ship yearns
> for its mate, tearing along under moon and cloud, sweating in
> oily tropic ports; rusting in dock; and so forth. At last comes the
> bridal night – wind, current and set of the sea aiding, while the
> eyes of men are held, and steamer meets steamer in a big kiss,
> and sink down to cool off in the water-beds. What I want to get
> at is the steamer's unconcern about the men who happen to be
> crawling about her innards at the time.[2]

This was fancy – and morbid fancy, not to be released in
published work; yet it goes only a little further than the
light-hearted animism of 'The Ship that Found Herself'.
That notion, of an engine acquiring a personality, by the
gradual adaptation of its parts to one another, was new and
strange to Kipling's contemporaries, though familiar
enough in these days when everyone is used to the effect of
running-in a new motor-car.

To write poety and prose about steamships, for the men
who worked in engine-rooms, was so new a practice that it
left the literary critics gasping, but Kipling's own public was
to be found among the makers of the world as it was at the
turn of the century. They found no difficulty in his vocabulary, no unfamiliarity in his subject-matter. The generation that bridged the Forth, built the Uganda Railway,
damned the Nile, laid the Pacific Cable, irrigated the
Punjab, sent radio messages across the Atlantic, crushed the
ore of the Golden Mile at Kalgoorlie, served with the
Mounties at the Klondyke, tunnelled through the Rockies,
revealed the last secrets of the earth's surface, and learned
to fly, had found its own laureate and not upon the advice
of the approved literary critics. 'What an interesting illus-

tration Kipling affords of the poetic imagination working under difficulties!' wrote Norton to a friend. 'There is little to nourish or quicken the spiritual side of his nature, but he has done a better work for his time than any other man in treating, through the poetic imagination, the material conditions which surround us all.'[3]

The image of the ship was to recur frequently in his later writings. Its origin may perhaps be traced to memories of childhood when a liner bore him away from the happy nursery-life at Bombay to misery and routine at Southsea. Whatever its origin, the image haunted Kipling's fancy for forty years. The Galley, or Galleon, or sometimes a modern ship – the ship of state – was his symbol for the material circumstances of a man's working life. In the relation between the galley and the galley-slave he pictured the antithesis between determinism and free-will. The ship was an expression of the Law, of that undefined *nomos* which provided him with a sort of stoical substitute for religion. His verses on 'The Derelict' (1896) personify the deserted ship as a heartbroken creature: 'Man made me, and my will is to my maker still,' he writes; but the seaman is the servant of the ship just as the ship is the prerequisite of the seaman's life. The seaman's duty to the ship is the measure of his manhood.

Life was a voyage; the profession he embraced was like a ship's routine; his farewell to India almost inevitably took the form of a ballad called 'The Galley-Slaves'. His delightful valediction to the outmoded three-volume novel was phrased as the passing of an old ship, 'The Three-Decker' (1894). His quarrel with the literary pirates of New York was transmuted into 'The Rhyme of the Three Captains' (1890), a ballad about sea-pirates. 'The Finest Story in the World' (1891), his tale about a masterpiece that could not get itself written, had for subject the adventures of a galley-slave, or rather a confusion between the adventures of two sorts of galley-slave. His Norman Knight who settled in Sussex after the Conquest (*Puck of Pook's Hill*, 1906), a story-hero described subjectively with some features of Kipling himself, made a voyage in a galley and toiled at the oar. One of the last stories he published ('The Manner of Men', 1930), thirty years later, told of the galley that carried Saint Paul to Rome. And in his posthumous autobiography he wrote of his unfulfilled ambition:

> Yet I dreamed for many years of building a veritable three-decker out of chosen and long-stored timber – teak, green-heart, and ten-year-old oak knees – each curve melting deliciously into the next that the sea might nowhere meet resistance or weakness ... a vessel ballasted on ingots of pure research and knowledge, roomy, fitted with delicate cabinet-work below-decks, painted, carved, gilt and wreathed the length of her, from her blazing stern-galleries outlined by bronzy palm-trunks, to her rampant figure-head – an East Indiaman worthy to lie alongside *The Cloister and the Hearth*.[4]

Since the true story of the British, fifty years ago, was the story of the British Overseas, in the age of Cromer, Curzon, Kitchener, Milner, Johnston, Lugard and Rhodes, it was Kipling's task to reveal the secrets of their actual life to his contemporaries. For a whole generation homesickness was reversed by Kipling's magic spell. Englishmen felt the days of England sick and cold and the skies grey and old, heard the East a-calling, fawned on the younger nations, learned to speak the jargon of the seven seas; while, in the outposts of empire, men who read no other books recognized and approved the glimpses of their own lives in phrases from Kipling's verse: the flying-fishes and the thunder-clouds over the Bay of Bengal, the voyage outward-bound till the old lost stars wheel back, the palm-tree bowing down beneath a low African moon, the wild tide-race that whips the harbour-mouth at Melbourne, the broom flowering above the windy town of Wellington, the islands where the anchor-chain goes ripping down through coral-trash.

He distinguished always the self-reliant labour of the pioneer, up-country and alone, from the ponderous remote bureaucracy of Whitehall and Simla. Kipling has been described as if he were the poet of orthodox conservatism. He was the very opposite of that; his admiration was always for the irregulars, the

> Legion that never was 'listed,
> That carries no colours or crest,
> But, split in a thousand detachments,
> Is breaking the road for the rest.[5]

In solitary places young Englishmen of the middle classes toiled and improvised at the task of civilizing backward countries, making wealth out of poverty and knowing very well that they would not get the profit of it.

> By the bitter road the Younger Son must tread,
> Ere he win to hearth and saddle of his own, –
> 'Mid the riot of the shearers at the shed,
> In the silence of the herder's hut alone –
> In the twilight, on a bucket upside down,
> Hear me babble what the weakest won't confess – ...

'The Song of the Banjo' was not written of the governing-class, the 'Sons of Mary' who accepted power and wealth as a right, but of the 'Sons of Martha', the middle-class adventurers who shrank from no responsibility and were never too proud for any task.

Even at sea, the engineer, down below, is his hero rather than the gold-laced captain on the bridge. Though all his own voyages were in liners, and it was with the eye of imagination that he saw the breaking waves as they towered over a tramp-steamer's hull, he could project himself into the skin of the drenched deck-hand:

> Once we saw between the squalls, lyin' head to swell –
> Mad with work and weariness, wishin' they was we –
> Some damned Liner's lights go by like a grand hotel;
> 'Cheered her from the *Bolivar* swampin' in the sea.*

* A comparison may here be drawn between Kipling, who sang the Song of Steam, and Conrad who, though a professional seaman, always harked back to the passing age, the age of sail. Conrad visited Kipling at 'Bateman's' and each was an admirer of the other's work.

Some extracts from early critical reviews of Kipling's work have been quoted in a previous chapter. It will now be proper to consider the maturer judgement of the reviewers, and the rise of hostile criticism as the eighteen-nineties drew to their close. There are times in the history of literature when the art of the approved masters is in harmony with popular sentiment, and times when it soars away into another sphere. In the eighteen-nineties, as again in the nineteen-twenties, popular art was a term of reproach, so that the painters and the poets in those two decades ignored and even despised the preferences of the great majority of their fellows, preferring to put out their work for the benefit of a small society of *illuminati*, sometimes, as it seemed, for the benefit of one another. The significant writers of the eighteen-nineties, according to the usual classification, are taken to be the group whose slogan was 'Art for Art's Sake'. There had been a change in literary fashion since the robust phase of Henley's *Scots Observer* which had led the fashion in 1889. 'Decadence' had triumphed, even in the persons of two or three writers who transferred their allegiance from Henley to the new group that surrounded Aubrey Beardsley.

It is in the numerous references of Henry James to Kipling (who remained his close family friend) that Kipling's decline from reputation with the leading critics can be traced. When in the spring of 1891 Kipling had circumvented Harper Brothers by producing a collection of stories in America, under the name of *Mine Own People*, Henry James had written a long adulatory preface.

His bloom lasts from month to month, almost surprisingly. This same freshness is such a very strange affair of its kind – so mixed and various and cynical, and, in certain lights, so contradictory of itself. At times he strikes us as shockingly precocious, at others as serenely wise. On the whole, he presents himself as a strangely clever youth who has stolen the formidable mask of maturity and rushes about making people jump with the deep sounds, the sportive exaggerations of tone, that issue from his painted lips. He has this mark of a real vocation, that different spectators may like him – must like him, I should almost say – for different things.

I hasten to add that the truly appreciative reader should surely have no quarrel with the primitive element in Mr Kipling's subject-matter, or with what, for want of a better name, I may call his love of low life. What is this but essentially a part of his freshness? And for what part of his freshness are we exactly more thankful than for just this smart jostle that he gives to the stupid superstition that the amiability of a storyteller is the amiability of the people he represents – that their vulgarity, or depravity, or gentility, or fatuity are tantamount to the same qualities in the painter himself.

He never arranges or glosses or falsifies, but makes straight for the common and the characteristic.

In his private correspondence James was not so flattering. The letters he exchanged with R. L. Stevenson contain several allusions to the newcomer whose genius both admired but both suspected. Was there some alloy of base metal in his composition? 'The talent enormous,' wrote James, 'but the brutality even deeper-seated.' 'He alarms me by his copiousness and haste,' wrote Stevenson; and again, 'He is all smart journalism and cleverness; it is all bright and shallow and limpid. No blot of heart's blood, no harmony to the music.'[6]

Another shrewd and subtle criticism appeared about the same time from the pen of Oscar Wilde, then known only as an aesthete and a wit, whose dramatic successes and personal catastrophe still lay in the future. In September 1890 Wilde wrote an insufferably drawn-out dialogue for the *Nineteenth Century* on contemporary letters. The reader who can stomach page after page of the verbal confectionary flavoured with synthetic perfumes that in the eighteen-nineties passed for fine writing will come towards the end to this comment on the young Kipling:

He who would stir us now by fiction must either give us an entirely new background, or reveal to us the soul of man in its innermost workings. The first is, for the moment, being done for us by Mr Rudyard Kipling. As one turns over the pages of his *Plain Tales from the Hills*, one feels as if one were seated under a palm tree reading life by superb flashes of vulgarity. The bright colours of the bazaars dazzle one's eyes. The jaded, commonplace Anglo-Indians are in exquisite incongruity with their surroundings. The mere lack of style in the story-teller gives an odd journalistic realism to what he tells us. From the point of view of literature Mr Kipling is a man of talent who drops his aspirates. From the point of view of life he is a reporter who knows vulgarity better than anyone has ever known it. Dickens knew its clothes. Mr Kipling knows its essence. He is our best authority on the second-rate.*

Realism in subject-matter was not Oscar Wilde's forte and he could hardly be expected to admire a man who went 'straight for the common and the characteristic', but, making allowance for that, his observations are telling. To a modern reader, whether he likes Kipling's style or not, the repeated statement that in Kipling's early stories there was a 'mere lack of style' reads strangely. It must be remembered that by 'style' Wilde meant high-falutin. Kipling was not the sort of writer, as Edward Shanks has pointed out, who wrote 'drops his aspirates' when he meant 'drops his aitches'. All these comments were made upon Kipling's Indian stories, which, with the *Barrack-Room Ballads*, produced a vast volume of criticism, all at first to much the same effect. The reviewers were fascinated, startled, and shocked. 'Idle people are beginning to ask each other idle conundrums about him,' said a writer in the *Saturday Review* on 14 May 1892. 'He is within measurable distance of the foundation of a Kipling Society.' Very soon, a reaction began against the undiscriminating praise given to all his work, copious and various as it was in his London years, by the less fastidious public. As early as 29 January 1891 a set of verses appeared

* Wilde's celebrated comment that Kipling had seen remarkable things 'through keyholes' does not appear in the essay as originally published.

in the *Cambridge Review*, over the signature 'J. K. S.', which the literary world knew to stand for J. K. Stephen, a brother of Kipling's early patron, Herbert Stephen. Would there never come a season, asked 'J. K. S.' –

> When the world shall cease to wonder
> At the genius of an ass,
> And a boy's eccentric blunder
> Shall not bring success to pass : . . .
>
> When there stands a muzzled stripling,
> Mute, beside a muzzled bore :
> When the Rudyards cease from kipling
> And the Haggards ride no more?

Kipling took no offence; he often used to chaff his friend Rider Haggard about it. They were stanzas, he said, which he would have given much to have written himself, which 'might survive when all but our two queer names are forgotten.' On the other hand, it is J. K. Stephen who is now remembered chiefly for his rhyme about Kipling and Haggard, but in 1891 anything written by a Stephen of Cambridge was admired, and while the world laughed at this amusing nonsense jingle it was hardly noticed that it was not criticism. To say that Kipling was an ass and should be muzzled was neither liberal nor polite; to couple him with Rider Haggard, a mere writer of romantic thrillers, did his reputation some undeserved damage. Though these two popular writers were contemporaries and lifelong friends, they had little in common, professionally.

A year or two after J. K. Stephen's jibe was published, a young man, who was to become Kipling's most malicious critic, arrived in London. Max Beerbohm published very little, and while he protested so prettily that his muse was no bigger than the servant-girl's baby, the literary world learned to wait expectant for each of his tiny little pronouncements, for Max had charm and talent. No one could deny, or did deny, that his work was polished, his wit penetrating – more penetrating with pencil than with pen. For fifty years anything spoken or written or depicted by Max called forth a shrill chorus of delight from the reviewers, and the present writer supposes himself almost the first to utter an unkind word about this incomparable master of the smirk and titter. Max was, as a rule, gentle, except when he touched upon one topic. He hated Rudyard Kipling. He set himself to destroy Kipling's reputation and later to assure the world that it had been destroyed, with no small degree of success among the literary coteries, but with no visible effect upon Kipling's ever-growing fame and influence in wider circles. At least nine caricatures, two critical articles, and a ferociously malevolent parody of Kipling's style have been recorded as the work of Max Beerbohm, and while he discharged these arrows, Kipling, for thirty years, remained entirely unmoved by them.* [7]

Among the hostile critics there was one who showed, as early as 1893, a disposition to love and hate together, a phenomenon not rare in writers on Rudyard Kipling. Francis Adams was a debunker who made a name (before his early death by suicide) for exploding the inflated reputation of the great Victorians. Tennyson was no sooner dead, in October 1892, then Adams belittled him, and then turned with gusto to attack the new young man who was succeeding Tennyson in popularity. He began with the handsome admission that *Barrack-Room Ballads* gave him 'the keenest pleasure had in reading a book of verse for years'; but the lapses from taste, he added, were unpardonable. 'The drop in Mr Kipling is always from the stars straight into the puddles.' Much of Adams's criticism consisted in a shrewd selection of weak episodes from early books, and weak lines from early poems which Kipling

---

*A sketch in the *Strand Magazine*, December 1892, seems to be Beerbohm's earliest caricature of Kipling. The boys of Horsmonden School induced Kipling to write a facetious article for their school magazine (*The Budget*, 14 May 1898). The following number, 28 May, contained a comment and a caricature by Beerbohm. Neither contribution is worth much, but they were reprinted in New York, 1899.

himself would have pruned away from his maturer work. Since no one now reads the early pieces which Francis Adams condemned, the substance of this criticism is largely irrelevant, yet the general impression persisted, and many of his judgements passed into the common stock of opinion in literary circles. Kipling's picture of life at Simla was 'duty and red tape tempered by picnics and adultery'. His view of the 'goodness of God in relation to Englishmen and "niggers" seems always to consist in the opportunity and ability of the former to give the latter "hell"'.

On Kipling's characters Adams had interesting observations to make. 'Description is his forte', but his characterization is weak.

He cannot escape from his own subjectivity. His *dramatis personae* melt away rapidly out of the memory, leaving us nothing but the impression of an admirably piquant and clever delineation.[8]

These notions were developed by Richard Le Gallienne, the editor of the liberal *Star*, who in 1900 wrote the first systematic study of Kipling's prose and verse. Le Gallienne was able to judge the *Barrack-Room Ballads* more adequately than some earlier writers because he was an enthusiast for the London music-halls. The ballads, he said, were perfect in their kind, like the art of Albert Chevalier; and the best of them, 'though made of the very refuse of language', was 'Mandalay'. 'Like Burns when he forsakes his dialect, Kipling is cramped and dull when he forsakes his cockney.' But here Le Gallienne is not quite ingenuous; he dislikes Kipling's later verses for their politics and so decries them as verses. 'A Song of the English' is a 'mild cantata'; 'Recessional' is a 'political catchword embedded in a hymn'. As for the technical songs and stories, he can make nothing of them, beyond noting Kipling's debt to Walt Whitman:

> In the labour of engines and the fields,
>   to show the developments and the eternal meanings.

As for Kipling's characters, 'the more pains he takes with them the less they live. He is deft at giving you sufficient notion of this man or that woman to last out the story. But mainly the story is the thing, and the characters are little more than pegs on which to hang an anecdote.' Kipling 'loves to pretend that he has no feelings', says Le Gallienne, and he must be blamed for a growing love of violence in the English character. 'As a writer he is a delight, as an influence he is a danger.'[9]

Early American criticism followed the same path as English criticism, at first a chorus of injudicious praise, varied by warnings against the author's 'smartness'. In America, too, the Simla stories were thought to be shocking. A writer in the *New York Herald* (1890) remarked: 'The most forcible impression which is left on the average mind by Mr Kipling's works is the dismalness, insincerity, brutality and utter worthlessness of all classes of British humanity in India.' William Dean Howells, who had deplored Kipling's 'jaunty' 'wink-tipping' manner in 1890, quite came round, as did gradually the Brahmins of Boston. A man who was praised by Henry James and Charles Eliot Norton must be taken seriously. The *Atlantic Monthly*, which had resisted the new enthusiasm for some years, capitulated in January 1897, by publishing Norton's long and laudatory article on *The Seven Seas*, the review which so delighted Rudyard and Carrie at Torquay.

It is now some six or seven years since *Plain Tales from the Hills* gave proof that a man who saw through his eyes was studying life in India and was able to tell us what he saw. And those who read the scraps of verse prefixed to many of his stories, if they knew what poetry was, learned that their writer was at least potentially a poet, not by virtue of fantasy alone, but by his mastery of lyrical versification . . .

The dominant tone of his verse is indeed the patriotic . . . it is this passionate, moral, imperial patriotism that inspires the first poem in the book, 'The Song of the English' . . . but if this be the dominant tone, the full scale which includes it and every other tone of Mr Kipling's verse is that of actual life seen by the imagination intensely and comprehensively, and seen by it always, in all conditions and under all forms, as a moral experience, with the inevitable consequences resulting from the good or evil use of it.

'What is a poet?' asked Wordsworth, and he answers the question: 'He is a man speaking to men. . . . He binds together by passion and knowledge the vast empire of human society.' And this vast empire of society includes the mean and the vulgar no less than the noble and the refined. The brutality of Tommy Atkins, the spirit of the beast in man, all appear in the *Barrack-room Ballads*, but not less his courage, his fidelity, his sense of duty, his obscure but deep-seated sentiment. The gist of all these Ballads is the display of the traits of human nature which make this semi-savage 'most remarkable like you'.

And so vivid are his appreciations of the poetic significance of even the most modern and practical of the conditions and aspects of sea life that in 'McAndrew's Hymn', a poem of surpassing excellence alike in conception and in execution, he has sung the song of the marine steam-engine . . . in such wise as to convert the clanging throbs and beats into a sublime symphony.

He has thus fulfilled a fine prophecy of Wordsworth's, that when the time should come, when the discoveries and applications of science shall become 'familiarised to men, and shall be ready to put on, as it were, a form of flesh and blood, the Poet will lend his divine spirit to aid the transfiguration'. The qualities which distinguish Mr Kipling's stories were not lacking in his poems. There was the same sure touch, the same insight, the same imaginative sympathy with all varieties of life, and the same sense of the moral significance of life even in its crudest, coarsest, and most vulgar aspects.

He continues the great succession of English poets . . . such a succession of poets as no other land can boast.

Norton had come nearer to appreciation of Kipling's technical songs and stories than had Richard Le Gallienne, but here Henry James quite failed. What was the song of steam to him? An oft-quoted letter of James should be read in this context, as a light-hearted flippancy by a friend writing about a friend, whose work he had praised both publicly and privately, for its other merits. If this letter is to be taken more seriously, it is a devastating admission of the limitations of its writer.

Henry James to Miss Grace Norton

Xmas Day, 1897

His talent I think quite diabolically great; and this in spite of the misguided, the unfortunate Stalky. His ballad future may still be big. But my view of his prose future has much shrunken in the light of one's increasingly observing how little of life he can make use of. Almost nothing civilised save steam and patriotism – and the latter only in verse, where I *hate* it so, especially mixed up with God and goodness, that that half spoils my enjoyment of his great talent. Almost nothing of the complicated soul or of the female form or of any question of *shades* – which latter constitutes, to my sense, the real formative literary discipline. In his earliest time I thought he perhaps contained the seeds of an English Balzac; but I have given that up in proportion as he has come down steadily from the simple in subject to the more simple – from the Anglo-Indians to the natives, from the natives to the Tommies, from the Tommies to the quadrupeds, from the quadrupeds to the fish, and from the fish to the engines and screws.[10]

But Kipling had yet something to say about 'natives' which would reveal James's aside to Miss Norton as shallow and frivolous indeed.

A far more serious blow was struck at Kipling's standing with the New England writers by the publication of 'The White Man's Burden'. Just as his South African pieces were an offence even to such dear friends as Aunt Georgie and Margot Mackail, so 'The White Man's Burden', which Theodore Roosevelt and his millions of supporters welcomed, made an end of Kipling's reputation in the stricter circles around Boston. William James and even Norton were much hurt by the tone of these verses, and liberals who had not known Kipling in America were quite disgusted. E. L. Godkin of the *Nation* wrote in a private letter:

Kipling has long been a most pernicious vulgar person. I only admire one thing of his, the 'Recessional'. He may have written other things as good but I don't read him. I think most of the current jingoism on both sides of the Atlantic is due to him. He is the poet of the barrack-room cads.[11]

It was only too common for critics of the left to condemn Kipling on hearsay evidence, without making Godkin's naïve admission that they hadn't read his works. Political passions then ran too high, in England and America, to allow justice to a writer who seemed to have given to party what was meant for mankind. Long afterwards a cooler view of his influence upon his generation could be taken, and a remarkable account of it was given by a man of the left wing – certainly no sympathizer with the views commonly attributed to Kipling. In his novel of Edwardian life, *The New Machiavelli*, H. G. Wells puts the following tribute into the mouth of his hero:

The prevailing force in my undergraduate days was not Socialism but Kiplingism . . .

It is a little difficult now to get back to the feelings of that period; Kipling has since been so mercilessly and exhaustively mocked, criticised and torn to shreds – never was a man so violently exalted and then, himself assisting, so relentlessly called down. But in the middle nineties this spectacled and moustached little figure with its heavy chin and its general effect of vehement gesticulation, its wild shouts of boyish enthusiasm for effective force, its lyric delight in the sounds and colours, in the very odours of empire, its wonderful discovery of machinery and cotton waste and the under officer and the engineer, and 'shop' as a poetic dialect, became almost a national symbol. He got hold of us wonderfully, he filled us with tinkling and haunting quotations . . . he coloured the very idiom of our conversation. He rose to his climax with his 'Recessional' . . .

He helped to broaden my geographical sense immensely, and he provided phrases for just that desire for discipline and devotion and organised effort the Socialism of our times failed to express, that the current socialist movement still fails, I think, to express. The sort of thing that follows, for example, tore something out of my inmost nature and gave it a shape, and I took it back from him shaped and let much of the rest of him, the tumult and the bullying, the hysteria and the impatience, the incoherence and inconsistency, go uncriticised for the sake of it:

Keep ye the Law — be swift in all obedience —
Clear the land of evil, drive the road and bridge the ford.
  Make ye sure to each his own
  That he reap where he hath sown;
By the peace among Our peoples let men know we serve the
  Lord!

To conclude this series of opinions we may select a still later verdict, by Desmond MacCarthy:

He made every character in his stories an artist in his lingo: the schoolboy, the engineer, the soldier, the bagman — even, by a stretch of imagination, different kinds of animals in the *Jungle Books*. But the most significant thing of all about him as a story-teller was that he put these gifts at the service *not* of the love-story, not of some adventure in sensibility, not of worldly success, but for the first time at the service of a man's relation to his work.

He wrote poems about what a farmer felt watching his fat cattle go through a gate, what an ex-soldier thought while mowing the vicar's lawn, what an engineer felt about his engine. He wrote poems not only about love and death — the eternal themes — but what the average man felt to be romantic in his daily life.

There is a feeling abroad that it is time the Muse ceased to repeat her ancient divinations and that she dealt with *everyday* emotions, with common not rare experiences. Who else has made anything like so spirited, so sincere, so unselfconscious an effort to do so? [12]

(2) Versification

If names were to be proposed for admission to the roll of English poets, during the last fifty years, the first choice of critical readers would probably be given to Yeats and Eliot, but not to Kipling who earned a wider fame than either of them in his lifetime, and whose works, as yet, have retained the affection of their readers for a longer period. Why is

Kipling not commonly ranked as a major poet? Both Yeats and Eliot have made considered pronouncements on this subject, and both, while expressing admiration for his achievement and technical proficiency, confess themselves baffled by the nature and purpose of his art. He was felt by his literary contemporaries to be out of the stream of English Literature, though the lettered, as well as the unlettered, were obliged to admit, even if they deplored the necessity of admitting it, that he was well in the stream – even for a time directing the current – of English life.

In his preface to the *Oxford Book of Modern Verse* Yeats permits himself to write with humorous nostalgia of literary London in the nineties, and to place Kipling among his fellows. No one could do it better than Yeats, who was also one of Henley's young men and a contributor to the *Scots Observer*. For Yeats there was but one whom all contemporaries accepted as the master of style – Walter Pater.

We poets [he says] continued to write verse, convinced that it would be disgraceful to take part in the social and political disturbances of the age. Then in 1900 everybody got down off his stilts; henceforth nobody drank absinthe with his black coffee; nobody went mad; nobody committed suicide; nobody joined the Catholic church; or if they did I have forgotten. Victorianism had been defeated, though two writers dominated the moment who had never heard of that defeat or did not believe in it; Rudyard Kipling and William Watson. Indian residence and associations had isolated the first, he was full of opinions, of politics, of impurities – to use our word – and the word must have been right, for he interests a critical audience today by the grotesque tragedy of *Danny Deever*, the matter but not the form of old street ballads, and by songs traditional in matter and form like *A St Helena Lullaby*.

Yeats's competence to write on Anglo-Irish folklore may pass without question, but he put himself out of court in writing of English folklore by his attitude to the English scene in the eighteen-nineties. With the other young writers of the 'decadent' period, he deliberately cut himself off from the English common people. He could not recognize the fact that Kipling had rejected his own Pre-Raphaelite upbringing and had renewed his strength by contact with red earth, the proof being in the very example, 'Danny Deever', that Yeats selected to disprove it. To be sure, Yeats and his young friends did not sing the living folklore of the proletariat at their literary parties. They were unaware that it existed, and when Kipling used that live idiom they supposed that he had invented it. 'Danny Deever' is instantly recognizable by anyone who has served as a soldier (a larger class today than it was sixty years ago) as actually and firmly composed in the style of the songs that the soldiers sang (and still sing) in the canteen. But what the soldier sang was not evident to Yeats.*

The theme was taken up far more intellectually by Mr Eliot in his introduction to *A Choice of Kipling's Verse*. At the end of his analysis Mr Eliot comes to no very clear conclusion. He defines Kipling's work with some exceptions, 'as verse and not as poetry', but as '*great* verse'; and it is worth noting that Kipling himself used the same terms, always referring to his own work as his Verses not as his Poems. 'Kipling', says Mr Eliot, 'employed rather simple rhythms with adroit variations.' The paternity of Kipling's verse eludes Mr Eliot's search because he looks in the wrong place.

Historically, a parallel may be drawn between the position in literary history of Kipling, and that of Sir Walter Scott. We do not now rank Scott very high as a 'pure' poet though much of his verse reaches a high level of accomplishment, and a ballad, here and there in his work, seems to be rather more than 'great verse'. He was immensely prolific, and often duplicated his effects by writing a succinct comment in verse on a theme he treated at greater length in prose. He enjoyed a vast popularity and made a great fortune by

* The 'St Helena Lullaby', a mature work of Kipling's middle age, is traditional in quite another sense; it is a Victorian drawing-room ballad, owing little to the folklore of the old street-singers.

his pen. Even when his name and influence dominated the British world he knew well that the unacknowledged legislators of mankind had shifted their ground. In an age when the enlightened were swinging sharply to the left, he was a Tory and not the sort of man to care much for changing fashions in the republic of letters. It was with conscious liberality that he handed on the laurels to Byron; it was beyond his comprehension to learn that he must hand them equally to Keats. For the mass of his own contemporaries Keats had no message at all; he was not of an age but for a continuing posterity. Scott was the writer of and for his age and as the interpreter of Scotland in the eighteenth century he is now remembered. His strength came right out of the soil of the Border dales; his style, vocabulary, metre, rhythm, lilt, and turn of phrase were effective just in the degree that they were close to that soil. The tradition in which he worked was a living tradition and the favour he won was from people who recognized his work as an indisputable aspect of real life as they knew it, as folklore. So were Rudyard Kipling's early ballads folklore, not pure poetry. Whether it is in any way a derogation of his work to make this assertion I shall leave to the professional critics to determine.

Walter Scott, like Robert Burns before him, used the traditional models of Lowland popular verse, never hesitating to adapt or borrow freely from his predecessors, according to the classic usage of folklore in all countries: such characteristics as the stylized imagery, the use of incantatory repetitions, the harmonics of a verse intended to be recited against a background of simple instrumental music, the turns of sentiment marked by a change of rhythm, the violent alternations of the grotesque, the horrible, and the pathetic.

But literary London in 1895 was occupied in turning its back on most of the things for which the rest of London cared, and when a young writer – an outsider from India – began to write in the living folklore tradition of the London streets, they could truthfully declare that they had never heard of it. When they discovered that the young Anglo-Indian was indifferent to their criticisms, scornful of their views, and devoted to a political cause they disliked, he was simply written off by critics.

'Kipling does not revolutionize,' says Mr Eliot.

He is not one of those writers of whom one can say, that the *form* of English poetry will always be different from what it would have been if they had not written. What fundamentally differentiates his 'verse' from 'poetry' is the subordination of musical interest.

If we consider him as a composer of ballads in the folklore tradition, we must examine what was the popular music of the English, in the year 1890 when Kipling abandoned his juvenile practice of writing facile imitations or parodies of Swinburne, Poe, and Browning, and began to write Ballads. Obviously he was strongly affected by the Scottish tradition, not least because his mother was a Macdonald. It is not difficult to trace a direct connexion between his narrative ballads and the similar work of Sir Walter Scott. A link between 'The Ballad of East and West' and 'Young Lochinvar' would not be hard to establish. The reader of Kipling's verse will not fail to notice a tendency to slip into Scotticisms (for example in 'Tomlinson') where there seems no need for that dialect in particular. The most impressionable of writers, Kipling seems unconsciously to have drifted into the style of the poet who gave him the momentary impetus to compose. It may be relevant to mention here an idiosyncrasy in his private conduct; he had a strange tendency, when writing an intimate letter to a dear friend, to vary his handwriting and to imitate the script of the person he was writing to.

We have seen that his early verse was largely imitative. His own account of his reading in 'Uncle Crom's' library at Westward Ho! gives the direction of his taste. The Jaco-

bean poets (not so fashionable in the eighteen-eighties as
they became forty years later) always interested him and
in his early manhood he made a special study of Donne;
Border Ballads have left their mark on his style in numerous
instances; but none of these influences was half as potent
in forming him as the evangelical teaching of his childhood. Both his father and his mother came of Methodist
families and, though not devout church-members, they were
born and bred in the evangelical tradition. They sent Rudyard, at his most impressionable age, to be brought up at
Southsea in a Calvinist household, where Bible-reading and
hymn-singing provided the standards for verse and prose.
This was the common fare of the great bulk of the English
people in the nineteenth century – of almost all of them, it
may be said, except the deracinated intellectuals. It was
precisely because Kipling's prose repeatedly echoes Biblical
rhythms and turns of phrase that it was accepted and understood by a public that read the Bible, but did not read
Walter Pater. When it came to verse, Kipling tended to
write in one of two styles. His more serious effects were
made in a sonorous and didactic style that directly derived
from *Hymns Ancient and Modern*, by far the most popular
volume of verse in nineteenth-century England. Here again
the intellectuals were out of tune with the national taste,
and it was left for Kipling to adapt this genre of the popular
hymn to the purpose of contemporary ballads. On his
voyage in 1891, when Kipling had 'General' Booth of the
Salvation Army for a travelling-companion, they struck up
an unexpected friendship. Kipling was much nearer to the
'General' in his approach to life than he was to the professional poets. The 'General's' appeal to the English people
was also made through the medium of hymns treated as
folklore, and he declined to let the devil have all the best
tunes.

Like 'General' Booth, Rudyard Kipling went into bar-
rooms and barrack-rooms and music-halls to find out the
songs the people were really singing, and fitted new words

to them. The tunes they knew best were hymn-tunes, and after that the range of popular songs, largely American in origin, that arose about the time of the Civil War and are still not forgotten – such songs as 'John Brown's Body', 'Marching through Georgia', and 'Tramp, tramp, tramp, the boys are marching', the songs that the boys had shouted in chorus at Westward Ho! Then there were the music-hall ditties, as strongly traditional as the evangelical hymns. At the end of the century, 'The Man that broke the Bank at Monte Carlo' and 'Knocked 'em in the Old Kent Road' were the direct successors of 'Vilikins and his Dinah' which dated back to the beginning of it. Since childhood Kipling had been fascinated by the London music-halls – too much fascinated his father thought – and when he returned to London in 1889 he told a friend that he found them more satisfying than the theatre. During his lonely year in London his solace was Gatti's, the same music-hall which Sickert was to 'discover' and depict in another medium a few years later. The *Barrack-Room Ballads* essentially are songs for the 'Halls', in which the 'patter' dominates the musical setting. Apart from Kipling, the greatest master in that art was W. S. Gilbert (whom Kipling several times imitated in *Departmental Ditties*); but Gilbert's method was to compose the 'patter' and then employ Sullivan, so long as he could hold him to the task, at writing tunes to it. Kipling once co-operated with Sullivan in this way, when producing 'The Absent-minded Beggar'; his usual method was just the opposite. When the substance of a poem was forming in his mind he found a tune – not a metre but a tune – and absorbed himself in its rhythm until the words arranged themselves, whereupon the poem was made.

I know of no writer of such great gifts [says Mr Eliot] for whom poetry seems to have been more purely an instrument. ... For Kipling the poem is something which is intended to *act* – and for the most part his poems are intended to elicit the same response from all readers, and only the response which they can make in common.

That is to say, the ballad is addressed to an audience not to an individual; it is to be sung, not read in an arm-chair; or, if not sung, it is presented in dramatic form as if it were being sung to an audience. The overtones which distinguish Kipling's verse from his prose are semantic rather than harmonic, getting their effect more from the associations of words than from the combination of sounds.

He experimented in almost every conventional verse-form, and wrote remarkably successful *vers libres* but, though the greater part of his verse is in regular rhymed stanzas, it will be found that the rules of scansion give little help in appreciating his rhythms. Take, for example, so celebrated a poem as 'Mandalay':

By the old Moulmein Pagoda, lookin' eastward to the sea,
There's a Burma girl a-settin', and I know she thinks o' me;
For the wind is in the palm-trees, and the temple-bells they say:
'Come you back, you British soldier; come you back to
  Mandalay!'

It will throw no light upon this poem to say that it is written in trochaic lines of eight feet, the metre of Tennyson's 'Locksley Hall', for the timing is entirely different.

Thro' the shadow of the globe we sweep into the younger day:
Better fifty years of Europe than a cycle of Cathay.

We shall come a little nearer if we notice that the rhythm of 'Mandalay' is similar to that of Poe's 'Raven'. The key-phrase, repeated with such powerfully nostalgic effect, 'Come you back to Mandalay', is identical in its timing with 'Quoth the Raven, "Nevermore"', and could be sung to the same tune, though it would not be appropriate. Kipling's method was to study the flow and timing of an air and to arrange his words accordingly. Instead of scanning his verses by setting them out in metrical feet with regularly recurrent accents, or stresses, it would be more significant to give them a musical notation since, actually, 'Mandalay' was written to the air of a popular waltz.

When Kipling was in America in 1889 he recorded his intention of composing a poem on the theme of the English Race, and of writing it to the tune of Handel's 'Dead March' in *Saul*. This project was not completed but, two or three years later, he wrote a *Barrack-Room Ballad* about a soldier's funeral, and used the *motif* he had intended for the other composition. 'Follow Me 'Ome', which was selected by Hilaire Belloc as one of Kipling's two best poems,[13] is singularly effective in the variety of time and tone which is achieved in a few lines, and it concludes with a sudden break into the rhythm of a slow march:

> 'Take 'im away! 'E's gone where the best men go.
> Take 'im away! An' the gun-wheels turnin' slow.
> Take 'im away! There's more from the place 'e come.
> Take 'im away, with the limber an' the drum.'

This, simply, is the tune of the 'Dead March' expressed in words, and suggests, inevitably to the reader, the slow thumping music of the military band in the distance. Kipling's ballads are not, as a rule, intended to be sung; but by giving the reader a hint of an old tune they provoke an unexpected emotional response:

> And the tunes that mean so much to you alone –
>   Common tunes that make you choke and blow your nose –
> Vulgar tunes that bring the laugh that brings the groan –
>   I can rip your very heartstrings out with those.

Sometimes he used a tune in this way, suggestively. An example is the savagely cynical-sentimental song, which he called the ' "Birds of Prey" March', about soldiers embarking in the rain for some colonial war. In a ribald, drunken style, the cockney song, 'Knocked 'em in the Old Kent Road', drifts in and out of the rhythm of the ballad:

> Cheer! An' we'll never march to victory.
> Cheer! An' we'll never live to 'ear the cannon roar!
>   The Large Birds o' Prey
>   They will carry us away,
> An' you'll never see your soldiers any more!

When Mrs Hill wrote her reminiscences of Kipling in India she claimed to have been present at the inception of the *Barrack-Room Ballads* in 1889.

We were on the British India steamer *Africa* sailing towards Singapore, standing by the rail when he suddenly began to hum 'Rum-ti-tum-tra-la' – shaking the ashes from his pipe overboard. I was used to this, knowing something was stirring in his brain. Humming in a musical tone, he exclaimed, 'I have it. I'll write some Tommy Atkins Ballads', and this idea kept simmering for months, with an occasional outbreak in soldier-like language.[14]

Kay Robinson described his method of composition in similar words: 'When he had got a tune into his head, the words and rhyme came as readily as when a singer vamps his own banjo accompaniment'. Kipling's phrasing is usually remarkable for its appropriateness, and his rhymes seem inevitable. Among his notebooks there is a tell-tale draft for a piece of society verse which he never finished. It is of no importance but for the form in which it is written down, in complete stanzas but with the rhyming last syllables left blank, to be filled in when the subconscious mind should provide them.

In one of his articles sent out to India[15] Kipling recounted his delight in composing a song for Gatti's music-hall and hearing it bandied across the footlights between the comedian and the chorus in the gallery.

> At the back of the Knightsbridge Barracks
> When the fog's a-gatherin' dim,
> The Lifeguard waits for the under-cook,
> But she won't wait for 'im.

Perhaps truth, perhaps fiction; but, truth or fiction, this is where the inspiration for the ballads comes from, and their execution recalls the technique of the old music-hall.

The orchestra strikes up a few bars of the air in unison; the singer comes forward and throws himself into the first verse of his song with a heavily orchestrated accompaniment *con molta espressione*. The second verse is light comedy, a patter-song spoken across the footlights in conversational tones, with a little gagging here and there, inserted so as not to break the rhythmical beat of the tune which the orchestra maintains, *allegro pianissimo*. The third verse is pure melodrama, rich with sentiment, and only bearable because it has been salted with the wit of the previous verse; and then the gallery is ripe for the conclusion, a release of emotion that has been uncomfortably stimulated. The singer gesticulates, the band crashes out in torrents of noise, the gallery sings and shouts, until even the genteel people in the stalls find their resistance broken down. The process is described by Kipling in his farcical story which turns on the promotion of publicity by means of a popular song, 'The Village that Voted the Earth was Flat'.

Imagine what its rage and pulse must have been at the incandescent hour of its birth! She only gave the chorus once. At the end of the second verse, 'Are you *with* me, boys?' she cried, and the house tore it clean away from her – '*Earth* was flat – *Earth* was flat – Flat as my hat – Flatter than that' drowning all but the bassoons and the double-basses that marked the word. 'Wonderful,' I said to Bat. 'And it's only "Nuts in May" with variations.' 'Yes – but *I* did the variations,' he replied.

Lower still in the social scale of literature were the bawdy songs that the soldiers sang in the canteen. Sailors' songs had already been collected by the literary, long before 1890, because sailors were 'romantic', but no one had thought of collecting genuine soldiers' songs, and when Kipling wrote in this traditional style it was not recognized as traditional. We must now return to 'Danny Deever', which Yeats and Eliot both selected for special notice. It is a question-and-answer ballad of a kind which has flourished in English folklore for many hundred years. Neither Yeats nor, more recently, Mr Eliot seems to have known that a grotesque bawdy song in much the same style was sung in the Army in Kipling's day, and is still to be heard. Like most folklore it exists in many versions, and had better be called, here,

'Barnacle Bill the Sailor'. In its earlier form, the alternate couplets in contrasted tones may well have served as a model for 'Danny Deever'.

A simple example of the use of a music-hall song for a music-hall theme is the ballad, 'Shillin' a Day', which goes to the tune of 'Vilikins and his Dinah', or any other Irish jig. The lover of Kipling's verse will no doubt be able to identify other basic tunes. 'Boots' may be assigned to the tune of 'John Brown's Body', with some confidence, and the irregular punctuation seems designed to point out the variations. 'Kabul River' has at least an echo about it of 'Tramp, Tramp, Tramp'; and if these assignments are not accepted as Kipling's actual use, there is still no doubt that these ballads were written to some familiar tunes of those days. Mrs Kipling's diary repeatedly used the expression: 'Ruddy was singing a new poem today ...' He would say 'Give me a hymn-tune' and, when someone suggested one, would go about for days humming it over, drumming it out with his fingers until words framed themselves to the tune, intent upon that and oblivious of the world, until he had finished his verse. It did not matter, for that purpose, that the song whose tune he borrowed was quite incongruous with the poem he intended; it was the rhythm he wanted and made his own. In an earlier chapter the haunting verses 'Let us now praise famous men' were quoted. They are like nothing else in the language in their strong unusual rhythm, except 'Pop goes the Weasel'. The assiduous student can find stranger incongruities.

(3) Kim

'He has come down steadily', said Henry James, 'from the less simple to the more simple.' If this was true of Kipling's middle period, the years of writing the *Jungle Books* and *Captains Courageous*, it was not to be true of the period into which he was moving. Kipling in the twentieth century was

certainly not a simple writer. His verse was to acquire new
harmonies and even to reveal those blots of heart's blood
which R. L. Stevenson had failed to find in the early
Barrack-Room Ballads; his prose stories which Henry James
had thought deficient in shades and subtleties were to become as richly polyphonic as Henry James's own. If the
reader will compare 'The Finest Story in the World' (1891)
with 'Wireless' (1903), or 'The Brushwood Boy' (1894) with
'They' (1904), the change will be apparent.

There was a turning-point in Kipling's life when his
youthful exuberance was put behind him, with much of his
youthful gaiety, when certain dreams had faded with the
loss of a beloved child, when he felt himself to be launched
into the bleak, unpromising sea of middle age. In the *Inclusive Verse* two poems stand side by side, dated 1902 and
1903. One of them, with the title of 'The Second Voyage',
seems to allude, defiantly and rather facetiously, to the process of settling down in middle life. Youthful enthusiasm is
discounted, adverse criticism is ignored, as life runs through
sunless seas, like a liner on its charted course, under the
serene guidance of married love.

> The sea has shorn our galleries away,
>   The salt has soiled our gilding past remede;
> Our paint is flaked and blistered by the spray,
>   Our sides are half a fathom furred in weed
>   (Foul weather!)
> And the Doves of Venus fled and the petrels came instead,
>   But Love he was our master at our need!

The other poem (of which some lines appeared as
chapter-headings in *Kim*) contains obscurities which have
baffled many readers.

> There walks no wind 'neath Heaven
>   Nor wave that shall restore
> The old careening riot
>   And the clamorous, crowded shore –
> The fountain in the desert,
>   The cistern in the waste,

> The bread we ate in secret,
>   The cup we spilled in haste.
>
> Now call I to my Captains –
> For council fly the sign –
> Now leap their zealous galleys,
>   Twelve-oared, across the brine.
> To me the straiter prison,
>   To me the heavier chain –
> To me Diego Valdez,
>   High Admiral of Spain!

It is a ballad set in the heroic age of Spain expressing the longing with which Diego Valdez the Admiral looks back to the buccaneering days of his youth, as Kipling the celebrity looks back with longing to his laborious boyhood in India. There can be no doubt about the allusion to the chain which still binds the Admiral, a galley-slave, in the servitude of duty.

The valediction to his old life was the publication of *Kim*, his last word on India, so many times laid aside, so long on the anvil. Ten years had passed since he had been an Anglo-Indian by right of service, ten years in which much had happened in India which he never appreciated. Lord Curzon invited him to Simla as a guest in 1899, but viceroys, he said, were not much in his line. India remained, in his eyes, the unchanging East, as he remembered it from childhood, and so he described it, lovingly, in *Kim*.

The new book owed something to his youthful romance, *Mother Maturin*, but how much cannot be told since no one now living has read the earlier work. Mrs Hill gave the following account of it:

> *Mother Maturin* I have read, which was never published because John Lockwood Kipling was not satisfied with it. It is the story of an old Irishwoman who kept an opium den in Lahore but sent her daughter to be educated in England. She married a Civilian and came to live in Lahore – hence a story how Government secrets came to be known in the Bazaar and *vice versa*.[16]

In London Rudyard had turned to *Mother Maturin* again, and then perhaps realized that his father had judged rightly in condemning it. The manuscript remained for years in the safe at A. P. Watt's office until in 1899 Rudyard brought it down to Rottingdean to ransack it for notions which he could work into *Kim*. Thereafter *Mother Maturin* vanished, probably destroyed by the author, though many years later Kipling prepared a draft for a film scenario which contained episodes from the old story.

The second plan for an Indian Romance took shape at 'Naulakha' in 1894. Now it was to be the life-story of *Kim O'rishti*, an Irish soldier's orphan, living foot-loose in India. Three times begun and laid aside, it was abandoned in favour of *Captains Courageous*. In the fall of 1899, having finished with *Stalky*, he turned again to *Kim*. Many times he took the draft down to Tisbury to be smoked over with the 'Pater' until in August 1900 Carrie wrote triumphantly in her diary that it was pronounced complete by a family council, which included the 'Pater' and Sallie Norton.

It grew like the Djinn released from the brass bottle [Rudyard wrote], and the more we explored its possibilities the more opulence of detail did we discover. I do not know what proportion of an iceberg is below water-line, but *Kim* as it finally appeared was about one-tenth of what the first lavish specification called for . . .

Kim took care of himself. The only trouble was to keep him within bounds. Between us we knew every step, sight, and smell on his casual road, as well as all the persons he met. Once only, as I remember, did I have to bother the India Office, where there are four acres of books and documents in the basements, for a certain work on Indian magic which I always regret that I could not steal . . .

At last I reported *Kim* finished. 'Did *it* stop, or you?' the Father asked. And when I told him that it was *It*, he said : 'Then it oughtn't to be too bad.' He would take no sort of credit for any of his suggestions, memories or confirmations – not even for that single touch of the low-driving sunlight which makes luminous every detail in the picture of the Grand Trunk Road at eventide.

The Himalayas I painted *all* by myself, as the children say. So also the picture of the Lahore Museum of which I had once been Deputy Curator for six weeks – unpaid but immensely important. And there was a half-chapter of the Lama sitting down in the blue-green shadows at the foot of a glacier, telling Kim stories out of the Jatakas, which was truly beautiful but, as my old Classics master would have said, 'otiose', and it was removed almost with tears.[17]

Kim was published at the end of 1900 about the time of the 'Khaki Election', when public opinion was sharply divided over the political views with which Kipling's name was linked, and so did not at first produce the chorus of applause which had greeted some of his earlier work. There was some hostile, and more of cool and grudging, criticism like that of Arnold Bennett, who said in an essay: '*Stalky* chilled me and *Kim* killed me.'[18] Since then the book has grown in stature and is often now selected as the Kipling book with the highest measure of artistry. It is, however, in the author's own words, not a novel but 'nakedly picaresque and plotless'.

Surely no other Englishman has written of India with such loving interest! Mr Forster's *Passage to India* is the only work which can be laid beside it, and in many respects *Kim* comes well out of the comparison. In this instance Forster, not Kipling, is the political writer, the observer of a passing phase. With his cool, sensitive regard Forster appraises the Indian character and the Indian scene, noting conscious and unconscious processes, analysing with a skill that Kipling did not and could not attempt to equal. In the cold light of Forster's observation all is clear and all unlovable.

Kim is not a political romance; the reader soon loses interest in a plot which the author does not trouble to elaborate. The education of a police spy – and that is what, superficially, *Kim* seems to be about – is hardly a subject for an *epos*; nor does it much matter. The hero, Kim, is thrown by this path into the vagabond life of India so that we may see, and smell, the hot scented dust and the people of the land. Here is a boy roving through India, loving it and causing us to love it. Politics, the Empire, the Law, are taken for granted. It is not 'Kim's' affair, nor the reader's, to question the credentials of the *Pax Britannica*, but to savour life within its borders. Nothing is explained or excused or justified.

Apart from a slight sketch of Lockwood Kipling ('the Keeper of the Wonder-house') in the opening chapter, Englishmen do not play a conspicuous part in the story. 'Bennett', the English Chaplain, is shown in an unfavourable light, and the Irish Chaplain, though less unpleasing, is merely a stock figure.* The drummer-boy who chums with 'Kim' in barracks is allowed none of the charm which, in spite of their depravity, was conceded to the 'Drums of the Fore and Aft'. 'Lurgan, the healer of sick pearls,' is a nondescript, not a true *sahib*. Kim's kindly patron, 'Colonel Creighton', is kept in the background.

The interest is all concentrated upon Kim's relation with four natives of India: the Pathan horse-dealer, Mahbub Ali; the Bengali, Hurree Chunder; the old dowager *sahiba* from Saharunpore; and the Tibetan lama who steals the limelight to become hero of the book. The lean ferocious Pathan and the suave sophisticated Babu seem at first to be stock characters, until they burst into life by showing the contradictions of living persons. The faithless, cruel Mah-

* Kipling's views on missionaries, when he was a young man, are expressed in a letter written from 'Naulakha' to the Rev J. Gillespie, on 16 October 1895. The original is in the Houghton Library.

'It is my fortune to have been born and to a large extent brought up among those whom white men call "heathen"; and while I recognize the paramount duty of every white man to follow the teachings of his creed and conscience as "a debtor to the whole law", it seems to me cruel that white men, whose governments are armed with the most murderous weapons known to science, should amaze and confound their fellow creatures with a doctrine of salvation imperfectly understood by themselves and a code of ethics foreign to the climate and instincts of those races whose most cherished customs they outrage and whose gods they insult.'

bub is gradually revealed as true and even tender; the volatile, timid Babu as discreet and courageous when put to the test; and the interaction of these characters illumines Kim's slow adolescence. This is a display of the novelist's art which Kipling rarely achieved in his other works (unless perhaps in that juvenile *tour de force, The Story of the Gadsbys*). There was a real Mahbub Ali, as Kay Robinson put on record; Babus looking like Hurree Chunder are plentiful in Calcutta to this day, but the *sahiba* and the lama were original inventions, new in literature. The *sahiba* was the first full-length in Kipling's gallery of elderly women, a group worth examining. The lama has no literary ancestry or progeny; he is Kipling's final comment on Buddhist Asia.

The author dwells lovingly upon some minor characters, the Jat, the Ressaldar, the 'Woman of Shamlegh' (who had made an earlier appearance as 'Lispeth' in *Plain Tales*); but all disappear from the scene before the end, leaving the stage to Kim and the lama, the two principals. The lama withdraws his mind into the world of reality, having rejected all the appearances of the world of illusion, even such symbols of infinity as his beloved Hills. Kim, too, has reached a stage of maturity and must take a decision. No longer a ragamuffin of the bazaars, but a beautiful godlike youth, he must choose between contemplation and action. Is he to follow the lama or to return to the chains which enslave the Pathan and the Babu to their material duties? Divided in loyalty, like Mowgli between the Village and the Jungle, living like the Brushwood Boy on two mental planes, he can be more conscious of the marriage of East and West than the Calcutta-trained Babu or the Pathan who has learned to outwit the English by their own devices. In the last stage of the lama's pilgrimage Kim quite forgets his own task in the world, while absorbed in the humble duty of love and gratitude.

He begged in the dawn, set blankets for the lama's meditation, held the weary head on his lap through the noonday heats, fanning away the flies till his wrists ached, begged again the evenings, and rubbed the lama's feet, who rewarded him with promise of Freedom – today, tomorrow, or, at furthest, the next day.

And when that day came, it was the lama who reminded Kim that he was a *sahib* with another course of life to pursue. Again the dilemma was presented, East or West, the Jungle or the Village, the world of dreams or the world of action; and, though it is not expressly stated, the reader is left with the assurance that Kim, like Mowgli, and like the Brushwood Boy, will find reality in action, not in contemplation.

With an almost audible click, he felt the wheels of his being lock up anew on the world without. Things that rode meaningless on the eyeball an instant before slid into proper proportion. Roads were meant to be walked upon, houses to be lived in, cattle to be driven, fields to be tilled, and men and women to be talked to. They were all real and true.

The desire to penetrate the occult exercised a strong fascination over Rudyard throughout life, an attraction which he resisted, not altogether successfully. In this respect Rudyard was a man of his day, interested in what interested his contemporaries, a reader of the numerous novels and poems that touched on these themes. His youth was passed in a circle where Madame Blavatsky and the early Theosophists had made no small impression. Later he was a friend of William James and acquainted with the speculations which, in 1902, were to be formulated in the *Varieties of Religious Experience*, the book which made a rational analysis of Eastern and Western mysticism.

The study of the irrational, the subliminal, the supernormal made great strides after the Viennese psychologists had found the key to the unconscious mind, with the consequence that many of the phenomena which the men of the eighteen-nineties regarded as supernatural were examined by the men of the nineteen-twenties in terms of the new psychology. Rudyard's later stories were to provide some evidence of his movement with this stream of thought.

From Sir Richard's Song (1906)

I followed my Duke ere I was a lover,
   To take from England fief and fee;
But now this game is the other way over —
   But now England hath taken me!

     *   *   *   *

As for my Father in his tower,
   Asking news of my ship at sea,
He will remember his own hour —
   Tell him England hath taken me!

As for my Mother in her bower,
   That rules my Father so cunningly,
She will remember a maiden's power —
   Tell her England hath taken me!

As for my Brother in Rouen City,
   A nimble and naughty page is he,
But he will come to suffer and pity —
   Tell him England hath taken me!

As for my little Sister waiting
   In the pleasant orchards of Normandie,
Tell her youth is the time for mating —
   Tell her England hath taken me!

As for my comrades in camp and highway,
   That lift their eyebrows scornfully,
Tell them their way is not my way —
   Tell them England hath taken me!

     *   *   *   *

from Sir Richard's Song (1800)

I followed my Duke ere I was a lover,
To take from England fief and fee;
But now this game is the other way over—
But now England hath taken me!

As for my Father in his tower,
Asking news of my ship at sea,
He will remember his own hour—
Tell him England hath taken me!

As for my Mother in her bower,
That rules my Father so cunningly,
She will remember a maiden's power—
Tell her England hath taken me!

As for my Brother in Rouen City,
A nimble and naughty page is he,
But he will come to suffer and pity—
Tell him England hath taken me!

As for my little Sister waiting
In the pleasant orchards of Normandie,
Tell her youth is the time for mating—
Tell her England hath taken me!

As for my comrades in camp and highway,
That lift their eyebrows scornfully,
Tell them their way is not my way—
Tell them England hath taken me!

[15]

A Home in Sussex

(1902–8)

In October 1899 Mr Harmsworth of the *Daily Mail*, for whom Rudyard wrote 'The Absent-minded Beggar', came down to see the Kiplings in a motor-car of his own. They were instantly converted to the new form of transport which released them from restraints that were beginning to bear heavily and in December Rudyard hired a motor from Brighton, with an 'engineer' at three and a half guineas a week. It was a

Victoria-hooded, carriage-sprung, carriage-braked, single-cylinder, belt-driven, fixed-ignition, Embryo which, at times, could cover eight miles an hour.[1]

The next summer, when they returned from Africa, they looked for something better in a market that was rapidly expanding. Rudyard bought a steam-driven American car of a long-forgotten type, called a 'Locomobile', and for two years drove it from end to end of Sussex, in a world still unprovided with petrol-pumps, spare tyres, or repair shops. Every motorist had to be his own mechanic and had to learn how to do running repairs as new problems arose. Two or three times a week Rudyard and Carrie set off for long drives with the 'engineer', and her diary gives the impression that few outings were completed without mishap.

Motoring misadventures play a large part in his stories during the next few years, and, once or twice, dominate the scene. The 'Locomobile' is faithfully described in 'Steam Tactics', a complex tale of sailors ashore, officious policemen, and Mr Loder's private zoo; the machine alone draws these diverse elements together. Rudyard often exercised his

mind with parodies in verse, and to this period belongs his
series, *The Muse among the Motors*, which first appeared in
the *Daily Mail*.

House-hunting was the ostensible reason for their drives
across the county. One day when the 'Locomobile' had
broken down, they went by train to Etchingham, then took
a 'fly' through woodland lanes to Burwash where there was
talk of a house named 'Bateman's'. It was a well-built square
Jacobean house of stone in a lonely valley, at the foot of a
steep lane running down from an unfrequented village.
'Bateman's' took their fancy so that for three days they
talked of little else, but while they hesitated, someone
stepped in and rented it. That was in August 1900, and
nearly two years passed before they heard that 'Bateman's'
was vacant again. It happened that again the 'Locomobile'
was out of order so that the second visit to Burwash, like
the first, was made by train and hired fly. There was no
doubt in their minds: this was the dream-house, the 'very-
own-house' of their private baby-talk, and they snatched it
out of the market.

When all was signed and sealed, the seller said: 'Now I can
ask you something. How are you going to manage about getting
to and from the station? It's nearly four miles, and I've used up
two pair of horses on the hill here.' A motor-car? 'Oh, those
things haven't come to stay.'

By this time the Kiplings had bought their second automobile, a Lanchester, and, so primitive was the motor-trade
in those days, Mr Lanchester in person delivered the car at
their door.

In three years [said Rudyard] from our purchase, the railway
station had passed out of our lives. In seven, I heard my chauf-
feur say to an under-powered visiting sardine-tin: 'Hills? There
ain't any hills on the London road.' [2]

The removal to 'Bateman's', on 3 September 1902 – it was
their last house-moving as they were sure it would be – was
taken easily by Rudyard and desperately hard by Carrie.

She rather thought the contractor's men were drunk, and the state of the house when she took charge was like 'chaos and black night', as she wrote in her diary. It was the end of the month before she began to enjoy the comfort of a fine mild autumn. Rudyard and the children had already taken the place to their hearts, and when the first family visitors, Stan and Cissie Baldwin and Hugh Poynter, were received, they too pronounced 'Bateman's' charming.

Rudyard then took his final decision to dispose of 'Naulakha'. He would never again now live in Vermont, never again visit the United States to stir the dreadful memory of 1899. He emptied 'Naulakha' of what they needed; invited Dr Conland to help himself to guns, rods, and sporting gear, and sold the estate to the Cabots for $8,000, much below cost price. It seems likely that Beatty Balestier had done his brother-in-law one more ill turn by hinting that he would dispute the title, and this may have been one reason why 'Naulakha' did not fetch a more adequate price.

Rudyard Kipling to C. E. Norton

30 November, 1902

We left Rottingdean because Rottingdean was getting too populated, though we didn't want to part from Aunt Georgie. Then we discovered England which we had never done before . . . and went to live in it. England is a wonderful land. It is the most marvellous of all foreign countries that I have ever been in. It is made up of trees and green fields and mud and the gentry, and at last I'm one of the gentry – I'll take a new pen and explain.

Behold us lawful owners of a grey stone lichened house – A.D. 1634 over the door – beamed, panelled, with old oak staircase, and all untouched and unfaked. Heaven looked after it in the dissolute times of mid-victorian restoration and caused the vicar to send his bailiff to live in it for 40 years, and he lived in peaceful filth and left everything as he found it.

It is a good and peaceable place standing in terraced lawns nigh to a walled garden of old red brick, and two fat-headed oast-houses with red brick stomachs, and an aged silver-grey dovecot

on top. There is what they call a river at the bottom of the lawn.
It appears on all maps and that, except after very heavy rains, is
the only place where it puts in any appearance. . . . Its name is
the Dudwell, and it is quite ten feet wide.[3]

He learned to know the River Dudwell better. Almost every
autumn it flooded the meadows, overflowed the garden on
several occasions, and at least once came into the house –
not always a 'Friendly Brook'.

In 1903 *The Five Nations*, his book of South African
verse, was sent to press, and with that he felt an instant
sense of relief. It was the end of an epoch for him as for
the Empire. A strong reaction was setting in against the
sentiments of wartime patriotism, and the prospects of the
imperialists in Parliament were blighted by Joseph Chamberlain's resignation in October. A day of great events was
over, and Rudyard recorded the fact oracularly:

> Things never yet created things –
> 'Once on a time there was a Man.'

Political urgency, gloomy though the outlook might be, was
shifting back from Africa to Westminster and, though he
continued to winter at the Cape for four years longer, Rudyard put South African affairs behind him with the publication of *The Five Nations*, as he had put India behind him,
long ago and far away, with the publication of *Kim*.

Never was the width of his interest more noticeable or
his power of assimilating new technical information more
astonishing than in the work he began at the end of 1903.
Among many celebrities who made it their business to
know him about that time were the two makers of Nigeria,
Sir George Goldie whom he met at the Cape, and Sir Frederick Lugard whom he met in Sussex. Though Rudyard had
never been in tropical Africa, he wrote one convincing
story, 'A Deal in Cotton', about the last days of the Arab
slave-trade, which must have been derived from his talks
with the two pro-consuls. He told it as if at a reunion of his

old school-friends, with 'Stalky' as one of the group; and Major Dunsterville of the 20th Sikhs had, in fact, re-entered Kipling's life. He visited 'Bateman's' in May 1904 and frequently thereafter.

This was a slight switch of interest but, as well as 'A Deal in Cotton', Rudyard wrote three other stories on widely differing themes in 1904. A settled way of life in Sussex, a home of his own with seclusion and privacy, stimulated a flow of new notions, as the first happy years in Vermont had done.

'Mrs Bathurst' is a strange and difficult tale. Rudyard had now quite outgrown the diffuseness and exuberance which marred some of the stories of his Allahabad period. He could afford to take his time, and let nothing go to press until it had been exhaustively edited and revised. It was not uncommon for the first draft of a story to be two or three times longer than its published form, as he whimsically explained:

In an auspicious hour, read your final draft and consider faithfully every paragraph, sentence and word, blacking out where requisite. Let it lie by to drain as long as possible. At the end of that time, re-read and you should find that it will bear a second shortening. Finally, read it aloud and at leisure. Maybe a shade more brushwork will then indicate or impose itself. If not, praise Allah and let it go, and 'when thou hast done, repent not'. . . . I have had tales by me for three or five years which shortened themselves almost yearly.[4]

He had not acquired this technique when he wrote 'The Drums of the Fore and Aft'; he perhaps overdid it when he shortened 'Mrs Bathurst', a complex story which would have supplied most writers with a full-length novel. It suffers from too much compression, so that in parts it is unintelligible. Nevertheless, for all its obscurity, 'Mrs Bathurst' is a powerful story, the account of a woman who is described as not very seductive or amusing or intelligent, but who was never forgotten by any man who made her acquaintance.

'Tisn't beauty, so to speak, nor good talk necessarily. It's just It. Some women'll stay in a man's memory if they once walk down a street.'

The original of Mrs Bathurst is said to have been a barmaid in Christchurch, New Zealand;[5] the setting of the tale is at Simonstown, the naval base at the Cape, but these are subsidiary matters. What the reader remembers is the glimpse of 'Mrs Bathurst walking down towards us with that blindish look in her eyes and the reticule in her hand', as the two sailors saw her in a cinema film. It is one of the earliest allusions to the cinematograph in fiction, as it is, perhaps, the earliest use of the word 'It' for feminine charm.

The critics had fallen foul of Kipling's early attempts to portray women, finding them all detestable, from 'the Colonel's Lady to Judy O'Grady'. The gently smiling, faithful, mature Mrs Bathurst was different indeed, but so elliptic is the process of her story that the reader is never plainly told what becomes of her. She is flashed on to the screen and off, with disastrous but undisclosed consequences to the sailor whom she has followed round the world. Such a tale could never be a popular favourite and it seems hardly credible that it should have been written by the author of 'The Absent-minded Beggar'.

It was no sooner finished than he set to work at 'They' (begun at Cape Town in February 1904), another story which some readers found obscure when it was first published. Since 'Baa, Baa, Black Sheep', he had made no direct personal revelations in his prose work, though many of his stories, of course, were founded upon incidents or characters that had come under his observation. When Rudyard himself appeared in these stories it was behind the mask he assumed to protect himself from publicity, not Rudyard as he was but Rudyard as he wished to be seen. Three times and, I think, three times only, he dropped the mask, revealing, in one instance, his unhappy childhood, in the others the unforgotten pain of his child's death. To early critics the story called 'They' was merely psychical fiction in his new style with a theme that was in the fashionable taste, another story like Henry James's *Turn of the Screw* (1898). The setting of the story is drawn from Rudyard's memories of motoring through Sussex, with many brilliant landscapes in his Pre-Raphaelite manner. The allegory is drawn straight from his own sorrow; the years of house-hunting, at last concluded, had been darkened by a shadow that never lifted from the heart of either parent. Soon after their return from America in 1899, Lockwood had written with unwonted openness to their old friend Sarah Norton:

Rud and Carrie, I may confide to you and Mr Norton who love them, found going back to the 'Elms' much harder and more painful than they had imagined. The house and garden are full of the lost child and poor Rud told his mother how he saw her when a door opened, when a space was vacant at table, coming out of every green dark corner of the garden, radiant – and heart breaking. They can talk of her, however, which is much, for Carrie has hitherto been stone-dumb. But to Mrs K. she softened and broke forth and they had long discourse, mingling their tears as women may and mothers must. Over every grave, at long last, the high road must run, and nobody wishes to hasten the time of indifference – but a sore heartache, I am sure, is relieved by sympathetic – (Lord! in the blue sky! What twaddle I'm writing). Of course, it is relieved by speech and friendly hands; all I meant to say was that those poor souls have got thus far with their burden – which will grow easier to bear with time.[6]

He and Carrie often went to visit his father's friend, St Loe Strachey, the editor of the *Spectator*, near Guildford in Surrey. They stayed a week-end with the Stracheys in June 1900 and on a Sunday morning walked together through the countryside, while their hosts went to church.

> There runs a road by Merrow Down –
> A grassy track today it is –
> An hour out of Guildford town,
> Above the river Wey it is.

Here, when they heard the horse-bells ring, ...

In the mind's eye Rudyard saw the long procession of the
dead who had walked the Pilgrims' Way throughout the
centuries, till time lost its significance. The transience of life
was its one persisting feature and a year as long to the grief-
stricken as a thousand years. From Merrow Down to Brookland in Romney Marsh there was no landscape, now, that
did not recall to Rudyard that slight figure, dancing through
the fern; and when, deep in woods of stilly oak, he found
his dream-house at last, it lacked one blessing only for him,
the child that might have taken his hand. It was not for
him to beat against the bars of space and time in so-called
psychical research. So, in his story, the blind woman in the
haunted house, whose second-sight reveals the presence of
the dream-children, was no true guide for him, who saw
with open eyes so deeply into the world of actuality. She,
too, recognized his vocation as craftsman not as mystic:
'For you it would be wrong,' she said, 'you who must never
come here again.' This prohibition lay upon the world of
dreams, not upon real Sussex and its living people.

A day or two after finishing 'They', his resilient intelligence had fastened upon a new subject which, wrote Carrie,
was 'a keen pleasure to him', a subject as far removed from
the enchantments of the occult as it could well be. He set to
work at an experiment in science fiction – as popular then
as now – a vision of the future called 'With the Night Mail'.
It is cast in the form of a journalist's account of an Atlantic crossing, by air, in the year 2000. Never before had
he allowed himself such a debauch of technical writing as
in this story, for which he invented thousands of words of
shop-talk to be put into the mouth of his 'M'Andrew' of
the future, and filled up pages with answers to imaginary
correspondents and advertisements for machines not yet invented.

Far more remarkable than his vision of the airship –
which was paralleled by the similar picture H. G. Wells
painted for *The War in the Air* – is his astonishing forecast
of the contrivances, the utilities, and the safety precautions

that airborne commerce would bring into being. Radio communication was new in 1904. Although a few ships were fitted with wireless telegraphy, there was no radio-telephony, no hint or suggestion of public broadcasting; but Kipling's air-liner moved through a world-wide network of radio services, supplying weather forecasts, and allotting safety-levels and landing priorities, thirty years before anyone else had dreamed of 'flying control'. His airship is engined with gas-turbines and is navigated on light-beams which pierce the clouds.

Three years later, in 1907, that is still before Wilbur Wright had come to Europe or Blériot flown the Channel, he wrote the draft of a sequel to 'With the Night Mail', calling it 'As Easy as A.B.C.', a political invention, filling out a sketch which he had lightly indicated in the first story.

It is not a Utopia: there is no suggestion that this is what Rudyard would have wished to come about; nor is it, like George Orwell's *1984*, a forecast of horror; it is a mere statement of what might occur when the technocrats should have made the progress which, to a seeing eye in 1907, they seemed likely to make. Broadcasting techniques were foreseen with uncanny accuracy and the transmission of energy by radio is carried to much greater length in his fantasy than has yet been achieved in real life, with the consequence that an international Utility Company of radio technicians, the 'Aerial Board of Control', has imperceptibly taken over the administration of the planet. The sovereign states have withered away, and political ideologies exist only as picturesque survivals or atavistic patches of superstition. The solution is 'as easy as A.B.C.'; power must pass to the organization that directs traffic through the world-wide radio network. Of its structure he has nothing to say except that it is cosmopolitan.

On the passing of politics, Kipling speaks clearly enough in his own voice. How gladly will the men of the future abandon the follies of Democracy, the slogans, the street-processions, the mob-oratory, the ancient corruptions, the corroding sentimentalities, in return for a system that secures privacy for private persons and adequate public services. 'Transportation is Civilization', and if the 'A.B.C.' takes responsibility for the 'traffic and all that that implies', politics may be forgotten.

The point of the story, the fable, is the emergence in Chicago of a group of political sentimentalists who alarm their neighbours by assembling in crowds, making speeches, and casting votes; and the solution triumphantly propounded by the Aerial Board of Control is to let them do it as a comic turn on the light programme of the London Broadcasting Service. Strangely enough, this situation is not treated as farce but as a narrow escape from social disaster, in an age when all sane men have realized the reckless cruelty of men in the mass. The future is not, in Kipling's view, a pleasant world to live in, but beset with neuroses, and doomed to extinction by a birthrate dwindling towards zero.

Radio techniques had engaged his attention since his cruise with the Channel Fleet in 1898, when the Navy was experimenting with Marconi's new devices; and Rudyard used their attempt to communicate through a half-comprehended medium (which physicists, in those days, called the 'aether') as a foil to communications of another sort, in his brilliantly constructed story, 'Wireless'. If messages could pass through the impalpable 'aether', as if material obstructions in space were of no account, why should not time be equally penetrable?

After writing 'With the Night Mail' he had swung back to the past, and in September of the same year sat down to a series of tales from English history. 'You'll have to look up your references rather carefully', said his father.

Something of the kind had been stirring in his imagination for a year or two. At Rottingdean he had consulted his 'Uncle Ned', a good medieval scholar, about historical reading, and had received a letter of advice couched in terms which give no hint of the mystical solemnity suggested by Burne-Jones's pictures. This reveals another side of life at 'North End House'.

Sir E. Burne-Jones to Rudyard Kipling

(Summer 1897?)

Sir,

I should like to caution you against the new-fangled bicycle you mention. I knew a gentleman most respectable on the Stock Exchange and connected by marriage with the Pocklington family who stand very high in the county as had a fatal injury in his *latissimus dorsi* in consequence of one of these bicycles. My advice would be if I might presume, Sir, stick to books.

The last volume of Mr Mommsen, a German gentleman, History of Rome, has about the state of Britain and other countries at the time of the withdrawing of the legions. The legionary system, Sir, had broke down some time before, in Constantine's time, but though short it is a very good account and would repay your perusal.

I will send you Geoffrey of Monmouth where is a lot of names – might prove useful – rum names, Sir, as ever was. He's a author as has been down in the market but is looking up now, and though his style is pomptious, being wrote in Latin he didn't understand, scholars is beginning to depend on him a good deal, as having got his stories out of old books, and not making them up himself as was for a long time supposed.

In the same humble volume is the writings of a cross old cove as ever lived, named Gildas, who didn't approve of the way people went on. Nennius, Sir, in the same volume is very skimpy but said to be all right as far as he goes.

Glastonbury and Iona was going it pretty strong in the Christian line, a good hundred years – I dare say – before the English come, as were Pagans of the most outrageous kind, though with great aptitude for religious teaching, as our glorious reformation shows later on.

Your tale, Sir, as I think you call the Best Story in the World, shows what the public might look for in your treatment of a ancient subject, and I think it about time the matter was took out of the hand of Canon Farrar – it's worse than rot, Sir, all that.

And I'll send you a book of costumes, civil and military, and anything else as I can lay hands on, in my limited libery. But I find, Sir, in getting up a subjeck, it's no good expecting a good book about it. The sort aren't written and that's the truth; get the lumber together, I say, and set fire to it yourself, if I may make so bold.

Yours very respectful

E. Burne-Jones.[7]

Rudyard's medieval studies led him to Domesday Book, and the first product of his invention after the removal to 'Bateman's' was the fable of the cat and the rat in Dudwell Mill, which he called 'Below the Mill Dam', an amusing piece of satire told to the accompaniment of the mill-wheel grinding out extracts from the Sussex Domesday.

The valley was alive with historic memories:

Just beyond the west fringe of our land stood the long, over-grown slag-heap of a most ancient forge, supposed to have been worked by the Phoenicians and Romans and, since then, uninter-ruptedly till the middle of the eighteenth century. The bracken and rush-patches still hid stray pigs of iron, and if one scratched a few inches through the rabbit-shaven turf, one came on the narrow mule-tracks of peacock-hued furnace-slag laid down in Elizabeth's day. The ghost of a road climbed up out of this dead arena, and crossed our fields, where it was known as 'The Gun-way', and popularly connected with Armada times. Every foot of that little corner was alive with ghosts and shadows.[8]

When Rudyard in October 1904 asked his friend Gwynne to buy a paper donkey's head for the children's play of Puck and Titania, the setting for the historical stories pre-sented itself. Their theatre was a fairy ring beside the brook, at the foot of a grassy slope which they knew as Pook's Hill.* By January 1905 Rudyard was hard at work with the historical stories that occupied the greater part of his atten-tion for the next five years. The first series, *Puck of Pook's*

* It is the long spur running up from the Dudwell Brook to Bur-wash Common, and is visible from the western windows of 'Bateman's'. There are several Pook's Hills in Sussex, but I can find no evidence that the name was attached to this hill before 1904.

Hill (1906), came rapidly off his pen. Then came a pause in
publication while he made a number of experiments. He
tried and rejected a story of Dr Johnson, a story of Defoe,
a story of King Arthur, but at last elaborated and approved
the eleven stories which were issued as *Rewards and Fairies*
in 1910. Much of the writing was done at the 'Woolsack',
and much of the research in the admirable South African
Public Library at Cape Town. In the summers the stories
were often taken down to Tisbury to be 'smoked over' by
Lockwood Kipling.

As these were primarily stories for children it is not surprising that their style changed as his own children grew
older. In 1904, when John and Elsie (the 'Dan' and 'Una'
of the books) acted their fairy play, they were no more than
seven and eight years old. When *Puck of Pook's Hill* was
published they were nine and ten, when *Rewards and
Fairies* was published, thirteen and fourteen. At a glance
the stories seem rather beyond the comprehension of children of these ages, but Rudyard wrote, as he wrote his other
'juvenile' works, on more than one mental level.

I worked the material in three or four overlaid tints and
textures, which might or might not reveal themselves according
to the shifting light of sex, youth and experience. The tales had
to be read by children, before people realised that they were
meant for grown-ups.[9]

Even making this allowance, the later stories are best suited
to adult readers; and the tale of Rahere the Jester ('The
Tree of Justice') may even be classed as one of Rudyard's
obscure psychological pieces.

The plan, of introducing historical incidents into modern
life as if in another dimension, was not original; Rudyard
never hesitated to borrow, and, in this instance, his model
was taken from the stories of the talented lady who wrote
under the name of 'E. Nesbit'. That autumn the children
had been delighted with her *Phoenix and the Carpet*, and
Rudyard had written to thank her for it. In 'E. Nesbit's'

tales, as in most others of magical intrusion into common life, the focus of interest is contemporary. *The Phoenix and the Carpet* is a story about shabby-genteel life in Camden Town, illuminated by the odd contrast of the supernatural episodes. The author scarcely troubles to make you believe in her magic; she is content to show you with awful clarity and delightful humour what Camden Town makes of it. In Kipling's 'Puck' stories the emphasis is reversed. The mechanism by which Puck confronts the two children with characters from English history, though skilfully worked, is a mere subsidiary device; nor are the historical episodes, themselves, at the heart of the matter. The Land and the People, persisting through Time and all its revolutions, are the theme of the two 'Puck' books.

> So to the land our hearts we give
>   Till the sure magic strike,
> And Memory, Use, and Love make live
>   Us and our fields alike –
> That deeper than our speech and thought,
>   Beyond our reason's sway,
> Clay of the pit whence we were wrought
>   Yearns to its fellow-clay.[10]

Striking his roots into Sussex, Rudyard now explored the dimension of time as, in his travelling days, he had explored the dimension of space. His old inquiry: 'What should they know of England who only England know?' was taking a new direction. What can they know of present-day England who do not feel its continuity with England's past? So, the hero of the two books is not Puck, not Dan or Una, not Parnesius or Sir Richard Dalyngridge; the hero is old Hobden, the yeoman who understands the whole story of the valley and the brook, by instinct and tradition. Proud as he was to become a landowner in Sussex, Rudyard's pride soon humbled itself before the historical figure of Hobden the Hedger, who is relevant to the life of the place in all its phases.

His dead are in the churchyard – thirty generations laid.
Their names were old in history when Domesday Book was made;
And the passion and the piety and prowess of his line
Have seeded, rooted, fruited in some land the Law calls mine.[11]

As newcomers, the Kiplings were naturally accepted with
reserve by the village people; and with their passionate love
of privacy, Rudyard and Carrie were content to keep themselves to themselves at 'Bateman's'. They nourished no
romantic illusions about the peasantry.

Of the little one-street village up the hill we only knew that,
according to the guide-books, they came of a smuggling, sheep-
stealing stock, brought more or less into civilisation within the
past three generations. Those of them who worked for us, and
who I presume would today be called 'Labour', struck for higher
pay than they had agreed on as soon as we were committed to
our first serious works. My foreman and general contractor, himself of their race, and soon to become our good friend, said:
'They think they've got ye. They think there's no harm in tryin'
it.' There was not. I had sense enough to feel that most of them
were artists and craftsmen, either in stone or timber, or wood-
cutting, or drain-laying or – which is a gift – the aesthetic disposition of dirt; persons of contrivance who would conjure with
any sort of material ...

There was one among them,* close upon seventy when we first
met, a poacher by heredity and instinct, a gentleman who, when
his need to drink was on him, which was not too often, absented
himself and had it out alone; and he was more 'one with Nature'
than whole parlours full of poets. He became our special stay and
counsellor. ... In his later years – he lived to be close on eighty-
five – he would, as I am doing now, review his past, which held
incident enough for many unpublishable volumes. He spoke of
old loves, fights, intrigues, anonymous denunciations 'by such
folk as knew writing', and vindictive conspiracies carried out with
oriental thoroughness. Of poaching he talked in all its branches,
and of pitched battles (guns barred) with heavy-handed keepers
in the old days in Lord Ashburnham's woods where a man might
pick up a fallow-deer. His sagas were lighted with pictures of
Nature as he, indeed, knew her; night-pieces and dawn-

* His real name was Isted.

breakings; stealthy returns and the thinking out of alibis, all naked by the fire, while his clothes dried; and of the face and temper of the next twilight under which he stole forth to follow his passion. His wife, after she had known us for ten years, would range through a past that accepted magic, witchcraft and love-philtres, for which last there was a demand as late as the middle sixties.

Rudyard did not search out historical episodes from books but drew them from the life around him. Never was his sense of dedication more clear, that in his best writing he surrendered himself to an impulse that came from without.

The whole thing set and linked itself. I fell first upon Normans and Saxons. Parnesius came later, directly out of a little wood above the Phoenician forge; and the rest of the tales followed in order. The Father came over to see us and, hearing 'Hal o' the Draft', closed in with fore-reaching pen, presently ousted me from my table, and inlaid the description of Hal's own drawing-knife. He liked that tale, and its companion piece 'The Wrong Thing', which latter he embellished, notably in respect to an Italian fresco-worker, whose work never went 'deeper than the plaster'.

Of 'Dymchurch Flit', with which I was always unashamedly content, he asked: 'Where did you get that lighting from?' It had come of itself. *Qua* workmanship, that tale and two night-pieces in 'Cold Iron' are the best in that kind I have ever made, but somehow 'The Treasure and the Law' always struck me as too heavy for its frame.[12]

In the whole range of Rudyard Kipling's work, no pieces have been more effective in moulding the thought of a generation than the three stories of the centurions defending Hadrian's Wall during the decline of the Roman Empire. 'There is no hope for Rome,' said the wise old father of the centurion. 'She has forsaken her Gods, but if the Gods forgive *us* here, we may save Britain.' The story of the centurion's task is told as a panegyric of duty and service, which press their claims all the more urgently when leaders fail to lead and statesmen study only their own careers. It strengthened the nerve of many a young soldier in the dark days of 1915 and 1941, and, if that was its intention, it mattered little that Rudyard's Roman soldiers of the fourth century too much resembled subalterns of the Indian Army.

To many readers the verses that accompany these stories mark the height of Kipling's literary achievement and here, if anywhere, he attained to the level of pure poetry, free from the cockney mannerisms, the occasional vulgarities and brutalities that the critics had been so quick to detect and to denounce in his earlier verse. *Puck of Pook's Hill* (1906) includes 'Puck's Song', the 'Harp-song of the Dane Women', 'Cities and Thrones and Powers', 'The Children's Song' ('Land of our Birth ...'), 'A Smuggler's Song'. The verses for *Rewards and Fairies*, written in the autumn of 1909, are even more remarkable; they include 'A Charm' ('Take of English Earth ...'), 'Cold Iron', 'The Looking-Glass', 'A St Helena Lullaby', 'Brookland Road' and 'The Way through the Woods'. And the series continues with the songs written in the following year for C. R. L. Fletcher's *History of England*, among them 'The Roman Centurion's Song' and 'The Glory of the Garden'.

Much as these verses have been admired and quoted, they were far surpassed in popularity by the four stanzas of 'If –' which first appeared in *Rewards and Fairies*. We have Rudyard's word that it was drawn from the character of Dr Jameson whom he had known for about ten years in Africa, and who visited 'Bateman's' in October 1909. The verses were written some time during the next six months. As Rudyard himself put it, they were 'anthologized to weariness', and translated into twenty-seven languages. Some day, when the sneers of the silly-clever, who suppose that what has become a truism is no longer true, have died away, these verses will renew their influence; and it will be noticed that their fluid rhythm and intricate rhyme-scheme make them a technical masterpiece.*

* I am obliged to Sir Maurice Bowra for pointing out to me that both the theme and the rhythm owe something to Browning's 'Epilogue' to *Asolando*.

The poem was printed as an epilogue to the story in which George Washington makes an appearance, a story beginning in Sussex but ending among the Quakers of Pennsylvania. This was his most sympathetic attempt to treat an American theme; and the introductory verses, 'If you're off to Philadelphia in the morning', recall clearly the fall of 1889 which he had spent in Pennsylvania with Mrs Hill and her parents. He had resumed his old correspondence with her and, when she wrote to him on the publication of each new book, he replied as old friends write, with no other emotional content than is implied by common memories of youth.

Otherwise, the 'Puck' stories are home-centred, sometimes moving away from Sussex but always returning to it with affection. The children, Dan and Una, are ingeniously drawn into each episode and not long overlooked. In the second book, each child has a particular, personal tale. John Kipling's story is of craftsmanship, 'The Wrong Thing', and is located in the village builder's workshop: Elsie Kipling's story, 'Marklake Witches', is shot through with level evening light over the pastures where the farmer's wife is teaching her to milk a cow, as Elsie actually was taught. The delicacy of 'Marklake Witches', a tale told by a young girl to a young girl, in the manner of the Age of Sensibility, is so penetrating that the reader might suppose himself to be listening to a minor character from Jane Austen; and the tale is perfectly set off by the haunting lyric, 'The Way through the Woods'. Rudyard had now attained to a mastery over his own technique that he never surpassed, and to a tenderness far removed from the emotional crudity of his Anglo-Indian tales.

In his quiet, secluded English home, surrounded by his family, wealthy, honoured by the world which yet he held at a distance, blessed with many friends, sought out by the men who did the world's work, he was almost happy. At Tisbury, his parents still li. d, aged and ailing, but, well as he loved them, it was not now to them that he turned for comfort. With his wife, his daughter, and his son, he had again based his life upon a 'family square', a reality which made all other social groupings seem vague and fluctuating. As the security and solidity of his life at 'Bateman's' was slowly strengthened, the pattern of the world outside was slipping into confusion. These were bad times for a Conservative in politics. Every winter, still, he went to South Africa, and his visits to the 'Woolsack', he used to say, were his political times.

The children were now old enough to make their own comments on the transition:

Every winter [wrote Elsie] the family left for South Africa just before Christmas, accompanied by large, black, dome-topped trunks, boxes of books, two faithful maids and the children's governess.

Things went according to a fixed routine. First the experienced appraisal of the ship and passengers by the two children, then the unpacking and stowing away of their travelling possessions in the tiny cabins of those days, and then their hunt to discover if any of their numerous friends among the stewards and crew were in this particular ship. A 'good trip' meant one on which several friends, from the captain downwards, happened to be on board. One special crony was a certain grizzled cabin steward, who could always be counted upon for escorted visits to otherwise forbidden parts of the ship, as well as plates of dessert after the grown-ups' late dinner.

The first few days through the Bay were generally chilly and sea-sick misery. But once Madeira was passed the sun gathered strength daily, the twilights shortened as the semi-tropical nights shut down swiftly, and the first lifting of the Southern Cross above the horizon was eagerly looked for. It was all familiar, yet ever exciting.

R. K. always worked during these voyages, mostly in a tiny cabin opening on to the noisy promenade deck, but sometimes seated at a small folding table on the deck itself. He was quite oblivious to the noise and movement round him, and would pace the deck, come back to his writing pad for a few moments, and pace the deck again, just as if he had been in his own study. His fellow-passengers interested him enormously and he invariably made many friends, specially with some young soldier or mining engineer just going out to start a career, or perhaps with a ship's officer. The delights of the captain's table were always courteously offered and as courteously declined, and the family had a small table just inside the door of the dining saloon.

R. K. was always quite unconscious of the interest that his presence aroused among his fellow-passengers. One chilly evening, going below to get his overcoat, he absent-mindedly put on the first thing that came to hand in his cabin, which happened to be a brown camel-hair dressing-gown. As he came on deck a young acquaintance diffidently drew his attention to the mistake; but R. K. simply remarked that the dressing-gown kept him very warm and that was what was needed! The young man went away muttering: 'Fancy being the sort of man who can do a thing like that and not have it matter.'

Often old friends were on board, Dr Jameson, Abe Bailey, Baden-Powell, mining engineers, and many of the big men who were shaping the destiny of South Africa at that time; endless talks and deck pacing went on in their company. Often after tea and before bed-time his children would collect various small friends, and sit in an enraptured circle round him on the sun-warmed deck in some quiet corner while he told them stories.

The end of the three-weeks' voyage to Cape Town meant the joyful arrival at the lovely, small, single-storied, white house, set under the shadow of Table Mountain, which Cecil Rhodes had given to R. K. for his life. A wide verandah or stoop ran on two sides of it, and there was an open court in the centre on to which all the rooms opened. Huge oak and pine trees sheltered the house, and the garden tumbled down the hillside, ending in a vast view across flat country to the Drakenstein mountains. Myrtle and plumbago hedges, oleander and fig trees, wild cannas and arum lilies, roses and violets grew under the lazy eye of Johnston, the Malay gardener, while a hedge of banana plants gave the children the daily fun of hunting for an unsplit banana leaf, the finding of which unknown treasure was never accomplished.

After lunch a siesta was the custom of the house, and R. K. was often read to sleep by his small daughter. Careful pronunciation of words was insisted upon, until he was too sleepy to bother about it; but when a specially long or difficult word had to be dealt with, the ruthless, wide-awake child would rouse her father to ask how it should be pronounced!

At an early age the two children were taught a proper respect for the use of words, and an appreciation of poetry. Very often in the evenings R. K. would sit in the nursery, intoning rather than reciting poetry by the hour. Wordsworth, Longfellow, the Sagas of King Olaf, the *Lays of Ancient Rome*, *Percy's Reliques*, and Border ballads became so familiar to the two small and eager listeners that quotations from them became part of their everyday talk. Misquotations were frowned upon, and the careful learning of verse insisted upon. 'The man took trouble to find the exact word to fit into the line; the least you can do is not to change it,' was his point of view. A feeling of fury at misquotation remains with his daughter to this day, and when a certain official of the B.B.C. in quoting four lines of verse by R. K. on the air managed to make three mistakes, it was with difficulty that she refrained from angry protest.

One of Rudyard's principal occupations at the Cape was the planning of the Rhodes Memorial, for which the contract was allotted to Herbert Baker. Should they erect a statue on the Lion's Head, to be visible from ships far out at sea? No, that could not be seen from the city. Should they place it near 'Groote Schuur'? It lay too low. Should they employ the sculptor Swan to cast a colossal bronze head, or an equestrian statue?

Having considered many schemes they agreed to use G. F. Watts's bronze statue of Physical Energy and to place a memorial verse by Ruydard Kipling in the shrine.

Rudyard Kipling to Herbert Baker

9 Feb. 1905

We both enormously like your sketch. Of course, being florid in my tastes, I should like, against the dark green, a vermilion entablature; and columns sheathed at the base in bronze – after the insolent Egyptian fashion. Something that to the vulgar suggested Cape to Cairo and to others – other things. No need to make it Dutch. Make it continental.

As to the statue, you are right in that Physical Force lies ready to our hands and will not delay the job. But that statue is the work of a great man grown old and – does it altogether jibe with the idea of a greater man cut off in his strength? But I can see that it is far better than the risk of a colossal error in bronze. Of course, somewhere on God's earth exists a sculptor who could give us, gigantically, the man as he was; half hitched round on his great horse, right hand laid on the beast's rump, the bootless flannelled legs flung anyhow, and in his left hand the bit of stick that he always used. To illustrate, let us say, these lines:

> As tho' again – yea, even once again,
>   We shall rewelcome to the stewardship
> The Rider with the loose-flung bridle-rein,
>   And chance-plucked twig for whip,
>
> The down-turned hat-brim, and the eyes beneath
>   Alert, devouring, and the imperious hand
> Ordaining matters swiftly to bequeath
>   Perfect the works he planned.

But if that statue were an hair's breadth wrong, or forced, what a sub-continental blister it would be! So it will be old Watts after all? [13]

The inscription on the monument, to which Rudyard gave much thought, spacing the letters with great care – 'it's bad enough,' he said, 'having to fit fluid things like tales into spaces' – was not this new verse but the old one written for Cecil Rhodes's funeral.

> The immense and brooding Spirit still
>   Shall quicken and control.
> Living he was the land, and dead,
>   His soul shall be her soul! [14]

Long before the completion of the memorial, affairs in South Africa had taken a turn which the Kiplings thought deplorable. Lord Milner's reconstruction of South African administration, begun before the end of the war, and financed by generous grants of money from the pockets of the British taxpayer, made admirable progress until 1905, when Milner returned to England, having completed his term of service. His design, to stimulate British emigration and so to create an enlightened, progressive, white Dominion in South Africa, needed time to mature, and it required that responsible self-government should not be granted to the two conquered Afrikaner states, until land-settlement and reformed administration were well advanced. But in England the Conservative Government, led by Arthur Balfour since Lord Salisbury's retirement, had outlived its mandate.

Balfour resigned in December 1905, and the General Election, in January 1906, returned the Liberals in an overwhelming majority. So malicious were the new Liberal members against the outgoing Conservatives, they revenged themselves by striking at Lord Milner, who was formally censured by a vote of the House of Commons. The Under-Secretary for the Colonies, whose duty it was to lead the debate, was a young man named Winston Churchill – then a Liberal – and Rudyard never forgave him for his part in this affair.

The cause was lost. Milner retired into private life. An immediate grant of self-government was made to the Transvaal, with the result that the Afrikaner General Botha became its first Premier, and the Boer nationalists resumed their traditional policy. To Chamberlain, Milner, Rudyard Kipling, and their friends, it seemed that the Boer War had been fought and won in vain. Rudyard wrote bitterly from Cape Town to his friend, H. A. Gwynne, now editor of *The Standard.*

Rudyard Kipling to H. A. Gwynne

7 Feb. 1906

Yes it has been a big turn over. ... To me it seems a savage protest against the infernal and eternal slackness of the last years of the Govt. – the years after J[oseph] C[hamberlain] left them. (For further details kindly read over *Below the mill-dam* and note where the miller threw the cat.) ... The fact that Gussy,

Teddy, Willy, Algy, etc., are knocked out seems to me a very cheering point and I notice that the *Standard* doesn't want Balfour to come back. Here I am with you altogether. What's happened to us [the Conservatives] is what happened to the nation in the Boer War, and we must change the quality of our recruits and demand more work from our officers. Moreover (like the Army) we mustn't be so dam' gentlemanly in future. Out here the Dutch naturally assume that the return of the Liberal party means '81 over again, and that the 'two republics' are going to be quietly put back in their old position.

Much worse news for the imperialists in South Africa was to come. At the provincial election of 1907 the same turn-over of votes was seen in Cape Colony, and Dr Jameson, who had been Premier since 1903, lost his majority.

Rudyard Kipling to H. A. Gwynne

1907?

Dear old man,

The cables will have told you how the elections have been a debacle for us. J. X. M[erriman] comes in, without a policy, and all South Africa goes voted Dutch. It ain't to be wondered at. The Imperial Government cut off the steam in the main boiler (the Transvaal) and the auxiliary engines, of course, follow suit and cease working. One advantage is that the 'Bond' don't much want to be led by Merriman. They prefer Malan. I fancy Jameson will soon resign.

The election of course was fought on fierce racial issues, and it is generally understood that all who were in any way loyal will duly come up for punishment. ... When it comes to unifying South Africa, you'll see things! I don't mind betting they'll monkey with the franchise. Remember that Rhodesia *must* be kept out of the federation and our ploy must be to develop Rhodesia as well as we can. It's the last loyal white colony.[15]

As Premier Dr Jameson had lived in Rhodes's house 'Groote Schuur' and, like Rhodes, had been on close terms of friendship with his neighbours at the 'Woolsack'. No letters survive, and little other evidence to show that for many years Jameson was one of Rudyard's few intimate friends. Apart from the one dramatic moment of his life, the 'Raid', Jameson was a quiet confident man who had emerged from tumults of abuse and flattery quite unmoved – treating those two impostors just the same. In his day there was a circle of friends, Fitzpatricks, Baileys, Strubens, all politically minded people, among whom he and Rudyard lived sociably. His leaving office, which Rudyard thought a disaster for South Africa, was at least a sore blow to the Kiplings' comfort. With 'Groote Schuur' occupied by an un-sympathetic Afrikaner of the opposition party, the life had faded from their society. There was no more company in that hospitable house, he wrote gloomily to Milner, no trade, no activity in Cape Town. Inefficiency and corrup-tion would soon prevail and the English would be *uitlanders* in South Africa again. To Gwynne he wrote, 'the handing over of a higher civilization to a lower is a heartbreaking job'.

It was time to be done with South Africa. The divided year, eight months in Sussex and three at the Cape, was be-coming difficult to adjust as the children grew older. John was now ready to go to boarding-school, the destiny of his class, and with great unwillingness the Kiplings bade fare-well to their dear 'Woolsack' for the last time in April 1908. Jameson, though out of office, was able to assure them that the house remained at their disposal, under provision made by the trustees of the Rhodes Estate. They never came back but, even twenty years later, at the end of his life, Rudyard rather tetchily refused to surrender his rights to the exclu-sive use of it.

Perhaps the children had the best of it. Among their visitors one sharp-eyed observer was a young girl who grati-fied a secret passion by meeting her favourite author. She was between ages, and sometimes sat with the grown-ups, sometimes played with the children on the beach at Mui-zenberg; she thus saw two different Rudyard Kiplings. When he was with the children, as he loved to be, the author of *Just So Stories*, she said, far surpassed her expectations, and his conversation excelled his printed books in its fascination for her. Indoors among the grown-ups she was not so sure, she felt that he was acting a part. It was only when a lady happened to mention that she had bought a new cooking-stove that his genius awoke. He would hear of nothing but technicalities about cooking-stoves, to the annoyance of the other guests who hoped for something higher.[16]

From The Fabulists (1917)

When all the world would keep a matter hid,
  Since Truth is seldom friend to any crowd,
Men write in fable, as old Aesop did,
  Jesting at that which none will name aloud.
And this they needs must do, or it will fall
Unless they please they are not heard at all.

When desperate Folly daily laboureth
  To work confusion upon all we have,
When diligent Sloth demandeth Freedom's death,
  And banded Fear commandeth Honour's grave –
Even in that certain hour before the fall
Unless men please they are not heard at all.

Needs must all please, yet some not all for need,
  Needs must all toil, yet some not all for gain,
But that men taking pleasure may take heed,
  Whom present toil shall snatch from later pain.
Thus some have toiled, but their reward was small
Since, though they pleased, they were not heard at all.

This was the lock that lay upon our lips,
  This was the yoke that we have undergone,
Denying us all pleasant fellowships
  As in our time and generation.
Our pleasures unpursued age past recall,
And for our pains – we are not heard at all.

*

[16]

At 'Bateman's'
(1908-14)

THERE is, among the Kipling papers, a thick file of letters recording his systematic refusal, throughout his whole career, of the titles and offices that were sometimes thrust upon him. He could not and he would not write to order, and he would not accept any public honour which might be construed as limiting his freedom to say what, as he thought, should be said. But he did not extend this rigidity of principle to his colleagues in the republic of letters, and often expressed his pleasure when they were rewarded with public honours. The knighthood given to his friend Rider Haggard gave Rudyard sincere pleasure, perhaps the more because it was a tribute to Haggard's services as an agricultural reformer rather than to his eminence as a novelist. As for himself, Rudyard had been offered a knighthood (K.C.B.) by Salisbury in 1899 and had refused it. Balfour repeated the offer (this time a K.C.M.G.) in 1903 and again it was refused. On this occasion Rudyard made the sardonic comment to Carrie that 'title-conferring is as slack as other Government business. Evidently they knew nothing of the K.C.B. of 1899.'

On the same ground – that he must be free – Rudyard refused many proposals to take part in public life. In 1904 he was pressed by the Conservative Party in Edinburgh to stand as their candidate for Parliament. He replied that he could serve them better outside Parliament as an independent writer. Later, two or three other constituencies offered to adopt him as their candidate, with the same result. Nor would he serve in official posts; he repeatedly refused to return to India in any public capacity. He declined an invitation to join the royal party when the Prince of Wales (afterwards King George V) went to India in 1903, and again when he went in 1911 after his accession to the throne. There were several occasions when Rudyard considered revisiting India as a private person, and might have gone if family affairs had allowed it; as a public personage he would not go.

The story of the Poet-Laureateship, after Tennyson's death, has been told in an earlier chapter. When Alfred Austin died, in 1913, there could be no doubt who ought to be the Crown's first choice as his successor. For many years it had been Kipling, not Austin, who had spoken for the nation on great occasions. Asquith, the Prime Minister, after considering Kipling's name, decided that it would be useless to approach him. I am permitted to repeat the following account given by Asquith's daughter, Lady Violet Bonham Carter, in a letter to Lord Baldwin:

> The vacancy occurred when we were on the Admiralty yacht in the Mediterranean as Winston's guests, and I remember very well my Father discussing the problem with me. The obvious choice was Rudyard Kipling. Bridges was the alternative choice in my father's mind. What weighed with him was the very reason you give – that Kipling was inspired and could not write to order. Bridges, with his classic chiselled gift would be more likely to be able to do so. He wrote, offering it to Bridges, I think, during our cruise or directly he came back.[1]

Nevertheless it was still Rudyard's occasional verses in *The Times* that made him the laureate of the people. His standing as a national figure was recognized in 1911 at the Coronation of King George V when places were reserved in the Abbey for Rudyard and his wife.*

He was somewhat less exclusive in respect of academic

---

* We have it on the authority of Sir Harold Nicolson that, when Bridges died in 1930, King George V desired to offer the laureateship to Kipling. No evidence survives that an offer was made. If made, it would certainly have been refused.

than of public honours, though here too he refused any
that might commit him to any class, or party, or coterie.
When Gosse, and some others of Kipling's friends, laid the
foundations of the British Academy in 1910, and pressed
him to become one of the original members, he applauded
their intention, he gave them helpful advice, but he would
not be one of their number. He had made it a rule never
to criticize any of his fellow-authors, and he could not join
a society that was to sit in judgement on them. There were
others, like Henry James, he suggested, who were better
qualified as critics. Having refused to join the British Academy, he made that a precedent for (twice) refusing nomination to the American Academy of Arts and Sciences.
Later in life, however, he showed gratification when elected
to the Institut de France.

His early talents had not been of a kind to attract the
notice of the universities. McGill University at Montreal was
the first to offer him an honorary degree, as early as 1899.
His later decision to revisit Canada and to accept a doctorate may perhaps be connected with the visit to 'Bateman's' in May 1907 of the distinguished McGill professor,
Stephen Leacock. In June Rudyard accepted the offer of a
doctorate from the University of Durham, and immediately
afterwards a similar offer from Oxford. Lord Curzon had
just been elected Chancellor of Oxford and according to
custom it was his privilege to nominate some eminent persons for admission to honorary degrees. Among the other
names he chose were those of Mark Twain and 'General'
Booth, both of them old friends of Rudyard. By chance, the
University of Cambridge also elected a new Chancellor,
Lord Rayleigh, a few months later, and he, too, brought forward Rudyard Kipling's name for a Cambridge doctorate.
Thus the following twelve months, 1907–8, were largely
taken up for Rudyard with visits of ceremony to universities.

Carrie and Rudyard spent two or three days sight-seeing
at York and Durham, in dark rainy weather, his first visit to
the north of England since boyhood. At Durham crowds of

students met him at the station and drew his carriage up the
steep narrow street which leads to the hilltop on which
stand the University and Cathedral. There was barely time
to complete the ceremonies before it was necessary to turn
southward, for Oxford. In unaccustomed gowns of grey and
scarlet which, said Rudyard, made him look like a West
African parrot, the visitors were kept waiting in the cloisters until, one by one, they were led into the Sheldonian
Theatre, to be greeted by the Chancellor in ceremonious
state, by the Public Orator who made a Latin speech, in
honour of each of them, and by the undergraduates in the
gallery who received them with cheers and ribald comments. As 'General' Booth, Mark Twain, and Kipling
awaited their turn, the 'General', magnificent as a Hebrew
patriarch in his scarlet gown, took note of his fellow-travel-
ler of seventeen years ago. 'Young man,' he said, striding
across the quadrangle to meet him, 'how's your soul?' Mark
Twain was a friend on a more material level; he had given
evidence for Rudyard Kipling in the Putnam copyright case,
and Carrie, who had met him in those days, had said he reminded her of Whistler. It was with Mark Twain that Rudyard slipped away to smoke under an archway, with guilty
apprehension, until they were summoned to the theatre,
Rudyard last of the batch. The Public Orator, no doubt
fluent in Latin, was deficient in eloquence, and mumbled an
inaudible address. 'Never mind, Rudyard!' shouted an
undergraduate from the gallery. 'You'll tell us all about it
afterwards.' But he didn't. It was said by spectators that the
ovation given him was more lively than any since Cecil
Rhodes had been given a doctorate.[2]

Political interests, joined with the invitation from McGill,
also induced him to look at Canada again. The Colonial
Conference of 1907 had been a deep disappointment to the
Conservative imperialists, and especially to Rudyard,
though he met all the Premiers from the overseas Dominions at a private party. At this conference a new concept
came into prominence, to which the name of Dominion

Status was afterwards given; it was sponsored by Sir Wilfrid Laurier, of whom Dr Jameson said bitterly to Kipling: 'that damned dancing-master bitched the whole show'.[3] The Commonwealth of free nations was in Jameson's view a poor substitute for a strong and federated Empire. South Africa seemed to be lost and the other Dominions discouraged, as Rudyard wrote in a letter to Deakin, the Prime Minister of Australia, who thus replied:

Alfred Deakin to Rudyard Kipling

21 March 1908

Your wish that I could realise what it means to 'live in a land without hope' awakens no response. After all one must not measure nations by the life span of individuals, and despite our endless blunders we cannot avoid being caught in the wider sweeps of the Empire's growth. Hold South Africa for another half century and people it with sufficient men and women of British blood and they will drag up the primitives in spite of themselves.

Melbourne in '90 looked stricken and was worse than any other part of Australia has ever been. But that crisis was almost confined to Melbourne and Sydney, and was simply a reaction against over-speculation at the moment. Since then, every institution and every individual that kept hold has emerged unscathed, without loss and in most cases with large profits. ... Australia today was never more prosperous. Our [trade] figures surpass those of Canada, although she is a million ahead of us and there is no boom here. Laurier is charming but he is not British in anything, and cares nothing for British interests outside the Dominion. Jameson is worth a hundred Lauriers, and will yet come to his own in a federated South Africa, if his health and patience endure. Very few statesmen in the Empire are better gifted for carrying on in a Dominion Parliament, or more capable of managing a small majority to advantage.[4]

But Jameson was out of office, and Rudyard turned for comfort to a Canada that prospered even under Laurier.

In the autumn of 1907 Rudyard and Carrie crossed the Atlantic again, she to visit her mother whom she had not seen for eight years, and he to receive his honorary degree

from McGill. He made a rare concession to Canadian enthusiasm by giving a series of lectures to the chain of Canadian clubs, the only occasion in his life when he submitted
to the compulsions of a lecture-tour. Canada as seen from
the railway renewed Rudyard's faith.

> Above all, I saw what had actually been achieved in the fifteen
> years since I had last come that way. One advantage of a new
> land is that it makes you feel older than Time. I met cities where
> there had been nothing – literally, absolutely nothing, except, as
> the fairy tales say, 'the birds crying, and the grass waving in
> the wind'. Villages and hamlets had grown to great towns, and the
> great towns themselves had trebled and quadrupled. And the
> railways rubbed their hands and cried, like the Afrites of old,
> 'Shall we make a city where no city is; or render flourishing a
> city that is desolate?' They do it too, while, across the water,
> gentlemen, never forced to suffer one day's physical discomfort in
> all their lives, pipe up and say, 'How grossly materialistic!' [5]

All his speeches were appeals to young Canadians to
realize and to accept their responsibilities:

> Your own labour, your own sacrifice have given you material
> prosperity in overwhelming abundance. ... There is no man,
> and here I must quote again, 'that can foresee or set limits to your
> destiny'. But any man, even I, have the right to remind you, that
> to whom much has been given, from them much – much – shall
> be required. [6]

The rancour which Rudyard sometimes showed against
the United States was strangely bitter at this time. He did
not cross the border but drew comparisons, perhaps over-
stated, between the disorderly 'Wild West' in the Republic
and the King's Peace in the Dominion:

> Always the marvel – to which the Canadians seemed insensible
> – was that on one side of an imaginary line should be Safety,
> Law, Honour, and Obedience, and on the other frank, brutal
> decivilisation; and that, despite this, Canada should be impressed
> by any aspect whatever of the United States. [7]

Though more than twenty years passed before Rudyard
set foot in Canada again, he maintained a copious corre-

spondence with many Canadian friends. Andrew Bonar Law and Max Aitken (Lord Beaverbrook) were shortly to introduce a Canadian flavour into English Conservative politics, and both became close friends of the Kiplings. Canada was a land of friendship and of hope when South Africa was written off, and Rudyard's enthusiasm increased three years later, when he and Aitken together heard of the overthrow of Laurier and the return to office of an imperialist government at Ottawa. After his return to England at the end of 1907, Rudyard wrote a long letter to Milner giving a more personal and candid account than is to be found in his *Letters of Travel.*

Rudyard Kipling to Lord Milner

[1908]

You will have to face the impact of young, callous, curious, and godlessly egotistical crowds who will take everything out of you and put nothing back. Their redeeming point is a certain crude material faith in the Empire, of which they naturally conceive themselves to be the belly-button.

Tell your bottle-holder to disconnect your bedroom telephone, so soon as ever you get to a hotel. Otherwise you will continue to enjoy the horrors of publicity in your bath and in your bed. Allah knows I have long since ceased to be a virgin, but I cannot help blushing when I am rung-up by women – with nothing on but spectacles and a bath-towel. Moreover I find it interferes with the peristaltic process, and Canada is a constipating land.

Sir William Van Horne's house at Montreal – it is a palace – is efficiently guarded against the world by an English butler of the gypsy name of Pharaoh. Outside that house there is very little peace except at Rideau Hall [the Governor's residence].

I am bringing out my Canadian *Letters to the Family* in a pamphlet for use in Canada where they are displeased with them. But I wrote them with a single loving wish to annoy the Radicals in England, and because I loved greatly I managed to irritate a little. I have just come out of a trough of blank bloody pessimism – a cold reasoned despair of the Republic – which has oppressed me for months. So I realise yet again the pits and gulfs you have been through.[8]

A horror of publicity and a dislike of making patriotic orations on public platforms were shared by Milner and Kipling, those two notable imperialists. They always spent Empire Day together, not, as might be supposed, in order to indulge in imperial rejoicings, but in order that each might be able to quote a prior engagement in the highly probable event of being asked to address a public meeting.

Soon after his return from Canada, Rudyard received a letter from the Secretary to the Swedish Academy offering him the Nobel Prize* for literature, the first time it had been awarded to an English writer. In this instance he accepted the honour, and crossed with Carrie to the Continent in severe wintry weather. Both were very seasick.

Even while we were on the sea, the old King of Sweden died. We reached the city, snow-white under sun, to find all the world in evening dress, the official mourning, which is curiously impressive. Next afternoon, the prize-winners were taken to be presented to the new King. Winter darkness in those latitudes falls at three o'clock, and it was snowing. One half of the vast acreage of the Palace sat in darkness, for there lay the dead King's body. We were conveyed along interminable corridors looking out into black quadrangles, where snow whitened the cloaks of the sentries, the breeches of old-time cannon, and the shot-piles alongside of them. Presently, we reached a living world of more corridors and suites all lighted up, but wrapped in that Court hush which is like no other silence on earth. Then, in a great lit room, the weary-eyed, over-worked, new King, saying to each the words appropriate to the occasion. . . .

Morning did not come till ten o'clock; and one lay abed in thick dark, listening to the blunted grid of the trams speeding the people to their work-day's work. But the ordering of their lives was reasonable, thought out, and most comfortable for all classes in the matters of food, housing, the lesser but more desirable decencies, and the consideration given to the Arts.[9]

After the last visit to South Africa, in 1908, Rudyard and Carrie decided to send John to a boarding-school at Rottingdean, with the knowledge that Aunt Georgie could be

* A gold medal, a diploma, and a sum of money estimated at £7,700.

kind to the homesick little boy as, thirty years earlier, she had been kind to his father. She was growing old and sometimes forgetfully called the boy 'Ruddy'.

During Rudyard's years in Sussex, his parents had aged rapidly. In particular his mother, a little older than her husband, had become an invalid, worn out partly by care for her unfortunate daughter, 'Trix' Fleming. After the first breakdown, Trix had recovered and had again joined her husband in India, until his retirement from the service. She was childless, and the charm and talent of her youth had wasted away with little to show in achievement, except a novel of Anglo-Indian life. Apart from this she was so other-worldly as to be hardly able to live a normal life, and her husband, John Fleming, a plain blunt man, was unable to give her understanding sympathy, though his patience was endless. The Flemings were, however, at hand when Alice Kipling's health collapsed. Rudyard, too, was summoned to Tisbury and Lockwood wrote bravely to a friend to say that the presence of his two children was a comfort to him. But Trix was too overwrought to give the least assistance and all the painful toil of supervising his mother's death-bed and funeral fell upon Rudyard. She died on 22 November 1910 and was buried at Tisbury.

Lockwood, old and tired, lingered a few weeks longer in a world which had lost interest for him. We have a last glimpse of him, paying a visit to Wilfrid Blunt at Crabbet and talking of the new political reforms in India, the Morley-Minto constitution, in terms of deep dejection. His last satisfaction in life was to see the appearance of *Rewards and Fairies* which he had watched over with loving care. In January 1911 Rudyard was recalled from his family holiday in Switzerland by bad news of his father. The old man had been taken ill while on a visit to the Wyndhams at 'Clouds' and there died of a heart attack before Rudyard's arrival. Again all the arrangements for the funeral and for disposing of his little property were left to Rudyard.

It was not only Rudyard that mourned the death of

Lockwood Kipling. His granddaughter wrote this of him:

> Lockwood Kipling was a short, rather square figure; bald even early in life and with a beard. His wonderful blue eyes beamed upon the world, with endless interest and kindly tolerance, and his voice was mellow and enchanting. People who met him only once, never forgot him. His knowledge of every art and craft, even the most unusual, was amazing, while his skill with his hands was a joy to watch. In his old age, he wrote long and charming letters to his ten-year-old granddaughter, instructing her in the best method of making and gilding gesso work. To further illustrate his meaning he decorated several delightful boxes for her in this way.
>
> His knowledge of many things was profound, his kindness and interest unending.

There comes a time in every man's middle age when his relatives and friends of the older generation seem to die in quick succession, leaving him naked against the cold blast of the passing years, when he feels himself alone, no longer protected by the comfortable guardians of his childhood. Rudyard's aunts and uncles, who had once meant so much to him, were slipping away: 'Ned' Burne-Jones long since, 'Aunt Aggie' Poynter in 1906, Alfred Baldwin in 1908; his old teachers, the beloved 'Crom' Price in 1910, William Crofts ('Mr King') in 1911; Dr Conland and Charles Eliot Norton dead in America, Henley dead in England. The death of his parents marked an epoch, but did not crush Rudyard as it would have done fifteen years earlier. His father, his dearest, most helpful, critic, had inspired his best work, and, still more, had restrained his exuberance, but the lesson was now learned, the style matured. Well as he loved his parents, he had cut loose from their control, and was devoted to his own new family square. Stan Baldwin's family renewed in the next generation the friendship of their parents; and Rudyard's debt to 'Crom' Price was repaid by his affection for 'Crom' Price's son and daughter, Ted and Dorothy. 'Crom' had left them ill-provided and among the friends who helped them it was Rudyard and

Carrie who saw to their education, and frequently invited them to spend their holidays at 'Bateman's'.

Rudyard was still a newspaper-man at heart. The printer's ink of the *Civil and Military Gazette* had left so permanent a stain that he was rarely as happy as when talking Fleet Street shop with others of the craft. Of his old associates, the 'Friends' of Bloemfontein, Julian Ralph was dead but two of the others were still near him. Perceval Landon, when not away on some assignment in Tibet or Turkey, saw much of Rudyard who built for him a cottage at Keylands on the 'Bateman's' estate. Landon was Rudyard's most intimate friend in middle life. There was also H. A. Gwynne who first managed Reuter's in London, then became editor of the *Standard*, a London daily that struggled to make headway against the new men who were converting journalism into a branch of high finance.

Rudyard Kipling to H. A. Gwynne

November 1904

There isn't in our minds the least doubt as to where you could best serve the Empire – i.e. in charge of a new, reconstructed, enthusiastic and wealthy paper. ... You have an unrivalled chance of preaching your Imperial Labour Party views; army and navy reform; protection and all the rest that is vital. You will be toadied to by all classes of men – and women – but that you won't mind – and you will be lied to a good deal. But that also is usual. Your strong pull should be knowledge of affairs. The business of an editor is not to write but to get the men who can, brigade them, and edit them.

18 October, 1905

I am having the *Army of a Dream* reprinted in pamphlet form, as there have been numerous requests from adjutants of volunteers etc. to get it to give to their companies. Hope to get it out for 6d. shortly. If you can make any use of it as a peg to hang more debate on, for goodness sake use it.[10]

To the *Standard* (29 April 1907) Rudyard gave the set of

verses which best summarize his social philosophy. He
called them 'The Sons of Martha'.

It is their care in all the ages to take the buffet and cushion the
shock.
It is their care that the gear engages; it is their care that the
switches lock.
It is their care that the wheels run truly; it is their care to embark
and entrain,
Tally, transport, and deliver duly the Sons of Mary by land and
main.

. . . . .

They do not preach that their God will rouse them a little before
the nuts work loose.
They do not teach that His Pity allows them to drop their job
when they dam'-well choose.
As in the thronged and lighted ways, so in the dark and the
desert they stand,
Wary and watchful all their days that their brethren's days may
be long in the land.

. . . . .

And the Sons of Mary smile and are blessèd – they know the
Angels are on their side.
They know in them is the Grace confessèd, and for them are the
Mercies multiplied.
They sit at the Feet – they hear the Word – they see how truly
the Promise runs.
They have cast their burden upon the Lord, and – the Lord He
lays it on Martha's Sons!

Ten years earlier he would have given these verses to *The
Times*, under the reign of Moberly Bell, but *The Times* was
about to change its ownership and policy, and Rudyard
transferred his influence to a grouping in politics and journalism that was sounder in allegiance to a traditional
morality. In 1911 Gwynne became editor of the *Morning
Post*, the organ of the right-wing Conservatives. Under his
control, as even its political opponents admitted, the *Post*
was the best edited and the best printed among the London

dailies. Rudyard maintained a regular correspondence with
Gwynne, not only on political questions but on the technicalities of journalism, often suggesting subjects for 'feature'
articles, and lines of action in matters of public interest.

In May 1909, at 'Bateman's', Rudyard was at work upon
'Marklake Witches' when Lloyd George opened his campaign to expropriate the rich and to destroy the power of
the House of Lords. Many wealthy households as well as the
household at 'Bateman's' took alarm. Rudyard usually left
financial affairs to Carrie, who had 'golden fingers', and she
usually took advice about their investments from Sir George
Allen, Rudyard's former employer in India, who had now
retired and was living in Sussex. They insured against death-
duties, bought some shares in America, and watched the
progress of politics with anxiety. From 1909 until 1914 he
threw himself into party activity on the extreme right wing,
attending party meetings in London and even speaking for
Max Aitken, at an election meeting. Rudyard Kipling lost
some of his popularity in those years; no longer the spokes-
man of the forgotten men, the soldiers and sailors, the
British overseas, he seemed to have become the propagandist of the Tory Party. This was not his intention, and
when a politician in Canada so described him he at once
threatened to bring an action for libel.

Rudyard Kipling to H. A. Gwynne

25 January, 1913

The *Morning Post* of the 24th has a quotation from M—'s
speech at Ottawa in which he alludes to the 'hired versifier and
Poet Laureate of the Unionist Party'. This is not pretty but I
think it may be useful. As I wired to you today I want you to
watch if any of the Rad. papers quote it. ... If they do it seems
to me that it would be sound business to jump on 'em for libel as
that kind of lie is apt to grow. ... I don't think the Unionist
party ought to be saddled with me as their 'hired versifier and
poet laureate' and my position is that I don't in the least intend
to have it said of me.[11]

His considered opinion on the routine of politics is to be found in 'The Village that Voted', a story completed and published in 1913. Politics, he said, was 'a dog's life without a dog's decencies'.

Kipling's method of accumulating material can be closely studied in the preliminaries of 'The Village that Voted'. The characters, though not drawn from the life, are reminiscent of the sort of men he knew. One of them was a specialist in bringing moribund newspapers to life like Gwynne, Kipling advised him, and occasionally spent evenings with him in his office. In the late summer of 1909 Kipling saw much of two friends in Parliament, his cousin Stanley Baldwin and Andrew Bonar Law, and attended one of the violent debates over the Budget, when Bonar Law, that calm unimpassioned man, displayed his skill at goading the Government into fury with violent and telling blows, delivered quite without emotion. In the following year, some political capital was made out of a police-court case at Croydon in which Bonar Law was fined for a motoring offence, under circumstances which suggested a vexatious prejudice against him on the Bench. Finally, in the summer of 1913 Landon and Kipling enjoyed themselves renewing their old acquaintance with the London music-halls. Here were all the ingredients which Kipling combined in his gigantic farce about 'the village that voted the earth was flat'. The subject is crowd-hysteria and the keynote is the anguished cry of the vulgar impresario: 'Curse Nature! She gets ahead of you every time.' Nothing could exaggerate the political hysteria of those days, and many years later Kipling had to confess the insufficiency of his own invention. In a letter to Frank Doubleday in 1920 he admitted that even his 'Village that Voted' had not made itself as ridiculous as Dayton, Tennessee, at the time of the Evolution controversy.

Any estimate of Kipling's work must take account of the series of elaborate farces, which he produced at intervals throughout his career. Four, at least ('Brugglesmith', 1891;

'My Sunday at Home', 1895; 'The Vortex', 1914; 'The Village that Voted', 1917), must be classed among his greater achievements and, like almost everything else he wrote, they have been described in flatly contradictory terms by various critics. Certainly, they are not meat for delicate stomachs. Kipling admitted to his friends, more than once, that comical outbursts gave relief to his own feelings, and these tales reveal a common pattern. They are all told in the first person, but the part he casts for himself is whimsical, puckish, malicious, not dignified or dominating. He is there to make sport and laugh at it. In each case an enormous practical joke is not so much induced as released, to develop by some law of its own, involving all sorts of innocent people but recoiling upon the head of the victim, a pretentious intruder. The punishment seems too heavy for the offence and, like many of the world's comic masterpieces, like the tale of Malvolio and the tale of Don Quixote, these stories reveal a strange streak of cruelty that almost spoils the fun, until all ends with a shout of gargantuan laughter that seems to purge away the hatred and resolve the tangle of emotion.

All Kipling's comic tales are strongly localized, and among his best landscapes are the backgrounds against which these farces are staged. In 'The Vortex', for example, when those portentous members of the Round Table bored him with their ideals, it was Kipling the lover of England who saw the reality of the scene on which they mouthed their irrelevant parts.

Well settled on the back seat, he did not once lift his eyes to the mellow landscape around him, or throw a word at the life of the English road which to me is one renewed and unreasoned orgy of delight. The mustard-coloured scouts of the Automobile Association; their natural enemies, the unjust police; our natural enemies, the deliberate market-day cattle, broadside-on at all corners, the bicycling butcher-boy a furlong behind; road-engines that pulled giddy-go-rounds, rifle galleries, and swings, and sucked snortingly from wayside ponds in defiance of the notice-board; traction-engines, their trailers piled high with road-metal; uniformed village nurses, one per seven statute miles, flitting by on their wheels; governess-carts full of pink children jogging unconcernedly past roaring, brazen touring-cars; the wayside rector with virgins in attendance, their faces screwed up against our dust; motor-bicycles of every shape charging down at every angle; red flags of rifle-ranges; detachments of dusty-putteed Territorials; coveys of flagrant children playing in mid-street; and the wise, educated English dog safe and quite silent on the pavement if his fool-mistress would but cease from trying to save him, passed and repassed us in sunlit or shaded settings. But Mr Lingnam only talked. He talked – we all sat together behind so that we could not escape him – and he talked against the worn gears and a certain maddening swish of the badly patched tire – *and* he talked of the Federation of the Empire against all conceivable dangers except himself.

It will be remembered that 'Mr Lingnam' was at last silenced by a swarm of bees. Rudyard had become an enthusiastic bee-keeper at 'Bateman's', and more than once made symbolic use of the social life of the bee in his comments on the contemporary human scene. His fable, 'The Mother-Hive', presaging the possible regeneration of society after a national disaster was a story which pleased its author. He quoted it in his letters to Gwynne as typical of his philosophy. Kipling was a technocrat, believing that the world of the future would be ruled by technicians, not by demagogues. Loose talk about liberty led only to disaster; what the age needed was economic organization by competent, and preferably silent, professionals.

His thousands of readers, themselves largely young technicians, found this a practical philosophy, but there was a rival attitude to life, most competently thought out, to which Kipling was almost blind. He had no appreciation of the practical administrative schemes of national organization which had been produced during his lifetime by the Fabian Society, the social gospel preached, in their respective styles, by his rivals for public attention, Wells and Shaw. The lunatic fringe of radical pacifists on the left wing disgusted him, and he saw nothing more in the Liberal schemes of social betterment than: 'Robbing selected Peter to pay for collective Paul'.

In the crisis of 1910 when Parliament was twice dissolved and the Liberals were maintained in power only by favour of the Irish Nationalist vote, and when the prerogative of the Crown was invoked to overrule the House of Lords, Kipling was among the group called the 'die-hards' who wanted the House of Lords to protest to the last. However, the majority of the Tory peers preferred to submit gracefully.

Rudyard wrote to Milner during the December Election to say that he had been 'slushing about in the wet with a car, taking voters to the poll'. 'I have a horrible fear,' he went on, 'that the Lords will now compromise – like "gentlemen" – out of some vague idea of saving the country, playing the game, pleasing the King, or some other devil's excuse for selling the pass.'[12]

Nineteen-eleven, Coronation year, with the hottest summer in living memory, was a year of strikes. The new doctrine of syndicalism – to force general reforms by 'direct action' expressed in nationally organized strikes of key industries – then first appeared in England. If the Lords could threaten to sabotage the constitution, why not the railwaymen?

Rudyard Kipling to H. A. Gwynne

21 April, 1912

How much foreign influence was there behind the coal-strike and how much foreign influence will there be behind the transport workers' strike? I want a temperate and lucid article ... on the benefits which an average working-man actually gets from joining a union. At present, it seems to me that he is confiding his cash to the only bank in the world whose cashiers may embezzle without punishment.

Rudyard Kipling maintained a long correspondence with

Duckworth Ford, an American friend serving in the Philippines, and pressed him repeatedly for technical details about the country: hygiene and sanitary measures, plague and cholera control, statistics of venereal disease, etc. In December 1911 he wrote:

Things in England are as mad as usual. If there were any logic in the English we should be steering straight for at least three revolutions at the same time, so I presume that they will neutralize each other. Meantime the Teuton has his large cold eye on us and prepares to give us toko when he feels good and ready. Our chances are not so slim as they look for the reason that the Teuton knows all about war as it should be waged scientifically, and my experience has been that when a man knows exactly how everything ought to be done under every conceivable contingency he is apt to be tied up by his own knowledge. But we ought to see in a few years now.[13]

The failure of the Tories to mobilize public opinion and to make their opposition effective provoked a revolution in the Party, engineered by the young Canadian, Max Aitken. In November 1911 Balfour was deposed, and Bonar Law, also a Canadian by origin, succeeded him. A cool, uncompromising politician, with none of the arts that bewitch the masses, Bonar Law concentrated, ruthlessly, upon a policy of maintaining the Union and consolidating the Empire by Tariff Reform. He and Aitken and Kipling were close friends in those years.

Rudyard Kipling to H. A. Gwynne

27 February, 1906

I can't tell you how highly I think of the work of the *Standard* during the past grave months: but I am glad you have seen the politicians at close quarters. They are a macaroni-backed crew, even the best of them, and they will follow only winning causes. You must wake up some of the young men on our side. Our great weakness, of course, is that we have no understudy to Chamberlain, and I think that is due to the way in which the inner caste of Conservatives has stifled and hampered the young blood. Can't you find a young 'un and enthuse him?

2 November, 1910

I very much like Aitken and I'm glad of what you told me about him. I wish I could manage something about Canada and U.S. reciprocity.

I got your betting list (most immoral). I say that Bonar Law will be leader. He's dead sound on Tariff Reform and it's a feather in Canada's cap! And mark my word, from now on, A. J. Balfour will give us no end of fireworks just to show that he can do it. His resignation speech was very fine.[14]

In the years when the strikers and the Ulstermen were resorting to 'direct action', another outburst of sabotage occurred in a form so irrational as to be rather ludicrous than tragic. In a declared democracy there seemed to be no logical answer to the claim that men and women should have equal political rights, and the steady opposition of a Liberal reforming Government against the concession of the franchise to women was indefensible. Kipling, with his lifelong devotion to two women, his mother and his wife, was no scorner of female intelligence, and his comment on the suffragettes was the set of satiric verses containing the well-known line:

The female of the species is more deadly than the male.

They appeared in the *Morning Post*, and stung a little. One lady who expressed her disapproval was his daughter Elsie, seventeen years old and endowed with a will of her own. He warned Gwynne that he would have to excuse himself to Elsie for publishing these verses, when next he came to 'Bateman's'. But she was to form her own opinion of the suffragettes, a few months later, when she was presented at Court. The débutante in front of Elsie was a suffragette, and repaid the royal hospitality by a display of ill-mannered exhibitionism before the King and Queen.

Rudyard Kipling to H. A. Gwynne

30 January, 1913

Doesn't all this suffragette racket remind you rather of Ladies' Sports on ship just before a heavy gale? When the men ought to be furling awnings or lashing boats they're told off to slice the potatoes, get out buckets, chalks and string for chalking the pig's eye and the officers who ought to be on the bridge are hanging around advising their respective females how to pick up eggs and spoons – specially spoons.[15]

At one moment the Liberal Government made a false step by condoning what looked perilously like political corruption. Kipling was quick to strike at them and with such force that future generations are likely to remember the name of Rufus Isaacs chiefly because he was Kipling's Gehazi, as they remember Hervey because he was Pope's Sporus and Buckingham because he was Dryden's Zimri.

> Well done, well done, Gehazi!
> Stretch forth thy ready hand.
> Thou barely 'scaped from judgement,
> Take oath to judge the land
> Unswayed by gift of money
> Or privy bribe, more base,
> Of knowledge which is profit
> In any market-place.

Though it was as a politician that Rudyard came before the public in the years before the First World War, he cared much less for politics than for his family and for the land. The process of setting root in a congenial soil is described, from alternative points of view, in two stories written in these years, 'An Habitation Enforced', which presents the return to England of an Anglo-American family, and 'My Son's Wife', which presents the return to the country of an urban intellectual. There would be no justification for describing either as an aspect of autobiography, but both are realized in terms of the Sussex landscape and society. The 'county' was more rapid that the 'village', and perhaps more whole-hearted, in accepting the Kipling, whose love of seclusion and dislike of intruders prevented them from mixing freely with their neighbours; yet the protective barrier which Carrie always built around Rudyard was not as insurmountable as some accounts have made it. The flow of visitors to 'Bateman's' was controlled by her determination that the merely inquisitive, the mere lion-hunter, the mere snobs should not waste his time. She was a captious, rather niggling housekeeper, who made a great to-do over her hospitality, but hospitable she was to those she wanted Rudyard to see, and a good friend to her friends. On the other hand, everyone wanted to meet the Kiplings.

Among the neighbours her closest friend was Lady Edward Cecil who had been at the Cape with them during the Boer War and shared their memories of Rhodes and his circle. While her husband was serving in Egypt, Lady Edward took a house, 'Great Wigsell', not far from Burwash. Her son, a little older than Elsie, and her daughter, a little younger than John Kipling, were among the neighbours that the children knew best, and Lady Edward was Carrie's closest friend in England. With the Baileys, the Bonar Laws, the Baldwins, the Cecils, Ted and Dorothy Price, and one or two of John's school-friends, John and Elsie began to make a social circle of their own.

Not far away were Sir George Allen at 'Free Chase', Perceval Landon at Keylands, and nearer still was Colonel H. W. Feilden, an old soldier who had retired after an adventurous life into a Queen Anne house in Burwash village street. His wife, an American from the Old South, makes a brief appearance in the story called 'The Edge of the Evening'. The Colonel played a larger part in the domestic life of 'Bateman's' than any other of the neighbours. He was Rudyard's frequent confidant and adviser on village politics, on developing the estate, on stocking the brook with trout. He fished with Rudyard on the summer evenings and rented the shooting in the winters when the Kiplings were away.

It was to the Colonel that the Kiplings turned in each domestic emergency, and Rudyard's letters to him, from South Africa or Switzerland, reveal his trust in the Colonel's tact and judgement.

When the children were younger they had been brought up by governesses, notably by Miss Blaikie, who remained a dear friend. Later, when more expert teaching was required, Miss Dorothy Ponton took charge since she could coach John in mathematics as well as Elsie in Latin and German. A memoir written by Miss Ponton gives a pleasant account of life at 'Bateman's'. It was in the autumn of 1911 that she arrived and went to live, with the private secretary and a maid, at Park Mill Cottage beside the Dudwell Brook.[16]

At this time Rudyard Kipling was forty-six years of age, short, but well-proportioned. He had a pronounced cleft in his chin and very dark, bushy eyebrows, beneath which his blue eyes glowed through his spectacles. In the country he usually dressed in 'plus-fours' with a remarkably shabby cap, or a Trilby hat. After working in his study most of the morning, he often did a little gardening before lunch. He was also fond of fishing and, in wet weather, usually donned leather gaiters and tramped across the fields with Mrs Kipling to inspect the farms on the estate. Mrs Kipling, in spite of a rather hard face, had a kindly smile. She was between forty and fifty years of age, short and stout and had very small feet. Her hair was almost white, and her eyes were greyish and shrewd. Elsie, the daughter, was a well-developed girl of sixteen years with nut-brown hair fastened loosely at the back with a black bow. Her dark hazel eyes were bright and intelligent. She had been brought up simply and, except for three months' holiday during the winter when her parents took her abroad, saw little of society. John, a typical schoolboy of thirteen [actually fourteen], was dark and thin and wore glasses.

During the school holidays there were usually young visitors at 'Bateman's'. Mr Kipling was fond of children and was adored by them, so they had great times together. But there were moments when Mrs Kipling found them rather too boisterous and exacting. As soon as Elsie had settled down to her term's work, Mrs Kipling asked me to give one hour's 'holiday work' to the other children [Oliver Baldwin and his sister], so that they might be kept quiet. The day when these lessons were to commence, Mr Kipling took his young relatives mushrooming, and I met them hilariously carrying back the harvest in his hat.

Elsie also wrote an account of life at 'Bateman's' in those days:

An average day at Bateman's was always a busy one. Breakfast was at 8 a.m. summer and winter, and the large morning post was dealt with immediately afterwards. Anything from sixty to a hundred letters came into the house daily, and were opened mostly by C. K. and her secretary – sorted out, discussed, torn up or answered as the case might be. The whole family developed an uncanny sense for knowing more or less what a letter might contain by its envelope, and R. K. would seize anything he thought promised to be interesting to open himself.

These letters, which always constituted a real task and which followed R. K. everywhere, were incredibly varied, came from every corner of the world, dealt with every subject, and contained every possible request and suggestion; Dr Marie Stopes asking that 'If' should be re-written to deal with women; H. G. Wells urging R. K. not to review a book of his (a thing R. K. never did) as their points of view were so different; or perhaps an unknown spinster wanting new words written for 'The Red Flag', though the Socialists were not to know who had done it! There were numbers of lunatics, and above all endless people wanting help and advice about writing. The latter were generally dealt with at length and with great sympathy, specially if the enquirers were young.

R. K. usually worked in the morning, if he had anything in hand, either doing the actual writing, or pacing up and down his study humming to himself. Much of his best known verse was written to a tune, the 'Recessional' to 'Melita', the tune usually sung to 'Eternal Father, strong to save'; 'Mandalay' to an old waltz tune: and so on; this was curious as R. K. was quite unmusical.

A walk or more work followed lunch, the second post was dealt with, and there would probably be visitors for tea. His interest in his garden was only mild, but on occasion he would take a swop hook or spud, and deal furiously with nettles and other weeds. In the early days at Bateman's he would sometimes fish for trout in the Dudwell, but his eyesight prevented him from doing much shooting. 'Farm walks' were often taken and while C. K. discussed with the foreman ditches to be cleaned out, barns to be repaired or crops to be sown, he stood by listening and only sometimes making a suggestion.

If he was really busy with a piece of work he was utterly absorbed in it and quite oblivious to anything else. Thus his children learned very early to keep any requests or plans until he had safely finished whatever was engaging him, until he 'came back' as they called it, and was again ready to enter their daily life.

It was for Carrie's sake that they went on to Vernet-les-Bains in the eastern Pyrenees after the usual family holiday in Switzerland in 1910. The cure here gave her some relief, and for several years the visit was repeated. Rudyard made friends among the numerous English visitors, and contributed 'Why the Snow falls at Vernet' to a magazine which was run by them. It was one year when Lord Roberts and his daughter were also at Vernet that Rudyard acted as interpreter at a formal meeting between the aged Field-Marshal (very worried because he was in plain clothes), the commander of the area garrison (very much in uniform), and the local Archbishop. This somewhat incongruous party was recorded in a stiff photo group, done by the excited hotel photographer.

Every January from 1909 until the outbreak of war they travelled by steamer and train to Engelberg or St Moritz. For a month or six weeks the children gave themselves up to ski-ing and skating and then, when John had returned to school, the other three toured the Continent, sometimes visiting the Château d'Annel near Compiègne, the home of Chauncey Depew, who had married their old friend, Julia Catlin.

Rudyard was by nature a lover of France, and of the French, who now read his books as avidly as the English. The childhood holiday which he had spent with his father in Paris in 1878 had started a tendency which motoring enabled him to cultivate in middle age, but his family used to say that he could never stay more than three days anywhere without being found out. When he visited a church the priest would recognize him and make an occasion of the visit; or some soldier in the street would accost him, challenge him, and carry him off in triumph to the officers' mess. By the third day there would be a call from the mayor with threats of a civic reception. All doors were open to Rudyard Kipling. No matter if it were closing-day, the management of any gallery or the owner of any historic house was willing – anxious – to show him round.

In the nineties, when rival imperialisms had forced a breach between France and England, Rudyard had passed through a short anti-French phase and in 1900 had written a story, 'The Bonds of Discipline', ridiculing the conduct of a French spy who introduced himself into a ship of the Royal Navy. There had also been an anti-Kipling outburst in France. Soon after the Boer War, a remarkable novel by Jean and Jérôme Tharaud was published under the title of *Dingley*, and was awarded the Goncourt Prize. It was plainly a hostile criticism of Rudyard Kipling presented in the form of a romance about his experiences in South Africa, written by someone who knew something about his domestic life and rather less about his writings. 'Dingley', the hero of the tale, was an English imperialist author who glorified war and was disillusioned when his own son was killed by the Boers. The treatment was topical and the book has now been forgotten.

After the Entente Cordiale of 1904, as England and France drew closer together, this short phase of antipathy vanished. Some of Rudyard's early works had long been issued in French translations (as in all the principal languages of the world). His vogue, in France especially, was much increased when his sympathy with French ideals became known. A link with French politics was Georges Clemenceau, an anti-imperialist but a man after Rudyard's heart, and a friend of Lady Edward Cecil who brought him over to 'Bateman's' more than once. Rudyard declared his devotion to the Anglo-French *entente*, a firm foundation of his political ideals for the rest of his life, by publishing his poem, 'France', in the *Morning Post*, on the occasion of the French President's state visit to London, 24 June 1913.

It was a tribute to the French national character in terms far different from the conventional English view:

> Furious in luxury, merciless in toil,
> Terrible with strength that draws from her tireless soil;
> Strictest judge of her own worth, gentlest of man's mind,
> First to follow Truth and last to leave old Truths behind –
> France, beloved of every soul that loves its fellow-kind!

A by-product of the Boer War, which men of good-will approved, was the extension of new and manly principles into popular education, in accordance with the active philosophy which Roosevelt called the Strenuous Life. All these and many other desirable qualities were fostered by the Boy Scout movement which Baden-Powell, the 'Hero of Mafeking', gradually brought into existence in 1907 and 1908. Rudyard was an early and enthusiastic supporter, proud to style himself 'Commissioner of Boy Scouts'. Just what is the debt of the Scout Law to Rudyard's concept 'The Law', which the *Jungle Books* had made familiar to a whole generation of boys, cannot be calculated; but Rudyard Kipling and Baden-Powell were friends and had discussed these questions. The debt is evident in *Scouting for Boys*, and when the 'wolf-cub' organization was provided for little boys, its origin in the 'Mowgli' stories was obvious. In the summer of 1909 Rudyard wrote his Boy Scouts' 'Patrol Song' (to the tune of 'A Life on the Ocean Wave') for Baden-Powell, and a few weeks later visited one of the early Scout camps in the New Forest. Thereafter he appeared more than once at Scout rallies.[17]

Furthermore, he was an active supporter of the National Service League to which old Lord Roberts devoted his declining years, but conscription in any form, even compulsory registration and training, was not regarded by any political party in those days as a policy for winning elections. In Rudyard's soldier-stories of this period there is always a note of bitterness against the military reforms of the Liberal Government, even against Haldane's Territorial Army which so nearly resembled his own 'Army of a Dream'.

Rudyard was more at home with the Navy than with the Army in those years. He had become a serious student of naval records, and he maintained his interest in naval techniques. From time to time he tried his hand at stories of life as seen from the lower deck, which might have been comparable with his earlier stories of life in the barrack-room. They are grouped round the character of his talkative petty-officer ashore, Pyecroft, who acts, like Mulvaney, as the author's mouthpiece. Though the virtuosity is immense, the stories themselves lack vigour and, while they have their admirers, there is not one of the Pyecroft stories which is likely to find its way into a selection of Rudyard Kipling's best six, or best twelve. Obviously they gave their author great pleasure, but this enthusiasm is rarely conveyed to readers who are not already familiar with naval jargon. The best of the series, perhaps, is the set of light verses, 'Poseidon's Law', which accompanies 'The Bonds of Discipline'.

Rudyard's devotion to the Navy was bound up with his hope that his only son should have a naval career. John Kipling had been dedicated to this service from birth, and his way was smoothed before him by the patronage of England's greatest living sailor. Sir John Fisher wrote to Rudyard offering to nominate John for a naval cadetship, thus giving him a historic line of succession because he, himself, had been nominated to a cadetship, fifty years earlier, by the last survivor among Nelson's captains. This offer was in vain, for when little John grew up into boyhood, his eyesight revealed a fault, and, like his father, he was obliged to wear spectacles. It became certain that he would never reach the rigorous standard of eyesight required for naval service, and hardly even the lower standard required by the Army. For a career as a regular soldier, or indeed for any professional career in those days, he must next be sent to a Public School. Westward Ho!, which Rudyard still regarded as superior to all others, was a memory of the past, a school no longer, and he decided to send John to Wellington College, another school with a strong military tradition. During the three years that John spent at Wellington (1911–13), Rudyard used frequently to drive over to Farnborough, not far away, where he stayed at the Queen's Hotel. He could visit his son and could meet many friends in the services, for the Queen's Hotel was much frequented by Army officers from Aldershot. He and Gwynne made it their headquarters while watching the Army Manoeuvres in the blazing heat of August 1913. Still more interesting was the rapid growth of something new, at Farnborough, the Royal Aircraft Establishment. Rudyard and John had first seen aeroplanes in France, in 1910, and during John's schooldays at Wellington grew familiar with them around Aldershot and Farnborough.

Rudyard Kipling to Colonel L. C. Dunsterville

10 December 1912

I've been down at Aldershot exploring a new world – the Royal Flying Corps. It's a rummy sensation to stand at the very beginning of things, as it might be with Primitive Man when he first launched his canoe. They don't know a damn thing but they are finding it out by experience – such of 'em as live. It's exactly like a kid rolling down a flight of steps and discovering the laws of gravity at the age of two. But they seemed to me to have already developed a typical eye and face. I noticed also that there is a New Smell in the Service – not Infantry (hot or cold) – not Artillery (which is horse-sweat and leather) – not motor transport which is petrol and oil, but a fourth and indescribable stink – a rather shrill stink if you understand, like chlorine gas on top of petrol fumes plus gummy calico in a shop. That's the stink of the aeroplane.[18]

John was a straightforward, popular and good-natured boy, with quick wit, a great sense of fun and much charm, but with no marked talents. At school he worked with moderation but played with spirit and energy, being a keen footballer. Rudyard was delighted when John brought home 'a piece of poetry that he had found in a book'; he had taken a fancy to it without knowing that his father had written it. When John joined a literary society at school, he easily prevailed on his father to read a paper to them, a privilege asked by much more distinguished societies in vain.

But John proved backward in his school-work, even with coaching from Elsie's governess in the holidays, and it seemed doubtful whether he could pass the examination for Sandhurst. In 1913 he left Wellington and went to a private coaching establishment at Bournemouth – one of those 'Army crammers' whom Stalky & Co. had so despised at Westward Ho!, and spent his last year there before the crisis of 1914 changed all their lives.

While at Bournemouth an event occurred which suggests that John Kipling was maturing. Though nominally members of the Church of England, neither Rudyard nor Carrie had made a practice of attending church services, except sometimes on ceremonial occasions. The children had been taught the elements of religion by governesses and had been taken to church but, it appears, John had never been baptized. There are signs that Rudyard, who had been rather strongly anti-clerical as a young man, was growing more disposed to accept the Christian revelation in middle age. Some of the stories in *Rewards and Fairies*, though far from orthodoxy, show a reverent religious sense which can hardly be paralleled in Kipling's earlier work, with its stoic cosmology, its impersonal deism, and its puzzling over mortality and immortality. The author of the verses headed 'Cold Iron' was in another mood. Whatever Rudyard's religious progress, his son John now made a decided step and, early in 1914, was baptized into the Church of England at the age of sixteen, with the approval of both parents who acted as sponsors.

In the spring of 1913 the Kiplings extended their usual tour as far as Egypt, their first visit to the East for twenty years. It was a renewal for Rudyard of the sights, smells, and sounds of Asia, which he faithfully recorded in a series of letters for *Nash's Magazine* (reprinted in *Letters of Travel*). It is strange to reflect how slight had been his earlier acquaintance with Egypt – that the author of *The Light that Failed* and of 'Little Foxes' set eyes on the Nile Valley for the first time at this late date. In Cairo they called on Lord Kitchener who made a bad impression on Rudyard. He was a 'fatted Pharaoh in spurs': he had 'gone to seed physically'; he was 'garrulously intoxicated with power'. Rudyard tackled the great man about Egyptian finances and supplied Gwynne with columns of statistics for use in denouncing Kitchener's agricultural policy.

When they returned home it was to find Ireland on the brink of civil war. The Ulster volunteers were equipping themselves with rifles obtained from Germany, and now the Catholic Irish of the south were forming a rival army. Rudyard and Carrie had visited Ireland in 1911 when they had found the 'dirt and slop and general shiftlessness of Dublin past belief' and had returned convinced that a firm stand by the Ulstermen could and should force the Liberal Government to abandon the Home Rule Bill.

Rudyard Kipling to H. A. Gwynne

2 December 1913

You talk of the German danger. Does it occur to you that a betrayed Ulster will repeat 1688 in the shape of direct appeal to Germany? And that in doing this she will have the sullen sympathy of a great many people in England who are suffering under intolerable misgovernment? Ulster is nearer than South Africa; and a betrayed Ulster is more dangerous than twenty southern Irelands in open revolt. The South Irish have no passion for Home Rule as such. They realize it would be against their business interests; their leaders know that the money to finance a new revolt could not come from Ireland but must come from the U.S. Which is the more dangerous enemy? The South playing a game it has not got its heart in, or the North in a blind rage, led by *its own leaders not by politicians*![19]

'Sullen sympathy' was not a strong enough term for the support already given to the Ulster cause by the Conservative Opposition in England. The Ulster Covenant, pledging resistance against any attempt to subject Protestant Ulster to the Catholic south, had been signed by thousands of English Protestants. Among the leaders of the Covenanting movement were Rudyard's close associates – Bonar Law, Milner, Gwynne – and none went further than he did in defiance. Throughout the early months of 1914 the Irish crisis grew more intense, blinding Rudyard's eyes, or so it seemed, to the imminent threat of a greater disaster, the European War against which he had, for so long, been warning his fellow-countrymen.

When the Government fumbled, in March, over the 'Curragh Incident', allowing their hands to be forced by a group of Army officers who sympathized with the Ulstermen and said so, it was clear that Ulster could not be coerced. The Government had lost control, and Rudyard had no doubt that the time was come to call their bluff. One day in April he sat down and wrote, for the journal of the Ulster party, his inflammatory verses:

> We know the wars prepared
> On every peaceful home,
> We know the hells declared
> For such as serve not Rome –
> The terror, threats, and dread
> In market, hearth, and field –
> We know, when all is said,
> We perish if we yield.[20]

A few days later, 16 May 1914, he made one of his rare public speeches, to ten thousand cheering Unionists on the

common at Tunbridge Wells, a bitter personal attack upon
the Liberal leaders, in terms that were virulent even by the
standard of those ill-tempered days. The Government, he
said, were like 'a firm of fraudulent solicitors who had got
an unlimited power of attorney from a client by false pre-
tences and could dispose of their client's estate how they
pleased'. He taunted them as common rogues for the Marconi scandals, saying flatly that, though they did not stick at
murder, money-getting was their strongest motive. They
were now reduced to the necessity of handing over Ulster
to a gang of criminals 'for no other reason than that they
might continue in enjoyment of their salaries'.

This 'wild outburst', as the *Manchester Guardian* described it in a headline, was reported at length in the newspapers. So crude an overstatement was an embarrassment
to Rudyard's own party and a self-inflicted wound to his
own reputation. Never, perhaps, had his reputation been so
low with all those good people of temperate opinions who
were sorely puzzled by the intricacy of the Irish problem.
This was the Kipling of the Beerbohm caricatures, a figure
far removed from the author of 'Recessional'.

Luckily, he had two sides still to his head. While the
Radical press took advantage of the joint in his armour
which he had exposed to their blows, another Rudyard was
corresponding in another vein with a friend at Oxford. Sir
William Osler, the Regius Professor of Medicine, was a
man of rare social accomplishment and wide reading – far
beyond his professional studies. Kiplings and Oslers were
connected on the distaff side, for Lady Osler was a Revere
of Boston and so related to the Balestiers. It was from Osler
that Rudyard acquired an interest in the history of medicine. To Osler he owed the story of René de Laennec the
inventor of the stethoscope ('Marklake Witches'), and to
Osler's judgement he submitted the story of Nicholas Cul-
peper ('A Doctor of Medicine'). In the second case Rudyard
was on his own ground, since botany had long been one of
his hobbies and old English herbals were his delight.

Sir W. Osler to Rudyard Kipling

9 May, 1914

Dear Kipling,

The Roger Bacon celebration is on June 10th. ... Bridges has promised to write a brief ode, in which he says he will deal only with philosophy and that he might not mention Roger Bacon at all. ... The Committee empowers me to ask you to write and recite something for us at the luncheon, dealing particularly with the personality and tragedy of Roger Bacon. Do please accept, and come to us, and bring Mrs Kipling.

Rudyard Kipling to Sir W. Osler

10 May, 1914

Dear Osler,

I can't tell you how shocked I am to find the practice of medicine at Oxford (Roger's own university) so grossly behind the age. It was Galen who laid down that 'anger at meat' (by which he meant all mental emotion save of the mildest) is the mother of evil; and here *you* are – Regius Professor – counselling me to recite my own verses 'at', not before or after, but *at* a bountiful meal. May I refer you to *Libellus R.B. etc. etc. de retardandis senectutis accidentibus et de sensibus conservandis* (Oxford 1590). But seriously, much as I should love to be of use to you I fear I am no good in the matter. I don't know Bacon except from the popular legend; I have no 'Brewer' and I can't get up to Oxford on the 10th and I am up to my eyes in work and arrears of work of all sorts.

Forgive me, and send me, as soon as you can, your paper on R. B. to file with my old doctors. Nicholas Culpepper, who could write even if he couldn't cure for nuts – says at the beginning of his Herbal, 'I knew well enough the whole world and everything in it was formed of a composition of contrary elements, and in such a harmony as must needs show the wisdom and power of a great God.' That seems to me to cover Roger Bacon's outlook and I present it to you for a quotation.[21]

The prospect of 'civil war in Ireland seems not to have imposed any change in the routine of the English upper classes. Rudyard attended meetings of political groups in London; Carrie was a prominent member of a ladies' com-

mittee which was to provide relief for loyal refugees from
Ulster; and these occupations did not prevent them from
taking their summer holiday, at Kessingland Grange, a
lonely house near Lowestoft, lent them by their friend Rider
Haggard.

While their eyes were set upon Ulster they paid small
heed to affairs in the Balkans which were of greater moment. Carrie's diary contains no mention of the Archduke's
murder at Serajevo or of any event in south-eastern Europe
until 31 July when Helen Cecil who had joined them at
Kessingland was sent for. Her father, Lord Edward, had
been recalled from leave 'because of the war'. For a few days
more the young people bathed, Carrie was 'possessed by' a
bad cold, and on 4 August Rudyard noted in her diary: 'Incidentally armageddon begins'.

It has been recorded in many novels and memoirs how
swiftly the world was changed in those few days of August
1914, yet no account is adequate to recall the alteration in
the magnitude of events, as if western civilization had gone
into another gear. Ulster, the Strikes, the Suffragettes,
shrank to insignificance. The tiresome jaded political
struggle with which the people, though they might not admit as much, were bored; the sham fights; the empty threats
in which no one quite believed, because no living Englishman had seen war or revolution on English soil; all this
vanished like a nightmare, leaving a clean issue, to resist
German aggression. Even the pacifists felt this relief from
the trivial, the second-rate. At least Mrs Pankhurst and Sir
Edward Carson could be forgotten. It was this sense of relief
that inspired those words of Rupert Brooke, a Liberal, which
have sometimes since seemed so hard to justify:

> Now God be thanked who has matched us with His hour,
>   And caught our youth, and wakened us from sleeping,
> With hand made sure, clear eye, and sharpened power,
>   To turn, as swimmers into cleanness leaping,
> Glad from a world grown old and cold and weary,
>   Leave the sick hearts that honour could not move. . . .

But that indeed was how it seemed in August 1914, and Rudyard's words for *The Times*, though more sombre than Rupert Brooke's, were in the appropriate key.

> Comfort, content, delight,
> The ages' slow-bought gain,
> They shrivelled in a night.
> Only ourselves remain
> To face the naked days
> In silent fortitude, ...[22]

MY BOY JACK (1916)

'Have you news of my boy Jack?'
  Not this tide.
'When d'you think that he'll come back?'
  Not with this wind blowing, and this tide.

'Has any one else had word of him?'
  Not this tide.
  For what is sunk will hardly swim,
  Not with this wind blowing, and this tide.

'Oh, dear, what comfort can I find?'
  None this tide,
  Nor any tide,
Except he did not shame his kind –
  Not even with that wind blowing, and that tide.

Then hold your head up all the more,
  This tide,
  And every tide;
Because he was the son you bore,
  And gave to that wind blowing and that tide!

[17]

The First World War
(1914-18)

At Kessingland, where the traffic route ran in deep water past the eastward promontory of Norfolk, some movement of warships could be seen, which stirred Rudyard's imagination, partly because he was better informed than most men about military and naval affairs, and had friends in Fleet Street who could tell him more. On 4 August, before the declaration of war, he wrote to R. D. Blumenfeld of the *Daily Express*.

Rudyard Kipling to R. D. Blumenfeld
Kessingland Grange, 4 August, 1914

Many thanks for your wire *re* ultimatum. I somehow fancy that these sons of Belial will wriggle out of the mess after all – or it may be worth Germany's while to avoid Belgium if we stay neutral. *How* the Teutons must despise us – and how justly! Meantime we look as if we were losing time. I'd be greatly your debtor if you could tell someone in the office to send me a wire, of evenings, when they have time, giving me the day's news.

The place we have taken here is for practical purposes the side of a ship. The garden runs about fifteen yards to a cliff – then the sea and all the drama of the skirts of war laid out before us. Destroyers going up and coming down in twos and fours – then a gunboat or so – then a N.Y.K. (Jap. boat) all white and disinterested going to London; then a Nelson liner with a sort of 'Mike, you're wanted', look on her; then steam trawlers and the usual procession of tows and barges.

The strain on *you* must be awful but there is the ancient text of the Rabbi (I think it was Hillel) to console one with. It says substantially that the worst that men and women meet in this world is just men and women and their notions. The old boy was a bit of a freethinker like so many of the Rabbis were at heart.

My father used to quote it to me as: – 'Nothing worse in the world than yourself – and nothing better.' [1]

Three days later, on the seventh, Kitchener made his first public appeal to the nation for voluntary recruitment in the New Army which was to bear his name and, on the tenth, John went up to London alone to offer himself for a commission, just before his seventeenth birthday. Forty years ago, when education beyond the primary stage was enjoyed only by a small minority, any reputable young man with a good education and a good character was eligible for appointment as 'Temporary Second Lieutenant', and might get a commission as soon as a regimental commander applied for his services. John had some training in his school Officers' Training Corps, but his poor sight would still prejudice commanding officers against him. He was rejected on his first application, and proposed to try his luck at enlisting as a private soldier, a more heroic decision in those class-conscious days than it would seem today, but Rudyard had another card to play. He asked their old friend Lord Roberts for a nomination to his own regiment, the Irish Guards, which was arranged in time for John to report for duty at Warley Barracks on 14 September. This was the last evidence of friendship between the Kiplings and Lord Roberts, who died a few weeks later while visiting the armies in France.

Meanwhile the other three had returned from Kessingland. In mid-August they were at Brown's Hotel among crowds of stranded American tourists whom Carrie described as 'noisy, restless and excited'. Then, at 'Bateman's' again, they busied themselves with aid to the Belgian Refugees and with work for the Red Cross, sending piles of linen to the London Hospital, and using for a greater purpose the organization they had formed in preparation for civil war in Ireland. They were avid for news and could get none or little, though Landon, Aitken, and Stanley Baldwin came to tell what they knew.

While the French and British drew back from Flanders

into France, Rudyard set himself to write his poem, 'For all we have and are'. Landon, who had offered some amendments which Rudyard accepted, took it to town on the last day of August for publication in the next day's *Times*. It was promptly pirated in America by the syndicated press.

The war news, as it came in, revealed a situation that grew more disquieting. One day in September Julia Depew arrived from Compiègne as a refugee, with a tale of German atrocities in France and Belgium, and the first gap in their own circle of friends came when Lady Edward had news that her son, George Cecil, was missing in the retreat from Mons. The strain of John's departure was increased for Rudyard by the renewed illness of his sister Trix for whom he had to make himself responsible, and his own health showed signs of giving way to these anxieties. As several times in his earlier life, nervous exhaustion showed itself in a partial paralysis of the facial muscles, which kept him at home for some days. Then in October he began a round of visits to hospitals and training-camps, so as to form his own impressions of the New Armies in training, of the veteran troops from Flanders, and especially of the Indian troops who had been brought to France. It was a peculiar pleasure to visit the hospital for Indian soldiers at Brighton.

Again and again he was invited to write official propaganda for the Government, and refused to do so, but when his friend Aitken (after 1916 Sir Max Aitken) was appointed official correspondent with the Canadian Army in Europe, Rudyard saw him frequently and gave him much help with his work. John had leave at Christmas which they all spent together with the Bonar Laws, at the Aitkens' house near Leatherhead.

Meanwhile the ferocity of the German war-machine grew more apparent. In January 1915 the first air-raids were made on undefended English towns; and in February the German Admiralty announced its policy of unrestricted submarine warfare. Rudyard's reaction took the form of three short stories written that winter, 'Swept and Garnished', written in October, 'Sea-Constables' in February, 'Mary Postgate' in March.*

'Swept and Garnished' is a rather horrid little story about the delusions of a German woman, lying in bed with a high fever, who sees the victims of the policy of 'frightfulness', dream-children who make a shocking contrast with the happy child-ghosts in 'They'. In the development of Kipling's art, the story is worth noticing as another example of his growing interest in the mental processes of elderly women.

The second story, 'Sea-Constables', like most of his sea-stories, is so technical as to be almost unintelligible to a landsman. Furthermore, its construction is so complex as to require the closest attention from the reader. Four men, all temporary naval officers, talking together over a good dinner enjoyed ashore, reconstruct, in snatches of dialogue, their relentless pursuit of a neutral skipper whom they know to be supplying German submarines. With good consciences and good digestions they recount their parts in hounding him to death.

Ethically 'Sea-Constables' is a deplorable tale, but war is a deplorable business, and Kipling was never the man to paint it in pretty colours. Perhaps because of its obscurity the detractors of Kipling have never condemned this story as roundly as they have condemned 'Mary Postgate', which somebody has described as 'the wickedest story ever written'. It is the tale of a plain, unloved, elderly governess and her secret maternal passion for her pupil, who is killed in the war. While she is engaged in disposing of the boyish possessions he has left behind, destroying them on a bonfire as a sacrifice to her vain and unrequited love, she has the opportunity of saving the life of a wounded German airman, after a bombing raid on the village. She deliberately, exultingly, lets him die, which, she says, 'no man would ever have

*Since there has been controversy on this point, it will be worth while to mention that Carrie Kipling's Diary describes Rudyard as working at 'Mary Postgate' on 8 March 1915.

done'. This is entirely personal, a tale about frustrated passion and vicarious revenge, not about any particular campaign. It is concerned with the quality of ruthlessness, an extension of the sardonic verse, 'the female of the species is more deadly than the male'.

One task that Rudyard willingly undertook in 1914 was to find a place for 'Stalky' in the New Armies. Times had changed since Dunsterville had been the leader in their enterprises and Kipling his admirer and lieutenant. Dunsterville had not achieved the career that Kipling had forecast for him. By some mischance he had missed, not only the campaigns in Burma, Egypt, and South Africa in which successful generals had made their names, but also the more spectacular events in campaigns on the Indian frontier. He had seen much hard service with his Sikhs but not in affairs which caught the public eye. Perhaps, too, the peculiar talents which impressed the other boys in Number Five Study at Westward Ho! were not so much esteemed by the bureaucrats in Simla and Whitehall. At any rate Dunsterville's career seemed to have come to an end after his term in command of a Sikh battalion and in 1914 he found himself in England, an unused, retired, Anglo-Indian colonel on a very small pension, while Kipling was rich and famous. Rudyard was kind to 'Stalky's' son – as to all children – and helped 'Stalky' from time to time with loans of money which were scrupulously noted and repaid. At forty-nine 'Stalky' was unlikely to get command of a battalion in the field and, having no friends in high places, he found no easy billet.

Among their contemporaries from the College, Aleck Godley was commanding the New Zealanders, Maclagan had a brigade of Australians, 'Potiphar' Rimington was Chief Engineer in Mesopotamia, Cunliffe was fighting a campaign of his own in the Cameroons, while 'Stalky' found no better job than conducting trainloads of soldiers up and down the line in France, one of the humblest tasks a staff

officer could be called upon to do, while his special qualifications as a Russian interpreter were overlooked. Rudyard,
who had many friends at the War Office, attempted to get
'Stalky' a brigade in Kitchener's Army, but the War Office
preferred to send him back to India as a brigadier on the
North-West Frontier, where in due course his long-awaited
opportunity appeared.

In the spring of 1915 it was still possible for Englishmen
to be optimistic about the war. They had survived the first
shock of the German onslaught and had made some progress in building up the resources which eventually must
bring victory. The war had settled down into its second
phase, the period of trench warfare, and in Sussex the life of
the countryside was adjusting itself to new ways. A party of
New Army officers (of the 'Loyals') were billeted for a time
at 'Bateman's'. Then came a day when the Kiplings offered
the house to the War Office for use as a hospital, and,
though this offer was not accepted, they spent less time
there. Rudyard was very busy with visits to camps and hospitals and seaports, and with writing descriptive articles
about them for the *Daily Telegraph*. On Salisbury Plain
there were Canadian troops, among whom several of his
friends were serving, and Carrie was an active member of
the committee of the 'Maple Leaf', the club for Canadian
soldiers on leave in London. The Rolls-Royce was laid up,
and, since there were now numerous occasions for visiting
London, they tended to save the awkward train journeys
by staying longer at Brown's Hotel, where John, from
Warley Barracks, could sometimes join them in the
evenings.

At seventeen John was a slim, good-looking boy, the tallest of
the family, with quick dark eyes behind his glasses, with a great
sense of fun and a passion for motor-bicycles. He found his life
in barracks interesting though hard, and made many friends. A
natural quickness and imaginative sympathy enabled him to get
on well with the men of his company, mainly Irishmen in those

early days; and it is said that his handling of a new draft of very drunken recruits from Dublin was masterly.

Scanty hours of leave in London were all his family saw of him that winter. John would arrive in his own car from Warley Barracks, sometimes alone but often with friends who would eat large meals and go to the theatre, or sit talking till late in the Kiplings' sitting-room at Brown's Hotel (always their London headquarters). Then, their few hours of leave over, they would pack into John's little car and rattle back to Warley.

His close friendship with his sister continued unshaken; they wrote often to each other and, when they met, discussed life with gusto and animation. He would criticise her frocks and give her errands to do for him at Fortnum and Mason's, while there was always a demand for the socks she knitted for him and his friends.[2]

But when May 1915 came, a month that brought news of heavy British losses in men on two battle-fronts, with small gains in ground, the shadow of John's departure overseas loomed nearer. Draft after draft went out from Warley Barracks to fill the gaps in the Regiment and, for his part, John was deeply humiliated at being left behind, though his name was put back only until he should reach his eighteenth birthday. In July his friend Oscar Hornung, who had often stayed at 'Bateman's', was killed in France, a shock that merely served to sharpen his impatience. Then plans were changed, the Brigade of Guards was expanded into a Guards Division and John was assured that he would be sent abroad with the newly formed Second Battalion, if his father should give permission.

On 10 August the Second Irish Guards were put under orders for France and on the following day Rudyard met his son in London to say good-bye, for he, too, was going abroad. Rudyard and Perceval Landon had been invited to pay a visit to the French Armies in the field. Father and son lunched together at the Bath Club, and then John had still three days of leave, which he spent with his mother and sister at 'Bateman's'. On the seventeenth, his birthday, he left them, looking, as his mother said, 'very smart and straight and young and brave' as he turned at the top of the stairs to say good-bye.

Rudyard was first of the two to see the realities of war.

Rudyard to Carrie Kipling

August, 1915

12 Aug. in the train between Abbeville and Amiens I was buttonholed by the Duchess of Rutland ... about a hospital that she wants to start. . . . Right in the midst of this clack a man with tinted spectacles passes. She says to me: — 'Ain't that Munthe – doctor to the Queen of Sweden?' As he passes she hails him – and Munthe it was. . . . I fell into talk with him at once and he tells me of all his grief and sorrow to find that Sweden is so – not pro-German but afraid of Russia – and how he has got himself into trouble in Sweden for his English and French leanings; and how he has dismissed himself from his Queen's service and how, but for the sad fact that our naturalization laws now insist that a man must put in twelve months' continuous residence in England, he would have 'already, my dear Mr Kipling, have been a British subject'. Of all of which you may believe as much as I did. He was immensely curious to know where I was going.

We left the pier with a quick stealthy turn and two destroyers came up out of the warm grey sea (or that was the effect of it) and fell in alongside us on either side, sort of lounging along to keep pace with our modest 22 knots.

13 Aug. Hotel Ritz, Paris

Back from that amazing human explosive. Clemenceau, who, on the instant of my coming held forth without break and so continued for forty coruscating minutes. All truth too, backed with very real power and the widest knowledge. I should say from what he said that *their* Government is the twin of ours, mentally and spiritually – same incompetence, same lawyer's explanations, same complete inability for anyone to admit that they were wrong in any particular, and the same furious intrigues . . .

He had no earthly doubt of the issue but – munitions, munitions was his cry throughout. I talked French. And talking of talking French, Mons. Ponsot at lunch said to me: 'If I had known you talked French so well, Mr Kipling . . .'

14 Aug. Hotel Brighton, Paris

I sent in my card to Briand, Minister of Justice, whom you remember we met at the Princess's. Now C[lemenceau]'s view of Briand is absolutely unprintable. He would endure, he says, a thousand Millerands sooner than one B. On that I can pronounce no opinion. He reminded me more of Lloyd-George than ever. It's a born demagogue with his mouth crammed with smooth things – but I can't help liking it ... the same L-G like shrug and lean forward of the shoulders at critical points, a sort of political bedside manner. A windbag, yes, but of the most un-scrupulous.

15 Aug. A villa (!) in Jonchéry

We were received on the château steps. It overlooked a heavenly valley and was surrounded on two sides by a platform of stone rather reminding me of Ewhurst. ... The General, who was called Nivelle, told me that his mother was English but he didn't talk good English for all that. He was a charming man of gentle manners. Lunch wouldn't be till one. Would I come out and see something? So we came ... to a tree – to a huge tree – an acacia, Landon says, about 60 feet high, with a ladder going up to a platform in the top branches. At last we came to a crow's nest in the tree, with a map under a little roofed table, a telephone and a man or two. ... Then, looking through the leaves and the branches, I saw the whole countryside falling away for miles in a long yellow slope. (The Boches had used gas weeks ago and the grass had perished for three or four miles). Twas like a stretch of lonely African veldt. ... Regularly all along the line of the horizon, three miles away, the shells from our guns in the discreet park raised clouds of white smoke precisely like the spouts of water up a breakwater in a storm.

Then we climbed down the ladder (which I loathed but I didn't bungle) and were taken to a set of enormous limestone caves or quarries where troops were resting. The General said to me with a wave of the hand: '*All* these men know your books.' I smiled politely. He turned on the nearest group and asked 'em. 'Yes, Yes,' said they, 'specially the Jungle Books.' ... The fuss about this tour is there's too much dam' R. K. in it. I have to lead all the processions.

20 Aug. Troyes

Yesterday was a somewhat full day. It began at 6 a.m. ...
among the wooded hills of Alsace. ... We stopped to look at a
battery of mountain guns; got out and walked under the gloom
of many trees ... thence we got into communication trenches
and walked and walked and walked, till we met a fatherly and
motherly Colonel who took us into the first line trenches which
are 7, or to be exact, 7½ metres – say the length of a cricket
pitch, from the Germans. They were Bavarians and had been
carefully attended to the night before, with the result that they
were *quite* tame, and I had peeps at 'em through loopholes
blocked with plugs. The Colonel pulled the plugs and bade me
look. I saw two green sandbags in a wilderness of tree trunks
and stones and no Bavarians saw me. ... The trenches were
beautifully clean and kept like a museum. There was no smell
save the smell of cookery. There was no noise because we were
so close and – nothing whatever happened.

22 Aug. Paris

I got here at 7.30 from Troyes – after a rather ludicrous time
about the passport, when we tried to buy our tickets to Paris.
The Commissary of Police ... knew nothing about us. ... Then
up rose a very dirty little corporal with a restless face and haled
us out. Once away from the presence of the officer his visage
changed. 'I knew,' said he. 'You are that Rutyar Kiplen of whom
we read. Our officers are all asses. Come along with me.' ...
When I owned to being 'Rutyar', he launched a long, friendly
and enthusiastic 'Ah God-dam!' which was the first I'd ever
heard of that much-described word.

Rudyard Kipling to John Kipling

Hotel Brighton, Paris. 22 Aug. 1915

Dear old man,

I hope you'll never get nearer to the Boche than I did. The
quaintest thing was to watch the N.C.O. gesticulating to his
Colonel and me to keep quiet – and to hear a hopefully expectant
machine gun putting in five or six shots on the chance and then,
as it were, stopping to listen. I don't mind trenches half as much
as going in a motor along ten or twelve miles of road which the
Boches may or may not shell – said road casually protected at
the worst corners with thin hurdles of dried pine-trees. Also, I

hate to be in a town with stone pavements when same is being bombarded. It's a grand life though and does not give you a dull minute. I found boric acid in my socks a great comfort. I walked 2 hours in the dam' trenches.

Don't forget the beauty of rabbit netting overhead against hand-grenades. Even tennis netting is better than nothing.[3]

After his return from France, strong pressure was brought on Rudyard by the Admiralty to write something about the Royal Navy. So firm were the traditions of the silent service that no one knew what the Navy was doing, and our allies supposed it was doing nothing. Here was a task that Rudyard could undertake and he spent September visiting ships of the Dover Patrol and the Harwich Flotilla. Having done this task, he arrived home out of sorts on 27 September. News had come through of a great attack in France, the Battle of Loos, which at first seemed likely to be a British victory; but Rudyard was ill with gastritis, unable to pay much attention to the news. The doctor saw him and put him on a strict diet.

The Battle of Loos was no triumph. Although the British had captured a section of the German front at great cost on 25 September, reserves were badly placed so that the first success was not exploited. An attempt by two fresh divisions to force their way through a narrow gap in the German front failed on the twenty-sixth. The Germans rallied and were regaining ground to the right and left of the gap when the last reserve, the Guards Division, was thrown in on the twenty-seventh to save a situation that was crumbling. The attack of the Guards was unsuccessful also; they made ground, lost it, recovered part of what they had lost, and then consolidated an unfavourable line, while the battle flickered out with little to show for all the valour expended, except 20,000 British dead. The picture of this fruitless struggle was beginning to take shape in the newspapers when on the morning of 2 October a telegram from the War Office announced that John Kipling was wounded and missing.

Elsie's friend Isabel Bonar Law (who was later to lose two of her brothers) was spending the day with her, and Carrie at once decided not to break the news until Isabel had gone. Somehow Carrie forced herself to go through with the day's routine. The next day it was fine after the rain – a 'beautiful, perfect day' she wrote in her diary – and action must be taken. She drove to Wigsell in the morning to share her sorrow with Lady Edward, who had lived through the same experience twelve months earlier, and before she had entered the house Lady Edward knew from her calm, set features what was the message Carrie had come to bring.

That afternoon Aitken arrived from France with such slight news as he had been able to gather, more than was known at the War Office. On the fifth Rudyard was well enough to work at his correspondence while Carrie and Elsie went to London to seek for news at the Guards Depot. They got very little beyond a word from the Colonel to say that John had been wounded while leading a small party of his men against the Germans. Only one of the party had returned wounded, to a hospital at Hythe where at last they found him, 'very sorrowful to hear the news about Mr Kipling who was good to us men and never downhearted'. The staff at Brown's Hotel, old friends of the family, were equally distressed.

Rudyard resolutely returned to work at *Sea Warfare* while awaiting further information. The routine went on as before except that Christmas, and Rudyard's fiftieth birthday four days later, passed without celebration. The War Office had urged him to write an account of the epic Battle of Ypres, 'M.I.5', to help them with propaganda; but such tasks as these he was unwilling to do. He was busy at writing accounts of his own visits to camps and ships, in his own time.

Meanwhile there was a faint chance that inquiry through neutral channels might discover John as a prisoner in Germany. Gwynne set up an inquiry through the British Minister to the Vatican. Walter Page, the American Minister, formerly a partner of Frank Doubleday, did his best, and Rudyard himself consulted the American Minister at the Hague, and a friend in the Swiss Red Cross, without much hope. All clues which seemed to offer a spark of promise were eagerly followed – to end in disappointment. The Kiplings continued to track down wounded men of John's battalion, seeking some hint of what had really happened that day, and for more than two years did not quite abandon hope. Carrie, at least, nourished a faint ray long after Rudyard with his greater knowledge of war had accepted his loss.

Rudyard Kipling to Brigadier L. C. Dunsterville

12 November, 1915

Our boy was reported 'wounded & missing' since Sep. 27 – the Battle of Loos and we've heard nothing official since that date. But all we can pick up from the men points to the fact that he is dead and probably wiped out by the shell fire. However, he had his heart's desire and he didn't have a long time in trenches. The Guards advanced on a front of two platoons for each battalion. He led the right platoon over a mile of open ground in face of shell and machine-gun fire and was dropped at the further limit of the advance, after having emptied his pistol into a house full of German m.g's. His C.O. and his Company Commander told me how he led 'em and the wounded have confirmed it. He was senior ensign tho' only 18 yrs and 6 weeks, and worked like the devil for a year at Warley and knew his Irish to the ground. He was reported on as one of the best of the subalterns and was gym instructor and signaller. It was a short life. I'm sorry that all the years' work ended in that one afternoon but – lots of people are in our position – and it's something to have bred a man. The wife is standing it wonderfully tho' she, of course, clings to the bare hope of his being a prisoner. I've seen what shells can do, and I don't.[4]

More than two years passed from the day of John's disappearance before a full account of his last hours came to light. Oliver Baldwin at last discovered Sergeant Farrell of

the Irish Guards who had been with John when the leading companies had forced their way into the gap between
Hill Seventy and Hulluch, the deepest penetration made by
any British troops in the Battle of Loos. They had fought
their way through Chalk-pit Wood, a copse of straggled
undergrowth, and had then encountered strong resistance
among some houses beyond the wood. John was using his
revolver when he was shot through the head and was laid
under cover in a shell-hole, by the Sergeant. Soon afterwards
the leading troops were driven back and years passed before
the further edge of Chalk-pit Wood again passed into British
hands. In this confused and bitter fighting among the slag-
heaps, and miners' cottages, more than ten thousand British
soldiers were reported missing and not seen again. There was
little doubt that John was one of the unlocated dead.

The time of uncertainty had been all the more agonizing
for the Kiplings because of their unspoken resolution to
maintain the ordinary routine of life unchanged. As the fact
of John's death became inevitable, the family – a square no
longer – became more withdrawn and self-sufficient. Neither
Rudyard nor Carrie ever talked much about their son, but
their life without him was never the same; it had lost a
motive force. Elsie now stood as the one barrier between her
ageing parents and their numbing sorrow, bearing a burden
of which they were hardly aware.

In those gloomy days, with the shadow never off his mind
– a son lying among thousands of other men's sons in an
unmarked grave – it was perhaps a slight consolation to
Rudyard to receive scores of letters bringing sympathy from
every part of the world. He had unknown enemies as well as
unknown friends, and among his letters were some which
reviled him with the brutal assumption that he deserved his
loss because, in some way, he had provoked the war. One
such letter that came through a neutral country from Germany was openly exultant. Letters that he found peculiarly
trying came from psychic mediums who offered to 'get in

touch' with John by occult methods, and it was to this suggestion that he replied in the verses called 'The Road to En-Dor', written in the wet summer of 1917 when the mutter of gunfire from the bloodstained swamps of Passchendaele, a hundred miles away, could be heard distinctly at Burwash. For a few months then he had the partial comfort of his sister's company; she stayed in the cottage at Dudwell Mill and every day they took long walks together. Dear as she was to him, since she shared his earliest memories, he could not share her flight from reality into the world of the psychic.

The Kiplings pressed on with their work, still going to London frequently. They took their place at more than one Memorial Ceremony, always a heartbreaking experience, even to iron-nerved Carrie, since 'Recessional' was always sung. Twice, at least, they were in London on air-raid nights, but no authentic account survives of any incident they did not share with millions of Londoners. Rudyard used to lunch regularly at the Athenaeum where he met many of the political leaders. A social honour he particularly appreciated was his election in December 1914 to one of the most exclusive societies in London, the dining-club that since Dr Johnson's day has been known simply as 'The Club'. On another social level, it was an equal delight to him to be made an honorary member of 'The Goat', the rendezvous of naval officers on leave in London.

Apart from two visits to quiet sectors of the war-front, in France and Italy, his closest contacts with fighting men were made in ships of the Royal Navy. He visited the Grand Fleet in Scottish waters and went more than once to Dover and Harwich. The ship's company of H.M.S. *Maidstone*, the depot-ship for submarines, were his special friends and for them he wrote several songs and epigrams.* One day at Harwich he went down in a submarine, and hated it since he was inclined to claustrophobia. His naval songs and bal-

---

* At the request of some naval friends Kipling designed crests and badges for several ships and naval units.

lads are perhaps the most firmly realized of his studies of active service, especially the sharply etched seascape in the poem 'Mine-sweepers' with its charming word-pattern of the ships' names:

Sweepers – *Unity, Claribel, Assyrian, Stormcock* and *Golden Gain.*

Rudyard could hardly fail to be gratified when in January 1917 a Coalition Government was formed to include all the resolute men who were determined to fight the war to a finish. If the hated Lloyd George was Prime Minister, it was some consolation that Milner was Secretary of State for War, while Bonar Law was Chancellor of the Exchequer and Stanley Baldwin his Financial Secretary.

On all questions of moulding public opinion Rudyard was now consulted, since his friends were in office, and when Sir Max Aitken (raised to the peerage as Lord Beaverbrook in 1917) formed the Ministry of Information he tried hard to draw Rudyard in.

Though Rudyard would never submit to any routine of writing sponsored propaganda, he undertook three tasks arising out of the war and gave the best of his time to them for about five years. The first was to write the history of the Irish Guards, his son's regiment. An approach was made to him in January 1917, and by March he was immersed in the task. It obliged him to hold frequent conferences with officers and to consult scores of wounded men in hospitals. The last hope that John might miraculously have survived as a prisoner did not flicker out until the end of the year, and by then the Kiplings had admitted, almost into their family circle, a group of John's young brother-officers who could tell him about their own battles and so enrich the history with the visual details that he loved. Rupert Grayson, John de Salis, Lord Castlerosse, Harold Maxwell, and other young ensigns came to 'Bateman's' to tell their story. These and other visitors continued to come to 'Bateman's' after the war, among them many soldiers and sailors from overseas, who became Elsie's friends as well as admirers of her father. A series of convalescent officers brought their families to stay as guests in one of the estate farmhouses which was re-furnished for their use and, besides, there were the Irish rank and file who had fought under John to be consulted. Rudyard diligently sought them out and his Regimental History is full of their sayings, as vivid and pungent as those of the Irish he had known long ago in India.

'Private Mulvaney', that once celebrated Irish soldier, had been out of mind for twenty years, while Rudyard in his Ulster Covenanting days had spoken with contempt of the Southern Catholic Irish. This was an attitude he could not maintain when writing of the men who had followed his own son to battle, and had suffered with him. He made amends, in the poem, 'The Irish Guards', written as a pro-logue to the history and as a tribute to those Irishmen who had fought in the old wars, for or against the English.

> Old Days! The wild geese are ranging,
>   Head to the storm as they faced it before!
> For where there are Irish their hearts are unchanging,
>   And when they are changed, it is Ireland no more!
>   Ireland no more!

The war dead presented their own problem: never in Europe's wars had so many thousands died, in campaign after campaign, crowded in so constricted a battlefield that war-cemeteries on a gigantic scale had to be constructed. It was this that suggested his whimsical fantasy, 'On the Gate', about the queue of flocking souls from Europe's battlefields and St Peter's improvisations to deal with the emergency. Herbert Baker and Rudyard had been considering it for some months – as had many others – when, in September 1917, Sir Fabian Ware came down to 'Bateman's' to invite Rudyard to become one of the Imperial War Graves Com-missioners. The scope of this undertaking ever widened, as a million British dead were found, exhumed, identified and re-buried in permanent cemeteries with headstones, inscriptions, gardens, and memorial crosses, by agreement with the authorities of many allied or formerly hostile countries. Rudyard used to say it was 'the biggest single bit of work since the Pharaohs – and they only worked in their own country'.[5] For the remaining eighteen years of his life Rudyard was a diligent member of the War Graves Commission, active in all its practical decisions. At one of the earliest meetings, with Lord Milner in the chair, he proposed the standard inscription – 'Their name liveth for evermore' – which was inscribed on the Stone of Sacrifice in each cemetery. The inscriptions for the British memorials in French cathedrals – in short, every inscription and almost every form of words used by the Commission was of Rudyard's drafting. He inspected many cemeteries and appeared at many functions on behalf of the Commission. He was one of the originators of the plan to bury an unknown British soldier in Westminster Abbey, a ceremony adopted by the other belligerent nations, and was responsible for the nightly ceremony of 'The Last Post' at the Menin Gate. Thus responsible for marking the graves of so many thousands, for providing a visible shrine at which so many bereaved parents could lay their grief, he identified no shrine of his own. John Kipling's fate was never surely known, his body never found.[6]

About the same time as the formation of the War Graves Commission, Dr Jameson came down to 'Bateman's' to ask Rudyard to become one of the Rhodes Trustees, thus involving him in the administration of millions of money for a purpose to which he was devoted. Rudyard and Carrie had been in Rhodes's counsels when the Rhodes Scholarships were initiated and, after Jameson himself, no one knew better than Rudyard what had been in Rhodes's mind. No public cause could lift up his heart more buoyantly than the provision of scholarships at Oxford for young men from the Dominions and the United States, and no task of reconstruction was more important than to revive the scheme after the war. The Graves Commission and the History of the Irish Guards turned his mind back upon old unhappy things; the Rhodes Trustees were guardians of the future.

He had no more than made up his mind to become one of the Trustees when in October 1917 Jameson died, leaving Rudyard to maintain the tradition that Rhodes had passed on to them. Their friends, the group of survivors from South African days, urged Rudyard to write Jameson's life, which he might have done if the *Irish Guards* had not engrossed his time. Instead, he suggested to Milner that the life should be written by Ian Colvin, a young journalist who had worked for Gwynne. This proved an unsatisfactory arrangement and Rudyard found himself obliged to edit the book.[7] In so doing he took pains to suppress allusions to himself, and no reader of the *Life of Jameson* would suppose that he and Kipling had been intimate friends who shared political confidences for fifteen years. That tale is now lost.

In 1917 Rudyard went off to Italy with Landon to write an account of the Italian campaign (*The War in the Mountains*). He attended the beatification of a saint in St Peter's, saw the Pope – who looked, he said, like Woodrow Wilson – and then had lunch in the palace of a cardinal in

a little wonder of a study full of priceless old prints and a genuine Holbein. . . . There was only Landon and I and the Cardinal and his domestic chaplain who was also general secretary. The latter was of quite a new type to me. I never knew before that domestic chaplains contradicted Cardinals. Well, we talked and we talked (the domestic chaplain talked most) for about two hours. I am a low-minded beast and I suspected from the first that we had not been asked for nothing. We hadn't; but that is a matter I must tell you *viva voce* when we meet. This land, rightly or wrongly, gives me the idea of being more full of eyes and ears than a peacock's tail . . .

And so we got away – much – oh much interested. This is the d—dest queerest trap-doorest world I've ever got into. . . . I shall be main glad to meet real plain soldier men again.[8]

He met the soldiers a few days later where the Italian
Army was fighting the Austrians on the mountain front.

Rudyard to Elsie Kipling

11 May, 1917

Oh Bird! I've just received your note of the 4th on my return
from war among the Alps. An inconceivable trip at the height of
4000 feet, in a country to which the Engelberg Valley is tame
and of no account. . . . And all the time guns were booming one
against another, lazily as they tried trial shots. They were 8″ and
11″ howitzers on our side; and when we climbed (or our car did)
up to the very bare tops of mountains behold the grass was all
pitted with shell-holes. It's a war of giants among mountains. I
looked into Tolmino and along 30 mile of Austrian front – wholly
different from all I saw yesterday. The immensity of the landscape
and the work dwarf all comparison. I don't know how on earth
or in the clouds I can describe it.[9]

During the years of American neutrality exasperation
against President Wilson's policy was widely spread in England. In his letters to American friends Rudyard wrote on
this with bitterness, and his low opinion of Woodrow Wilson was shared by at least one old friend in America, Theodore Roosevelt, whom the vagaries of Republican party
policy had thrust into the obscurity that ex-Presidents often
experience. Roosevelt told Kipling that Wilson was a hereditary shirker, he came of an old Virginian family of which
no member had fought on either side in the Civil War.
What could one expect from such a breed?[10]

On his part, Woodrow Wilson had no such prejudice
against Kipling. He wrote, through a mutual friend, to ask
Rudyard for an autographed copy of 'If –', which, he said,
had been a constant inspiration to him.[11]

When, at last, Wilson felt able to bring the United States
into the war, the decision resolved in Rudyard's mind the
dilemma which had so long embittered him. A grand alliance of England, France, and America (that doubtful part-

ner, Russia, had just fallen away into chaos) united all that he thought worthiest in the civilized world. But this was an alliance of men as colleagues in action, not a politician's compromise, and his contempt for the political leaders, in England and America alike, was unmitigated.

The arrival of American ships in European waters, of American soldiers in British training-camps, aroused his enthusiasm. He went at once to Winchester to visit them – was even persuaded to make a speech of welcome to a parade of 7,000 men; and when a correspondent [12] wrote from America asking for leave to reprint some of his verses, he gave it only on condition that all profits should be given to American Army charities. Later, he collected some news of the American Navy for Roosevelt.

I have been seeing one of our Naval Officers . . . and he brings me first hand news . . . of the almost comically good relations between the two Navies. Your destroyers shine especially in convoy and anti-submarine work. Both sides groan together over the enormous amount of unnecessary paper-work. The American reports are held up to our people as models of what concise and accurate reports should be. . . . All our young men speak very highly indeed of the U.S.N. and are getting on as sociable as a 'basket of kittens', to quote Uncle Remus. I've heard a good deal about your airmen – their competence, modesty, and insatiable zeal.[13]

Rudyard transferred to Roosevelt some of the confidence and devotion that he had formerly given to Rhodes, and for the same reasons. He approved the things that Roosevelt did, and had not the least objection to his hero's occasional roughness and violence in speech. They met only once in twenty years, in 1910 when Roosevelt was honoured at Oxford, but through those years exchanged many letters which are now in the Library of Congress.

War-work and war-journalism left little time for imaginative writing in prose. *A Diversity of Creatures*, Rudyard's volume of stories including all that was outstanding since 1912, was published in 1917. Two or three more stories which he had in draft were laid aside for five years, while he concentrated on the tasks he had set himself. In verse he was more productive, and these years saw the publication of many finely imaginative pieces, often barbed with some political message. The 'Epitaphs of the War' belong to this period.

Even more forceful were his diatribes in verse against those whom he held responsible for the errors of the war, notably his poem on 'Mesopotamia'. It was the Government of India that so mismanaged the first Mesopotamian campaign, especially the medical services, and in denouncing this incompetence Rudyard returned to the criticisms he had passed upon Simla thirty years before.

They shall not return to us, the resolute, the young,
  The eager and whole-hearted whom we gave:
  But the men who left them thriftily to die in their own dung,
  Shall they come with years and honour to the grave?

Shall we only threaten and be angry for an hour?
  When the storm is ended shall we find
How softly but how swiftly they have sidled back to power
  By the favour and contrivance of their kind?

A reading public, that was learning to expect from Rudyard Kipling these harsh and uncompromising sentiments, opened *The Times* one day in May 1918 to find a new poem printed over his name at the foot of the middle page, in that place where 'Recessional' and 'For All We Have and Are' had once appeared. It was called 'The Old Volunteer' and quite lacked the least spark of fire or spot of venom; it was mild and silly. Though no critical reader could doubt that this was some kind of hoax, *The Times* plunged itself into deeper confusion by an unwillingness to laugh it off. They almost refused to accept Rudyard's indignant repudiation, and Scotland Yard failed to discover who was responsible. This was the most absurd and the most annoying of the many occasions in Rudyard's literary life when sentiments he had not uttered, or verses he had not written, or ephemeral work which he had tried to suppress, were published over his name without his permission. He could never free himself for long from the hateful publicity that these episodes brought him.[14]

When the war news was at last favourable, Rudyard was slow in turning to optimism. As late as 13 October 1918 he and Landon ruefully agreed that they had 'no conviction of the prospect of peace', but rather some anxiety lest there should be a compromise without exemplary victory. This was the theme of the poem 'Justice', which was syndicated in 200 newspapers during October, a plea for the disarmament of Germany and the punishment of war-criminals. It was with no exultation that the Kiplings faced the end of the war. There was as yet no radio-broadcasting and, at 'Bateman's', they had not even installed a telephone.* Quietly they spent 11 November at home and learned only by the ringing of the church bells that the armistice was signed.

The activities of President Wilson still filled Rudyard with alarm. He wrote to Roosevelt (7 November 1918) in the hope of mobilizing Republican opinion against the President.

The guts of Europe are sliding into our laps, day by day, but at the one moment when we allies ought to have our hands free to deal with a continent *in extremis* we are tied up by Wilson's idiotic Fourteen Points. They open the door to every form of evasion and quibble. . . . England takes her victories very grimly.

Roosevelt replied amicably. But, revealing the mistrust of Kipling's judgement that can often be observed in their correspondence, he warned him not to overstate the case. Roosevelt also was bitterly opposed to Wilson, 'a mere doctrinaire with no ideals'. He hoped for an Anglo-American alliance but did not hold with the American anglophiles

*It was not installed in Kipling's lifetime. He rarely used a telephone, disliked it, and much more disliked intrusive calls.

and English americanophiles 'who do more harm than good'.[15] Rudyard took this correspondence to Milner, the Secretary for War, but there was little to be done. Though Republican gains in the elections might weaken Wilson, they would not tend to an American alliance with France and England. In any case the President had come to Europe to solve its problems, by a mere announcement of some liberal sentiments. On 27 December 1918 Rudyard was commanded to Buckingham Palace to meet the President, who 'impressed him not at all'. He was 'arid – first, last, and all the time a schoolmaster'.

The President's moment of triumph was followed by a blow that struck Rudyard to the heart. In January 1919 Theodore Roosevelt died. Rudyard, who had lately been reading his *Pilgrim's Progress* and applying it to the times, wrote of him as Great-Heart:

> Oh, our world is none the safer
> Now Great-Heart hath died!

The outlook for the family at 'Bateman's' was no brighter: 'and now a world to be re-made', wrote Carrie bleakly in her diary, 'without a son'.

A CHARM (1910)

Take of English earth as much
As either hand may rightly clutch,
In the taking of it breathe
Prayer for all who lie beneath.
Not the great nor well-bespoke,
But the mere uncounted folk
Of whose life and death is none
Report or lamentation.
    Lay that earth upon thy heart,
    And thy sickness shall depart!

It shall sweeten and make whole
Fevered breath and festered soul.
It shall mightily restrain
Over-busied hand and brain.
It shall ease thy mortal strife
'Gainst the immortal woe of life,
Till thyself, restored, shall prove
By what grace the Heavens do move.

Take of English flowers these —
Spring's full-facèd primroses,
Summer's wild wide-hearted rose,
Autumn's wall-flower of the close,
And, thy darkness to illume,
Winter's bee-thronged ivy-bloom.
Seek and serve them where they bide
From Candlemas to Christmas-tide,
    For these simples, used aright,
    Can restore a failing sight.

These shall cleanse and purify
Webbed and inward-turning eye;
These shall show thee treasure hid
Thy familiar fields amid;
And reveal (which is thy need)
Every man a King indeed!

[18]

After the War

(1919–24)

WHEN Dorothy Ponton, who had once been Elsie's governess, returned to 'Bateman's' in 1919 as Rudyard's secretary,
she noticed some small but ominous changes in the family
routine. 'Mr Kipling had lost his buoyant step, though his
genius and courage remained unabated.' His physical health
had deteriorated, after recurrent attacks of gastric trouble,
which Miss Ponton attributed to suppressed anxiety rather
than to any physical cause.[1] Carrie relaxed none of her
diligent watchfulness over his well-being. Visitors noticed
that she habitually followed him about the room with her
eye. Not only did she guard his health; she opened his
letters, dictated replies to the secretary, corresponded with
the literary agent, managed the household, and eventually
farmed the land, watching all expenditure with a prudent
eye; and it was commonly said in the neighbourhood that
she would have got more out of the estate if she had put
more into it. She paid the bills. There had been a time
when Rudyard found his accounts disordered because his
cheques were often retained as souvenirs instead of being
presented for payment. His autograph was now so strictly
guarded that no unauthorized scrap of his handwriting was
allowed to leave the house; even his personal letters were
checked in and out by the secretary, a precaution which has
enabled the students of his work to detect several forgeries.*
So dependent was he upon Carrie in money matters, there
came a day when his own bank denied knowledge of its

* The 'Dorian' correspondence, now in the Houghton Library, which
Mrs Livingston pronounced a forgery, is condemned on these grounds
(and on other internal evidence).

most celebrated client. He had run short of cash and dropped in casually to draw a cheque, but, not having been seen there before, he was treated as a stranger until the manager came to identify him.

Carrie's life was devoted to guarding and cherishing the husband whom she had married when he was a young man with precocious talents and Bohemian habits, and the protective crust she formed around his life grew harder as she grew older. Even more than Rudyard she hated prying eyes. When Carrie's mother died in 1919 her last personal link with America was snapped. Though she had seen her mother only once in twenty years, at Montreal in 1907, Carrie had written her long weekly letters (now, it seems, no longer extant), and had never quite thrown off her mother's guidance. Rudyard, too, judging by a few surviving letters, respected and liked his mother-in-law. It was unpleasant to discover, when Mrs Balestier's estate was valued, that Beatty had been sponging on her for years, so that she had been obliged to use up her capital in gifts to her scapegrace son. The same charming, drunken, good-for-nothing, he was still the scandal of the strait-laced, the admiration of the wilder set in Brattleboro, still disposed to boast in his cups of victory over the Kiplings. It was quite in character that when he came to die in 1936, he expressed regret for the harm he had done them, and a wish that they could have met again in friendship. His name had been mentioned so rarely in the Kipling household that Elsie hardly knew she had an uncle in Vermont.[2]

The sister, Josephine Dunham, was never intimate with Carrie, though the two were on terms of civil acquaintance. When the Dunhams visited England, their young family found a key to Rudyard's affection, especially since the eldest boy so much resembled his uncle Wolcott Balestier, the long-lost friend.

Rudyard's own relatives often visited him at Burwash and, for a man who was reputed to be an inaccessible recluse, he lived a sociable life. The Visitors' Book contains the names of half the people in England who were eminent in the world of action, not merely the fashionable or the literary. A stream of visitors came, averaging in the nineteen-twenties a hundred and fifty a year, of whom many were invited to stay the night; and many more would have come if they had got past Carrie's scrutiny. As time passed, the numbers tended to increase, especially the number of children. The descendants of 'Aunt Louie' Baldwin, through three generations, came regularly and the book sometimes records an exclamation of delight when a new youngster appears for the first time. Names of relatives and family friends, Sussex neighbours, and young men who had known John in the Brigade of Guards recur frequently, as do certain old-faithfuls, bound to the Kiplings by some personal tie: Aleck Watt and Frank Doubleday, Ted and Dorothy Price, Miss Anderson, who had once been Rudyard's secretary, Miss Blaikie, who had once been Elsie's governess, 'Ellen' a beloved and retired housemaid.

To take as an example the casual visitors in a single year, they included for 1921 – as well as Perceval Landon back from the Far East and Oliver Baldwin back from Armenia – William Nicholson the painter and Siccard the sculptor, Burton Hendrick who was writing the life of Walter Page, Fabian Ware of the War Graves Commission, Sir Hugh Clifford the Governor of Nigeria, Eveleigh Nash the publisher and Randolph Lewis the script-writer, the Princess Christian, Admiral 'Blinker' Hall, Charles Scribner from New York and Sallie Norton from Boston, the Rector of Strasbourg University, Mr Tompsett the porter from Brown's Hotel, and Dr Frank Buchman with a team of young men who gate-crashed and sang hymns on the lawn. This is a group picked at random, and another year might show 'Stalky' back from the Caspian, Sir William Willcocks, who damned the Nile, Cameron Forbes from the Philippines, Kermit Roosevelt, Bishop Gwynne from the Sudan, or Jarvis Bey the Governor of Sinai.[3]

The flying men in this new generation turned to Rudyard

as their fathers had done in the nineties when he was known as the poet of *The Seven Seas*. One great airman, Sir John Salmond, traced on the globe in his study at 'Bateman's' the air-routes which, twenty years later, were to encircle the earth; which, twenty years earlier, Rudyard had already foreseen. When the first Atlantic flight was achieved, by the British airship 'R.34' in 1919, the crew took with them a single book, *Traffics and Discoveries*, so that they could refer to his story, 'With the Night Mail'. Then, autographed by each member of the crew, the book was presented to the author.

The daily correspondence at 'Bateman's' included many letters from would-be authors asking the Master's advice, which he often gave, if they seemed young and modest. In later life, when his contemporaries had done their work and made their names, he urged them sometimes to write their reminiscences. Sir John Bland-Sutton's entertaining book, Sir Walter Lawrence's *The India We Knew*, and 'Stalky's' *Dunsterforce* owe much to his advice. As in the case of the *Life of Jameson* and the *Milner Papers*, the price of Rudyard's help was the suppression of his own name. We are the poorer for not knowing what Lawrence might have written about the young Kipling at Simla.

Rudyard's fame, and the public work in which he was engaged, brought an inevitable result. The admission to the Cabinet of his friends, Bonar Law and Baldwin, during the last years of the war had meant that he would again be pressed to accept some public honour. Stanley Baldwin brought a message from the Prime Minister in May 1917 to say that Rudyard might have 'any honour he will accept'. His reply was that he would accept none. Even after this private communication, he heard a rumour that he was to be one of the first knights in the new Order of the British Empire, and hastily warned Bonar Law that 'it must not be'. And again, in spite of that, he received an official notification a few days later, that without his knowledge he had been appointed a Companion of Honour. This third time his temper was ruffled and he wrote to Bonar Law: 'how would you like it if you woke up and found they had made you Archbishop of Canterbury?'

The Order of Merit, which had no political significance, seemed the appropriate mark of distinction to offer to Kipling the poet and story-teller, and his name had more than once been canvassed when vacancies occurred in earlier years. The strongest recommendation came from the Poet Laureate, Robert Bridges,* in a letter written to the Palace in 1916.

It is plain that he is the greatest living genius that we have in literature; and it is generally thought that he has been passed over on account of his politics. The only other reason I could think of would be that he has written so much in slang and low dialect. But much of his later work is altogether above any such reproach and some of it is extremely beautiful on any standard.

In December 1921 the new offer was made. One morning at 'Bateman's' Rudyard, looking through his letters, passed one of them over to Carrie 'with characteristic lack of interest'. It was a proposal from the King's Private Secretary, Lord Stamfordham, that he should accept the Order of Merit: 'in recognition of the eminent services you have rendered to the Science of Literature and of the almost unique estimation in which your works are regarded throughout the British Empire'.

It was a grand letter, noted Carrie in her diary, adding that she felt sure he would decline it even though it seemed to come direct from the King. 'The fact that the King has been pleased to signify his approval of my services to Literature,' he wrote, 'will be, to me, the great honour of my life. But I would ask you, while presenting my humble and loyal duty ... to pray that His Majesty may hold me excused.'

* See also footnote on p. 460.

It was felt due to the King, in whose personal gift the Order of Merit lay, to make a discreet announcement to the press of this rejected offer. As Rudyard was not consulted and as he had shown the correspondence to no one but his wife, he was deeply distressed at the publication of his decision, which seemed to imply a discourtesy to the King. He was mollified only when further explanations had been made by Lord Stamfordham, and when he had again been able to assure the King that he could do better service without a title or award than with one. From this time, Lord Stamfordham, whom Rudyard met occasionally dining at 'The Club', was one of his friends, and his association with the Royal Family and Household became closer. Yet even this friendship did not save Rudyard from further pressure to accept some honour. In 1924 the Order of Merit was again offered to him, since it was believed that he had changed his mind; and again he was obliged to refuse while assuring the King of his loyalty and gratitude.[4]

Academic honours he did not refuse. In 1920 the University of Edinburgh awarded him a doctorate.

Rudyard Kipling to Colonel H. W. Feilden

9 July 1920

In the evening I went to my dinner. . . . I strictly remembered your injunction about my speech, eschewed prolixity and the Scotch accent and got a good reception. . . . The Moderator (*such* a Scot) in replying to my speech for the University expatiated on Edinburgh having annexed an Englishman! I said nought but watched him deliver himself deeply into my hands. Next morn he comes to me and says: 'Am I rightly informed that your grandmother was a MacDonald?' 'No,' I said. 'It was my mother but – how should you lowlanders know these things?' He was out of Midlothian, and in a temperate way I danced on his carcase. Selah!

The Degree giving began at 9.30 and endured without a break till 11.45, when we went to St Giles and were prayed over for an hour by the clock; and then to lunch at the Union. . . . What I admired most were the faces of the boys and girls as they came up to be capped. It was a cross-section of the Scottish race. They made rather a row when my turn came.[5]

In the autumn of 1920 the Kiplings were at last able to resume the motoring-tours in France which had given them such delight in the happy years before 1914. But every visit to France, after the war, had the character of a pilgrimage, because Rudyard's duty as a War Graves Commissioner obliged him to visit and report upon the cemeteries where the million dead of the British Armies were reburied. To drive or wander across the waste ground, bought with dear blood in five long campaigns, was an enterprise that touched his own heart-strings. As well as his stories of the battle-fields, he left other fragments:

> 'I plough deep' said the car,
> 'I plough old wounds afresh –
> 'What you thought was a scar,
> 'I will show you is stricken flesh . . .'[6]

He made careful inspections of more than thirty cemeteries in northern France and, on his first tour, turned aside to see the battlefield of Loos and to identify the shattered stumps and brambly undergrowth of Chalk-pit Wood.

The next visit to France was very different in character – a personal triumph. A message was brought to him by André Chevrillon that the University of Paris wished to give him a doctorate, and this was followed by a similar message from Strasbourg. In Paris and in Alsace during November 1921 he was welcomed with the acclamation due to a national hero, fêted by the Chamber of Deputies, received by the President of the Republic, and overwhelmed with invitations. From this time, his frequent visits to Paris brought him often into contact with the leaders of French political and social life, especially in the circles where he was introduced by his old friend, Clemenceau.

Rudyard had a gift for penetrating the undertones of conversation. His own French was fluent though inaccurate, and powerfully helped out by gestures; his skill at extracting the sense of what was said to him seemed uncanny. Not only could he fall into casual talk with some patois-speaking peasant in France, and come away after five minutes, equipped with minute technical knowledge of his farming methods and family history; there were occasions when he achieved the same result in Spain and even Czechoslovakia by signs and gestures, without pretence of knowing the language at all. In Parisian society the language was no barrier to him and, at a pinch, he could make a short speech in French. In his addresses to the Sorbonne and to the University of Strasbourg, however, he spoke in English after careful preparation. Each of these deliberate speeches was a variation on a theme that was the foundation of his politics for the rest of his life, the necessity for Anglo-French co-operation. 'The whole weight of the world at the present moment lies again, as it used to lie in the time of our fathers, on the necks of two nations, England and France.'[7]

By the spring of 1922 the construction of cemeteries in France was so far advanced that the King and Queen decided to make a solemn pilgrimage to them on behalf of the whole nation. This was a State occasion, in which Rudyard took part, not as a national poet but as a Commissioner for War Graves.

The Kiplings were already touring the battlefields when on 11 May 1922 they were instructed to meet the King at Vlamertinghe near Ypres. Rudyard arranged to change into clothes of ceremony in a peasant's cottage, then waited in the lee of a wall – it was bitterly cold – for the arrival of the King with Field-Marshal Haig, an incident that suggested to him the charming little tale which he wrote some years later and called 'The Debt'. This was a preliminary meeting and on the thirteenth he and Carrie were present at the great ceremony at Terlincthun, near Boulogne, under the shadow of Napoleon's Colonne de la Grande Armée. There were many graves of Indian soldiers in this vast cemetery and, while waiting for the King's arrival, Rudyard happened upon a memorial to 'Gunga Din, Stretcher-bearer'.

The King spoke his words, as Rudyard noted, 'with splendid delivery and dignified bearing'. 'In the course of my pilgrimage,' he said, 'I have many times asked myself whether there can be more potent advocates of peace upon earth than this massed multitude of witnesses to the desolation of war.' It was his hope, he concluded, that these visible memorials would 'serve to draw all peoples together in sanity and self-control as it had already set the relations between our Empire and our Allies on the deep-rooted basis of a common heroism and a common agony'.[8]

After the Queen had laid a wreath on the memorial, the Commissioners were presented to the King, who had a short private conversation with Rudyard and Carrie, the first occasion, it appears, on which they spoke freely together. Since fanciful accounts of this meeting have been put about, it may be as well to set down the only authentic record, Rudyard's own. The King spoke to Carrie Kipling about her son John, and Rudyard took proud notice of her graceful curtsey. Rudyard was then presented 'and the King said what was seemly'. 'I praised his delivery,' said Rudyard, 'which was also seemly.' They then spoke a little 'about the politicians' and Rudyard noticed that the look in the King's eye was that of 'a decent man who suspects he is being carted'. There was no talk of honours or awards. A few days later, when both had returned to England, Rudyard was asked to meet the King again, at a private party, the first evidence that a link of personal affection was growing up between these two elderly men.

The summer of 1922, even after a happy trip to Spain in the spring, had been exhausting to Rudyard's vitality. His work for the War Graves Commission had reached a climax, and *The Irish Guards in the Great War*, the most sustained of all his literary efforts, was at last finished. As always,

mental fatigue reacted on his physical condition which now
began to give Carrie much anxiety. She watched his weight
with solicitude, noting that it had fallen below 130 pounds.
He looked old, yellow, and shrunken. Since the gastric
trouble of 1915, he had long suffered from intermittent pain
which the local doctor treated with purging and dieting but
could not diagnose. The great surgeon, Sir John Bland-
Sutton, who had been a friend of the family for many years,
was frequently consulted – to no effect – and by August there
was no doubt that Rudyard was seriously ill. He withdrew
to London into a nursing home in Fitzroy Square, for a
prolonged course of X-ray examination by several specia-
lists. No conclusion was reached except that there was no
sign of the cancer he had always dreaded.

Carrie, much exasperated by servant troubles, the common
complaint of the post-war world, brought him home to
'Bateman's', an invalid, on a strict diet and strangely listless
in manner. He was bed-ridden, did no work, and took little
interest in the political crisis of that autumn. A few weeks
earlier he had drafted a political manifesto for the Conservative Party. Now he hardly noticed the progress of the intrigue which overthrew Lloyd George's Coalition and made
Bonar Law Prime Minister, with Stanley Baldwin as his
Chancellor of the Exchequer.

Carrie suddenly found herself in the middle of a storm of
hostile publicity, which she had to weather alone, since
Rudyard was too ill to bear his part. On 11 September 1922
the *New York World* published an account of a supposed
interview with Rudyard Kipling, which was at once repeated, as front-page news, by the press of England, France,
and America. It purported to be a statement made by Rudyard to Clare Sheridan on Anglo-American relations, which
at that time were in a delicate state. Rudyard, like many
well-informed Europeans, was indeed distressed by the
triumph of the isolationists. The callous withdrawal of President Harding from Europe seemed as irresponsible in one
way as the pontifical meddling of President Wilson had

seemed in the other; and it is not unlikely that Rudyard had let slip some casual remarks to that effect in private conversation.

Clare Sheridan was the married daughter of a family, who were near neighbours of the Kiplings – the Frewens of Brede Place. When she invited herself to tea at 'Bateman's', with her two young children, she was welcomed, and it had never occurred to Rudyard that an old friend, for he had known her almost since her childhood, could sink to the vulgarity of selling his tea-table conversation to the American press. His distaste of interviewers, and his unwillingness to make general statements to reporters, were notorious and, if he had talked freely, she must have known his words were not for publication. He was alleged to have said that America had come into the war too late and had pulled out of it too soon with the satisfaction of cornering all the gold in the world, and that the American nation was corrupted by low-class immigrants since her best blood had been spilt and wasted in the Civil War. The isolationists made so much capital out of this tirade that official disclaimers were made both by the French and the British Governments. While they took pains to explain that the point of view expressed was not their own, it was left for Rudyard to make his own explanations. Rather late and grudgingly, he issued a notice to the press, which gave it no priority: 'I did not give Mrs Sheridan an interview. I did not say the things which I see she ascribes to me, and have not discontinued the habit of saying what I wish to say over my own signature.'[9] Though Clare could hardly repeat her allegations after this disclaimer, she consoled herself by sneering at the Kiplings' domestic life, in her next book.*

In October Rudyard was well enough for a visit to Lon-

* 'R. K.,' she said, 'a jolly little man with a school-boy humour, would not have seemed anything much if his eyebrows had been shaved and one had not known his name.' He was 'wrung dry by domesticity. When he had a good story to tell, Mrs K. always intervened to tell it better.' (*Nuda Veritas.*)

don, where Stanley Baldwin came to see him at his hotel immediately before going to Buckingham Palace to receive the seals of office. A few days later the gastric pains returned, more violently than before, and the specialist Sir Humphry Rolleston was sent for. He recommended an operation which was performed by Bland-Sutton on 15 November.

Again, as in New York in 1899, Carrie took charge of everything, and again Frank Doubleday – on a visit from America – stood by his friends. But this time publicity was kept under control, and, by mighty efforts on the part of Carrie, the reporters were held at bay. No crowds waited at the Kiplings' door; and only the well-informed, among them the King and the Queen, sent their sympathy. Rudyard, though very ill indeed, survived the operation and was able to return to 'Bateman's' for Christmas, 'very low and depressed' but, as Carrie thought, 'improving'. In February 1923 there was a relapse, but when the spring returned he rapidly grew stronger.

In April Rudyard and Carrie went by sea to Cannes. As they bucketed through the Bay they saw a ship called the *Bolivar*, behaving just as Rudyard's *Bolivar* did in the ballad, to his great delight and to that of all the other passengers. They stayed on the Riviera and there a new access of strength came to him. He wrote 'The Janeites' and a 'Stalky' story, the beginning of his last great burst of literary activity.

In October 1923 Rudyard's election as Lord Rector of the University of St Andrews gave him the opportunity to speak to the rising generation, in an address which was afterwards published under the title of *Independence*. The author of 'If—' and 'The Sons of Martha' here succinctly expressed his social philosophy, which attracted much notice and some hostile criticism in a world that had grown unaccustomed to that message. He began with a quotation from Burns:

> To catch Dame Fortune's golden smile
>   Assiduous wait upon her,
> And gather gear by every wile
>   That's justified by honour –
> Not for to hide it in a hedge
>   Nor for the train attendant,
> But for the glorious privilege
>   Of being independent.

He made a side-glance at thrift, which, he supposed, needed little encouragement at a Scottish university. 'You, for the most part, come, as I did, from households conversant with a certain strictness,' he said, 'which has taught us to look at both sides of the family shilling – we belong to stock where present sacrifice for future ends was accepted, in principle and practice, as part of life.' To people of such an upbringing the desire for Independence, 'the singular privilege of a man owning himself', comes naturally, and, though the world of 1923 was unstable, there were hard facts that the young should remember.

Except for the appliances we make, the rates at which we move ourselves and our possessions through space, and the words we use, nothing in life changes. The utmost any generation can do is to rebaptize each spiritual or emotional rebirth in its own tongue ... and ... no shortcomings on the part of others can save us from the consequences of our own shortcomings.

Yet in all ages the younger generation, besides its own burden, must bear the burden imposed upon it by the past and the present. The past few years have so immensely quickened and emphasized all means of communication, visible and invisible, in every direction, that our world ... is not merely 'too much with us', but moves, shouts, and moralizes about our path and our bed through every hour of our days and nights. Partly through a recent necessity for thinking and acting in large masses, partly through the instinct of mankind to draw together and cry out when calamity hits them, and very largely through the quickening of communications ... the power of the Tribe over the individual has become more extended, particular, pontifical, and, using the word in both its senses, impertinent, than

it has been for many generations. Some men accept this omni-
presence of crowds; some may resent it. To the latter I am
speaking.

Nowadays, to own oneself in any decent measure, one has to
run counter to a gospel, and to fight against its atmosphere;
and an atmosphere, so long as it can be kept up, is rather cloy-
ing. ... Thanks to the continuity of self-denial on the part of
your own forbears, the bulk of you will enter professions and
callings in which you will be free men – free to be paid what your
work is worth in the open market, irrespective of your alleged
merits or your needs. Free, moreover, to work without physical
molestation of yourself and your family as long and as closely
as you please; free to exploit your own powers and your own
health to the uttermost for your own ends.

At any price that I can pay, let me own myself. And the price
is worth paying if you keep what you have bought. ... A man
may apply his independence to what is called worldly advantage,
and discover too late that he laboriously has made himself dependent on a mass of external conditions for the maintenance of
which he sacrificed himself. So he may be festooned with the
whole haberdashery of success, and go to his grave a castaway.
Some men hold that the risk is worth taking. Others do not. It is
to these that I have spoken.[10]

THE STORM CONE (1932)

This is the midnight – let no star
Delude us – dawn is very far.
This is the tempest long foretold –
Slow to make head but sure to hold.

Stand by! The lull 'twixt blast and blast
Signals the storm is near, not past;
And worse than present jeopardy
May our forlorn to-morrow be.

If we have cleared the expectant reef,
Let no man look for his relief.
Only the darkness hides the shape
Of further peril to escape.

It is decreed that we abide
The weight of gale against the tide
And those huge waves the outer main
Sends in to set us back again.

They fall and whelm. We strain to hear
The pulses of her labouring gear,
Till the deep throb beneath us proves,
After each shudder and check, she moves!

She moves, with all save purpose lost,
To make her offing from the coast;
But, till she fetches open sea,
Let no man deem that he is free!

[19]

The Last Phase of
his Work

THE publication in 1923 of *The Irish Guards in the Great War* released Rudyard from an obligation; he had paid a debt, but he had also snapped a link with his past days of happiness. While his house was frequented by young men who had been John's friends, who came and talked in the language of soldiers about the Regiment and its experiences, John's world was still alive in his imagination. It was never Rudyard's habit to hanker back towards the past, and, having put the *Irish Guards* behind him, he moved with characteristic resilience into a new creative phase, as he slowly recovered health after his illness. In this respect he was more fortunate than Carrie, who had no such secret resources and never quite reconstituted her life after the loss of her only son.

In 1924 he sent 'The Janeites' to press and followed it up by a succession of effective tales, several of which were psychological studies of the war. They were collected in 1926 with a variety of other pieces under the general title, *Debits and Credits*. Nine years had passed since the appearance of *A Diversity of Creatures*, which had included 'Mary Postgate' and the other early war-stories. Meanwhile the literary fashion had changed and Kipling, if he was remembered at all in literary circles, was remembered as a political writer whose politics were sadly out of date. This estimate took no account of one important factor in judging his status in the world. The sale of his books, in England, in America, and in those many countries where they were sold in translation, never flagged but increased year by year, even though they were never issued in cheap editions.*

The new book, *Debits and Credits*, was at first received coolly by the critics, though rapturously by the Kipling fans. It has had the experience, rare in the chronicle of his career, of steadily rising in favour with students of literature. I would venture the assertion that if Kipling had published nothing but 'The Bull that Thought', 'The Eye of Allah', 'The Janeites', 'The Wish House', 'A Madonna of the Trenches', and 'The Gardener', his name would stand high among the world's story-tellers. It would be hard to find such variety of subject, such richness of treatment, in the work of any contemporary, and, when compared with his own earlier work, these stories will be found to express a more delicate sensibility and a deeper penetration of motive. The other stories in the book, and even these six, display also Kipling's characteristic faults; some passages which gave offence to the thin-skinned, some almost incomprehensible jargon, and some lapses into obscurity. 'A Madonna of the Trenches' must be grouped among his 'difficult' stories. It was typical of his indifference to public opinion that he began the book with an allegorical tale ('The Enemies to Each Other') that seemed to be a kind of private joke. In form it is a version of the legend of Adam and Eve expanded at great length in a pseudo-oriental style like a stilted version of the *Koran*. It is remarkable that he published it, not that he wrote it.

Kipling's stories are sometimes cryptic, sometimes obscure, sometimes allegorical. Quite early in his career he developed a technique of leaving the story half-told and so maintaining the suspense. This is the traditional method of the ghost-story, which is spoiled if an explanation is offered, a

---

*During Kipling's lifetime Macmillan's, who held the English rights of his collected volumes of stories, sold about seven million copies, Doubleday's, who held the American rights, nearly eight million.

method used by Poe in *Tales of Mystery and Imagination*, which Kipling imitated as a young man.

He was not, strictly speaking, a writer of adventure-stories except in his books for children. The form of his stories for adults is usually a descriptive comment on a group of characters in a dramatic situation. For example, even so romantic a tale as 'The Man who Was' tells next to nothing of the hero's adventures, which are left to the reader's imagination; but presents, almost visually, the effect of his sudden reappearance. In this instance enough is revealed, though in some others the narrative never emerges. 'At the End of the Passage', for example, is a problem-story in the same mode as the problem-pictures which were so popular at the Academy in Kipling's younger days. This is all I am going to tell you, says the author. Make what you can of it. His 'knowingness' which infuriated some critics, his hints that he could say a great deal more if he chose to, were marks of juvenility which he grew out of. In later life the hints were of what he did not know, the esoteric, the subliminal, the occult. There are cryptic elements in 'They', in 'The House Surgeon', in 'A Madonna of the Trenches', in 'The Gardener', but here they are dictated by humility in presence of the uncomprehended.

Other stories are found difficult for the reason that they seem to be wilfully obscure, through strangeness of vocabulary or complexity of construction. His love of jargon for its own sake (delightfully exhibited in *Just So Stories*) sometimes betrayed him, as it betrayed Rabelais, into mere avalanches of words. Sometimes the composition of his narrative, partially and gradually revealed in dialogue, is confusing. 'The Devil and the Deep Sea' appears to have been written out of sheer delight in the terminology of marine engineering. Those parts of the narrative which concentrate upon this main theme are, in their way, a triumph of virtuosity, while the rest of it is so compressed, so pruned and cut, chopped off so short, that I, for one, have never been able to discover what happens at the end. The sea stories in general are the most technical, and 'Sea-Constables', a dialogue between four characters, all of them talking naval 'shop', is, if not the most obscure, perhaps the most difficult story Kipling ever wrote. By contrast, 'The Bonds of Discipline', also told in dialogue by two characters alternately speaking different jargons, is quite clear.

The cryptic and the obscure styles are combined in several stories and are carried to their greatest length in 'The Dog Hervey' which presents more puzzles, the more it is examined; it abounds in literary, masonic, psychological, and canine clues which lead nowhere. Like 'Mrs Bathurst', 'The Dog Hervey' seems to have been made incomprehensible by ruthless cutting. Perhaps the themes of both are too complex for treatment within the limits of a short story.

Yet another group of difficult stories are the allegories or fables. In November 1891 he had published 'The Children of the Zodiac', a long fable of which no satisfactory explanation has been offered by any commentator. All that can be said about it with conviction is that it deals with the marriage of a young poet, who dreads death by cancer of the throat, and that in 1891 Kipling was a young poet contemplating marriage, and ill with an affliction of the throat. We have his word for it elsewhere that he regarded cancer of the throat as the 'family complaint'.[1] The fable, then, is personal – something between himself and the woman he was about to marry.

A problem piece in which the obscurity is gradually and skilfully made plain, is 'The Gardener', his story of the unmarried mother and the war-graves in Flanders. It is told with such tenderness as to efface the memory of the parallel tale of 'Mary Postgate'. This is quite another view of the soul of a hard, efficient, loveless woman. All these war-stories – as the name *Debits and Credits* implies – turn upon loyalties, the part played in love or friendship by the one who gives and the one who takes, a relation often seen in reverse when seen with intimate understanding. In war who bears the greater burden, the one who lives or the one who dies? Kipling's obsession with the war-dead dwelt upon his understanding that the soldiers were initiates, admitted to a higher degree of the suffering which is the law of life, and so separated from the lovers at home.

The strongest continuing motive in his work throughout his whole career was the sense of comradeship among men who share a common allegiance because committed to a common duty. His love of technical jargon, though partly a mere delight in the richness of language, was strengthened by a conviction that the best talk is 'talking shop', the kind of conversation which lives and is genuine because it is based upon a secret shared between those who know how something is done, a secret conveying that kind of knowledge which is power. Freemasonry, with its cult of common action, its masculine self-sufficiency, its language of symbols, and its hierarchy of secret grades, provided him with a natural setting for his social ideals. In India, when very young, he had been a keen and loyal mason, and the ritual of masonry had first revealed to him the underlying unity of Indian life in the one context where race, religion, and caste were overlooked. Even a non-mason can point out scores of allusions to masonic ritual, dispersed through the whole of Kipling's verse and prose, proving how deeply the cult affected his mode of thought. Yet it does not appear that the circumstances of his later life allowed him to attend lodge-meetings frequently, or to pass through the course of office that leads to the higher degrees of the craft. He is said to have been a member of the Authors' Lodge and to have occasionally attended its meetings, but no evidence has been brought forward that there is any foundation in fact for the irregular war-time lodge which he used as the background for several of his later stories.* Perhaps some single occurrence at a lodge-meeting was enough to set his mind at work.

---

* Kipling was a founder member of two lodges connected with the War Graves Commission, 'Silent Cities' No. 4948 in England and No. 12 in France.

His avowedly masonic episode, 'In the Interests of the Brethren' (written in 1917), was a demonstration to his brother-masons of what they might do to help soldiers on leave from the front, if they would take some liberties with masonic rules; and whether they accepted this advice his fellow-masons will know best. To the general reader 'Lodge Faith and Works, 5837' is merely the scene set for the narration of some powerful stories in his later manner, notably 'The Janeites' (begun in 1922) and 'A Madonna of the Trenches' (1924).[2]

'The Janeites' is a cunningly contrived story written with as many skins as an onion. It is told in the first person by Kipling himself, who begins with a description of the masonic lodge, in elaborate and loving detail. Within this frame the hero is introduced by another mason, Anthony, whose comments, interjected from another point of view, serve as a foil to those of Kipling the narrator. Humberstall, the hero of the tale, a gentle bewildered giant unaware of his own strength and reduced by shell-shock almost to witlessness, is persuaded by Anthony to talk of his experiences in France. Between these three men there is a sympathetic bond, the comradeship of Freemasonry which, says Humberstall, is all the religion he has got, the faith to which he clings, and which, as it seems to the reader, preserves his sanity.

But Kipling the narrator knows that Anthony and Humberstall have another bond of sympathy which they can never fully reveal to him, the secret sympathy that unites soldiers who have been on active service in the war. The comradeship of the trenches constitutes, as it were, a second degree with its own passwords and ritual, a degree to which no mere civilian can be admitted.

Then the mild and puzzled Humberstall modestly reveals that he has graduated, almost unconsciously, to a still higher degree. Though he understands imperfectly what are its implications, he has become a 'Janeite'. Now it is Kipling's turn to give the password and talk the secret language, because he too is a 'Janeite', while Anthony, quite unaware of this ritual, limps forlornly behind a conversation he cannot keep up with.

What is the subject of this curiously involved story? In a sense, of course, it is Kipling's tribute to the genius of Jane Austen (he would never pass through Winchester without reflecting that, after Stratford, it was the holiest place in England, for the sake of Jane Austen and Izaak Walton). But the story would have the same point if it had been called 'The Trollopians' and if the password had been 'Hiram's Hospital' instead of 'Tilneys and Trap-doors'. Where the action strikes home is revealed in the character of Humberstall the innocent, who can fulfil himself only in loyalty to a dedicated group of friends.

Unless 'Jane' herself is to be counted one of the characters, 'The Janeites' is a masculine story. Let us turn to another written entirely about women. 'The Wish House' demands of the reader a willing suspension of disbelief. Two old villagers, each of them aware that one of the two is stricken with cancer and condemned to death, sit and gossip about their past. How far Kipling had advanced in his craft, since the slick stories of his boyhood with their condescending attitude to women, is nowhere seen more clearly than in his study of 'Mrs Ashcroft', the dying woman. Not the least effective feature of her conversation is the mixture of suburban smartness with traditional peasant cunning. She knows her way about London, she listens to the wireless; but she remains at heart a countrywoman and a believer in the ancient lore. It was typical of Kipling's method that he borrowed several of her features (and admitted doing so) from Chaucer's 'Wife of Bath'.

Gradually 'The Wish House' takes the shape of a ghost-story about a curse which is lifted from the back of one who is beloved but unworthy, and is faithfully borne by one who loves and forgives. A generation had passed since 'Tomlinson' at Hell-gate had received the Devil's warning:

The sin that ye do by two and two ye must pay for one by
one!

which had then seemed audaciously original. At sixty years
old Kipling had acquired a deeper understanding of life's
retributive processes, and knew that 'Mrs Ashcroft' might
well pay the reckoning for her lover's sin as well as for her
own, and do it gladly; nor was it necessary to call in a supernatural mechanism for transferring the burden. Yet 'Mrs
Ashcroft' believed, and the reader finds himself also believing, that she deliberately took up the burden of her
man's troubles by a magical device, by trafficking with an
evil spirit, potent with curses though not with blessings. The
effect is gained by Kipling's careful rejection of all the trappings of romance. The 'Wish House' is no picturesque
haunted grange but a dingy villa in a suburban street, infested by a shabby, wheezing, down-at-heel, fumbling
elemental, the dregs of ghosthood. It serves, and the
story-teller makes his point.

... she built an Altar and served by the light of her Vision –
   Alone, without hope of regard or reward, but uncowed,
Resolute, selfless, divine.
   These things she did in Love's honour ...
What is God beside Woman? Dust and derision.[3]

The impulse to write was not exhausted when *Debits and
Credits* was published in 1926. Hugh Walpole has preserved
in his diary a pleasant word-picture of 'a wonderful morning with old Kipling in the Athenaeum. He was sitting
surrounded by the reviews of his new book, beaming like a
baby.'[4] He was already hard at work upon a new set of
stories to succeed it. The last volume, however, *Limits and
Renewals*, mostly written in 1927 and 1928 though not 'collected' until 1932, shows some falling away in the author's
skill; it is the book of a tired and ageing invalid. Professor
Dobrée, in his penetrating study of Kipling's later style,
has pointed out his obsession with the problem of pain,
natural enough in a man who was never free from pain, for

more than a few weeks at a time, during the last twenty years of his life. A theme in all the war-stories was the 'breaking- strain', the amount of pressure human beings can stand from physical tortures and mental terrors without a psychological collapse; and his favourite treatment of this problem is the salvation of a personality by devotion to another personality, by loving rather than by being loved. Yet love may seem too strong a word for a mere clinging to life at whatever point an emotional attachment can be secured. It may be simply gratitude as in 'A Friend of the Family', or love of animals as in the story significantly named 'The Woman in His Life'. The fear of fear, the knowledge that mental hells are more racking than physical hells, the unwillingness of even the bravest to face ultimate and hideous realities, may even reduce wretched mortals to a state where physical pain brings relief by numbing the mind.

> Dread mother of Forgetfulness
> Who, when Thy reign begins,
> Wipest away the Soul's distress,
> And memory of her sins.[5]

That last shrinking from the ultimate and the inevitable is the subject of the war-poem 'Gethsemane' which many readers have found difficult.*

> The Garden called Gethsemane,
> It held a pretty lass,
> But all the time she talked to me
> I prayed my cup might pass.
> The officer sat on the chair,
> The men lay on the grass,
> And all the time we halted there
> I prayed my cup might pass.

*R. K. gave this explanation to F. N. Doubleday (Doubleday Papers). The verses, he said, referred to 'the horror that overtakes a man when he first ships his gas mask. What makes war most poignant is the presence of women with whom he can talk and make love, only an hour or so behind the line.'

His 'Epitaphs of the War', 'naked cribs of the Greek Anthology' he called them, include much comment on this theme; one that Rudyard Kipling thought good of its kind was 'The Coward':

> I could not look on Death, which being known,
>   Men led me to him, blindfold and alone.

These were his final comments on the First World War: to every man his own private terror, his own vein of courage, his own breaking-strain, his own salvation by a loving attachment to life; and the other aspect of the picture may be seen in the strange, elaborate – not quite successful – allegories of the after-life, 'On the Gate' and 'Uncovenanted Mercies'. The reader is not expected to believe in them unreservedly.

Limits and Renewals includes one *comédie humaine* in Rudyard's happier style, the study of the village *curé* and the village atheist which he called 'The Miracle of Saint Jubanus', based upon an incident he had once seen when visiting a Spanish Cathedral. The book also includes an ill-natured anecdote, 'The Tie', written long since and dredged up from the bottom of his notebooks where it might better have been allowed to stay. But the strength of the book lies in the stories about doctors and disease, topics which now meant more to him than the life of soldiers and sailors that he had written about in his youth.

On any count, 'Dayspring Mishandled' is an astonishing performance, a profound, obscure, and singularly unpleasant story about a vindictive feud between two expert bibliophiles, or rather the vindictive persecution of a sham expert by a genuine expert. Revenge goes so far that the victim is not spared further taunts and triumphings when dying of a painful disease. But more engaging than the revenge-motive is the virtuosity with which a spurious poem by Chaucer is composed, a fifteenth-century manuscript faked, and the specious scholar is deceived.* As if this involution were not

* It was just like R. K. to go through the whole process of faking a medieval manuscript with his own hands before writing the story.

enough, the progress of the plot is contrasted with the degeneration of the victim, as disease wears him down, until the combined assaults of pain and disillusion reveal his breaking-strain.

The progress of an incurable disease is also the subject of 'Unprofessional', a story that repays study. Sir John Bland-Sutton said Kipling had here foretold the course of medical research, as far ahead as his 'Easy as A B C' had foretold the progress of aviation. An early draft had borne the name 'Stars in their Courses', which suggested its theme, the revival of an old notion that had stimulated the astrologers in antiquity but had led them astray. When reconsidered in a modern laboratory, this notion might reveal, or so the author's fancy suggests, recurrent and rhythmical changes in the cells of the body – 'tides' in the tissues produced by influences from without, 'the main tide in all matter'.

Rudyard's later writing, ever more involved, compressed, and elaborate, had lost nothing in force or in range. While he reached out continually to master new technologies and to bring them within the scope of his art, he seemed less able to visualize a scene in a few unforgettable words. We are given situations rather than scenes, conversations rather than characters. The faking of the manuscript in 'Dayspring Mishandled' is not likely to be forgotten, but one cares little about the two bibliophiles, and less about the victim's wife who is given an illicit love affair, by way of underplot.

It is an old joke in the book trade that two classes of books will always find a market in England, books about doctors and books about dogs. After his medical stories Rudyard indeed turned to the other category and enjoyed his last success with dog stories in a new mode. He had always been a dog-lover and, from his earliest days as a writer, had introduced some favourite dogs into his stories about people. In 'Garm, a Hostage' and 'The Dog Hervey', the dogs had been among the leading characters, but dogs seen through the human eye. His beasts, in the *Jungle Books* and elsewhere, had been treated allegorically, in another traditional

style, as characters personified appropriately, like Circe's
swine, in some animal garb that suited them. *Thy Servant a
Dog*, published in 1930, was not a beast fable in the conventional form, but a genuine attempt to present a dog's point
of view, in a simplified vocabulary which seemed adequate
to a dog's intelligence, an experiment in the rudiments of
language.

Since the marriage of their daughter had left Rudyard
and Carrie alone in their house, he had submitted to a
dynasty of Aberdeen terriers, the companions of his solitary hours, giving 'his heart to a dog to tear'. His dogs were
the last creatures on whom he turned his exact and penetrating gaze, to the renewed delight of his readers who
bought 100,000 copies of *Thy Servant* in six months. The
author of that book was a student of life on a familiar level;
the author of 'Dayspring Mishandled' was no mean scholar.
Not much information survives of Rudyard's reading habits
and some of the critical remarks ascribed to him are spurious.
There was, however, one friend with whom Rudyard habitually discussed literary matters, the American novelist, Edward Lucas White. They had first met as fellow-masons
and for more than thirty years they corresponded, using
masonic phrases, and commenting on one another's books.
Rudyard told him much about the origin of his own stories
and in so doing revealed something of his literary technique. 'How far is a man justified', he had once asked
White, 'in using onoma – (I can't spell it) – topoeic metres
reproducing the beat of engines and so on? Where does
legitimate art end and trick-work begin?' And again: 'I
have been experimenting with divers metres and various
rhymes. The results serve excellently to light fires with.' It
was to White that he first confided his interest in the
poems of Donne, many years before they became a literary
fashion. Donne, he said, was 'Browning's great-grandfather'
and no small singer, 'a haughty proud-stomached individual
in his life, with Browning's temperament for turning his
mind upside-down as if it were a full bottle and letting the

ideas get out as best they could'. Another Jacobean they discussed was Phineas Fletcher, 'who sat down before the human carcase and hammered out God knows how many lines of high and disposed allegory'. Not of the first rank, Rudyard admitted, but, like Drayton and Drummond, he 'worked largely' and gave all he had to his verses.[2]

Rudyard confided to White a number of facts about the origin of the 'Puck' stories, particularly an account of the song sung by 'Philadelphia' in 'Marklake Witches'.

Shenstone has somewhere or other, about the end, I think, of a long and dreary ode, four lines of pure tears thus:

> Yet time may diminish the pain.
> The flower and the bud and the tree
> That I reared for her pleasure in vain
> In time may bring comfort to me.

– or words to that effect. I quote without the book but my heart knows it too well. Well! of course they were the words for my Philadelphia only they wouldn't have been set to music. So I had to invent a new sort of parallel passage of about the same age and appearance; and if you look closely you'll see that they in turn owe something to the meditation of Alexander Selkirk, 'I am Monarch, etc.' The actual effect comes out of 'desolate', 'rare', and 'change'. I'm rejoiced that you spotted it.[6]

In his letters to another literary friend, George Saintsbury, he could assume that his correspondent needed no prompting. From 1916 onwards Carrie Kipling went at intervals to Bath to be treated for her rheumatism, while to Rudyard these visits meant renewing his friendship with Saintsbury who lived at Bath in retirement. Sending him a set of his collected verse, Rudyard wrote: 'Look at some of the smaller ones in the third volume. *You'll* know the heifers I've ploughed with, from Herrick to Donne.'[7]

In his later life Rudyard accepted Saintsbury as a sort of literary patron to fill the place once held by Charles Eliot Norton. He treated the old critic with deep respect and was inordinately proud when Saintsbury dedicated to him his *Notes from a Cellar-Book*. He consulted Saintsbury about

Frank Doubleday's plan for a *de luxe* edition of Lesser English Classics (Skelton, Christopher Smart, Crashaw, Tourneur, Raleigh, Tusser, Coryat), for which Stanley Morison was to lay out the typography; he ventured to question Saintsbury's comments on the English novelists. 'Thackeray', said Rudyard, 'had the bit of Victorian convention uneasy in his mouth and champed on it.' Hence the restlessness of his 'interjected moralities'.

Their discussions turned mostly on French literature, and when Saintsbury produced his standard work on the French novel, Rudyard wrote:

> I've had a superior sort of Whitsuntide holiday. My cousin who is Financial Secretary [Stanley Baldwin] came down very tired for a rest. *He* bagged the 2nd Volume first because he wanted to know your faith about Balzac and I got the first (not without heat) to see about Rabelais. Then he curled up in the house and garden, and I browsed in my room and we didn't do anything else at all on Saturday and Sunday except read and compare notes. . . . I haven't had as good a time for years . . . till I almost felt I'd made my own researches. (Well, I *did* once bite pieces out of the *Grand Cyrus*.)
>
> Then I got on to the second, especially Maupassant . . . and the result . . . an earnest resolve, which I shall never have time to fulfil, to renew my old French readings.

Later he made a separate comment on a French contemporary. 'I've been reading the Anatole France estimate at the end of the volume. Ages ago, my Dad introduced me to Anatole in the *Reine Pédauque*, etc. No, he ain't a serious thinker. (Hell's too full of that class of fraud.)' But Rudyard added with pride that, when they met, Anatole France had embraced him.[7]

Rudyard's interest in French novels has been recorded from another aspect by a French writer with whom he sometimes corresponded. When they first met, wrote M. Joseph-Renaud, at a dinner of the Authors' Club, 'this little dark man with the blinding gold spectacles and the enormous eyebrows, came up and shot a rapid fire of questions at me, without any sort of introduction. 'Are the duels in Dumas correct in detail? Are there any such Bretons as those described by Pierre Loti? Is it true that Madame Bovary was a real person? Tell me about this Colette whose animal stories are so much better than mine! And so on, and so on.' The questions followed one another so fast that I had hardly time to answer.

As he listened to me, he stroked his bald head with a hand so brown that you might have thought him a Hindu (he was so dark that some people put about a rumour – quite false – that he was a half-caste), and when he was sure he had drained me dry he turned abruptly away with a quick 'good night'. I had never met so tenacious an interviewer. A few minutes later, I told my story to Frank Harris who replied: 'Ruddy is a journalist still: he always wants to know a little more.'[8]

Comments on his contemporaries are rare in Rudyard's private letters and almost unknown in his published works. He wrote with freedom to C. R. L. Fletcher, the Oxford historian with whom he had collaborated in a *History of England* for schools, and in these letters one or two critical comments may be found, for example, some early contempt for that overrated author, Lytton Strachey. 'I've been reading *Eminent Victorians*. . . . It seems to me downright wicked in its heart.' Or on R. G. Collingwood's *Speculum Mentis*: 'I've read Collingwood. It's the old finale to most things in this world – the *dénouement* is that there isn't any *dénouement* – only deliquescence. But Collingwood's tremendously interesting.'[9]

Rudyard was a rapid reader who skimmed through whole parcels of newly published books, sent him by A. P. Watt, and then returned to his English Classics. While he was writing dog stories he wrote to a friend: 'I haven't been doing much outside reading of late. Beaumont and Fletcher mostly, and some Dekker, and Evelyn's Tree-book and John Milton.'

John Evelyn's 'Tree-book' (*Sylva*) was evidence of Rudyard's long interest in systematic botany. He travelled always with a well-used copy of that old classic, *Flowers of the Field* by C. A. Johns, and noted observations in its margins. He arranged the ninety-three orders of British plants in a mnemonic rhyme for easy mental reference and, as might be expected of a writer who so much enjoyed 'baiting his hook with gaudy words', he was avid to acquire new rustic names for flowers and herbs.* In France he made a point of collecting French varieties of English wild flowers and recording their French rural names.

The other book that accompanied him wherever he went was one of his many editions of Horace, in his later years the handsome vellum-bound volume which he 'grangerized' with glosses, translations, parodies, and comments beautifully written in the margins. If space permitted, a critical essay might be written on Kipling's devotion to this Master. It would begin with his schooldays when his teachers at Westward Ho! laid the foundation of his studies, making him 'loathe Horace for two years, forget him for twenty, then love him for the rest of his days'. His version of *Donec gratus eram tibi* suggests that, even as a schoolboy, he did not hate it as much as he supposed. Horatian allusiveness and compression, Horatian overtones, are to be found in all Kipling's national hymns, and it is clear that his interest had been completely recaptured by 1917, when he wrote 'Regulus', the story of the boys who wrestled with the fifth ode of the Third Book and understood it better than they knew. When the volume, *A Diversity of Creatures*, containing 'Regulus', was published it also included a parody, or perhaps we should say an imitation, of one of Horace's slighter, wittier poems. It was put out as a translation of the 'third ode of the Fifth Book' with a catch-title from the Latin, *Ubi Lollius, etc.* Some reviewers in the less academic

* 'Eyebright, Orris, and Elecampane –
Basil, Rocket, Valerian, Rue,
(Almost singing themselves they run) . . .'
                                        'Our Father of Old.'

organs of the press fought a little shy of this ascription. Might it be genuine? And Kipling began to build up an elaborate joke, with his friends at the Universities, based upon this 'translation'.

Rudyard Kipling to C. R. L. Fletcher

21 April 1917

Kindly supply me with the original of that Horatian Ode which I have so inadequately translated. As a matter of fact I only came across the second (Urbino's) copy of the missing Fifth Book in the Library of the Vatican a few years ago quite by chance, and transcribed the Third Ode in haste, by very indifferent light, in the Crypt of the Dogale. There is another copy of the Fifth Book at Upsala – as you of course know – but it is in a bad condition and the marginal notes of Clavesius add nothing to its value. The third copy – if Sir James Urquhart's statement to the Spanish Ambassador can be trusted – should be in the Bodleian. ... My excuse for troubling you is that I have already been attacked in a private letter, by a so-called scholar, who asserts that no such book as the Fifth ever existed.[10]

The letters to Fletcher and Saintsbury thereafter contain many allusions to this imaginary work which actually appeared in print in 1922: *Q. Horatii Flacci Carminum Librum Quintum a Rudyardo Kipling et Carolo Graves Anglice Redditum...*' The Latin versions, by A. D. Godley who, as Public Orator at Oxford, was skilled in such learned witticisms, were much admired by scholars. It was a true collaboration and, while Kipling wrote most of the English versions, he had his say in the Latin versions also.

Some readers may think that his best versions of Horace are the marginal glosses – hitherto unpublished – in his favourite copy. Yet they are not versions, but commentaries, sometimes facetious commentaries, on the poet's character and method. He translates a line or two as the starting-point for an epigram of his own or, as if Horace were not already the most concise of authors, he adds a version of his own which is still more concise.

Beneath the beautiful

> *Vides ut alta stet nive candidum Soracte . . .*

he writes:

> 'Tis cold! Heap on the logs – and let's get tight!
> The Gods can turn this world for just one night.
> I will enjoy myself and be no scorner
> Of any nice girl giggling in a corner.

Inter vitae scelerisque purus moved him to no such enthusiasm as the Regulus Ode aroused in the breast of Mr King, but to this flippancy:

> The Pure and Perfect Bore
> Goes scatheless evermore,
> Arrows and Poison never yet destroyed him.
> Such is the Mantle thrown
> By Dulness on Her own
> That when he sings the very Beasts avoid him.
>
> So he pervades the Earth
> Absorbed in his own Worth,
> No Tact restrains – no Grace – no Humour move him,
> And yet – Oh Womankind!
> This God's Own Ass can find
> Some long-enduring Lalage to love him!

He was not always so flippant; here is an epigram based upon: *Quis desiderio sit pudor aut modus . . .*

> They pass, O God, and all
> Our grief, our tears,
> Achieve not their recall
> Nor reach their ears.
> Our lamentations leave
> But one thing sure.
> They perish and we grieve
> But we endure.

There are signs that these Horatian fragments were but sketches and studies for something Rudyard did not live to complete.

'NON NOBIS DOMINE!'
(Written for 'The Pageant of Parliament', 1934)

Non nobis Domine! –
  Not unto us, O Lord!
The Praise or Glory be
  Of any deed or word;
For in Thy Judgement lies
  To crown or bring to nought
All knowledge or device
  That Man has reached or wrought.

And we confess our blame –
  How all too high we hold
That noise which men call Fame,
  That dross which men call Gold.
For these we undergo
  Our hot and godless days,
But in our hearts we know
  Not unto us the Praise.

O Power by Whom we live –
  Creator, Judge, and Friend,
Upholdingly forgive
  Nor fail us at the end:
But grant us well to see
  In all our piteous ways –
Non nobis Domine! –
  Not unto us the Praise!

[20]

The Last Years
of his Life
(1924–36)

IN October 1924 Elsie Kipling was married to Captain George Bambridge, who had served in the Irish Guards. She was to live abroad, since he was in the diplomatic service, and without her Rudyard found the grey old house at Burwash, 'resonant, silent, and enormously empty'. Still, as Rudyard and Carrie grew older – both in poor health – he clung to his young friends and, until the end of his life, continued to make new ones among the youngest present in any company. Carrie's diary never fails to record his pleasure in the visits of the children of his old acquaintances. Rudyard would have no party manners and, when inviting his friends to bring their children, always insisted they should come in their oldest clothes, fully prepared to fall into the pond.

Those of his own contemporaries who still survived were as dear as ever, but Colonel Feilden died in 1922, Rider Haggard in 1925, Perceval Landon in 1927, and these he never replaced in his affections. Rider Haggard, the only professional novelist in the small circle of his intimates, was endeared to Rudyard, as Henley had been, by a common sorrow: each of the three had lost a beloved young child. To Haggard he extended the signal honour of allowing him to work at his own table when he came to stay at 'Bateman's'. Rudyard would make suggestions to him for names and picturesque episodes, and one of Rider Haggard's later romances (*Red Eve*) owes much of its fantastic quality to suggestions from Rudyard Kipling. He was prolific of notions for stories which he did not write, this one, for example, which he offered to Lord Dunsany:

30 May 1935

Dear Dunsany,

Here is a thing which has come up in my head, which I can't handle because I don't know present-day Irish (Mick) language and backgrounds. So I send it for you to consider. Substantially, I have made it boil down to three or four young I.R.A. – Rebels – Mountainy Men, or cattle of that kidney who, for their own purposes – revenge, politics, a row about a girl or what you please – have fired into – set light to – bombed – or otherwise terrorized a neighbour's house. Or, alternatively, they have waylaid and hammered a man in the dark, or cut off a girl's hair (you have large choice in the matter, I believe). Anyway, they find themselves landed with a dead or dying person who must be disposed of before the dawn breaks.

They discuss the situation among themselves, and finally, pick up the corpse and bear it off with intent to dispose of it in a kindly bog. En route, they find that there has attached himself to their little procession, an odd-looking person in some sort of clerical garb that they can't identify. He seems to have taken on himself charge of the whole situation – even to the extent of turning round and furiously (*sic*) bidding them, in dumb show, (*sic*) go on when they (Irish fashion) begin to waver in their precise objective.

It is his amazing eyes that they notice first of all. Then it dawns on them that he is not of this earth, and, further, that he is mad – a mad ghost.

In great fear they follow his signals, to the lip of the bog where he takes charge of the committal, and delivers a sermon on the dead, on them, on Ireland at large. It is rather a notable sermon – as you will find when you try to write it; he being, or, rather, having once been, Dean of St Patrick's in whose crypt his body, he tells them, lies. Cut it off at that point, or, if you like, add frills and grace-notes at discretion – such as one of the lads telling his priest the tale at Confession, or something of that kind.

You are the only man who can do it with comprehension and venom.[1]

Another surviving friend was Sir John Bland-Sutton, not only a celebrated surgeon but an original investigator into pathology, and a diligent collector of odd scraps of learning. His hobby was comparative biology, and, expert as he was in human anatomy, he did not disdain to draw parallels from the digestive organs of birds. It was remarked in Burwash that Rudyard and his distinguished visitor spent a Sunday afternoon catching domestic fowls and listening to the digestive noises in their gizzards. Bland-Sutton gave Rudyard much delight in the way of friendship but failed altogether to master his illness. Watching over Rudyard for twenty years, he could never relieve his abdominal pain.

After the war Rudyard used often to motor to Oxford on business for the Rhodes Trust. Through Sir George Parkin, the administrator of the Rhodes Trust, he would arrange to receive parties of Rhodes Scholars at his hotel. As an honorary doctor of both Oxford and Cambridge, as Lord Rector of St Andrews, Rudyard had shaken off a certain uneasiness he had once shown in academic society, and now had many friends in the Universities. It was Oxford that he knew first and best, as a Rhodes Trustee, but it was Cambridge that admitted him to full membership as Honorary Fellow of Magdalene College. For each of the old English Universities he wrote a ballad – two variations on one theme, the almost unnatural regression from manhood to boyhood of the postwar students.

The merry clerks of Oxenford they stretch themselves at ease
Unhelmeted on unbleached sward beneath unshrivelled trees ...

It was his perpetual theme in the nineteen-twenties when the return of peace seemed an incredible fantasy after the reality of war.

There was one man in Oxford in 1919 who, more than all his generation, was aware of these contrasting atmospheres. Rudyard met T. E. Lawrence in London before the Armistice and later at Oxford. He was able to do Lawrence a slight service by introducing him to his own American publisher Frank Doubleday, and in the correspondence between Frank and Rudyard there are some remarks upon the inscrutable 'T. E.', a greater puzzle to his friends in 1919 than he became later after the publication of the *Seven*

Pillars. Lawrence 'fusses about himself too much', wrote Rudyard, and gave Frank his opinion that there 'must be a woman at the back of it'.[2]

There came a day, after Lord Milner's death in 1925, when Rudyard refused to adapt himself to new modes of thought at Oxford. As internationalism prevailed he stuck grimly to the lost cause of sheer conservatism. The times had passed him by and it was a crucial point in political progress as he saw it, when Philip Kerr (afterwards Marquess of Lothian) was appointed to the vacant place in the Rhodes Trust; for Kerr was a Liberal and an internationalist. When the British Empire itself was changing its shape to become a liberal commonwealth, Rudyard found the new concept mightily different from Rhodes's Dream. He accordingly resigned from the Rhodes Trust and dismayed his colleagues by insisting that his resignation should be publicly announced, as made on principle.[3]

The following year, 1926, saw the General Strike, which revealed at once the leftward swing of English opinion and the weak irresponsibility of the Socialist leaders. In this crisis Rudyard played no part and contributed no message for the hour, since his health had collapsed again. In December 1925 he had again been struck down with pneumonia, and at the time of the Strike was convalescing in France. There followed another long period of ill-health, for the abdominal pains returned as soon as he left the regimen of the sick-room.

His cousin Stanley, leader of the Tory Party for most of Rudyard's later life, was Prime Minister in this critical year but, fond as Rudyard was of his cousin as a man, he progressively thought less of him as a politician. It was Stanley Baldwin's destiny, perhaps his strength, that for a large part of his career he acted in concert with men of very different views and principles. He served in Lloyd George's Coalition Government (1917–22) as a junior minister, and in Ramsay MacDonald's Coalition Government (1931–5) as a senior minister; and in his own three terms as Prime Minister

(1923–4, 1925–9, 1935–7) his policy was easy and accommodating. In Ireland and in India he loosened imperial ties with a willingness that was shocking to Rudyard, who used to say: 'Stanley is a Socialist at heart'. Carrie Kipling mistrusted him and thought him spoiled by power. Nevertheless, the close family friendship was maintained; the Kiplings often stayed at Astley, the Baldwins' home in Worcestershire; were regularly invited to Chequers, the Prime Minister's official country house; often dined in Downing Street. Rudyard's remarks upon the allies with whom Cousin Stanley worked in political coalitions were often unprintable. He was not alone in noticing that Baldwin was born rich and gave away much of his fortune anonymously to the nation, whereas Lloyd George was born in poverty and grew rich on politics. When an old friend, Philip Gosse, sent Rudyard a copy of his book on *Pirates*, it elicited the comment:

  On the whole, as you almost hint in your opening remarks, I don't suppose that the pirate did much more harm than the politician. And no pirate that I ever heard of came out of his business with a couple of millions 'personal fund' for which he absolutely refused to account! Nothing like modern science after all! [4]

A little later he was using the same analogy of a Socialist Chancellor of the Exchequer. 'If you re-read *Treasure Island*', he wrote jocularly to a friend at Oxford, 'substituting Viscount Snowden for Long John Silver, you'll be amazed.' [5]

An event which saddened Rudyard and Carrie was the breach with Stanley Baldwin's son, Oliver, who had meant much to them when they lost their own son. Carrie had regarded him almost as one of the family and had spoken more affectionately of him than of any of her other nephews or nieces; and Rudyard had been proud of Oliver's enthusiasm as a young soldier. That he should change sides in politics was his own affair, but conduct which they thought unfilial they could not forgive.

Another friendship that began to cool was that with Lord Beaverbrook, as Rudyard came to realize that there were many things which they no longer saw in common, and after Beaverbrook's admission of certain of his political ambitions, they never met again.

Like many another elderly Conservative in the nineteen-twenties Rudyard reacted to the news of events in Ireland, Egypt, India, by moving further to the right in politics. The *Morning Post*, superbly edited by H. A. Gwynne, continued to fight its rearguard action, and Rudyard continued to urge Gwynne to take stronger stands. He was for years closely associated with the editorial policy of the *Post* and on terms of friendship with Lady Bathurst, the proprietor. The Kiplings spent many week-ends at Cirencester with the Bathursts; and in other country houses frequented by the High Tories: at 'Chevening' with the Stanhopes, and at 'Whiteladies' with Sir W. Johnson-Hicks. At these houses they met, for the most part, political and 'service' friends, such men as Sir Roger Keyes, Sir Archibald Montgomery-Massingberd (an old friend from the South African War, who became the Chief of the General Staff), and Lord Lloyd, the last hope of the stern unbending Tories. When Lloyd was Governor of Bombay he again urged Rudyard to revisit India, but Rudyard replied that Carrie's health would never stand it, and to go without her was out of the question.

House-parties at the Cazalets' in Kent were drawn from a wider section of society and always included some celebrities from the world of art and letters. Here Rudyard met P. G. Wodehouse and challenged him : 'Tell me, Wodehouse, how do you finish your stories? I can never think how to end mine.' On this occasion Hugh Walpole was one of the guests, and thus described the party :

Kipling at Fairlawne is like a little gnome. All sorts of people about. The Athlones – she with her funny old German governess who says not a word but suddenly breaks out once with 'Ach, Thomas Mann – he's a splendid writer' and looks across the table scornfully at Kipling as though she'd like to tell him how inferior she thinks *he* is. And J. H. Thomas suddenly putting his arm confidentially through mine after lunch, although he scarcely knows me, and chuckling : 'You're a novelist. Well, keep your eye on me, my boy, for I'm your next P.M. 'Ow's that for a prophecy?' And then catching Kipling's arm and chuckling in *his* ear some rather dirty joke about Labour Gentlemen of the Bedchamber. Not that Kipling cares in the least about any of them. He is kindly, genial, ready apparently to be friends with anyone but keeping all the time his own guard.

I asked him at luncheon whether he approved of censorship (apropos of this tiresome stupid *Well of Loneliness*). No, he doesn't approve of the book. Too much of the abnormal in all of us to play about with it. Hates opening up reserves. All the same he'd had friends once and again he'd done more for than for any woman. Luckily Ma Kipling doesn't hear this. . . . She's a good strong-minded woman who has played watch-dog to him so long that she knows now just how to save him any kind of disturbance, mental, physical, or spiritual. That's *her* job and she does it superbly . . .

He really, I think, has no vanity. He's a zealous propagandist who, having discovered that the things for which he must propagand are now all out of fashion, guards them jealously and lovingly in his heart, but won't any more trail them about in public.

He walks about the garden, his eyebrows all that are really visible of him. His body is nothing but his eyes terrific, lambent, kindly, gentle and exceedingly proud. Good to us all and we are all shadows to him.

'Carrie,' he says turning to Mrs K., and at once you see that she is the only real person here to him – so she takes him, wraps him up in her bosom and conveys him back to their uncomfortable hard-chaired home. He is quite content.[6]

General Dunsterville ('Stalky'), with whom Rudyard remained on terms of affection throughout life, was in a special position. It was a powerful comfort to Rudyard that his early faith in his friend was, at last, justified, when Dunsterville leaped at one of the few opportunities for brilliant initiative offered in the dreary routine of slaughter that constituted the First World War. His audacious expedition to

save North Persia from the Bolsheviks was an exploit surpassing anything the young 'Stalky' could have imagined.
Rudyard had been right and 'Stalky' only needed scope. But,
after the war, as a retired major-general on a small pension,
with no private means and no employment, what could
Dunsterville do but exploit his own publicity? First, of
course, he could write an account of his campaign and go for
a lecture tour; and then, since all the world knew he was
'Stalky', there was nothing for it but to cash-in on his
reminiscences of Rudyard Kipling. This was not so popular
at 'Bateman's' where 'Stalky' became, perhaps, suspect. Furthermore, he was an early worker for the formation of a
Kipling Society, which the object of attention regarded
with gloomy distaste, disliking these monumental tributes
while he was still alive – none more than the books by Sir
George MacMunn, who as a British officer should, he
thought, have known better. There was no stopping the
formation of the Society.

Since 1919 at least, Mr J. H. C. Brooking had been trying
to bring enthusiasts for Kipling's works together. In 1922 he
persuaded 'Stalky' to lend a hand, though 'Stalky' expected
opposition from the Kiplings. A convening committee,
Brooking, 'Stalky', and 'Ian Hay' (Major J. H. Beith), met in
1923, but it was not till 1927 that the Society was formally
constituted, with about a hundred members, and 'Stalky' as
their first president. The difficulty had been that the keen
members expected some leading 'Kipling-ites' to lend their
names, and the obvious leaders were deterred by Kipling's
dislike of the whole affair. 'Stalky' was persuaded to become
president, and the first committee included Brooking, Beresford ('M'Turk'), and MacMunn. There are now (1954) more
than 700 members in the United Kingdom and active
branches in the United States and other countries, and the
quarterly *Kipling Journal* has passed its hundredth number.[7]

Even more than the flatteries of the Kipling Society, he disliked the activities of bibliophiles who trafficked in his
private letters, draft manuscripts, rejected trifles, and un-

authorized editions. All this was what he called the 'Higher Cannibalism'. When his old friend, Mrs Hill, offered some of his early manuscript fragments for sale he wrote a letter of remonstrance; and when an American devotee formed a classified study of all his works, authorized and unauthorized, he disliked the intention. The devotee, Admiral L. H. Chandler, made several approaches to Rudyard, and was repulsed more than once, with letters in the coldest terms from Rudyard's secretary, before his persistence was rewarded with an interview. The Kiplings liked him, and the Chandler Index (now in the Library of Congress) is the most complete analysis that exists of Kipling's writings. When a *Summary* of its conclusions was published Rudyard annotated a copy in his own hand.

After Admiral Chandler came Mrs Flora Livingston, the Houghton Librarian from Harvard. She forced the defences of 'Bateman's', with recommendations on the ground of sheer scholarship, was received with civility, and became a friend. Her Bibliography, based upon the immense collection of Kiplingiana now in the Houghton Library, is a model of its kind.

In London his clubs provided him with the variety of talk that he loved. He lunched usually at the Athenaeum until, upon the proposal of his publisher, Sir Frederick Macmillan, he was elected to the smaller and more private Beefsteak Club. A man who was always on a diet of more or less strictness could take little pleasure in the luxuries of the table. He rarely dined out, never ate more than a little of the plainest food, and always left early, so that he attended dining-clubs, Grillion's or 'The Club', for the conversation rather than the food and drink. Sir William Osler has preserved an account of a dinner at 'The Club' in 1919 with the Archbishop of York in the Chair and John Buchan, Henry Newbolt, Charles Oman, H. A. L. Fisher, and Kipling among the company. 'Kipling was in very good form, and told many good war-stories. He said he would not be surprised if in a few years the monastic life was revived – as men were seeking relief from the burdens of a hard world and turning more and more to spiritual matters.'[8]

From time to time Sir Abe Bailey gave vast dinner-parties to forty or more guests, all men at the head of their professions, and to these parties Rudyard was usually invited. But the circle of his intimates was small and the functions he attended were few. So long as his uncle Edward Poynter was alive, he was regularly invited to the Royal Academy Banquets. He enjoyed the London theatres and – in the old silent days – occasionally visited the cinema. To get Kipling to speak at a public function was no small achievement, and when he undertook to speak, his address was always prepared many days in advance with as much care as if it were a poem or short story. As his academic connexions were strengthened he was frequently asked to give more formal addresses, and there can be few other men who have declined to deliver the Gifford Lectures at Edinburgh, the Romanes Lectures at Oxford, the Leslie Stephen Lecture at Cambridge, and the National Lectures of the B.B.C. He was proud to be a member of the Stationers' Company and a freeman of the City of London, but refused to be president of the Authors' Society. In 1926 a signal honour, which he accepted, was conferred upon him by the Royal Society of Literature – the gold medal which had been awarded only three times before, to Walter Scott, George Meredith, and Thomas Hardy. At this point in his life, perhaps, Rudyard Kipling came nearest to the frigid altitude of being an accepted classic, and in consequence was all the more out of fashion with the *avant-garde*.

In January 1928 the death of Thomas Hardy at a great age marked a turning-point in English literature, which was recognized by the solemnity of his funeral in Westminster Abbey on a wet dark day. Among the pall-bearers were a group of Hardy's younger contemporaries, all of them revered in the republic of letters, and all doomed to pass, before many years, into the temporary eclipse that marks a change of fashion. The coffin was escorted by the Prime Minister and the Leader of the Opposition, by the Heads of the Oxford and Cambridge Colleges which had given honorary fellowships to Hardy, by Gosse and Barrie, Galsworthy and Housman, Kipling and Shaw. This was the first and only occasion when those two 'essentially good-hearted men', Rudyard Kipling and Bernard Shaw, came together. They were introduced at the Abbey door by Edmund Gosse but, genial as both could be, they found nothing to say to one another. Gossips noted with malicious glee that in the procession Rudyard tried to pair himself with Galsworthy, and Shaw remarked afterwards that it was ludicrous to marshal so little a man as Kipling with so tall a man as himself.[9]

A few months after Hardy's funeral the King and Queen were guests at a private party in a London house. King George had no sooner made his entry than he caught sight of Rudyard, sent for him, remained all the evening in conversation with him in a corner of the room, and when it was time to go, felt obliged to apologize to his hostess for neglecting her other guests. A few weeks later Rudyard was invited to Balmoral for a week-end. The friendship was now ripening so that Rudyard felt more than a loyal dismay when, at the end of the year, the King was struck down with pneumonia. The Kiplings were staying at Chequers with the Prime Minister, who was supplied with bulletins sent directly from the Palace; and when the crisis was past Rudyard still got private reports from Lord Stamfordham. When the spring returned the King went down to recuperate by the sea at Bognor, in quiet seclusion. Rudyard was one of the few who were invited to visit him there – it was no more than fifty miles from 'Bateman's'. What Rudyard could then do for his sovereign was to prescribe him a course of light reading. He sent the King parcels of novels by Edgar Wallace, which were read and carefully returned, marked 'R. K.' in the King's hand. He said it was his rule to return borrowed books, most scrupulously, which was more than others did when they borrowed books from him.

King George V was the first sovereign of England to

travel widely throughout the British Dominions, as Kipling was the first English poet to do so. Their experience had endowed both men with a devoted love for India and the Indian peoples; and both retained a marked distrust for those professional politicians, in England and in India, whose projects for solving India's problems seemed to be guided by other motives than love.*

All who personally knew the two men remarked upon their fundamental humility. King George's strength was that he knew himself to be just an ordinary man; and it was a feature of Kipling's greatness, too, that he would never allow admirers to pay him compliments. He was a craftsman who sometimes felt that words were put into his mouth, by a daemon or genius that came from without, not from within. In this way only was he distinguished from other men, and by this sense of inspiration was dedicated to a duty. The King, also, was a dedicated man and each of them recognized this quality in the other.

Even before his cousin became Prime Minister, Kipling had often been consulted about an epitaph, an inscription, or the phrasing of a formal statement, by the discreet organizers of public ceremonies. It was no new thing when Baldwin appealed to him for help in such matters, and it is no secret that several of Baldwin's most eloquent addresses, notably those delivered at functions where party politics would have been out of place, were revised and polished, if not actually composed, by Kipling. When called upon to advise the sovereign, in his constitutional capacity, about forms of words, Baldwin made a practice of taking his cousin's advice.

Since there was so great a natural sympathy between King George V and Rudyard Kipling, who had so many likes and dislikes, so many virtues and prejudices in common, it was not surprising that the King's celebrated Christmas broadcasts, which so widely extended the influence of the Crown

* For an appreciation of Kipling by a talented Indian nationalist see the *Memoirs of Aga Khan* (p. 226), on Mrs Sarojini Naidu.

and drew the nations of the Commonwealth so close together, echoed Kipling's message.

Twenty years back he had foreshadowed the technical broadcasting services which were to encircle the earth; and it was with quiet satisfaction that he listened on the afternoon of Christmas Day 1932 to King George's words. He never thereafter alluded to his part in this achievement. It was a personal triumph for the King, whose honesty, simplicity, and kind-heartedness instantly impressed themselves upon a world of listeners, not less because his rich, low, unaffected voice – the voice of a sailor – revealed his natural talent for broadcasting. It was something of a triumph for Rudyard Kipling, too.

Life at 'Bateman's' was diversified by many motor tours. Whether they turned north for the road to Scotland, or southward from Calais for the Latin lands, the adventure was always new and uplifting. Rudyard kept careful records of his journeys, with notes on mileage, the state of the roads, and the comfort of hotels, and duly reported defects to the Automobile Association.[10] Often his motoring journals provide comments on scenery, and architecture, with word-pictures of landscapes or wayside happenings which might reappear one day in a story. Such notes as these were the raw material he packed away in his memory for future use, sketches which happen to have survived from thousands.

For me this land, that sea, these airs, those folk and fields suffice.
What purple Southern pomp can match our changeful Northern skies,
Black with December snows unshed or pearled with August haze –
The clanging arch of steel-grey March, or June's long-lighted days?

Yet in the dark days of January and February the south called him, not only into the sunshine but into a land of

warmer temperaments where he need not record, as often
in England: 'the waitress scornful and abstracted'. The contrast of north or south was never put more lovingly than by
his own centurion:

You'll take the old Aurelian Road through shore-descending
    pines
Where, blue as any peacock's neck, the Tyrrhene Ocean shines.
You'll go where laurel crowns are won but – will you e'er forget
The scent of hawthorn in the sun, or bracken in the wet?[11]

One tour of France may be described from a long letter
written by Rudyard to Rider Haggard:[12]

14 March 1925. All the landscape round Havre looked like a
new (& rather cheap) bridecake with its light powdering of snow.
Just enough not to hold up the car, and the Seine looking like
pewter between the glittering banks. Too cold for comfort as we
ran into Rouen. Went off at once to Rouen Cemetery (11,000
graves) and collogued with the Head Gardener and the contractors. One never gets over the shock of this Dead Sea of
arrested corps.

That evening in his hotel he began to write what he describes as 'the story of Helen Turrell and her nephew and
the gardener in the great 20,000 cemetery'. He worked at it
every evening and finished it at Lourdes on 22 March.

We crashed into Evreux whose Cathedral is a wonder – but
not *the* wonder; and thence to Dreux – more Gothic and sparser;
and at last, in the tail of a dripping day to Chartres – the great
blue-grey bulk of the Cathedral dominating, it seemed, half
France. Our old hotel had been modernized, to our immense
wrath, and was full of *ouvriers*, paint, petrol, and noises. Got into
the Cathedral on the very last fading of the twilight and it was
as though one moved within the heart of a jewel . . .

At Perigueux, you strike the real, overbearing, brute, Byzan-
tine of the 10th century; and one realises what a toss-up it was
that our creed hadn't taken a dominantly oriental twist (might
have been better if it had, p'haps). I liked the naked convention
of strength and rigidity which doesn't lend itself to internal
haberdashery . . .

I like the Spaniards for not worrying about the rest of the world, but I can't love 'em . . .

Consider now a day that gives you a couple of hours in the morning above the caves of the Dordogne – incised and painted Cro-magnon piccys of bison, horse, wolf, and rhino traced on the irregularly dimpled roofings and sides of those limestone grottoes, as smooth as candle-drippings. All you hear is now and then the one wee drop of water from the tip of a stalactite. The rest is all warm, stone-walled stillness and those inexplicable figures. Well, one steps outside and beyond one's own notions of time in such places.

Then a couple of hours later you are at Lourdes – same sort of smooth bluish-white rock grottoes in a hillside but instead of incised totems, a lavender and white presentation of Our Lady just in the spot where Bernardette, the peasant girl, had the visions. And all the smooth nodular scarped rock below smeared and covered and runnelled with the gutterings of countless candles – lighting up and going out like the children of man. . . . Huge gardens and public spaces round the church, flanked by huger hospices where the many sick of the summer can wait and lie up when they come to be healed. Miracles do not occur in the winter.

On a later holiday he crossed the Channel with a shipload of pilgrims returning from Lourdes and noticed with pity the many for whom there had been no miracle. 'It was like watching the return of the damned to Hell after a few breaths of hope.' [13]

In the winters, as they grew older, they went farther afield to avoid the cold, often for a short sea-voyage which revived and rested Rudyard but weakened and exhausted Carrie. Their later travels usually ended in illness for one of the two, since the changes of diet – on motor tours which he so much enjoyed – usually upset his digestion. The search for sunshine took them to Algiers, Sicily, and Spain to find that these countries had no certainty of warmth in early spring, and even Egypt proved chilly. Twice they went up the Nile as far as the First Cataract, to seek at Assouan the comforting heat they both needed. In Egypt Rudyard could

pursue his tasks for the War Graves Commission, the more
pleasantly since he had made a friend of the Australian
soldier, Colonel C. E. Hughes, who was in charge of war
graves in the Middle East. Together they visited the cemeteries and battlefields of the Palestine campaign, and made
an expedition into Sinai with Major Jarvis the Governor.

An unpublished poem, written to the tune of a bawdy old
song, expressed Rudyard's views on the imbroglio of Jews
and Arabs under the British mandate:

> In ancient days and deserts wild
> There was a feud – still unsubdued –
> Twixt Sarah's son and Hagar's child,
> That centred round Jerusalem.

Tracing the progress of the feud down the ages, he discovered it still smouldering in the land of Israel:

> For 'neath the Rabbi's curls and fur,
> (Or scents and rings of movie-kings)
> The aloof, unleavened blood of Ur
> Broods steadfast at Jerusalem.[14]

The most rewarding winters were spent on the Riviera,
where they could be sure of the regular, simple diet they
both needed, and could enjoy sunshine and scenery in the
company of their friends, without losing access to good doctors in case of illness. Elsie, too, would often join them, coming from Madrid or Paris. Carrie had always been, and
Rudyard became as he grew older, a creature of habit so
that, having found the landscapes and the lodgings that
suited them, the two were inclined to return to them again.

Most of their journeys began or ended in Paris where they
stayed at least once in every year after the war. A friend of
very long standing, who as Julia Catlin had met them first
in Bermuda, and then as Mrs Depew had entertained them
at Compiègne in the old happy days, was often their hostess,
and made for them what was almost a second home, in
Paris. She was now married to General Taufflieb, one of

Rudyard's many friends in the French Army, and when Julia's daughter married Peter Stanley, an English surgeon practising in France, the friendship was extended to the younger generation.

After Rudyard's illness in 1926 Bland-Sutton recommended a long sea voyage, which enabled him to realize an old dream. He had written in *Just So Stories*: 'I'd love to roll to Rio, some day before I'm old' and, after nearly twenty years of absence from the tropics, he crossed the line again in 1927 on a voyage to Brazil, taking the deepest interest in his fellow-passengers, mostly Spaniards and Portuguese. With some firmness he detached himself from publicity, declining to become a guest of the nation; and revelled in the prospect of a race of Europeans, at home in a tropical climate, and busily engaged in pioneering a new country. *Brazilian Sketches*, written for the *Morning Post*, had the gusto of his early *Letters of Marque*, and were lightened with verses in his simplest, sincerest style.[15]

In 1929 it was Carrie who was ordered abroad for her health. That indomitable woman, never relaxing her care for her husband, now had no daughter at home, no one to nurse and tend her own ailments.

> If you can force your heart and nerve and sinew
> To serve your turn long after they are gone,
> And still hold on when there is nothing in you
> Except the Will that says to them: Hold on!

The verse might have been written for her when, her eyesight failing, racked with rheumatism, and now diagnosed as a diabetic, she pursued her unaltering routine. In February 1930 the two of them again broke new ground, sailing for the West Indies and taking with them Helen Hardinge, Lady Milner's daughter. It was an uneventful voyage which Rudyard spent restfully, working only a little at the dog story called 'The Woman in his Life'. In Jamaica, after refusing an invitation to be the guests of the Governor, they started a tour of the islands, which was spoiled by Carrie's

sudden collapse with appendicitis. At first they pressed on
hopefully and had reached Bermuda when she was obliged
to go into the hospital, seriously ill. Helen Hardinge could
stay no longer and Rudyard was left in solitary lodgings
from March to June, his longest separation from Carrie in
forty years of married life.

He had his own resources, and was witness of a scene (the
sailor and the parrot that misbehaved) which he worked up
into the story, 'A Naval Mutiny;' and, harking back to observations made, years previously, into the background of
Shakespeare's *Tempest*, he made a ballad of them. Otherwise it was a blank period with little to do beyond watching
the cruising liners put ashore their crowds of American
tourists, who had come to Bermuda in those days of Prohibition solely to get drunk as soon as possible.

With a wife seriously ill, and no medical care he could
rely on, Rudyard's anxiety was when and how to escape
from Bermuda, since the regular shipping lines ran only to
the United States. He wrote anxiously to Frank Doubleday
for advice, with the proviso that even if an operation was
necessary, Carrie could not face a visit to New York, which
would bring back dreadful memories to her. The mental
strain would kill her. In any case, Rudyard went on, the
United States was 'not a civilized country for the sick'.
They must arrange to return by way of Canada.[16] Carrie
grew worse, and it was only on 1 June that he got her
aboard a ship for Halifax, Nova Scotia, and so to England.
This was their last experience of the New World, and left
him less in sympathy with America of the nineteen-thirties
than before. In Canada they still had good friends but, apart
from Frank Doubleday – and he, like Rudyard, was elderly
and ailing – there were few left of their acquaintances from
the old days. Thirty-five years had passed since they had
left Vermont, and Carrie now retained few links with her
old home.

Rudyard's last serious work was done in the early months

of 1932, the charming conversation-piece called 'Proofs of Holy Writ',[17] in which Ben Jonson and Shakespeare are shown discussing the Authorized Version of the Bible. It appeared just too late for inclusion in *Limits and Renewals*, and has not been reissued in any popular collection of his stories. Thereafter, as if he knew his life-work was over, he turned to collection and recollection. He took pains over arranging a new volume of *Collected Verse*, concluding it with an appeal to biographical writers to respect his private life.

> And for the little, little, span
> The dead are borne in mind,
> Seek not to question other than
> The books I leave behind.

It was in vain; a man who endears himself to a whole generation by his art cannot reject their natural desire to know more of his life. He had made himself their friend and had to accept the demands of friendship.

He prepared for the American market a select volume of verse and prose with the title, *A Pageant of Kipling*, and supervised the preparation of the gigantic Sussex Edition, luxuriously bound in thirty-five red leather volumes. Then he began to write a book which, said Carrie, was to 'deal with his life from the point of view of his work'. As its title, *Something of Myself*, suggested it was hardly an auto-biography but a reluctant release of what little he wished his readers to know; it contains no mention of Flo Garrard or of Mrs Hill, of Wolcott or Beatty Balestier, no allusion to the deaths of Josephine and John Kipling. There are few dates and those not always accurate. But, as a picture of the mood in which he approached his work at each period of his life and as a record of self-criticism it is worth much, and without it this book would have been poorer.

Meanwhile his growing distrust in the social tendency of the nineteen-thirties was expressed in his address to the

Royal Society of St George. It was the time of King George's Silver Jubilee, and Rudyard spoke on the 'immemorial continuity of the nation's life under its own sovereigns'. The burden of his speech, as of so many of his later utterances, was the weak and negative policy of the lesser men who were left in charge of the nation's affairs, since their worthier contemporaries had sacrificed themselves in the First World War. Not these men's half-hearted self-delusions but enduring springs of vitality drawn from the nation's past would save us in the new perils that frowned upon the world. These men

were not happy. There was a necessity laid upon man to justify himself. . . . It was in accord with human nature that a theory should have sprung up that the War had been due to a sort of cosmic hallucination. . . . The theory absolved those who had not interested themselves in the War and, by inference, condemned those who had. . . . It was what men said and did to prove to themselves that their errors were really laborious virtues that built up the whole-time hells of life.[18]

The summer of 1935, which had begun with a visit to the Stanleys in Paris, passed pleasantly for Rudyard though poorly for his wife. He contributed a belated Just So Story, 'Ham and the Porcupine', to the gift-book for the little Princess Elizabeth, and wrote a poem, 'The King and the Sea', which was published in all the newspapers. A friend of whom he saw much was Sir Percy Bates, the shipowner, with whom he went to the Naval Review, and with whom he corresponded in a welter of technicalities about the launching of the giant Cunarder, the *Queen Mary*. He went to the Academy (and thought it 'rotten'); he dined at 'The Club'; he attended the annual reunion of the Old Boys of his school. Carrie's ill-health dictated their movements, and for her sake they went to Marienbad for the cure. To pass through Germany was an unpleasant ordeal, by their way of thinking, but at Marienbad Rudyard was supremely happy. He had not seen such woods and hills, he wrote to

Frank Doubleday, since leaving Vermont. He made good progress with his autobiography, but Carrie made no progress in health; she had 'hoped so much of the visit and nothing came of it'.

In the autumn they were home again and Rudyard frequently in London, busy with Hollywood agents. A film of *Thy Servant a Dog* was projected, shown to the Trade, and dropped, but at last two Kipling films went into production, *The Light that Failed*, and *Elephant Boy* which the genius of Sabu, the Indian boy actor, made into a work of art as well as a commercial success.*

The Kiplings voted at the general election of 1935, which established Stan Baldwin in office with a sure majority, though Rudyard had never been more out of sympathy with his cousin. The liberal policy of the Cabinet towards India was not of a kind to enlist Rudyard's support and the policy of sanctions against Italy during the Abyssinian War seemed to him sheer lunacy. We were making the Italians our enemies for three generations by threats, which we could implement, he said, with no weapon 'more formidable than a surplice'. In December he wrote one of his political poems for *The Times* on the subject of Sanctions. It was in the post on the day, 20 December 1935, when the story of the Hoare-Laval negotiations came to light. Whatever it was that Rudyard had written, it was vitiated by the ensuing political crisis so that he had some difficulty in suppressing and destroying his poem before publication. About the same day, he worked for the last time at *Something of Myself*.

Rudyard was now nearing his seventieth birthday, an event he said, that 'somehow seems to lack charm'. To another friend he wrote, 'You have my acutest sympathy over what you delicately call the "nuisance" of growing old. A

---

*Neither film was released before R. K.'s death. Many experiments were made at filming his early stories in the 1920s, but rarely with success. A script for a silent film of 'Without Benefit of Clergy', in which 'Mother Maturin' appears as a character, is in the Kipling Papers. It has little merit. *The Light that Failed* has been filmed at least three times.

train has to stop at some station or other. I only wish it wasn't such an ugly and lonesome place, don't you?'[19] He was engaged in redrafting his will and, when his birthday came, 30 December, in a dark wet winter at 'Bateman's', with the Brook in high flood, neither he nor Carrie was in a mood for jubilation. Rather to their surprise, the event made a stir in the world, and critics who had ignored Rudyard's existence for years paid him unwonted tributes. Carrie noted grimly that she celebrated her birthday (her seventy-third) on the following day 'by dealing with Rud's mail. So far 108 telegrams and 90 letters.' It gratified her, in spite of illness and fatigue, that there was a personal letter from the King as well as the pile of congratulations from the unknown – 'all very nice and cordial and affectionate, and many from quite simple folk telling of what he has meant to them'.

One letter that Rudyard wrote on his seventieth birthday was to an American friend, Mrs Jackson Stoddard, who had charged him with misunderstanding her country. His last word on that theme may be worth recording. 'Remember,' he wrote, 'that I lived in the land for four years just as a householder. ...' 'As the nigger said in Court: "If Ah didn't like de woman, how come I'd take de trouble to hit her on de haid?"'[20]

In a very different mood he wrote to Edith Macdonald, the last survivor among his aunts, to whom since childhood he had given confidence and affection.[21]

2nd Jan. 1936

Dearest Aunt Edie,

Bless you for your note which has just come in. He who put us into this life does not abandon His work for *any* reason or default at the end of it. That is all I have come to learn out of my life. So there is *no* fear.

I was hoping for your letter, my dear; and it makes me feel better to have got it.

Ever your loving

Ruddy.

The Kiplings had planned to go to Cannes early in January 1936 and came up to Brown's Hotel for a few days before leaving.

On 12 January they both went to Hampstead to visit George Bambridge who was ill in bed with bronchitis. Rudyard was in good health and spirits and looking forward to going to France, but Carrie seemed far from well, as indeed she had been for some time. The last phase is told in the words of her daughter:

Early on 13th Elsie was rung up from the Middlesex Hospital and told that her father had had a sudden and violent haemorrhage in the night, and had been rushed to hospital, where a dangerous operation had been performed.

She went at once to the Middlesex, where she met her distracted mother and the surgeons, and learnt how serious things were. Anxious as she was for her own husband, ill at home, and yet feeling that she should be with her mother, Elsie finally decided to join her at Brown's Hotel, making visits to the Hospital and dashes home to see how George was progressing.

Carrie was very brave, and, after the first shock, calm, but the strain of anxiety and publicity were very great. Varying bulletins, as Rudyard fought for his life, grew worse and then rallied, were reflected on the posters in the streets, while press photographers haunted the entrance to the Middlesex and Brown's, and letters, telegrams and telephone calls poured in. The see-saw of hope and anxiety went on but – on 16th he grew rapidly worse and Carrie and Elsie were warned to be ready to return to the Hospital at a moment's notice. When they left after their last visit to him in the evening of the 16th they lay down, fully dressed, and tried to rest, but at 2 a.m. on 17th the urgent call came, and they left the hotel in falling snow and chilly darkness for their final vigil.

All that day they never left the Hospital, where the thoughtful kindness they received made these dreadful hours as bearable as possible. When night came they were given rooms in which to rest. Soon after midnight Rudyard died, having been unconscious for some hours, and his body was placed in the beautiful little chapel of the Hospital. It was 18th January, 1936, the 44th anniversary of his marriage. Now, for the first time Carrie broke down utterly, but not for long; her usual courage soon reasserting itself. She and her daughter left the Hospital, to face a barrage of cameras on the doorstep, and a nightmare day of telephones, telegrams, letters and callers at their hotel. Stanley Baldwin spoke most movingly on the wireless about his cousin.

Weak and ill as he still was, George Bambridge came to the hotel to help deal with the flood of correspondence from all over the world, and with arrangements for the cremation at Golder's Green. Just as his coffin arrived, covered with the Union Jack, the followers of Saklatvala, the Indian Communist who had been cremated just before Rudyard Kipling, were singing the Red Flag.

In the falling dusk of January 22nd, Elsie and George went to the Middlesex Hospital chapel, to go with the urn to Westminster Abbey. From Dean's Yard the little procession of clergy and the two mourners moved through the dimly lit cloisters and Abbey to the Warrior's Chapel, where, after a short service, the urn was left to await the funeral next day.

The newspapers, which so recently had celebrated Kipling's 70th birthday, were cramped for space on 18th and 19th January by news of the King's illness. It was generally known that he, too, was dying and, before preparations could be made for Kipling's funeral, the King's death plunged the whole nation into mourning, Nevertheless, before the Abbey was put in order for the royal ceremony, the writer whose devotion had been rewarded by the King's friendship was buried in Poets' Corner. The last occasion of that kind had been the burial of Hardy who was borne to the grave by an escort of poets and dramatists. Not so was Kipling; his pall-bearers were the Prime Minister, an Admiral, a General, the Master of a Cambridge College, Professor Mackail for his family, Sir Fabian Ware, and two old friends, H. A. Gwynne and A. S. Watt; and the congregation consisted of men of action, the men with whom he had spent his life, rather than men of letters.

The funeral service in Westminster Abbey was thus described in George Bambridge's diary:

When Carrie, Elsie, and I followed the ashes into Poets' Corner and stood on the edge of the grave above the urn I feared C. K. would fall, as she was swaying to and fro. Elsie and I had her arms and she recovered gradually to some extent. The service was long and the ordeal great, but music was good and arrangements quite flawless. Every seat in choir and lantern and both transepts were filled and the general public was admitted as well; thousands could not obtain entry. The scene was wonderful, the mourners represented every branch of the Services, every art and craft, a more distinguished gathering could not be imagined.

My sorrow at losing R. K. is great. He was wonderfully kind to me and I shall miss him much. He was far away the greatest living Englishman to-day, wonderfully far-seeing and great-hearted, and his work will live. I like to think he will lie all Tuesday so near his late King to whom he was devoted and who was devoted to him. After the service a procession past the grave of all those present took place and the singing of the 'Recessional' and 'Abide With Me' (he chose this hymn) was most affecting.

Never was any man buried in Poets' Corner with more clear a title as master in the craft of letters, never any man more worthy to lie beside Charles Dickens and Thomas Hardy. His impact upon the age he lived in had been greater than that of any writer since Dickens, and like Dickens Rudyard Kipling had always been a man of the people. Neither had forfeited even a fraction of a vast publicity by reason of the strictures of the fastidious. There had always been critics who said that Dickens was 'vulgar' because sentimental, and Kipling 'vulgar' because brutal, but the people knew better. Kipling, except in one or two immature pieces written in youth, had never lapsed into the sentimental optimism with which Dickens deceived himself; the puritan strain in his ancestry preserved him from that error, placing him rather in the same company with Thomas Hardy, the Hardy – that is – who wrote the final choruses of *The Dynasts*. From early middle age Kipling had been a pessimist, if to face unpleasant truths with candour and resolution is pessimism. His greatest poem looked to the end of an epoch not to a Utopian future, and was rightly called 'Recessional'; his firmest message to his generation – to take up the 'White Man's Burden' – offered them no hope of easy triumph.

The impulse and the circumstance of his own life were important only in relation to the Law, that temple built to the design of the Great Overseer.

> If there be good in what I wrought
> Thy Hand compelled it, Master, Thine –
> Where I have failed to meet Thy Thought
> I know, through Thee, the blame was mine . . .
>
> The depth and dream of my desire,
> The bitter paths wherein I stray –
> Thou knowest Who hast made the Fire,
> Thou knowest Who hast made the Clay.[22]

Though compounded, like all men, of two elements, one akin to clay and one to fire, it is not in this mingling of opposites that we can account for his two soul-sides, the 'separate sides to his head', of which he had once written so buoyantly. There was one side which the world knew well, for he was one of the few in his generation whose name and face and message were universally familiar. Streets and terraces and frontier townships were named after him, branches of the Kipling Society flourished in five countries, the sale of his books, in many languages as well as in English, maintained his rank as a bestseller throughout his life and for twenty years after. His admirers in every land were numbered by scores of thousands; he was by far the most frequently quoted of contemporary authors, as the Dictionaries of Quotations demonstrate. To this day, in allusion, quotation – and misquotation – the Kipling Tradition is revived almost daily in the newspapers. Whether liked or disliked, he was the only poet of his day whose verse was known by men and women of all classes, all creeds, all walks of life.

His message was addressed to his generation in its active

mood, and was accepted. The sailors and the soldiers, the engineers and artificers, the administrators and pioneers – all who knew the Secret of the Machines, all the 'Sons of Martha' were on Kipling's side, all those, that is to say, who were concerned with what was being done, rather than what was being said – or thought – in the modern world. But, before his death, the word-spinners, for the most part, had passed him by, despising his adherence to the old Law and to the Gods of the Copy-book Headings.

So much for that side of his soul which he exposed to the world, but what has been revealed of his soul on its other side? 'Seek not to question other than the books I leave behind,' he pleaded to posterity: question, then, the last story in the *Jungle Books*, where Mowgli is torn between the jungle and the village, that is to say between the world of fancy and the world of fact. Or question Kim who overcame his inclination to follow the higher path with his beloved lama and returned to the service of the *raj*. Or question 'The Children of the Zodiac', his allegory of a poet who rejects the life of an immortal in order to work among men with the certainty of pain and death, the probability of loneliness and disrepute.

His solution of these problems was found by intuition, not by reason. His genius – or, as he preferred to say, his *daemon* – showed him the heart of the matter by a sort of second-sighted faculty, that he himself mistrusted. By preference he aligned himself with his hard-headed Anglo-Saxon father, called himself a Yorkshireman, and sometimes spoke slightingly of the Celtic blood derived from his Macdonald mother; all the more because his mother and his mother's family meant so much to him. An otherworldly Celtic seer he would not consent to be. The dreams and delusions that afflict and stimulate the adolescent had sometimes rapt him away, out of himself, into occult imaginings, which he repelled, while his sister, lacking his earthy fibre, surrendered to them. Though he never doubted the actuality of the unseen world, from which there came to

him the words he was bound to speak, he could never accept
the rationalized formulas of any church or sect. His contacts were immediate, and best stated in his own words: [23]
'I expect that every man has to work out his creed according to his own wave-length, and the hope is that the Great
Receiving Station is tuned to take *all* wave-lengths'.

Epilogue

MEMOIR BY MRS GEORGE BAMBRIDGE

THE sunlit months we spent every winter in South Africa seem to dominate the memory of my early childhood rather than our English summers. The hot, pine-scented days and cool nights were delightful, and I know that, in later years, my father was often homesick for that lovely country.

The *Just So Stories* were first told to my brother and myself during those Cape winters, and when written, were read aloud to us for such suggestions as could be expected from small children. The illustrating of the stories gave their author immense pleasure, and he worked at them (mostly in Indian ink) with meticulous care and was delighted when we approved of the results.

The 'Woolsack' seemed constantly full of grown-up visitors, one of whom (we only knew him as 'Dr Jim') was especially delightful, while a rather ponderous and silent man, we were later to realize, was Cecil Rhodes.

About this time a lunatic took it into his head that my father was the reincarnation of someone he did not like and that it was his duty to shoot him. To this end he followed us from England to the Cape, arriving at the 'Woolsack' late one hot night. Hearing a banging on the heavy teak side-door, my father went to investigate and was confronted with the business end of a revolver held in the shaking hand of an excited and voluble man, obviously with a grievance. Talking to this madman gently but without pause, my father enticed him into the house, where they sat talking for hours, until many strong whiskies and the endless drone of his unwilling host's voice at last sent the man to sleep. At intervals during several years, and in various places the same lunatic (whose family announced that he was not mad enough to certify) reappeared, and finally he fired a revolver at my father one day as he came out of the Athenaeum. This was too much even for the most patient of men, and the reluctant relatives were at last induced to have their kinsman shut up. When he died some time later, my father himself ordered, and sent to his funeral, a large wreath, with his card attached.

From our earliest years my father's relations with us children were close and intimate, and his patience in answering our questions was immense. Because I knew that I should always receive a careful answer, my stream of queries was endless and earned me the nickname of 'Elsie Why'. The verses 'I keep six honest serving-men' are a memory of those ceaseless questions.

One summer in the early 1900s we children and my father acted scenes from *A Midsummer Night's Dream*. Our stage was an old grass-grown quarry, and there my brother as Puck, myself as Titania, and my father as Bottom, rehearsed and acted happily. A most realistic cardboard donkey's head had been donned by Bottom for his part, and the village policeman, passing along the lane, was amazed to see the familiar tweed-clad figure of my father topped by this extraordinary headgear.

This was the first beginning of the stories that afterwards became *Puck of Pook's Hill*.

The affectionate, but firm, discipline of our lives was in my mother's hands and we were brought up with a strict sense of obedience to parental authority, and a simplicity which verged on the austere. There was no question of regarding my father as an aloof genius, or of having any special reverence for his writings; indeed, for many years most of his books remained unread by his children, and it was only after his death that I first read *Kim*. From an early age his bookshelves were open to us, and the only attempt to restrict our reading was the advice that certain books might interest us more when we were older. He read aloud to us for hours in his expressive and flexible voice, and it was in this way that, as we grew older, we came to know Scott, Jane Austen, much of Thackeray and endless poetry: Dickens we none of us much cared for. His great knowledge of both English and French literature made him a wonderful guide to reading, and he would draw up elaborate lists of the classics in both languages for me to read. An elderly and long-suffering French governess had given both us children a firm and fluent grounding in French, so that we became almost bilingual at an early age.

Switzerland for winter sports replaced our Cape voyage after 1908, when my brother had gone to school. There my father cautiously took to ski-ing, a sport at which his cousin, Stanley Baldwin, was more ambitious and successful. Some weeks in France or Italy usually followed, and then back to Sussex in the early spring.

Visitors were frequent at 'Bateman's', often total strangers who came from all the corners of the world to discuss their work and problems, to ask advice or help, or merely to tell of their adventures and experiences. The visitors' book, kept in my father's small handwriting, is a strange medley of names, which sometimes had notes against them, such as 'cold rice pudding' or the initials 'F.I.P.' The former note was a reminder that a certain Colonial Administrator liked cold rice pudding instead of early tea, while the latter meant 'Fell in pond'. These letters come after a surprising number of distinguished names, as boating on the square, shallow pool in the garden was a favourite summer amusement which often ended in an overturned boat and dripping figures on the lawn.

'Bateman's' lies in a steep valley, its formal yew-hedged and flag-pathed garden going down to the little River Dudwell, with oak and chestnut woods rising on the slope to the south. Inside the house is darkly panelled and with small latticed windows, the effect (except on a bright day) being

of a certain sadness. The stiff furniture is very much of the
period of the house – about 1630 – with a resulting lack of
comfort which my parents never seemed to notice. Many
of the things were beautiful in themselves, but the whole
effect was rather sparse and, in the winter, chilly, in spite of
the huge wood fire in the hall. The study, a large square
room on the first floor, facing south and east, is lined on
two sides with ceiling-high book shelves. The desk, a large
birch-wood table, with a wooden-seated chair and an enormous waste-paper basket, faces the eastern window looking
down the valley. He wrote on large pale-blue pads that were
specially made for him, and for many years used a thin,
silver penholder, Waverley nibs, and a large pewter inkpot.
During the last few years of his life he took to using a typewriter, though he was never very expert with it. During my
father's life a large canvas-covered case labelled 'Notions'
lay on the desk, containing unfinished stories and poems,
notes and ideas, collected through the years. After his death
my mother burnt this, though the interest of its contents
would have been immense. A hard sofa is at right angles
to the small fireplace. Lying on his side, his head propped
on his right hand, my father spent many hours on this sofa
while he brooded over the work he was busy with at the
moment. From time to time he would jump up and go to
the desk, write a line or two, make a note or correction,
then resume his place on the sofa. When writing verse, he
usually paced up and down the study humming to himself.
He was never disturbed while at work, but at intervals he
would call over the stairs for either my mother or myself,
to 'come and listen' while he read part of a story or poem,
and to discuss it with him. When something was too obscure, I would protest that it was impossible to understand
and we would argue the best way of rewriting it to make it
clearer. When deep in some piece of work he was so utterly
absorbed as to be quite absent-minded, even when away
from his desk. As children, we learned to recognize these
periods as ones in which he must not be bothered with the

things of everyday life. When he 'came back', as we put it to each other, he would quickly again enter into our lives and interests.

His only attempt at play-writing was in 1913, when he and I together wrote a one-act play called *The Harbour Watch*, of which Pyecroft was the hero. Vedrenne and Eadie produced it in a series of matinées at the Royalty Theatre, but it was not a great success.

When in 1914 I duly 'came out' and went to the stately London balls of that last summer of the old world, my father would often come with me, talking to chaperones and eating late suppers with other parents of his generation. Invitations to the large week-end parties of those days would be accepted by my parents if I wanted to go. There was an evening at one of these gatherings at Cliveden when my father, acting in charades with convincing horror, made his fellow-guests' flesh creep.

The strain of the first war (the coming of which he had so long predicted) and my brother's death, left both my parents in poor health in 1918, and my father subject to severe attacks of internal pain. Numbers of doctors tried to cure him, but with little success, though endless treatments were prescribed. The courage and patience with which he bore the recurring pain and the cures that were tried were truly heroic. His self-control was superb and the sweetness of his temper unfailing; he would only ask to be left alone until the pain was over. It was not till 1933, when he was terribly ill while in Paris, that a French doctor found that for some fifteen years he had been suffering from duodenal ulcers. What endless pain and suffering he could have been saved had this conclusion been arrived at earlier; now he was too exhausted to undergo an operation.

During the years following my brother's death in 1915 until my marriage in 1924, I was hardly ever away from my parents, and my father and I were close and constant companions; the three of us went everywhere together. Visits to France, Algiers and Spain he always enjoyed, though the inevitable publicity which accompanied his travels abroad sometimes made it difficult for him to have a quiet holiday. But, though the recognition by strangers in every country ranged from the eager request for an autograph from the customs official who had opened his luggage in Czechoslovakia to the Mayor of some smart Riviera resort asking us to a Gala banquet at the Casino, the kindness and interest were always the same. He was always happy in France and knew much of the country well from our many long motor trips there.

The honorary degrees given him in Paris and Strasbourg pleased him very much, though the speeches, banquets, and parties that went with them were rather an effort. He gave so much of himself while meeting people that he was often exhausted after a big dinner or reception, though a short rest quite restored him.

One evening in Paris, while staying at the Meurice, he was asked by the leader of the hotel orchestra if there was any piece he would like played. Without any hesitation he asked for 'Sambre et Meuse', to the delight of the band and the amazement of the other guests. The rococo hall of the hotel was so splendidly unsuitable a place to hear the swinging strains of this most stirring of marches.

After the 1914–18 war his work with the War Graves Commission took him often to the devastated regions. This work was very close to his heart, and I think the feeling that his own son had no known grave made him take an intense interest in the laying out of the cemeteries.

My mother introduced into everything she did, and even permeated the life of her family with, a sense of strain and worry amounting sometimes to hysteria. Her possessive and rather jealous nature, both with regard to my father and to us children, made our lives very difficult, while her uncertain moods kept us apprehensively on the alert for possible storms. There is no doubt that her difficult temperament sometimes reacted adversely on my father and exhausted him, but his kindly nature, patience, and utter loyalty to her prevented his ever questioning this bondage, and they were seldom apart. She had great qualities; a keen, quick mind and ready wit, a business ability above the average and loyalty and kindness to old friends; but above all, an immense and never-failing courage in pain and sorrow, both of which she bore unflinchingly. My father's much exaggerated reputation as a recluse sprang, to a certain extent, from her domination of his life and the way in which she tried to shelter him from the world. To a certain degree this was a good thing and enabled him to work without too much interruption, but he needed also the stimulus of good talk and mixing with people, and as the years went on and his life became more restricted, he missed these keenly.

My father inherited a great deal of his own father's artistic ability and was often busy with pencil and paint-brush illuminating, for instance, his various copies of Horace's Odes with designs and pictures. His knowledge of lettering of all ages and his skill in reproducing it was great, and he took infinite pleasure in the drawing of the delicate and fantastic letters for 'How the Alphabet was made' in the *Just So Stories*. Sometimes to amuse himself he would fake old documents, and the results, having been 'aged' by careful rubbing with soot and dust, were marvels of convincing antiquity. If painted masks or gilded paper crowns with splendidly real-looking jewels were wanted for theatricals or fancy-dress parties, he made them with the greatest skill and endless trouble. The writing of limericks delighted him, and there exists an old copy of Lear's Nonsense Book on the blank sheets of which appear many verses, illustrated with spirited little drawings of the Old Maid of Zug, the Young Lady of Brie, the Three Young Ladies of Nice and many more.

Deftness and certainty of movement were characteristics of his. The way he handled things, lit a cigarette, made a gesture or movement, was compact of neatness and energy. He never fumbled, and his gestures were always expressive.

Up to the time of his death at seventy his slim and upright figure moved surely and lightly.

The gift of being able to talk to anyone about the things that interested them was peculiarly his, and the shyest person would respond quickly to the quite genuine interest he always took in people. On one of the rare occasions when he was being interviewed, the young reporter chatted happily about his own life and ambitions at some length and only realized after he had left that my father had said nothing about himself.

He was interested in food and wine to a certain extent, and enjoyed reading old cookery books, such as Mrs Glass's. I remember a time in France when we made a long detour in a day's motoring to sample the pigs' trotters in a town noted for this delicacy, and which a French general had said should not be missed. At home he mostly drank cider out of a pewter tankard. The strict diets of his later years made his meals very dull, and his smoking was much curtailed. At one time he had smoked some 30–40 cigarettes a day, but this was firmly rationed by his doctors, to his great annoyance, though he was still allowed his pipe.

He was quite uninterested in his clothes, and his collection of aged and battered hats was large. When my mother thought he needed another suit, he went obediently to his tailor, who provided him with a new one of the same cut and much the same material as the previous one. He never grumbled, however, when he had to wear formal clothes for a special occasion, and always changed for dinner at home.

Card games were a mystery to him, though there was a legend that he had played poker in his youth. Cribbage and Patience were the only games I ever saw him play, except Mah-Jong, which fascinated him for a time.

Though great honours were offered to him, he refused to accept any but literary or academic ones, holding that accepted honours would mean the loss of that complete independence to say, in prose or verse, what he thought should be said. An instance was his speech to the Society of St George in 1935, with its urgent warning that Germany was again preparing for war. This was resented as being 'unsuitable for Jubilee Year', and was hardly reported in the press. The poem, giving the same warning in 1932 and called 'The Storm Cone', was criticized as being 'exaggerated and gloomy'.

The two great sorrows of their lives, my parents bore bravely and silently, perhaps too silently for their own good. My mother hardly ever spoke of her two lost children, but sometimes my father would talk of them to me. There is no doubt that little Josephine had been his greatest joy during her short life. He always adored children, and she was endowed with a charm and personality (as well as enchanting prettiness) that those who knew her still remember. She belonged to his early, happy days, and his life was never the same after her death; a light had gone out that could never be rekindled. My brother, John, took after his American forbears in looks, with brilliant hazel eyes, dark eyebrows and hair, and a slim figure. A quick and vivid personality of much charm was evident, even before he was eighteen. My father was devoted to him, and his pride and interest in his son's short time as a soldier were intense. The long drawn-out agony of the years during which his fate was uncertain left its mark on both my parents, though outwardly they remained calm.

Among the young officers who had given my father their account of many episodes in France for the regimental history of the Irish Guards in the first war was Captain George Bambridge. His exploits (he was several times wounded, won the M.C., and was mentioned in despatches) are duly noted in the history. His friendship with us continued when peace came in 1918, and he often visited 'Bateman's'. After leaving the Army he became Honorary Attaché at the Embassy in Madrid, and during a visit we made there in the spring of 1924, he and I became engaged.

Though my father was delighted by my obvious happiness and was fond of George, something like despair filled him as he looked forward to life at 'Bateman's' without his only remaining child. The years since John's death had brought us very close together, and he had come to depend on my constant companionship. Now, not only was I to marry, but to live abroad. My mother, who was always more reserved, filled the time before my wedding with busy plans for clothes, furniture, and house linen. But I think that she, too, was sad at my leaving home, besides having grave doubts of my housekeeping abilities!

We were married at St Margaret's, Westminster, in October 1924 and left at once for Brussels, where George had now been appointed. That winter was a dreary one at 'Bateman's'; the house seemed 'very large and quiet' my father wrote me. His abiding interest was now to be everything that concerned my new life. The house, furniture, domestic arrangements, friends, social doings, and above all my health, everything interested him. He wrote me long letters, demanding details of every kind, from the description of a court ball to our plans for improvements in the kitchen. My parents visited us in Brussels, afterwards in Madrid (where we returned in 1926) and later in Paris. They enjoyed, I think, the parties we gave for them, as well as the more formal entertainments at the Embassies, and our various homes were a constant source of interest to them. When I was asked (by a not-to-be-ignored personage) to urge my father to make a speech at a big dinner in Paris, he undertook the task to please me without question.

In 1933 we returned to England, and our life in the delightful old house and garden which we rented in Hampstead was a source of happiness to him to the end of his life.

After his death, a destroyer was named after him, which I launched at Greenock just before the war. There is an epic story of the *Kipling*'s heroic rescue of the survivors of the *Kelly* during the battle off Crete, of her terrible four-hundred-mile journey, crowded with wounded, listing heavily and ceaselessly attacked by German bombers, of her arrival at Alexandria with the rescued men, wounded, dirty, and exhausted, lined up on deck, to be greeted by a great roar of cheers echoing across the harbour. All this might have been one of my father's own stories.

All my life I have been surrounded by the kindness and interest of people, from many countries and in many walks of life, who knew my father personally, or felt they did so through his writings. In out-of-the-way corners of the world his name has brought me new friendships. Often still, I have letters from complete strangers saying how a poem or story had helped and encouraged them, or remembering some quiet kindness he had done them, long ago.

Sources

(a) BIBLIOGRAPHY OF PRINTED SOURCES
(b) UNPRINTED SOURCES

REFERENCES to Rudyard Kipling's works in the Notes are given (in *italic*) by their titles, as in the *Bibliography* by F. V. Livingston. *Something of Myself* is abbreviated as *S of M*. References to printed works if listed in (a) are given under their author's names and, if not listed, in full. References to unprinted sources are given under the abbreviations listed in (b), or in full.

(a) PRINTED SOURCES

F. Adams: *Essays in Modernity.*
L. S. Amery: *My Political Life.*
The Athenaeum, November–December 1890.
Sir H. Baker: *Cecil Rhodes.*
G. C. Beresford: *Schooldays with Kipling.*
Wilfrid Blunt: *Memoirs.*
The Bookman, May 1901.
E. J. Buck: *Simla Past and Present.*
G. B.-J. [Burne-Jones] – *Memorials of Sir Edward Burne-Jones.*
D. Chapman-Huston: *The Lost Historian* (Memoir of Sir Sidney Low).
A. Chevrillon: *Rudyard Kipling.*
H. Cushing: *Life of Sir William Osler.*
John Connell: *Life of W. E. Henley.*
Daily Mail, London, October 1899 to March 1900.
Daily Telegraph, London, April 1900.
Bonamy Dobrée: *Rudyard Kipling.*
Dufferin and Ava, Marchioness of: *Our Viceregal Life.*
L. C. Dunsterville: *Stalky's Reminiscences.*
T. S. Eliot: Introduction to *A Choice of Kipling's Verse.*
The Friend, Bloemfontein (complete set in the Carpenter Collection).
Sir E. Gosse, article in *Century Magazine*, April 1892.
Sir Ian Hamilton: *Listening for the Drums.*
R. Hart-Davis: *Hugh Walpole.*
(Mrs) Edmonia Hill: article in *Atlantic Monthly*, April 1936.
R. Thurston Hopkins: *Rudyard Kipling.*

G. Ireland: *The Balestiers of Beechwood* (unpublished).

H. James, article in the *Cosmopolitan*, May 1892.

I. Kaplan: *Rudyard Kipling in America*, 1889 (unpublished).

The Kipling Journal, Nos. 1–112.

Margaret Lane: *Life of Edgar Wallace*.

Richard Le Gallienne: *Rudyard Kipling*.

W. R. Lawrence: *The India we Served*.

B. Lee-Booker: *Yesterday's Child*.

F. V. Livingston: *Bibliography of the Works of Rudyard Kipling*, and *Supplement*.

Sir D. MacCarthy: *Memories*.

J. H. McCarthy: *Reminiscences*, vol. ii.

Edith Macdonald: *Annals of the Macdonald Family*.

F. W. Macdonald: *As a Tale that is Told*.
Letters of James Macdonald.

J. W. Mackail: *Life of William Morris*.

Sir G. F. MacMunn: *Rudyard Kipling, Craftsman; Kipling's Women*.

Guy Paget: *Letters from Rudyard Kipling* (privately printed).

B. Patch: *Thirty Years with G. B. S.*

The Pioneer, Allahabad. 75th anniversary number, 1940.

Dorothy Ponton: *Rudyard Kipling at Home and at Work*.

Julian Ralph: *War's Lighter Side*.

H. C. Rice: *Rudyard Kipling in New England*.

E. K. Robinson: article in *McClure's Magazine*, July 1896.

The Scots Observer, 1889–90.

G. Seaver: *Francis Younghusband*.

R. L. Stevenson: *Complete Works*, vol. xxv.

H. A. Tapp: *The United Services College, 1874–1911*.

Angela Thirkell: *Three Houses*.

The Times: History of the War in South Africa.

The United Services College Chronicle (complete set in Houghton Library).

F. F. van de Water: *Rudyard Kipling's Vermont Feud* (an amusing account from Beatty Balestier's point of view).

Sir F. Ware: *The Immortal Heritage*.

Arthur Waugh: *One Man's Road*.

H. G. Wells: *The New Machiavelli*.

W. B. Yeats: *Introduction to the Oxford Book of Modern Verse*.

(b) UNPRINTED SOURCES

(1) The Kipling Papers, the property of Mrs George Bambridge (K P). They include his press-cutting books, Mrs Kipling's diaries, and many portfolios of correspondence.

(2) The Kipling and other collections founded by Mrs F. V. Livingston at the Houghton Library, Harvard (Houghton). Notably the Henry James and C. E. Norton letters.

(3) The Berg collection in the New York Public Library (Berg). They include several early drafts of Kipling MSS.

(4) The Carpenter collection in the Library of Congress (Carpenter), including the Conland letters and many documents formerly belonging to Mrs S. A. Hill.

(5) The Theodore Roosevelt Papers in the Library of Congress (Roosevelt).

(6) Private papers of Mr F. Cabot Holbrook, Brattleboro, Vermont (Holbrook).

(7) Private papers of Mrs Nelson Doubleday, Oyster Bay, Long Island (Doubleday).

(8) The Kipling–Henley correspondence, the property of Mr 'John Connell' (Henley).

(9) Letters of Kipling to Rhodes and Herbert Baker at Rhodes House, Oxford (Rhodes).

(10) The Milner Papers at New College, Oxford (Milner).

(11) The Kipling–Barry correspondence in the Toronto Public Library (Barry).

(12) Papers in the possession of Mr Howard Rice, Junior, Princeton University (Rice).

Other sources are acknowledged in full.

Notes

THE Quotation on page 5 is from a letter to Sir H. Baker (Rhodes).

Chapter 1 (p. 31) – Kiplings and Macdonalds

(1) K P. (2) This is conjectural. The date and place of J. L. Kipling's birth are uncertain. (3) K P.

Chapter 2 (p. 41) – Childhood: Bombay and Southsea.

(1) *Daily Gazette*, Karachi, 19 January 1936. (2) Dates identified by the P. & O. Company. (3) *S of M*. (4) Capt. P. A. Holloway, 4 Campbell Road, Southsea. (5) *Letters to Guy Paget*. (6) and (7) *S of M*. (8) 'Baa, Baa, Black Sheep'.

Chapter 3 (p. 55) – Public School

(1) G. C. Beresford. (2) L. C. Dunsterville. (3) *Souvenirs of France*. (4) *Land and Sea Tales*. (5) *S of M*. (6) *Stalky & Co*. (7) *Sussex Edition, vol*. xxxv. (8) Memorandum by A. M. ('Trix') Fleming (K P). (9) Berg.

Chapter 4 (p. 79) – Lahore and Simla

(1) *The Light that Failed*. (2) *Letters of Travel*. (3) K P. (4) *From Sea to Sea*. (5) KP. (6) *Plain Tales from the Hills*. (7) *Sussex Edition*, vol. xxxv. (8) K P. (9) *S of M*. (10) K P. (11) and (12) R. K.'s diary for 1885 (Houghton). (13) *S of M*. (14), (15), and (16) K P. (17) *Kim*. (18) *S of M*. (19) and (20) K P. (21) *McClure's Magazine*, July 1896. (22) K P. (23) *From Sea to Sea*. (24) K P. (25) *McClure's Magazine*, July 1896. (26) 'My First Book', *The Idler*, 1892. (27) *S of M*. (28) 'A Song in Storm'.

Chapter 5 (p. 127) – Simla and Allahabad

(1) Photograph in Carpenter Collection. (2) *Atlantic Monthly*, April 1936. (3) Carpenter. (4) 'Three and an Extra' (*Plain Tales*). (5) 'Miss Youghal's Sais' (*Plain Tales*). (6) K P. (7) *S of M*. (8) G. F. MacMunn; also N. W. Bancroft, *From Recruit to Staff-Sergeant* (reviewed by R. K. in *Civil and Military Gazette*, 5 February 1886); G. F. Younghusband, *Story of the Guides; Civil and Military Gazette*, 1 January 1887 (for 'Taking of Lung-tung-pen'); *Glasgow Herald*, 14 August

1889 (for 'Namgay Doola'). (9) 'The 'Eathen'. (10) 'Drums to the Fore and Aft'. (11) 'Rikki-tikki-tavi'. (12) K P. (13) *The Pioneer*, 75th anniversary number; *The Bookman*, May 1901. (14) K P.

Chapter 6 (*p. 163*) – *A Return to London*

(1) Authorities for the voyage: *From Sea to Sea*; *Atlantic Monthly*, April 1936; papers and photographs in Carpenter Collection. (2) For travels in Western America the published version in *From Sea to Sea* is not wholly reliable. Corrected from letters to Mrs Hill (K P). (3) *From Sea to Sea*, corrected from Hill letters; also I. Kaplan. (4) Reviews from press-cutting book (K P). (5) Letter from L. de Forest (Houghton). (6) K P. (7) *Kipling Journal*, December 1950; Livingston. (8) *S of M*. (9) D. Chapman-Huston. (10) Tennyson to C. V. Stanford (K P). (11) *Kim*. (12) *Kipling Journal*, December 1930. (13) 'In Partibus', *Sussex Edition*, vol. xxxv. (14) *S of M*; 'One View of the Question'. (15) *Letters to A. P. Watt*.

Chapter 7 (*p. 197*) – *Kipling in London*

(1) Henley correspondence; F. Harris, *Contemporary Portraits*; *Time and Tide*, 20 February 1937; *Kipling Journal*, December 1939; *S of M*. (2) Memorandum of A. M. ('Trix') Fleming (K P). (3) Hill letters (K P). (4) *S of M* is inaccurate here. Corrected by press-cutting book (K P) and Lyall, Sir A., *A Life of Lord Dufferin*. (5) Henley correspondence. (6) R. Le Gallienne. (7) *Saturday Review*, 14 February 1903. (8) C. P. Trevelyan, *Life of Mrs Humphrey Ward*.

Chapter 8 (*p. 221*) – *Kipling and the Balestiers*

(1) For the Balestier family: G. Ireland; Howard C. Rice; Holbrook Papers; Registers of St Luke's Church, Rochester, N.Y.; personal information. (2) E. Gosse; J. H. McCarthy; H. James (in *Cosmopolitan*, May 1892); Arthur Waugh; Holbrook Papers; 'The Book of Gosse' (Cambridge University Library); personal information. (3) *S of M*. (4) 'The Three-Decker'. (5) Personal information. (6) Press-cutting book (K P). (7) F. W. Macdonald. (8) *S of M*. (9) K P. (10) Letters of Henry James (Houghton); R. L. Stevenson, *Complete Works*, vol. xxv. (11) *S of M*, corrected by courtesy of the editor, the *New Zealand Herald*; *Kipling Journal*, Nos. 47, 52, 56, 57, 85. (12) R. H. Croll in *Australian National Review*, November 1937. (13) 'William the Conqueror'; correspondence with George Allen (K P); personal information from Mr F. H. Andrews. (14) Letters of Henry James (Houghton). (15) C. K.'s diary; personal information. (16) Personal information. (17) An early draft of 'The Long Trail' (Berg Collection); Lawrence Hutton, *Talks in a Library*. (18) Henley correspondence; C. K.'s diary; D. Chapman-Huston.

Chapter 9 (p. 249) – A Home in Vermont

(1) *Letters of Travel*. (2) R. W. Emerson, 'Monadnoc'. (3) Reprinted in *Letters of Travel*. (4) 'Rhyme of the Three Sealers'. (5) *S of M*. (6) C. K.'s diary. (7) *S of M*. (8) C. K.'s diary. (9) R. K. to Rider Haggard, 20 October 1895 (Houghton). (10) C. K.'s diary, 11 November 1893. (11) Henley correspondence. (12) 'The Coiner'. (13) U.S. College *Chronicle*, December 1894. (14) K P. (15) R. K. to Mrs Twiss, 24 August 1896 (Berg Collection). (16) Personal information. (17) *S of M*. (18) 'An American'. (19) Houghton. (20) *S of M*. (21) *Letters of C. E. Norton*, vol. ii, p. 236. (22) Houghton. (23) *S of M*. (24) S. S. McClure, *Autobiography*; C. K.'s diary. (25) The trial from a transcript in the Holbrook Papers; files of the *Vermont Phoenix*; personal information. (26) K P. (27) Houghton.

Chapter 10 (p. 297) – At Torquay

(1) Carpenter. (2) Holbrook. (3), (4) and (5) Carpenter. (6) Houghton. (7) R. K. to Stephen Wheeler, 1 February 1897 (K P). (8) R. K. to Mr Rockhill, 1 March 1897 (Houghton). (9) Personal information. (10) Many authorized and unauthorized editions of 'The Vampire' in Houghton and Carpenter Collections. (11) Carpenter.

Chapter 11 (p. 313) – The White Man's Burden

(1) Houghton. (2) K P. (3) A collection of letters to Earl Baldwin on Kipling and the laureateship is in K P. (4) R. T. Hopkins. (5) 'What the People Said.' (6) *The Times*, 20 December 1937, confirmed by C. K.'s diary. (7) Letters to R. K. about 'Recessional' in K P. (8) K P. (9) and (10) Personal information. (11) 'Song of the Wise Children', 1899(?). (12) 'The Fairies' Siege'. (13) *S of M*. (14) 'The Elephant's Child'. (15) *Kipling Journal*, December 1947. (16) 'Kitchener's School', and letter in K P. (17) *S of M*. (18) 'The Truce of the Bear'. (19) Roosevelt. (20) *Stalky & Co.* (21) Roosevelt.

Chapter 12 (p. 343) – Last Visit to the United States

(1) A. Thirkell. (2) 'Song of the Wise Children'. (3) *Evening Sun*, New York, 2 February and 12 February 1899. All letters and other papers relating to R. K.'s illness in 1899 were preserved by C. K. in K P; F. N. Doubleday's letters and other papers are in the Doubleday Collection; also letters of A. Woollcott (Library of Congress). (4) Papers relating to the Putnam lawsuit in the Carpenter Collection. (5) *The Times*, 4 April 1899, and many other newspapers. (6) Carpenter. (7) L. C. Dunsterville; *Kipling Journal*, No. 23; *Cambridge Gazette*, 18–19 January 1900.

Chapter 13 (p. 359) – The South African War

(1) 'The Voortrekker'. (2) *S of M*. (3) K P. (4) *S of M*. (5) Julian Ralph.

(6) *Daily Telegraph*, 13 April 1900. (7) *S of M*. (8) *Tribunal de Genève*, 18 January 1901. (9) *S of M; A Book of Words*. (10) *Journal of the African Society*, October 1932. (11) and (12) Carpenter. (13) Rhodes Papers. (14) K P. (15) Rhodes. (16) Margaret Lane. (17) H. Baker and Rhodes Papers. (18) *The Echo*, Brighton, Sussex, 17 June 1902.

Chapter 14 (p. 393) – Kipling and his Contemporaries

(1) Houghton. (2) R. K. to Henley, 31 December 1896. (3) *Letters of C. E. Norton*, vol. ii; to S. Weir Mitchell, 31 January 1907. (4) *S of M*. (5) 'The Lost Legion', 1895. (6) H. James to E. Gosse, 6 August 1891 (Houghton); and letters of R. L. Stevenson (*Complete Works*, vol. xxv, p. 213). (7) Max Beerbohm; *Poet's Corner, Christmas Garland, Things Old and New, Around Theatres, Fifty Caricatures*, etc. (8) Francis Adams. (9) R. Le Gallienne. (10) Houghton. (11) R. Ogden, *Life of E. L. Godkin*, letter dated 23 December 1899. (12) D. MacCarthy. (13) Personal information. (14) *Atlantic Monthly*, April 1936. (15) 'My Great and Only' (*Civil and Military Gazette*, 11 January 1890). (16) *Catalogue of English and American Authors*, issued by the American Art Association, 30 April 1921. (17) *S of M*. (18) A. Bennett: *Books and Persons*, 1917.

Chapter 15 (p. 431) – A Home in Sussex

(1) and (2) *S of M*. (3) Houghton. (4) *S of M*. (5) *Kipling Journal*, No. 85. (6) Houghton. (7) K P. (8) and (9) *S of M*. (10) 'Sussex'. (11) 'The Land'. (12) *S of M*. (13) Rhodes. (14) 'The Burial'. (15) K P. (16) Personal information.

Chapter 16 (p. 459) – 'At Bateman's'

(1) and (2) K P. (3) *S of M*. (4) K P. (5) *Letters of Travel*. (6) *A Book of Words*. (7) *S of M*. (8) Milner Papers. (9) *S of M*. (10) and (11) K P. (12) Milner. (13), (14) and (15) K P. (16) D. Ponton. (17) Unfortunately no documentary evidence has come to light on this point. (18) and (19) K P. (20) 'Ulster', wrongly dated in *Inclusive Edition*. (21) H. Cushing. (22) 'For All We Have and Are'.

Chapter 17 (p. 497) – The First World War

(1) *Daily Express*, 18 January 1926. (2) Personal information. (3) and (4) K P. (5) and (6) Sir F. Ware. (7), (8), (9) and (10) K P. (11) R. K., letter to E. Bok, 15 November 1920 (K P). (12) K P. (13) Roosevelt. (14) *S of M; The Times*, 27 May 1918. (15) Roosevelt.

Chapter 18 (p. 523) – After the War

(1) D. Ponton. (2) Personal information. (3) The 'Bateman's' Visitors' Book, written and annotated in R. K.'s hand, is in K P. (4) R. K.'s correspondence with members of the Royal household, and other rele-

vant letters, are quoted by gracious permission of H.M. the Queen.
(5) and (6) K P. (7) *A Book of Words.* (8) Sir F. Ware. (9) *The Times,*
11, 13 and 14 September 1922. (10) *A Book of Words.*

Chapter 19 (p. 539) – The Last Phase of his Work

(1) R. K. to Mrs Hill, 29 June 1906 (KP). (2) Masonic certificates in
K P; *Freemason's Magazine,* No. 678; *Kipling Journal, passim*; per-
sonal information. (3) 'Late Came the God'. (4) R. Hart-Davis. (5)
'Hymn to Physical Pain'. (6) and (7) K P. (8) *Le Figaro Littéraire,* 19
September 1953. (9) and (10) K P.

Chapter 20 (p. 559) – The Last Years of his Life

(1) K P. (2) Doubleday. (3) Rhodes. (4) R. K. to Dr Philip Gosse,
21 December 1927. (5) R. K. to C. R L. Fletcher, 24 June 1932 (K P).
(6) R. Hart-Davis. (7) *Kipling Journal,* No. 8; personal information.
(8) H. Cushing. (9) B. Patch: *Thirty Years with G. B. S.*; personal information. (10) K P. (11) 'The Roman Centurion's Song'. (12) K P. (13)
R. K. to J. W. Barry, 14 September 1935 (Toronto). (14) British Museum
MSS. Add. 45680W. (15) *Brazilian Sketches* were reissued as a book
in America but not in England. They are in the *Sussex Edition.* (16)
Doubleday. (17) *Strand Magazine,* April 1934, and *Sussex Edition.* (18)
The Times, 7 May 1935. (19) R. K. to Ernest Snow, December 1935
(Houghton). (20) R. K. to Mrs Jackson Stoddard, December 1935 (Car-
penter). (21) K P. (22) 'My New-cut Ashlar'. (23) R. K. to Henry Arthur
Jones (Houghton).

General Index

Characters in Rudyard Kipling's works are collected together under the general entry Characters

Index of Kipling's Works

Readers who despair of finding the story ·007 in our alphabetical list are hereby informed that there are references to it on pages 261 and 302.

FOR THE BEST IN PAPERBACKS, LOOK FOR THE

In every corner of the world, on every subject under the sun, Penguins represent quality and variety – the very best in publishing today.

For complete information about books available from Penguin and how to order them, write to us at the appropriate address below. Please note that for copyright reasons the selection of books varies from country to country.

In the United Kingdom: For a complete list of books available from Penguin in the U.K., please write to *Dept EP, Penguin Books Ltd, Harmondsworth, Middlesex, UB7 0DA*

In the United States: For a complete list of books available from Penguin in the U.S., please write to *Dept BA, Viking Penguin, 299 Murray Hill Parkway, East Rutherford, New Jersey 07073*

In Canada: For a complete list of books available from Penguin in Canada, please write to *Penguin Books Canada Limited, 2801 John Street, Markham, Ontario L3R 1B4*

In Australia: For a complete list of books available from Penguin in Australia, please write to the *Marketing Department, Penguin Books Australia Ltd, P.O. Box 257, Ringwood, Victoria 3134*

In New Zealand: For a complete list of books available from Penguin in New Zealand, please write to the *Marketing Department, Penguin Books (N.Z.) Ltd, Private Bag, Takapuna, Auckland 9*

In India: For a complete list of books available from Penguin in India, please write to *Penguin Overseas Ltd, 706 Eros Apartments, 56 Nehru Place, New Delhi 110019*

PENGUIN LITERARY BIOGRAPHIES

ABOUT THE AUTHOR

Alex Riley is an award-winning science writer .... ries of evolution, conservation, and human health. A ....ness is his first
book. In 2019, he received a best feature .... e Association of
British Science Writers for his report ....riendship Bench, a
project that began in Zimbabwe in 2006 ....since provided mental
healthcare to disadvantaged communities around the world. His articles have been published by *New Scientist*, Mosaic Science, Aeon,
PBS's *NOVA Next*, and the BBC, among others. He lives in Bristol.

Praise for *A Cure for Darkness*

'Boldly ambitious, deeply affecting, and magisterial in scope, *A Cure
for Darkness* is a milestone in the literature of clinical depression,
humanizing the global quest to unlock the secrets of a profoundly
disabling disorder . . . It's a masterpiece' Steve Silberman, author
of *Neurotribes: The Legacy of Autism and the Future of Neurodiversity*

'Breezily written, personal and accessible . . . a valuable addition to a
literature that will be especially needed as the pandemic recedes' *The
Times*

'Offers a rich and generous picture of research into depression to
date . . . Riley's own postgraduate brush with depression structures his
book, but the most striking thing about *A Cure for Darkness* is its
acknowledgment of disparate experience – for patients, as well as their
physicians or therapists – and extreme complexity' *Financial Times*

'Interweaving memoir, case histories, and accounts of new therapies,
Riley anatomizes what is still a fairly young science, and a troubled
one' *New Yorker*

'A substantial and revealing history of [depression] . . . grappling with
the opposing psychological and biological therapies of pioneering
psychiatrists Sigmund Freud and Emil Kraepelin, and their divided
successors' *Nature*

'Expansive and thoughtful, [*A Cure for Darkness*] illuminates the complexity and elusiveness of [Riley's] subject' *New Statesman*

'*A Cure for Darkness* is both a compelling intellectual contribution and an act of generosity. Alex Riley combines meticulous reporting and evocative storytelling to reveal scientists' evolving understanding of depression and the many ways it can be treated. In this candid, accessible, era-spanning book, Riley brings rare sensitivity and lucidity to a topic that has defied comprehension for centuries, weaving a story that is both sweeping in scope and intensely personal' Siri Carpenter, science journalist and editor of *The Craft of Science Writing*

'Alex Riley explores the long shadow of depression that winds through human history with intelligence and insight and – equally important – with courage and compassion. The resulting, remarkable book shines like a light against the night itself' Deborah Blum, author of *Love at Goon Park: Harry Harlow and the Science of Affection*

'A splendid read and a stunning debut, imbued throughout with warmth, intelligence, authority, and regard for the reader' David Dobbs, author of *Reef Madness*

'Alex Riley knows what depression is personally. Here he explains for the general reader what it means, and its story in psychiatry, in one of the best overall books on depression that I've seen' Nassir Ghaemi, author of *A First-Rate Madness*

'[An] eye-opening survey of the many shapes and forms of depression, from ancient history to today. As science writer Riley notes in his concise, refreshing debut book, depression is a vastly complex collection of overlapping mental states, the product of genes, neurotransmitters, upbringing, health, trauma, diet, lifestyle, and other factors . . . The author delves into these moments with notable vigor, insight, and scientific background information' *Kirkus*, starred review

'In his broadly researched and compassionate debut, Riley traces the history of treatments for depression and our changing understanding of the human brain . . . An essential book that brings much-needed awareness to depression and the lingering stigma and misinformation surrounding it' *Library Journal*, starred review

A
Cure
For
Darkness

1. the story of depression
and how we treat it

Alex Riley

EBURY
PRESS

I

Ebury Press, an imprint of Ebury Publishing,
20 Vauxhall Bridge Road,
London SW1V 2SA

Ebury Press is part of the Penguin Random House group of companies
whose addresses can be found at global.penguinrandomhouse.com

First published by Ebury Press in 2021
This edition published by Ebury Press in 2022

www.penguin.co.uk

A CIP catalogue record for this book is available from the British Library

ISBN 9781785039027

Printed and bound in Great Britain by Clays Ltd, Elcograf S.p.A.

The authorised representative in the EEA is Penguin Random House Ireland,
Morrison Chambers, 32 Nassau Street, Dublin D02 YH68

Penguin Random House is committed to a sustainable future
for our business, our readers and our planet. This book is made
from Forest Stewardship Council® certified paper.

To Lucy

This book is a work of non-fiction based on the life, experiences and recollections of the author. In some cases names of people, places, dates, sequences and the detail of events have been changed to protect the privacy of others. The information in this book has been compiled as general guidance on the specific subjects addressed. It is not a substitute and not to be relied on for medical, healthcare or pharmaceutical professional advice. Please consult your medical advisor before changing, stopping or starting any medical treatment.

Contents

Today, an estimated 322 million people around the world live with depression, the majority in non-Western nations. It's the leading cause of disability, judged by how many years are 'lost' to a disease, yet only a small percentage of people with the illness receive treatment that has been proven to help. An estimated 15 per cent of people with untreated depression take their own lives.

'... while we see sadness, unhappiness, and grief as inevitable in all societies we do not believe that this is true of clinical depression.'

George Brown & Tirril Harris, *Social Origins of Depression* (1978)

Introduction

On a chilly December morning in 2019, I walked to my local doctor's office in south Bristol, just as grey clouds passed overhead to reveal a patchwork of clear blue sky. Unlike my previous appointments, some booked in an emergency, this one felt hopeful, like a milestone in my recovery. I told the doctor, a middle-aged woman with a kind smile who leaned forward in her chair as she listened, that I wanted to come off antidepressants. I had been taking sertraline – a selective serotonin-reuptake inhibitor or 'SSRI' – every day for over two years, and I wanted to see what life was like without them. Could I be rid of the side effects that had become so normalised that I had forgotten what life was like before? Would my energy levels be any different? My feeling of connection to others? My libido? SSRIs are known to take some of the intimacy of life away, and I wanted to be reunited.

The doctor asked me whether I was sure I was ready to come off these drugs. I told her that I was, adding that my partner Lucy was supportive of this decision. My bouts of depression had become so brief and infrequent that we hoped that I didn't need these drugs any more. Although my thoughts still turned to suicide now and again, I felt confident that I could control them. The suicide plan that I had once sketched out didn't just seem like a distant memory, but the memory of a different person. In addition to antidepressants, I had been through two rounds of cognitive behavioural therapy (CBT) and seen therapists who practised mindfulness and psychodynamic approaches. Consequently, I felt like I was better able to rationalise the extremities of negative thought that could make it feel like others would be happier, healthier, more content without me.

While therapists can come and go within a few weeks, antidepressants often need to be taken for years to keep depression at bay. Before sertraline, I had been on citalopram (another SSRI) for two years. Chemically accustomed to their effects, coming off these drugs can be a tortuous experience for many people. Withdrawal symptoms include dizziness, sweating, confusion, brain zaps, and – if recent anecdotal reports are confirmed – a heightened risk of suicide. That's why I met with my doctor and agreed to reduce my dose gradually, over months and not the two weeks that psychiatric guidelines once recommended. After four years of elevated levels of serotonin, I was introducing my brain to a new equilibrium.

At the same time, thousands of miles away in Wuhan, China, a novel coronavirus was spreading through its new home in the lungs of humans. Silent and unknown to science, this was the germination of a pandemic that would thrive on proximity, bring healthcare systems to their knees, and demand widespread quarantines in the general public. Had I known all this, I might have changed my decision to decrease my dose of antidepressants. After all, the consequences of a pandemic and the social triggers for depression overlap with frightening acuity. There's the death of loved ones. Unemployment and poverty. Major life transitions. Trauma. Divorce and domestic violence. Loneliness. All are known risk factors for depression. And all followed in the wake of Covid-19, a virus that could kill and debilitate, that led to some of the highest rates of unemployment since the Great Depression, and that forced billions of people to transition into a new and uncertain world. I reminded myself that anxiety and distress are natural responses to a global catastrophe. But if the depression returned – the crippling lack of motivation and the mental pain that can make suicide appealing – I knew I could just as easily increase my dose as decrease it.

My doctor recommended regular meditation and exercise to help with any withdrawal symptoms. I had been researching this book for two and a half years by this point and knew that both can have potent antidepressant effects. The practice of meditation is based on the positive acceptance of the present, leaving little space for the negative thoughts about the past and the future that often define depression. There is some evidence that it can even recalibrate the immune response. As low-grade chronic inflammation – the same bodily process that underlies rheumatoid arthritis and Crohn's disease – is a common contributor to depressive symptoms, these moments of silent contemplation might be seen as a form of mental medication. As long as depressive thoughts aren't allowed to spiral and grow, meditation is an antidepressant without side effect. Excepting the risk of injury and muscle tiredness, the same is true of exercise. But there is also a sense of mastery that comes with jogging, practising yoga, or weightlifting. Both the psychological and physiological benefits of exercise are valuable parts of staying mentally healthy. The latest studies show that running three times a week, for example, can be as effective in reducing depressive symptoms as first-line treatments such as SSRIs and CBT.

And so, with these studies in mind, I made sure to don my running trainers and jog to the woodlands and parks near our home in south Bristol. With our dog Bernie chasing squirrels through the undergrowth or quietly trundling along by my side, I felt my daily concerns start to fade away with every mile. My breathing slowed and felt effortless. My mind started to wander as my muscles flexed in rhythm. It was fluid. Meditative. I didn't have my phone and I don't own a smartwatch, so I didn't know how far I'd travelled. But when I got home, a banana tasted like heaven and a cup of tea was pure indulgence. I felt a warm glow throughout my body that could last for the rest of the day. On other days, I made sure to sit, cross my legs, breathe with my diaphragm, and let my thoughts flow through my mind as neutrinos pass imperceptibly through the Earth. My favourite place to meditate is anywhere with trees. Listening to their leaves rustle, their boughs creak, reminds me of life outside of myself, wondrous products of evolution that barely move even in the fiercest winds. They even share nutrients with their neighbours through their entangled roots, just as we might reach out and offer someone a helping hand.

After three months of tapering my dose toward zero, I swallowed my last chunk of sertraline on 6 March 2020, a time when the number of deaths from Covid-19 were higher in Europe than in Asia. Based on sertraline's half-life, I knew that it might take a few days for the drug to be out of my system. I was expecting the worst. Indeed, by the second day, I felt fatigued, had the occasional cold shiver down my back, and felt so tired that I had to curl up in bed and sleep in the afternoon. When I woke up an hour or so later, I didn't feel any better. Sleep wasn't restorative. As I noted in my diary, 'Today (Monday), feeling groggy, like my thoughts are flowing through treacle. Brain heaviness. Goose pimples, chills, flu-like symptoms? Confused, nauseous.' I decided to go for a walk. With Bernie snuffling along next to me, I passed through city streets, boggy parks, woodlands, and across the Clifton Suspension Bridge, which was illuminated against the evening sky like a floating shelf lined with fairy lights. Fine rain filled the air. After an hour or so, I was drenched but my head had cleared. I was returning to a life soon to be placed in lockdown.

While the world adapted to life behind a screen, I remained vigilant for any symptom or sign that I might be collapsing, just as I had done so many times before.

*

Like thick curly hair, mental illness runs in my family. Psychosis and mood disorders, the two major groups of psychiatric classification, can both be found in its last three generations. Rumours and realities of institutionalisation have been passed down my maternal line. My mum remembers the day when my grandmother Renee was taken away to a mental institution in the 1970s. 'That is one of my worst memories,' she told me over the phone in August 2017. 'We didn't know whether she was going to come back.' Called High Royds, it was just one so-called asylum within a short van drive from their home in Thornton, a village just outside of Bradford in northwest England. But this memory is blurred in its details and may not have even happened. She was a child then and memories can be manufactured like nightmares. There's no doubt that Renee struggled with depression, especially after her husband Eric, my grandfather, died of lung cancer in 1975. At a time when SSRIs like sertraline hadn't yet been put into prescription, she was given diazepam (Valium) to calm her anxiety and dampen her grief. When at her worst, she described her mental anguish as 'tearing down the wallpaper'. But no one else in the family remembers Renee being taken away for any period of time. The patient reports from High Royds, although incomplete with whole years missing, hold no trace of her.

I never met Eric or Renee. Lung cancer also claimed Renee's life in April 1987, just a few months before my mum gave birth to her first child, my elder brother. Renee had named the bump 'Rupert' and, after she died, my brother couldn't be called anything else. His middle name is Eric. Her parents' passing left a dark shadow over my mum's future, one that she would never truly recover from. She pined for her parents as she became a parent herself. In her mind, it was the greatest tragedy that Renee and I were never able to meet. She always said that I was a lot like her. There was my love of nature. My studiousness and passion for science and literature. Today, I also wonder whether we suffered similarly.

Whatever our life experience, the main difference between Renee and myself is the treatments that were available to us. While she was prescribed a mild tranquilliser, I had the option of a range of SSRIs and evidence-based talking therapies such as CBT and interpersonal therapy. These two options – the biological therapies such as antidepressants and the psychology-based talking therapies – have been a central theme in the treatment of depression for decades.

With the image of Renee being taken away from her, my mum has always held a deep mistrust of psychiatric treatment. She has never reached out for professional help for her own mental struggles. Her own depression was a common feature of my childhood. There was the lack of sleep, the waking up at three in the morning and pacing downstairs. There was the drinking. The thoughts of being better off dead. Looking through old family photographs, I can see the hallmark signs that have followed me through my adulthood. In the rare photograph in which she appears – her long, dark, and curly hair like that of her girlhood crush Marc Bolan, the lead singer of the glam rock band T. Rex – she seems distant, as if there is a gulf between her and the child sitting on her lap. Her thick glasses frame a glazed expression. As a child, I often felt like there was an impenetrable gap between us. Today, I know that we share more than we care to imagine. I wish I could reach back into my childhood to tell her that it's okay to be struggling. That not feeling a connection to her children at times is perfectly normal for someone who's been through the trauma she has. After years with barely a word between us, we can now speak over the phone, and I can think of all the things, despite her past, that she taught me. My cooking, my northern twang, the comfort of making do with what you have: I hold them all dear, and they all came from her.

My own experience with depression has provided a new perspective on my mum's past. Thinking of the years just before I was born, I now wonder whether her move from a flat in the city of Bradford to an old farmhouse in the sticks of the Yorkshire Dales was her way of starting afresh, hoping to leave the past behind her. Moving with my dad – then a skinny, half-marathon running, mullet-sporting Queen fan who wore tight white trousers – she helped transform a dilapidated house into a home. With rotten floorboards, moss growing in the dining room, and only one fire for heating and cooking, they were spartan beginnings. For two years, Dad tried his hand at raising and milking goats, ending up losing money, and returned to his former occupation in construction. Mum was a mobile hairdresser who would drive through twisting country lanes to reach her clients. (There was also a fish-and-chip van that similarly brought one of the norms of towns and cities into remote villages.) She was also skilled on the sewing machine, fashioning trousers for me and my brother out of odd bits of material and old curtains. For family weddings, she would make waistcoats and smart trousers that were strange combinations of tailored and ill-fitting.

It was a healthy upbringing, but there was a shadow following all of us during these times. Although it isn't infectious like a virus, depression thrives on proximity; travelling down familial attachments, especially from mother to child. The latest studies show that having a depressed parent increases the risk of depression in children threefold. This predisposition isn't destiny, however. Nature, as far as depression is concerned, is nearly always bound by nurture. Only in the presence of environmental triggers is this underlying risk activated.

In 2015, after years of mistrust, arguments, and silence, my parents separated after 30 years of marriage. It wasn't unexpected, but it shattered the life I once knew. The family home – the only place I had called home – was put up for sale. I visited my parents separately in their unfamiliar rented accommodation. At the same time, I was transitioning into a new career. I had left a PhD at the University of Sheffield and was working as a researcher at the Natural History Museum in London. Using the latest CT-scanning technology, I studied the teeth and skeletons of sharks and rays, both living and extinct. There were aptly named cookie-cutter sharks, rays with whip-like tails, and deep-sea oddities known as chimeras or 'ghost sharks' with translucent skin. After a childhood of scrapbooks filled with dinosaurs and other megafauna from different continents and geological eras, this was a dream job. On my breaks, I walked around the museum's maze of corridors and came to know each specimen like an old friend. Giant marine reptiles splayed out on a wall, stuffed lions and pandas with fur faded by time, and the skeletons of dinosaurs that I had learnt the names of when I was so young that I couldn't yet tell the time or ride a bike. A giant sloth stood at the entrance to our Earth sciences department.

After seven months at the museum, the first – and only – scientific paper I co-authored was published: 'Early development of rostrum saw-teeth in a fossil ray tests classical theories of the evolution of vertebrate dentitions.' Quite a mouthful. Peer-reviewed research is the bedrock of science, but I didn't think much of my contribution. Although I had worked hard – writing sections of the study, analysing the CT-scan data, and creating digital schematics of our theories – I didn't think my name should grace the paper. Any positivity in my life didn't seem to sink in. I wasn't worthy. Like the fossils that I studied, I felt delicate and brittle, capable of breaking at the slightest drop.

A few months later, I was sitting in my supervisor's first-floor office, ancient fish fossils, cardboard boxes, and paleontological journals covering every surface. She was a prolific writer, a respected name in palaeontology. I told her that I was struggling, that I couldn't continue. I began to cry. I thought I was a failure. We agreed that I needed to take some time off. I never returned to academia.

Unemployed and trying to make ends meet as a freelance writer (a hobby that I had started in 2012), my motivation waned and my interest in love and life ceased. My first long-term girlfriend told me that I was depressed and that I needed to talk to a doctor or a therapist. She couldn't support me any more. We broke up soon afterwards and, although I had seen it coming for months, I was devastated. Shortly after, the old farmhouse was finally sold. I felt unwanted, unloved, unmoored: drifting into a dark place that threatened to swallow me whole.

Ever since then, I have sought a deeper understanding of my own experience with depression. Where did our fixation on SSRIs and CBT come from? Are there alternatives that might be better suited to my symptoms? Rather than handing out antidepressants through trial and error, can we predict who is likely to respond to a certain treatment before they are prescribed? Can depression be prevented before it arises? What novel treatments might be available in the future?

As I learnt, my experience is not representative of depression as a whole. Just as I had once studied the diversity of the animal kingdom, I soon discovered a similar diversity of depression, the many shapes and forms it can take, and treatments that I once thought to have been long dead and buried were transformed into modern miracles. What's more, I learnt that the word depression is almost meaningless when viewed from a global perspective. Other idioms of emotional suffering are better suited to this particular form of mental illness. Whether it's known as heart pain or thinking too much, a person's language and culture need to be taken into account before talking therapies can be effective. While I personally sought reassurance that more effective treatments were on the horizon, I found that one of the most important missions for psychiatry is expanding the reach of current therapies to people who have no access to mental healthcare. As well as invention, the treatment of depression depends on investment.

It is hardly surprising that a single diagnosis doesn't capture the reality of depression. It is a product of upbringing, trauma, financial uncertainty, loneliness, diet, behaviour, sedentary lifestyles, neurotransmitters, and genetics that cannot be encapsulated in a word. It can be mild or severe, recurrent or chronic. It can emerge once and never appear again, or it can cast a dark shadow throughout adulthood. Some people sleep too much, others suffer from insomnia. Some eat too much while others shrink toward starvation. Depression can emerge alongside cancer, heart disease, obesity, and diabetes, and can make these diseases more lethal; it is a catalyst of mortality.

But it is also highly treatable. From antidepressants, to talking therapies and electroconvulsive therapy (ECT), to some of the more novel treatments such as exercise, diet, and psychedelic substances, there are a range of options that can lead a large percentage of people back to a healthy state of mind. Current treatments are far from perfect, and some remain unproven, but when faced with such a diverse disorder as depression, it's amazing that there are a range of options that are effective. 'We should be aiming towards complete remission for everyone with depression,' says Vikram Patel, professor of global mental health at Harvard Medical School. 'The problem is that these treatments are seen as competing with each other, which is not the case.' They work for different severities or symptoms of depression. Even the most debilitating forms of depression, mental disorders that come with high risk of suicide and crippling delusions of guilt, can be treated within a few weeks. For people who have failed to respond to every type of treatment available, experimental methods such as deep brain stimulation have the potential to lift decades of suffering in seconds.

Another problem is that current treatments aren't always used correctly. Talking therapies are often restricted to four or five sessions that can be insufficient when dealing with the deep-set complexities of depression. Antidepressants aren't given at the right dose or for a long enough course. A healthy diet and exercise can be as effective as SSRIs and CBT but aren't prescribed alongside these first-line treatments. And many psychiatrists are no longer trained to provide electroconvulsive therapy, a potentially life-saving treatment that has been used for decades. History teaches us to learn from our mistakes, but it also reminds us not to leave our successes behind.

Although I feel comfortable talking about my experience with depression, there is still a lot of stigma and misinformation about the treatments that are available. If you see a therapist, you are weak, unable to cope with the stresses and strains of everyday life. If you take antidepressants, you're a machine with broken parts. Even if ECT saved your life, you can't discuss – never mind celebrate – the reason for your recovery for fear of being judged, or, worse, abused and bullied. All treatments have the potential to do more harm than good, but each one has to be seen as a balance between the potential benefits and the risk of side effects. Does the pain of depression or the chance of suicide make any side effects relatively unimportant? Treatments also have to be seen in the context of history: why were they initially developed, what other options were available, and how have they evolved over time? When seen through this temporal prism, stigma can vanish, and treatments that were once seen as barbaric can be welcomed back into medical practice.

When I first started writing this book in the summer of 2017, I was torn about where it should start. Should I allow history to unfold from the dawn of medicine and move forward – century by century – into the modern age? While this would be a logical structure, I thought that it didn't capture the essence of the story I wanted to tell. Instead, before travelling back into Ancient Greece and the booming civilisations of Mesopotamia, it seemed more appropriate to begin with two figures who have shaped modern psychiatry. Born three months apart in 1856, Emil Kraepelin and Sigmund Freud would come to embody two opposing fields in the treatment of depression. Was it a biological disease in need of physical treatments such as surgery, electrical stimulation, or drugs? Or was it an illness of environmental influences – upbringing, trauma, social bonds – that was in need of psychological therapy? From antidepressants to CBT, and from ECT to psychoanalysis, the work of these two patriarchal figures in psychiatry flows through this history like two rivers feeding into the same ocean. Often kept separate but occasionally crossing paths, the biological and the psychological themes of depression have formed the basis of my own treatment since I first walked into my doctor's office in south London in 2015, four years before I decided to withdraw from sertraline.

PART ONE

Cutting Steps into the Mountain

'The day will come, where and when we know not, when every little piece of knowledge will be converted into power, and into therapeutic power.'

Sigmund Freud (1915)

'If a fright or despondency lasts for a long time, it is a melancholic affection.'

Hippocrates

'The time has gone by ... when the unhappy insane could be cast into mismanaged Hospitals and, as too often is the case, left in jails and poor-houses, festering in heaps of filthy straw, chained to the walls of dark and dreary cells ... Much has been done, but more, much more, remains to be accomplished.'

Dorothea Dix (1848)

The Anatomists

Strolling through the port town of Trieste, 19-year-old Sigmund Freud passed women in elegant English dresses carrying small white dogs and smelling of patchouli. The wives of rich merchants, their fragrance and finery were in stark contrast to his study subjects inside the Trieste Zoological Station, a research institute that was 'five seconds from the seashore'. Wrested from the dark recesses of the Adriatic Sea – a thumb-shaped lobe of the Mediterranean between the western coast of Italy and the Balkan Peninsula – the young Freud spent his hours dissecting hundreds of slimy, stinking eels. Mouth agape, eyes glazed in the blank stare of death, and lacking the scales that define other species of fish, it was like slicing through a particularly long, and wholly unappetising, sausage. A fresh-faced student at the University of Vienna, Freud had been given a project that had stumped many great anatomists since Aristotle: did eels have testicles?

In 1874, a couple of years before Freud's student project, another researcher, Simon Syrski, also working in Trieste, had claimed to have found these highly sought-after testes. He called them small 'lobed organs'. Freud, already a confident and gifted researcher, wasn't convinced. In a letter to a childhood friend, he wrote, 'Recently a Trieste zoologist claimed to have discovered the testicles, and hence the male eel, but since he apparently doesn't know what a microscope is, he failed to provide an accurate description of them.' Freud certainly knew what a microscope was and, during his time on the Adriatic coast, honed his skills even further as he subjected a total of 400 dead eels to intense scrutiny, his hands 'stained from the white and red blood of the sea creatures'. Later in life, Freud's intense gaze would become a trademark – along with circular spectacles, cigars, and a rug-covered chaise longue – that could penetrate deep into the soul of any interlocutor.

Sat at his workbench with a view over the seashore, he couldn't penetrate the mystery of eel testicles, however. The life of an eel was far more secretive and mysterious than he, or any other scientist, could have dreamed of. Although found in rivers and streams across Europe, *Anguila anguila* reproduce en masse somewhere in the Sargasso Sea, a 3,000-mile migration that crosses the boundary of freshwater and saltwater, the Mediterranean, and passes over the Mid-Atlantic Ridge. As they journey to this communal tryst males develop their testes, just as deer and elk only grow antlers before their seasonal combat. For the rest of their lives, they don't need them or have them. Freud was looking for something that, at that specific time and place, didn't exist.

Although he had failed in his task, Freud shouldn't have been too hard on himself. Even with modern science's ability to 'see' the inner components of an atom (such as the Higgs boson) or detect the subtle vibrations from the collision of black holes billions of lightyears away in space, the minutiae of eel reproduction still remain uncovered. Although small eel larvae have been found in the Sargasso Sea, no one has observed their courtship rituals. Eel sex has held onto some of its most intimate secrets that have been millions of years in the making.

Disgruntled, disappointed, and questioning his future as an anatomist, Freud returned to the city of Vienna, the so-called 'Mecca for Medicine', and probably never looked at eels the same way again. They were a delicacy to some – delicious when baked in a pie. To him, however, they were nothing but a reminder of failure. Having excelled at school and university (often at the top of his class), learnt seven languages in addition to his native German, and read Shakespeare from the age of eight, it must have been an unfamiliar feeling. But his time in Trieste wasn't a complete waste. Freud had honed his skills as an observer, a scientist: someone who reaches into the unknown and hopes to bring back something new.

The cosmopolitan city of Vienna was an exhilarating place to be for a young scientist. And nowhere was this more the case than in Ernst Brücke's physiology department. Before they were cleared away for lectures, table tops were covered in devices for the measurement of physics and chemistry: 'kymographs, a myograph, compasses, ophthalmometers, scales, air-pumps, induction apparatus, spirometers and gasometers formed the normal equipment of an institute in which all rooms were dominated by Galileo's command: to weigh all that was weighable and to measure all that was measurable,' wrote the historian Erna Lesky in her book *The Vienna Medical School of the 19th Century*. '[T]he work,' she added, 'even in deprived conditions, attracted students of all nationalities.' People from Germany, Hungary, Russia, Romania, Slovakia, the Czech Republic, Greece, and even the United States came here to study, all speaking in different tongues and accents but still communicating their latest discoveries in science.

Away from the lens of a microscope, however, Vienna was a relatively unpleasant place to live. For much of the nineteenth century, it was an overcrowded city with shortages in housing and where sewage flowed uncovered. At high tide, the River Vienna – a tributary of the Danube that flows through the capital cities of Hungary, Serbia, and Romania – would overflow, forcing filthy water into the streets. Infectious diseases such as

tuberculosis spread quickly and easily. Although an aqueduct
had been built when Freud was a university student, the city
was still in need of a good clean. The heavy traffic of horse-
drawn carts and trams chipped away at the roads and kerbs like
stone mills through wheat grains, emitting a fine dust of granite into the air and residents' lungs. 'In the streets, in the
squares, in the public buildings, everywhere we can smell and
breathe in quantities of dust, garbage, and discharged gas,' one
researcher at the University of Vienna wrote. While England
had introduced a Nuisances Disposal Act as early as 1846,
Vienna had no such progressive public-health legislation.

Pollutants weren't just in the air and water: anti-Semitism
cast a dark shadow over the crowded city. As one author later
wrote, the discrimination against Jews was like 'an evil-smelling
vine that twined about the whole social structure of Vienna,
choking so many green hopes to death'. Freud had zero tolerance for anyone who might insult his Jewish heritage, and it
was a constant battle, one that made him want to pack up his
things and leave town for good. He dreamt of England, the
place where his stepbrother had settled when he was a child.
He imagined that discrimination wasn't as prevalent there as it
was in Germany or Austria, that England was a country where
a Jew could walk down the street and not have his hat flung
into the gutter.

Long before he created the field of psychoanalysis, Sigmund
Freud's primary tool of observation was the table-top microscope. Crafted from brass and steel with a horseshoe-shaped
stand, the microscopes built by Edmund Hartnack in Paris
were his particular favourite. With a mirror to reflect sunlight, a few corrugated knobs to focus the sample into view,
and the all-important curved lens that looks down onto the

microscope's stage like a telescope points towards the stars, anatomists like Freud could zoom into previously unseen worlds. It was a cornerstone of scientific enquiry – and of psychiatry – in the late nineteenth century. Freud spent most of his waking hours looking at slices of life blown up to 300 or 500 times their normal size. After his time in Trieste, he worked in Brücke's physiology laboratory on the outskirts of Vienna. It was a cramped room in a building once used as a rifle factory and, before that, a stable. It was here that Freud moved from eel testicles to the nervous system of fish, crustaceans, and humans.

It sometimes felt like he was looking back in time. The delicate nerves of animals were like spindly road maps into our ancient ancestry. Whether he was peering down at the stained nerve cells of river crayfish, sea lampreys, or brain samples from human cadavers, they all showed a remarkable consistency in form. '[N]othing else than spinal ganglion cells,' Freud laconically wrote of his fish samples. Although different shapes and sizes, they shared ancient anatomical threads, and he could see them when he looked closely enough.

Next to his bronze microscope were sheets of paper and a sharp pencil. At this time before microphotography, anatomical drawings were the only means of conveying what one saw down the microscope, providing the basis of science communication between peers and colleagues. Freud was particularly talented at translating his observations. In his study of crayfish, for example, one writer admiringly states that 'the cell bodies [are] shaded so carefully that they appear three-dimensional, alive, alien eyeballs bobbing in space'. Art, science, and a sense of awe merged on the page in front of him.

Keen observation, detailed translation, patience: these were qualities that would remain with Freud through the twists and turns of a long career. Another was revealing the unseen, making the invisible visible.

Nerves, the individual units of nervous systems, are delicate and often invisible to the human eye. They are also the same colour as the tissue that surrounds them. In short, they stick out as much as brown rivers surrounded by mud. Freud developed his own method of tissue staining – known as his 'golden stain' for its use of gold chloride not its colour – that not only kept the delicate nerves intact but made them observable under the microscope. '[B]y this this method,' Freud wrote, 'the fibres are made to show in pink, deep purple, blue or even black, and are brought distinctly into view ... it is believed that it will prove of great service in the study of nerve tracts.' After viewing Freud's tissue slices under the microscope, Brücke, a balding man with wispy whiskers over his pale cheeks, was impressed. 'I see your methods alone will make you famous yet,' he said.

Despite his hopes for its dissemination and success, Freud's golden stain didn't make it far beyond the walls of the laboratory in Vienna. Ten years previous, Camillo Golgi, an Italian anatomist and future Nobel laureate, had developed a silver-based stain that was far simpler and, therefore, more popular. Freud had come so close to a scientific discovery that he could almost reach out and touch it. Unfortunately, it wouldn't be the last time. Near-discoveries would be a leitmotif of Freud's early career. In 1884, for example, he came excruciatingly close to the theory that nerves weren't interconnected like a huge net within the body but were separated by tiny gaps. As he wrote, 'the nerve cell becomes the "beginning" of all those nerve fibres anatomically connected with it,' and then 'the nerve as a *unit* conducts the excitation, and so on.' A few years later, Ramon y Cajal, a neuroanatomist in Barcelona, would publish his foundational theory that stated each nerve was a separate unit – a 'neuron' – separated by a space called the synapse, thus ushering in a new era of neuroscience. Both Camillo Golgi and Ramon y Cajal would share a Nobel Prize in 1906 for their research 'in recognition of their work on the structure of the nervous system'. In his publications, Cajal cited Freud's work.

Fame often comes with fortune, and Freud desperately needed some money. Ever since he was a child growing up in Leopoldstadt, the northeastern district of Vienna that attracted Jewish immigrants from across Europe, he was accustomed to an impecunious way of life. As a young adult, however, he had grown tired of not knowing whether his parents and his seven younger siblings were going to go hungry from one day to the next. He sent them some cash when he could afford to and splurged any remainder on his two luxuries in life: books and cigars. He regularly borrowed money from his colleague, friend, and member of the Viennese aristocracy, Josef Breuer, someone who was, thankfully, willing to support him when he could. With each gulden spent, Freud sunk deeper into debt. As he once wrote in his characteristically sarcastic manner, 'It increases my self-respect to see how much I am worth to anyone.' Even with Breuer's donations, the stains on young Freud's suit remained unchallenged, and his diet of corned beef, cheese, and bread unchanged. He sought a scientific discovery not only for his personal curiosity as a scientist but for the money it might bring him.

Freud's frustrations with money reached a tipping point in 1882, the year he turned 26 years old and fell in love with Martha Bernays, a close friend of his sisters. Two months after their first meeting in his family home, Freud and Martha were engaged. But he couldn't afford a wedding. Miserably, he couldn't even afford the two-day train journey from Vienna to

Wandsbek in Hamburg, the town that Martha had recently moved to with her mother. The first four years of their relationship unfolded underneath their pens. In a world where telephones weren't yet a regular feature in the home, the young couple wrote letters to each other nearly every day. Freud used scraps of paper, pages torn from his lab notebook, and old envelopes to express his frustrations over not being with his love and having the chance to kiss. Penniless, all he had to offer was his devotion. 'Do you think you can continue to love me if things go on like this for years: I buried in work and struggling for elusive success, and you lonely and far away?' Freud wrote. 'I think you will have to, Marty, and in return I will love you very much.'

Together with his financial struggles, his long work hours, and the regular undercurrent of anti-Semitism in Vienna, Freud's isolation from his fiancée certainly took its toll on his health. He was frequently struck with bouts of fatigue, irritability, and a crippling low mood. These spells would appear out of the blue and leave him unable to work. 'I have been so caught up in myself, and then I have days on end – they invariably follow one another, it is like a recurring sickness – when my spirits decline for no apparent reason and I tend to get exasperated at the slightest provocation,' he wrote to Martha in January 1884, describing a common experience of depression. 'I just can't stop worrying today.' Lovestruck, he thought that his only cure was to be with Martha. 'I think I can feel happy nowadays only in your presence,' he wrote, 'and I cannot imagine that I shall ever be able to enjoy myself again without you.'

In the nineteenth century, the modern view of depression was taking shape. From the 1860s onwards, the idea of a 'mental depression' was being forged into a standalone diagnosis. Before this, there was a diversity of interchangeable terms – vapours, spleen, hypochondriasis – to describe depressions without delusions of guilt or sin, the kinds that might be seen in the community and not in mental institutions. And then there was melancholia, a word that had initially been used to describe a state of prolonged fright and dejection that was centred on a single delusion. People thought they were dying of an unknown disease, had committed some unforgivable sin, or that the world was about to fall on top of them. But in the wake of the Enlightenment period in Europe, the term melancholia became associated with the idea of poetic insight, of men who were gifted in the arts and sciences for their ruminative pastimes. To be melancholy was to be gifted and damned. Melancholia became a vague term and was almost lost from medical parlance.

By the nineteenth century, there were numerous attempts to replace the term entirely. 'The word melancholia,' the famed French psychiatrist Jean-Ètienne Dominique Esquirol wrote, 'consecrated in popular language to describe the habitual state of sadness affecting some individuals should be left to poets and moralists whose loose expression is not subject to the strictures of medical terminology.' He proposed a new term: lypemania, 'a disease of the brain characterised by delusions which are chronic and fixed on specific topics, absence of fever, and sadness which is often debilitating and overwhelming'. While it became quite popular in some French institutions, lypemania didn't catch on in other European countries and melancholia remained as current as ever. Benjamin Rush, the so-called father of American psychiatry and a signatory of the United States Declaration of Independence, suggested the diagnosis of 'tristimania' (meaning 'sad' and 'madness'), but even his impressive accolades and political clout couldn't budge melancholia from its perch.

While melancholia remained a common description of severe depression in mental institutions, the idea of 'nerves' was sweeping through western communities, blurring the lines between the body and mind. Someone might be anxious, depressed, fatigued. They might be suffering from an inexplicable paralysis of their arm or leg. Their hands might shake, or their sense of smell or sight might temporarily disappear. Everything that was unusual could be explained by a fault in their nervous system, the electrical circuitry of life.

Freud's low moods and irritability were seen as a mental by-product of his nervous system. It was constitutional. But, like any physical ailment, it could also be exacerbated by a person's environment. The fast-paced modern lifestyle, the need to compete in the growing urban centres around the world, was thought to be the main trigger for nervous disorders in men. Freud, and thousands of people like him, felt worn-down and exhausted from within, as if the rush of modernity was abrasive to the delicate innards of the body. For women, meanwhile, caring for sick relatives or educating themselves in matters for which they were supposedly unsuited – science, politics, economics – were at the core of this illness.

The tendency to link emotional distress with the nervous system was particularly common in the middle and upper classes of Europe and the United States. Since it handily replaced looser diagnoses like insanity and madness, it made a visit to mental asylums – historically, places of chains, mistreatment, and disgraced family names – unlikely. Those were places for the melancholic, the raving, and the poor. But with a diagnosis of an unknown nervous disease, people with depression could be seen by a doctor, just like someone who had the flu or a broken leg. Noticing this, the directors and doctors of mental asylums started to rebrand their institutions to keep pace with this surge in socially acceptable patients. Places of insanity became hospitals of 'nerves' and 'nervous diseases'. One asylum in Bendorf, western Germany, for example, changed from a 'Private Institution for the Insane and Idiots' to a 'Private Institution for Brain and Nervous Disease'.

Although there was no evidence that nervous diseases existed, and no microscope powerful enough to bring such maladies into view, this idea still influenced how depression was treated in the nineteenth century. Freud, for example, spent his time resting, indulged in warm baths, and played chess to give his strained nerves time to strengthen. In the United States, such a restful approach was medicalised to extremes.

The so-called 'rest cure' was an unusual mix of spa treatment and torture. Created in Philadelphia by the neurologist and former war-time surgeon Weir Mitchell, it was as excruciating as doing nothing whatsoever. 'At first, and in some cases for four or five weeks, I do not permit the patient to sit up or to sew or write or read, or to use the hands in any active way except to clean the teeth,' Mitchell wrote. 'I arrange to have the bowels and water passed while lying down, and the patient is lifted onto a lounge for an hour in the morning and again at bedtime, and then lifted back again into the newly-made bed.' Coddled beyond compare, the patients were separated from their family and friends, and even their mail was carefully checked and censored. In this therapeutic seclusion, they were fed and cleaned as if they were infants, but they were also subject to strict punishments if they did not acquiesce. Forced feedings, rectal enemas, and even lashings were used. Meals consisted of mutton chops, pints of milk, dozens of eggs, and Mitchell's own recipe for raw-beef soup laced with a few drops of hydrochloric acid to help with digestion. With greater reserves of fat, fragile patients were thought to be bolstered against the damaging effects of their weak nervous systems. To reduce muscle wastage, a mild electric current was applied all over the body. Regular massages helped encourage blood flow.

In the 1880s, Charlotte Perkins Gilman, author and social activist, wrote that her treatment made her spiral 'so near the borderline of utter mental ruin that I could see over'. Her experience inspired *The Yellow Wallpaper*, a harrowing short story published in 1892 in which the female protagonist gradually becomes psychotic within the tight confines of her nursery, often seeing a woman trapped behind prison bars that lay underneath the foul-smelling, off-yellow-coloured wallpaper. A classic that was largely ignored at the time, *The Yellow Wallpaper* is a chilling reflection of Perkins's own experience, and where the rest cure nearly led her.

Virginia Woolf, the British novelist, was equally damning about her rest cure at the fashionable Harley Street doctors in central London. 'I have never spent such a wretched eight months in my life,' she wrote to a friend in 1904. Her husband Leonard Woolf, meanwhile, wrote that her 'doctors had not the slightest idea of the nature of the cause of her mental state ... all they could say was that she was suffering from neurasthenia and that, if she could be induced or compelled to rest and eat and if she could be prevented from committing suicide, she would recover.' The founder of Hull House (an educational community centre for women in northern Chicago) and future Nobel laureate Jane Addams not only criticised the rest cure but questioned its theoretical basis. Her depression wasn't caused by a faulty nervous system, she wrote. And it certainly didn't stem from her literary interests or her pursuit of gender equality. 'She credited her own depression to feeling that she lacked a goal and an appropriate vehicle with which to confront a harsh, unsympathetic – masculine – world,' wrote Susan Poirier, medical historian at the University of Illinois in Chicago. 'What she needed [was] a means of humanitarian action in the political, social, and moral mainstream of the world.' Exactly the opposite, that is, to the domestic 're-education' that depressed women were being subjected to.

Meanwhile, inspired by the rest cure, the 'west cure' was basically a ranching holiday in the badlands of the western states of America. The artist Thomas Eakins, the poet Walt Whitman, and a future president of the United States, Theodore Roosevelt, were all prescribed this masculine getaway. As they herded cattle, rode horses, and slept under the stars at night, they thought it was the best time of their lives.

As with Sigmund Freud in the physiology laboratory of Ernst Brücke, Emil Kraepelin received a standard introduction into psychiatry in the nineteenth century. Working under the genial director of the mental asylum in Munich, Bernhard von Gudden, he was told that insanity was rooted in some physical aberration in brain tissue. The only window into its nature and potential diversity, therefore, was through the lens of a microscope. '[von Gudden] thought that the only entrance into the psychiatric labyrinth could be found by anatomical dissection, and by penetrating into all the fine details of the brain's constructions,' Kraepelin wrote. Not only did von Gudden advocate brain anatomy over all else, he invented one of the major tools that made it possible: a coffee-table-like machine that would become known as the 'von Gudden microtome'. After placing the brain sample in a hollow tube in the centre of the table, the researcher guided a blade neatly over its upper surface, tightening a screw underneath the table to push the specimen upwards before each cut. It was not too dissimilar to a butcher slicing through a chunk of cooked ham.

The ability to neatly slice through a squishy specimen such as the brain was a breakthrough. '[I]n eight days almost an entire rabbit brain can be sectioned and beautifully stained,' von Gudden wrote, 'something that twenty years ago I would have not considered possible; our knowledge will now be potentiated.' While other students were given birds, moles, or fish to understand the basics of brain anatomy, Kraepelin was handed the brains of reptiles. Could these simplified models help reveal some of the fundamental elements of our own anatomy? Kraepelin would never know. He didn't care how quickly or finely someone could slice up a brain like salami, or how beautiful the staining techniques were; he did not believe these methods would reveal the root causes of mental disorders in his lifetime. He didn't publish any studies on neuropathology, not one paper on reptile brains.

Although he lacked enthusiasm for this particular project, Kraepelin didn't disagree with his supervisor. He also believed that mental disorders were a psychological response to changes in brain tissue. Like von Gudden and the majority of nineteenth-century psychiatrists, he was a biologist at heart. He just thought that this scientific pursuit was a little premature in an era when microscopes were still rudimentary and a microtome table was seen as a sensation. 'With the means available,' Kraepelin later wrote, 'it was almost completely impossible to identify changes caused by disease processes.' Plus, he had poor eyesight, and looking down a microscope to tease apart subtle differences in brain matter was unlikely to be fruitful.

Moving from Munich to the University of Leipzig, from the south of Germany to the north, Kraepelin discovered a different way to reveal hidden mental processes. In 1881, sat at his wooden desk in the experimental laboratory of the famed psychologist Wilhelm Wundt, he started drinking, injecting, and inhaling different drugs, hoping that they would each provide a new view into the mind. 'In spite of the Spartan simplicity of the furnishings an industrious scientific life and great enthusiasm ... reigned in these rooms,' Kraepelin wrote.

A short, stocky man with a yellowish complexion and a thick Van Dyke beard, Kraepelin's primary tool was alcohol. Diluting laboratory-grade ethanol in water, he made foul-tasting cocktails of precise strengths and drank every drop. Although he added a dollop of raspberry syrup to the cocktail, watching as the clear liquid swirled into pink, there was no masking the burning sensation of pure ethanol. As bad as it tasted, Kraepelin was excited to start his latest experiment. With the help of a colleague, he tested his reaction times, his short-term memory, and the speed at which he could read basic German literature, each result recorded by a wooden, clock-like timer on the tabletop that could stop time to the millisecond.

It didn't take long for his response times to lengthen. He became more forgetful. Reading took longer and he struggled to keep still. He was getting drunk – intoxicated for science.

In total, Kraepelin managed to persuade 14 volunteers to drink the same awful mixture but in slightly different concentrations. Some were more alcoholic than others. With these simple variables, Kraepelin concluded that 'higher doses caused an earlier onset and more extended occurrence of impairment'. It was a simple equation: more booze equals drunker for longer. This had been known for centuries, ever since early civilisations had discovered the wonders of fermentation, but experiments like these had never been conducted before. As an attempt to isolate the effect of alcohol from the basic action of drinking, Kraepelin also gave some volunteers carbonated water as a control. He was using an early equivalent of a placebo. No one had created such a standardised method to quantify and, importantly, compare inebriation.

His work wasn't limited to alcohol. Using the same measures of response times, Kraepelin tested caffeine in tea, tobacco in cigarettes, and more medicinal drugs such as morphine and ethyl ether, a potent tranquilliser. Without exception, he was the first test subject. Only after his own 'safety' test did he request help from volunteers. All but one drug passed the test. An injection of morphine, he found, was both unpleasant and potentially dangerous: 'I personally tolerated it so badly that proper experimenting was completely impossible in my case. And the danger of developing morphinism [addiction to morphine] precluded me from persuading other people.' Tea, on the other hand, was a much more pleasant experience for everyone involved. In this experiment, rather than slowing his volunteers' reactions, like alcohol, the caffeine in the tea heightened them. 'There was a clear and longer lasting facilitation of sensory and intellectual processes,' wrote Kraepelin. People were focused, more responsive. Plus, too much tea only led to an edgy restlessness and a headache.

Basic in formula, Kraepelin's work held enormous potential. With such systematic and accurate observations, he hoped that his research would begin to align psychology – the study of how the mind works – with the serious and respected disciplines of the natural sciences, such as chemistry and physics, fields rooted in measurements, quantification, theories that could be tested in the laboratory with experiments. Just as chemistry was built on concentrations, catalysts, and changes over time, Kraepelin wanted to make the study of the mind more scientific. By introducing healthy volunteers to a single variable – alcohol, for example – he sought to under-stand how everyday consciousness responds to a change in the environment.

Working at a time when German was the language of sci-ence, he had high hopes for success. 'We felt that we were trailblazers entering virgin territory,' Kraepelin wrote about himself and his supervisor Wundt, 'creators of a science with undreamt-of prospects.' He named this new science 'pharmaco-psychology', a definition that reflected his focus on how drugs (pharmacology) could influence the mind (psychology). His work was one of the earliest roots of Big Pharma and the drugs – such as antidepressants and tranquillisers – that revolution-ised mental healthcare in the wake of the Second World War. Although the methods have changed over the decades, the same principles are found in Kraepelin's experiments and con-temporary pharmacological research: placebo controls, precise concentrations (doses) of drugs, and the repeated observations of behavioural changes over time.

Although his experiments were certainly scientific, Kraepe-lin knew that they fell well short of a robust science. His sample sizes were too small. Just over a dozen people drinking alcoholic cocktails isn't going to be representative of every-one. Age, sex, and current drinking habits could all influence the end result. To account for such inevitable variability, large sample sizes were needed. Although Kraepelin would con-tinue to add to his datasets for the next ten years – working from three different cities in two countries – he never felt like he achieved his initial hopes for his new science. Indeed, Wundt didn't even mention his experiments in a comprehen-sive review of his laboratory's contributions to psychology, written in 1910. This part of his life – these primordial stages of psychopharmacology – is considered insignificant compared to his major contribution to the study of the mind and mental disorders. Kraepelin found his true calling when he moved from the labratory to the bedside of mentally ill patients, from psychology to clinical psychiatry. With the same penchant for precision and systematic observation, he would start to create a grand classification system on which the field of modern psychiatry would be built.

The origins of this work began in the Easter holidays of 1883. Over three weeks, Kraepelin sat down to compile a text-book on the current state of psychiatry. Though he was hesitant to write anything at first (it was Wundt's idea), his *Compendium of Psychiatry* provided a creative outlet for his experimental observations and, he hoped, would bring in some much-needed money for a young researcher. In its 300 pages, Kraepelin expressed his frustration with the current state of psychiatry, how a student such as himself could become so quickly dissatisfied with the anatomical approach and the embarrassing lack of effective treatments. In Munich and else-where, he felt helpless when treating the 'confusing mass' of mental illness that he saw daily. Litres of alcohol were used as both a stimulant and a sedative, a balm for the manic and the depressed. Over the years, Kraepelin's *Compendium* would grow in size and popularity, becoming the go-to guide of clini-cal psychiatry for generations to come. With flowing prose and case studies that sometimes read like science fiction, he slowly revealed the alien worlds of the mentally ill.

Über Coca

Sigmund Freud sat in an overcrowded laboratory, looking down at his latest staining experiment, and mused over his own weakened nervous system. If only he could see what a weakened nervous system looked like, understand its biology in detail. Would he then be able to find a way to make it stronger? Might he reverse his nervous spells? In 1884, he believed he had found a solution: chemistry. Freud read that a military doctor had given his troop of fatigued soldiers a new drug that quickly restored their stamina. A white powder that dissolved easily into water, this drug was called cocaine. 'A German has tested this stuff on soldiers and reported that it has really rendered them strong and capable of endurance,' Freud wrote to Martha in April 1884. 'Perhaps others are working at it; perhaps nothing will come of it. But I shall certainly try it, and you know that when one perseveres, sooner or later one succeeds. We do not need more than one such lucky hit to be able to think of setting up house.'

As he moved from Brücke's laboratory to the adjacent medical hospital, from tissue specimens to sick patients, Freud saw cocaine as a significant side project, one that had the potential to bring him fame and fortune while also easing his mental troubles. If it could increase the endurance of soldiers, could it reverse his fatigue and low mood? If his name was associated with a medical discovery, would that mean regular royalties and scientific renown? Although it is well known to be a dangerous and addictive drug today, cocaine was a relatively new addition to the pharmaceutical arsenal of the nineteenth century. Not much was known about it other than it had some stimulating qualities. Many pharmacologists thought that it was very similar to the caffeine in tea.

Purchasing his first batch of the drug from the German pharmaceutical company Merck, Freud dissolved one part cocaine to ten parts water and drank the viscous solution. The first sensation was the taste: floral and not at all unpleasant. His lips then felt furry and numb. A sensation of heat spread through his skull just as a shot of whisky warms the heart. Lightheaded and dizzy, he felt a rush of energy, a feeling of activity and purpose. It was stimulating, refreshing, and restorative. 'In my last severe depression I took coca again and a small dose lifted me to the heights in a wonderful fashion,' Freud wrote to Martha on 2 June 1884. 'I am just now busy collecting the literature for a song of praise to this magical substance.' Given access to a colleague's well-stocked library in Vienna, Freud read every book he could on the topic of cocaine, from its historical significance to its burgeoning use in Western medicine.

A month later, rain was pouring outside Freud's bedroom window as his comprehensive review 'Über Coca' was published. Over two dozen pages, he wrote with excitement and adoration about this 'treasure of the natives'. The leaves of E. coca, Freud noted, had been chewed by Native Americans for centuries. According to Peruvian mythology, the coca leaf was a gift from the sun god to the rising Incan Empire. Generations of people in South and Central America were strengthened against long walks in the pursuit of prey, fruiting trees, or new territory. With coca in the mouth, mountains became molehills. Days without food generated no pangs of hunger. Even in death, coca leaves were placed in the mouth to help the deceased journey into the afterlife. 'It was inevitable that a plant which had achieved such a reputation for marvellous effects in its country of origin should have been used to treat the most varied disorders and illnesses of the human body,' Freud wrote.

In 1860, a young graduate student working in the university town of Göttingen isolated a single molecule from the oval-shaped leaves of *E. coca*. Cocaine was just one among many compounds that might have held some medicinal properties of the whole leaf, but it was the one with the most obvious effects. In the blink of an eye, thousands of years of cultural traditions were boiled down to a crystalline white powder.

In addition to exhaustion and fatigue, Freud noted that cocaine had been used in the treatment of digestive disorders, addiction to alcohol and morphine, asthma, diabetes, and was also used as an aphrodisiac. As the pharmaceutical company Parke, Davis, & Co. reported, 'An enumeration of the diseases in which coca and cocaine have been found of service would include a category of almost all the maladies the flesh is heir to.' In addition to Freud's own limited experience, people with severe melancholia were shown to benefit from this new drug. Patients who had been unresponsive for weeks or months, held down in a depressive stupor, started talking again. Jerome Bauduy, a professor of diseases of the mind at Missouri Medical College, said that he 'frequently witnessed the morose, silent, taciturn patient, a prey to the most profound grief or sadness, recover his normal self, begin to talk about his case and wonder how he could have ever experienced such gloomy ideas'. Four minutes after an injection of cocaine, a 17-year-old boy referred to as 'W.H.' from St. Vincent's Hospital in St. Louis, Missouri, started to openly discuss his troubles with his doctor. 'Cocaine changed the scene as if by magic,' one witness wrote.

Freud thought that such 'magic' should be found inside pharmaceutical cabinets around the world. Nearly a year after his first taste of cocaine, he had a rare opportunity to make this into a reality. Smartly dressed, with his beard trimmed and hair slicked into a perfect parting, he stood before a meeting of the Vienna Psychiatric Society. Some of the best medical minds in the city – perhaps in the whole of Europe – were there, watching. Eloquent but exposed, Freud was like an insignificant specimen placed underneath the lens of his tabletop microscope. He told his audience about cocaine, a substance that, he thought, they urgently needed. 'Psychiatry is rich in drugs that can subdue over-stimulated nervous activity,' he said, 'but deficient in agents that can heighten the performance of the depressed nervous system. It is natural, therefore, that we should think of making use of the effects of cocaine.' His underlying message was simple, if a little muddied by medical jargon: there are sedatives to calm the manic or violent patient, but nothing for those who are depressed. Although the term wouldn't be used for another 70 years or so, Freud was offering psychiatry the first antidepressant.

A popular and oft-used portrait of Freud shows a besuited, grey-haired man with one arm held akimbo while his free hand cradles a thick brown cigar. His thick white beard surrounds a straight-lipped mouth, while his famously dark eyes seem to peer out of the photo, out of history, and deep into the thoughts and feelings of whoever meets his gaze. He is an unmistakably acute observer of the human condition. Although it is a static image, a single frame from one of the many photo shoots his son-in-law provided over his lifetime, it nonetheless captures the confidence and nonchalant demeanour of a paternal figure of psychiatry. Along with a pair of circular glasses and a rug-covered chaise longue, this is the image of Freud that would become instantly recognisable as the creator of psychoanalysis, a field of dreams, repressed memories, and the unconscious.

The name Sigmund Freud is so closely aligned with psycho-analysis – like Santa Claus and Christmas – that it is easy to forget that he was a biologist for much of his early adulthood. During his years at the University of Vienna and his medical training at Vienna General Hospital, there was little if any dis-cussion of the unconscious, no interpretation of dreams, and the Oedipus complex – the theory that young boys are sexually attracted to their mothers and repress their innate desire to kill, and usurp, their fathers – would have sounded bizarre even to Freud himself. He published his first article on psycho-analysis in 1896 when he was 40 years old, and only became widely known for this work 20 or so years later when he was in his 60s.

There wasn't a neat division between one career path and the other. There was no T-junction at which Freud turned away from medical science and towards psychoanalysis. It was a gradual process dictated by chance encounters. His first step away from anatomy and cocaine took place outside of Vienna in 1885, the year he was awarded a research grant to study in Paris. It was probably the most important break of his life, a trip that would open a whole new world of opportunity in the treatment of psychiatric diseases.

It was a far cry from the physical-chemical teachings of his former tutor, Ernst Brücke. In Paris, doctors studied and employed hypnosis, a mesmeric method of therapy that was closer to magic than the microscopes other psychiatrists used on a daily basis. Drinking cocaine to calm his insecurities over his rudimentary French, Freud was placed under the wing of Jean-Martin Charcot, a man who he later described as 'one of the greatest physicians' he knew and a 'genius'. '[He] simply uproots my views and intentions,' Freud wrote. 'After some lectures I walk away as from Notre Dame, with a new perception of perfection.' Charcot was a solitary figure in the increasingly international world of medical science, one that Freud would soon emulate. His isolation was largely due to his theories on hysteria, a mysterious disorder of convulsions, speech impediments, paralysis, euphoria, hallucinations, and a dizzying array of other symptoms that seemed to defy any logical explanation. The only thing that had been considered gospel was that it was a disorder of women. 'Hysteria' comes from the Greek *hystera*, meaning 'uterus', a hangover from the days when it was thought that this female organ could move around the body like a homegrown parasite, making mischief wherever it settled. First, an arm might stop working. Then speech degrades. Finally, the patient starts seeing things that no one else can.

Confident, thick-skinned, and with a certain Parisian nonchalance, Charcot had the audacity to suggest that men, absent of a uterus, could suffer from hysteria. (He wasn't the first doctor to propose this; the French physician and psychologist Paul Briquet wrote about male hysteria in 1859.) Charcot moved between the physical and psychical realms of medicine, between the brain and mind, at the Salpêtrière Hospital, causing his own mischief as he did so. For six weeks, Freud worked in his pathological laboratory, using his adept microscopy skills to study cerebral paralysis and aphasia (a loss or impairment in speech) in children. But it was his observations on hypnosis and the treatment of hysterical patients that made the biggest impression. As Charcot soothed some of his patients into a trance-like state, he could introduce an idea that would become fixed into their bodies after they came to. If he explained that their arm was paralysed, for example, his patient would 'wake' up and make this into a reality. Their otherwise healthy arm would be paralysed. It was as if, through hypnosis, Charcot had reached into a part of their minds that was usually locked away, a mental safe house of some sort, and managed to place a rogue thought inside before the gates closed with the return of consciousness. Freud was stunned. 'I had the profoundest impression of the possibility that there could be powerful mental processes which nevertheless remained hidden from the consciousness of man,' he wrote. This was known as the unconscious, a place where repressed thoughts, traumatic memories, and the ancestral urges of our species were thought to play out behind bars, a psychical labyrinth locked away from everyday life. The word 'unconscious' predated Freud. He didn't coin the term. But it would nonetheless make him famous.

Moving back to Vienna in February 1886, Freud didn't keep in contact with his French contemporaries. Charcot died a few years later in 1893. Freud held the lessons he had learnt, the things he had seen, close to his chest, shielding them from his medical supervisors and peeking at them when they weren't looking. Theodor Meynert, Freud's guide to psychiatry at Vienna General Hospital, thought that hypnotism 'degrades a human being to a creature without will or reason and only hastens his nervous and mental degeneration ... It induces an artificial form of alienation.' He called its growing use a 'hobby of nonmedical charlatans ... which was not even worth thinking about'. To Meynert, psychiatry was still a branch of anatomy. 'The more psychiatry seeks, and finds, its scientific basis in a deep and finely grained understanding of anatomical structure [of the brain], the more it elevates itself to the status of a science that deals with causes,' he wrote.

Freud would soon be creating his own science, his own hypotheses on the causes of mental disorders.

By the late 1880s, an epidemic of drug addiction was spreading through Europe, and many doctors blamed Sigmund Freud, the passionate and persuasive author of 'Über Coca', for the growing public-health crisis. According to Louis Lewin, a pharmacologist from Berlin, and one of Freud's most vocal critics, cocaine dens of 'unimaginable depravity and filth' had started to coagulate in the recesses of European cities, including his own. 'These unfortunate beings lead a miserable life whose hours are measured by the imperative necessity for a new dose of the drug,' Lewin wrote. 'Those who believe they can enter the temple of happiness through this gate of pleasure purchase their momentary delights at the cost of body and soul. They speedily pass through the gate of unhappiness into the night of the abyss.' Albrecht Erlenmeyer, another leading doctor from Germany, blamed Freud directly for introducing the 'third scourge of humanity', a drug just as damaging as morphine and alcohol.

There had been warning signs from the beginning. After buying his first batch of the drug in April 1884, Freud had sent cocaine packages to his favourite sister Rosa, to Martha, and provided the first few grams that his good friend Ernst von Fleischl-Marxow used in order to wean himself off morphine (a drug he had become dependent on after a painful surgical operation to his thumb). Long into the night, Freud would watch his friend sitting in the bathtub as he injected more and more cocaine into his bloodstream. Freud held firm that he wasn't just substituting one addiction for another but that the cocaine infusions acted like nicotine strips for people trying to quit smoking today. Soon, Fleischl-Marxow was injecting over a gram of cocaine into his body every day, a tremendous amount compared to the twentieth of a gram that Freud occasionally swallowed during his episodes of irritability, fatigue, and depression. Some nights the two doctors were able to discuss exhilarating topics of philosophy and science together. On others, Fleischl-Marxow became delirious in the bathtub and saw white snakes and insects crawling over his skin. Freud had once described his friend as 'a thoroughly excellent person in whom nature and education have combined to do their best'. But this once bright light was starting to fade.

Fleischl-Marxow's hallucinations didn't dent Freud's belief that cocaine could provide some magic to medicine. Still in debt and struggling to make ends meet, he was determined to show that it had a golden future. Stubborn, emotionally explosive, and unmoved by the evidence in front of him, he was beginning to isolate himself from the field that had made him into a promising young anatomist. He was turning his back on science and medicine. In response to his critics in Europe, Freud wrote a short rebuttal entitled 'Craving for and Fear of Cocaine', a title that sounds like an unpublished Hunter S. Thompson novel. It was similarly outlandish. Published in July 1887, Freud stated that only morphine addicts became addicted to cocaine, as a result of an already 'weakened will power'. 'Cocaine has taken no other victims from us, no victims of its own,' he wrote. He decried Albrecht Erlenmeyer's statement that cocaine was the 'third scourge of humanity', while insisting that, for him, after years of drinking his cocaine solutions, the drug still showed no sign of having addictive qualities. 'On the contrary,' Freud wrote, 'more often than I should have liked, an aversion to the drug took place, which caused the discontinuation of its use.' He accepted, however, that not everyone had his agreeable disposition and that the risk of misuse – especially among addicts and those who injected the drug – was greater than that of morphine.

This paper was largely ignored. 'It made no impression on his contemporaries,' wrote Siegfried Bernfeld, an early biographer of Freud. 'The paper was probably judged and discarded as the stubborn reiteration of one who could not admit error frankly.' To everyone but Freud the conclusions were clear: cocaine was no wonder drug for psychiatry, no cure for weak nerves or its concomitant bouts of depression.

Criticised and pushed to the fringes of academia, Freud nevertheless achieved one of his goals in life. On 17 June 1886, after four long years of engagement, he and Martha were married in Wandsbek. 'Freud had at last reached the Haven of happiness that he had yearned for,' wrote his colleague and biographer Ernest Jones. The majority of the money for the ceremony came from Martha's wealthy aunt and uncle. In 1890, the young couple moved into Berggasse 19, a second-floor flat in the northern district of Vienna, where Freud would live and work for the next 48 years. He hung reproductions of Rembrandt's anatomy lesson and Fuseli's nightmare, and covered every surface with ancient artefacts from Greece and Egypt. As a housewarming gift, one of his patients, Madame Benvenisti, bought him a chaise longue, a piece of furniture that would become a centrepiece of his future.

Although he didn't publish any more papers on the drug, Freud continued to drink his cocaine solutions up until the mid 1890s, over a decade of use. He no longer sent packages to friends and family, and he certainly didn't prescribe cocaine injections to his patients. Nevertheless, his interest in this drug still led to one of his most prescient insights into the potential cause of depressive disorders. If a drug could lift a person back into well-being, he reasoned, then the underlying cause of depression must be rooted in some 'unknown central agent, which can be removed chemically'. In the late nineteenth century, before anyone knew about the existence of neuro-transmitters in the brain, before any antidepressant had been put into prescription, Freud was flirting with a theory of depression that wouldn't gain traction for another 80 years or so. As he dove deeper into more psychological matters – away from the fine neurons of the brain and into the strata of the mind – Freud never truly lost his faith in drug therapy, even as Emil Kraepelin became the figurehead for biological psychiatry, the field that saw depression as a bodily disease in need of physical treatments.

'Psychiatry's Linnaeus'

Kraepelin had dreamt of becoming a professor of psychiatry by the time he was 30 years old. And he achieved it – just. Thanks to his psychological experiments and the unexpected popularity of his *Compendium of Psychiatry*, he had moved from Leipzig to become the professor of psychiatry at the University of Dorpat (also known as Tartu) in Estonia in 1886, continuing his experiments into the effects of drugs on the mind. He was greeted at the railway station by a fellow professor from the university and, in a cart drawn by two brown horses, he was taken through town, over the river Embach, to his new home. In contrast to this warm reception, Dorpat was a miserable, isolating place with bitingly cold winters and heavy snowfalls. Kraepelin would later say that it was five years in a 'kind of exile'. 'Going for walks offered little attraction, because the surroundings were monotonous,' he wrote. 'It was not worth going for trips by rail [either], because the trains came so rarely and were slow.' The deaths of his children compounded his misery. In 1890, his third daughter, Vera, died of diphtheria at 18 months. A year later, Hans, his first son, died of sepsis. Out of four births in five years, only Antonise, his second daughter, survived.

To distance himself from grief, Kraepelin buried himself in his work, adding to the textbook he had started in 1883. From its 380 pages, his 'little book', as he called it, would grow into a 3,000-page tome by 1915, each volume dedicated to the memory of his former teacher Bernhard von Gudden, who had mysteriously died – along with the so-called 'Dream King' of Bavaria, Ludwig II – in Lake Starnberg in June 1886.

On 9 November 1890, just as winter started to grip the city of Dorpat in its vice, Kraepelin received an offer of employment from Heidelberg University, an academic hub back in Germany. Would he be interested in becoming the new chair of psychiatry? Kraepelin gratefully accepted and moved in March 1891 with his wife and daughter. It was a huge step forward in his career and provided a healthier lifestyle for his family. 'My wife and I are fine now,' Kraepelin wrote in the autumn, 'the marvellous landscape and the joy of being in Germany again as well as a long vacation have gradually soothed the pain and made us more and more enjoy the great luck of our return from grim fights.' Compared to Dorpat, Heidelberg was more clement in its weather and offered tree-lined walks around an ancient castle and hiking routes over two neighbouring mountains, each as smooth and green as two heads of broccoli.

Heidelberg is a city steeped in philosophy and academia. For much of the eighteenth and nineteenth centuries, famed poets and physicists walked up and down its streets and, particularly, the path – known as Philosophers' Way – that ran behind Kraepelin's house. When not working at the hospital clinic, he would follow in their footsteps with his Great Dane in tow. (The two of them, a short, stocky man and his gangly dog, must have made quite the sight.) 'As long as my professional life allowed, I fled into the fresh air,' he later wrote. In a city known for its unusually tropical climate, he was surrounded by an ordered display of sun-loving plants such as the bulbous-leaved stonecrop, purple flowered ivy-leaved toadflax and the glossy teardrop-shaped leaves of spreading pellitory. Among this botanical backdrop were ruby-tailed wasps, iridescent wild bees, and wall lizards.

As a boy growing up in northern Germany, Kraepelin had walked through the countryside with his older brother Karl, analysing plants according to the classification system of the Swedish botanist Carl Linnaeus. Different leaf shapes, colours, and habitats could identify a single species, each one formalised with two Latin names. A bright explosion of azure petals, for instance, often defined cornflowers (*Centaurea cyanus*), the national flower of Germany. From his earliest days, Kraepelin learnt that even the endless forms of evolution could be put into neat groups. In his 30s, he attempted to furnish psychiatry with a similar system. For his efforts, he would later become known as 'Psychiatry's Linnaeus'.

Kraepelin's days were filled with a diversity of mental disorders at the university clinic. Slowly, judiciously, and with the same respect for accuracy that he had shown in his laboratory experiments, he started to document what he saw on a standardised set of counting cards or *Zählkarte*. Although similar *Zählkarte* had been used in German hospitals for decades, they had never been so treasured by one man before. Rather than taking a snapshot of a patient's symptoms and jumping to conclusions, Kraepelin monitored their progress over months and years. If they were discharged from the hospital, he tried to keep in touch through their doctor or local psychiatric clinic. If they were transferred to another mental asylum, he would take note of where they were going and how he could receive updates of their health. Collectively, his counting cards created a timeline. As new details were added to the original notes, they became an invaluable insight into a patient's unique mental state and how it changed – for better or worse – over time. From his millisecond experiments in the laboratory to the months of his patients' mental illness in the clinic, Kraepelin turned to time as a valuable resource.

After amassing thousands of such cards, Kraepelin would pack up his boxes and travel to his 'place in the country', a villa on the tranquil shores of Lake Maggiore, Italy. Like working on a huge jigsaw puzzle, he was constantly trying new combinations until a pattern seemed to click into place. As one of Kraepelin's colleagues recalled, 'again and again [he] worked through thousands and thousands of his patients' files in order to group and re-group them'. Were there a few core similarities that linked them? Was there a final stage, a terminus, for a common set of symptoms? In short, did they fall into discrete categories based on similarities and differences, just as plants and animals can be sorted into different kingdoms, families, genera, and species?

Meticulous, obsessive, and often frenetic in his desire for new information, Kraepelin soon became convinced that there were two main groups of mental disorder. One group he deemed incurable. He called this disorder 'dementia praecox', a disease of hallucinations and paranoia that would be renamed schizophrenia in 1909. Once diagnosed, usually in adolescence, Kraepelin was sure that it was a downwards slope towards dementia (this is now known not to be the case). The disorder that he frequently saw patients recover from he called 'manic-depressive insanity'. He noted that the first episode arose in young adulthood (before the age of 25), it was more common in women (especially in those who were pregnant or recent mothers), and each bout ran a finite course, often lasting a few months to a year. Although commonly mistaken for the modern diagnosis of bipolar disorder, Kraepelin's term actually represented a collection of states that included depression, mania, and the cyclical disorder that flipped between both these extreme lows and highs of mood. (Bipolar wouldn't be classified as a distinct mood disorder until 1957.) 'During the course of years,' Kraepelin wrote of manic-depressive insanity, 'I have become more and more convinced that all the pictures mentioned are but manifestations of one disease process.'

Manic-depressive insanity, Kraepelin thought, was a disorder primarily of the body. Of all the potential causes, he wrote, 'defective heredity is the most important, occurring in seventy to eighty per cent of cases'. In a time before the discovery of DNA, Kraepelin believed that any traits – even those acquired during a person's lifetime – were passed on from parent to offspring. '[S]o-called psychic causes – unhappy love, business failure, overwork – are the product rather than the cause of the disease,' Kraepelin added. '[T]hey are merely the outward manifestation of a pre-existing condition; their effects depend for the most part on the subject's *Anlage*,' their cellular development and constitution.

As he embraced the biological theory of depression, Kraepelin also practiced elements of counselling. Chatting with his patients at the university clinic in Heidelberg, he learnt about their previous life experiences, when their symptoms first arose, and any problems they were experiencing back home. He advised his depressed patients to live a quiet life, avoid the stress of marriage, and, for those women who were suffering from postnatal depression (a sizeable chunk of his patients), not to have any more children. He believed that all 'sources of emotional disturbance should be avoided, such as the visits of relatives, long conversations, or [the sending or receiving of] letters. Attempts to comfort the patient in the height of the disease seem to be useless,' he added.

Despite his influential contributions to psychiatric theory and classification, Emil Kraepelin isn't a household name like many other historical figures of his field. Unlike Alois Alzheimer or Hans Asperger, there are no diseases that bear his name. Unlike Elisabeth Kübler-Ross (the creator of the five stages of grief), he has no eponymous model of psychological behaviour. He doesn't have anywhere near the global fame of Sigmund Freud. But he was no less influential. Many would argue that he is the most influential of all. 'Modern psychiatry begins with Kraepelin,' one textbook from 1969 states. As two historians wrote in 2015, Kraepelin was 'an icon who helped guide us to the now dominant view of psychiatry that is medical in orientation, diagnostic in focus, and predominantly based on the brain'. His great divide between psychotic disorders and mood disorders still exists today, both in how we diagnose and treat them. Schizophrenia is often kept separate from depression, for instance, one being treated with antipsychotics, the other antidepressants. As the Swiss psychiatrist Eugen Bleuler wrote in 1917, by 'cutting steps in the mountain', Kraepelin created a path for other psychiatrists to climb into the future.

In 1899, however, his importance wasn't in how his work would shape the future but how it had provided a break from the past. First published in the sixth edition of his popular *Psychiatry* textbook, Kraepelin's manic-depressive insanity had succeeded where other terms had failed: he added a vital update to nearly 2,000 years of melancholia.

A Melancholic Humour

Just as the natural world was made up of the four elements earth, fire, air, and water, Hippocrates, the famed philosopher of ancient Greece, thought our bodies were composed of just four basic components. 'The Human body contains blood, phlegm, yellow bile, and black bile,' he wrote in the third century BC. 'Health is primarily that state in which these constituent substances are in the correct proportion to each other, both in strength and quantity, and are well mixed.' Hippocrates viewed the body as a system of fluids, pumps, and valves, like a well-oiled machine, that needed to be kept in check. Too much or too little of one particular fluid – or 'humour' – risked damaging the cogs that maintained this harmony, ratcheting a person away from the smooth ride of health and into a breakdown of disease and disorder. Influenced by the three *doshas* of ancient India, the underlying theory was rooted in balance and imbalance, health and disease.

People with too much phlegm, for example, were resigned to life or 'phlegmatic'. Too much blood imbued a sanguine character. Yellow bile was associated with aggression. Finally, an excess of black bile led to two of the most feared diseases. If it became clogged in the body, it formed cancerous tumours that sent thin tendrils through the body like the spindly legs of a crab. In an unhealthy abundance, meanwhile, black bile led to the desolate and hopeless state known as melancholia.

In ancient Greek, black bile literally translates as *melan khōle*, and there are significant overlaps between this state and the more severe forms of depression known today. In fact, melancholia is still used to describe a state of depression that is generally defined by a key set of symptoms: early morning waking, insomnia, severe weight loss, a sluggishness that borders on physical disability, and delusions of wrongdoing or guilt that are often repeated like a daily confession of sin. This isn't your everyday case of the blues. It is a life-threatening disorder that responds remarkably well to biological treatments such as antidepressants and ECT and has historical roots that reach back to the dawn of medicine.

Aristotle, Plato, Socrates, and Pythagoras: these household names all had an influence on generations of philosophers who tried to explain how the the mind worked in both health and disease. But the most important writer on the topic of melancholia lived in Rome in the first century AD, four centuries after Hippocrates. Claudius Galen of Pergamum started his career as a physician to gladiators. As he patched up their wounds, he also provided individual dietary regimens to keep them at their fighting best. He then moved to Rome and became the personal physician to the emperor Marcus Aurelius and his family. No matter where he settled, he was a prolific writer, reportedly publishing 400 books before he died in AD 200 when he was in his 70s. Most of the ideas weren't his own, however. 'He was a great borrower,' Franz Alexander and Sheldon Selesnick write in their 1966 book *The History of Psychiatry*. 'He plagiarized, synthesized, embellished, and copied. The perpetuation of his influence was due to his staunch advocacy of Hippocrates and his acceptance of a Creator to whom he frequently dedicated his works. Christianity in the Dark Ages could find no exception to Galenic monotheism.' As religion became the ultimate truth in place of medical science in the Middle Ages, Galen's works were seen as gospel for 1,500 years of Western thought.

What is left of his medical writings (or their translations) shows that Galen thought that melancholia wasn't a single disease. There were at least three types of melancholia that could be classified according to their symptoms and presumed location in the body. First, there was the imbalance of black bile within the blood. Second, a condition in which the black bile had poisoned the brain. And third, a gut-based disease that he called 'melancholia hypochondriaca' that was associated with flatulence and stomach pains, constipation and indigestion. This was also called the 'gassy disease'. As future scientists would discover for themselves, the link between the brain and the gut, particularly when discussing depression, is a vital one.

Galen knew that different diseases require different treatments. For his blood-based melancholia, he aimed to reduce the amount of black bile in a person's body by draining some of their blood. By cutting a vein on the inside of the elbow joint, Galen hoped that such bloodletting would bring his patients back to reason, even those cases in which the black bile had poisoned their brain. In a world without antibiotics, sterile practices, or any knowledge of bacteria or viruses, this was a very dangerous approach. Any cut could be fatal, every blade a potential vehicle for infection.

In cases of the gassy disease, however, bloodletting wasn't suitable. In fact, Galen actively argued against its use. Instead, he recommended herbal remedies, such as black hellebore, that induced vomiting, or emetics that helped flush the disease from both orifices. As he purged his patients, Galen also advised them on what they should put back into their bodies. As in Ayurvedic medicine in India, diet was an integral part of every treatment. In particular, the avoidance of foodstuffs that were thought to increase the black bile, or, in Galen's terminology, 'atrabilious blood' in the body. 'I can tell you,' Galen wrote, 'that atrabilious blood is generated by eating the meat of goats and oxen, and still more of he-goats and bulls; even worse is the meat of asses and camels ... as well as the meat of foxes and dogs. Above all, consumption of hares creates the same kind of blood, and more so the flesh of wild boars ... so do all kinds of pickled meat of terrestrial animals, and of the beasts living in the water, it is the tuna fish, the whale, the seal, dolphins, [and] the dog shark.' It wasn't just a meat-based diet that he presumed was problematic, but certain vegetables including cabbage and sprouts, as well as pulses such as lentils. Red wine was a luxury best avoided for those at risk of melancholia.

Galen much preferred dietary changes to bloodletting. But he often found himself torn between the two. Without any reliable markers of the different types of melancholia – blood, brain, or gut – he sometimes wasn't sure which line of treatment would be most suitable. In such cases, he undertook a tentative course of bloodletting at the elbow. 'If the outflowing blood does not appear to be atrabilious, then stop at once,' he wrote in his book *On the Affected Parts*. 'But if the blood seems to be of this kind, then withdraw as much as you deem sufficient in view of the constitution of the patient.' It was as if he could see the dark and gloopy humour drain out of his patients' arms, each atrabilious drop bringing them closer to health and harmony, and away from the dreaded melancholia.

Before the texts of Hippocrates and Galen crumbled into dust like the columns of the Greek and Roman empires, a few Christian missionaries made copies of their rolls of parchment and fled to the booming civilisations of Mesopotamia. Located in the middle of the Silk Roads that connected East to West, countries that are now called Iran, Iraq, Saudi Arabia, Afghanistan, Syria, and Turkey became vital lifelines for modern medicine. The Dark Ages – the medieval period between the fall of Rome in the fifth century and the Enlightenment of the seventeenth – were only dark in western Europe. Although this was an era defined by Islam, it was a bustling fusion of cultures from around the world. Christians and Jews learnt and wrote in Arabic. Cities such as Damascus, Cairo, and Baghdad attracted immigrants from all over the world, if not to stay then to visit and learn from some of the great polymaths that resided in these centres of civilisation.

In AD 849, Abu Zayd al-Balkhi was born in a small village in what is today Afghanistan. Home schooled by his father, he was a precocious child with interests as varied as the culture that surrounded him. As a young adult, he moved to Baghdad and spent eight years researching any topic that was worthy of his attention. During the so-called 'Golden Age of Islam', there was a lot to take in. Shy, introverted, and with a preference for isolation over any form of socialising, Abu Zayd wrote at least 60 books in his lifetime, one of which merged the bodily theories of ancient Greece with psychological treatment. Although he didn't doubt that some depressions came from within, from an imbalance of black bile, say, he also put forward the view that this illness could arise from purely mental processes. Negative thinking was at the heart of this condition. Abu Zayd recognised that how we view and interpret the world can be far more important than the world itself. Our reality can be shaped by our own perception, preconceived expectations, and thought patterns. Something that might be neutral or even slightly positive can be twisted into an experience that was negative and personally detrimental. This 'cognitive theory' of depression would be made famous by Aaron Beck, a psychiatrist working in Philadelphia in the 1960s. Although each came to their theories independently, we can say that Abu Zayd predates this modern treatment by ten centuries. 'No scholar before him had written a medical treatise of this kind,' Malik Badri, a historian and psychologist from Sudan, writes.

In his book *Sustenance of the Soul*, Abu Zayd separated depression into three types. First, there was sadness, a normal reaction to life. Second, there was depression triggered by stressful life events. And third, a form of the illness that was heritable and seemed to be unrelated to external circumstance. In short, Abu Zayd used a classification system that would only become popular during the twentieth century: he saw depression not only as a spectrum from sadness to disease, but that there was a 'reactive' type and an 'endogenous' type. The former was treatable with psychotherapy and guidance to a more positive outlook. The latter was not. Abu Zayd thought that bloodletting was a barbaric treatment and vaguely described a form of 'blood purifying' that may have included dietary changes or herbal remedies.

Although progressive in his thoughts on depression, Abu Zayd was largely ignored in subsequent centuries. His texts were only recently rediscovered. In the 1970s, they were translated into German and, in 2014, into English. Today, you can read a section of *Sustenance of the Soul* on your eReader.

This could have been a very different history if Abu Zayd's works were better known. Bloodletting might have stopped here. Instead, the most influential philosopher working in the city of Baghdad was Ibn Sina or 'Avicenna'. It was his *Canon of Medicine* that cemented the humoral theories of Galen in the Middle East and then transported them back into western Europe. In the eleventh and twelfth centuries, two missionaries, Constantinus Africanus and Gerard of

Cremona, translated this Arabic text into Latin, the language of the Western world.

The works of Avicenna were used as educational tools in medicine for centuries. As his words were passed on and reprinted, they were also merged into the prevailing Western worldview of the time: Christianity. In her twelfth-century *Book of Holistic Healing*, Hildegard of Bingen wrote that black bile was a marker of the original sin, one that stretched right back to Adam in the Garden of Eden. Black bile, she wrote, 'came into being at the very beginning out of Adam's semen through the breath of the serpent since Adam followed his advice about eating the apple'. Melancholia, she added, 'is due to the first attack by the devil on the nature of man since man disobeyed God's command by eating the apple ... it causes depression and doubt in every consolation so that the person can find no joy in heavenly life and no consolation in his earthly existence.'

This mix of theology and medical theory would remain little changed up until the seventeenth century. In his epic treatise *The Anatomy of Melancholy*, Robert Burton added that 'spirit' was also an important determinant of disease. 'Spirit is a most subtle vapour,' he wrote, 'which is expressed from the blood, and the instrument of the soul.' To him, melancholy was a habitual state of sadness that arose from astrological signs, curses from the Gods, and changes in the weather, and could only be cured by simple diet, regular exercise, and mental occupation. 'There can be no better cure than continual business,' Burton wrote, a statement that would soon be brought into a therapeutic reality in mental asylums.

At around this time, in the era of Enlightenment, skilled anatomists had sifted through the fluids and fibres of the human body – sometimes stealing dead criminals from the gallows to use as cadavers – and found no evidence of a gloopy black substance anywhere. Blood, phlegm and yellow bile, yes. But nothing of *melan kholē*. Black bile, a focal point of medical science for so long, didn't exist. As one author wrote in 1643, 'we cannot here yield to what some Physicians affirm, that Melancholy doth arise from a Melancholick humour'.

How did this theory of melancholia endure for so long? For one, the understanding of how the body works was rudimentary in the West. It was only in the seventeenth century that the circulation of blood was starting to be understood, for example. The notion that humans are made up of microscopic cells hadn't yet been proposed. In fact, the first microscopes were only just being invented. Finally, and perhaps most importantly, the human body is awesome in its complexity, and it demands centuries and millennia to understand in detail. Nowhere is this more obvious than depression, a disorder that has an almost comical talent of evading biological definition. Whether it's caused by an imbalance of bile or chemicals in the brain, it has a history of duping those who try and pin it to a unifying theory.

Instruments of Cure

The eighteenth century was the beginning of a seismic social change in the Western world. From 1760 onwards, the industrial revolution fed the sprawl of factories and agriculture, fuelling a population boom. Between 1800 and 1850, for example, the number of people living in Britain doubled, from 10.5 to 21 million. The country was becoming an empire, one forged in the furnace and fed with coal wrested from deep below the earth. Especially in the north of the country, chimney smoke covered the landscape in soot. The black veneer on buildings and trees was so ubiquitous that a species of moth became dominated by its darker form, a 'melanic' mutant that was better camouflaged in this new human-made environment. Known as the peppered moth (*Biston betularia*), those moths that were paler in colour were easily picked off by hungry birds.

With any revolution there are winners and losers; inequality is the norm. While a select few got rich from fossil fuels, millions of workers stayed poor. Anyone strolling through the British cities of the eighteenth century would soon stumble upon the disease, dirt, and depravity that thrived in areas where humans congregate. Poor houses, prisons, and workhouses were places for those who failed to make a living. And with financial troubles, the death of loved ones (either from disease or accidents at work), and a very raw feeling of helplessness, insanity thrived. Mania and melancholia, the violent and the desolate, were the two diagnoses used, as different as chalk and cheese. But, in the growing number of so-called mental asylums, all inpatients were similarly chained and bled.

The non-existence of black bile barely changed the view of melancholia and its treatment. After all, there was nothing better, no alternative explanation. The suggestion of 'animal spirits' or the soul didn't offer anything concrete about the origin or treatment of depression. The terms vapours, hypochondriasis, and spleen were used for states of mental agitation, all still rooted in the notion of black bile being burnt in the spleen and infusing the brain with darkness. Bloodlettings and purging were still part and parcel of many therapeutic regimen. As the superintendent of Bethlem Royal Hospital in London wrote in the eighteenth century, 'that has been the practice invariably for years, long before my time, it was handed down to me by my father, and I do not know any better practice'. People with mental disorders were often chained – sometimes for their own protection – as they bled. Seen as lower animals rather than fellow humans, punishment was viewed a suitable form of therapy. 'Old and young, men and women, the frantic and the melancholy, were treated worse, and more neglected, than the beasts of the field,' one asylum director wrote.

This callous approach to insanity was slowly changing, however; shifting towards methods of psychotherapy, individualised care, leisurely activity, and a healthy diet.

In the walled city of York in the north of England, William Tuke built a cottage-style 'Retreat' that banned physical restraint and replaced it with entertainment, education, and empathetic conversation. A 60-year-old tea merchant, Tuke felt an obligation to create The Retreat after Hannah Mills, a local widow and Quaker, died in suspicious circumstances shortly after being admitted to the Mental Asylum of York. A Quaker himself, he believed that God spoke directly through him and thought that news of Mills's death reached his ears for a reason. He began designing an institution in York that could live up to the word 'asylum'.

One of the first patients to walk over The Retreat's wooden floorboards and gaze upon its flower-filled gardens was Mary Holt. Described as 'low and melancholy', she wasn't chained or bound in a straitjacket. Instead, she was fed a healthy meal three times a day, drank fresh milk from the asylum's cows, and was offered porter or wine with lunch. Her depressed state was met with compassion, and any morbid ideas or delusions were guided, through conversation with her carers, towards more peaceful thoughts. Sewing, knitting, and reading were thought to be suitable occupations for people like Mary. Mathematics and the classics, meanwhile, were touted as the most beneficial literature. As evidenced by The Retreat's bills, opulent delicacies such as oranges and figs were a part of a therapeutic environment that would have seemed completely alien to people who would have once been detained in workhouses, poorhouses, or prisons that dotted the English countryside, sweeping up any vagrants that were sleeping rough on the soot-covered city streets.

A cottage in the middle of nowhere is a strange place for a revolution, but that was indeed the case here. The Retreat was the physical manifestation of what became known as 'moral treatment', a form of care that would spread from northern England and alter centuries of abuse masquerading as medical science. Once seen as beasts only responsive to punishment, the manic and the melancholic started to be treated as humans who were unwell and in need of protection and support.

Born in 1732, William Tuke was a pertinacious man whose life was defined by loss. When he was a child, he fell out of a tree and was trephined – a procedure in which a small disc of bone is cut from the skull – to ease any swelling of his brain. Throughout his life, people would touch this boneless part of his head and feel the soft spring of his scar tissue. Both his parents died when he was an adolescent, and Tuke was raised by his aunt and uncle, Mary and Henry Frankland, who owned a grocery shop. Working as their apprentice, he would soon be given the business after Henry died and Mary, a widow without any children of her own, could no longer look after it. In 1754, when he was in his early 20s, Tuke married Elizabeth Hoyland from Sheffield, a nearby city in northern England. She died giving birth to their fifth child in six years. 'I was on the brink of destruction when my dear wife was taken from me,' Tuke wrote.

Tuke turned to his religion for comfort, always attending the annual meeting of the Society of Friends (the traditional term for Quakers) held in London and even serving as their treasurer for 20 years. Running a tea business while the East India company had a monopoly on the import and distribution of most goods from the British colonies, he was business savvy and money-minded. Thankfully, in the late 1700s, tea drinking was growing in popularity. No longer a pastime of the wealthy, it was quickly becoming an everyday beverage for an entire nation. In 1784, the British government reduced the amount of tax on tea from 100 per cent to 12 per cent. Tuke profited hugely, expanding his business into coffee from Turkey and chocolate from the West Indies.

Dogged in everything he did, Tuke was also hugely empathetic and civil to anyone he met. As one of his patient's poems states:

> What tenderness with strength combined,
> Dwelt in his energetic mind.

Initially limited to local 'Friends', The Retreat at York was soon admitting new residents from as far away as Bristol and Penzance, in southwest England, the opposite side of the country to this new asylum. Travelling by horse and cart, the journey was long and arduous. But upon entering the garden through a row of beech trees and stepping towards a farmhouse in full bloom, it was worth it. For the family member who had accompanied their manic or melancholic kin, it might have seemed like they were dropping them off at a luxury holiday destination with free booze, an island of peace and pleasure where there was once only shackles, seclusion, bloodletting, brutality, and despair.

The Retreat at York was used as a model for dozens of new asylums being planned across the country. Physical restraints were thrown out, and mental asylums in England and across Europe were built with moral treatment in mind. Hanwell Asylum in north London, for example, was filled with the fresh air of optimism. When John Conolly became medical superintendent in 1839, there were 600 instruments of restraint. Iron manacles, leather straps, chains, and locks: he threw them all out. 'Darkness and bonds are, even in [the most] difficult cases, never applied,' he wrote in 1856, 'hasty and reproachful words are forbidden; punishment is a word unknown; and as far as can be done in intervals of calmness, the patient is the object of soothing attentions; whilst during the worst paroxysms of his disorder, he is never abandoned and left to his wretched-ness.' To replace the methods of restraint, Conolly hired a larger troupe of trained nurses and medical attendants, and made sure that isolation was only used for the most dangerous or violent patients. Those with melancholia, now freed from their shackles, were supervised and supported, even through the long dark night if necessary. 'The old prison-air has departed, and asylums have really become ... instruments of cure,' Conolly wrote. 'Not only to the maniacal patient, who comes tied up because he is violent, [but] to the melancholic creature who is also tied and bound, because he desires to end his existence, does the non-restraint system bring deliverance and comfort.'

Once freed from physical restraint, patients were sur-rounded by activities and entertainment. 'Recreation, when it is essentially innocent in its tendency, is so necessary to the preservation of mental health, that it has always formed a part in the treatment pursued in all well conducted asylums,' one medical director wrote in 1844. Backgammon, billiards, and boardgames were available indoors. Outside, there was cricket, kite flying, and other leisurely activities on the gardens' lawns. Musical instruments, literature, and art classes provided a crea-tive outlet for people whose every moment had once been censored and subjugated. The transformation was striking. 'The convalescent wear an expression of the most serene satis-faction,' Conolly wrote, 'and a smile, seldom seen before, plays on the countenance of the melancholic.' Anything to distract these patients from their morbid thoughts was seen as therapeutic.

As with the practices of Galen in Rome, diet was a key ingre-dient of moral treatment. Those melancholics who were admitted into asylums half-starved were initially fed a diet of beef tea and arrowroot. When they could stomach it, they were given three meals a day, the largest for lunch, including healthy portions of meat and vegetables and a few glasses of booze to wash it down. Sherry, brandy, and wine were all seen as suitable tonics. The Stanley Royd Hospital in northwest England brewed its own beer onsite. Instead of emetics or bleedings, rhubarb was often given as a natural laxative that helped ease the constipation often associated with this mental disorder. As with Galen's 'melancholia hypochondrica', the digestive system was seen as a circuitous path towards a cure.

By the early nineteenth century, moral treatment had crossed the Atlantic, and institutions in the United States were designed according to the religious and moral code of The Retreat at York. In 1817, the 'Friends Asylum' was built according to the beliefs of two leading figures of the moral-treatment movement: Thomas Scattergood, a 'mournful prophet' who suffered from frequent bouts of melancholia and visited William Tuke in England, and Benjamin Rush who sought freedom for his mentally ill patients. Inspired by the work of Rush and Scattergood, the social reformer Dorothea Dix helped to spread the values of moral treatment throughout the mental asylums of the United States. After a nervous breakdown in 1836, Dix was treated at the Retreat in York in England and became a living example of the benefits of respect, leisure, light occupation, and a gradual realignment with reason and reality.

Did moral treatment actually work? Were people more likely to recover from melancholia – or mania – if they were treated with generosity and fed a healthy diet? Without chains and enforced punishments, it certainly wouldn't have been detrimental to people's mental health. But it's difficult to know what was responsible for any recovery, especially those that occurred 200 years ago. A healthy diet and entertainment might have helped. Or, alternatively, time spent away from the outside world might have been just what a person needed to break their cycle of depression. Precise conclusions are an impossibility. The one thing that is clear is that depression can resolve on its own given time, a fact that can make any treatment appear to be curative.

As with mania, the depressed and melancholic have long been known to spontaneously recover. (This might be the only time a depressed person can be called spontaneous.) No one knows why or how this happens, just that it does – often. It might take months or years, but a large majority of patients will get better if left alone, even if they spend a long time getting worse beforehand. Like a bout of flu or shifting seasons, depression usually has a finite and cyclical course. This might seem like a good thing, and in many ways it is. But this phenomenon has also provided an accidental platform for abuse. Without controlling for these spontaneous recoveries, many doctors and psychiatrists of yore were tricked into thinking that their methods were effective. Whether they were given the rest cure, bloodletting, purging, or a change in diet, a patient's recovery might have happened anyway, without any intervention whatsoever. Without taking spontaneous recoveries into account, anything could be deemed to have a positive effect.

This does not mean that the treatments used today are a waste of time – far from it. Those months or years with depression can be so inexplicably painful that anything that can reduce their duration is to be lauded. Between 10 to 15 per cent of people with depression die by suicide, a risk that is seven times higher for men than women. And not everyone spontaneously recovers. Chronic depression can be an endless state of despair, especially for the elderly who may be suffering from other diseases such as cancer, diabetes, or dementia. An effective treatment for depression, therefore, can be seen as anything that can shorten the time to recovery. A remission in a few days or a few weeks, for example. Not in a few months or years. This pursuit of early remission is captured by the term 'efficacy', once defined as 'the capability of an agent, demonstrably and measurably, to alter the statistically predictable natural history of the disease'. But in the asylums of Britain and elsewhere, there were few options but to wait and hope that the patient recovered on their own.

In the nineteenth century, the size of mental institutions exploded and left the initial hopes of moral therapy in their ashes. While the average asylum housed just over 100 patients in 1827, this number had risen to more than 1,000 by 1910. 'Our numbers have increased out of all proportion to our accommodation,' one worker at a county asylum in Staffordshire wrote. 'We have 36 males sleeping without beds.' Similar patterns were seen across Europe, in particular in France and Germany. In 1904, a total of 150,000 people were living in mental institutions in the United States. The number of medical attendants didn't increase at the same rate. The ratio of patients to carers became so small that neglect and isolation were commonplace. 'The treatment is humane but it necessarily lacks individuality,' one doctor wrote in the medical journal *The Lancet*, 'and that special character which arises from dealing with a limited number of cases directly.' Even The Retreat at York, a house originally designed for a maximum of 30 patients, was eventually home to over 100. As one patient said, 'to one that has always been used to a small family, this is just like being in a show'.

By the end of the nineteenth century, well-kept gardens and cottage-like buildings were replaced with high fences, long, tree-lined driveways, and brutal architectural design that made for easy surveillance. A central bell tower provided a 360-degree view of the grounds, while long corridors allowed hundreds of patients to be monitored at a glance. A mental institution in Liverpool was famous for a corridor that was over half a kilometre long. Homely asylums with specific diets and entertainment were replaced by cold and monotonous institutions. The food was the same no matter your condition. Medical attendants wore matching uniforms and a jangle of keys hung from their belts, as if they were prison guards.

The future seemed bleak for melancholics and their mentally ill neighbours. With overcrowding only getting worse, the hopes of moral treatment were fading. Plus, there was still no insight from anatomists either. In the 1840s, the German psychiatrist Wilhelm Griesinger had famously proposed that 'patients with so-called "mental illnesses" are really individuals with illnesses of the nerves and the brain', but there had been no breakthroughs to confirm his statement. The autopsies of deceased patients found no brain abnormalities consistent with mania or melancholia. There was no black bile. But there was still nothing to replace it with.

There was one discovery that suggested that this faith in neuroanatomy wasn't misplaced. General paresis, a fatal blend of depression, mania, delusions, and dementia that had been dubbed 'one of the most terrible maladies that can afflict a human', was associated with clear lesions in the brain, small pockmarks where neurons had died. It was as if a tiny but voracious organism had been munching on a patient's soft brain tissue, slowly sending them into madness. The modern name for general paresis is neurosyphilis, a bacterial infection that has reached into the nervous system. (This disease would help to revolutionise biological psychiatry in the early twentieth

A Cure for Darkness

century, leading to the first Nobel Prize awarded to a psychiatrist.)

Melancholia, meanwhile, was still no clearer than it had been in Galen's day. 'Without wishing to discourage younger men from following up this line of work,' George Savage, the medical superintendent from Bethlem Royal Hospital in London and author of the popular 1884 textbook *Insanity and Allied Neuroses*, wrote, '[w]e are groping in the dark for what we do not yet know. There is at present a deep ditch of ignorance between us and the true pathology, and for that matter, physiology of the mind.'

Ten years later, Sigmund Freud had started to craft his own physiology of the mind, a science rooted in strata of the psyche rather than anatomical dissection. At the same time, in Heidelberg, Emil Kraepelin was similarly discouraged by anatomy and would later come to doubt the psychiatric classification that he had created.

The Talking Cure

The field of psychoanalysis wasn't the creation of one man. Biographies and historical accounts have long painted Sigmund Freud as a maverick theoretician who dared to explore topics that others shied away from. That he was a depressed loner in an uncharted world of the human psyche was taken as fact, a testament of his courage and determination in the face of impossible odds. But the first biographers of Freud, Ernest Jones and Siegfried Bernfeld were also his colleagues and close friends. The person in charge of his legacy, his private letters, and his unpublished documents was his daughter Anna Freud, one of the most faithful Freudian psychoanalysts of the twentieth century. In short, the story of psychoanalysis and how it became one of the most popular fields of psychology has long been biased and airbrushed.

As new documents and details have emerged, historians of the twenty-first century have drastically changed the story of how psychoanalysis came to be. 'It can be said that Sigmund Freud did not so much create a revolution in the way men and women understood their inner lives,' George Makari, historian and professor of psychiatry at Weill Cornell Medical College, wrote in his 2008 book *Revolution in Mind*. 'Rather, he took command of revolutions that were already in progress.' As Freud himself wrote to his colleague in Budapest, Sándor Ferenczi, 'I have a decidedly obliging intellect and am very much inclined toward plagiarism.' Evolutionary theory, Newtonian physics, sexology, hypnotherapy, experimental psychology: Freud utilised them all. Theories of inhibition, the unconscious, innate sex drives, and even the idea that dreams might offer an insight into insanity were being debated long before Freud began his move from brain anatomy to the strata of the psyche. Freud's true gift, Makari concludes, was his ability to attract those ideas that were flourishing around him and condense them into his own towering edifice of thought.

This was certainly the case for his development of psychoanalysis as a form of talking therapy. Inspired by his trip to Paris and the power of hypnosis, Freud co-authored *Studies in Hysteria* in 1896 with Josef Breuer, a mentor, financial benefactor, and close colleague who had provided an insight into how mental symptoms can be removed with words. Based on a now famous case study of Bertha Pappenheim ('Anna O.'), Breuer set the foundations on which psychoanalysis was later built.

Raised in a wealthy traditional Jewish family in Vienna, 21-year-old Bertha Pappenheim first met Breuer in December 1880, a time when Freud was still a budding anatomist who hadn't yet met Charcot and his hysterical patients in Paris. After nursing her dying father, Pappenheim was exhibiting some highly unusual symptoms. 'She spoke an agrammatical jargon composed of a mixture of four or five languages,' the psychiatrist and historian Henri Ellenberger wrote. 'Her personality, now, was split into one "normal", conscious, sad person, and one morbid, uncouth, agitated person who had hallucinations of black snakes.' Pappenheim described her two personalities as 'a real one and an evil one'. She remained in bed for nearly four months between the end of 1880 and the spring of 1881. Breuer, a bearded man with a domed forehead and deep-set eyes that curved downwards like the dark facial markings of a sloth, was the only doctor she would speak to.

Her father's death in April 1881 made Bertha spiral further into idiosyncrasy. She only spoke in English and didn't understand German. She became deeply suicidal and, for her own safety, was transferred to a country house – Breuer initially called it a 'villa' – that was within walking distance of Inzersdorf mental asylum on the outskirts of Vienna. There, she soon felt calmer, her agitation subsided, and she enjoyed playing with a Newfoundland dog and meeting the local residents. Breuer travelled from Vienna every few days and would spend hours talking to Pappenheim. He noticed that when she explained her symptoms, the contents of her hallucinations, for example, they seemed to dissipate, just as discussing problems at home with a close friend might help relieve some of the stress they have caused. It was cathartic.

In December 1881, a full year after her symptoms first started, Pappenheim's illness took an unexpected turn. She reverted back to those first days and relived them, hour by hour, all over again. It was as if her body clock had been set back 365 days. Every tomorrow was a repeat, as if Breuer's medical notes were now being played out like a dramatist's script. 'Breuer was able to check that the events she hallucinated had occurred, day by day, exactly one year earlier,' wrote Ellenberger. Breuer, a valued member of the aristocracy and one of the most respected doctors in Vienna, noticed that among this repetition was another opportunity for catharsis. When he asked Pappenheim to explain when and where her symptoms had taken hold of her, he could slowly uncover their original source. Like a detective pushing pins into a city map to determine the location of a wanted criminal, Breuer could track down the offending moment and, he hoped, prevent further harm.

It was a long and tiring process, one that was made even more drawn out by Pappenheim's mercurial mental state and Breuer's busy schedule back in Vienna. It could take hours of discussion (sometimes aided by hypnosis), often through a distressing chain of memories, before the original experience was brought out into the open. But the rewards were clear to see. Her recollections were restorative. By reliving the memory that inspired the symptom, Pappenheim was able to defuse each situation and the damage it was doing to her body. While nursing her father, for example, she had a vision of a black snake slithering from the walls of the room and killing him. She felt an overwhelming urge to beat it away with her right hand, but it would not move – her arm was stiff, stationary, and, to add insult to injury, her fingertips had transformed into little snakes, a terrifying hand puppet of the mythical creature Medusa. At that moment, she prayed to herself in English. After discussing this memory with Breuer, her repetitive spells were broken. The black snakes vanished. She could move her arm. Her English gave way to her native German.

The healing power of words and recollection was remarkable. Pappenheim's symptoms gradually lessened and sometimes disappeared altogether. It was as if, by returning to these traumatic emotions that she had feared and suppressed, she was able to relieve some pent-up energy that was powering her unusual disabilities. While Breuer called this technique the 'cathartic method', Pappenheim said it was a 'talking cure'.

But it was no cure. Bertha Pappenheim didn't recover from her illness. Although she may have felt better after discussing her problems with a trusted doctor, Pappenheim would spend the next few years institutionalised and dependent on regular injections of morphine. Only after she found her true calling in campaigning for social equality – becoming one of the most famous feminists of the late nineteenth century – was she able to live a life outside of the institution. Although she was diagnosed as hysterical and included as one case study in Freud and Breuer's *Studies in Hysteria*, her illness has more recently been tied to her pious and sexually restrictive upbringing, her later subjugation by a patriarchal society, and her unconscious striving for meaning and purpose. '[Her] illness was the desperate struggle of an unsatisfied young woman who found no outlets for her physical and mental energies, nor for her idealistic strivings,' wrote Ellenberger. As a woman raised in a traditional Jewish family, she wasn't allowed to even apply to a university. As was the case for women prescribed the rest cure, her social niche was set within the household. Perhaps caring for her dying father had brought this expectation into an uncomfortable reality, a glimpse into a future that she feared more than any number of snakes.

Bertha Pappenheim's case reports added a fertile seed to Freud's growing interest in the psyche and, in particular, the unconscious. In Paris, Jean-Martin Charcot used hypnosis to paralyse someone's arm with words. With his cathartic method, Breuer showed that extracting painful memories could make a paralysed arm move again. Whether it was a limb, speech, hallucinations or morbid fears, the mind seemed to be in ultimate control of the body. Only by making the patient aware of these connections could they be guided towards the relief of their symptoms. '[Breuer] found a method of bringing into her consciousness the unconscious processes which contained the meaning of her symptoms and the symptoms vanished,' Freud later said.

After publishing *Studies in Hysteria*, Freud started to separate himself from Breuer. He thought that his use of hypnosis was outdated, largely ineffective and only worked on a select few patients. He no longer relied on catharsis – the retelling of a story. Freud became an interpreter, suggesting causal connections between memories and a person's mental state. As with his golden stain that made the invisible visible, it was Freud's task to find what his patients were hiding away, to fill it with colour and meaning.

In 1899, the same year that Emil Kraepelin first presented his all-encompassing 'manic-depressive insanity', Freud published *The Interpretation of Dreams*, a book that, he thought, was his most original and important work. 'Insight such as this falls to one's lot but once in a lifetime,' he wrote. While Charcot had reached into the unconscious of his patients in Paris with hypnosis, Freud argued that a person's dreams provided a 'royal road' into this otherwise locked cargo of the mind. By interpreting the content of a patient's dreams, Freud sought to reveal his patients' repressed memories, wishes, and desires, allowing them to relive an appropriate emotional response. No longer restricted to the idiosyncrasies of hysterical patients, dream interpretation was a means of alleviating those conflicts, perversions, and traumas that everyone hides away from their family, from their doctor, and even from themselves. Crucially, everyone dreamt at night, even if they didn't think twice about what their dreams meant.

Dream interpretation was just one component of the nascent field of psychoanalysis. The other was free association. Inspired by a favourite book from Freud's childhood that advised writing 'without falsification or hypocrisy, everything that comes into your head', it was a slow and protracted process in which his patients spoke, uninterrupted, about any memory, thought, or feeling as they lay down on his couch in the consulting room at Berggasse 19. Famously attentive and constantly looking for hidden meanings, Freud thought he could hear the subtle whispers of the unconscious as his patients spoke. It was as if the mind's cargo was shaking its cage and screaming to be set free. In isolation, these mutterings might be considered meaningless. But through years of analysis and interpretation, Freud thought he could connect them into a neat line of associations that might bring understanding – and relief – to his patients' suffering. He called this 'a resolute pursuit of the historical meaning of a symptom'.

'In every one of our patients we learn through analysis that the symptoms and their effects have set the sufferer back to some past period of his life,' Freud later said. 'In the majority of cases it is actually a very early phase of the life-history which has been thus selected, a period in childhood, even, absurd as it may sound, the period of existence as a suckling infant.'

His patients complained of aches and pains, loss of senses, obsessional thoughts, strict routines, and a list of unusual symptoms that seemed to have no physical basis. They were known as 'neurotics'. In its earliest years, psychoanalysis was focused on three main forms of neurosis: anxiety-hysteria, conversion-hysteria, and the obsessional neurosis. 'These three disorders, which we are accustomed to combine together in a group as the transference neuroses, constitute the field open to psycho-analytic therapy,' Freud said. He met with few, if any, depressed patients. To him, they were boring. As one psychotherapist later wrote, a depressive was someone 'who interacts sparsely with others, is dull and unproductive, sees the world in an impoverished and stereotyped way, and really wants to be left alone'. It didn't have the idiosyncrasies of hysteria or the psychological whodunnits of the 'Rat Man' (a case in which the memory of being told about a form of torture involving rats was associated with obsessional neurosis) or the 'Wolf Man' (a famous dream of white wolves in a tree that Freud interpreted as the early moment of anxiety when boys and girls become aware of the other sex). By this point, the diagnosis of 'weak nerves' had been separated from its psychological symptoms of anxiety and depression and was largely seen as a case of chronic fatigue, a physical state that Freud pinned to a depletion of sexual energy from too much masturbating.

Freud was sailing into uncharted seas and felt like he was sometimes speaking to the waves. His once-in-a-lifetime insight, *The Interpretation of Dreams*, sold terribly. Over six years, only 351 copies were sold, many to people who would provide scathing reviews on its contents. 'The attitude adopted by reviewers,' Freud wrote, 'could only lead one to suppose that my work was doomed to be sunk into complete silence.'

Early in November 2015, I cycled through the growing chill of winter to a psychiatric hospital near Brixton in south London. My bike's gears didn't work, and the chain fit loosely around its rings, clunking forward with each pedal. It wasn't a smooth journey, and what should have taken 15 minutes took around half an hour. I got lost. When I arrived at the gates to the hospital – a low, red-brick building with colourful signs detailing the different psychiatric departments – there were a few speed bumps, a final test of the assault course. But I had made it. I locked my bike up in the car park, put my elasticated lights into my bag, and walked into the building. I was ready for my first session of group therapy.

My doctor had put me forward for this four-week course of CBT a few months earlier. After leaving academia and focusing on my writing, I was still having thoughts of suicide and had a crippling lack of interest in once enjoyable activities. He initially offered me an antidepressant, an SSRI called citalopram. I declined. I worried that such a drug would make my mind blur. My writing too. I was just beginning to be published in magazines and didn't want to sacrifice the progress I had made. Only later would I realise that an antidepressant could be a necessary tool in my career, especially when the alternative is depression. Instead, we agreed that a group therapy 'workshop' might be a better place to start. And so, every Wednesday, I would force myself out of the flat, cycle to the hospital, and join 20 or so other people who were also struggling with their mental health.

We were a diverse bunch. Some people sat in their comfy trousers and trainers while others were in their smart-casual work attire. One guy turned up still in his flashy cycling gear (clip-in shoes included), and stored one of his bike wheels behind his seat. Some of us were young, in our early twenties, while others were middle-aged and greying. There were men and women, wealthy and poor, and a range of ethnicities. A cursory glance around the room provided a quick insight into the non-discriminatory nature of depression: it affects us all.

I didn't know it then, but these four sessions of psychotherapy were built on the work of Sigmund Freud and Emil Kraepelin. Although it wasn't confidential or one-to-one, and there was no chaise longue in sight, it was still a platform in which an insight into mental processes – thoughts instead of memories – is used to treat depression. Plus, it was a psychoanalyst, a disciple of Freud, who had created the core elements of this psychotherapy in the 1960s. Then there was the health questionnaire on my lap, a systematic method of tracking how my symptoms changed over the course of the four-week treatment. A form of psychotherapy with a set of counting cards, this was a convergence of history, a modern meeting of two forefathers of psychiatry.

Sitting down on a slightly padded chair, I filled out the Patient Health Questionnaire (or PHQ-9) before the therapy session began. I have filled out this same questionnaire many times since then – both over the phone and in person – and it isn't a difficult or time-consuming task. There is a list of nine common symptoms of depression and, for each one, a question: how often in the past two weeks have you felt like this? Not at all? Several days? More than half the days? Or nearly every day? Each answer is given a value from zero to three so that the number of symptoms is easily added up and the duration of life that they encroach upon can be quantified. It's a quiz you ideally don't want to score high on. For me, as I looked down at the A5 piece of paper, four symptoms really stood out as descriptions of my recent self:

1. Little interest or pleasure in doing things. (Nearly every day, three.)
2. Feeling down, depressed, or hopeless. (Three.)
6. Feeling bad about yourself – or that you are a failure or have let yourself or your family down. (Two.)
9. Thoughts that you would be better off dead or of hurting yourself in some way. (Two.)

I don't know why, but I tried to shield my paper as I wrote down my scores. Perhaps I felt a deep shame in admitting my problems, even if it was just a number on a piece of paper while I was sat next to a complete stranger. Perhaps I didn't want anyone to have a quick insight into this part of my identity. After all, I was still coming to terms with it myself.

The aim of any treatment, whether it is a talking therapy or drugs, is to reduce the severity of depression. When using the PHQ-9, this is gauged by the sum total of your nine scores. Score below five and you aren't considered to be depressed. Score above six, however, and you creep up through mild, moderate, moderately severe, and severe depression. (At this time, in November 2015, I was between the moderate to moderately severe range.) It's far from a perfect system. Everyone is likely to be biased to some degree and skew the results. In my case, I felt an urge to exaggerate my symptoms as a way to ensure further treatment. I didn't want to score below a threshold and be turfed out of the therapy I had waited months for. Other people, meanwhile, might trivialise their problems, as they don't think they have depression or need therapy. Either way, the PHQ-9 – and other tools like it – is a quick and handy insight into emotional suffering.

With a dark November night at the window, our therapist – a broad-shouldered, smartly dressed man with a short black beard – wrote the word 'RUMINATION' on the flip board in large red letters. It was a word I knew – to think about something deeply. Charles Darwin, for example, ruminated on the topic of evolution for a long time before writing his magnum opus, *On the Origin of Species*, in 1859. I have ruminated on the title of this book. But in CBT this word takes on a slightly different meaning: it is to cycle through negative thought patterns and become so consumed by them that you feel trapped. You become ensnared by your own mind, shackled by a world that you have created inside. Like training a muscle, the more you think that way, the stronger the cycle is, and the harder it is to break free.

The therapist then drew the face of a cartoon clown on the flip chart. It had a big looped smile, a red nose, and untamed hair. He asked everyone around the room to think of a word to describe clowns. They are funny. Happy. Colourful. But they are also terrifying, sad, and dark, the stuff of nightmares. All were correct, he said, it just depended on the context: the person who was answering the question. So, the field of CBT asks, why not choose the more uplifting options? If clowns are funny and happy, then you'll have a better time when you see one. Such a simple thought experiment reveals the basis of CBT. If you can choose how you think about objects and experiences in life, you can change the way you feel about yourself, the world around you and the future.

I found these lessons to be interesting, but they made little impact on my mental health. I was silent throughout the group exercises and didn't want to share those problems that were most troubling to me. As in school classrooms or university lecture halls, there were a few outspoken people who seemed to speak for the rest of us, even though our problems might be very different. I wanted to talk about my self-doubt and feelings of guilt. I wanted to understand my suicidal thoughts, my separation from friends and family. I had turned 25 years old the previous month, and I remembered sitting at my birthday drinks feeling completely alone. I felt hollow, halfway to death on a day that celebrates birth. I didn't know then that these thoughts would later lead me so close to suicide that I shiver at the thought of not being here now.

After the four sessions of group CBT, I returned to my doctor and explained that I was still feeling depressed. We spoke for five or ten minutes; providing the briefest of insights into my symptoms, and the course of my illness and its potential triggers. We decided that I should take the antidepressant originally offered: citalopram. This drug would tinker with the neurotransmitters in my brain and, I hoped, make me stable again. I wasn't told of any side effects. I wasn't told that coming off these drugs could be very difficult for some people. All I knew was that I was desperate for change, willing to do anything to move away from pain and back towards pleasure. For the next four years of my life – as I started dating my partner Lucy, moved from London to Berlin to Bristol, continued to write science articles for various magazines, signed a book deal, became an uncle, and adopted a dog – I would swallow an SSRI every day before bed.

Love and Hate

The first significant psychoanalytic theory of depression was proposed by Karl Abraham, a promising psychoanalyst from Berlin who Freud initially kept at arm's length while trying to pull his protégé, Carl Jung, closer. A smooth-faced, stoic, and often sardonic man who, like Freud, was born into a Jewish family, Abraham felt a duty to understand and help his oft-ignored depressed patients. 'While the conditions of nervous anxiety have been treated in detail in the psychoanalytic literature, the depressive conditions have not found similar consideration,' he told an audience at the Third International Psychoanalytic Congress in Weimar, Germany, in 1911. 'And yet depressive affect is just as widespread.' His first insight into depression came from Giovanni Segantini, a famous Swiss painter whose *oeuvre* he much admired. (It was not uncommon for Freud's followers to use pieces of art, literature, or mythology to illuminate their theories of human psychology.) One of Segantini's compositions stood out from the rest. Known as *The Wicked Mothers*, it depicts a chilling backdrop of ice-capped mountains, frozen snow, and, in the foreground, a pallid mother entangled into the trunk of a gnarled tree. A fierce, red-haired baby feeds at her breast. Abraham looked at this painting and saw a window into the roots of depression.

As he learnt more about Segantini, Abraham's two-dimensional ideas of a 'wicked mother' figure were given shape and substance. When Segantini was a baby, his mother was depressed after grieving the death of her first child (Segantini's older brother). Then, when he was five years old, his mother died. Raised by his grandparents, he suffered from severe bouts of depression and was often institutionalised or living on the streets. Abraham interpreted Segantini's story – and his painting – as a universal metaphor for depression. Although Segantini loved his mother and longed for her affection and attention, she was unable to satisfy his emotional needs. When she died, Abraham believed that Segantini's infant mind interpreted this as a form of abandonment. It was as if she had simply packed up her bags and ran out on him. Hatred welled up inside, pushed love aside, and clouded his world as an adult. This unconscious hatred tainted everyone and everything in his surroundings. Not only did he himself hate, but it felt like everyone else hated him back. Segantini felt alone, castigated, and judged from every angle for his incapacity to love, the core features of many experiences with depression.

Love and hate are opposing forces in psychoanalysis. Eugen Bleuler, an early advocate of psychoanalysis working in Zurich, called the continual battle between these two emotions 'ambivalence'. Adopting this phenomenon into his own practice, Abraham proposed that his depressed patients didn't love their mother when they were children and that hatred had been victorious in their emotional war of ambivalence. Absent of affection, feelings of hostility found an empty space in which to thrive. Abraham summarised his patients' experiences with the maxim, 'I cannot love people; I have to hate them.' In his private practice, he noted how his depressed patients' dreams were often full of masochistic desires and seething with anger and frustration.

Abraham saw his own life reflected in his analysis of Segantini. 'A recurring theme in Abraham's work is traumatic early abandonment by the mother, of the kind he experienced when he was two,' the psychoanalyst and historian Anna Bentinck van Schoonheten writes in her 2015 biography of Karl Abraham. After a tragic fall down a flight of stairs, his mother miscarried her second child, a daughter, and a moment of intense grief turned into unshakeable despair. 'His mother was still physically present, but unreachable because of her depression,' wrote Bentinck van Schoonheten. Too young to empathise with her loss, little Karl felt like his mother had abandoned him, sapping his childhood of the warmth and comfort that he most desired. Although Abraham kept much of his personal life private, Bentinck van Schoonheten concludes that he suffered from depressive episodes for much of his adult life, periods when his letters become infrequent, impersonal, and nihilistic.

Juggling his growing private practice and the thrice-weekly meetings of the Berlin Psychoanalytic Institute, Abraham studied Segantini for two years between 1908 and 1910. As he learnt of their similar childhoods and experiences with depression, he was unaware that this project was also a deathly view into his own future. Segantini had died from an infection in 1899. He was 41 years old. Likewise, Abraham would die from septicaemia and wouldn't live to see his 50th birthday.

Just as the gravitational forces of planets can slingshot passing asteroids into the icy hinterlands of space, the people who Freud brought closest to himself were often destined to be pushed furthest away. Alfred Adler, Wilhelm Stekel, and even his 'crown prince' Carl Jung were all shown the door after they contradicted his dogmatic theories of an innate sexuality. His closest friends, Josef Breuer and Wilhelm Fliess, became his most-hated former acquaintances. Abraham, on the other hand, was a harmonious force in the history of psychoanalysis. Where his leader was mercurial, he was level-headed. Instead of disparaging any diversion from Freudian doctrines, he welcomed a broad range of views and insights from his peers. When mentally well, he was also a model psychotherapist. 'He spoke little, but his silence was justified and in an extraordinary way urgent and encouraging,' one patient recalled, 'his voice, with its dark timbre, was calm and calming. Cool and detached, but when necessary humanely intimate, he was certain of the trust of his students and patients.'

After their first meeting in December 1907, Karl Abraham and Sigmund Freud wrote nearly 500 letters to one another, a slightly greater number coming from Berlin than Vienna. Reading through their correspondence, it is clear that Abraham deeply admired his commander in chief and often expressed his desire to meet face to face. Whenever Freud was travelling away from Vienna for work or on holiday, Abraham never failed to remind him that he would be thrilled to host him at his Berlin home, even if it was just for a few hours. Freud, meanwhile, was awkward and standoffish in his responses. Even when he did pass through Berlin on his way back from England in September 1908, he informed Abraham that he had not found the time to pop in to see him and his wife. 'I was actually in Berlin for 24 hours and did not call on you,' he wrote. 'I could not, because I crossed from England with my aged brother and visited my sister who lives in Berlin, and between the two camps of fond relatives I saw as little of Berlin as I did of you.' A few days later, Abraham replied, 'Now, I must beg you, dear Professor, not to imagine that I took offence at your passing through Berlin. If you reproach yourself for this reason, there is a simple way to make amends. When next you come to Berlin, please give my wife and myself a good deal of your time.' When Freud was invited to Clark University in the United States to present his introductory courses to psychoanalysis, Abraham only asked whether he was able to pay him a visit on his way back. 'That is what interests me particularly in this matter,' he wrote. After Freud mentioned that he might be able to provide a 'brief reunion', Abraham couldn't contain his excitement. 'What gave me most pleasure in your letter was the hope of seeing you here in the autumn. Perhaps I may ask you already now to be generous in apportioning your time! I am so looking forward to it, and in the course of time such a great deal has accumulated that I want to discuss with you!'

Like two courting teenagers destined for a break-up, there was a disparity in affection between Abraham and Freud. Over the years, however, their relationship would become one of the most productive in the early history of psychoanalysis. 'This was a partnership that paid rich scientific dividends,' the psychoanalyst Edward Glover wrote. 'Freud writing with magisterial clarity on the essentials of the science he had founded [and] Abraham, optimistic and sanguine as ever, reaching boldly into new territories.'

His boldest territory was depression, a black hole of human psychology that few of his peers dared to contemplate. If Freud's friends, family, or colleagues suffered from depression, they were advised to travel to see Abraham in Berlin. His home – a spacious apartment opposite a fire station with a sand pit and playground in the back garden for the children – became an international hub for the psychotherapy of depression. For people who were often unwilling or unable to speak, never mind waxing smoothly through the practice of free association, psychoanalysis was often a painful experience for both the analyst and the patient. But Abraham found a way past these problems. As with Emil Kraepelin, he noticed that depressions came and went, that they were often separated by lucid periods in which the patient was more open to discussion, more motivated to dig into their dreams, thoughts, and painful memories. Just as the worst of the depression was subsiding, Abraham explained and interpreted his patients' symptoms, how they were the product of their ambivalence between love and hate, their relationship to their mother, and their inability to love.

He observed some significant improvements, even claiming that he had cured someone with melancholia – sometimes seen as a more chronic, less cyclical condition than depressive insanity – before it became permanent, 'something which had never happened before'. 'By the help of psychoanalytical inter-pretation of certain facts and connections,' Abraham added, 'I succeeded in attaining a greater psychic rapport with the patients than I had ever previously achieved ... Psychoanalysis [is] the only rational therapy to apply to the manic-depressive psychoses.' There was one patient, his sixth case of depression, that he thought exemplified the power of this talking therapy. Before entering Abraham's practice in Berlin, the patient had spent time in mental asylums and had only found partial relief from his depression through such palliative care. But Abraham was able to analyse and interpret his depression, uncovering long-lost memories and linking them with his present state. Slowly, step by gradual step, the symptoms were removed as if this 'talking cure' was slicing through the psychological shack-les that had long held his patient down. 'His severe depression began to subside after four weeks,' Abraham wrote. '[H]e had a feeling of hope that he would once again be capable of work.' After six months, the patient's analysis came to an end. His friends noticed a positive change in his character and, 12 months later, the depression hadn't returned. 'I am happier and more care-free than I have ever been before,' he reported.

Abraham knew that this was a promising start and nothing more. Six patients was hardly a representative sample of all depressed people. Plus, perhaps these patients would have recovered anyway, without psychotherapy of any kind. 'Naturally,' Abraham wrote, 'a definite opinion as regards a cure cannot yet be given for after twenty years of illness, interrupted by free intervals of varying length, an improvement of [a few] months' duration signifies very little.' Still, he believed that the improvement was in step with the success or failure of his therapy. With every memory he analysed, every dream interpreted, he believed that his patient looked slightly more stable, happier, and less governed by feelings of shame and hatred. As with his patients, the future for psychoanalysis in the treatment of depression was looking much brighter in Berlin. 'Although our results at present are incomplete,' Abraham wrote, 'it is only psychoanalysis that will reveal the hidden structure of this large group of mental diseases.'

Although he rarely saw it for himself, Freud was pleased with his colleague's efforts. 'Berlin is a difficult but important soil,' he wrote, 'and your efforts to make it cultivable for our purposes deserve every praise.' And by setting up shop in the booming capital of Germany, Abraham was infiltrating a country dominated by biological psychiatrists led by Emil Kraepelin.

Freud and Kraepelin never met. Like particles of matter and antimatter, perhaps the whole world of psychiatry would have collapsed if they did. Although the figureheads of two rival factions – the psychological versus the biological – they might actually have found many similarities to discuss. Born in the same year, both Freud and Kraepelin were trained by leading neuroanatomists of the nineteenth century. Their first scientific pursuits were influenced more by money and the opportunity of marriage than basic curiosity. And they each were interested in drug therapies and forms of counselling. History is never as simple as two opposing silos.

It is clear from their writings that they weren't overly fond of one another. In the eighth edition of his psychiatry textbook, published in 1909, Kraepelin wrote that 'Freud and [Carl] Jung are nonsensical,' adding that 'the fundamental features of the Freudian trend of investigation [are] the representation of arbitrary assumptions and conjectures as scientific facts ... the tendency to generalisation beyond measure from single observations. As I am accustomed to walk on the sure foundation of direct experience, my Philistine conscience of natural science stumbles at every step on objections, considerations, and doubts, over which the likely soaring tower of imagination of Freud's disciples carries them without difficulty.' In short, this so-called 'science' of psychoanalysis ran counter to the fundamental components of what Kraepelin would consider scientific.

In response, Freud wrote that Kraepelin was the leader of the 'enemy camp' in the 'blackest clique of Munich'. In his famous *Introductory Lectures on Psycho-Analysis*, he added several scathing comments on the lack of understanding of such 'scientific psychiatry', tying the biological approach to routine family histories and vague notions of heredity. 'Psychiatry has given names to various compulsions; and has nothing more to say about them,' he told his audience. 'He has to content himself with a diagnosis and, in spite of wide experience, with a very uncertain prognosis of its future course ... it is but a miserable contribution ... a condemnation instead of an explanation.' Defective heredity, strict diagnosis, long-term prognosis without treatment: although he didn't mention Kraepelin directly, he was criticising the very core of his scientific contributions.

Psychoanalysis offered something that biological psychiatry badly needed: an understanding of a person's illness. Whether theories of love, hate, and sexual longing were correct hardly mattered. If someone believed that they were being heard, that their unique personal history was the reason for their tumultuous present, then the therapeutic gains could be wondrous. It wasn't an easy skill to learn, and psychoanalysts had to tailor their approach for different situations. Psychotherapy with a depressed person, for example, was a delicate balancing act. 'There must be a continuous, subtle, empathetic tie between the analyst and his depressive patients,' Edith Jacobson, a German émigré and disciple of Karl Abraham, wrote. 'We must be very careful not to let empty silences grow or not to talk too long, too rapidly, and too emphatically; that is, never to give too much or too little.' Such patients are emotionally unstable, so prone to swing back into a depression that any disappointment or misconstrued comment can undo any progress made in the analysis. 'For this reason they usually need many years of analysis with slow, patient, consistent work,' Jacobson added. 'With these patients, we are always between the devil and the deep blue sea.'

The most basic elements of psychoanalysis – sitting down and talking with another human – were revolutionary, a model that subsequent psychotherapies would replicate. 'Words and magic were in the beginning one and the same thing, and even to-day words retain much of their magical power,' Freud explained in one of his lectures in 1915. 'By words one of us can give to another the greatest happiness or bring utter despair; by words the teacher imparts his knowledge to the student; by words the orator sweeps his audience with him and determines its judgements and decisions. Words call forth emotions and are universally the means by which we influence our fellow creatures. Therefore let us not despise the use of words in psychotherapy.'

A First Sketch

In addition to his *Psychiatry* textbooks and the neat classifications they contained, Kraepelin had guided the construction of a new scientific hub of biological psychiatry at the University of Munich. Built in 1904, the facility – a white-washed, horseshoe-shaped building on a tree-lined street in central Munich – was replete with laboratories dedicated to experimental psychology, chemistry, serology (the study of blood), and genealogy, and contained a vast archive for books and the storage of all of his *Zählkarte*. He had assembled an impressive roster of experienced staff from across Germany. Of note was Alois Alzheimer, a former student from his days in Heidelberg. Designing his own pathology laboratory – a well-lit room with 15 workspaces, tabletop microscopes, and a separate room for microphotography, on the third floor of the clinic – Alzheimer would become famous for his discovery of a 'strange and serious' form of dementia. Kraepelin, in the eighth edition of his *Psychiatry* textbook, named it 'Alzheimer's disease', a much-needed reminder that brain anatomy could offer something to the study of mental disease, even if manic-depressive insanity and dementia praecox were still unwilling to reveal their innermost secrets. Everywhere scientists cared to look – in blood sugar, measures of metabolism, gastric juices, nitrogen levels in exhaled breath, brain slices – there were no insights into the causes of depression.

It was away from the laboratory where Kraepelin and Alzheimer had their greatest influence on psychiatry. In addition to their written works, their lectures and workshops were legendary. 'Whoever has listened to the lessons of Alzheimer and Kraepelin,' the Italian physician Gaetano Perusini wrote in 1907, 'wherever they came from, will not have found the journey too long.' And wherever someone lived and worked, Kraepelin's *Psychiatry* textbook came to be seen as a bible of biological psychiatry. His diagnosis of manic-depressive insanity was a necessary update from notions of black bile and melancholia. But there were still heated debates about whether it was overly simplistic, and if there were other forms of depression that weren't depressive insanity. There were those who thought distinct disease states in psychiatry didn't exist and any attempts to classify patients were merely satisfying a basic human need for order. To Alfred Hoche, a German psychiatrist also working in Munich, the work of Kraepelin and his followers was flawed; 'a kind of thought compulsion, a logical and aesthetic necessity, insists that we seek for well defined, self-contained disease entities,' he wrote, 'but here as elsewhere, unfortunately, our subjective need is no proof of the reality of that which we desire, no proof that these pure types do, in point of fact, actually occur'. He added that the recent surge in excitement over classification, or 'nosology', in psychiatry wasn't creating new understanding but was like 'clarifying a turbid fluid by pouring it busily from one vessel to another'.

Kraepelin was his own worst critic. He cautioned that his classification system still didn't reflect a biological reality. 'We are still so far removed from a real knowledge of the causes, phenomena, course, and termination of the individual forms [of mental disorder] that we cannot yet dream of a surely established edifice of knowledge at all,' he stated at one of his famous lectures on clinical psychiatry. 'What we have formulated here is only a first sketch, which the advance of our science will often have occasion to change and enlarge in its details, and perhaps even in its principal lines.' He was remarkably candid when it came to his work's shortcomings.

Kraepelin had tried his utmost to find a true map of mental disease and ended up feeling like he hadn't done enough. As two historians of Kraepelin, Eric Engstrom and Kenneth Kendler, wrote, 'Experience had shown that what at first appeared to be sharp clinical boundaries had become ever more blurred and that a "thorough differentiation between normal and pathological conditions" was an impossibility'. In lieu of certainty and fact, Kraepelin had created an introduction and a guide into the confusing, irrational, and often extraordinary minds of the mentally ill. Although psychoanalysis would come to dominate psychiatry by the middle of the twentieth century – especially in the United States – Kraepelin would have the last laugh.

In 1980, an emergence of 'neo-Kraepelinian' philosophy resulted in the third edition of the *Diagnostic and Statistical Manual for Mental Disorders*, or *DSM-III*, a booklet created in the United States and used as a 'Bible' in the classification of mental illness around the world. As Edward Shorter, a historian of medicine from the University of Toronto, wrote, the '*DSM-III* represented a massive "turning of the page" in nosology, and it had the effect of steering psychoanalysis toward the exit in psychiatry and the beginning of a reconciliation of psychiatry with the rest of medicine'. Rather than trying to reveal a person's repressed memories or interpret dreams, psychiatrists argued that there were neat disease states – diagnoses – that could be tracked through time. In place of manic-depressive insanity, there was another all-encompassing diagnosis: major depressive disorder. But such a simplification belies the diversity of depression. Throughout the twentieth century, treatments would be developed that were specific to certain symptoms or severities of depression, a few beams of light to illuminate a once dark and endless forest.

In September 1915, Freud sent a letter to Karl Abraham, then working as a surgeon's assistant on the Eastern Front of the First World War. Situated in Allenstein, a bucolic setting of lakes and trees, his characteristic stoicism was put to the test. '[I] have found confirmation of the solution of melancholia in a case I studied for two months,' Freud wrote. Abraham was stunned. He couldn't believe that anyone, not even 'the genius' Freud, had dipped into his field of expertise and found something that he had not. Freud's claim that he had solved the puzzle after two months of analysis seemed to belittle Abraham's years of careful observation, his thorough analysis of Giovanni Segantini, and two lengthy publications on this very topic.

As with many of his other theories, Freud had absorbed the ideas around him and added a subtle modification that he could call his own. Although hatred was a key part of depression, Freud wrote, it wasn't because of an absent or uncaring mother, as Abraham had argued. It was much broader. The causal factor was similar to mourning. But instead of the death of a loved one, the patient suffers from the loss of any type of 'love-object', a family member, a relationship, or an unfulfilled expectation of the self. The mental energy that was once focused on this object, Freud wrote, was then branded by its departure. In depression, this negative energy was turned inwards (not outwards as Abraham had proposed), straight back into the person's own mind – their 'ego'. This would become known as 'retroflected hostility', a process that showed itself through intense periods of self-reflection, critical judge-ment, and, ultimately, hatred. The depressed person, Freud wrote, begins to feel 'worthless, incapable of any achievement and morally despicable ... he reproaches himself, vilifies him-self and expects to be punished. He abases himself before everyone and commiserates with his own relatives for being connected with someone so unworthy.'

Reading through Freud's scribbled draft over and over, Abra-ham felt like his work had just been appropriated without credit. Love, loss, hate. It was all uncomfortably familiar.

For the first decade of their friendship, Abraham was punc-tual in his correspondence with Freud. While the latter would often take days or weeks to respond, Abraham would reply almost as soon as he had opened the latest envelope. With this particular letter, however, he waited a month to reply. It wasn't because he was busy learning how to patch up injured soldiers on the Eastern Front. And it wasn't due to the delays of the postal service caused by the disruptions of war. It was because he was writing one of the longest letters he would ever send to Berggasse 19, Vienna.

When he finally posted his response to Freud's theory of depression, Abraham's letter was respectful and delicately bal-anced, much like the man himself. Although he hadn't experienced it first hand, he knew that Freud was prone to vol-atile outbursts and had swiftly made enemies of anyone who had contradicted his theories in the past. 'I should like to remind you – not in order to stress any priority but merely to underline the points of agreement – that I also started from a comparison between the melancholic depression and mourn-ing,' he wrote. Fearing that even this was a little too bold, Abraham sheepishly added that, although he hoped that his work could be more clearly referenced, he was 'able to accept all the essentials' of Freud's theory. 'It seems to me that we ought to agree easily.' Even those elements that he still couldn't accept, he wrote, 'as you know, dear Professor, I am ready to re-learn'.

Over a month later, Freud told Abraham that he had just finished writing the second draft of his grand treatise on depression. As requested, he credited Abraham, 'to whom we owe the most important of the few analytic studies on this subject'. He wasn't saying that his theories were inspired by his colleague's research. Freud was merely informing his readers that Abraham had also done some work in this area.

Published in 1917, Freud's essay 'Mourning and Melancholia' wasn't the first psychoanalytic interpretation of depression and neither was it the last. Nonetheless, it was a foundational text that crystallised a blurry set of ideas that Abraham had published and gave budding psychoanalysts the confidence to treat depressive disorders. Through the method of free association and the analysis of dreams, thoughts, and memories, it was the psychoanalyst's job to reveal what 'love-object' their patient had lost. Abraham, Freud, and their followers were palaeontologists of the mind, digging through their depressed patients' unconscious layers, hoping to uncover the old bones of a pathological monster.

By 1925, Abraham had fully adopted Freud's theory of object-loss and merged it with his former ideas of maternal abandonment. Depression, he wrote, is

connected to an event with which a person in their mental state at the time was not able to cope ... a loss that caused a profound inner shock and was experienced as unbearable. It was always the loss of someone who was the centre of the person's life. Loss did not necessarily mean death, but an intense relationship with another person was suddenly destroyed, for example by a disappointment that could never be set right. The feeling of total abandonment that resulted would then trigger depression. A disappointment of such magnitude could only happen in early childhood with regard to the mother and it would cause a desire for revenge that was hard to control. Deep beneath that vengefulness was a nostalgia for the original mother, for the earliest sense of satisfaction at the mother's breast.

While Freud was focused on the Oedipus complex, a stage of psychosexual development that arose between the ages of three and five, Abraham pushed the origin of depression back into the earliest moments of human attachment. During the so-called 'oral phase', Abraham reasoned, the baby develops its first love-object: the warm, nourishing, and comforting milk, and the breast from which it suckles. With this early love-object as a template, humans are then primed to seek other attachments as they grow into adults. Healthy relationships that provide comfort, for example. But when these relationships break, the loss can feel like the world is ending, like a baby hungry for milk and screaming for its next feed. For those people who had passed through the 'oral phase' of their infancy with frustration and disappointment, Abraham thought, this same feeling emerged once more in later life whenever a love-object was lost. Depression was the result.

'Abraham's [ideas] about a pre-Oedipal mother-son relationship,' Anna Bentinck van Schoonheten writes, 'gave a whole new direction to psychoanalysis.' While Freud was still focused on the importance of father figures, penis envy, and death wishes, Abraham's disciples provided some of the most exciting avenues for psychological therapies to follow. From the

1920s onwards, Melanie Klein, a former student of Abraham in Berlin, studied the behaviour of newborns and young infants in order to understand the earliest stages of psychological development and how they might give rise to depression later in life. As one textbook on psychoanalysis and depression states

> it was Melanie Klein who first elaborated the theory that this predisposition depends not on one or a series of traumatic incidents or disappointments but rather on the quality of the mother-child relationship in the first year of life. If this is of a type which does not promote in the child a feeling that he is secure and good and beloved, he is, according to Klein, never able to overcome his pronounced ambivalence toward his love-objects and forever prone to depressive breakdowns.

In the 1950s, John Bowlby, a British psychoanalyst, would add to Abraham and Klein's work and create his 'attachment theory' of depression that made physical contact and comfort essential resources for a person's mental health. It is important to remember that it wasn't Freud who first initiated this field of study. It was Karl Abraham.

Before the Armistice of 11 November 1918 was signed and the First World War ended, Abraham returned to Berlin from the sylvan hillsides and lake-filled valleys of eastern Europe. After a few shock deaths in the family, he sunk into a deep depression that turned his hair grey and his body thin. But he still remained in regular correspondence with Freud in Vienna and continued to be his most-loyal servant. Along with five other members of the so-called 'Committee', he wore a golden ring containing a small Grecian stone from Freud's personal collection of treasures and antiquities. After years of service, Abraham was twice elected president of the International Psychoanalytic Association and, from this vantage point, was a shrewd force in the promotion of Freudian psychology around the world. 'Abraham will in future be recognised as one of those men of outstanding ability who helped fertilise and stir into movement the, till then, paretic science of psychiatry,' the psychoanalyst Edward Glover wrote.

On 7 June 1925, Abraham wrote a letter to Freud while he was resting in his bed in Berlin. His throat was swollen and sore. His body temperature swung up and down with feverish ferocity. He believed that he had caught the flu from his recent sojourn to Holland. In fact, he had a fish bone lodged in his throat that had become infected. In a time before antibiotics, such an unlikely and unfortunate injury could be lethal. Over the coming months, Abraham would exhibit the hallmark symptoms of septicaemia: fevers, inexplicable recoveries, and even moments of euphoria. At those conferences that he managed to attend, he looked emaciated, a shadow of his former athletic self. When he was younger, Abraham was the first to conquer two mountains in Switzerland. He named the second peak after a climber who had failed in his attempt. Only in his late 40s, he was now taking a mountain railway in Bernese Oberland up to an altitude of 1,270 metres, this time in the pursuit of fresh air. Reclining in a deck chair at the Hotel Victoria, unaware that he was about to die, he read his favourite philosopher, Aristophanes, a writer of dark comedies in ancient Greece.

Upon hearing of Abraham's illness, Freud joked that he didn't know that he was capable of staying in bed. 'I like to think of you only as a man continually and unfailingly at work,' he wrote. 'I feel your illness to be a kind of unfair competition and appeal to you to stop it as quickly as possible.' Two years earlier, Freud had learnt that the pain in his jaw was cancerous and spent large amounts of his own time recuperating from painful surgeries, radiotherapy, and frequent adjustments to his new prosthetic jaw.

Karl Abraham died on Christmas Day in 1925. Freud's last letter to Abraham's flat in Berlin was to Hedwig, his colleague's wife of nearly 20 years and the mother of his two teenage children, Hilda and Gerd. Freud, writing in February of 1926, was still unable to process his grief. 'I have no substitute for him,' he confessed to Hedwig, 'and no consolatory words for you that would tell you anything new.' The great translator of human misery was lost for words. Ernest Jones, an English psychoanalyst and fellow commitee member, found the appropriate interpretation. 'There is no way of meeting this blow,' he wrote in a letter to Freud, 'it cannot be dealt with, for nothing can ever cure it – not even time. The loss is quite irreplaceable.'

Several months later, in October 1926, the field of biological psychiatry also lost a father figure. After a short bout of pneumonia, Emil Kraepelin was laid to rest in Heidelberg, the clement city where his family first found happiness in 1891. Buried in a graveyard that sat at the foot of Königstuhl (King's Chair), the mountain that he had walked up and down so often in life, his name was engraved into a smooth lump of granite that looked like the upturned nose of a canoe. There was no date, no flashy accoutrements or religious maxims of any kind. Under his name, there was only a single sentence:

> Dein Name mag vergehen
> Bleibt nur dein Werk bestehen.

> Your name may vanish
> Only your work will continue.

PART TWO

'The Biological Approach Seems to Be Working'

'... the extent to which a treatment flourishes is directly dependent upon the specific features of the day's clinical landscape. In the long haul, viability is a matter of ecology, not virtue.'

Jack Pressman, *Last Resort* (1998)

'... for those patients who respond to a particular tranquilliser or antidepressant, old or new, that one drug is invaluable; it means for them the difference between sickness and health ... humans and not statistics suffer.'

Pierre Deniker

'Depression, which was once thought to be merely an unfortunate state of mind for which the depressed patient was largely responsible, is now recognised as a very common and painful disease – for which, fortunately, highly successful types of medical treatment have become available.'

Nathan Kline

Fighting Fire with Fire

A decade before his death, Emil Kraepelin's legacy had reached outside of Germany, crossed the English Channel, and settled in a new psychiatric stronghold in south London. After visiting Munich, Frederick Mott, director of the London County Council's Central Pathological Laboratory, was so impressed with what he saw that he returned to Britain intent on planning something similar, a psychiatric hospital that was a hub of scientific research. He knew someone who would be interested in such a project: Henry Maudsley, a world-famous psychiatrist who wrote essays, novels, and rubbed shoulders with Charles Darwin and other members of the nineteenth-century intelligentsia. Maudsley thought it was a project long overdue. He offered £30,000 for the construction of a hospital that put science and research at the centre of British psychiatry, a sizeable sum at the time. By the end of the project, his donation had doubled. The language of psychiatry was changing from German to English.

Built in 1917 and looking more like a city hall than a mental institution, the Portland stone and red bricks of the Maudsley Hospital brought the treatment of mental illness into the community. There were few beds and most patients could come and go with as little as 24 hours' notice. This buzzing outpatients' department was frequented by a diverse set of patients that would previously have been hidden away at home.

The first superintendent here, Edward Mapother, hoped to continue what Emil Kraepelin had started: to align psychiatry with medicine, a field of strict diagnoses and cures. The son of a former president of the Royal College of Surgeons in Ireland, Mapother followed in his father's footsteps and trained in medicine, specialising in neurology before working as a military doctor during the First World War. As part of the Royal Army Medical Corps, he was positioned in northeastern France during the Battle of Loos, a two-week conflict in which Britain lost twice as many soldiers as the oncoming German army. Mapother saw first hand what shock and stress could do to the mind, and how little he could do to help ease the pain. Some days it felt like he shared the 'thousand-yard stare' of these shell-shocked soldiers, peering into the abyss.

In the late 1920s, Mapother was at the centre of a debate concerning the diagnosis of depression. More specifically, manic-depressive insanity, the all-encompassing diagnosis of Kraepelin. Was it a true reflection of the patients who were seen as outpatients and those who spent time in institutions? Some psychiatrists argued that there were actually two major groups of depression. The first was caused by environmental influences, either childhood trauma, as many psychoanalysts posited, or reactions to war or misfortune. This was known as 'neurotic' or 'reactive' depression. The second was more biological in origin and was known as 'psychotic' or 'endogenous' depression. (Confusingly, the terms neurosis and psychosis had previously been used to describe the complete opposite conditions. Neurotic was a term for physical nervous ailments such as neurasthenia. A psychosis was a disorder of the mind that often came with hallucinations. As psychiatry became anglicised, it was as if the language used became increasingly contradictory.) The terms were vague and often relied more on metaphor than scientific reasoning. One doctor, for example, explained that someone with neurotic depression 'looked on a beautiful garden [and] obtained as much pleasure out of it as anyone else', while the psychotic 'could see it was beautiful but ... could not feel it'.

In 1926, at the annual meeting of the British Medical Association held in Nottingham, Mapother argued that there was only one depression: manic-depressive psychosis. It was a spectrum, a condition that varied 'infinitely in degree', that each person could move up or down depending on the duration, severity, and potential recovery of their condition. Mild or severe, long or short, neurotic or psychotic, there 'is no constant or specific cause, and no distinctive bodily change recognisable during life or after death,' Mapother said. 'The range of the term [depression] is a matter of convention.' The only division that he could see was whether someone was institutionalised or not. People seen in the community were more likely to be called neurotic while those in institutions were labelled as psychotic. 'I can find no other basis for the distinction,' Mapother said, 'neither insight, nor cooperation in treatment, nor susceptibility to psychotherapy will serve.'

Shy, introverted, and sometimes so nervous that he vomited before big presentations, Mapother filled the lecture hall with despair and frustration when it came to treatments. 'A patient with serious emotional disturbance should be kept in bed as in the case of a feverish tuberculosis patient ... [O]pen air and sunlight are nearly as important in [depression] and massage is a useful substitute for exercise,' he said. A balanced and nutritious diet kept the worst of the weight loss at bay, while sedatives were prescribed to soothe troubled minds into a deep – but hardly refreshing – sleep. The treatment, in other words, was much the same as it was in William Tuke's days at The Retreat in York in the late eighteenth century. Over a hundred years had passed with little change. The one exception was the emergence of psychoanalysis, but Mapother was a vocal critic of its use in depressions. '[A]ctive psychotherapy, especially analysis of any kind, is merely harmful,' he said.

It was a desperate situation, one that was made worse by the economic depression that encircled the globe for much of the 1930s, sapping funding from most studies into mental illness. 'At the time,' Heinz Lehmann, a German psychiatrist working in Montreal, Canada, wrote, 'a clinician was almost helpless when faced with a depressed patient.' A range of treatments – nitrous oxide inhalation, testosterone injections, X-ray irradiation, opium, the removal of teeth that were presumed to be infected – had been tried and failed. Doctors and patients shared a feeling of hopelessness. Inside mental institutions, forced feedings and 24-hour suicide watches were still common practice for the most severely ill patients. 'Even in the more neurotic types of depression, and despite all the psychotherapy given, suicides were frequent, and patients often took months or years to get well no matter what one tried to help them,' one psychiatrist working in London recalled. The only evidence-based finding came from who was most likely to suffer from depression. Based on the records from Kraepelin's clinic, Helen Boyle, an English doctor who studied the thyroid and its associations with mental illness, said in 1930, '70 per cent are women – a large preponderance of women.'

In lieu of effective therapy, the staff at the Maudsley collected as much information on their patients as possible, hoping to uncover some link between their history and their current situation. Like psychoanalysts digging through the unconscious, biological psychiatrists reached back through the years in the hope of finding an explanation for a person's present. Ultimately, however, it was a means of keeping busy. After filling out 30 pages on a patient, one psychiatrist wrote that such an exercise 'gave us a feeling that we were doing something for the patient by learning so much about him, even if we could not yet find any relief for his suffering'.

The one success story in psychiatry came from an unlikely source: malaria. Injecting this infectious microbe into the blood of patients with the dreaded neurosyphilis, Julius Wagner-Jauregg, a moustachioed psychiatrist working in Vienna, found that this once fatal disease could be cured if caught early enough in its course. Caused by an infection of syphilis that had cork-screwed into the delicate neurons of the brain (hence 'neurosyphilis'), the disease would normally progress through a series of familiar stages, each a stepping stone further into despair. First, a person's speech would start to degrade. Then muscles in the face and around the eye would begin to quiver and twitch uncontrollably. Finally, delusions of grandeur – the ownership of untold riches, unparalleled fluency in foreign language, or hundreds of sexual partners – were common as patients rocked between depression and mania. Some people died believing they were immortal.

For over a century, a range of treatments had been tried. Low-calorie diets, bloodletting, leeching, cupping, purgatives, mercurial ointments, diuretics, proteins from tuberculosis, boiled milk: all had failed. Once a diagnosis of neurosyphilis was confirmed, one doctor wrote, 'it is the duty of the physician to say at once that the case is without hope'. But the fires of a malarial infection, Wagner-Jauregg found, could cleanse the body of this disease. Out of his first 400 patients, 60 per cent achieved remissions within two years and were able to return home and to work. In 1923, one doctor pushed this figure to over 72 per cent. After eight to 12 rounds of fever, a three-day course of quinine – an antimalarial drug extracted from the bark of Cinchona trees that grow on the slopes of the Andes Mountains in South America – rids the body of the *Plasmodium vivax* cells. Although milder than other types of malaria (such as *Plasmodium falciparum*), this so-called 'tertiary malaria' was still very capable of killing. Indeed, patients did die from this treatment.

In 1927, Wagner-Jauregg was awarded a Nobel Prize for his work, the first psychiatrist to receive the honour. Although antibiotics such as penicillin were soon introduced into the treatment of syphilis (preventing the disease from entering the nervous system in the first place), Wagner-Jauregg's legacy could still be found in the message his work sent to other biologically orientated psychiatrists: with daring effort and justified risk, even the most hopeless cases can be cured. With few other options than to sit and wait, treatments for depression – the embodiment of hopelessness – began to follow Wagner-Jauregg's risky example. 'In this therapeutic and theoretical vacuum, almost any treatment was tried, providing it had the potential for treating large numbers of patients with a minimum of highly trained staff,' Elliot Valenstein wrote in his book *Great and Desperate Cures*. 'For many physicians, risking any therapeutic possibility was preferable to confessing helplessness.'

Unfixing Thoughts

For most of her adult life, Becky was prone to extreme emotional outbursts. She screamed and wailed when she experienced the slightest disappointment in her day. She flailed her arms, knocking over anything within reach. Sometimes, she'd throw her own faeces. Becky was, after all, a chimpanzee. But, one day in 1934, she suddenly stopped going – for lack of a better word – apeshit. She appeared to be a completely different chimp. She could endure endless disappointment, failing to open a box that contained treats hundreds of times in a row, for example, and remaining unfazed. In fact, she was more likely to be euphoric than angry. Fail or succeed, Becky seemed like a very content, happy chimpanzee.

Carlyle Jacobsen, a 33-year-old psychologist from the Primate Research Centre at Yale University, New Haven, presented Becky's story at the second international neurological Congress at King's College London in August 1935. The significant change in her character, he explained, was related to a change in her brain. Along with his supervisor and director of the research centre John Fulton, Jacobsen explained how they had removed Becky's frontal lobes, the regions of the brain that sit just above the eye sockets. After this operation, Jacobsen thought that Becky had joined a 'happiness cult'.

By this time in the 1930s, it was well established that different parts of the brain had different functions. Like a children's jigsaw puzzle composed of several large pieces, scientists had started to separate what looks like a homogenous mass of soft tissue into a complex organ with regions dedicated to memory, movement, and hearing. Even speech could be mapped to a specific blob of tissue – known as Broca's area – that was located on the underside of the temples. But did this 'brain localisation' theory hold true for traits as abstract and individual as emotion, temperament, personality? A few remarkable case studies seemed to suggest that this was indeed the case.

The most famous example, both now and in the 1930s, was the so-called 'American Crowbar Case'. In September 1848, a 25-year-old railroad worker called Phineus Gage was hammering his tamping iron (a metre-long rod that was used to pack explosives into a drilled hole) when a spark ignited and, in the blink of an eye, propelled the iron out of the hole and through Gage's head. Landing 30-metres down the Rutland and Burlington Railroad, it was smeared with greasy bits of brain and blood. Although the tamping iron had entered his face just underneath the cheekbone and exited from the top of his forehead, a large chunk of his frontal lobes being destroyed in the process, Gage survived and seemed coherent soon after the accident. After his physical injuries healed, however, he wasn't the same person. His doctor noted that he was 'fitful, irreverent, indulging at times in the grossest profanity (which was not previously his custom), manifesting but little deference for his fellows, impatient of restraint or advice when it conflicts with his desires'. His friends simply thought that he was 'no longer Gage'. His employers found his change of character so marked that they refused to offer him another job. Unable to return to the railway lines, Gage became a curiosity of Barnum's Circus.

Similarly intriguing insights into the function of the frontal lobes emerged after brain surgeries. In 1930, an American man known simply as 'Patient A.' had large sections of his frontal lobes removed as a result of a brain tumour. After the operation, he was reported to be emotionally rigid and often euphoric – two traits that seemed out of character when compared to his former self. Amazingly, the only thing that seemed to remain constant was his intelligence. Even without his frontal lobes, it was reported that he suffered no decline in IQ.

Egas Moniz, a 60-year-old neurologist from Lisbon in Portugal, was in the audience that day at King's College London, listening to Jacobsen's descriptions of Becky the chimpanzee. Tall and besuited with a shiny toupee covering his balding pate, Moniz asked Jacobsen whether such results might be used to develop new treatments for mental disorders. Could the frontal lobes be modified in some way to control the emotional extremes of psychiatric patients? Jacobsen replied that he hadn't given it much thought – he was an experimental psychologist, not a clinical psychiatrist. In truth, neither had Moniz until he heard this lecture. Still, he was excited to put such experiments into practice back home. He didn't have any chimpanzees to work with. But he knew where he might be given access to institutionalised mental patients.

Born on 27 November 1874 in the small coastal village of Avanca, northern Portugal, Moniz grew up hearing stories about his country's colonial past, how this once great empire had spanned the globe from Asia to South America and from Africa to Oceania. Moniz's own family history reached back 500 years in Avanca alone. But, as with the Portuguese Empire, these riches were slowly lost, and after the unfortunate and unrelated deaths of his parents, his brother, and his beloved uncle, Egas Moniz became the sole survivor and heir to a once powerful aristocracy.

After graduating from Coimbra University in 1899, Moniz accepted a position of lecturer at the medical school, trained in neurology in Paris, and became the Portuguese ambassador to Spain. During his political duties, he met the Nobel laureate Ramon y Cajal. Working in Barcelona, Cajal had published some of the most intricate and beautiful maps of our nervous system and, through a series of similarly intricate experiments, provided the best evidence for synapses, the tiny gaps that separate one neuron from another. He didn't know it at the time, but Moniz would follow in Cajal's footsteps; he too would be awarded a Nobel Prize, the first Portuguese scientist to receive the honour.

Moniz's first breakthrough in science came late in life. In his early 50s, working at the University of Lisbon, he published the first scan of cerebral angiography, an early brain-imaging technique that involved injecting an opaque fluid into the bloodstream and detecting its flow through the brain with X-rays. Areas of the brain where blood was blocked or diverted through other vessels indicated the presence of an anomaly such as a brain tumour. It was an exciting and state of the art brain imaging technique, just like the functional MRI scans of today. Single-minded, daring, and determined to add to his rich family history, Moniz published over 100 articles and two books on angiography. He was hailed as one of the leading neurologists of the twentieth century, a person who other scientists could look to for guidance.

Moniz attended the 1935 congress in London to present his work on angiography. His photos were plastered over an entire wall. But, as he sat in the lecture hall and listened to Carlyle Jacobsen discuss Becky the chimpanzee, he thought that he had just discovered his next project. Instead of visualising blockages in a person's brain due to cancerous tumours, he wondered whether he could introduce blockages of his own. 'Seldom in the history of medicine has a laboratory observation been so quickly and dramatically translated into a therapeutic procedure,' one psychiatrist later said.

On 12 November 1935, three months after the congress in London, a woman with severe depression and paranoia was placed under general anaesthetic and prepped for her operation in a surgical room at Hospital Santa Marta, a long two-storey building with a baroque, tiled interior. With swollen hands from the gout that had painfully erupted when he was just 24 years old, Moniz lacked the dexterity for precise surgical procedures. But he guided his neurosurgeon, Pedro Almeida Lima, as best he could. The patient's hair had been shaved from the forehead to behind the ears. Pure alcohol was rubbed onto the bald scalp to avoid contamination. Then Lima bored a couple of holes through the unconscious woman's skull, each a few inches from the midline, like two upward-facing eye sockets. Swapping his drill for a sharp scalpel, he then cut through the liquid-filled cavity, known as the 'dura', that cushions the delicate brain inside the skull. Draining the overflowing fluid and cauterising the blood vessels, he was faced with the shiny pink folds of the cerebral cortex, the outer region of the brain that holds our most human characteristics: abstract thought, consciousness, the self. To access the bottom of the frontal lobes, an area that sat just above the back of her eye sockets, Lima used a hypodermic needle to reach through the cortex and squirted a few drops of pure ethanol to dehydrate, and destroy, any neurons in this region. Moniz called this site of destruction a 'frontal barrier', one that he thought would release this patient from her fixed thoughts.

After the woman came to, Moniz declared the surgery a success. Her depression and restlessness had cleared, and he said it was a 'clinical cure'. Over the next four months, Moniz and Lima performed similar operations on patients provided by

José de Matos Sobral Cid, professor of psychiatry at Miguel Bombarda mental hospital in Lisbon. Nine of the patients (seven women and two men) were diagnosed with depression, six had schizophrenia, two had panic disorders, and one person suffered from what would later be called bipolar disorder. After the seventh patient, ethanol was swapped for a sharp metal instrument that Moniz called a 'leucotome', after the Greek words *leukós* for white (as in white matter) and *tome* for a cutting instrument. About the size of a chopstick, the leucotome had a retractable wire loop near one end that, when rotated, made a circular cut in any soft tissue it touched. To sufficiently disconnect the frontal lobes from the lower parts of the brain, Moniz advised Lima to make four to six cuts, two or three on each side of the brain. This became known as the 'core operation'. The operation itself – a slicing of the white matter that sits just behind the frontal lobes – was called a prefrontal leucotomy.

Soon after the neurology congress in London, Moniz wrote that 'true progress in this science [of psychiatry] will only be made with an organic orientation'. A strict biological psychiatrist, he was no disciple of Freud's theories of the psyche, the ego, or the unconscious. Mental disorders were rooted in the delicate concatenations of the brain, just as a broken leg is the product of a fractured bone. To Moniz, diseases such as depression and schizophrenia were the result of 'fixed connections', pathways in the brain that were overused like congested motorways. This biological traffic was replicated in a person's obsessions and certain thoughts or behaviour. People suffering from severe depression, Moniz wrote, 'live in a permanent state of anxiety caused by a fixed idea which predominates over all their lives', adding that 'these morbid ideas are deeply rooted in the synaptic complex which regulates the functioning of consciousness, stimulating it and keeping it in constant activity'. To Moniz, this relationship between anatomy and actions led to a single therapeutic option: 'it is necessary to alter these synaptic adjustments and change the paths chosen by the impulses in [an attempt] to modify the corresponding ideas and force thoughts along different paths'. Could Moniz block or redirect the flow of pathological thoughts in a depressed person's brain? Could he free their fixed thoughts with a simple surgical operation? Just as Becky was made happy and stoic after surgery, Moniz argued that severing the frontal lobes from the rest of the brain could turn a depressive character into a member of Becky's 'happiness cult'.

Moniz later argued that he had been thinking about prefrontal leucotomies long before he had even heard of Becky the chimpanzee, but there doesn't seem to be any good evidence for this claim. Even a cursory glance through the scientific literature of the time would have revealed that the function of the frontal lobes was far from clear. The chimpanzee research from Carlyle Jacobsen and John Fulton at the Primate Research Centre at Yale University, for instance, provided a valuable insight into the unpredictability of frontal-lobe surgeries. Becky's pen-pal Lucy (also a chimpanzee) had the same operation but was transformed from a calm character into a cantankerous, poo-flinging alter ego. It was the same operation with completely opposite outcomes. 'In his review of the literature on the frontal lobes,' the neuroscientist and historian Elliot Valenstein wrote, 'Moniz simply extracted what was useful to his argument and ignored the rest.'

On 26 July 1936, at the Parisian meeting of Société Médico-Psychologique, one of Moniz's students explained how 14 out of 20 patients had improved after their prefrontal leucotomies. Sobral Cid, the professor from Miguel Bombarda mental hospital, who was in attendance, argued that his patients were severely 'diminished' and had exhibited a 'degradation of personality' after the surgery. 'As for the hypothesis of functional fixation by which [Moniz] explains the good results of his method,' he added, 'it rests on pure cerebral mythology.'

In spite of such immediate first-hand criticism, leucotomies were soon performed in Romania, Italy, Brazil, and Cuba. But, even in these countries, the procedure was rarely used. Many psychiatrists were hesitant to take up such a radical and permanent approach to the treatment of mental disorders such as depression. Then, in the spring of 1936, an American psychiatrist from George Washington University opened a copy of Egas Moniz's first manuscript on leucotomy and thought that every page was bursting with a psychiatric revolution. His name was Walter Freeman, a goateed man who often walked with a cane. He was as charismatic as he was controversial.

'The Brain Has Ceased to Be Sacred'

Walter Freeman was the kind of doctor who could fill a lecture hall on the weekend. Even though they could be socialising or sleeping, his students would instead attend his classes on brain anatomy and psychiatry, and some would even bring their dates. He was both a lecturer and a performer. 'In the gloomy and tight days of the Great Depression, Freeman's lectures substituted for entertainment,' wrote his biographer Jack El-Hai. Stood at the front of the hall, Freeman would draw on the blackboard with both hands, not only to save time but as a dazzling accoutrement to his act. When he used patients from the university's psychiatric wards as living case studies, he treated each one as just another educational tool, largely insensitive to their feelings or confidentiality. To his audience, Freeman treated the bodies from the morgue and people from the hospital with the same level of respect, slicing through their brains with either a scalpel or his sharp tongue.

Often described as a genius, Freeman was an influential figure in psychiatry from a young age. In 1926, when he was just 31 years old, he was appointed as the head of his own department at George Washington University, an institution in the centre of Washington DC. A year later, he became a secretary of the American Medical Association, an academic perch that allowed him to oversee and support developments in the field. Like Egas Moniz, he presented his own work on brain imaging at the neurological meeting in London in August 1935, the first time the two met. A year later, after reading that Moniz had put his theory of 'fixed thoughts' into practice in Lisbon, Freeman started collaborating with his own skilled neurosurgeon at George Washington University. Tall, clean-shaven, and taciturn, James Watts shared a passion for brain science and the potential of neurosurgery. A former student of John Fulton at the primate laboratories at Yale, he had met Becky the chimpanzee before her operation. In contrast to her usual cantankerous nature, she vaulted over a few rows of seats to greet him and wrapped her arms around his neck in a loving embrace. Fulton, meanwhile, wasn't so enamoured by Watts. His student's seriousness contrasted with his own jovial character. But he couldn't help but admire his skills as a surgeon. As he once commented, Watts had 'the most beautiful pair of hands that I have ever seen at work at an operating table. It is really quite extraordinary.'

Even the most skilled surgeon is only as good as his tools. Soon after they met, Watts and Freeman ordered a few leucotomes from the same French supplier that Egas Moniz used and started practising his method of prefrontal leucotomy on pickled brains in the morgue. A promising collaboration between the sharpest mind and the most skilled hands was forming in the chilly basement of the hospital.

In the autumn of 1936, after they were satisfied with their 'coring' accuracy, Freeman and Watts operated on their first patient. Alice Hammatt was a 63-year-old housewife from Topeka, Kansas. Following her first pregnancy in her twenties and the death of the child, she had a long history of mental anguish. She struggled to sleep, felt constantly agitated and worried, and suffered from crushing bouts of depression. She was suicidal. Her main worry when it came to the operation was that her long curly hair had to be sacrificed in order to bore holes into her skull. After the operation, Freeman noted, she 'no longer cared' about her appearance. In total, Hammatt had six cores cut into her brain, two more than Moniz's standard operations and an early sign that Freeman and Watts were keen to develop their own method of prefrontal leucotomy. Indeed, they soon renamed the operation a 'frontal lobotomy', as they didn't just cut through the white matter of the brain (as in a leucotomy), but also took cores from the frontal lobes themselves. (A 'lobectomy' is a complete removal of the frontal lobes.)

Although hesitant to jump to conclusions, Freeman felt that Hammatt's operation was, on the whole, successful. 'Whether any permanent residuals of frontal lobe deficit will be manifested is uncertain at the present time,' he wrote, 'but the agitation and depression that the patient evinced previous to her operation are relieved.'

Although more commonly known for its use in chronic cases of schizophrenia, many of the first patients to receive lobotomies were suffering from what was then called involutional melancholia or agitated depression. They suffered from a devastating medley of delusions and morbid fears during their later years. People who had shown no sign of mental illness in their lives would, upon reaching their late 40s or 50s, fall victim to a disease that was a common sight in mental institutions. As one author wrote in the 1930s, 'the involutional melancholic would be a thin, elderly man or woman, inert, with the head lifted up off the pillow. There were some sort of Parkinsonian-like qualities, mask-like face sunk deep into misery ... If you could get them to say anything, it would be something about how hopeless things were, how they were wicked, doomed to disease, death, and a terrible afterlife, if there was one.'

Whether involutional melancholia was different than manic-depressive insanity was debatable. After all, similar delusions of guilt and wrongdoing could be found in younger patients.

But there was something about this variety of depression that warranted its own classification. There was the late onset without any previous record of psychiatric illness. The endless hand-wringing. Even the personality of the patients seemed widely different before their attack. While younger depressives were often described as outgoing, equable extroverts before and in between their depressive episodes, involutional melancholics were often introverted, sensitive, and lived day to day according to a strict routine. One author listed the classic traits as 'a narrow range of interests, poor facility for readjustment, asocial trends, inability to maintain friendships, intolerance and poor adult sexual adjustment, [and] also a pronounced and rigid ethical code'. This obsessive compulsion for order was seen as an important predisposition to their later decline. After reaching middle age, their well-choreographed routines were thrown out of whack by the natural transitions of life. The kids grew up and left home. Friends and family fell sick and sometimes died. Divorce or stale marriages can make someone dwell heavily on the past, on the opportunities missed, and the future that can never be. 'The mind is occupied with the "might-have-beens",' one textbook from 1956 states.

Before he eventually incorporated involutional melancholia into the diagnosis of manic-depressive insanity, Emil Kraepelin made some characteristically astute observations of such patients under his care. 'Remote and often insignificant facts are recalled, such as the stealing of fruit in childhood, disobedience to parents and neglect of friends,' he wrote, 'which now cause them the greatest anxiety. They are perfectly wretched about it.' He noticed that such delusions had a strong religious element that emerged in repetitive mantras or agitated moments of personal reverie. 'All wickedness is due to them,' Kraepelin wrote, 'they have desecrated the communion bread, or have spat upon the image of Christ. They are totally unworthy, should be buried alive ... hanging is too good.' While thinking so little of themselves, involutional melancholics also raised their actions and former deeds to the highest level of religious wrongdoing. They were equally derogatory and self-important.

With their repetitive symptoms – hand-wringing, pacing, the preoccupation with a few recurring thoughts – involutional melancholics were the biological incarnation of Egas Moniz's theories. They were rigidly fixed in body and mind. And because they were often chronically ill, not cycling between depression and lucid moments, even the most drastic forms of treatment were deemed necessary to halt their suffering. Desperate for relief and in very real danger of death from suicide or starvation, the prefrontal lobotomy soon became the treatment of choice for involutional melancholics, a quick surgical operation that could release them from their morbid obsessions. 'They all responded remarkably to prefrontal lobotomy,' two psychiatrists working in Boston, Massachusetts, wrote in *The New England Journal of Medicine*, the leading medical journal in the United States.

By 18 November 1936, just over two months since their first operation, Freeman and Watts had performed a total of six lobotomies. Again, their reports were a mix of positivity and caution over its use and potential misuse. '[T]he patients have become more placid, content, and more easily cared for by their relatives,' they wrote. 'We wish to emphasise also that indiscriminate use of the procedure could result in vast harm. Prefrontal lobotomy should at present be reserved for a small group of specially selected cases in which conservative methods of treatment have not yielded satisfactory results.' Moreover, they warned, 'every patient probably loses something by this operation, some spontaneity, some sparkle, some flavour of the personality'.

From the outset, that is, neither Freeman nor Watts thought that this was a cure for chronic depression or other mental disorders. A lobotomy couldn't bring a person back to health. It couldn't rewind time. But it could make people more peaceful, stoic, and content. Rather than suicidal, a patient was likely to be insensitive to their surroundings. A lack of emotional depth replaced constant worrying. A restless character was transformed into someone who sat in the same seat every day and stared out of a window. 'These patients are not only no longer distressed by their mental conflicts but also seem to have little capacity for any emotional experiences – pleasurable or otherwise,' one author later wrote. 'They are described by the nurses and the doctors, over and over, as dull, apathetic, listless, without drive or initiative, flat, lethargic, placid and unconcerned, childlike, docile, needing pushing, passive, lacking in spontaneity, without aim or purpose, preoccupied and dependent.'

Family members – the people who often knew patients best before their operations – reported haunting transformations in their loved ones. 'My husband may be better, but he is not the same,' the wife of a schizophrenic patient said. 'He is much inferior to what he was.' A parent said that her daughter was 'a different person. She is with me in body but her soul is in some way lost.'

As with the chimpanzee experiments at Yale and the few examples of frontal-lobe damage in humans, the operation's effect on personality was anyone's guess. 'We could fairly accurately predict relief of certain symptoms like suicidal ideas,' Watts later admitted during an interview in the 1970s. 'But we could not nearly as accurately predict what kind of person [they were] going to be.'

Late in 1937, Freeman and Watts replaced Moniz's 'coring method' with what they called the 'precision method'. Instead of using a retractable wire loop to cut small spheres in the brain, they designed a cutting tool that looked like a butter knife crossed with a knitting needle. Flat and with a ruled edge to measure the depth of an incision, this tool enabled a clean cut rather than a rough core. (Their Washington-based manufacturer engraved both their names into their handles.) To guide his blade, Watts orientated himself with a series of landmarks on a person's skull. First, the squiggly line where the frontal bones of the skull fuse together (known as the coronal suture) was a natural marker for where to cut the two boring holes, each drilled along this line and just above the temples. Second, an arch of bone that sits above the nasal cavity provided an estimate of how far into the frontal lobes to cut.

This change in method was soon followed by a change in theory. In 1939, three years after the first lobotomy in the United States, Freeman proposed that this operation didn't just disrupt 'fixed thoughts' (as Moniz had proposed) but disconnected the frontal lobes from the emotional centre of the brain, known as the thalamus. The more connections they cut, he thought, the less emotional oomph the thalamus provided to a person's thoughts. For the more severe or 'incurable' cases of schizophrenia, Watts performed a 'radical' lobotomy, disconnecting larger sections of the frontal lobes from the thalamus below. The common side effects – headaches, incontinence, confusion, and apathy – were also more likely and more severe. For the agitated, involutional melancholics, however, they performed a 'minimal' or 'standard' lobotomy, slicing a smaller section of the frontal lobes and still finding that the depression and anxiety often lifted. 'Long-standing depressions disappear as if by magic,' one doctor noted.

*

The immediate reaction to prefrontal lobotomy was as divisive as the operation itself. While some thought that it was the future of biological psychiatry, a much-needed addition to the paltry selection of treatments that it offered its patients, others thought that it was a reversion to the radical bloodlettings of yore. 'This is not an operation, this is a mutilation,' one psychiatrist said shortly after its introduction.

In April 1941, at a meeting of the American Psychiatric Association held in Cleveland, Ohio, a heated discussion on lobotomy took place around a single table. Walter Freeman, as expected, was at the centre of attention, sitting on a six-person panel that discussed the merits and limits of neurosurgery, the umbrella term for any surgical operation on the brain. He started by defining what the frontal lobes were. They were linked to foresight, he said, 'that is, with looking into the future and with the consciousness of the self'. It was these traits, he thought, that a lobotomy disrupted. A person lost interest in themselves, became uninterested by any prior delusions of guilt or persecution, two traits at the core of those depressions experienced by people who were prime candidates for a lobotomy. Without foresight, patients lived in the present and failed to worry about the future. 'The past and future seem telescoped for them into the present,' the psychologist Mary Frances Robinson wrote. 'They meet each situation as well as they can and then are ready for the next one.'

Another panellist, Dr Lyerly, then described 24 of his patients with involutional melancholia. Although they weren't always discharged, he said that over 70 per cent had improved. 'By "improvement", I mean that the patients came out of the severe mentally depressed states and became happy, cheerful and slightly elevated,' he said. 'The patient frequently wakes up with a smile on his face ... and they were no longer such a problem in the hospital.' Along with the reduction in suicidal actions, forced feedings became a thing of the past. Everyone ate. And ate. And ate. While some argued that this increased appetite was due to the damage done to the brain, Freeman said that it was a by-product of their well-being. '[T]he gain in weight is merely an expression of the contentment with existence as it is,' he told his fellow panellists.

M.A. Tarumianz, the superintendent of the Delaware State Hospital at Farnhurst, added to Lyerly's positive results. Shortly after Freeman and Watts created their 'precision method', Tarumianz operated on eight patients with severe depressions. Between the ages of 37 and 66, seven had been suicidal and two had attempted to end their lives several times. After the operation, however, all of them had shown remarkable transformations. Two were even able to return to work.

The economic benefits of lobotomies seemed obvious. If institutionalised patients were able to return to their homes, their families, and even their former jobs, they were no longer an expense of the state. Trained psychiatrists, doctors, medication, and custodial care can quickly add up to costly medical bills. And since mental institutions were funded by taxpayers' money, everyone could benefit from any treatment that could reduce the inpatient population. With a back-of-the-envelope calculation, Tarumianz told his fellow panellists that lobotomies could save the average mental institution $351,000 every year.

But these calculations translated into an uncomfortable reality. Tarumianz's reduced costs of care didn't just encompass those patients who had been sent home, but also those who had died from their treatment. And with lobotomy this wasn't an insignificant number. With a skilled surgeon, between 2 to 4 per cent of patients died during or shortly after the operation, usually from a major blood vessel being accidentally cut in their brain. But hidden away in unpublished cases, these numbers could increase to 10 or even 20 per cent. Tarumianz used the conservative estimate of 10 per cent mortality. This number – a fully grown male elephant in the room – was flicked aside as if it was an unimportant speck on case reports. 'So far I have not seen a single case that has not responded favourably except in which death occurred,' Tarumianz said.

Roy Grinker, a psychoanalyst from Chicago who had been trained by Sigmund Freud in Europe, added a voice of reason to this panel. Although he wasn't against the use of lobotomy, he refused to jump to any conclusions given the lack of experience and empirical data. The economic costs were meaningless, he said. Any saving to the mental institution would simply be taken up by the patient's household or community. 'In the long run it makes very little difference,' he told his fellow panellists. His main concern, however, was the possibility that the patients would have recovered without any operation whatsoever. Although he didn't use the term, he was concerned about the placebo effect. 'The amount of attention and interest in the long hospitalised [patient] is practically nil,' Grinker said. 'Now you have a new operation and you are enthusiastic about it. You bring your patient into the hospital ward. You operate on him. You supply him with nurses. You pay a lot of attention to him. You have brought to bear on this patient a tremendous amount of psychologic care which he did not have before and you get some results.' How could anyone determine whether a successful operation was due to the lobotomy or all of the other elements of the treatment? Grinker also raised the important point of spontaneous recoveries. 'I have previously expressed my surprise that patients have been operated on after only a few months of mental illness,' Grinker added. 'It is obvious that even the natural process of recovery has not been allowed to take its effect ... But, once one cuts, there is no return.'

Although similar critiques appeared in scientific journals in 1941, few of these words seemed to filter through to the public. In the early 1940s, journalists were largely positive when writing about prefrontal lobotomy. If newspapers and magazines were to be believed, a cure for mental disorders had just been discovered, and Walter Freeman was akin to Jesus Christ, a bearded man dressed in white robes who could perform miracles. On 24 May 1941, a month after the conference in Cleveland, the *Saturday Evening Post* ran a three-page feature on Freeman and Watts. 'The brain has ceased to be sacred,' the science writer and editor Waldemar Kaempffert wrote. 'Surgeons now think no more of operating upon it than they do cutting out an appendix.' This wasn't a criticism of an overly gung-ho approach to psychiatry. It was a statement of celebration, a comment on how far psychiatry had come in the treatment and understanding of mental disorders. The patients were the true benefactors of this daring approach. 'A world that once seemed the abode of misery, cruelty and hate is now radiant with sunshine and kindness to them,' Kaempffert wrote. Wearing face masks, surgical gowns, and pointing to an illuminated X-ray of a skull, Freeman and Watts were pictured as intrepid explorers ushering in a bright future of precision medicine.

In *Psychosurgery*, their 1942 textbook on lobotomies and similar operations, Freeman, Watts, and their colleague Thelma Hunt, an associate professor of psychology at George Washington University, dedicated their work to Egas Moniz, the man who 'first conceived and executed a valid operation for mental disorder'. In 1939, Moniz had been shot four times by a delusional patient in Lisbon. Although he survived, he was badly injured, permanently disabled, and went through months of arduous rehabilitation. He never fully recovered. In his letters to Freeman, he updated his younger disciple on his health. Already retired and approaching 70 years old, Moniz focused on his writings and only occasionally supervised the operation he had invented.

Psychosurgery was a pivotal turning point in the history of the prefrontal lobotomy. It solidified a growing realisation in the psychiatric community that the procedure had moved away from its leucotomy roots to become the specialty of American psychiatry, of Walter Freeman and his surgical sidekick. Largely written in Freeman's flowing prose, the book provided a captivating journey from the skull trepanations of antiquity, through the theories of frontal-lobe function, and into the prefrontal lobotomy and its origin at the International Neurological Congress in London, where Moniz heard the reports about Becky the chimpanzee. After performing 80 surgical operations between 1936 and 1941, Freeman concluded that the best results were found in depressions that came with severe agitation or fixed delusions. Overall, roughly two-thirds (63 per cent) of such patients could be expected to improve after a lobotomy.

Miss E.G., a 59-year-old housekeeper who suffered bouts of depression every ten years, was a classic case study for the operation. She was also the first patient mentioned in *Psychosurgery*. Before the operation, she constantly fidgeted, rubbing her hands together as if massaging them with moisturiser. Her mind was elsewhere, her attention span short. And although she had no intention to kill herself, she wished that she would die soon. 'The mood was one of enormous depression,' Freeman wrote. On 17 April 1937, with her consent and that of her family and her priest, Miss. E.G. was injected with morphine and an anaesthetic, and given a lobotomy. 'As the operation progressed, she dropped off to sleep and snored gently,'

Freeman wrote. 'Very little bleeding was encountered and the patient left the operating table in excellent condition.'

Two weeks later, Miss E.G. was discharged from the hospital. After the initial confusion and incontinence had cleared, her incisions healed, and the scars were covered by a shock of new hair. 'They tell me that I look ten years younger,' she reported. 'When I'm tired, I still get the circles under my eyes, but they don't seem to be as deep as they used to be.' Although she spent most of her time at her sister's home, continuing her work as a housekeeper, she enjoyed visiting the local cinema. Previously such an excursion was torture, the depression making any trip out meaningless and painful. 'But last night I went and really enjoyed it,' she reported to Freeman. 'I forgot myself during the movie, and when I came out, I felt refreshed rather than harassed like I used to.'

Miss. E.G. was content within her domestic lifestyle, but other patients were not so lucky. One person with depression died during the operation, a casualty caused by an accidental cut to the anterior cerebral artery that nourishes the frontal lobes with oxygenated blood. And although Freeman never mentioned her by name, Rosemary Kennedy – the younger sister of the future president of the United States, John F. Kennedy – was permanently disabled after a botched lobotomy in November 1941. In *Psychosurgery* she was simply labelled as one of the 'poor' results. This was a tragic understatement.

As a wealthy businessman, investor, and politician, Joe Kennedy Sr had built his life on his own success. But for more years than he liked to think about, he was at a loss with his eldest daughter. In many ways, Rosemary was the perfect child – pretty, with long curly hair and a straight-toothed smile. But inside, Joe thought, she was a torrent of unsuitable emotions, a young woman who was set to tarnish the family name. She would not conform to the family's social norms; rather than being placidly well-mannered, she was rebellious and prone to staying away from home overnight. Joe thought that puberty had caused a change in her personality. But even as a baby Rosemary had seemed different. Compared to her eight siblings, she didn't take to reading or writing so easily. While his other children excelled at school, Rosemary always remained a few years behind her age group. Her condition – what would today be termed 'learning difficulties' but was then known as 'feeble-mindedness' – was thought to have been a result of a lack of oxygen during the final stages of her birth.

Despite her disability, Rosemary rose to any occasion that she faced. When her father became US ambassador to Great Britain in 1938, she strolled through Buckingham Palace in the presence of royalty, turning heads as she walked past with her bright smile and trailing white dress. She had no problems in attracting the attention of the opposite sex. Like many young girls, she became fascinated by boys and started to enjoy their flirtations. As a pupil at a convent school in Washington DC, she would sneak out at night, freeing herself from the expectations of her family, and drink alcohol into the early morning. According to one biographer of the Kennedy family, the nuns at the school 'feared that she was picking up men and might become pregnant or diseased'.

It was when Rosemary turned 21 years old that her behaviour became most alien to the Kennedys. She threw and smashed objects in the house. She would scream and storm up to her room after the slightest provocation. Once, she kicked her grandfather in the shin. On top of her irritability and anger, she was often depressed, a mental state that might have been rooted in the isolation she felt from her own family. Rosemary was one of nine siblings, and it was made obvious that she was not like them.

Her parents worried that her behaviour was the result of some 'neurological disturbance [that] had overtaken her, and it was becoming progressively worse'. Without consulting his wife, Joe Kennedy Sr spoke to a Boston-based doctor and asked whether the latest psychosurgery operations might 'fix' his daughter. He was told that such action wasn't merited. Then he met with Walter Freeman and James Watts in Washington DC, at their offices not far from Rosemary's school. Watts told Joe that Rosemary suffered from 'agitated depression' and that lobotomies had shown great promise in reducing the intense mood swings and outbursts of this affliction.

In November 1941, Rosemary was strapped to a table with only Novocain, a local anaesthetic, for comfort. The pain was softened but she was conscious throughout. The hard bone of her skull vibrated as the drill went in – twice, once on either side of her forehead. The experience was defined by 'a grinding sound that is as distressing, or more so, than the drilling of a tooth'. As James Watts pushed the leucotome in, Freeman knelt down next to Rosemary, asking her to complete simple cognitive tasks. Can you count backwards from ten? Can you state the Lord's Prayer? What about 'God Bless America'?

'We made an estimate on how far to cut based on how she responded,' Freeman would later say.

After her scalp was stitched back together and the anaesthetic had cleared, Rosemary's mental capacity was compared to that of a two-year-old. She couldn't walk properly, and her right arm hung motionless at her side. She was incontinent. After a short stay at a private psychiatric hospital north of New York City, Rosemary lived the rest of her life in a small outbuilding – nicknamed 'Kennedy Cottage' by her carers – at

St. Coletta School for Exceptional Children in Jefferson, Wisconsin. 'The nurse who attended the operation was so horrified by what happened to Rosemary that she left nursing altogether, haunted for the rest of her life by the outcome,' wrote Kate Clifford Larson in her 2015 biography of Rosemary.

Even with such blatant risks, lobotomies were soon performed in countries that were initially hesitant to accept this new treatment. The first lobotomies were performed in Britain in 1943. A year later, a few psychiatry departments in the Soviet Union started their own psychosurgery programmes. As it spread, the operation was adapted by surgeons into a dizzying array of techniques. The angle of the incision, the region of the brain that was severed, and the type of tool used: all were modified to suit the patient or, more commonly, the latest theories of mental disorder. Some surgeons preferred to open up the skull rather than blindly cutting through two bore holes. Unswayed by this technique, Freeman wrote, 'The surgeon sees what he cuts but does not know what he sees.' While brain tissue was being frozen, cauterised, or sucked up like spaghetti, Freeman and Watts stuck to their trusted precision method. 'We claimed ours was the best,' Watts said, 'but it's hard to know.'

In the UK, Wylie McKissock, a leading surgeon from Atkinson Morley Hospital in Wimbledon, southwest London, became a vocal advocate for the Freeman-Watts lobotomy, performing over 3,000 operations during his career. 'This is not a time-consuming operation,' he once wrote. '[It] can be done by a properly trained neurosurgeon in six minutes and seldom takes more than ten minutes.' Bore, prod, swivel, stitch – a personality changed for ever.

In the mid 1940s, Walter Freeman replaced his 'precision method' of lobotomy with a procedure that required little skill, few instruments, and zero surgical training. '[I]t proved to be the ideal operation for use in crowded mental hospitals with a shortage of everything except patients,' Freeman wrote. He called it the transorbital lobotomy, but it would become more widely known as the 'ice-pick method'.

Unlike the prefrontal procedure that required two bore holes in the skull, the transorbital method entered the brain through the back of the eye sockets. Using a hammer and a metal implement that looked like a sharp ice pick, Freeman accessed the brain cavity with a forceful tap and then moved his blade back and forth, blind to what and where he cut. Its simplicity made the operation faster and, therefore, open to more patients. Its indiscriminate use spread throughout mental institutions and into the surrounding communities in the United States. Freeman would even go 'on tour', driving over 11,000 miles in a station wagon to perform his transorbital lobotomies. 'Some of the "black eyes" are beauties,' he wrote in the same callous manner he had once shown in his university lectures. 'I usually ask the family to provide the patient with sunglasses rather than explanations.'

Freeman's mother once called him the 'cat who walks by himself'. He was independent, a loner, someone who thrived in his own company and didn't require any external input for motivation. But with transorbital lobotomy he was pushing his innate tendencies to their limits. Not just a maverick, he became a heretic. This procedure was not supported by even his closest peers. 'What are these terrible things I hear about you doing lobotomies in your office with an ice pick?' John Fulton, the primate researcher from Yale wrote to Freeman. 'Why not use a shotgun? It would be quicker!' From its first use in 1946, James Watts refused to adopt or condone this method. 'In both mental and physical disease, surgical intervention should be reserved for cases in which conservative therapy has been tried and failed or in cases where such treatment is known to be ineffective,' he wrote. 'It is my opinion that any surgical procedure involving cutting of brain tissue is a major surgical operation, no matter how quickly or [easily] one enters the intracranial cavity. Therefore, it follows, logically, that only those who have been schooled in neurosurgical technics, and can handle complications which may arise, should perform the operation.' In response, Freeman wrote, 'I am equally insistent that it is a minor operation since it involves no cutting or sewing, and that it should be performed by psychiatrists.'

Freeman had not only estranged himself from his closest colleague but the field of biological psychiatry as a whole. While he used his transorbital method on a whim, other leaders in the field had begun to acknowledge the need for a conscientious selection of patients before conducting any form of psychosurgery. 'The more one employs and studies this method of operation, the more clearly one realises that in individual, carefully selected cases it can yield much of value,' Snorre Wohlfahrt, a psychiatrist working in Stockholm, Sweden, said in 1947. Selecting the wrong patient, however, could lead to permanent damage or exacerbation of the initial problem.

How did such a radical treatment become so popular? Why did so many respected psychiatrists put their faith in such an irreversible, and ultimately unproven, surgical operation? It was as if they were probing every possibility and hoping that something – anything – would turn out to benefit their patients. And lobotomies certainly had the potential to change lives. It was an operation that could induce a state of harmony to a once hectic mind. 'In several of the greatly improved cases the effect of the operation has been sensational,' Wohlfahrt said.

'Whereas they had previously been depressed, inhibited, ego-centrically self-pitying individuals, or tormented by obsessive thoughts and confined in their activities, they have recuperated, become cheerful, active persons, freed from inhibitions and needless worry ... If time permitted, much might be said about these case histories and the revolutionary changes in character through which these patients have passed.' The therapeutic goal for a lobotomy was focused on introducing a more manageable mental state and hoping that it was an improvement on what came before. (This approach was once likened to taking the 'sting' out of mental disorders.) Although a patient's personality might be irrevocably altered, they were, hopefully, no longer a threat to themselves or their family. They could return home and might even return to work. 'If the reward of the physician is the satisfaction of alleviating distress,' one psychiatrist wrote, 'we have felt that the operation brought this reward. Patients were more comfortable and families gratified.' Rather than spending years on an overcrowded ward, tormented, sleepless, and kept in questionable conditions, the appeal of returning to their community would have been obvious to any patient (and their family). Plus, this operation was undoubtedly effective in reducing the number of institutionalised patients, a popular metric for the success of any medical treatment. Regardless of how functional patients were after the operation, psychiatrists and doctors believed that the more people out of mental hospitals the better.

In 1949, Egas Moniz was awarded the Nobel Prize in Physiology or Medicine for 'his discovery of the therapeutic value of leucotomy in certain psychoses'. Controversial and hotly debated into the present, this honour no doubt helped to cement lobotomy as a real scientific discovery for the field of biological psychiatry. In reality, however, the wheels had already started to turn against this popular form of psycho-surgery.

In 1953, Nikolai Oserezki, director of the psychiatric institute at the IP Pavlov Leningrad Medical Institute told a meeting of the World Federation for Mental Health that every lobotomy 'violates the principles of humanity'. Arguing that it was only good for turning patients into 'vegetables' or 'intellectual invalids', he voiced concerns that had been fuelling active debate for years in the Soviet Union. Although only a few hundred operations had been performed there since the end of 1944, there were many who advocated the use of lobotomies in chronic or otherwise incurable cases of mental disorder. Even so, based on the outspoken criticism and research of the psychiatrist Vasili Giliarovskii, the Soviet Minister of Health signed a decree on 9 December 1950 that banned the procedure across the entire Communist state.

The initial positivity and hope that surrounded lobotomies was replaced with widespread caution or outright condemnation. An article published in *Scientific American* in 1950, for example, stated that 'it is certainly an exaggeration to refer to all lobotomized patients as "human vegetables", as one author has done. Yet the results are serious enough to give us considerable concern.' After the Soviet Union, many other countries banned the operation entirely. Its declining use in depression, however, was largely due to another treatment, a competitor that was invented two years after Walter Freeman had first heard of Moniz's prefrontal leucotomy. It was cheaper, required no surgical training whatsoever, and didn't merely flatten the emotional reactivity of agitated patients. But it wasn't a newly discovered drug that revolutionised the field of biological psychiatry. It was the redirected flow of electricity from a light switch.

The Most Powerful Reaction

Ugo Cerletti, chair of the Clinic for Nervous and Mental Disorders at the University of Rome La Sapienza, was brought to the slaughterhouse on a rumour. In the spring of 1937 – a time when Italy's fascist dictator Benito Mussolini was in crazed cahoots with Adolf Hitler – one of Cerletti's colleagues had told him that pigs were killed with powerful bursts of electricity. 'Electrical slaughtering,' he called it. Welcomed to the slaughterhouse in Rome by the thick smell of manure and the din of snuffling grunts, Cerletti soon found that the rumour was false. The electric shock – 125 volts delivered to the sides of the head with a large calliper-like contraption – instantly made the pigs freeze, fall onto the stone floor, and convulse as if they were having epileptic fits. Unsightly and brutal, this was the humane part of slaughter. It ensured that the pigs, a large white breed from England, were unconscious before their throats were cut. If left untouched, Cerletti noticed, they soon got back onto their hooves and trotted back to their pen pals. They seemed dazed, confused perhaps, but altogether unharmed.

'It occurred to me that the hogs of the slaughterhouse could furnish the most valuable material in my experiments,' Cerletti wrote. Swapping his laboratory coat for some grubby overalls, Cerletti, a broad-chested 60-year-old with slick black hair and thick bushy eyebrows, picked up the large calliper-like contraption with both hands and placed it around a pig's head. A quick burst of electricity was all that was needed to induce the epileptic-like fit, he found. Only when he left the electricity running for over a minute – 600 times longer than the usual tenth of a second – was the electric shock fatal. This was a huge margin of safety, Cerletti thought. 'These observations gave me convincing evidence of the harmlessness of a few tenths of a second of application through the head of a 125-volt electric current, which was more than sufficient to insure a complete convulsive seizure.'

While Cerletti was shocking pigs at the slaughterhouse, his student Lucio Bini was busy at the university's clinic, a three-storey, ochre-coloured concrete building, studying how brief electric shocks affected the brains of dogs and other laboratory animals. The use of stray dogs in laboratory research, collected by the municipal dogcatcher, was normal in the 1930s, an era of biological science before the introduction of specific strains of mice and rats (today's go-to lab mammals). After each experiment, the dogs were euthanised and their brains were sliced and stained. Peering down his tabletop microscope at these tissue sections, Bini was looking for signs of nerve damage. Is that fibril out of place? Is that cell's nucleus disintegrated? Are there signs of haemorrhage? When he found time away from his other duties, Cerletti would pop in for a look. At the microscope, one of his students thought that he looked 'like a falcon high in the sky, searching for prey on the ground below'. Neither Cerletti nor Bini saw anything that might prevent brief electric shocks from being used in humans. It was a huge moment for Cerletti. '[W]e had at our disposal, for the first time, the possibility of inducing in man, at will and without harm, convulsions,' he wrote, 'this most powerful reaction of the nervous system.'

Epilepsy, and the convulsions that it can cause, winds a long and dark path through human history. Before it was given a medical name, this mysterious disease was explained in entirely supernatural terms. Demons, gods, or otherwise: the fits were the mark of the unearthly, a person who had been seized by an invisible spirit and left the confines of natural law. For their supposed curse, people with epilepsy have long been shunned, shamed, and isolated from their families or communities. It was once thought that the convulsions were contagious and people would step away from this so-called 'Sacred disease'. Philosophers and physicians, however, inquisitive souls that they are, often stepped closer. For them, epileptic fits were a curiosity. Rather than a curse, many found them to be a potential cure for many diseases of the mind.

In his 1758 book *A Treatise on Madness*, one of the first textbooks dedicated to mental illness, the English physician William Battie wrote, 'as ignorant as we are and perhaps shall always be of the reason, experience has shown that ... one species of spasm however occasioned seldom fails to put an end to that other [malady] which before subsisted'. In 1828, G. Burrows, a doctor working in London, found that two scruples of camphor oil – a gloopy liquid used for candle wax or embalming bodies – could induce a convulsive seizure in his patients with insanity. 'A complete cure followed,' he wrote. One of his contemporaries agreed, writing, 'When the patient awakes from the epileptic attack his reason will return.' In the 1930s, Ladislas von Meduna, a neurologist at the Brain Research Institute in Budapest, bolstered these broad observations down to a microscopic level. Slicing up hundreds of pickled brains from patients who had died from a variety of diseases, he found that those from epileptic and schizophrenic patients were opposites of each other. Those from epileptic patients were packed with glial cells, the putty or 'glue' of the brain's tangled network of neurons. In contrast, schizophrenic brains were deficient in these cells. 'To explain the difference,' von Meduna later wrote, 'I developed the hypothesis that the [cause of] epilepsy has a stimulating effect upon the growth of the glia cells, while [that of] schizophrenia has an opposite, a paralysing, effect of the glia system.' In short, there was a 'biological antagonism' between epilepsy and schizophrenia.

Although this theory would turn out to be wrong, it would still lead von Meduna to a grand therapeutic conclusion: if he could find a way to induce an epileptic fit, he might find a cure for schizophrenia, a disease that Emil Kraepelin had once deemed incurable.

As with malaria and neurosyphilis, could one disease treat another? Von Meduna tested various drugs on laboratory animals to see if any could reliably induce a convulsion. Strychnine, thebaine, nikethamide, caffeine, absinthe – all were unsatisfactory. In June 1934, he settled on camphor oil, the same convulsant that doctors had used centuries before his time. Injecting this dark and viscous substance into his patient's muscle, an epileptic-like fit would normally begin within a few minutes. Sometimes, however, it took half an hour – and the waiting was agony for the patient. Knowing that the fit was about to happen, but not knowing exactly when, left each person in a panicked state before they succumbed to the inevitable. The feeling would later be described as 'impending doom'. Sometimes the convulsion didn't even occur.

When the injection had the intended effect, the grand mal seizure progressed through its familiar stages. For the first few seconds, in what is known as the 'tonic phase', the muscles of the body jerk into a state of contraction. The spine arches backwards. The jaw clamps upwards like a vice. With every sinew straining, vomit, urine, faeces, and, for men, semen are sometimes ejected from the body. After this brutal beginning, the 'clonic phase' takes over. For the next 30 to 40 seconds, the limbs and trunk of the body start to gyrate as if the person is lying down in the back of a van being driven over a cobbled street. Frothing at the mouth is not unusual.

It wasn't a pleasant experience or a pretty sight. But von Meduna's patients seemed much healthier in the convulsion's wake. Out of his first 24 patients in Budapest, he found that ten were rid of the hallucinations, delusions, and inexplicable paroxysms that defined their condition for so long. Publishing his results in 1934, von Meduna found that once-catatonic patients started to get out of bed, dress themselves, eat food without forced feedings, and – for the first time in years – start talking. Soon after this, he found a replacement for camphor oil, a drug known as cardiazol (marketed as Metrazol in the United States). Faster in its action, it reduced the level of anxiety before the convulsion. This 'convulsive therapy' would soon encircle the globe, spreading from Budapest to other countries in Europe and into the Americas. Feeling like he had just found the source of the Nile, von Meduna wrote 'a new art and possibility of cure opens up for us'.

After a few of his students returned from a training course in convulsive therapy in Vienna in 1936, Ugo Cerletti had one question: why didn't they use electricity instead? Before he visited the slaughterhouse, he had been using short bursts of electricity to induce epileptic seizures in his laboratory animals for years, studying the effects on the hippocampus, a region of the brain involved in memory. It was a project driven more by curiosity than any urge to develop a new medical treatment. 'I never thought that these experiments would have any practical application,' he wrote. But the link between electricity and convulsive therapy seemed too obvious to ignore. After centuries of using toxic injections like camphor oil, he wondered whether his research could offer something more humane.

*

In March 1938, police officers brought a new patient into Cerletti's clinic. In his late 30s or early 40s, the man had been found wandering through the central station in Rome in a confused state, muttering to himself in a language that no one else understood. As one of Cerletti's students later wrote, he 'was unemotional, living passively, like a tree that does not give fruit ... We concluded that we were dealing with a mentality that was completely unraveled, and gave little hope, even for a partial recovery'. This patient was exactly what Cerletti had been waiting for. He asked Bini to set up their electroshock machine – a shoebox-sized, cream-coloured cube of metal with a few dials, knobs, and switches on its top surface – in a quiet backroom on the first floor of the clinic. Used by a laboratory technician who took naps between shifts, it was empty but for a small metal-framed bed in the corner. It was unlikely that they would be disturbed or, as Cerletti feared, discovered by his peers. Just in case, he asked one of his younger students to poke his head out of the door now and again, just to check if anyone might be coming.

The air in the room was thick with anticipation. In a few seconds, Cerletti's reputation could be destroyed. A former student of Emil Kraepelin and Alois Alzheimer in Munich, Cerletti was a gifted teacher in his own right and, upon returning to Italy, was nicknamed 'the Maestro' for his didactic approach to psychiatry. He exuded warmth and empathy, a humanism that later became known as the 'Cerletti atmosphere'. This academic standing took decades to amass. But it could all be lost in an instant. Cerletti knew that what happened in this disused room was on his head. What if the patient died? What if he and Lucio Bini had missed something in their brain autopsies? He had been concerned about the answers to such questions ever since he'd first heard of von Meduna's convulsive therapy. Inspired by the 'youthful enthusiasm' of Bini, he also couldn't help thinking that this could be the spark that fuels a revolution in biological psychiatry.

Bini, a portly 30-year-old with a thick moustache, stood next to the machine he had helped build. Plugged into a nearby light switch, a couple of thick black wires snaked into a device that looked like a huge pair of headphones. Inside each of the two thick pads of brown cloth was an electrode, a flat piece of metal where the electric shock would jump into the patient's skull. Dipped in a saline solution, these pads were placed over the patient's temples and, when all was set, Cerletti gave the signal for the treatment to begin. As the switch was flicked on, an automatic stopwatch inside the machine allowed the electricity to flow for a fraction of a second. Almost immediately, the patient's body tensed up, he let out a groan, and his back arched upwards from the bed. His mouth opened wide and then clamped down on a piece of pipe wrapped in rubber that protected his tongue from his teeth. After a few seconds, the tonic phase of the convulsion ended and the patient progressed into the clonic phase. His legs and arms thrashed wildly.

Then he turned blue. He wasn't breathing, and his blood and brain were being deprived of oxygen. The room was silent except for Bini's voice. He had started counting. Soon, his colleagues were counting along with him. It became a ceremonial chant of sorts, one that they all hoped would culminate with a sign of life. At the 48th second – a period that seemed like an eternity – the patient sighed heavily and everyone took a long, deep breath. It wasn't particularly hot in the room, but one student, Ferdinando Accornero, noticed that his forehead was beaded with sweat. 'Now the patient was breathing regularly, was sleeping, and was calm,' Accornero later wrote. 'We

A Cure for Darkness

glanced at each other; in our eyes, there was a new shining light.' Cerletti confirmed that the session was a success.

Although it is often cited as such, this wasn't the first time this patient received electroshock therapy. The details of the first session – what happened, who was there, whether it worked – have been lost over subsequent decades. Memories are fallible. Biographies are often biased. And stories are reshaped every time they are told. For a touch of clarity, it is necessary to go back to Lucio Bini's original notebooks. Reading through these documents, Roberta Passione, a historian from the University of Bologna, discovered a slightly different story. In black scribbles across A5 lined paper, Bini recorded that the first 80 volts for one tenth of a second ended in the patient singing at the top of his voice. The subsequent shocks were then increased in duration to half a second and then three quarters of a second. The voltage remained constant, and so did the result – there was no convulsion. 'The patient is freed, gets up immediately, walks quietly back to the ward, talking in his usual loose way,' Bini wrote. 'In the afternoon and the following day, he did not present any phenomenon of particular mention.' He hadn't been harmed. But he also wasn't showing any signs of improvement.

Over the next few weeks, however, this first patient would be given 11 sessions of electroshock therapy – 11 successful convulsions – and would show such an improvement that he'd be discharged from the university's clinic on 17 June 1938, returning home to his wife in Milan and continuing his work as an engineer. Three months later, however, his symptoms slowly reappeared. In bed, he would whisper to himself and begin to distance himself from his wife. It was the first sign that this was no miracle cure. Electroshock therapy could boost a patient back to health, but it couldn't keep them there for ever.

As Cerletti and Bini gained more experience with this new form of convulsive therapy, they began to share their results and methods. On 28 May 1938, just over two months since their first patient had been brought into their clinic, they presented their observations at a meeting of the Royal Medical Academy of Rome. Cerletti began by describing the previous form of convulsive therapy: the Cardiazol method of von Meduna. It was costly, involved a painful injection, and the fear of impending doom before the convulsion understandably made patients hesitant to be treated a second time. Even after the convulsion had passed, the remaining Cardiazol in the patient's body caused an agitated state that could last for a number of hours. Electroshock didn't come with these drawbacks. 'Loss of consciousness instantaneously follows delivery of the current,' Cerletti told his audience. 'Afterwards, there is a phase of muscular relaxation with stertorous breathing. The state of unconsciousness lightens gradually and the patient becomes more alert, relaxes the jaw, moves the eyes and begins to answer to verbal stimuli. After five minutes he can talk but remains clouded. After eight to ten minutes the patient is completely himself. If not disturbed, he falls asleep and after a few hours wakes up completely restored.'

'The advantage of this method,' he added, 'is the immediate and absolute loss of consciousness of the subject, lasting for all the length of the treatment. The patients, if asked about their experience, state they do not remember anything but having slept.'

Back in the clinic at the University of Rome La Sapienza, scenes of secrecy transformed into loud celebration. Three to four times a week, one of Cerletti's assistants, Spartaco Mazzanti, would blow an out-of-tune trumpet through the wards to signal that the next session of this revolutionary treatment was about to start. The once disused backroom on the first floor became packed with curious onlookers, students, and a suite of psychiatrists recording the heart rate, blood pressure, brain activity, and other quantifiable measures of a patient's health.

Despite communications between fascist Italy and the rest of the world being stymied, news of Cerletti's work nevertheless reached across the Atlantic. 'Although physicians were reluctant to earmark the new treatment as particularly beneficial for any specific type of insanity,' an article in the *New York Times* stated in June 1940, 'it was said that it had been used successfully in [the] treatment of schilzophrenia [*sic*].' This was already an outdated conclusion in Cerletti's clinic in Rome. In his first manuscript on the topic, entitled 'L'Elletroshock' and published in the Italian journal *Rivista Sperimentale di Freniatria* in 1940, he wrote, 'Even more brilliant results than in schizophrenia were obtained in manic-depressive insanity, particularly in depressive episodes.' From the 180 or so patients who had received electroshock therapy in Rome since April 1938, he found that depressed patients required fewer convulsions to bring about a recovery. In some cases, only four sessions, spread over a week or so, were all that was needed. In comparison, schizophrenic patients might need 20 sessions or more. 'We seem to be able to state that the morbid [depressive] episodes are actually halted or at least considerably shortened in their presumable duration,' Cerletti concluded. 'A series of complete remissions was obtained.'

Ugo Cerletti's detailed manuscript on electroshock therapy – a product of two years of research, detailed methodology, and over 180 patients – was seldom read outside of Italy. Even today, it hasn't been translated from its original Italian. Appropriately for the Maestro, it was his cherished students and colleagues who helped spread his invention around the globe. And none of his former students had a larger influence than Lothar Kalinowsky, a German neurologist who witnessed the second patient to ever receive electroshock therapy in 1938 and vowed to never see it again. That evening, when Kalinowsky arrived home to his wife Hilda, she thought he looked as 'white as a sheet'. Perhaps it was the involuntary, high-pitched yelp as the air was forced from the patient's lungs by the brief electric shock. Or it could have been its speed, an instantaneous fit triggered by the flipping of a switch. And while the chemically induced convulsions weren't too dissimilar from an injection of other drugs, such as anaesthetics, this electrical procedure seemed altogether unnatural, forced, manufactured by a machine. Whatever his reasons, Kalinowsky soon saw the potential of this new treatment and broke his vow, performing 1,000 sessions during his time in Rome. 'It is amazing to see most depressions of various depths and duration clear up with the same number of three to five treatments,' he later wrote. The great value of electroshock therapy, he continued, 'cannot be questioned when we realise how much human suffering is prevented by shortening the [depressive] episode.'

After working directly underneath Cerletti for five years, Kalinowsky was forced to move in 1938 as Mussolini signed the 'Pact of Steel' with Nazi Germany, joining the two nations together like two metals melded into a formidable alloy. Upon hearing that all Jewish émigrés from Germany were to be apprehended and imprisoned, 37-year-old Kalinowsky and Hilda rushed onto the next train to Zurich, leaving behind their home, their possessions, and even their two children. The girls would be picked up from school by family friends and taken to a safe (non-Jewish) household. Kalinowsky had planned for this. In 1933, he had fled from his home in Berlin following the Reichstag Fire. With anti-Semitism spreading across Europe like a poisonous vine, emigration was always likely.

Inside his small briefcase, Kalinowsky packed what would be his future. Tucked away among his clothes and other essentials was a blueprint of Bini's electroshock machine. As Kalinowsky travelled from one city to another, he would become a psychiatrist, a salesman, and an international champion of electroshock therapy. In Paris and Amsterdam, he showed Bini's designs to directors of mental hospitals and helped guide their construction and subsequent use. Not everyone was sold on the procedure, however. Aubrey Lewis, an Australian psychiatrist and director of the Maudsley Hospital in London, met Kalinowsky with stern indifference. But slowly his peregrinations spread the work of Cerletti and Bini into Europe and beyond. In 1940, Kalinowsky arrived with his family in New York. Finding work at several mental hospitals – including the New York State Psychiatric Institute, a largely psychoanalytical institution on the Upper West Side of Manhattan – Kalinowsky attracted psychiatrists from all over the United States. For his central role in its dissemination, one historian called Kalinowsky the 'Johnny Appleseed' of electroshock therapy.

There was immediate resistance to electroshock therapy in the United States. Since the late nineteenth century, the only other method of applying electricity to a person's skull in this country wasn't an attempt to cure a patient but to kill a prisoner. The electric chair was an infamous form of criminal punishment. In reality, electroshock therapy and the electric chair were as different to each other as licking a nine-volt battery is to being tasered in the face. While the electric chair can deliver up to 2,000 volts to the head and leg (flowing through the heart and causing a cardiac arrest), Bini's electroshock machine – and other machines like it – only delivered between 70 and 120 volts to the temples. (A small fraction of this actually reached the brain.) The former was switched on for upwards of a minute while the latter only lasted for a few milliseconds. Despite this unfortunate comparison, electroshock therapy was widely adopted in the US in the early 1940s. As Renato Almansi and David Impastato, two psychiatrists working in New York at the time, recalled, '[the] doubts and obstacles were soon dissipated and replaced with typical American enthusiasm'.

If someone seemed to be living in a confusing state of slow motion, suffered from anorexia, woke up early in the morning without much sleep, and had depressive symptoms that gradually improved throughout the day, then electroshock therapy was almost guaranteed to help. If delusions or psychosis were present – as had been one of the defining features of involutional melancholia – then figures near to 100 per cent effectiveness were reported. 'The fundamental fact remains that a new uniformly successful treatment, introduced into psychiatry, effectively terminates depressive psychoses,' one psychiatrist said in November 1944, 'whereas all previous methods have failed to produce such spectacular results.' Another psychiatrist wrote that it was nothing short of a miracle: 'Patients with severe depressive disorders and stuporous states that had disconnected them from the real world for months and even years came back to life.' Like a forest fire vital in liberating the seeds from inside tough pinecones, a quick burst of electricity – and, more importantly, the convulsion that it caused – seemed to reanimate a person from the thick psychological shell in which they were encased.

Not all depressions responded equally well to electroshock therapy. It was rarely as effective in the milder depressions that were found in the community. And this was puzzling. Why would a medical treatment be more effective in the worst cases while hardly influencing the milder versions? Imagine a drug that kills cancer only when it has metastasised around the body and not before. It didn't make much sense. The explanation, many psychiatrists thought, was that electroshock therapy was specific to severe depression because it was a distinct disease. This was 'endogenous' depression (coming from within), the more biological form of the disease and a diagnosis that would continue to be used for much of the twentieth century. The idea that manic-depressive insanity was a spectrum – the argument that Edward Mapother had staunchly held at the Maudsley in the 1920s – was starting to break apart.

The other form of depression, the one that didn't respond to electroshock therapy, was termed 'reactive depression'. Rather than being biologically determined, this form of illness was related to stressful life events, personality types, and a more responsive (or reactive) mental state to changing conditions. If the stresses of life disappeared or ameliorated, people with reactive depression had a good prognosis. They were likely to recover. Those with endogenous depression, meanwhile, would remain tormented no matter how good their lives seemed to everyone else. These two categories weren't perfect reflections of reality, and a great debate between biological psychiatrists ensued for much of the twentieth century regarding their accuracy and clinical utility. There were huge grey areas between the two. Endogenous depressions could be triggered by environmental stressors such as divorce, unemployment, and death of loved ones. Reactive depressions might not dissipate even with the greatest reversals in fortune. But this division was nonetheless useful in predicting who might respond to the different treatments available. Without biological markers from brain slices or blood samples, knowing that electroshock therapy worked in more severe, often delusional, depressions was a boon to psychiatry. It meant that a life-threatening condition now had a good prognosis. 'The greater the loss of contact with reality,' Kalinowsky wrote, 'the better the treatment.'

Psychoanalysts were never in doubt that there were two major types of depression. In 1917, even Sigmund Freud wrote that so-called psychotic depressions – those with delusions and a better response to electroshock therapy – had some biological basis. It wasn't purely a disorder of unconscious conflicts. The idea of at least two main types of depression were widely shared throughout psychiatry.

The main difference was in the treatment they received. Whether someone was given electroshock therapy or sat through endless sessions of psychoanalysis depended less on their depression – its symptoms, severity, or supposed biology – and more on which office they walked into. The psychoanalyst believed that patients required insight into their unconscious conflicts and repressed desires, a deep dive that no amount of electroshock therapy could provide. As a report from New York State Psychiatric Institute noted, 'There was a tendency for the residents to prefer to delay all forms of organic [biological] treatment until extensive trials of psychotherapy were exhausted.' But, once exhausted, there was no arguing with the efficacy of electroshock therapy. As one biological psychiatrist said, 'The analysts denigrate me, but when their mothers get depressed, they send them to me.'

Legacy

In 1938, the year that electroshock therapy was still being performed in secrecy, Sigmund Freud's life was threatened by the same fascist ideology that had forced Kalinowsky to leave Berlin. Although he was an atheist, Freud was raised in a Jewish household and married to a Jewish wife. Because of the violent anti-Semitism in the Nazi Party, psychoanalysis was labelled as a 'Jewish science' and, therefore, worthy of destruction. In Berlin, the Gestapo removed Freud's books from the public library and burnt them in the street. With his hallmark dry wit, Freud wrote, 'What progress we are making. In the Middle Ages they would have burnt me, nowadays they are content with burning my books.' After his home in Vienna was raided, Freud decided to leave the city he had lived and worked in for 79 years. When he was just a toddler, his mother and father had fled from anti-Semitism in Germany and settled in Vienna. Now, with his family under threat, it was Freud's turn to flee.

After a brief stopover in Paris, he took the night ferry to England and found a welcome party of friends and family at Victoria Station in London. Although he had hoped to see out his last days in Vienna, he had always admired England from afar. In August 1939, a month before Germany invaded Poland and the Second World War began, he sat in his study, surrounded by his antiquities and furniture that had been delivered from Vienna. Having experienced the violence and hatred of Nazism first hand, he hoped that he wouldn't live to see its domination in Europe. Gazing out at the flowers that lined his accommodation's garden, Freud knew that he wouldn't see this latest war unfold. His enemy – the squamous cell carcinoma which had first been diagnosed in 1923 – had defied years of painful surgical operations, electric cauterisation, and radiation therapy. After his last surgery in early 1939, he wrote to his friend Marie Bonaparte, 'My world is again what it was before – a little island of pain floating on a sea of indifference.' On 22 September 1939, Freud's island of pain was flooded with three centigrams of morphine. He fell asleep and didn't wake up. He took his final breath early the next morning. Unlike four of his five sisters who were murdered in concentration camps, Freud chose euthanasia.

Psychoanalysis would grow to its zenith after his death. By the middle of the century, it was said that a psychoanalyst sat at the top of every psychiatry department in the United States. Not only was this study of the unconscious and repressed memories used in treatment but also in classification, the field most commonly associated with Emil Kraepelin. In 1952, the first *Diagnostic and Statistical Manual for Mental Disorders (DSM-I)* was published, based on psychoanalytic concepts. Rather than neat clinical groups like Kraepelin had advocated in his textbooks, each patient was often classified according to a supposed underlying mental cause. Depressive reaction, for example, was a 'psychoneurosis' caused by repressed anxiety. In such patients, the *DSM-I* reads, there was 'no gross distortion or falsification of external reality'. Depressive psychosis, meanwhile, was, as Freud had suggested, a more biological disorder that often came with delusions and hallucinations, and was rarely tied to a stressful life event. These groupings would remain popular, especially in the United States, for the next three decades.

*

It was a fatal twist of irony. In 1940, as electroshock therapy was providing a few remarkable scenes of recovery across the world, biological psychiatry was also leading thousands of mentally ill people to their doom. Emil Kraepelin's popular *Psychiatry* textbook was also popular within the ranks of the Nazi Party. In its most expansive eighth edition, published in three volumes between 1909 and 1912, Kraepelin wrote, 'The relatives have often suffered from the same form of the disease.' Depression begets depression. This idea of 'defective heredity' aligned with the themes of eugenics, the field of science that had swept through Britain and the United States and led to the mass sterilisations of thousands of people with disabilities or severe mental illnesses. Men underwent vasectomies. Women had their tubes tied or their ovaries blasted with ionising radiation. Only in Germany, however, was eugenics taken to its most extreme ends. Before the Holocaust claimed the lives of millions of Jews, thousands of mentally ill inpatients were murdered. Those with 'manic-depressive insanity' were killed because of a diagnosis, one that Emil Kraepelin had pushed into the zeitgeist.

In 1916, a colleague of Kraepelin's at Munich, Ernst Rüdin, had provided solid evidence that mental disorders were heritable. If Kraepelin was a tireless hoarder of patient reports, Rüdin was an avid collector of family histories. Both were obsessed with big data and even bigger ideas. Rüdin had collected information on the families of 701 patients at the Munich clinic who were diagnosed with dementia praecox. Using large sample sizes and the latest statistical methods, he provided the first conclusive evidence that severe mental disorders were often passed on from parent to offspring. It ran in families. He even created an equation that could estimate the likelihood of the disorder emerging in the future: the 'empirical heredity prognosis'.

After dementia praecox, Rüdin turned to manic-depressive insanity. Once again, he collected detailed information from the families of 650 patients who had been diagnosed with the disorder since 1904. He used the same statistical methods as before, refining them where he could. But he didn't get the same result. There wasn't a strong heritable component. No matter how he played around with his data, it was a weak connection at best. '[Rüdin's] demands for negative eugenic measures against patients with [mood] disorders and their families could not be justified on the grounds of the heredity figures he had calculated,' Hubertus Himmerich and his colleagues from the University of Leipzig wrote in 2017.

But Rüdin never published this study. He was a co-founder of the Society for Racial Hygiene and an editor of the Archive of Biological Hygiene for Race and Society, and his findings didn't align with that of his – or his country's – worldview. Manic-depressive insanity remained in the realm of heritable diseases along with dementia praecox, learning disability, epilepsy, Huntington's chorea, and hereditary blindness. All were eventual targets of extermination. Kraepelin may have created the classification system on which psychiatry was built, but by claiming that 'defective heredity' was the key ingredient of mental disorders, he also provided the basis for some of the greatest tragedies in human history.

Like the British mathematician Francis Galton who coined the term 'eugenics' in 1883, Adolf Hitler was a radical Social Darwinist. 'The *völkisch* state must see to it that only the healthy beget children,' he wrote. 'Here the state must act as the guardian of a millennial future ... It must put the most modern medical means in the service of this knowledge. It must declare unfit for propagation all who are in any way visibly sick or who have inherited a disease and can therefore pass it on.' 'National Socialism,' another Nazi leader added, 'is nothing but applied biology.'

Although eugenics had its critics – the psychiatrists Oswald Bumke in Germany and Henry Maudsley in Britain, for instance, cautioned how the complexity of mental illness couldn't be so neatly pruned from a population – over 410,000 people with mental or physical disabilities were surgically sterilised in the 1930s.

As the German military pushed eastwards into Poland in 1939 and then up into Russia the year after, the residents of mental institutions were herded up and gassed, shot, drugged, or blown up with explosives before being buried in mass graves by Polish prisoners (who were then shot). Between 1939 and 1941, a network of six killing centres was set up across the expanding German Reich as part of the Aktion T4 programme for the extermination of the mentally ill and the disabled. In less than two years, an estimated 70,000 people were murdered. At Hartheim Castle, 'one of Upper Austria's most beautiful and most significant Renaissance castles', over 18,000 people were killed, most by carbon monoxide poisoning inside a tiled room with shower heads in the ceiling. Their remains were burnt into ash. This ash was tipped into the river or simply scattered on the surrounding castle grounds. In 2001, these human remains were discovered at Hartheim Castle and buried in an ecumenical ceremony. The ash inside each urn was a nameless mixture of people who had all shared the same fate.

Aktion T4 was soon put to a halt. Relatives learnt about the fate of their parents, siblings, or children. The sweet smell of burning bodies filled the air around killing centres and locals noted how the large grey buses were always dropping people off at these sites but never picking anyone up. (Staff at Hartheim

Castle used these buses to go to the cinema in nearby Linz.) Bookkeeping errors – such as the death certificate of a man who'd had his appendix removed long ago stating that he'd died from appendicitis – made the widespread rumours of killing centres into a shocking reality. But the killing didn't stop there. Although Aktion T4 was officially terminated in August 1941, the Nazi Party found other ways to kill those people infamously labelled 'life unworthy of life'. As the Second World War continued, supplies of food and medicine were shuttled to the front lines and mental asylums were left empty. An unknown number died from starvation and disease. This was known as 'decentralised euthanasia', or 'wild euthanasia'.

In 1944, a year before the Second World War ended and the true devastation of concentration camps had been revealed, Emil Gelny, the director of two psychiatric hospitals in Austria, killed 300 mentally ill patients with an electroshock machine. But this wasn't electroshock therapy. He had bought an Elkra II, a black machine that looked like a portable speaker on a small Christmas-tree stand, and adapted it so the voltage could be increased, the duration of the shock extended from milliseconds to minutes, and added four more electrodes that could be attached to a person's wrists and ankles. Patients were individually treated with electroshock therapy by the routine method (two electrodes on the sides of the head), and then, while they were unconscious, the four electrodes were attached and the machine was switched on. They were dead in less than ten minutes. Gelny performed his form of euthanasia for visiting psychiatrists, detailing how it was preferred to injecting sedatives. It was cheap, quick, and patients died thinking that they were receiving electroshock therapy, a common treatment in psychiatric hospitals at the time. This was later referred to as 'the darkest chapter in biological psychiatry'.

Although Emil Gelny's euthanasia was an extreme case, even the standard practice of electroshock therapy could be easily misused. It was then adopted as a method of control, a means of punishing unruly or loud patients. Although it was relatively painless and a person lost consciousness before the convulsion, patients would become drowsy, confused, and quieter in the wake of the treatment. In what became known as 'regressive shock therapy', treatments were given to chronic schizophrenic patients several times a day for a week or more, a terrifying frequency that made a patient 'so regressed that he is bedridden, does not know his name, is doubly incontinent, and is unable to swallow'. More commonly, electroshock therapy was given to people with mental disorders who would never benefit from its use.

But, for this story, a journey in and out of depression, its potential benefits were clear to anyone who used it properly. In the right hands and on the right patients, it was amazing, revolutionary, a treatment that saved lives. 'The recovery of the severe, long-standing, agitated depressions makes a profound impression,' one psychiatrist said in 1941. 'The morale of the personnel [at the hospital] has been improved by the feeling of active service and treatment for such a large percentage of patients.' With electroshock therapy, between 80 and 90 per cent of patients were lifted from their depression, a figure that remained largely constant as Lothar Kalinowsky travelled from one country to another. Without electroshock therapy, one psychiatrist working at the Maudsley Hospital in London recalled, 'I would not have lasted out in psychiatry, as I would not have been able to tolerate the sadness and hopelessness of mental illnesses before the introduction of convulsive therapy.'

Kalinowsky had read reports of 10,000 sessions of electroshock therapy, performed in doctor's offices, in patients' homes, and even in hotel suites. Despite such widespread use, he found that there had been no serious complications. 'To date in the hands of various investigators,' he wrote, 'the electric shock method seems relatively harmless.' As one of his contemporaries put it, 'in an era in which hypothermia, hyperthermia, lobotomy, and lobectomy are being carried out for the treatment of mental diseases, electric shock is, relatively speaking, a mild approach.'

Cerletti's Monster

While lobotomies were still being used for more chronic states of depression, particularly those in elderly patients, the introduction of electroshock therapy largely removed the need for this drastic surgical operation. The exceptions to this general rule were soldiers returning from the Second World War. After joining the war effort in December 1941, thousands of American men were flown back to their families and their homes, but they often weren't the same as when they left. They were panicked and fearful. Some talked to themselves or believed they were being pursued. Nightmares reached into reality. Others were depressed and unable to resume the active lives they had once lived. Electroshock therapy was used and frequently found wanting. Deep anxieties and neuroses, fears and frights, were never part of its forte. (As Kalinowsky once wrote, 'It cannot be emphasised enough that contrary to psychotics, some neurotics may be harmed by [electroshock therapy]. Anxiety, as the most frequent symptom in neurotics, is often aggravated.') These veterans needed another option.

'By August 26th, 1943, many relatives and guardians of patients who had failed to improve with shock therapy began to demand more rapid and drastic treatment,' wrote Fred Mettler, a neurologist from Columbia University, New York. Just as the spouse of a cancer patient might request the details of the latest drug trial, families of war veterans were willing to try anything that might bring their fathers, husbands, and sons back. In response, the Veterans Health Administration issued information about lobotomies, a 'last resort' for those who had failed to respond to electroshock therapy.

It was these patients who Mettler would use to try and understand whether the broad field of psychosurgery could be made more precise, to disentangle which parts of the brain could be excised for greater effect. 'Could we find, for example, that only one cortical area need be removed to achieve a particular result?' he asked. '[Could] an essentially uncertain operation be reduced to a proper surgical technique and its unnecessary damage eliminated?' It was such investigations that would usher in a new wave of surgical techniques – cingulotomies, topectomies, amydalotomies, and tractotomies – that would continue to be used for the rest of the twentieth century. A survey from 44 neurosurgical centres in the UK in 1978, for example, found that 431 such operations were performed over a two-year period. Depression was the most common diagnosis recorded, accounting for 63 per cent of patients. With greater medical safeguards such as the UK's 1983 Mental Health Act, which stipulated the use of brain surgery only after the consent of the patient, their psychiatrist, and two other representatives from the Mental Health Act Commission, such treatments would decline in popularity, being used only in cases of depression, obsessive compulsive disorder, or anxiety that were chronic and resistant to other treatments.

From this history of greater precision, a technique that used electrical stimulation rather than surgery emerged. Today, deep brain stimulation (DBS) is a promising treatment for people with severe depressions who have failed to respond to all other options. As Jack El-Hai, the biographer of Walter Freeman, wrote in 2005, 'Freeman's career may seem bizarre to many people today, but it is playing out again – with better technology, a better understanding of the functioning of the brain, and better ethical guidelines – in the burgeoning world of the new psychosurgery.' We will travel to this new world later in this story.

Although it wasn't as drastic or permanent as a prefrontal lobotomy, the side effects of electroshock therapy in the 1940s were still severe and numerous. Fractures in the bones of the limbs, spine, and pelvis were found in around 23 per cent of patients (for chemically induced convulsions this figure could be as high as 43 per cent). This was the most pressing concern during the treatment's early years. 'If shock treatment is to survive,' one author wrote in 1940, 'the incidence of fracture complications must be reduced to a minimum.' Most commonly, the middle region of the spine suffered from compression fractures as a result of the back muscles contracting powerfully in the first few moments of the convulsion. Although these were often hairline fractures, the type only seen in X-rays and which healed quickly, they were still an undesirable side effect, both for the patient and the image of electroshock therapy. Nonetheless, some patients were willing to sacrifice their skeleton for their mental health. As one study reported, 'The patient felt greatly improved and was content to have his shoulder broken rather than suffer the depression.'

By 1941, Lothar Kalinowsky had developed a quick fix that substantially reduced the risk of fractures: sandbags. By placing three heavy sand-filled sacks underneath the spine of his patients, he enforced a posture – known as hyperextension – that stretched the internal edges of their vertebrae away from each other. As it was these edges that were most likely to be compressed, this position could reduce the risk of fractures significantly. Using X-rays to scan the vertebrae of 60 patients before and after their treatment, Kalinowsky found no evidence of damage.

Sandbags were far from a fix-all, however. Many people were unable to benefit from electroshock therapy, as the risks were still too high. The elderly, for example, often had bones too brittle to undergo a grand mal seizure. If they did, their hips and limbs might snap like dry twigs. In such cases, even the best-placed sandbags would be insufficient.

Then there was the memory loss. Although often temporary, this was hugely disorientating for a large percentage of patients. Some forgot what they did in the days preceding their electroshock-therapy sessions. Others lost years of their life. Even memorable events such as their own weddings, family holidays, or military service could be forgotten. In the 1940s, there was a theory that this 'retrograde amnesia' wasn't a side effect but was actually the curative element of the treatment, as if patients simply forgot that they were ill. (This is now known not to be the case; there is no relationship between memory loss and the treatment's effectiveness.)

A minority of patients lost more than memories. Studies in the 1940s found that around 0.06 per cent of patients died during or following their course of electroshock therapy. One psychiatrist wrote that this was 'negligible', especially when compared to the figures of 2 to 20 per cent for lobotomies. The most common cause of death was heart failure, but there was one account of a ruptured intestine in a 28-year-old 'aggressive schizophrenic'. Although many deaths couldn't be directly attributed to the treatment (they may have been coincidental), this last example seemed causative. 'There would not appear to be any reason for the condition other than the electrical treatment administered to the deceased,' the pathologist wrote. These potential complications needed to be taken into account for each patient and their underlying conditions: 'A psychiatrist, because he so often has to deal with patients incapable of making their own decisions, has an even greater responsibility to bear in this respect and must accept it.'

As antibiotics were being mass produced for the first time, making once-lethal infections vanish within a few weeks, electroshock therapy became a staple of psychiatry. By 1944, the first controlled study into its efficacy had been published. Kenneth Tillotson and Wolfgang Sulzbach, two psychiatrists working at McLean Hospital in Belmont, Massachusetts, compared the rate of recovery in 70 depressed patients who were given electroshock therapy to 68 comparable patients who received the standard care (essentially no care) within the hospital wards. With this simple difference – one group with and one group without electroshock treatment – they hoped to investigate a well-known complication in any treatment for depression: patients often recovered on their own. 'The efficiency of convulsive treatments is frequently minimised or entirely disputed on account of the generally favourable prognosis in depressions,' Tillotson and Sulzbach wrote. 'Our evidence, however, argues against this.'

Over four years of study, not only did 30 per cent more patients recover in the electroshock therapy group compared to controls (80 per cent versus 50 per cent), but they were also half as likely to relapse back into a depressive state a year in the future. Perhaps most spectacular were four patients who had suffered from unremitting depression for upwards of 15 years who then recovered in a matter of weeks or months. Two years later, they were still depression free. And although short-term memory loss was still a common complaint, over long periods of time electroshock therapy actually had cognitive benefits. Rid of the sluggishness of depression, they 'displayed a far more efficient intellectual as well as emotional adaptivity to their environment than ever before in their life,' Tillotson and Sulzbach wrote.

While Kalinowsky saw electroshock therapy as a safe, effective, and profitable profession, his former supervisor, Ugo Cerletti, grew ever more critical of his creation's wanton usage. '[I]n private practice,' he told an audience at the first Congress of the Society of Italian Psychiatry since the end of the Second World War, 'progress cannot be made ... since not all the apparatus, the tools and the analyses which are commonly available in a modern clinic can be used.' More than just a lack of equipment, he added that the financial incentives of treating private outpatients was tempting many budding researchers away from curiosity-driven medical research.

As with Mary Shelley's Dr Frankenstein, Cerletti thought he had created a monster that wasn't only damaging his profession but also the patients he felt a duty to help. 'I came to the conclusion that we must get away from the use of electroshock,' he later wrote. 'When subjecting unconscious patients to such an extremely violent reaction as these convulsions, I had a sense of illicitness and felt as though I had somehow betrayed these patients.' Worried that he had also inadvertently aided in the demise of laboratory research, Cerletti, now approaching 70 years old and with his eyebrows bushier than ever, worked even harder to undo the damage he had done.

He didn't lose faith in the efficacy of electroshock therapy. He was as convinced as anyone of its therapeutic potential, especially for certain severe forms of depression. He just didn't think that a convulsive treatment always required a convulsion. Surely all the thrashing of limbs, crunching of vertebrae, and clamping of jaws wasn't necessary if the brain was the focus of the therapy? Why should the body go through so much trouble as a side reaction? For Cerletti, the path forward was clear as the stained slices of brain tissue under his microscope. 'The future lies in the domain of biochemists,' he wrote.

As a student at the University of Turin in the late nineteenth century, Cerletti had failed chemistry. Even when he retook the test, he still only scraped through. Even so, it would be this world of molecules, test tubes, pipettes, and graded solutions to which he turned in his later years. Cerletti became obsessed with a family of chemicals that he called 'acroaganines'. Taken from the Greek words *akros* (extreme) and *agon* (struggle or defence), they were the chemical basis of electroshock therapy, he thought. Just as an immune response leads to the release of antibodies, he proposed that a convulsion released its own 'highly vitalising substances with defensive properties' against depression and other mental illnesses.

As with his early tests into the safety of electroshock therapy, Cerletti looked to pigs for answers. He returned to the slaughterhouse in Rome. After administering electroshocks several times before they were killed, Cerletti would extract the solution that bathed the pigs' brains. It was these foul few millilitres, gloopy and sickly yellow in colour, that Cerletti thought contained the coveted acroaganines. Once distilled, he hoped to inject this solution into his patients, removing the need for electricity or a convulsion. Could these brain chemicals lead to a less catastrophic form of therapy? Would this discovery attract the next generation of psychiatrists back into the laboratory, a place where medical revolutions emerge from such daring theories?

Young or old, Cerletti didn't succeed in chemistry. Acroaganines were in the same chemical family as fairy dust and black bile – they didn't exist. His final experiments were all dead ends.

Psychoanalysts had their own theories about how electroshock therapy worked. Fear of imminent death, punishment from a parent-like figure, enforced regression into an infantile state: all were proposed as potential mechanisms for this treatment's efficacy. Ultimately, Edith Weigert, a leading psychiatrist in the United States, wrote, 'the effect of the different [shock] treatments is a breaking through of the patient's autism, making him more affectionate, more interested in the outside world, more manageable, more sociable.' Although it was an invention of biological psychiatry, psychoanalysts still turned to electroshock therapy as a tool that could 'open up' their patients and make them more amenable to psychotherapy. '[W]hatever doubt may exist about the dynamics of improvement,' one psychotherapist wrote in 1943, 'there can be no doubt of the empirical fact that electro-shock therapy is an important contribution to the art and science of mental healing.'

From its underlying biology to its effects on the mind, no one knew how electroshock therapy worked. 'It is true that no adequate theory for [electroshock therapy] is available,' Kalinowsky wrote in 1949, 'but this is no valid reason against its application. The patient who needs help cannot wait until empirical knowledge has found a satisfactory theoretical basis.' To him, the important thing wasn't how it worked. Just that it did.

Although it came with disabling side effects, Kalinowsky argued that any psychiatrist who refused to employ this treatment for the most severe mental disorders was guilty of medical malpractice. Refusing to adopt a treatment that can relieve months of suffering in patients, he argued, was like withholding food from someone who is starving. 'The surgeon does not refuse a necessary operation because of its impending risks,' he wrote in *Somatic Treatments in Psychiatry*, a textbook he co-authored with a colleague at the New York State Psychiatric Institute. 'Mental disorders are as destructive as a malignant growth and far more terrible in the suffering they may cause. Risks are therefore justified.'

Ugo Cerletti was right about the potential for biochemistry in electroshock therapy. It just wasn't acroaganines. As early as the late 1930s, muscle relaxants were removing the need for the violent convulsions that defined the procedure. With an injection of curare (pronounced 'coo-rah-ree'), the muscles of the body would remain relaxed while the brain still went through the classic electrical fluctuations of the clonic and tonic phases of a grand mal seizure. But it was a dangerous practice that blurred the lines between life and death. Made from the boiled stems of climbing plants, curare had been used to kill prey in the Amazon rainforest since time immemorial. Painted onto spear tips or arrowheads, this viscous paste quickly entered the bloodstream and stopped the muscles that surround the lungs from expanding and contracting. In a few minutes, animals as large as deer would fall to their knees and suffocate. At one tenth of a lethal dose, however, curare was used to reduce the contractions of convulsive therapy. Paralysing the muscles for 15 to 20 minutes, the convulsion was restricted to the brain and hidden from the body. With artificial respiration reducing the risk of suffocation, the problem of fractures became a distant memory.

Lothar Kalinowsky, however, refused to use curare. 'I had my first and only fatality ... in a patient where I used curare,' he confessed years later. Although fatalities were rare, there was no doubt that, in the wrong hands, curare could paralyse a patient's breathing or even their heart. To Kalinowsky and others, it was 'more dangerous than the complications it is supposed to prevent'. Symptomless fractures were better than accidental suffocation.

Curare was nevertheless an insight into a safer future for electroshock therapy. It shined a light on the essential organ of a convulsion: the brain. The body needn't move at all; as long as the electroencephalogram (EEG) – the readout of brain activity from electrodes placed on the head – showed the steep scribblings that define a grand mal seizure, then the session could be deemed a success. Such 'modified' electroshock therapy also injected a sense of hope for those people who were once thought to be unsuitable for this treatment – people with medical problems such as osteoporosis, slipped discs, and previous fractures. Even the brittle bones and dwindling reserves of cartilage of the elderly were no longer contraindications for this treatment. This was a boon, not only for psychiatry but general medicine. Late-life, or 'geriatric', depression not only coincides with other chronic diseases such as diabetes, cancer, hypertension, and cardiovascular problems, but can exacerbate them. It makes cancer more likely and more lethal. It reduces a person's adherence to pills that help keep diabetes at bay, thereby reducing their efficacy. And people with depression are far more likely to die from heart complications compared to someone who isn't depressed. In late life, that is, untreated depression is a dangerous and potentially lethal co-traveller. As early as the 1940s, however, electroshock therapy had the potential to shunt the ageing process toward a healthier path.

In 1952, a time when psychiatrists were still learning how to harness the potential of electrically induced convulsions, a safer relaxant entered the field of medicine. Appropriately for this story, a chemist working just a stone's throw from Ugo Cerletti's laboratories in Rome began his work on a fast-acting, rapidly dissipating muscle relaxant that was initially termed 'curare of short action'. Its formal name, succinylcholine, or 'sux', was a vital development in the treatment of depression. Even Kalinowsky accepted this new drug and pushed his sandbags out of his methods and his private practice. Along with general anaesthesia and artificial respiration (a requirement for any use of general anaesthetic), sux helped transform a dated shock therapy into a modern medical procedure. To complete the break from the past, electroshock therapy went through several rebrands. Over the coming decades, it would be referred to as electroplexy, cerebroversion, central stimulation (CS), brain stimulation therapy (BST), and, wait for it, central stimulation with patterned response (CSPR). But the name that stuck was electroconvulsive therapy, and its famous initialism, ECT, a potentially life-saving treatment that had the potential to both help and harm mentally ill patients.

From the 1960s onwards, however, it would nearly drop out of psychiatric practice altogether. 'It was as if penicillin had somehow vanished from the medical armamentarium,' wrote Edward Shorter and David Healy, two medical historians, in their 2007 book *Shock Therapy*, 'and a generation's memory of its very existence had been somehow erased.'

The Psychic Energisers

It had smooth white fur and a little pink nose that wiggled a set of whiskers from side to side, and it lived in a wire cage. It looked like every other mouse Nathan Kline had ever seen. But as he watched this particular mouse, Kline, director of psychiatric research at Rockland State Hospital in New York, noticed that it was behaving differently to most of its laboratory kin. It was more active, more aware of its surroundings, than a run-of-the-mill mouse. It seemed to buzz with energy, powered by some invisible force within the confines of its enclosure. If it had a wheel, it might have been able to run nonstop for hours without food or water. This mouse – nameless, just one of hundreds – was just what Kline had spent years searching for.

Kline, a smartly dressed man with thick horn-rimmed glasses who was once described as having a 'twinkle in his eye that spoke of something extraordinarily curious', was visiting the laboratories of Charles Scott, a leading pharmacologist in the United States. Before his arrival, the mouse had been injected with reserpine, a drug extracted from the root of a plant that had been used in Indian medicine for centuries. Known as sarpaghanda, or snakeroot, it was used for a variety of ills. Snake bites and scorpion stings. Asthma. High blood pressure. Insomnia and insanity. Mahatma Gandhi used snakeroot to 'attain states of introspection and meditation'. Kline was very familiar with reserpine. In 1954, two years before his visit to Scott's laboratory, he had helped introduce the drug into the United States as a treatment for calming the manic, often destructive highs of some of his patients. On one of the psychiatric wards that Kline first trialled the drug at Rockland State Hospital, it became much quieter and the furniture, windows, and people weren't in need of repair as often. Even the hospital's glazier noticed that he wasn't spending as much time working on that particular ward.

Reserpine was one of the first 'tranquillisers', a class of drugs that didn't come with the lethargic side effects or addictive qualities of strong sedatives such as barbiturates and opium, both of which had been used for decades in mental hospitals.

In 1952, a similar chemical trialled at Saint-Anne Hospital in Paris, known as chlorpromazine (marketed as Thorazine in the United States), was found to be even more effective in the treatment of schizophrenia than reserpine. Thomas Ban, a clinical psychiatrist and historian, was working in Austria when chlorpromazine was first released. He thought that it was nothing short of a miracle drug. 'I could sleep through the night, and patients whom I never really thought would come back, came back,' he recalled, his face beaming with delight at the memory. 'It was unbelievable. The whole psychiatric establishment didn't believe it.'

The effect of these two drugs – known as neuroleptics or, later, antipsychotics – was far greater than fewer smashed windows on hospital grounds and a better night's sleep. For the first time in human history, severe, life-threatening mental illnesses could be targeted with drugs, allowing outcasts of society to become outpatients with a prescription and regular medical supervision. For the first time in their adult lives, people were able to live in their community, in a home or halfway house, outside the walls of a mental hospital. 'This was, I think, one of the most exciting periods that I've ever had in my life,' Joseph Barsa, a stocky, balding, and conservative colleague of Nathan Kline at Rockland State Hospital, recalled. 'People who had been in the hospital for twenty or thirty years began to improve, and we were able to discharge them. And the thing is, the joy, the excitement, and the enthusiasm spread throughout the staff. It was a different environment.'

Reserpine wasn't perfect and sometimes didn't work at all, but it nonetheless provided a shift in how Kline thought about the treatment of mental illness. He started to wonder whether there was a chemical opposite to such tranquillisers. 'If one compound could swing the emotional pendulum down,' he wrote, 'then there should be another compound that could swing it up.' He had no idea what this hypothetical chemical would look like, where it would come from, or how it would work. He just knew it had to exist.

In the spring of 1956, three years after his first trial with reserpine, he thought he had found it in Scott's laboratory in New Jersey. Even though the mouse had been injected with reserpine, a tranquilliser, it was full of energy. The mouse should have been dozing and fatigued. It should have been stationary, not endlessly seeking. This paradox had a chemical explanation. The day before Kline's visit, the mouse had been given a different class of drug. It was called iproniazid, a chemical that seemed to reverse the depressing effects of reserpine. Kline thought that this could be the upward swing of his emotional pendulum.

From their source, reserpine and iproniazid were very different drugs. While the former was extracted from the root of a plant that blooms in white flowers across India, the Himalayas, and throughout most of Indonesia, the latter was a product of

Nazi rocket fuel. One was a chemical wrested from nature, the other forged in modern warfare.

Hydrazine is a clear, highly combustible liquid that was used by the Nazis toward the end of the Second World War, propelling their V2 missiles into Britain and France. After the war ended, pharmaceutical companies in the United States bought these redundant reserves at low cost, poring through their properties for anything that could be put to use in the postwar world. Needless to say, it was dangerous work. A single spark could fuel an explosion. But great risk can reap great reward. In 1951, one chemical showed promising antitubercular activity in the Petri dish. It was called isoniazid, soon marketed as Rimifon. Then, by adding a clump of carbon and hydrogen atoms to this drug, Herbert Fox, a chemist working at the pharmaceutical giant Hoffman-LaRoche, created iproniazid. It was his finest creation, superior to its mother molecule, and succeeded where many of the strongest antibiotics – such as streptomycin – had failed. It killed *Mycobacterium tuberculosis*.

From Fox's laboratory in New Jersey, the drug was sent around the United States and given to various animals infected with tuberculosis. Guinea pigs, rabbits, rhesus monkeys: all showed promising improvements or even a complete recovery from their infection. When the same result was found in humans, the mass media exploded with hyperbole. WONDER DRUG FIGHTS TB, the *New York Post* wrote in two-inch type on its front page. During a 15-minute radio broadcast that was aired across 12 American networks in February 1952, listeners were told, 'Tuberculosis – the disease which destroyed more than five million lives last year, whose indiscriminate path through man's recorded history has filled more graves than war, famine, or pestilence – has been stopped. Scientists and clinical physicians have reported "amazing results" in the treatment in New York hospitals of some 200 tuberculosis patients ... for whom all hope had been abandoned.'

There were also reports of patients feeling a little too good, euphoric even. At Seaview Hospital on Staten Island – a $4 million complex that the *New York Times* called 'the largest and finest hospital ever built for the care and treatment of those who suffer from tuberculosis' – patients started to feel better the day after taking the new pills, even though their lungs were still pocked with painful lesions filled with bacteria. 'A few months ago, the only sound here was the sound of victims of tuberculosis, coughing up their lives,' one news article stated. After iproniazid, however, formerly terminally ill patients were 'dancing in the halls tho' there were holes in their lungs'. 'No bed cases remain,' the doctors at Seaview confirmed. 'The wards have a completely new appearance.' Each room was a scene of celebration.

Intrigued, pharmacologists soon started to tease apart what these drugs actually did inside the body. Even at a molecular level, iproniazid and reserpine were opposites of one another. While reserpine reduced the levels of serotonin in the brains of rabbits and rats, iproniazid increased them. But what did this mean? In the mid 1950s, little was known about serotonin's role in the brain. After all, it was only in 1952 that Betty Twarog, a 24-year-old PhD student working at Harvard University, first found evidence of this molecule in brain tissue. (Independently, researchers in Edinburgh discovered serotonin in brain tissue and presented their work to the British Pharmacological Society in July 1952, a month after Twarog submitted her paper.) Prior to this, serotonin was studied in the blood serum (hence 'serotonin') and the gut (where 90 per cent of serotonin is produced). But even without any definite explanations, the modulation of serotonin became a hot topic of research. Was serotonin of prime importance in mood regulation? Did the tranquillising effects of reserpine and the euphoria of iproniazid centre around this single molecule? When Nathan Kline thought that there might be a chemical opposite to his tranquillisers, he didn't expect it to be so neatly packaged.

If it could reverse the depressing effects of reserpine in mice and make critically ill patients dance, could iproniazid also reverse mental depressions? Shortly after he saw the hyperactive mouse in New Jersey, Kline tested iproniazid on some of his resident patients at Rockland State Hospital. Along with his colleagues Harry Loomer and John Saunders, Kline chose 17 schizophrenic patients who were also suffering from severe bouts of depression. One such patient, a 42-year-old woman known as 'E.S.' who had been hospitalised for 20 years and hadn't responded to convulsive therapy or reserpine, was 'quiet, withdrawn, and unresponsive to questions'. Her attendant said that 'she just wasn't there'. She remained this way, silent and in the dark, for the first five weeks of her iproniazid treatment. During the sixth week, however, some invisible barrier seemed to have been lifted between herself and those around her. 'She is loud and talkative,' Loomer reported, 'some of her verbalisations are quite sensible.' In total, 70 per cent of inpatients showed some sign of improvement after taking iproniazid.

This was a promising start. But the most remarkable findings were to be found outside the hospital's walls, across the Hudson River, and down into the lively heart of Manhattan, a place where depression seemed to thrive. Every afternoon at around four-thirty, Kline drove his black Thunderbird soft-top into the city to meet his private patients, sometimes staying until after 11pm. His offices were on the ground floor of an

East Side greystone that contained so much artwork that it was likened to a 'metastasis from the Museum of Modern Art'. With five nurses and three psychiatrists in attendence, four patients could be seen every hour, a turnover that made Kline's clinic the McDonald's of clinical psychiatry. Over two thirds of his patients were suffering with depression. Although, as Kline later wrote, 'Suffer is often too mild a term for the wracking agony and raw pain [of depression] which cries out for relief.' In early 1957, the cries of many of his patients were met for the first time – with iproniazid.

'You see, Doctor,' one patient told Kline, 'the pills have worked ... I am not depressed or frightened anymore. I go everywhere and talk to everyone. I am full of energy ... I knew that I was in for another year of depression. I shall be eternally grateful.' The depression of another patient, a 30-year-old housewife who had been given seven years of psychoanalysis, started to lift for the first time after taking iproniazid three times a day for three weeks. Out of 31 patients, Kline found that 30 'responded with complete remission of symptoms'. If such reports could be replicated elsewhere, nothing in the history of psychiatry could compare to iproniazid.

'There is a revolution in psychiatry,' wrote Earl Ubell, the science editor of the *New York Herald Tribune*. 'The biological approach seems to be working.'

Kline called iproniazid a 'psychic energiser', the chemical opposite of tranquillisers such as reserpine. Its formal name, however, is monoamine oxidase inhibitor or, in short, MAO inhibitor. It's not as catchy, but MAO inhibitor is certainly more accurate. A 'monoamine' is a single molecule that is derived from an amino acid, the building blocks of proteins that make up the bulk of every living thing, from microscopic bacteria to massive blue whales. Serotonin, for instance, is a monoamine created from tryptophan, an amino acid found in most protein-rich foods such as tofu, chocolate, and mushrooms. Dopamine and noradrenaline, two other well-studied monoamines, stem from tyrosine. Each monoamine is a crucial signalling molecule in the body's tissues, sending messages from one neuron to another, or from a neuron to a muscle or organ. Your every thought, memory, and move is founded on a well-choreographed dance of monoamines.

Let's recreate their dance floor. Imagine clenching your fists in front of you and moving them towards each other, right hand to left hand, knuckle to knuckle. Leave a small gap in between. Don't let them touch. This is a gigantic and hugely simplified model of two neurons meeting in your brain. The gap between your knuckles is important because that represents the synapse, a place where monoamines flow from one neuron (your right hand) to the other (your left hand). At this junction, the electrical signal that flowed through this neuron is translated into a complex chemical signal. Whether it's serotonin, dopamine, or any of the other monoamines found in the body, vital information is relayed through the brain's neural networks in an instant. For this reason, monoamines are called 'neurotransmitters', chemicals that transmit information between neurons. Our brains aren't just electrical organs (as was thought up until the middle of the twentieth century), they are fluent in the language of chemistry too.

All chemical reactions need an off switch. Whether it is temperature regulation or the amount of oxygen in the blood, everything needs to be kept in check. This is called homeostasis, roughly meaning the same thing (homo) kept constant (stasis). For monoamines in the body, this control comes from an enzyme called monoamine oxidase that can grab hold of serotonin and noradrenaline and temporarily disable them by altering their chemical structure. MAO puts an end to whatever message the monoamine was sending. Without this 'off' switch, the brain would be awash in a confusing abundance of signals, all vying for space in the synapse and causing an overload for our everyday consciousness.

To different degrees, iproniazid stops this 'off' switch from working (hence MAO inhibitor). By preventing the MAO enzyme from doing its job, it keeps monoamines such as serotonin and noradrenaline as they are – signalling molecules in the brain's synapses. (The first monoamine oxidase, discovered by Mary Hare a chemist at the University of Cambridge, in 1928, interacted with tyramine, another monoamine.) It's a cascade effect: by blocking the enzyme that normally breaks down serotonin and noradrenaline, these monoamines are free to increase in number. Iproniazid in the brain is like the introduction of wolves into Yellowstone National Park. These large predators indirectly increase the growth of grass and trees by reducing the feeding activity of deer. Iproniazid, by similarly blocking the activity of MAO, increases the amount of monoamines in the brain, the fundamental basis of our own internal ecosystem. At the right dose, a new homeostasis – one with slightly higher levels of serotonin and noradrenaline – can take root.

With iproniazid and reserpine, an energiser and a tranquilliser, Kline dreamt of a day when mood could be tinkered with like body temperature or blood-sugar levels, guiding people away from pathological extremes towards a healthy norm.

Drug therapy didn't sit well with psychoanalysis, the dominant psychiatric worldview at the time. The theories put forward by Karl Abraham, Sigmund Freud, and Melanie Klein were still seen as the one true insight into the cause and treatment of depression. Nathan Kline, originally trained by a leading psychoanalyst in the United States, was well-versed in the latest revisions of theories that focused on loss and feelings of deprivation that were first experienced in childhood. 'One supposed mode of development [for depression] is that a child somehow fails to receive from the parents the love and support it needs,' Kline wrote. 'The child resents this bitterly but cannot express it openly because of guilt and so turns the anger inward.' He added, 'In effect, the child enters into a kind of subconscious alliance with the parents, rejecting himself as he believes they reject him and forming toward himself feelings of inadequacy and unworthiness. Thus created is a pattern of responses that becomes deeply embedded in the individual's personality. He will be plunged into depression, so the theory goes, whenever some stress situation brings out his buried feelings of rejection and failure.'

Depression was the emotional aftershock of object-loss and the conflicts that lay hidden in the unconscious. Only by extracting them – through hours of analysis 'on the couch' – could a patient start the process of recovery. It could take years and thousands of dollars until they were freed from their affliction. There was no place for iproniazid in this technique. If any benefits were reported from drug therapy, psychoanalysts argued, it was because they simply masked the deeper causes of depression, just as drinking alcohol can be effective at covering up stress. Such a deep-seated conflict as depression wasn't amenable to simple changes in chemistry. To say otherwise was close to heresy, a viewpoint that could end a once-promising career in psychiatry. 'So intense were the feelings that some good friends and respected colleagues took me aside to warn me that I was making a fool of myself,' Kline wrote. 'I was told that if I persisted in pursuing such an eccentric course, it could jeopardise my career.'

'Such warnings, of course, were both well-meaning and sincerely motivated,' he continued. 'They came from men who believed drug treatment of mental disturbance was, by definition, a dangerous quackery.' As one of his contemporaries later remarked, 'No one in their right mind in psychiatry was working with drugs. You used shock or various psychotherapies.'

Kline grew up along the boardwalk and busy streets of Atlantic City, New Jersey, a place that seemed to be – and often was – governed by its own rules. Under the jurisdiction of Enoch 'Nucky' Johnson, a man who, according to the *Atlantic City Press*, 'had flair, flamboyance, was politically amoral and ruthless', and had turned the city into a hub of drinking, sex work, and gambling during a time of prohibition and economic austerity. 'We have whisky, wine, women, song and slot machines,' Johnson once said. 'I won't deny it and I won't apologise for it. If the majority of the people didn't want them, they wouldn't be profitable and they would not exist. The fact that they do exist proves to me that the people want them.' It was as if Atlantic City had broken away from the mainland and floated adrift from the rigid work ethic that founded the American dream.

For Kline, a resident here, the endless mesh of entertainment and hedonism wasn't a holiday. For all he knew it was life itself. Although the cast in Atlantic City was in constant motion – people moving in and out like the ocean's tide – the characters remained the same. Drunken, disorderly, criminally extravagant. 'I thought everyone lived that way all the time,' Kline later wrote, 'and, naturally, I did the same. Money was meant to be spent, objects were in stores in order to be purchased, and life was there in order to be lived.' As his teenage interests in literature and poetry shifted towards medicine and psychiatry, he knew that he would never outgrow his childhood in Atlantic City.

Kline seemed to make up his own rules and live by them. When the medical director of a pharmaceutical company rejected his bid to test iproniazid, for example, Kline circumvented his decision by inviting the company's president to lunch at Theodore's Restaurant in New York City and, 'in the flush of excellent food and wine', was able to sweet talk his way to what he wanted. He was known for his womanising and would separate from his wife after nine years of marriage. He intentionally antagonised his peers at international conferences and would give experimental drugs to mentally ill patients without consent or approval from medical-ethics committees. In short, he lived life as if it were a game and he was the protagonist

Nathan Kline was no saint. When it came to depression, however, he would do more than anyone to push its treatment into the mainstream, not only providing relief for millions of people but changing the scientific perception of what depression is. During a time of psychoanalytical obsession, he stuck his neck out for biological psychiatry and seemed to relish the attention that it brought him. The front cover of his bestselling book, *From Sad to Glad*, made his confidence plain to see: 'Depression: You Can Conquer It Without Analysis!'

The Shoes That Prozac Would Fill

Ten years before Nathan Kline gave his patients iproniazid, another class of drugs was widely used to treat depression. Originally created as a potential decongestant to replace ephedrine (a chemical extracted from the ephedra plant that had been used in Chinese medicine for millennia), Benzedrine sulphate was shown to make withdrawn patients at the Maudsley Hospital in London more outgoing, even chatty. 'Almost everybody showed an increased tendency to talk, but the effect was most striking in depressive patients,' the psychiatrists wrote. '[T]hey overcame their [depression] and several of them talked spontaneously to other people for the first time since their admission.' As they spoke, they felt better about themselves and the world around them. One patient declared that she was an 'exulted being'. Another compared Benzedrine to a double shot of whisky, a feeling of 'energy and self-confidence'. The main difference, he added, was that whisky was only enjoyable when he was feeling healthy. When he was depressed, it made his situation even more miserable. But Benzedrine didn't.

In 1937, a study from researchers at the Mayo Clinic in Minnesota found that out of 30 patients who were given Benzedrine sulphate to take with breakfast and before lunch, 21 showed an almost immediate response. 'As soon as I started taking Benzedrine the depression and feeling of fear left me at once,' a 45-year-old man who had suffered from bouts of depression for almost 26 years said. '[I]n other words it made me feel like I have felt before under normal conditions when I have been at my best of vigour.'

Benzedrine sulphate is an amphetamine, a drug in the same family as ecstasy, speed, and crystal meth. In the late 1930s, however, it was most likened to caffeine, as if patients were being lifted from a depression with a particularly strong coffee. 'Benzedrine is a stimulant,' Erich Guttmann, a researcher from the Maudsley Hospital told the Royal Society of Medicine in October 1938, 'and although it does not appear to alter a depression fundamentally, it can lead to a symptomatic improvement which may tide the patient over a critical period, or it may provide that final impetus which is so often necessary in a depression that drags on.' Drugstores in the United States and pharmacies in Britain stocked the growing variety of amphetamines that followed in Benzedrine's footsteps, offering relief from narcolepsy, fatigue, and general tiredness. University students could purchase 'Pepper-upper (Pep) pills' and stay awake for days, allowing prolonged periods of study that were previously impossible. Soldiers on both sides of the Second World War gulped down amphetamines to keep their minds alert, their eyes focused, and their bodies ready to fight even after sleepless nights or long marches. While the British army gave Benzedrine to their infantry and aviators, the Nazis preferred Pervitin, a brand name for methamphetamine (a form of crystal meth).

Although there were warning signs from the beginning – there were reports of students fainting and dying after taking Benzedrine to keep them awake during exam season – amphetamines were marketed as a treatment for 'mild depression' in 1939. The pharmaceutical company that produced Benzedrine – Smith, Kline & French – showcased its product into the mainstream. One poster from 1945, for instance, shows a besuited man standing proud, his chest pushed outwards and his hands on his hips. He is smiling and gazing into the distance. Behind him, his enlarged countenance is in a state of confusion and despair, the shadow of his former self. The poster makes it clear: his transformation is due to a new drug. 'Only in the last decade has there been available – in Benzedrine sulphate – a therapeutic weapon capable of alleviating depression,' it reads.

Amphetamines provided an alternative to psychoanalysis and electroshock therapy, a quick fix for 'mild' depressions that could boost a person's energy and feeling of well-being. Amphetamine therapy, Abraham Myerson, a leading psychiatrist from Boston and famed author of the 1925 book *When Life Loses Its Zest*, wrote, 'is not in any sense curative and its effects are not permanent, but it helps to dissipate the morning apathy and depression. [I]ts ameliorative effect is sufficiently important to recommend it while the process of natural recovery is taking place.' For the restlessness, insomnia, and anxiety that often came from taking regular doses of a stimulant, sedatives were commonly prescribed in the evenings. 'Clinically, the effects of the two kinds of drug, when given in combination, seem to be regarded as "mutually corrective",' the pharmacologist Hannah Steinberg wrote. While one drug lifted a person slightly closer to agitation and euphoria, the other brought them back down for a sleep.

Financially, these drugs were a huge success. In 1949 alone, Smith, Kline & French earned over $7 million from their sales in amphetamines. At their peak, pharmaceutical companies produced 800 metric tons of amphetamine pills every year, the equivalent of every person in the United States taking 43 doses of amphetamine per year. Before the designer drugs like Valium, Prozac, and Xanax, there was Benzedrine sulphate. 'It established the "profile" that subsequent antidepressants would have to match,' the historian Nicolas Rasmussen wrote, 'the shoes that Prozac would ultimately have to fill.' The difference is that modern antidepressants actually work, even in severe cases of depression.

My first week on citalopram was awful. It was spring, and I sat on the sofa wrapped in a duvet feeling like I had the flu. Confused, nauseous, dipping in and out of a sleep, I swallowed my daily pill and waited for my brain to get used to its new injection of serotonin. The flu-like symptoms soon stopped, but my depression did not. In fact, it only got worse. The nausea was a daily occurrence, a constant reminder that I was a depressed person taking prescription drugs. This would have been a price I was willing to pay if the drugs worked, if the depression stopped. I could live with nausea. But the depression didn't abate, and I tried to run from my demons.

I was 25 years old and thought that a freelancer could, and should, live anywhere he wanted. I had been in London for two years and wondered whether it was the reason for my anguish. After all, there was the extortionate cost of rent, the constant buzz of traffic, sirens, and the inability to escape to more tranquil places without an expensive train ticket. Although most of my friends were living in the city, it was rare that we met up and saw each other. I decided that I wasn't happy living in London and made plans to move to Berlin, a city that I had visited three times and thought would be a perfect place to start afresh. I had been dating Lucy for a few months, and she had been thinking along similar lines. We moved in the summer of 2016, found a studio flat that a friend was subletting for a few months, and thought that this might be the beginning of a healthier future.

There were good times, moments of a new relationship that I will forever cherish. We learnt German together, walked through ancient woodlands filled with birdsong, and wrapped ourselves up against the dry continental winter that could dip to minus 15°C. But, despite the distractions, it was soon evident that I was getting worse. My depressive episodes were becoming more frequent and more dangerous. I always made sure I had enough citalopram to last me until we returned to the UK to visit friends, but the drugs didn't seem to be doing anything except chopping one long depression into small, but severe, depressions. One day, I decided to stop taking them.

Although citalopram and other SSRIs are not addictive, they can come with some pretty horrendous withdrawal symptoms if you suddenly stop taking them. I wasn't told this. I quickly wished I had been. There's a German word for depression: *Weltschmerz*, or world pain. And this withdrawal certainly felt apocalyptic. I locked myself in our bedroom and rocked myself into a stupor, sitting on the floor with my head in my hands. That weekend, one of my friends was visiting for a few days, but I barely saw him. He must have heard my crying and screams. When he was leaving to catch his flight home, I hugged him and apologised. He left on a positive note: he admitted that he hadn't realised how bad depression could get. In that moment of departure, he became a closer friend.

'I feel trapped by a drug that I hate,' I wrote at the time. If both group therapy and antidepressants hadn't made a dent in my depression, then what point was there? Why go on when both fields of psychiatry – the psychological and the biological – had tried and failed to make a difference? As Lucy was working for a start-up in Berlin that demanded 11-hour days, I sat in our one-bedroom flat and thought about an end. This world pain had to stop. I noted in my diary how Winston Churchill named his depression the 'black dog', a pet name that had helped to separate his mental state from himself. As my first group therapy classes had taught me, I'm not a depressed person but a person with depression. But as it took away more and more of my days, I couldn't see it like that any more. I felt like a depressed person. I couldn't call my depression by a pet name. As I wrote in my diary, 'Looking into the future – a difficulty at this time – I worry that others, my family, the media, Lucy, would know exactly what to call my depression. It would be my killer.'

It was then, only six months after arriving in Berlin, that we decided to move back to the UK and reach out for the support of friends and family, and to look for the next stage of treatment. I was put on a waiting list for one-to-one CBT, and my dose of citalopram was doubled to its maximum. Anything higher would lead to dangerous side effects, such as the so-called 'serotonin syndrome'. In mild cases, too much serotonin in the body can lead to vomiting, diarrhoea, and muscle twitching. But it can also cause convulsions and, as one case report published in the *Journal of Medical Toxicology* in 2014 states, 'fatalities may occur'. 'The clinician,' the authors of this report added, 'must be aware of the potential for large ingestions of citalopram to produce life-threatening effects and monitor closely for the neurologic, cardiovascular, and other manifestations that, in rare cases, can be fatal.'

The doctor, a compassionate middle-aged woman who kept calling me Alexander, suggested that Lucy keep hold of my pills. Did we have a safe for which only she knew the code? Could she hide them somewhere I would never think to look? In that moment, we all agreed that I was a danger to myself. This prescription could be used for two purposes: for stability or for suicide. Unfortunately, it was the latter that seemed more likely.

For me, citalopram is a drug of side effects. After my dosage was doubled, my anxiety increased beyond what I knew was possible. I spent nights obsessing over thoughts that would never have troubled me in the past. My heart palpitated and a feeling of sickness extended from the back of my throat to the pit of my stomach. I knew that SSRIs worked for many people. But, after two and half years without relief, I also knew that citalopram wasn't for me.

In 2015, 7.2 per cent of the adult US population were taking antidepressants. In 2018, 16.6 per cent of the UK population had received an antidepressant in the previous 12 months, half of whom had taken these drugs for the entirety of that year. In Australia, these figures stand at 15 per cent, a proportion that has doubled since 2000. In all countries, prescriptions are increasing year on year.

These data are striking. It could be argued that pharmaceutical companies have a grip on a large percentage of the population, and their pockets. But high uptake of prescription drugs could also be a sign that people are more willing to reach out for professional help, whether it is for their depression, anxiety, or any of the other illnesses for which these drugs are effective. These treatments have been stigmatised for a long time, and people have had difficulty accessing them. The only problem is that antidepressants are not always brilliant at treating depression. Some studies have found that they are only worth a patient's while if they are severely depressed, someone who experiences a broad range of symptoms for a long period of time. In such cases, antidepressants can do wonders, living up to the claim of miracle cures that made the headlines with the introduction of Prozac in the late 1980s. For milder depressions, the evidence for their efficacy has led to heated debates and round after round of contradictory reviews.

In 2018, a meta-analysis – a kind of review that lumps similar studies together, filters through their differing methods, and takes an average of their results – published in the journal *The Lancet* seemed to provide some much-needed clarity. Reviewing studies into 21 different antidepressants, Toshi Furukawa, Georgia Salanti, and their colleagues found that they were all more effective than a placebo, but only just. In some cases, the gap between treatment and placebo was so small that the clinical benefit of prescribing these drugs remained inconclusive. Would patients actually *feel* such a slight reduction in their depression's severity? Would the side effects of these drugs make other parts of their life worse in the process? These are questions that continue to fuel arguments at international conferences and between psychiatrists in medical journals. I have sat and watched such debates and felt exasperated at the growing gulf between what psychiatrists study and the patients who they aim to treat.

Clinical trials have a long history of cherry-picking patients who aren't representative of depression as a diverse collection of mental disorders. Usually more chronically depressed and not actively suicidal, they fit neatly into the DSM III's criteria of major depressive disorder. They have suffered with five or more symptoms for at least two weeks. Such patients are a specific subset of people with depression. But when someone reaches out for support, the doctor or psychiatrist doesn't get to decide whether they can choose another patient. They have to make a decision. Should this person receive an antidepressant or not? With limited time and resources, they have to make a call – and that call is usually an SSRI like citalopram, the drug I was prescribed in 2016.

I have often felt betrayed by this common practice. I thought that an SSRI was pushed into my life unnecessarily. But a study published in November 2019 provided a refreshing sense of understanding and clarity. Conducted across 179 general practices in four UK cities, this 'pragmatic' randomised-controlled trial followed the health of 640 people who weren't cherry-picked before the trial began. 'Participants in our study ranged from those with very few depressive symptoms to those with severe depressive symptoms, therefore our results are more readily generalisable to the population currently receiving antidepressants in primary care,' Gemma Lewis, a lecturer of psychiatric epidemiology at University College London, and her co-authors wrote. For me, the results were reassuring. Even with such a broad sweep of depression, the SSRI sertraline outperformed the placebo on a range of measures. At six weeks, self-reported mental well-being and 'quality of life' was significantly improved in the SSRI group. Similarly, levels of anxiety – a common experience for people living with depression – were significantly reduced. At the 12-week mark, a significant number of patients were in remission from their depression (51 per cent) compared to placebo (31 per cent). Importantly, there was no correlation of clinical improvement with severity of depression; both mild and severe depressions responded similarly. The superiority of the SSRI over placebo, therefore, was unlikely to be simply a product of the more severely ill patients responding to antidepressants.

Reading through this study, I found comfort in knowing that antidepressants are able to help support such a diverse group of patients suffering from very different experiences of depression. It provides some important reminders that an SSRI can make people feel better and reduce the anxiety that often can initiate and maintain a depressive episode, while also guiding half of these everyday patients into remission. Far from perfect and still prescribed through trial and error, it shows that antidepressants are an effective weapon in our psychiatric arsenal.

G22355

In the mid 1950s, a meeting of psychopharmacologists was being planned for the Second International Congress for Psychiatry. Held in Zurich, a charming city of bridges, cobblestone paths, and church steeples that perch above the tranquil Limmat River, it was supposed to be a small gathering, not too different from a dinner with colleagues. But, as one of the organisers wrote, 'the "speck" of drugs to treat mental illness [had] developed into a small cyclone', and they had to make time and space for over 90 participants. More than a dozen pharmaceutical firms provided the financial support for a three-day meeting, one that was separate from the general psychiatry conference. Nathan Kline was one of the introductory speakers. On the page, Kline was an eloquent and enthusiastic writer. In person, he was flamboyant and captivating, an orator who could cause waves of laughter in an otherwise sterile medical symposium. Some people loved him. Others detested him, thinking that he was narcissistic and would be more successful as a stand-up comedian than a serious academic.

Along with his growing art collection of Haitian sculptures, Kline amassed a vast archive of jokes over his lifetime. He often couldn't wait to return home from his private practice in Manhattan to test his latest quip on his daughter. At the international conference in Zurich, Kline started his plenary lecture – a talk that is scheduled for a time when the whole conference can attend – with his latest gag. He had isolated the cause of schizophrenia, he said. It was a bacterium all along – *the crafty*

Schizococcus! A cure would soon be on the way. Whether any-one laughed was not recorded.

Over the next two days, Kline regaled his audience with his work into reserpine and iproniazid, two drugs that would twice lead him to the coveted Lasker Award in medicine. (Kline is one of only two people to have received two Lasker Awards.) Although there had been reports of harmful side effects in patients taking iproniazid, such as dizziness, fainting, and a few cases of liver damage, Kline thought that these were unsub-stantiated or, if they were real, part and parcel of this line of work. 'It is almost a truism that a pharmaceutical [drug] that does not have side effects is a useless one,' Kline told his audi-ence in Zurich. There is always a trade-off between cost and benefit, a middle ground between how much is taken away and what is restored. Every drug is a chemical compromise. For iproniazid, as it would later turn out, the costs were just a bit *too* costly.

Kline wasn't the only person in Zurich with a promising new drug for depression. After a decade without any advance on the existing amphetamines such as Benzedrine sulphate, two antidepressants were discovered within a few months of each other. Roland Kuhn, a psychiatrist from the bucolic town of Münsterlingen in Switzerland, presented his work on the last day of the general psychiatry conference. Largely unknown on the international scene, Kuhn hadn't been invited to the psychopharmacology section. Taciturn, sober, and with a whisper-soft voice, he was a very different character to Kline. He didn't have a plenary slot at the congress, nor any jokes for his small audience. All he had was an exclusive window into one of the greatest discoveries in the treatment of depression, one that would not only add to Kline's work but, in time, replace it.

But no one knew that in September 1957, not even those dozen people who stuck around and listened to his talk. Kline didn't even know who Kuhn was.

An unhurried town of a few thousand people, Münsterlingen sits on the southern shores of Lake Constance, the third largest body of water in central Europe, which laps at the borders of Switzerland, Germany, and Austria. During the cooler months of the year, a thick fog blankets the streets at dawn, only lifting with the heat of the sun. By late morning, one can once again look out from the shore and see the sand-coloured speck of Meersburg Castle in southern Germany, the invitingly blue and still lake in between. Working at Münsterlingen's psychiatric hospital, a trio of tall buildings that perch on the edge of Lake Constance, it was this view that Roland Kuhn saw most of his working life. For a time, he lived on the hospital's grounds, opening the window of his apartment to the moist air and the din of waterfowl. It was like working where others might choose to holiday. It was so calm, picturesque, and peacefully quiet that Kuhn rarely left.

He hoped that his research would put Münsterlingen firmly on the map. (Switzerland was a central hub of biological psychiatry and nearby Kreuzlingen was famous for its psychoanalytic institute, the Bellevue Sanatorium led by Ludwig Binswanger, but Kuhn and Münsterlingen were little known.) Since 1953, Kuhn had been working with a chemical called G22355, a direct descendent of chlorpromazine, the famed tranquilliser first discovered in Paris. These two chemicals shared the same three-ringed structure, a trio of honeycombs in a row. The only difference was in a few hydrogen and carbon atoms in place of an atom of sulphur. This slight change in structure, however, had dramatic effects in function. G22355 was useless, Kuhn found, for his hallucinating or manic patients; it either did nothing or made their symptoms worse. But it was brilliant for a subset of people who were depressed.

On 21 January 1956, Kuhn noted how Paula J., one of the first people to be given this chemical, had 'undergone a transformation'. 'All of her restlessness and agitation has vanished,' he wrote. 'It is not entirely clear how the medication could have been responsible for such an abrupt change within a week's time, or whether this depressive phase abated spontaneously.' This latter explanation seemed unlikely to Kuhn, however. She seemed like a completely different person after taking G22355. She slept better, was more sociable, friendly, energetic, and enjoyed reading books quietly.

Kuhn wanted to know more. Was Paula J.'s experience just a one-off? A placebo effect? After testing the drug on 100 patients with schizophrenia who were also depressed (a diagnosis of schizoaffective disorder might be given to such patients today), Kuhn found that G22355 could elevate mood in 40 of them. It wasn't a miracle by any means, but it was still a significant result in such a diverse mix of severely ill patients. On 31 August 1957, in an article in his local bulletin *Swiss Medical Weekly*, Kuhn wrote: 'Feelings of guilt, delusions of impoverishment or culpability simply disappear or lose their affective importance, move into a distance, and the patient becomes indifferent and unconcerned with respect to these feelings.' Previously bed-bound patients started getting up early in the mornings, initiated conversations for the first time in months, and wrote letters to people outside of the hospital's walls. In the wards, these formerly withdrawn individuals became social and even popular, elevating the mood of others. Just as the sun burned through the fog that blanketed Münsterlingen in the winter mornings, G22355 seemed to dissipate whatever had clouded his patients' minds.

A week after his publication in *Swiss Medical Weekly*, Kuhn travelled to the psychiatry conference in Zurich, a 50-mile journey into the south of Switzerland. 'The depression,' he said in his native German, 'which had manifested itself through sadness, irritation and a sensation of dissatisfaction, now gave way to friendly, joyous and accessible feelings.' While Nathan Kline used terms like 'psychic', 'ego', and 'id', to describe iproniazid, bridging the gap between psychoanalysis and drug therapy, Kuhn was fluent in medicine and scientific reasoning. Verbose and boringly thorough, he spoke with a philosophical monotone that made his once-in-a-lifetime discovery no more than a speculative whisper among the hubbub of other biological psychiatrists. When he had finished his presentation, the room remained quiet. The dozen or so people who turned up to this last-minute talk were wholly indifferent to the latest revolution in the treatment of depression.

Heinz Lehmann, a good friend of Nathan Kline, didn't make it to Kuhn's talk. He only became aware of the Swiss psychiatrist's work as he was flying back from the conference in Zurich to his home in Canada. In 1937, Lehmann had escaped from Nazi Germany by asking a friend to invite him on a skiing holiday in Quebec. Arriving at the airport with skis and a suitcase of clothes, he left all his other possessions behind and settled in Montreal, becoming the clinical director of Verdun Protestant Hospital in 1947. A decade later, he shared the Lasker Award with Nathan Kline (and others) for his research into chlorpromazine and its subsequent introduction into Canada and the United States. Returning from Zurich in September 1957, Lehmann read Roland Kuhn's article in its original German and couldn't wait to order some samples of this drug for his patients. Could he aid in this drug's dissemination, just as he had done with chlorpromazine? While Kuhn believed that qualitative observation was enough to determine whether a drug worked or not, Lehmann was a psychiatrist of the scientific method. He required quantitative evidence. He started a clinical trial, using a change in symptoms over time as a measure of recovery, improvement, or decline. Out of 84 patients with various forms of depression – endogenous or reactive, chronic or acute – he found that, roughly, two out of every three (60 per cent) either fully recovered from their depressive symptoms or improved to such an extent that they could leave the hospital and return to their home or community.

Using different methods and styles of psychiatry, Kuhn and Lehmann both found that this drug was best suited to endogenous depression. In these cases, on average, three out of four people (75 per cent) improved. 'The effect is striking in patients with a deep depression ... associated with fatigue, heaviness, feeling of oppression, and a melancholic or even despairing mood,' Kuhn wrote, 'all these symptoms being aggravated in the morning and tending to improve in the afternoon and evening.' After a few days or weeks on G22355, Kuhn continued, 'the patients express themselves as feeling much better, fatigue disappears, the feeling of heaviness in the limbs vanishes, and the sense of oppression in the chest gives way to a feeling of relief.' Those who had been shrinking in size for months started to enjoy their food and, over time, were able to maintain a healthy weight. Those who suffered from insomnia or woke up in the early hours of the morning and struggled to get back to sleep found that they not only slept, but they felt refreshed. They weren't 'fatigued ... as that so often produced by sleeping remedies,' Kuhn wrote.

In 1958, two years after Kuhn's first trials, G22355 became a licensed drug. It lost its codename and became known as imipramine (marketed as Tofranil in the United States), the first member of a new family of drugs named tricyclic antidepressants after their three-ringed molecular structure. Prescribed in the United States and across Europe, imipramine represented another milestone in the treatment of depression: a drug that worked through a different chemical pathway to MAO inhibitors. 'The pharmacological uniqueness of imipramine is of special significance,' wrote the pharmacologist Fritz Freyhan in 1960, 'since on the one hand its action cannot be explained in terms of enzyme inhibition, while on the other hand it appears to be the most effective antidepressant drug which is now available.' Although imipramine also increases the concentration of monoamines in the brain's synapses, it doesn't block MAO or any other enzymes. Instead, it wedges itself into the channels used by monoamines to return to the neuron that originally released them. These channels are like nanoscopic travellators that allow these neurotransmitters to be reabsorbed, recycled, and reused. Its technical term in biochemistry is 'reuptake'. In particular, later studies found, imipramine was particularly good at blocking the reuptake of noradrenaline, a neurotransmitter associated with sleep, appetite, and response to stressful situations. In our imaginary model of the synapse, this process occurs along the sides of the clenched right hand, completing the circuitous flow of chemistry from the knuckles. Reuptake, rather than MAO inhibition, would prove of great importance in the future of drug therapy. It didn't lead to the same side reactions that would nearly doom many MAO inhibitors in the 1960s.

While imipramine was a great addition to the biological psychiatrist's medicine cabinet, there were doubts over whether it offered anything above existing treatments. 'It should be noted,' Heinz Lehmann wrote in 1958, 'that the effects of the drug are much less spectacular than the therapeutic action of electroconvulsive treatment as regards both immediacy and intensity of its results. A deeply depressed patient who is suicidal might still require electroconvulsive therapy in order to control the situation rapidly, particularly if the patient is not hospitalised.'

Although its use would sharply decline in the 1960s, ECT was still seen as the yardstick that any new therapy had to be measured against. 'Electroconvulsive therapy (ECT) is considered by many clinicians to be the most effective treatment for depression,' one study from 1966 states. 'It is therefore important that any treatment suggested as a replacement for it be shown objectively to be at least equal if not superior in therapeutic efficacy.' In the middle of the 1960s, two large-scale studies (incorporating over 500 patients from four cities) in the United States and England put imipramine to the test, and ECT came out victorious in both. While the drug therapy led around 50 per cent of patients into remission, ECT stood at 70 or even 80 per cent. If delusions were present, as was the defining feature of melancholia, it was even more effective. More commonly known as 'psychotic depression' today, this is a life-threatening illness that has a higher rate of suicide than depressions without delusions. But, amazingly, it is highly treatable. Studies in the 1970s and 1980s that used simulated-controls – a form of placebo where an anaesthetic and muscle relaxant are used but without an electric shock or convulsion – added further evidence that ECT is particularly effective in this type of depression. 'Indeed, the significance of the original results, which show that real ECT is a more effective antidepressant than simulated ECT, depends very largely on the presence of 22 patients with delusions,' a study of 70 patients concluded.

While these studies are now decades old and can't be repeated due to modern ethical standards (high-risk suicidal and psychotic patients can't be given simulated treatments), they all point in the same general direction: 'a clear and significant advantage for ECT over medication,' wrote Nancy Payne from New York University and Joan Prudic from the New York State Psychiatric Institute in 2009. 'In fact, no study has found any treatment, including other forms of brain stimulation currently in development, to be superior to ECT in the treatment of major depression.'

In the 1960s, however, imipramine was still seen as a viable replacement for ECT. Although it came with its own set of disabling side effects, such as muscle tremors, dizziness, and dry mouth, these were often temporary or reversible with a slightly lower dose. If the unquenchable, clacking dry mouth persisted, Nathan Kline recommended glycerine based lozenges such as Pine Bros cough drops. '[O]ther candies become cloyingly sweet after a short while,' he wrote. Imipramine was also easier to administer than ECT. There was no need for general anaesthetic, injections of sux, and no risk of memory loss (a worrying side effect to most patients, even if it was usually temporary). But there were still concerns over whether imipramine was any safer.

The first reported case of an overdose of imipramine came less than a year after its release onto the pharmaceutical market. At 10pm on 19 February 1959, a 29-year-old nurse who had previously been treated with ECT picked up her bottle of imipramine tablets and swallowed them all. She felt nothing for three quarters of an hour and then fell asleep. As she was nodding off, she hoped that she wouldn't wake up again. Two doctors from Barrow Hospital in Bristol investigated what happened next and published their report, 'Suicidal Attempt by

Imipramine Overdosage', in the *British Medical Journal*. 'She has no recollection of any dreaming, and woke at 6:30 a.m. the next day in an agitated state, with gross involuntary movements of all her limbs, head and neck, which she described as being just like those of a fit and of a violent and terrifying nature,' they wrote. 'She remained in this state for some time, being unable to shout for help. Eventually her mother brought her a morning cup of tea, and, seeing the gross movements, asked what was wrong.' Her daughter was unable to respond but managed to gesture towards her empty bottle of pills.

This first overdose on imipramine didn't result in its first death. But tricyclic antidepressants still had the potential to kill. Although the risk was small – one study found that, on average, four people died from an overdose for every million prescriptions, or 0.0004 per cent – it meant that these drugs had to be monitored and administered with care, especially when giving them to patients already at high risk of suicide. It was a paradox in a pill: imipramine could save lives from depression but could also be used for suicide, the most tragic consequence of this mental disorder.

Iproniazid, meanwhile, wasn't as effective as Nathan Kline first thought. Although he originally reported that 30 out of 31 patients responded favourably to the drug, larger trials weren't so successful. While some studies found a response rate of 75 per cent, others produced figures as low as 25 per cent. This huge disparity demanded an explanation. Why would the same drug help three quarters of depressed people in one study and then only a quarter in another? Was it the dose? Was it the length of time it was prescribed? As it turned out, the most likely explanation was that a group of depressed patients actually included people with a variety of different disorders, all lumped together as depression. Some might have endogenous depression, others might be more reactive. But iproniazid seemed to stretch the definition of depression until it broke off into a new term altogether.

Atypical depression is, as the name suggests, an unusual form of illness. It is defined by its complete reversal of some of the defining features of endogenous depression. While this latter, more physical depression was characterised by weight loss, insomnia, and a cognitive dulling that negated any significant amount of anxiety, atypical depression was associated with eating too much (hyperphagia), sleeping more than usual (hypersomnia), and hyperactivity that manifested itself in tremors, restlessness, and crippling amounts of anxiety. Although these two conditions seemed complete opposites of one another, they were often lumped together under a single diagnosis: unipolar depression. (By 1959, bipolar disorder – a cyclical disease of mania and depression – had been separated into its own diagnosis and its own chemical treatment: lithium carbonate.)

For much of the twentieth century, doctors and psychiatrists weren't oblivious to the existence of an atypical subtype of depression. They met with countless patients who exhibited these symptoms. The problem was that they were often the most difficult to treat. Michael Shepherd, a psychiatrist from St Thomas' Hospital in London, called atypical depression the bane of his psychiatric career. 'For two years or more, [these patients] may have been complaining of vague depression, increased emotionality, diffuse anxiety, and sometimes of phobic fears of going out in the street, of traveling alone, etc.,' he said at a conference held in Cleveland in 1960. 'They may also have become bad tempered, irritable, hyperreactive and aggressive; quite unlike so many of the more endogenously depressed patients ... In my twenty years' experience, this sort of [depressed] patient has been one of the most impossible and difficult to treat by any method.'

Atypical depression usually responded to iproniazid within five to eight days. The only problem was that when a patient came off the drugs, either by accident or to see if they had fully recovered, the depression returned like air being sucked into an area of low pressure. Relapse, as well as recovery, was a defining feature of MAO inhibitors such as iproniazid. People had to take these drugs for a long time to remain healthy. The same is true of both tricyclics and the third family of antidepressants, SSRIs, that were first used to treat depression in the 1980s.

Imipramine wasn't completely useless in atypical depression. It just took longer to have an effect. Rather than a few days, drugs like imipramine might take four or more weeks to lift someone out of this type of depression. ECT, meanwhile, made the anxieties that defined atypical depression worse and was best avoided for such patients.

More than a diagnosis, atypical depression was a lesson in how we study disease. It showed that clinical trials don't always fail because the drug doesn't work. Even if the large majority of patients didn't respond to a treatment, there might be a hidden minority that did. If the potential diversity of depression isn't taken into account, Peter Dally and Eric West, two doctors from St Thomas' Hospital, wrote in 1959, 'dramatic improvement in a few cases within the larger group may not reach statistical significance and may be ignored. Yet such improvements may be of greatest importance'.

Just as Emil Kraepelin came to doubt his neat classification, these diagnoses weren't seen as a perfect guide to the diversity of depression. Atypical, endogenous, psychotic, reactive: they all had their own variations and overlapped with one another in their key features. Even if they were artificial constructs, they were also useful tools that helped sick people get the treatment most suited to their symptoms.

As it would turn out, this was particularly important for drugs like iproniazid. Appropriately for a chemical extracted from rocket fuel, this MAO inhibitor was soon found to kickstart a cascade of chemical explosions inside the human body. To prescribe this drug to someone who was unlikely to feel any benefit, therefore, could be catastrophic. Roughly one patient in every 500 suffered from liver damage after taking the drug and became jaundiced – their skin turning a sickly yellow – from hepatitis. One in five of these patients died. Nathan Kline, who had been promoted to director of the recently created Rockland Research Institute (formerly Rockland State Hospital), argued that there was insufficient evidence to support these claims. 'Among those first 400,000 Marselid [the brand name for iproniazid] patients, there were some who got married, some who had ski accidents – and some who got jaundice,' he wrote. 'The marriages and ski accidents were not blamed on the drug, but the jaundice was. In fact, the case was never proved statistically, but the mere raising of the question created serious doubts.' In 1961, a decade after it was first given to terminally ill tuberculosis patients on Staten Island, iproniazid was withdrawn from the medical cabinets of most countries around the world.

In one of his final pieces of writing, Kline recalled how it took six years for this anti-tubercular drug to be 'discovered' by psychiatry. 'The whole iproniazid story was one of these "acres of diamonds" affairs,' he wrote, 'in which medicine kept stumbling over a treasure that had all along been lying there on its own neglected backyard.' Although Kline had a personal attachment to this treasure, it wasn't a huge loss to psychiatry. By the early 1960s, there were already three new

MAO inhibitors, phenelzine (Nardil), isocarboxazid (Marplan), and tranylcypromine (Parnate), that could be prescribed. These were the drugs that would remain a part of the treatment of depression into the present day. As is the case for all drugs, they are not without risk. But tranylcypromine – pronounced TRAN-il-SIP-roe-meen – was considered the safest because of its familiar chemistry. Although it functioned as a MAO inhibitor, it was actually a member of the amphetamine family and was therefore more recognisable, somehow safer – a drug that was unlikely to cause liver damage and could be prescribed with confidence.

The Mysterious Case of the Lethal Headaches

On 23 June 1962, a 27-year-old man walked into the Maudsley Hospital, slowly making his way past the Grecian columns that shadow its entrance. He felt giddy and off-balance, and he suffered from a painful headache at the back of his head, right at the point where the nape of the neck meets the underside of the skull. It pulsed with every heartbeat. Any movement made his head feel as rigid as wood. A nurse took his blood pressure. It was high but nothing out of the ordinary. Soon after, he passed out. His blood pressure suddenly plummeted. A few hours later, he was dead. A post-mortem examination revealed a burst artery, a haemorrhage, at the back of his head, right at the point where his headache had once pulsed.

Though the consequences were less severe, three other patients at the Maudsley reported the same story: a 'devastating headache' and, intriguingly, a prescription of tranylcypromine. Each case was reported on and written up by J.L. McClure, chief resident at the Maudsley and supervisor of a 29-year-old man called Barry Blackwell. A recent medical graduate, Blackwell listened to the reports and quickly lost interest. Three headaches and one death ... So what? Thousands of people in the UK were taking tranylcypromine to combat their depression. They weren't having any troubles. Further, there were no such reports from the United States, a country where even more tranylcypromine was prescribed than in Britain. If there was a problem with this drug, surely it would emerge there first.

As a medical student at the University of Cambridge in the early 1950s, Barry Blackwell spent more time at the local pubs and playing rugby than reading his textbooks. Having grown up fleeing from war in India and Nepal, and then being moved to a rural boarding school in the south of England to avoid German missile strikes aimed at urban centres like London and Bristol, his time at university was a welcome relief, a period of freedom and socialising. After he graduated – without distinction – he moved to Guy's Hospital in London, a soot-darkened set of buildings just south of London Bridge. It was a leading institution for medical teaching, plus they had the oldest rugby team in the world. Over the next few months, he rotated as an intern in surgery, emergency medicine, and internal medicine. Although he published no case studies or reports during these early days, he did discover what he loved about being a doctor: chatting to patients, listening to their stories, and linking personal history to current health. 'I was transformed by contact with patients,' he would later say. 'That unleashed both my energy and curiosity.' Only when he discovered the people behind the abstract world of illness did he truly become a doctor.

Whether he liked it or not, Barry Blackwell seemed almost fated to unlock the medical mystery that was sweeping through the Maudsley's wards. As he was eating in the hospital canteen, a long rectangular room with rows of pendant lights hanging from the ceiling and the smell of coffee infusing the air, a group of doctors were discussing a young female patient. She had recently suffered from a haemorrhage following a very painful headache. Blackwell was sitting within earshot, listening to their every word.

'Was she taking tranylcypromine?' he asked, recalling his supervisor's report.

Yes, they said, she was.

From this chance encounter over lunch, Blackwell decided to spend some time investigating tranylcypromine and these painful, potentially lethal, headaches. Was this drug definitely to blame? With such few cases, could it all just be a coincidence that people were taking tranylcypromine? Was there a missing link between their prescription and these peculiar headaches? Blackwell sat down in the hospital's medical library and scoured through previous volumes of *The Lancet*, looking for any sign of headaches and tranylcypromine from the last 20 months. He found six patient reports. But he couldn't see any obvious pattern in the pages in front of him. The headaches affected both men and women, young and old, and didn't discriminate by job or location. The only whisper of a clue came from when these headaches occurred: they were most common in the evening. It wasn't enough to crack this mystery, but this temporal pattern would make sense when all the other pieces of the puzzle came together.

Without any firm conclusions, Blackwell published a short letter in *The Lancet* in which he proposed that these headaches might be far more common than previously thought. Were more people suffering – and potentially dying – from a drug that was supposed to help treat their depression? Although Blackwell had found a mere six cases, he was only looking in one journal and its recent publications. What about the other medical journals? More significantly, were similar headaches and deaths going unreported? While he didn't have any answers to such questions, Blackwell was hoping that someone else might.

In the days before instant text messaging and email, he still didn't have to wait long for a response in the mail. Reading through the latest copy of *The Lancet* in his local library, a pharmacist working in Nottingham read Blackwell's article and thought he knew what the missing link was. Posting his own letter directly to Dr Blackwell at the Maudsley Hospital in London, he explained how his wife had suffered the same back-of-the-head headache that the doctor described, not once but twice. In each case, he wrote, she had eaten a cheese sandwich for supper. 'No effects are caused by butter or milk,' he wrote. 'If cheese is indeed the factor, it could perhaps explain the sporadic nature of the incidence of the side effect.'

Could cheese react with tranylcypromine to cause such blinding pain and, in rare cases, kill someone? Blackwell didn't believe it – it was, well, unbelievable. But as he was made aware of more cases and had time to reflect on the topic, the conversation he had overheard in the canteen suddenly ballooned in significance, almost making him burst with the potential thrill of discovery. Perhaps that one case held the answer all along. As he had flicked through the pages of medical journals in the library, he rummaged through the kitchen's records (a sizeable archive that was stored for monitoring patient allergies and other side effects), and found the menu from that day, the evening the woman's headache started. He knew she was vegetarian and wouldn't have chosen the meat option. She had eaten a cheese pie.

The next step seemed obvious to Blackwell, a young intern with equal parts confidence and naivety. He prescribed himself 20 milligrams of tranylcypromine from the hospital's pharmacy and took it daily for two weeks. Then, when he felt that he was sufficiently dosed up, he sat down to a breakfast of cheese.

Through their ability to elevate the number of neurotransmitters in the brain's synapses, tricyclics and MAO inhibitors led to the most popular theory about depression: that it is an imbalance of brain chemicals. It was a logical conclusion. If these drugs worked – and they did for a large percentage of patients – then, by extrapolating backwards, depression was ultimately a deficiency in brain neurotransmitters. First proposed in the mid 1960s, there were two imbalance theories for depression: one for noradrenaline and one for serotonin. Both were modern reversals of Galen's humoural theory. In place of too much black bile, a lack of neurotransmitters was considered the key determinant of low mood.

There were several observations that supported this idea. After taking drugs that reduce the amount of noradrenaline in the brain, for instance, people with no history of psychiatric illness developed a depressive-like condition that sometimes necessitated treatment with electroconvulsive therapy. (Subsequent studies would cast doubt on this association.) Research groups in Scotland and the Netherlands found that people with depression had lower levels of metabolic products of serotonin in their spinal fluid, an indication that serotonin itself was in short supply. And, finally, people who had died from suicides had less serotonin in the hind regions of their brain than people who had died in car accidents or from old age. Such patterns could be explained by many other mechanisms that weren't taken into account. Indeed, the authors of both imbalance theories were rightly cautionary in their conclusions. 'It must be stressed that this hypothesis is undoubtedly, at best, a reductionist oversimplification of a very complex biological state,' wrote Joseph Schildkraut in 1964, a then 30-year-old research psychiatrist from Bethesda, Maryland, and author of the noradrenaline imbalance theory.

Both theories of chemical imbalance, in other words, weren't seen as scientific truths. Not in the beginning, at least.

They were put forward as guides or frameworks on which the research community could build more conclusive experiments and assessments. By the end of the twentieth century, however, these putative theories would be raised to the heights of scientific facts thanks to the third class of antidepressants that had few of the side effects of MAO inhibitors or tricyclics. Although they offered no improvement in efficacy, their main contribution to drug therapy was greater safety.

Even so, the first SSRI to reach public prescription was a dangerous failure. From its first studies in rat brains in 1978 to its eventual ban in 1983, zimelidine had a short life. Although early trials conducted in Sweden found no serious side effects other than nausea and headaches, more comprehensive studies found that the drug was associated with a 25-fold increased risk of Guillain–Barré syndrome, a neurological disorder that leads to muscle weakness and, eventually, total paralysis. Over a year and a half of Swedish health records, there were 13 reports of this otherwise rare disease.

Next came fluoxetine hydrochloride – Prozac. First created from an antihistamine-like molecule in 1972, it would take 15 years for this drug to be released onto the market as a specific treatment for depression. As with zimelidine, there were safety concerns. There were also doubts over whether it was actually effective. Plus, it takes time to fashion a popular brand that would change the course of history. Prozac, as it would turn out, isn't as effective in treating depression as most other antidepressants – MAO inhibitors, tricyclics, or even other SSRIs. Lacking in efficacy, it was pushed into the mainstream with the help of a shift in US legislation. Previously limited to posting their leaflets and booklets to general practitioners and psychiatrists, pharmaceutical companies – such as Eli Lilly, the company behind Prozac – could create ads for their consumers, circumventing doctors. On radio, television screens, and on the nascent sites on the internet, SSRIs swept through the American populace along with ads for smoking cessation, lowering cholesterol, and hair-growth formulas for men. Eli Lilly hired a marketing mogul who had worked for McDonald's, Kelloggs, and Pillsbury.

Antidepressants were normalised with the introduction of Prozac and other SSRIs. As an article in *Newsweek* put it, 'Prozac has attained the same familiarity of Kleenex and the social status of spring water.'

SSRIs similarly popularised the monoamine hypothesis of depression. 'These antidepressants will correct for a chemical imbalance in the brain,' is a common mantra of doctors. While such a statement isn't categorically wrong, it is still a far cry from being right. This can be plainly seen in how long it takes for these drugs to have an antidepressant effect. SSRIs, tricyclics, and MAO inhibitors all increase the level of monoamines in the brain surprisingly quickly, sometimes peaking within just 30 minutes. But a person's depression might not budge for three weeks or over a month. The action of these drugs, in other words, doesn't match their effect. If there was an imbalance of serotonin in the brain, why don't patients respond to antidepressants in half an hour? Wouldn't that make more sense? Wouldn't that be fantastic?

This 'lag phase' has been a glaring hole in psychiatry for decades, and many researchers have rushed to fill it with a suitably sized theory. Most persuasive, perhaps, is the idea that serotonin leads to the regrowth of brain regions that have been damaged from the stress of depression. Studies in mice have shown that parts of the hippocampus – a central part of the brain involved in memory – can regenerate new neurons after prolonged antidepressant treatment. But mice are not humans, and there is still an active debate over whether neurogenesis, the cellular process of brain regrowth, is even possible once we reach adulthood. Further, the recent work on fast-acting anti-depressants such as ketamine, an anaesthetic that targets glutamate and not serotonin, has shown that drugs needn't take three weeks to have an effect but can lift someone from depression within hours.

Despite the name, antidepressants aren't the opposite of depression. 'People like this idea of whatever an antidepressant does then the converse of it must be what was wrong to cause depression,' says Lisa Monteggia, a professor of pharmacology at Vanderbilt University in Nashville, Tennessee. 'What I think we are studying is an antidepressant response.' By understanding how current drugs work, Monteggia hopes to develop even more precise and effective treatments that come with fewer side effects. If there's a pathway in the brain that they are all using to lift people out of depression, then perhaps a drug can be developed that targets that pathway specifically while leaving the rest of the brain unaffected. 'What we're currently doing might not tell us much about depression and that's okay,' says Monteggia.

Instead of precise mechanisms, we are left with the collective reports of what it feels like to be on antidepressants. 'What antidepressants do is that they buffer you against the stresses of life,' says David Nutt, a pharmacologist at Imperial College London. 'So, when you're on them, stress is less stressful. And therefore you can emerge from the depression slowly, as you're less pounded by waves of stress.'

All SSRIs – Prozac, sertraline, Paxil, Wellbutrin – are a blessing and a curse in pill form. The risk of overdose is so low that they have been handed out to almost everyone who had the slightest hint of depression. Who wants to talk about their problems and reveal their pathological thought processes when they could just take a pill every day and feel, in the famous words of a patient of the psychiatrist Peter Kramer, 'better than well'?

In early 2018, I started taking a new antidepressant: sertraline, or Zoloft. While Prozac had risen to fame in *Newsweek* and had its catchy slogans – 'Welcome Back' – sertraline came with an egg-shaped mascot and some lessons in basic chemistry. During a television commercial first aired in the early 2000s, a simple schematic of a synapse shows how monoamines travel from nerve A to nerve B. In depression, the soothing narrator explains, this flow is reduced. But sertraline corrects for this imbalance: 'When you know more about what's wrong, you can help make it right.'

I was unaware of such commercials (both because I would have been ten years old when they aired, and I didn't live in the United States), but I still hoped that sertraline was an improvement on citalopram. Drugs that are similar in structure can have dramatically different effects. One SSRI might not have any impact on someone's depression while another can lead them into complete remission, so I slowly reduced my dose of citalopram before starting my new prescription.

One hundred milligrams a day. One white pill. Then a 50-milligram booster – two pills. The improvement was gradual, the pace of a glacier. Then, after weeks or months of feeling emotionally flattened, I started to notice things that I thought I had for ever lost. I felt the basic desire to move again, the pleasure of activity and purpose. I felt moments of comfort and warmth inside my chest that I decided to call love. Such awakenings didn't happen all at once, and I barely noticed that I was changing. But I was slowly becoming stronger over time, more resistant to change. Lucy noticed my recovery before I did. But we were hesitant to celebrate. We both knew it wasn't over. Every day we remained vigilant, looking for any sign that I might be struggling.

I have spoken to many people who are also taking sertraline. Friends, family, the local tradesman who was incredibly open about his experience on the drug as he worked on our house. The side effects often circle around a single topic: sex. As well as reducing levels of anxiety and depression, sertraline – and other SSRIs – can make a person's libido shrink. In some cases, it not only makes sex unappealing but uneventful. It can make orgasms stop entirely. For people who might already feel crippled by loneliness or their failures in life, this can put an enormous strain on relationships. One psychiatrist told me that one of his patients chose his depression over taking these drugs. The loss of intimacy was too much for him to bear. Unfortunately, he killed himself as he thought that neither option was a life he wanted to live.

My side effects were minor. The sickness of citalopram disappeared altogether. But it still wasn't a perfect fit. Out of the blue, my depression would still return with a vengeance. These episodes were less frequent than they had been, and that was a relief. But it was still a return of my suicidal thoughts, the mental anguish that gripped my brain in a swirling vortex of activity, the lack of motivation that could leave me fatigued and listless for week after week after week. Were these drugs doing anything? Was I simply experiencing a placebo effect in the first few weeks of my treatment? Had I been seduced by a sertraline honeymoon? Such questions would follow me through the next two years of my life. Only when I decided to come off sertraline, in March 2020, would I realise the influence this drug had on my life.

To understand what something does, scientists often remove their topic of interest from their experiments. It is a common method of enquiry in genetics and ecology. What happens to the growth of a mouse without a particular gene? How does an ecosystem fare without a single species? In my personal experiment, removing sertraline from my body made me realise how much it supported me.

After eating cheese for breakfast, Barry Blackwell made sure to stay within the hospital's wards so he could be treated quickly in case of emergency. Half an hour passed without symptom, then hours. Nothing happened. Frustrated and confused, he returned to his patients.

With two young children at home and another on the way, Blackwell was moonlighting as a medical officer in an ambulance at weekends. He needed the extra money. One evening, a man called the emergency services and said that his wife was suffering from a severe headache after eating a cheese sandwich. The ambulance pulled up outside, and they entered the house to find that she was in the midst of a hypertensive crisis. For the next half hour, Blackwell watched as her blood pressure peaked and then fell back to a healthy state, her headache slowly subsiding. Just as his motivation was waning, this mystery seemed to offer another glimpse of discovery for Blackwell, pulling him back into the story.

He decided to try another test, not on himself but on a willing patient at the Maudsley who was already taking tranylcypromine. After she ate some cheese, Blackwell sat by her bedside, checking her blood pressure and pulse. After two hours, she showed no unusual activity and he left the room.

His buzzer beeped. A nurse was requesting a painkiller for his patient, the woman he had just left. She had developed a terribly painful headache and needed aspirin. Then, as he was walking through the Maudsley at night, one of his colleagues rushed through the corridor to attend to two patients who were both suffering from headaches. Both were taking tranyl-cypromine. And the cheese dish had made its weekly rounds in the cafeteria. It was the cheese! Blackwell wrote up these cases and published a paper in *The Lancet* in October 1963. Over nine months, he reported, there had been 12 cases of hypertension and headaches in patients that had taken tranylcypromine at the Maudsley Hospital. Eight had definitely eaten cheese.

His paper was peer-reviewed and then ridiculed. His colleagues laughed at his ideas. 'In a small way, the idea that a common dietary substance might kill someone was as ridiculous as it once was to consider the earth round or that man was descended from a monkey,' Blackwell later wrote. One representative of a pharmaceutical company wrote that his findings were 'unscientific and premature', which they definitely were. But Blackwell was no longer a lone investigator in this medical mystery. A few weeks after he published his first report in *The Lancet*, a research group at the Westminster Medical School in London provided a missing slice of the story: a molecule called tyramine, a product of tyrosine, an amino acid that takes its name from *tyros*, the ancient Greek word for cheese.

Tyramine was a key monoamine, one that worked alongside the better-known serotonin, dopamine, and noradrenaline. Its main function is to constrict blood vessels, a so-called vaso-constrictor, reducing the amount of space for blood to flow in our circulation systems. Like nipping the end of a hose pipe with your fingers, the pressure increases. When cheese is digested in the gut, this reaction is usually undetectable and reversible. But when taking a MAO inhibitor, a substance that blocks the enzyme that breaks down monoamines such as tyramine, the message to constrict the blood vessels isn't switched off. Homeostasis is knocked off balance. The pressure can escalate until blood pulses through the body and bursts through the delicate vessels at the back of the head.

From his office at Rockland Research Institute in New York, Nathan Kline read the worrying reports of the cheese reaction and soon realised that history was repeating itself. First iproniazid, now tranylcypromine. Although the risk of a headache was low (0.0001 per cent) and the risk of dying even lower (0.00001 per cent), tranylcypromine was withdrawn from US markets by the Food and Drug Administration (FDA) on 24 February 1964, a decision backed by the evidence that Barry Blackwell had accrued. Out of three and a half million prescriptions, 500 people suffered from the devastating headaches that were first recorded at the Maudsley. Forty people died from brain haemorrhages.

Unlike with iproniazid, however, Kline and other psychiatrists campaigned for tranylcypromine's use in hospital settings, and the drug was reintroduced into the pharmaceutical canon later that same year, this time with strict dietary guidelines.

It wasn't just cheese. After Barry Blackwell's first reports from the Maudsley, a whole smorgasbord of foodstuffs were found to be high in tyramine and high-risk for people taking MAO inhibitors. There were cases of hypertensive crises after eating pickled herrings and other tinned fish such as anchovies. A few headaches were thought to arise from poorly kept meat and game that had started to ferment. Yogurt, packet soups, yeast extract, beer, mushrooms, and even banana skins (when stewed as in some Caribbean recipes) were added to the growing list of restricted substances.

When patients were warned of such dangers, the risk of headache, haemorrhage, or dying was negligible. MAO inhibitors are still used to treat depression today, albeit rarely and only in exceptional circumstances. 'The people who really benefit [from MAO inhibitors],' says Ted Dinan, a professor of psychiatry at University College Cork, 'who you can really pick up from day one, are the people who are hypersomnic (or oversleeping), hyperphagic with carbohydrate craving, or very anxious when they're depressed.' In other words, people presenting the signs of atypical depression. Several clinical trials in the 1980s and 1990s found that roughly three quarters of patients with atypical features – such as gaining at least ten pounds in weight, sleeping over ten hours a day, and suffering from anxiety reactions such as panic attacks – responded to the MAO inhibitor phenelzine. Only half of such patients responded to a tricyclic antidepressant. Over 30 years of his career, Dinan says that he has had no problems with MAO inhibitors. Used for the right people with the necessary upfront precautions, he has only found success. When he meets someone with an atypical depression, he doesn't wait till all the other options have been exhausted. He uses them from day one. '[And] they respond' – Dinan clicks his fingers – 'like magic.'

In 1970, eighteen leaders in biological psychiatry gathered at Taylor Manor Hospital in the city of Baltimore and discussed their lives' work. Barry Blackwell began the proceedings with a speech on serendipity, scientific discovery, and cheese. Lothar Kalinowsky, now in his 70s and more skeletal than ever, provided a historical background of what came before both chemical convulsions and electroshock therapy. Nathan Kline and Roland Kuhn pontificated on their chosen family of antidepressants – MAO inhibitors and tricyclics – and made it quite clear that they could both claim the title for the first person to discover an antidepressant. Referring to iproniazid, Kline said, 'No drug in history was so widely used so soon after announcement of its application in the treatment of a specific disease.' Given to 400,000 people in the United States in 1957, it was put into prescription a whole year before imipramine. But, Kuhn told his audience, his trials started in January 1956, nearly a year before Kline gave iproniazid to his hospital patients.

There was no doubt who was the face of antidepressant therapy, however. With two Lasker Awards, a bestselling book on depression, and his obvious *joie de vivre* on radio and television, Nathan Kline embodied the excitement and discovery of drug therapy. In the 1960s, he was featured on the front cover of *Fortune* magazine and was referred to as one of the ten best-known men in the United States. During a time when the tensions of the Cold War fuelled global interest in scientific research, space exploration, and technological innovation, Kline convinced governments and non-governmental organisations (NGOs) that mental health was worth investing in. In 1955, Kline was one of three psychiatrists who persuaded Congress to donate \$2 million to the study of new drug therapies in psychiatry every year. 'The amount involved ... in the 1950s was vast – so much so that those charged with administering it found it difficult to give it away,' wrote the historian and pharmacologist David Healy in his book *The Antidepressant Era*. 'By most accounts the figure who did most to extract this money was Kline ... his efforts at lobbying were probably the single most important input to the establishment of a new psychiatry.'

Throughout his career, Kline met with world leaders in medical research, such as the deputy director general of the

World Health Organisation Thomas Lambo and the famed philanthropist and activist Mary Lasker. He was twice a guest on the popular *The Dick Cavett Show*, sitting in the same seat as Orson Welles, Janis Joplin, Truman Capote, and Stevie Wonder once had. He even met the Dalai Lama.

At the 1970 meeting in Baltimore, Kline gave his talk on MAO inhibitors an unusual title: 'An Unfinished Picaresque Tale'. Barry Blackwell, 36 years old and a recent immigrant to the United States, didn't know what 'picaresque' meant and looked it up in his *Oxford English Dictionary*. Picaresque ... 'Relating to an episodic style of fiction dealing with the adventures of a rough and dishonest but appealing hero.' Blackwell wondered whether Kline was referring to the drugs or to himself. Like iproniazid and other MAO inhibitors, Kline certainly had some toxic reactions to his personality, and his approach to science.

With MAO inhibitors often a second-choice treatment for depression, Kline became obsessed with his next project: endorphins. Naturally produced by the body, this family of 'feel-good' molecules were seen as the starting point for a new class of painkillers. Literally meaning 'endogenous morphine', scientists hoped that endorphins – in particular beta-endorphin – could lead to the same level of relief as morphine without the risk of addiction. Nathan Kline and Heinz Lehmann, his old friend who would stay with Kline in his luxury apartment in Manhattan, wanted to test this substance on mentally ill patients. Could this be an alternative form of drug therapy, one that would replace imipramine just as it had replaced MAO inhibitors? It was novel, untested, and had no name to attach itself to – a scientific discovery up for grabs. Kline, as one author noted, 'moved onto new ideas with a wheeler-dealer's arrogance and a cavalier manner'. He invited the only supplier of beta-endorphin, C.H. Li, to his 13th-floor apartment, a zebra-skin rug on the wall and sliding glass doors that led onto a balcony, and 'sweet-talked' his way to what he wanted. Li thought his host was 'courageous' and agreed to provide him with some synthetic beta-endorphin, a hard-to-come-by commodity.

But psychopharmacology was no longer the Wild West it once was. In the 1950s, the main challenge for people like Kline had been getting their hands on new drugs such as reserpine and iproniazid. Once they had a sample, they could give it to anyone they wanted, both hospitalised and in the community (as Kline did in 1957). But since the thalidomide disaster that led to 10,000 babies being born with severe developmental defects (half of which died within the first few months of life) in the 1960s, the laws surrounding drug testing had become much tighter. Although thalidomide wasn't certified by the Food and Drug Administration in the US (thanks largely to FDA inspector Frances Kelsey), it nonetheless epitomised the damage experimental drugs could do if they were handed out like aspirin. New experimental drugs now required official certification from the FDA – usually after being tested for safety in at least two different laboratory mammals – and signed consent from the patient and their family. But, in his cavalier attempt to race ahead, Kline sometimes did neither. Li worried that he was moving too fast, later adding that Kline 'liked the limelight too much. He wanted to make a big noise.' According to a later lawsuit, Kline gave 23 hospital patients an unregulated, uncertified drug that, in the end, showed unremarkable effects.

In December 1977, Kline presented his early trials on six patients at an international conference at the Caribe Hilton in San Juan, Puerto Rico. As music and laughter from a wedding ceremony filtered into the room, Kline resolutely claimed that beta-endorphin was antipsychotic, anxiolytic, and antidepressant. Wearing a grey chequered blazer, he had curly white hair and a matching beard that, as one author later noted, gave him a 'slight resemblance to Charlton Heston's Moses'. But Kline was no longer a leader of his people. The man who had made jokes in Zurich and helped usher in a new era of biological psychiatry was gone. Standing at the podium, he was seen as a dangerous throwback, more Old Testament than New. One attendee, Avram Goldstein, a leader in endorphin research, stood up after Kline's presentation and spoke for ten minutes. He called Kline's work 'a nonsense study' that could jeopardise public trust in scientists if it were to continue. There was no control group, too few patients, and by claiming that this drug was a miracle cure before the trial began – which Kline did – any positive result was likely down to a placebo effect. 'A considerable supply of the rare and expensive synthetic beta-endorphin was committed to an experiment that could not, in principle, have yielded positive results,' Goldstein added. '[To] raise public hopes without sound scientific evidence ... will serve science poorly in the long run.'

Kline described the next five years as a kind of 'slow agony'. An audit of his files took three months. Representatives from the United States Department of Health and Human Services 'hounded' him. He spent $100,000 on lawyer fees. Then, in March 1982, he sat in a courtroom in downtown Manhattan and signed a form that prevented him from studying 'in any manner whatsoever any investigational new drug'. His days as a scientist were over. In December, he retired from a 30-year career at the Rockland Research Institute. But he still had his private practice in Manhattan. 'With this unfortunate matter behind me,' Kline said in a statement, 'I will serve my patients and the medical community with a continued commitment to relieve the suffering from the debilitating effects of psychiatric disorders.' A few months later, Nathan Kline was dead. Aged 66, his aorta – the main artery that carries blood out of the heart – ruptured. He died on the operating table on 11 February 1983. After his death, the Rockland Research Institute was renamed the Nathan Kline Institute. Today, the golden statuettes and certificates from his two Lasker Awards are still found there, boxed away in a disused room next to a photocopier. Handwritten in crisp gold and blue calligraphy, his 1964 certificate looks like a royal script taken straight out of a children's fairy tale. 'Dr. Kline, more than any other single psychiatrist, has been responsible for one of the greatest revolutions ever to occur in the care and treatment of the mentally ill,' the award reads. 'Literally hundreds of thousands of people are leading productive, normal lives who – but for Dr. Kline's work – would be leading lives of fruitless despair and frustration.' Rough, dishonest, but appealing, Nathan Kline's life was itself an unfinished picaresque tale.

PART THREE

Getting Therapy

'We live in secular and mobile societies ... where the extended family and close communal ties of the immediate neighbourhood are little more than nostalgic images to be revered at Thanksgiving and Christmas ... Thus, although the traditional forms of family and neighbourhood are less important, substitutes are being developed to provide the emotionally relevant equivalence in modern urban life. Psychological attention to interpersonal relations and the growth of professional psychotherapies offer secular, scientific, and rational responses to these needs.'

Gerald Klerman, Myrna Weissman, and colleagues, *Interpersonal Psychotherapy of Depression* (1984)

'Unlike surgery, psychotherapy cannot be expected to have universally uniform techniques. This is because psychotherapeutic techniques are not pieces of hard technology but ways of soft communication. They have to be culturally relevant. Hence the idiom of any psychotherapeutic system has essentially to conform to the myths, legends, beliefs, and languages of the people with whom it is to be practiced.'

J.S. Neki

'we ought to encourage the old to act as surrogate grandfathers and grandmothers to the community at large.'

Nathan Kline

In Your Dreams, Freud

'He will *not* die!' Lizzie Temkin Beck yelled. 'My son will *not* die!' Only seven years old, her youngest child Aaron had been playing in the playground when he was pushed from the slide, broke his arm, and within a few days had contracted a bacterial infection that spread through his bloodstream. He was put on the hospital's 'danger list'. Such cases of septicaemia, the doctors said, had a 90 per cent mortality rate. Put another, slightly less pessimistic, way: Aaron Beck had a 10 per cent chance of surviving.

And he did. Although he spent his eighth birthday in the hospital, his infection cleared, and he was soon back at school. And though he was behind his year group, Beck quickly caught up. In fact, he felt so determined to make up for lost time that he actually overtook his classmates and skipped a year. From an early age, Beck faced disadvantage and flipped it on its head. 'Psychologically,' he later admitted, this experience showed 'that if I got into a hole, I could dig myself out, [and] I could do it on my own.'

Artistic, tenacious, and quietly confident, Beck made a success of everything he put his mind to. He finished top of his class at high school, graduated with honours from Brown University in English and Political Science, and then decided that he wanted to study medicine. He was told that a Jewish boy wouldn't be accepted onto a medical programme without studying medicine or biology at university. After he completed a foundation year, however, he did precisely that. Between 1946 and 1948, he rotated between internships in surgery, dermatology, infectious disease, and neurology, the latter piquing his interest for its precision in diagnosis and the ability to see disease states under the microscope, just as Alois Alzheimer once had in Emil Kraepelin's clinic in Munich.

Beck thought that psychiatry was a bit of a joke. Hospitals and universities across the United States were dominated by psychoanalysis in all its different flavours, and Beck thought that this approach lacked any sort of accuracy or scientific rationale. 'Everything that we would see in patients would be interpreted in terms of some deep, dark invisible forces,' he said. When he did meet with mentally ill patients, he felt very uneasy providing any half-baked interpretation of their mental woes and what stage of their sexual development they might stem from. 'I thought it was nonsense,' he later admitted. Like it or not, Beck was forced into a six-month psychiatric rotation at Cushing Veterans Hospital in Framingham, Massachusetts. At this time, there were so few budding psychiatrists that this career move seemed like an opportunity too good to pass up. He could either stick to the overprescribed, competitive field of neurology or try his hand at psychiatry and have room to flourish. As months turned into years, he even started to put his faith in psychoanalytical theories and train as an analyst himself. His colleagues 'had answers for everything,' he said. 'They could understand psychosis, schizophrenia, neuroses, every single condition that came in, you could get a good, sound – [or] apparently sound – psychoanalytic interpretation. And [psychoanalysis] also held out the promise that it could cure most people's conditions.'

It wasn't long after he finished his training in psychoanalysis that he realised that these promises were sometimes paper thin, that the theories they were based on weren't always supported by scientific evidence.

From 1959 to 1961, Beck investigated one of the hallmarks of Freud's theory of depression: that it was a product of hatred turned inwards, or 'retroflected hostility'. If this was the case, Beck reasoned, then his patients' dreams would be filled with themes of hate, masochism, or self-flagellation for their perceived failures in life. What he found was, in truth, quite banal. One patient dreamt of a pair of shoes she adored but frustratingly found that they were both for the same foot. A man dreamt about a vending machine that accepted his coins but never released a drink or snack no matter how long he waited. Although the specifics of the dreams changed, themes of slight disappointment and mundane worries seemed to be common for many of Beck's depressed patients. They didn't dream of hating themselves.

For Beck, this was the first sign that Freud might have been wrong. The second came from a simple experiment. Beck started to play a rigged card game with his patients. He decided who won, himself or the patient. If people with depression were slouching torrents of self-hatred, Beck hypothesised that they wouldn't enjoy winning. They would feel like they deserved to be punished. Losing was more in line with their worldview. Again, this wasn't what Beck found. Compared to people who didn't suffer from depression, his depressed patients relished their wins and their self-esteem blossomed more than any other group of patients. To Beck, this meant one thing: his depressed patients had a negative worldview, an irrational idea that life was rigged against them. When this was shown not to be the case (as in the card game), they felt much better about themselves.

Just as the mythical figure Oedipus kills his father, Beck was providing a death knell for Freudian psychoanalysis. But a card game wasn't going to overturn decades of psychological dogma. A few dreams weren't going to nullify retroflected hostility. What Beck required was a theory of his own. Only then could his findings be tested, scrutinised, and compared to the Freudian era that he was hoping to leave behind.

As with his card game, he started playing more of an active role with his patients. Rather than sitting back and allowing their thoughts and memories to flow freely – as was the case for psychoanalysis – Beck asked them questions about what they were thinking of as they dipped into their emotional depths. As they did so, they came to contradictory, and often comical, conclusions. 'A brilliant academician questioned his basic intelligence, an attractive society woman insisted she had become repulsive-looking, and a successful businessman began to believe he had no real business acumen and was headed for bankruptcy,' Beck wrote. These were extreme cases. But they exemplified a mould that most of his depressed patients could fit into. Whenever they thought of anything – whether it was about themselves, how others see them, or predictions of the future – they were almost always negative and often irrational.

'In making these self-appraisals the depressed patient was prone to magnify any failures or defects and to minimise or ignore any favourable characteristics,' Beck wrote. What's more, these thoughts (no matter how comical or paradoxical) were perceived to be as factual as the gravitational force that kept their feet on the ground. 'Intrinsic to this type of thinking is the lack of consideration to the alternative explanations that are more plausible and more probable,' Beck wrote. Through delicate questioning, Beck tried to reveal a depressed person's 'distortions of reality' and tried to guide them back to a more rational view of themselves, others, and the future.

Beck called this technique 'cognitive therapy', an offshoot of a field of cognitive psychology that was spearheaded by Albert Ellis, an American psychologist who developed Rational Emotive Behaviour Therapy. In the 1950s, Ellis posited that it was our thoughts and preconceptions of life events that were important rather than the events themselves, a train of thought that reached back to the stoic philosophers of ancient Greece. In ninth-century Mesopotamia, Abu Zayd al-Balkhi fashioned his own cognitive theory of therapy in his book *Sustenance of the Soul*. Only in the 1970s, however, did the so-called 'cognitive revolution' gather momentum.

Albert Ellis, Aaron Beck and everyone else who stepped into this revolution were soon at the centre of a lively debate that largely took place in medical journals. Since the 1950s, it was widely thought that behaviour therapy would be the next psychotherapy to replace classical psychoanalysis, not cognitive therapy. Initiated by Ivan Pavlov's salivating dogs and then diversifying into pigeons pecking at levers and rats pressing at pedals, behaviourism argued that a two-way system between a stimulus (a bell ringing for food) and a physical response (salivating) could explain our own lives. Although far more complex than the conditioning with a bell ringing, human behaviour was thought to be shaped by an endless series of interactions with our environment that determine our social connections, language, perception, and memory, and our likes and dislikes.

Depression, for example, was seen as a learnt trait in response to negative situations. One of the most famous depictions of this was called the 'learned helplessness' model. In the late 1960s and early 1970s, Martin Seligman, a psychologist from the University of Pennsylvania (the same institution where Beck worked), performed one of the most famous experiments into depression. It wasn't for the fainthearted. Medium-sized 'mongrel dogs' were suspended in a harness with a hole for each of their legs. They were then given a series of 'severe, pulsating' electric shocks through a couple of copper plates touching their hind paws. No matter how much they wriggled or whimpered, these shocks didn't abate for 50 seconds. When they were then placed in a muslin-covered cubicle with a wire mesh floor that could be electrified with the same intensity, they stood still, vibrating with the waves of the electricity that were out of their control. They didn't try to jump over a barrier that was easily jumpable. They were symbols of helplessness. From their time in the harness, they had come to believe that there was no point in trying to escape.

Dogs that hadn't been placed in the electric harness, who hadn't been conditioned that the electricity was unavoidable, were far more likely to try anything to escape from the electric shocks under their feet. They would bark, crash into the sides, and eventually find their way over the barrier and to safety. The only way to achieve this with the helpless dogs was to drag them across the barrier with a long lead. Seligman called this 'directive therapy'. 'The initial problem seems to be one of "getting going",' he wrote.

The parallels with depression were obvious and hugely appealing. Seligman even found that rats that had been forced into this state of helplessness also suffered from weight loss, anorexia, and had lower levels of noradrenaline in their brain, the same monoamine that was the basis of the first chemical-imbalance theory of depression in humans. As with his directive therapy in dogs, behavioural therapy for depression was based on countering negative stimuli in the environment with positive experiences. Rather than sitting at home or lying in bed, it was the therapist's job to try and drag their patients back to former activities that they once enjoyed. 'Although the extreme distress felt by the depressed person needs to be the first point of contact in therapy,' one psychologist wrote in the *American Psychologist* in 1973, 'the long-range objective needs to emphasise those positively reinforced behaviours that are missing.' By countering helplessness with hope, some studies claimed that behaviour therapy was effective in over 80 per cent of depressed patients.

Behaviourists thought they had the psychological field at their fingertips. Then, in the 1970s, cognitive therapy was lauded as the next big thing. They weren't happy. 'The cognitivists reject the conditioning theory of [mental illness] on the ground that they have a better theory which embodies an advance of such magnitude that they characterise it as "the cognitive revolution",' Joseph Wolpe, a behaviourist working in South Africa, wrote. 'They see themselves as the bearers of a new paradigm that has the same relation to conditioning as [general] relativity has to Newtonian physics.' Wolpe thought it was a sham. To him, cognitive therapy was already a part of behaviour therapy, a field that he had helped build since publishing his 1958 treatise *Psychotherapy by Reciprocal Inhibition*. Highlighting irrational thoughts and countering negativity with positivity: to him, it still sounded like conditioning. As Wolpe once wrote, 'Cognitive therapy is a subclass of behaviour therapy ... no matter how complex the contents may be.'

Burrhus Frederic (or B.F.) Skinner, a leading behaviourist in the United States who claimed that everything we do is a product of conditioned responses and, therefore, free will is an illusion, shared Wolpe's frustration. In 1977, three years after retiring from his professorial position at Harvard, Skinner wrote an article entitled 'Why I Am Not a Cognitive Psychologist'. After providing a detailed insight into how behaviourism can explain everything from sexuality to street crime, he added that the focus on internal thoughts and processing of information that defined cognitive psychotherapy was a dangerous game. To him, depression and other mental illnesses were a conditioned response to an environment. By ignoring this external element, Skinner feared, there would be no political pressure to change, say, unemployment, poverty, poor housing, or diseases that take their toll on the mental health of a population. 'The appeal to cognitive states and processes is a diversion which could well be responsible for much of our failure to solve our problems,' he wrote. 'We need to change our behaviour and we can do so only by changing our physical and social environments. We choose the wrong path at the very start when we suppose that our goal is to change the "minds and hearts of men and women" rather than the world they live in.'

For Beck and his students, it was as if they were stuck in the middle of two opposing forces, each unwilling to budge an inch. On one side were the biological psychiatrists with their ever-growing collection of tricyclic antidepressants and their startling statistics of remission and recovery. On the other: behaviourists who had their own association (the Association for Advancement of Behaviour Therapy, or AABT) which was so inhospitable to cognitive psychologists such as Beck that he was forced to create his own association. Some cognitive psychologists received 'cease and desist' letters from their behavioural peers. 'We felt very much on our own, that there was a need to kind of fight for our place in the department and fight for prerogatives in the department, fight for fair treatment,' Ruth Greenberg, a psychologist and graduate of the University of Pennsylvania, recalled. 'I don't have the sense that anybody necessarily discouraged [Beck], but I don't think there was a lot of support.' Other students found these early years to be thrilling. 'There was the excitement of being the underdog and coming up with something that was really challenging the establishment,' Brian Shaw, one of Beck's students and colleagues, said.

History is sometimes primed for humour. Once rival factions, cognitive and behaviour therapy would soon merge into one of the most popular treatments for depression: cognitive behavioural therapy, or CBT. While rationalising negative thought patterns, depressed patients are also advised to fill in a diary of activities for each week and take note of positive experiences. '[B]ehavioural techniques are used to promote cognitive change,' wrote the cognitive therapist Marjorie Weishaar in 1993. 'Increasing the daily activity of a depressed patient may directly contradict beliefs of ineffectiveness or predictions that he or she is more contented in bed.' Internal thoughts and the external environment were seen as being equally important in recovery.

There's an adage in cognitive therapy that Aaron Beck cured his mother's depression the day he was born. After his sister Beatrice died during the 1918 flu pandemic – a global tragedy that killed between 50 and 100 million people worldwide – his birth two years later put an end to his mother's agony, albeit temporarily. With three boys at home, his mother was protective of her youngest son. He wondered whether she would have preferred a girl instead of another boy, but she never voiced these thoughts or made him feel like a disappointment. While his father, a stoic shopkeeper, nurtured his interest in bird watching and botany, his mother was a mercurial presence in the home, for ever shaken by the experience of losing a child.

With such a beginning, it was almost as if Beck was destined to make a living from helping people who suffered from depression. It was in his blood. Unlike many other psychotherapists, however, he wanted to provide evidence that his cognitive approach was effective and to what extent. He sought confirmation that his theories weren't just logical on paper but actually worked in practice.

To begin, he needed a way of measuring a person's depression. Rather than using qualitative metrics such as 'I'm feeling better today and I am sleeping more', he wanted to be able to quantify depression's severity over time. Only then could he assess whether his psychotherapy was working or not. In 1961, he published his 'Beck Depression Inventory' (BDI), a health questionnaire that has been used in thousands of studies over the decades since and, according to a review from 2011, is the third most-cited paper in psychiatry. The BDI contained 21 facets of depression. Upon entering his outpatient clinic in Philadelphia, his depressed patients chose which options best described their current state. The first topic was mood, and there were five answers to choose from:

0. I do not feel sad.
1. I feel blue or sad.
2a. I am blue or sad all the time and I can't snap out of it.
2b. I am so sad or unhappy that it is very painful.
3. I am so sad or unhappy that I can't stand it.

After 20 more topics – such as pessimism, lack of satisfaction, crying spells, irritability, feelings of guilt, social withdrawal, sleep disturbance, and loss of appetite – Beck was handed a quick insight into his patient's depression. 'As I look back on my life all I can see is a lot of failures,' one statement reads.

Another: 'I used to be able to cry but now I can't cry at all, even though I want to.' And, reaching into the very core of severe, endogenous depression, 'I wake up early every day and can't get more than five hours sleep,' and, 'I have lost interest in sex completely.' With the different levels of severity for each symptom, Beck could then track the patient's depression over time, and see whether they were getting better (or worse) over the weeks and months of their treatment, whether it was psychotherapy, drug therapy, or otherwise.

As he continued to develop his theory, Beck trained himself to highlight his own cognitive distortions. Between 1962 and 1967, during a five-year 'splendid isolation' from psychiatry, Beck spent each morning and afternoon at home writing down all his thoughts, their percentage of importance on his mind, and how each one could be rationalised or adjusted to better fit with reality. He used every piece of paper, notebook, and envelope he could find, scribbling down his thoughts in between playing tennis, napping, and going to the cinema with his wife Phyllis. (His mother had also enjoyed visiting the cinema during times of stress and passed this on to her youngest son.) He toyed with different colour schemes in his notes, constantly reorganising and re-evaluating his cognitions on paper. 'It is difficult to describe in words the explosion after 1962 of spiral-bound notebooks, inside front and back covers of notebooks, pocket notebooks, steno pads, 3x5 notecards, and random pages on which line after line of his "negative" thoughts are jotted down systematically,' wrote the historian Rachael Rosner. 'The template Beck used in his self-analysis became the foundation for the entire treatment protocol of cognitive therapy.' He told Phyllis everything and, with her background in journalism, she was the perfect first editor to his ideas. 'She was my reality tester,' Beck said. 'She went along with the newer ideas I had, and that gave me the idea that I wasn't in left field.'

Nearly a century before, Sigmund Freud had similarly isolated himself to analyse his unconscious desires before treating patients in his flat in Vienna. Beck similarly developed his own characteristic look. Just as Freud had his circular-framed glasses and thick cigar, Beck was rarely seen without a bow tie (a bright red one for special occasions) around his neck. His friendly demeanour and his cool, pale blue eyes were in stark contrast to the piercing gaze of Freud.

As he distanced himself from psychoanalysis, both in theory and appearance, Beck moved closer to Emil Kraepelin. By combining empirical symptom profiles (Kraepelin) with talking therapy (Freud), Aaron Beck paved the way into a more collaborative future, one in which combinations of therapies – drugs and psychotherapy, for instance – would be used to help patients recover from depression. For Beck, however, there was only one treatment fit for the task. 'We're not saying that patients can't respond to drugs,' Beck told a journalist from the *New York Times* while sitting in his Cognitive Mood Clinic, a set of rundown offices with tattered chairs in Philadelphia. 'We're simply saying that cognitive therapy is more effective.'

More Than One Psychotherapy

In the late 1960s, Myrna Weissman, a soft-spoken but straight-talking social worker from Boston, found a new job working at Yale University with Gerry Klerman, one of the leading biological psychiatrists of the twentieth century. While he had spent his career studying pharmacological methods – becoming an expert on tricyclic antidepressants such as imipramine, for example – Klerman was hoping to branch out into psychological treatments. One question was dominating his mind, and he hoped Weissman could help provide an answer. Did talking therapy – whether it was marital therapy, group therapy, or psychoanalysis – actually make antidepressants less effective? Did they undo whatever good they were doing inside the brains of his patients? In a famous review of the scientific literature, the famed British behaviourist Hans Eysenck certainly thought so: there 'appears to be an inverse correlation between recovery and psychotherapy,' he wrote. 'The more psychotherapy, the smaller the recovery rate.'

Klerman wanted to test this idea in a clinical trial, just as he had tested tricyclic antidepressants in the past. For that, he needed a manual that could be used by different therapists to provide the same methods time and time again. Just as imipramine can be given in precise doses, he sought a talking therapy that could be replicated and compared to other treatments. Weissman worked two days a week and regularly met with Klerman to discuss and refine their growing manual.

This was the beginning of interpersonal therapy, a form of talking therapy that emerged at roughly the same time as cognitive therapy but was inspired by a more holistic view of depression. While Beck concerned himself with the internal workings of the mind, Weissman and Klerman focused on our ability to form strong social bonds, and what happens when they start to weaken and break. They were inspired by the work of Harry Stack Sullivan, the psychoanalyst who wrote, 'The field of psychiatry is the field of interpersonal relations, under any and all circumstances in which these relations exist … [A] personality can never be isolated from the complex interpersonal relations in which the person lives and has his being.'

Today, as professor of psychiatry at Columbia University, Weissman has a framed photograph of Aaron Beck on her second-floor office's window ledge, a view of George Washington Bridge and the Hudson River in the background. 'We were friends,' she says. 'We were not competing.' There were no grounds for competition. Neither Weissman nor Beck knew whether their theories were accurate, that their methods would be effective in the treatment of depression. Still, during her time at Yale University, Weissman was bolstered by some of the most celebrated minds to ever contemplate the origins of depression.

In the 1960s and 1970s, any social theory of depression had to mention the work of John Bowlby, a British psychoanalyst who was still an active researcher when Weissman began her work. She remembers sitting in a lecture theatre listening to Bowlby, a balding man with drooping jowls and a wheezing voice, and thinking that he was God. (He was also good friends with Gerry Klerman.) Taking inspiration from evolutionary theory and ethology (the study of animal behaviour), Bowlby was a new breed of psychoanalyst, one who was guided by science and its pursuit of objective truth. Instead of focusing on the Freudian dogma of erotogenic zones (oral, anal, genital), he proposed that the most important development in a child's early life was one of basic attachment. Babies cling, grasp, and like to be rocked. They cry for attention and smile when smiled at. They pine for their mother and follow her every move. From birth, Bowlby reasoned, we are primed to make strong attachments. If we weren't, we wouldn't survive. Born helpless and with underdeveloped brains compared to other primates, humans require years of dedication and maternal care. 'It is fortunate for their survival that babies are so designed by Nature that they beguile and enslave their mothers,' Bowlby wrote in his 1958 paper 'The Nature of the Child's Tie to Its Mother'. This behaviour, he added, is 'as much the hallmark of the [human] species as the red breast of the robin or the stripes of a tiger'.

Mental disorders, Bowlby wrote in his 1969 book *Attachment and Loss*, are the cost of our biological need for attachment. It needn't be the loss of a mother. It could be any of the strong social bonds that we make throughout our life, all of which follow in the footsteps of our initial maternal bond. As this book was published, Gerry Klerman and his colleagues at Yale University were providing some of the best evidence to support Bowlby's theories. Through several surveys and questionnaires, they had found that, in the six months prior to the onset of symptoms, 'departures from the social field' were three times as common in people with depression than those who were not depressed. Divorce, disease or death of loved ones. Unemployment, a change of job circumstance, or a new job. Family members leaving the home. Stillbirths and pregnancy. All these events were seen as breaks in attachment, confirmation of Bowlby's theories into the social origins of depression.

Support also came from London, the city where Bowlby had been trained and worked for much of his professional career. In the 1970s, the sociologist George Brown and his colleague Tirril Harris were finding similar ties between loss and depression in Camberwell, south London, a catchment area that included rich women with titles to their name and families living in dank Dickensian conditions. This diversity in setting was matched by a surprising variety of life events. 'Some [events] were unexpected but others had been eagerly sought; some were major catastrophes but others involved no more than a change in routine,' Brown and Harris wrote in their book *Social Origins of Depression*. 'The message is again that it is loss and disappointment rather than change as such that is important.' Whether it was called loss, disappointment, or an exit from the social field, depression was being seen as a product of our social connections, an imbalance within our communities rather than just chemical communication across a synapse.

Interpersonal therapy started with common sense. As with drug therapy, a diagnosis seemed like a logical place to begin. Did the patient meet the criteria for depression? Were their symptoms numerous and frequent enough to warrant treatment at all? Second, as guided by the work from New Haven and London, could Myrna Weissman and Gerald Klerman pinpoint what might have triggered the episode? 'It made sense that when people come in [for therapy], we find out what is going on in their life,' Weissman recalls. Who are they dependent upon? Do they have someone who is giving them trouble or causing stress? Has anything happened recently that was unexpected or disruptive? 'You find out the problems that are associated with the onset of symptoms,' Weissman says. 'Although it may be apparent to the world what's going on, it may not be apparent to the person. So it's first clarifying that.' Only by understanding the problem areas could they then be worked on and remedied. Over 12 to 16 weeks, interpersonal therapy provided the stage for an intimate conversation about the present stresses of life, and how they might be resolved or accepted.

Most of the manual was a collaboration, but Klerman added an important piece that he thought was missing. Every patient, he said, should be told that they were ill: that they were not a depressed person, but a person with depression. They weren't defined by their illness. As with someone with a virus or a bacterial infection, they could get better. This so-called 'sick-role' was first theorised in the 1950s and granted ill people a greater amount of freedom to focus on their well-being, even at the expense of long-held plans. No one would expect someone who had pneumonia (a non-contagious bacterial infection) to attend a wedding or have friends over for dinner. The same should be true for people with depression.

In 1979, the National Institute of Mental Health (NIMH) decided that the time was right for a large-scale trial into psychotherapy. As part of the Treatment for Depression Collaborative Research Program, cognitive therapy and interpersonal therapy were chosen as the two leading therapies used in the United States. Both would be compared to imipramine, the gold-standard drug therapy at the time. All three were then compared to a more basic level of care or, in the drug trial, a placebo pill. Conducted at three sites (George Washington University, University of Pittsburgh, and Oklahoma University) and using the same methods and health questionnaires, the only real difference was which treatment the 260 patients would receive. How would they compare after 16 weeks? What about 18 months after the trial had finished? Taking nearly two years to plan and peer-review, this multi-site trial was the best way of finding out.

Aaron Beck believed that this was the opportunity for cognitive therapy to show its true value. In 1977, he and his colleagues had published their first clinical trial and found that, compared to 12 weeks of imipramine treatment, cognitive therapy helped three times as many patients into full remission from depression (79 per cent versus imipramine's 24 per cent). What's more, these benefits were maintained over the next three to six months. By this point, 13 out of 19 (68 per cent) of patients given imipramine had returned to drug therapy, while only three out of 22 patients (14 per cent) given cognitive therapy required further treatment. Beck hypothesised that these long-term benefits were due to the patient learning about their disruptive thought patterns and being able to apply new techniques to their management. Just as someone might be made aware of a glaring grammatical mistake they had been making for years, they would learn from their therapeutic lessons and rarely repeat the same errors in the future. Beck called it a 'sense of mastery' over one's emotions. No drug could offer such mastery.

There were problems with this study. It was a small sample of people with depression: only 41 patients (22 for cognitive therapy and 19 for imipramine). Perhaps people who were somehow primed to respond to cognitive therapy just happened to be in that group. Only when greater numbers were included could these random biases be reduced. However, the most problematic element of the paper wasn't its content, or that Aaron Beck was a co-author, but where it was published: *Cognitive Therapy and Research*, a journal he had just created. The centrepiece of its inaugural volume, this paper kick-started Beck's new journal with a bang. Everyone in the trial wanted to believe that this therapy would work. And such excitement can be infectious.

The Treatments for Depression Collaborative Research Program was more neutral. It took place away from the buildings affiliated with either cognitive or interpersonal therapy, and the therapists were trained as part of the trial. This took three months. Beck complained that this wasn't sufficient. He needed a year to train anyone up to a level required for cognitive therapy, he said. This would allow them to learn not only the theory but also how to practice it in a way that was human, empathetic, supportive, and, if necessary, jovial. 'Some of the beauty,' said Jeffrey Young, a close colleague of Beck and one of the trainers in the trial, 'got lost in the translation into a manualized therapy.' With only three months of training, Beck worried that this trial would be a test of the individual therapist rather than his cherished therapy. Frustrated, he compared the therapists in this trial to a set of junior doctors performing delicate heart surgery.

The NIMH had their reasons for this brief opportunity for training. They wanted to test cognitive therapy as it would be performed in the real world, often by people who were recent psychology graduates and who didn't have a complete grasp of Beck's therapeutic repertoire. If this therapy was to be adopted nationally – or even internationally – it had to be scalable. 'The immediate goal of the training programs was to efficiently and effectively train therapists at the different research sites to attain specified levels of mastery in their respective treatment approaches,' the coordinators of the trial, Irene Elkin and Tracie Shea, wrote. Training every single therapist up to Beck's preference might have resulted in more effective practitioners, but it wasn't seen as an efficient approach.

Beck resigned from the study. 'I think his underlying feeling was "this won't [turn] out that well",' Young recalled, 'which is what did happen.' While all three forms of therapy were superior to placebo, only interpersonal therapy and imipramine excelled in the more severe cases of depression. Cognitive therapy was significantly less effective in reducing depressive symptoms in this group of patients.

Why might this have been the case? Cognitive therapists argued that because interpersonal therapy was rooted in psychoanalytical theories of loss, these therapists were better placed to deal with these more severely ill patients. They had decades of practice in a very similar form of talking therapy. The freshly trained cognitive therapists, meanwhile, didn't have the same depth of experience that was crucial when dealing with the most challenging patients. Elkin and Shea acknowledged this discrepancy: 'the most intensive training program is that for CB therapy, in which a new (or relatively new) framework is taught for conceptualising and treating the problems of depressed patients. Somewhat less intensive is the IPT training programme, in which the selected therapists already share a fairly common framework, and in which the training, although providing them with some new procedures and strategies for treatment, mainly serves to focus, channel, and sometimes restrict their usual treatment approach.'

And yet, for Beck and his colleagues, there was still one positive outcome of this trial. A year after treatment had ended, the number of patients who relapsed back into depression or who returned to treatment was lowest for those who had received cognitive therapy. As with their first study in 1977, Beck and his colleagues put this down to the lessons that the patients had learnt about how their thoughts influence their conditions, and how they could control them. A drug might make someone feel better through increases in monoamines, but cognitive therapy was like a tutorial in mental healthcare, a set of tools that could be used long after the last therapy session had finished. 'I think cognitive therapy is likely to compare quite nicely with other existing interventions like pharmacotherapy in terms of short-term effects,' said Steven Hollon, a close colleague of Beck and a lead researcher in cognitive therapy since the 1970s. 'But I think it's in the long-term effects – the prevention of relapse, the prevention of recurrence, and possibly the prevention of the initial onset in the first place – that's cognitive therapy's major contribution.'

Cognitive behavioural therapy is the most frequently prescribed psychotherapy for depression for good reason. 'Problem-solving does work and interpersonal does work,' says Helen Christensen, the director of the Black Dog Institute in Sydney, Australia, 'but there's no doubt the strongest evidence is for CBT.'

In the autumn of 2017, two years after my group therapy sessions, I caught the bus from our rented flat in Bristol to a mental health centre on the outskirts of the city. I filled in my PHQ-9 as I waited for my therapist to collect me from the waiting room. In a tiny office with little more than a desk, a computer chair, and a padded chair for me to sit on, we went through the familiar choreography of CBT.

I wrote down my 'personal summary', a list of thoughts or events that were making me feel low. We would then spend the next six weeks working through these key areas. I filled a 'behavioural activation' diary every week, detailing what I was going to do each day and making sure I made time for pleasurable activities as well as chores. If anything made me feel good about myself or my current situation, I jotted it down in my 'positive data log'. With homework and photocopied printouts, this was a far cry from lying down on a sofa and speaking about any dreams or anything else that came into my mind. Unlike psychoanalysis, CBT is rigidly focused on the realities of the present. Through discussions and paperwork, negative thought patterns are tested against reality and, hopefully, retrained towards a viewpoint that is more healthful. I doubted my abilities as a writer, for example, even though my pitches were still being accepted by science magazines. Making this latter point clear in my head, I felt more confident that I had a future in this career of my choosing. When I thought that my family was in tatters, I was reminded that I lived with Lucy and that we were happy together.

As I left each session, I felt a slight buzz that we were making progress. I felt that I could train myself away from depression. As I caught the bus back to our flat, I watched as the trees were shedding their yellowed leaves. They were changing, ensuring that they could make it through the coming winter.

The sixth and final session of CBT was a recap. What had I learnt over the last few weeks? What could I still work on? Could I implement the behavioural activation diary and the positive data log into my everyday life? I felt like I needed less reviewing and more training. After the first session was spent introducing my problems, I only had four 50-minute therapy sessions to work through a mental illness that I had struggled with for over two years. It was as if a doctor had given someone a cast for their broken leg and then, before the bone had healed, taken their support away again. The bone might hold, or it might break and lead to an even longer rehabilitation.

My PHQ-9 scores were still showing that I was moderately depressed at the end of this 'low-intensity CBT'. I was honest in my review. I wanted more time, the option of high-intensity CBT in order to continue any progress we had made. Before we said goodbye, my therapist told me that she would refer me for a phone review. I should expect the call in two weeks or so, and it shouldn't last more than 45 minutes. If they decided that prolonged treatment was necessary, then the waiting list was two months at least.

The next week I received a letter from my therapist. It was sent with good intentions but made me feel much worse about my future. 'I would encourage you to continue practicing the techniques that you have learnt throughout your treatment,' she wrote. 'Should your situation worsen, or if you feel like you are in a crisis, you should seek support from your GP or the emergency services. It has been good to meet you and I wish you every success in your ongoing recovery.' In my head, it was a confirmation that I was being abandoned. I wasn't important enough to continue with the therapy that I had found useful. When it was invented, CBT was meant to last between 12 and 16 weeks, and I thought that my low-intensity course was just a means of ticking boxes, of covering the health system's back if I were to kill myself.

My disappointment is reflected in the scientific literature; low-intensity CBT doesn't fare well in the few clinical trials that have assessed its efficacy. Although it has similar effects as SSRIs or 12 weeks of CBT in the short term, these benefits aren't maintained over the subsequent months. In 2017, for example, a study of 400 people living in northeast England found that over half (54 per cent) of patients who had responded to low-intensity CBT had returned to their depressed state 12 months after the trial had finished. They had relapsed. In comparison, the rate of relapse for normal CBT practice – as taken from the average of seven clinical trials – is only 29 per cent, nearly half the number of people. In fact, high-intensity CBT has some of the longest-lasting effects of any treatment for depression. In 2016, a study encompassing 469 patients from 73 general practices in the UK found that the benefits of 12 to 18 sessions of CBT are maintained for at least four years when compared to a 'treatment as usual' group. What's more, the majority of these patients had suffered from severe depression that had been unremitting for at least two years. They were terribly unwell, suffered from various long-term health conditions, and had failed to respond to a course of antidepressants. And yet with a full course of CBT they were able to stay healthy long after the treatment had ended.

The long-term benefits of CBT have been known for decades. It is this longevity that separates this psychological therapy from antidepressants. Drugs such as SSRIs only work for as long as a person takes them. Take them away, even slowly, and the depression is likely to return. Although the reasons are still unclear, this difference has been explained by the educational element of psychological therapies that Aaron Beck first noted in the 1970s. A patient learns how to deal with some of the causal mechanisms of their depression. They notice their negative thoughts that might spiral into despair and a feeling of helplessness. Just by noticing and rationalising such thoughts – 'I'm not a failure at everything' – they gain some element of self-sufficiency, a means of controlling their mental health that an elevation of serotonin cannot provide. If this is the case, perhaps the five or six sessions of low-intensity CBT don't provide enough time for such lessons to be learnt.

Low-intensity CBT isn't pointless. For some people, it can have lasting benefits. But six weeks of therapy shouldn't end abruptly, especially if someone shows signs of improvement in their mental health. Rather than being told to expect a further phone review a few weeks in the future, an immediate continuation of the therapy should be offered. After bravely reaching out for professional help, a person with depression shouldn't have to go through that process again.

In my case, I skipped my phone interview for further therapy as I thought I was wasting everyone's time by even asking for more CBT. Someone else might need it. Plus, who knows what state I might be in after two months? I had heard that some people waited eight months for treatment. I wondered how bad things would have to get before someone took my case seriously. When Lucy booked me in for another emergency doctor's appointment – calling my GP as I was advised to do – the doctor recommended a type of antidepressant, known as venlafaxine, that doesn't just change the serotonin levels in the brain but also noradrenaline, another neurotransmitter. I had heard of this drug and had read reports that its withdrawal effects were notoriously severe. After my experience in Berlin with citalopram, I felt terrified about becoming stuck on this drug too. Lucy and I agreed that this was a bad idea, a medical version of trial and error that we didn't want to get involved in. After hearing that I was suicidal, the doctor finished our conversation by saying, 'I hope I don't have to worry about you tonight.'

I ignored him and walked out. Lucy and I made the slow journey home together, arm in arm. She wanted to scream as much as I did.

Healthcare systems aren't built for depression, or mental illness more generally. This is a problem of funding rather than a lack of knowledge. To avoid unnecessary side effects and patients becoming stuck on their prescriptions, the sensible option would be to treat depression with CBT first and only if that fails try antidepressants such as SSRIs. But this doesn't reflect the clinical reality. A prescription of antidepressants is cheaper, and easier, than a full 12 to 16 weeks of patient-focused CBT.

Around the world, mental healthcare is criminally underfunded. In the UK, for example, only 1 per cent of the £3.5 billion healthcare budget is allocated for adults with depression or anxiety disorders. That's £500, roughly, per person. In comparison, the investment for physical rehabilitation in a person's last year of life amounts to £60,000. As the psychiatrists Richard Layard and David Clark write in their 2014 book *Thrive*, 'We spend so much on trying to extend the *length* of life (often by very small amounts), and yet so little on improving its *quality*.'

There are many ways to argue that mental health is worth investing in. There's the economic argument (it is cost effective to treat depression so that people are more efficient at work), the scientific argument (these treatments work when given to the right patients), and the global argument (depression is a leading cause of disability around the world and requires significant action). But even the best statistical models amount to nothing compared to the moral argument: people with depression are suffering and at high risk of suicide, and families are affected over generations. It is a tragedy of incalculable proportions that they don't receive the treatment they need.

'If Mom Ain't Happy Ain't Nobody Happy'

CBT is often what people mean when they say they are 'getting therapy'. But it isn't the most suitable option for everyone. Interpersonal therapy, for example, can work for those people who require guidance through problematic life events. Whether someone is trapped by their own thoughts or stuck in a tricky social situation, psychotherapy should match the concern. 'There shouldn't be one psychotherapy,' says Myrna Weissman. 'I think that people who say, "This is *the* psychotherapy," are doing a disservice to patients. It's like saying there should only be Prozac.'

Interpersonal therapy was just one element of Weissman's work. After completing her PhD in 1974, she was first and foremost an epidemiologist, an academic who tracked diseases through time and populations, just as cartographers keep up to date with the growth of cities. Weissman turned to academia at the right time and in the right place. She studied at Yale University when a vocal civil-rights movement was campaigning for equal opportunities at work for everyone, regardless of their race, sexual orientation, or gender. 'I applied for the PhD program, in the 1970s, as a young, married mother of four children under the age of seven,' Weissman later wrote. 'I did not fit the historical picture of a Yalie.' Without the constant push for equality, a mother of four was unlikely to be seen as a potential candidate for any PhD programme.

Weissman's doctoral research focused on chronic diseases such as cancer and cardiovascular disease, some of the best-known and well-studied epidemiological subjects. Depression, and other mental illnesses, weren't studied in such detail. The few surveys that had been conducted were based on abstract terms such as 'well-being' or 'social functioning'. With the arrival of the *DSM-III* and Beck's inventory for depression, symptom clusters and strict diagnoses were becoming staples of psychiatry, replacing the Freudian notions of depressive neurosis or anxiety reactions. It was a watershed moment for depression. In one go, a medley of different diagnoses that biological psychiatrists had used were all lumped together underneath the term major depressive disorder (MDD). Involutional, atypical, reactive or endogenous – it was all the same: MDD. The only detail was whether there were melancholic features present. Was the depression significantly worse in the morning than the evening? Did the patient show excessive guilt or marked slowing in thought and movement? Had they lost a significant amount of weight recently? This wasn't a separate disease entity, not according to the *DSM-III* anyway. It was a more endogenous *subtype* of major depression.

Although major depression was no doubt an oversimplification of the true nature of depression, the *DSM-III* was an excellent tool to help find people who might require psychiatric care. As it was the same diagnosis no matter where it was used, populations across the United States could be studied and, importantly, compared. Already in contact with the psychiatrists – known as neo-Kraepelinians – working on the *DSM-III*, Weissman saw an opportunity to branch out from physical diseases and study the patterns of mental illnesses in the American population.

*

Psychotherapy and epidemiology, the two silos of Weissman's work, were deeply connected. How can you treat depression if you don't know how common it is? How can you deliver therapy of any kind, chemical or psychological, to the people who need it if you don't know who they are? In her first survey, encompassing 511 people living in the New Haven area, Weissman suggested that psychiatrists had been focusing on the wrong demographic. At this time, in the 1970s, there was a widely held theory that depression was predominantly a disorder of menopausal women. From her survey, Weissman didn't find any evidence to support this claim. Yes, women were twice as likely to suffer depression compared to men. But they certainly weren't menopausal. They were more likely to be in their 20s or 30s – the prime of their reproductive lives. Even adolescents, a demographic that were thought to have insufficient 'ego' development to suffer from depression, were found to show the hallmark signs and symptoms of major depression.

This was a small study. Just over 500 people living in New Haven might not be relevant to other communities, both in the United States and around the world. Perhaps there was another reason that the first episode was occurring at younger ages in this sample. To support (or refute) these preliminary results, Weissman needed larger samples from multiple sites across the United States.

As with her academic induction at Yale, Weissman found a political atmosphere that was highly conducive to her ongoing research. Jimmy Carter, the president of the United States, and his wife Rosalynn Carter were investing millions of dollars in mental-health research and the dissemination of evidence-based therapies. Weissman sent the handwritten drafts of her small New Haven survey to the Secretary for Health, Education, and Welfare, Joseph Califano, highlighting the early onset of depression. If confirmed, could adolescents and young women in particular be targets of either psychotherapy or antidepressants? The funding for what would become the largest survey of depression in the United States came shortly thereafter.

The Mental Health Epidemiologic Catchment Area (ECA) programme, published in October 1984, included 17,000 people from five different study sites across the United States (St. Louis, Baltimore, Los Angeles, Durham, and New Haven). Weissman, then director of the Depression Research Unit at Yale University, and her colleagues focused on the local region of New Haven, a leafy city in Connecticut where 126,000 people lived. Familiar patterns emerged from the data. With help from Priya Wickramaratne, a statistician who could make sense of the large stacks of raw data, Weissman found that, on average, women were indeed twice as likely to have depression than men. The first onset was in the young, on average at 27 years old, and these rates gradually declined after middle age and menopause (in contrast to the previous theories). On average, nearly 5 per cent of American people would experience, or were currently experiencing, a depressive episode. As Weissman walked down the tree-lined streets of New Haven, in other words, one in every 20 people she passed were, on average, either suffering from a current depressive episode, were in recovery from a previous episode, or were likely to become depressed later in life.

Weissman's surveys soon spanned state lines and crossed national borders. Hundreds of individuals became thousands. Although the prevalence differed from country to country (the rates of depression in Taiwan and Korea were significantly lower than in New Zealand and France, for example), the same patterns were found no matter where in the world she looked.

Depression was roughly twice as common in women than in men. It had a first onset in adolescence to early adulthood. And the risk of depression was two to four times higher in people who had been divorced or separated.

In October 1985, Richard Glass and Daniel Freedman, two leading psychiatrists in the United States, found such epidemiological work both exceptional and deeply worrying. Not only were the rates of depression and other mental illnesses higher than expected, the majority of people weren't receiving support or psychiatric care of any kind. '[D]ata from the ECA, as well as previous epidemiologic surveys, indicate that most persons with psychiatric disorders in the community are untreated,' they wrote in the *Journal of the American Medical Association* (*JAMA*). 'The costs of untreated illness are unknown, but may be astronomical in terms of lost productivity alone.' Absenteeism, lack of motivation at work, and fruitless visits to the general practitioner who thought aches and pains had nothing to do with the patient's mental state – it all added up. In the United States alone, Glass and Freedman wrote, the cost of untreated mental-health conditions could be as high as $185 billion per year.

Merging her expertise in interpersonal therapy and epidemiology, Weissman saw an opportunity to do something about this mental-health gap. In addition to the NIMH Treatment for Depression Collaborative Research Program, this form of talking therapy had been tested alongside antidepressants and found to provide a significant reduction in symptoms compared to just using the drugs on their own. In particular, while tricyclics seemed to target the sluggish cognition, sleeplessness, and bodily complaints such as constipation, interpersonal therapy provided a boost to a person's self-esteem while reducing thoughts of guilt, suicide, and helplessness. 'Our data,'

Weissman told the *New York Times* in 1978, 'show that the combination of drugs and psychotherapy has an additive effect. And we have seen that at the end of the treatment, usually four to 12 weeks, there is a noticeable difference. People function better. They feel better. They eat better. They can sleep. And most important, when the crisis is over, they can begin to work at identifying the problem that led them into the depression in the first place.'

Today, interpersonal therapy is a first-line talking therapy for depression. Based on multiple, large scale clinical trials, it is generally seen as being similarly effective as CBT and antidepressants. On average, roughly half of patients who receive this form of psychotherapy improve to such an extent that their depressive symptoms fall into a healthy threshold. Due to its focus on social ties and understanding of life transitions, interpersonal therapy has been shown to be particularly useful for depression in mothers.

Myrna Weissman has experienced many of the departures from the social field that define her work on interpersonal therapy. Divorce, transitioning into a new career and city, but it was only in 1992 that she had to stop what she was doing and focus on her own health. On 3 April of that year, after a long battle with diabetes, Gerry Klerman died of kidney disease at the age of 63. After both of their first marriages had ended in divorce, Weissman and Klerman had been married for seven years.

It felt as if an entire field of academia was in mourning. 'The world of medicine has lost a distinguished, energetic, and prolific member of its community,' Martin Keller, a psychiatrist from Brown University, wrote. '[Klerman's] ability to challenge and stimulate trainees was extraordinary and although this often created some performance anxieties in his students, his style was greatly admired and emulated.' At his funeral in New York, Daniel Freedman, the editor of the journal *Archives for General Psychiatry*, said that 'Gerry always brought a kind of cleansing clarity to anything he touched. We all grieve him, but the things that he made happen really are happening now and will be in the future.' His influence reached out from biological psychiatry and stimulated the field of psychotherapy.

Although it wasn't unforeseen (Klerman had been on dialysis for years), his death turned Weissman's life upside down. They shared much of their social space. He was a mentor and a close colleague, a friend and the stepfather of her four kids, a loving husband. 'I put [interpersonal therapy] aside,' she says. 'I had to.' After publishing the first edition of *Interpersonal Psychotherapy of Depression* in 1984, and finding this treatment's efficacy replicated by her own research group and elsewhere, this was no longer a professional hobby that she could devote herself to. John Markowitz and Lena Verdeli, two colleagues from Columbia University, took the reins. Since then, interpersonal therapy has been adopted and adapted by psychiatrists from around the world. Her manual has been refined through four editions and translated into seven languages. The latest edition was published in 2018. Gerry Klerman is credited as an author of all of them.

As is the case in interpersonal therapy, Weissman's approach to life is to focus on the problems of the present and not to dwell so heavily on the past. Divorce and widowhood are labels that no longer define her. Today, she is a married woman with four adult children and seven grandchildren. She has grieved two husbands and a first marriage that ended in divorce. But these were natural responses, and only if they continued for many months or even years would such pain become something that might require psychiatric treatment. The line between grief and depression is diffuse and impossible to define. But Weissman knew that an incomplete grieving process was a dangerous precursor to mental-health problems. 'Depression [can be] associated with abnormal grief reactions that result from the failure to go through the various phases of the normal mourning process,' the first *Interpersonal Psychotherapy of Depression* textbook states. 'A delayed or unresolved grief reaction may be precipitated by a more recent, less important loss. In other cases, delayed reactions may be precipitated when the patient achieves the age of death of the unmourned loved one.'

In order to feel stronger and return to work, Weissman knew she had to accept the rumination, guilt, anger, and obsession that followed Klerman's death. As she stepped aside and allowed others to take interpersonal therapy into the future, Weissman moved from studying how depression spans continents to how it gets passed on in the home.

For decades, Weissman has been investigating one of the most intriguing patterns in psychiatry: the children of depressed parents are at particularly high risk of depression. Although the reasons are still foggy, the most obvious explanation for this pattern is that a depressed parent is less able to nurture, care for, and generally take interest in their child as they grow. 'That's not rocket science,' says Weissman. 'That was obvious. If you have children and realise how much energy it took, how could you be depressed and take care of kids?' Using her New Haven surveys, Weissman quantified this risk over the decades, as the cohort of children became adults and parents themselves. At the ten-year mark, the risk of depression was three times as high for people who had lived with depressed parents compared to those who hadn't. (This figure has remained relatively constant at the 15, 20, 25, and, most recently, 30-year marks.)

The next step screamed from her datasets. 'In epidemiology there's the concept of the "modifiable risk factor",' Weissman says. 'And the modifiable risk factor was the depressed parent: you can modify that, by treating them.'

As she was waiting for a flight back to New York from a conference held in Hawaii, Weissman started chatting to a psychiatrist who told her about the results of an impressive trial about to be published. Known as STAR*D, it was a test of modern drug therapy and how quickly it could lead to remission (a near total absence of symptoms of depression) in over 4,000 people. If one drug failed, another was immediately tried. If that also failed, a third option was prescribed. Weissman asked whether she could study the children of these patients. By treating the parent, would the depressive symptoms of the child also improve? With the help of several research groups around the United States, this is exactly what Weissman found. Just as a keystone species might allow neighbouring life to flourish, the health benefits of being free from depression seemed to trickle down from parent to child. The crucial element was remission, not just treatment. Only those parents who were rid of their depression seemed to benefit their children (as judged by questionnaires that assessed symptoms of depression, anxiety, and disruptive behaviour disorder as well as their social functioning).

Weissman's study was covered in the *New York Times*. To celebrate its publication, her children – all adults at this point – bought her a customised T-shirt. Across its front, it read IF MOM AIN'T HAPPY AIN'T NOBODY HAPPY.

Published in 2006, it was a foundational study that provided a parental focus for the prevention of depression. But it also created some confusion in the psychiatric community, even among the co-authors of the study. 'We do not know from this study that treating parents causes the children to do better,' says Judy Garber, a clinical child psychologist at Vanderbilt University, Tennessee, who led one of the sites for the STAR*D trial. 'It is simply that the parents are doing better, and so are the children. And it can be for a massive number of reasons.' The parents of the children who got better could have been less depressed to begin with, Garber says. It could be due to shared life events that weren't taken into account in the sample. Perhaps the correlation was the other way around: The kids getting better facilitated to the parents' response to treatment.

Although Weissman could see that the sequence of events was from parent to child (and not the reverse), she knew that the study needed to be refined and replicated. 'So we did another study, which was a clinical trial,' Weissman says, a laconic statement that makes the process of scientific publication – planning the study, applying for funding, selecting the patients, conducting the trial, analysing the results, and editing the manuscript following peer-review – sound quick and easy. Published in the *Journal of American Psychiatry* in 2015, the study found that children of depressed mothers treated with the antidepressant escitalopram (Lexapro) showed significant improvements in their social functioning and mental health. 'We showed the same thing [as before],' Weissman says. 'If the mother got better, with treatment, the kids got better.' A few hundred miles west of Weissman's office in Manhattan, at the University of Pittsburgh, some of her former colleagues at Columbia had continued to study interpersonal therapy. In

2008, they replicated Weissman's results with the therapy that she had helped to create. Treating depressed mothers with interpersonal therapy led to improvements in the mental health and social functioning of their children.

As with vaccinations and dental care, the responsibility of mental healthcare in children shouldn't be wholly on their parents. In an ideal world, national governments should provide evidence-based therapies for families. These can either be universal (given to everyone regardless of risk) or targeted (given to those in high-risk demographics), the two main forms of preventative medicine. According to Helen Christensen, universal prevention is the only way forward. 'You don't know who's going to get depressed,' she says. 'We might have risk factors and so on, but that's not actually going to tell us which particular person on the ground is likely to get depressed ... So you've got to actually provide these sort of prevention interventions for everybody.'

For children and adolescents, the classroom has been seen as the most logical place for universal psychotherapy, delivered by visiting therapists or using internet-based programmes. Currently, however, the evidence supporting such initiatives is weak at best. Large school-based clinical trials in Chile and the UK have failed to find significant reductions in depressive symptoms compared with other approaches such as attention control or Personal, Social, and Health Education (PSHE) lessons. In fact, the latter study, led by researchers at the University of Bath, found that children given CBT in schools were *more* likely to show signs of low mood 12 months after the trial had finished. As Robyn Whittaker, associate professor at the National Institute for Health Innovation, University of Auckland, and her colleagues succinctly wrote in 2017, 'Universal depression prevention remains a challenge.'

The bulk of the evidence currently supports targeted prevention. In 2009, for instance, Judy Garber and her colleagues provided a cognitive-behavioural programme for adolescents who either had symptoms of anxiety or hopelessness (known antecedents of depression) or their parents had a history of depression. 'What we found was what we call a moderator effect,' Garber says. 'Those teens whose parents were not currently depressed benefited from the intervention. With the programme, they had fewer depressive episodes. But when we looked at the teens whose parents *were* currently depressed, the intervention didn't make a difference.' The reasons why are still unknown. 'It could be genetics, it could be that [those] parents were more ill,' Garber says. 'To some extent, we found that there was a slightly lower attendance rate. So maybe the parents were having trouble getting the kids to the intervention.' Whatever the case, it's clear that depression is a disorder that arises within the family and should be treated as such. Whether its cognitive behavioural or interpersonal, psychological intervention is a powerful tool in the long-term treatment of depression. The main challenge for psychiatry is getting these services to people who need them, no matter where they live.

'Happier Than We Europeans'

During her psychiatric training at the Maudsley Hospital in London in the late 1980s, Melanie Abas was faced with some of the most severe forms of depression known. 'They were hardly eating, hardly moving, hardly speaking,' Abas, now a professor of global mental health at King's College London, says of her patients. '[They] could see no point in life,' she says. 'Absolutely, completely flat and hopeless.' Any treatment that might lift this oppressive disease would be life-saving. By visiting their homes and their general practitioners, Abas made sure that such patients were taking their prescription of antidepressants for long enough for them to take effect. Working with Raymond Levy, a specialist in late-life depression at the Maudsley, Abas found that even the most resistant cases could respond if people were given the right medication, at the correct dose, for a longer duration. When all else failed, she turned to ECT. 'That gave me a lot of early confidence,' says Abas. 'Depression was something that could be treated as long as you persisted.'

In 1990, curious to expand her horizons, Abas accepted a research position at the University of Zimbabwe's medical school and moved to Harare, the country's capital city. Unlike today, the country had its own currency, the Zimbabwean dollar. The economy was stable. Hyperinflation, and the suitcases of cash that it necessitated, was over a decade away. Harare was nicknamed the 'Sunshine City', a bright centrepiece of a country only liberated from British rule a decade before. Called Southern Rhodesia (after Cecil Rhodes, a British businessman who lived in South Africa) until 1980, Zimbabwe had taken hold of its own future. Yet, although there was sunshine in Harare, the country was descending into a painful period of decolonisation. After instilling the people of Zimbabwe with a sense of national pride and individual freedom, the political activist Robert Mugabe soon became a tyrant who was closer to the cruel colonial elites whom he had replaced than a home-grown saviour of his people. From 1983 to 1987, an estimated 20,000 Ndebele citizens were slaughtered in the western region of Matabeleland North, a political stronghold for the rival ZAPU party. Carried out by the government's North Korean-trained military, this became known as Gukurahundi, a name that translates as 'the early rain that washes away the chaff before the spring rains'. In the parlance of international law, it was genocide.

Execution was only one of the fatal products of Mugabe's regime. While he remained wealthy and well-fed, the majority of people in the country struggled to get by. What was described as 'the worst drought in living memory' struck the country in 1992, drying up river beds, killing over a million cattle, and leaving cupboards empty. Malnutrition and a lack of medicine against infectious diseases such as tuberculosis, cholera, and malaria meant that children – the most vulnerable demographic along with the elderly – struggled to survive. For every 1,000 live births in Zimbabwe around 87 children died before the age of five, a mortality rate 11 times higher than that in the UK. The death of a child left behind grief, trauma, and, as Abas and her team found, a husband who might abuse his wife for her 'failure' as a mother. Then there was HIV, a virus that would infect a quarter of the population by the mid 1990s.

With such loss, poverty, and disease, it was surprising that depression, a mental disorder that thrives on such disruptions in the social sphere, was rarely found in Zimbabwe. A survey from the City of Harare reported that fewer than one in every 4,000 patients (0.001 per cent) who visited the outpatients department had depression. 'In rural clinics, the numbers diagnosed as depressed are smaller still,' Abas wrote in 1994. In comparison, around 9 per cent of women in Camberwell, the southern region of London where Abas was working at the Maudsley Hospital, were depressed. Essentially, she had moved from a city where depression was prevalent to one in which it was so rare it was barely even noticed. It was a complete reversal of the research she was accustomed to. From busily treating the most severe cases of depression with drugs or ECT, her research in Harare had to start at the very beginning: finding people who might need her help.

This low rate of depression fit snugly with a racist dogma that had first taken root during the Enlightenment era of the eighteenth century. At this time of Eureka moments and insightful musings, the Genevan philosopher and composer Jean-Jacques Rousseau eloquently proposed that civilisation was the scourge of our species. He romanticised the notion that historically humans had lived in peaceful union with nature. '[N]othing is so gentle as man in his primitive state,' he wrote, 'this period in the development of human faculties ... must have been the happiest and most durable epoch.' As such, people who lived outside of the so-called 'civilised' world were viewed as cheerful, peaceful, and, in a term wrongly credited to Rousseau, 'noble savages'. This Western worldview soon encircled the globe. Upon meeting the aboriginal people of Australia, for example, James Cook, explorer and captain in the British Royal Navy, wrote that they 'live in a Tranquillity which is not disturb'd by the Inequality of

Condition: The Earth and sea of their own accord furnishes them with all things necessary for life, they covet not Magnificent Houses, Household-stuff ... they live in a warm and fine Climate and enjoy a very wholsome Air, so that they have very little need of Clothing ...' They were, in short, 'happier than we Europeans'.

Australian Aborigines, African bushmen, Native Americans, and the Inuit were all thought to resemble the pure spirit of humankind. Untouched by the ways and words of civilised society, they were free of the stresses and strains of modern life. Unhappiness, never mind depression, was as alien to these cultures as the woollen stockings, petticoats, and ruffles that men of the Enlightenment found so fashionable. Rousseau believed that our species was originally destined to remain in this state of peaceful union but had been enchanted by the promise of individual expression, industrial revolution, scientific breakthroughs, and the overall prosperity that civilisation would bring. This 'progress,' Rousseau wrote, 'has been in appearance so many steps toward the perfection of the individual, and in fact toward the decay of the species'. Civilisation was a poisoned apple that Western society had consumed with relish. There was no cure, no turning back. Other, less-developed cultures were in danger of being similarly corrupted and pushed out of their peaceful ignorance.

This view was reversed during the nineteenth century's 'Scramble for Africa'. As European nations sought ever-greater geopolitical power, Africans were recast as so-called savages who were in desperate need of civilisation and, most commonly, the guiding faith of Christianity. It was an enforced alignment with the values of their colonial masters. There was nothing peaceful about living in a colony. Natural resources such as gold, diamonds, rare dinosaur fossils, and sometimes entire villages were stolen and transported back to Europe for sale or exhibition. Tens of millions of Europeans travelled to see the mock mud huts, ceremonial dresses, drums, dances, black skin, and curly hair of these 'savages'. Any rebellion or violent uprising was quelled with an inequality in weaponry; spears and bows and arrows were no match for rifles and bullets. The cost of colonialism is incalculable.

Whether a colonialist spoke French or English, German or Italian, Spanish or Portuguese, the same rhetoric was taken as fact. Before the colonisation of African countries, they said, there was no civilisation there. It was a continent of sparse populations, rudimentary dwellings, and illiteracy. Small villages, tribal leaders, and subsistence farming was the rule through centuries and over thousands of miles of coastline, savanna, desert, and forest.

Psychiatrists – the western equivalent of traditional healers and shamans – adopted this worldview into the middle of the twentieth century. Depression, it was said, was a Westernised disease, a product of civilisation. It wasn't found on, say, the plateau of eastern Africa, the shores of Lake Victoria, or anywhere else south of the Sahara Desert. 'In general, it seems,' the psychiatrist Geoffrey Tooth wrote in 1950, 'that classical depressive syndromes are seldom seen, at least in Africans untouched by alien influences.' These aliens – Western people – might not have been from outer space, but they were seen as products of other worlds: urban life and the stress that modernity brings. '[T]he very notion that people in a developing black African nation could either be in need of, or would benefit from, western-style psychiatry seriously unsettled most of my English colleagues: their skepticism was rampant,' a psychiatrist working in Botswana in the 1980s wrote. 'They kept saying, or implying, "But surely they are not like us. It is the rush of modern life, the noise, the bustle, the chaos, the tension, the speed, the stress, that drives us all crazy: without them life would be wonderful."'

In Zimbabwe, the grip of colonial psychiatry had to be particularly tight. While still called Southern Rhodesia, the country provided indisputable evidence that, if made public, could overturn the Rousseau-esque notion of happy people untouched by modern life who lived peacefully with nature. Since the first Portuguese explorers journeyed through the region in the sixteenth century, there had been reports of huge cities of granite in southern Africa, local populations that reached into the thousands, and evidence of former trade networks with China, India, and the Middle East. Nowhere was this more obvious than in Southern Rhodesia, a place where hundreds of ruins speckle the landscape in every direction, none more impressive or controversial than the drystone walls of 'Great Zimbabwe'. Before the colonial missionaries, explorers, and psychiatrists of Europe arrived, civilisation had thrived here. Built in the eleventh century and inhabited for the next 400 or 500 years, Great Zimbabwe comprises a trio of fortress-like structures that are spectacular in both their scale and architectural fluidity. Constructed atop a hill and snaking into the valley below, a series of impressive drystone walls – 11 metres tall and five metres wide in places – were built entirely from granite mined from the local bedrock. The 'Hill Complex' blends into a natural crag of granite rocks that perch atop a raised mound of earth. A stairway in this African acropolis leads to a natural balcony among the boulders. Below, an oval structure known as the 'Great Enclosure' stands as the centrepiece of a former city. At its height, archaeologists and mathematicians have estimated that between 10,000 and 18,000 people lived at Great Zimbabwe, a few hundred behind its curved walls while the rest eked out an existence in wooden huts outside.

But no colonial country wanted to admit to the true origins of this forgotten city. Reuniting Southern Rhodesia with its history could lead to a resurgence in pride and individuality, revolution, and, ultimately, independence. And so, since the 1870s and into the twentieth century, colonial journalists and archaeologists had argued that the local Bantu people were incapable of building such walled fortresses and, instead, proposed that Great Zimbabwe was the work of the mythical Queen of Sheba, the 'Erythraean' people of southeast Asia, travellers from southern India, or Arabs from the Middle East. 'Censorship of guidebooks, museum displays, school textbooks, radio programmes, newspapers and films was a daily occurrence,' a former curator at the Museum of Great Zimbabwe recalled. 'Once a member of the Museum Board of Trustees threatened me with losing my job if I said publicly that blacks had built Zimbabwe ... It was the first time since Germany in the thirties that archaeology has been so directly censored.'

As with architectural competency, presumed levels of intelligence have long been tied to the predisposition to mental illnesses such as depression. In 1953, the recently created World Health Organisation based in Geneva published a report entitled 'The African Mind in Health and Disease'. Written by John Carothers, a British doctor who had worked at Mathari Mental Hospital in Nairobi, Kenya, in the 1940s, this report set the tone for other psychiatrists working across sub-Saharan Africa to follow. He quoted several authors who compared African mental states to those of Western children and to immaturity. A black person, Carothers wrote, 'has but few gifts for work which aims at a distant goal and requires tenacity, independence, and foresight'. In an earlier paper, he compared the 'African mind' to a European person's brain that had undergone a lobotomy. The lack of depressive cases at his mental hospital seemed to confirm these views. How could someone be depressed if they lacked foresight and the pursuit of distant goals? How could someone worry or feel guilty about past deeds when they are so embedded in the present? Out of the 1,508 patients Carothers saw between 1939 and 1948, there were only 24 cases of depression, a mere 1.6 per cent of total admissions. 'Even allowing for the fact that other cases have doubtless been missed,' Carothers wrote, 'the condition as a whole is relatively rare.'

Carothers's views were becoming outdated soon after he had written these words. Thomas Adeoye Lambo, a psychiatrist, author, and member of the Yoruba people of southern Nigeria, wrote that Carothers's conclusions were nothing but 'glorified pseudo-scientific novels or anecdotes with a subtle racial bias'. Refraining from calling out blatant racism, Lambo was a calm and impressive character in everything he did. 'Nobody could meet him without coming away with a powerful impression of being in the penumbra of a force-field that radiated power and presence,' the psychiatrist and novelist Femi Olugbile wrote. Lambo wore his traditional blue robes to otherwise besuited global health conferences and would later become the deputy director general at the World Health Organisation. Carothers's studies, Lambo concluded, contained so many gaps and inconsistencies 'that they can no longer be seriously presented as valuable observations of scientific merit'.

The tide was turning fast. From the late 1950s, colonial states in Africa were giving way to independent nations. With this shift in cultural identity and freedom from foreign emancipation, it was as if a veil was slowly being removed from an entire continent. This was even seen in the shift in psychiatric epidemiology: rates of depression soared as decolonisation spread. Studies in two Ugandan villages – places of rolling hills, fields of crops, and quietude – found that the rates were twice as high there as in south London. Among the Yoruba tribe of Nigeria, the rates were four times as high as a population in Stirling County, Canada. This didn't mean that decolonisation had caused the increase in depression. It was simply that representatives from Western countries began communicating with people from other cultures, not seeing them as underlings but as equals. The same phenomenon was being recognised the world over. 'For one trained in one's own culture and by those familiar with the patients' culture ... it becomes evident that the mood of sadness in oriental depressives is no less frequent than in the western co-sufferers,' Venkoba Rao, a professor of psychiatry at Madurai Medical College, India, wrote in 1984. Speaking the local language, living in communities rather than in mental hospitals – the hallmark signs of mental suffering revealed themselves in ways that were unmistakably familiar to the Western term 'depression'.

Kufungisisa

Following in the footsteps of researchers in Uganda and Nigeria, the reality of depression in Zimbabwe was revealed a decade after it gained independence in 1980. Between 1991 and 1992, Melanie Abas, her husband and colleague Jeremy Broadhead, and a team of local nurses and social workers visited 200 households in Glen Norah, a low-income, high-density district in southern Harare. They contacted church leaders, housing officials, traditional healers and other local organisations, gaining their trust and their permission to interview a large number of residents. They wanted to know whether depression even translated into the local Shona language. What if there was no word for depression? Could this be another reason why this so-called Western disease had been so neglected in sub-Saharan Africa? Through discussions with traditional healers and local health workers, Abas and her team found that *kufungisisa*, or 'thinking too much', was the most common descriptor for emotional distress. This is very similar to the English word 'rumination' that describes the negative thought patterns that often lie at the core of depression and anxiety. 'Although all of the [socioeconomic] conditions were different,' Abas says, 'I was seeing what I recognised as pretty classical depression.'

It wasn't just a case of thinking too much, however. There was also the lack of sleep and appetite. A loss of interest in once enjoyable activities. And a deep sadness (*kusuwisisa*) that is different from a normal state of sadness (*suwa*). Using culturally appropriate terms such as *kufungisisa* to help identify mental suffering, Abas and her team found that depression was nearly twice as common in Harare as in a similar community in Camberwell. In direct contrast to the previous surveys that found a rate of one in every 4,000 (0.001 per cent), Abas's community surveys found that it was closer to one in every five people (20 per cent).

As with the epidemiological studies in the United States and England, Abas wondered whether stressful life events were associated with depression in Harare. Even if the words were different, did the same social triggers transcend cultural and national boundaries? Adopting the methods of George Brown and Tirril Harris, famed sociologists who studied the relationship between life events and depression in Camberwell, she found a strong pattern emerge from her surveys. '[We found] that, actually, events of the same severity will produce the same rate of depression, whether you live in London or whether you live in Zimbabwe,' she says. 'It was just that in Zimbabwe there were a lot more of these events.' Poverty, malnutrition, unemployment, cholera, HIV: all took their toll. In particular, HIV and depression fit together into a tight spiral that slowly twists toward mortality. Not only are people who are HIV-positive twice as likely to be depressed than a HIV-negative person, but the depression then makes the virus more lethal. The same is true for poverty: it is both a trigger for depression and made worse by being depressed.

These cyclical relationships were also an opportunity. Would treating the depression, Abas wondered, have knock-on effects for other facets of a person's life? Would they take their antiretroviral medication and feel less stigmatised by their HIV status? Would they find employment and earn a living for themselves? At the time, in the 1990s, over 100 million people around the world were said to suffer from depression but only a select few were receiving treatment. Even today, 90 per cent of people living in low-income countries don't have access to evidence-based therapies like antidepressants and psychotherapy. In high-income countries, this figure hovers around 60 per cent. As Shekhar Saxena, the former director of the Department of Mental Health and Substance Abuse at the World Health Organisation, once put it, 'when it comes to mental health, we are all developing countries'. Little did Abas know that her work wouldn't just help treat depression in Harare or even Zimbabwe. It would eventually lay the foundations for a revolution in mental healthcare that would reach out of sub-Saharan Africa – a place previously thought to be absent of depression – and across the world.

In 1992, inspired by the work of David Ben-Tovim, a doctor working in Botswana, Abas helped introduce a form of psychotherapy that nurses and doctors could provide to their patients in health centres across Harare. Known as the 'seven-step plan', it was a mixture of Myrna Weissman's interpersonal therapy and Aaron Beck's cognitive therapy, and it could also include antidepressant treatment. Starting with questions about patients' personal lives and what they might be thinking too much about, nurses were advised to listen and empathise. 'Try and share their sadness,' Abas wrote. In the first meeting, they would also evaluate the risk of suicide, and after a few days they'd repeat the same steps and discuss potential support networks – friends, family, church, or a welfare agency. If symptoms persisted for three or more weeks, a prescription of amitriptyline, a tricyclic antidepressant, was advisable. The patient should be informed of the potential for dry mouth, sedation, constipation, and the lag time between taking the pills and the relief of the depression (or *kufungisisa*). Three months later, any patients with persistent or severe depression should be referred to one of the ten psychiatrists serving a country of 10 million.

The most revelatory element of this seven-step plan was its most basic: the knowledge that *kufungisisa* was a common and treatable illness revealed the potential for a healthy future. Brochures and posters were displayed in health centres across the city to reduce stigma and increase understanding of this common disorder:

> Thinking too much makes people ill.
> We call this illness *kufungisisa*-depression.
> It is a mental illness but it is different from madness
> or *kupenga* and it is not caused by *Ngozi* [evil spirits].

But who takes notice of posters and pamphlets, especially when they are busied by their own thoughts? To really drive home the message, a drama group transformed these words into a song and dance that they hoped would resonate with a culture more attuned to live performances, music, and rhythm than an audience trying to avoid eye-contact with strangers in the stuffy waiting rooms of the Western world.

Over her two and a half years in Harare, Abas had developed a soft spot for the Sunshine City. It was a place of intriguing contrasts. In areas of great poverty, there was a shared feeling of camaraderie and joy. The roads were filled with potholes, but they were lined with flowers and, in the summer months, the violet blossoms of jacaranda trees. It was welcoming. A second home. But Abas had to complete her training as a psychiatric epidemiologist and return to England, accepting a permanent position at King's College London. Over the next decade, the political and economic situation in Zimbabwe continued to spiral into crisis. The number of psychiatrists in the country dropped to just one or two. And with a health service already stretched to breaking point, the nurses and doctors more focused on HIV, cholera, and tuberculosis than *kufungisisa*, Abas worried that her work would be forgotten, dismissed as just another casualty of Robert Mugabe's authoritarian regime.

The study of mental health – its prevalence, diagnosis, and treatment – around the world has many names and origins. John Carothers, for example, was one vocal member of the field of transcultural psychiatry, a colonial practice built upon ethnocentric ideologies, racism, and the construction of Western-style mental institutions in foreign lands. In 1995, this antiquated field underwent a much needed rebrand with the publication of a book. Coordinated and co-written by Arthur Kleinman, professor of anthropology and psychiatry at Harvard University, *World Mental Health* put forward an agenda that could tackle the high prevalence of depression and other psychiatric disorders around the globe.

It was a time of fresh insight and hope, an era in which common mental disorders were understood as the real threats we now know them to be. At one time, the metric used to gauge whether a disease required action and attention was its overall mortality. How many people did it kill and how quickly? By this count, cancer, heart disease, and infectious diseases took centre stage in any policy decisions relating to the allocation of funding for health services. Even when a patient dies from depression it is often labelled as 'suicide', a blurred view of the true cause of death.

But diseases don't just exist on the line between life and death. They influence our lives in myriad ways and aren't always fatal. Just before the publication of *World Mental Health*, the mortality-based conception of diseases changed with the introduction of the disability-adjusted life year (DALY) in the early 1990s, a metric that took into account not only death but also the number of lost healthy years. 'One DALY can be thought of as one lost year of "healthy" life,' the World Health Organisation states. Based on this more accurate model of the way disease encroaches upon health, depression and other mental disorders immediately became some of the most-costly diseases. In 1992, for example, a study by the World Bank estimated that mental-health problems accounted for over 8 per cent of all healthy years lost. This was more than cancer (6 per cent), heart diseases (3 per cent) and malaria (3 per cent). 'Yet despite the importance of these problems, they have received scant attention outside the wealthier, industrialised nations,' Kleinman and his colleagues wrote in *World Mental Health*. '[A]llocations in national health budgets for preventing and dealing with these problems are disproportionately small in relation to the hazards to human health that they represent.'

In his mid 70s, goateed and focused more on writing books than conducting research, Kleinman says that his initial optimism after the publication of this book was quickly replaced with frustration and the dreadful feeling of being pushed to one side. As the 1990s turned into the early 2000s, the concerns over world mental health were replaced by another health crisis: HIV. 'I watched us being knocked off the agenda by the AIDS movement,' Kleinman says. This isn't to say that the AIDS movement didn't require urgent action and funding. It did. The production of antiretroviral drugs that kept HIV loads down and their dissemination around the world is one of the greatest success stories of modern medicine, one that continues today. It was once thought to be impossible to provide antiret-roviral drugs to people living in sub-Saharan Africa in order to stem the HIV crisis. Although HIV is still an international problem, viral loads are decreasing, and with the correct treatment and advice, people can live happy, productive lives while being HIV-positive.

It is time for the same success for the treatment of depression, Kleinman says, an illness that is far more widespread and common than HIV and has a suite of effective treatments available. Psychotherapy, antidepressants, electroconvulsive therapy: they all work for different severities or subtypes of the disease. But even if modern, evidence-based therapies were made universally available, they still wouldn't reach everyone. In some parts of the world, psychiatrists are highly stigmatised and few people might want to see them. Even if they did, they might not be able to afford them. Others might prefer to see a local religious leader or a traditional healer. Many more wouldn't want to speak about their problems outside of their home for fear of shaming or discrimination from their friends or family. An effective therapy is often a compromise, a blend of the scientific model of medicine and the local customs and culture that allow such a model to be accepted if and when it is made available. Lastly, in order to tackle a mental-health crisis that numbers in the hundreds of millions of sufferers, treatments must be scalable. If they are too costly, require too much time for training, or are so specific that they can't be implemented both in sprawling cities and isolated villages, then they won't work. In order to ensure sustainability, the allocation of treatment has to be a part of the public-health system, and initiatives must not be governed by short-term contracts from universities or NGOs but instead require a regular slice of the national-health budget year on year. 'That's the only way to go,' Vikram Patel, professor of global mental health at Harvard University and co-creator of Sangath, a community health service in Goa, India, said in June 2018 at a global mental-health workshop held in Dubai.

Sitting in his second-floor office at Harvard University in Boston, Arthur Kleinman doesn't know when this shift will happen. 'I'm 77 years of age,' he says. 'Let's say that I live to 95, that would be optimistic. So that's 18 years. In 18 years will we see substantial monies come into this field? I hope so, I sincerely hope so. I have no idea if it will or not. So I'm not planning, necessarily, to see the victory. But will there be a victory in this area? Absolutely. Will it happen in the twenty-first century? Absolutely.'

Helen Verdeli, a clinical psychologist and colleague of Myrna Weissman at Columbia University, travelled to southwest Uganda in February 2002. It was her first visit to Africa, and she travelled away from the capital city of Kampala and began her work in dozens of villages in the southwest of the country. Surrounded by fields of crops, she met with village elders and the next counsellors in interpersonal therapy for depression. Without trained psychiatrists or psychologists in this area, her plan was to train employees from World Vision International, an NGO that worked in the area, providing aid and education to the local communities. But, at the last minute, they told Verdeli and her colleagues that they were too busy. They couldn't take on any more responsibilities. As an alternative, they asked their relatives if they could help instead.

Initially a problem, this change of plan became the beginning of the latest approach to global mental health: training the local community in psychological therapy. With zero experience and no medical degrees, could laypersons be effective therapists? A few little-known studies from the 1970s and 1980s suggested that this might be an understatement. Although not limited to depression, one review found that, out of 42 published studies, 13 showed that community-health workers (or 'paraprofessionals') were more effective than trained professionals. Only one study found professionals more effective, while the remaining 28 studies found no difference between the two. 'The clinical outcomes that paraprofessionals achieve are equal to or significantly better than those obtained by professionals,' the author, Joseph Durlak from Southern Illinois University at Carbondale, wrote in 1979. 'The provocative conclusions from these comparative investigations is that professionals do not possess demonstrably superior therapeutic skills, compared with paraprofessionals. Moreover, professional mental health education, training, and experience are not necessary prerequisites for an effective helping person.'

Nine people living in the Rakai and Masaka provinces of southwestern Uganda fit the criteria Verdeli, Weissman, and their colleagues were looking for. They had grown up in the local area and had at least a college-level education. Plus, they all spoke English and Luganda (the most common indigenous language in Uganda), and could communicate with both the American visitors and their neighbours. Over an intensive two weeks of training, Verdeli and her colleague from Columbia University Kathleen Clougherty taught them the ins and outs of interpersonal therapy.

The identification of causal life events and their solution isn't an easy task in any therapy session. But these difficulties were raised to frightening extremes in a low-income country like Uganda. As Abas had found in Zimbabwe, the same life events were found here as anywhere else on Earth. Death, divorce, disease, unemployment, natural disasters, poverty. It is their frequency that is unavoidable. Throughout the 1990s, nearly a quarter of people living in Uganda were infected with HIV. Not only did the virus usually come with a death sentence, it also led to social isolation, stigmatisation, and the death of loved ones. The loss of breadwinners was particularly devastating, leaving families without the financial support they once depended on. Widowed, the wife or wives (polygamy is common in Uganda) of the deceased had few skills to earn a living and fell further into poverty. Civil wars, political repression, and widespread malnutrition stirred depression into every corner of the country. A survey from Paul Bolton, a cross-cultural psychiatrist from Johns Hopkins University in Baltimore and a colleague of Verdeli, found that 21 per cent of people in southwest Uganda met the criteria for major depression. A previous study had found a similar rate. Roughly one in four people required psychiatric care, whether it was psychotherapy or antidepressants. But few received any. Even traditional healers in Uganda expressed their inability to help people with depression-like illnesses. For people with depression, the isolation and helplessness were crushing.

As was the case in Shona, there wasn't a word for depression in Luganda. But there were close equivalents, Bolton found. *Yo'kwekyawa* and *okwekubazida*, roughly translating as self-loathing and self-pity, overlapped with Western diagnoses of depression. Since it came with suicidal ideation, *yo'kwekyawa* was seen as the more severe form of the two depression-like illnesses. As well as the usual symptoms of fatigue, lack of interest, and feelings of hopelessness, *yo'kwekyawa* and *okwekubazida* also included a few nuances of their own: people with these illnesses tended to not respond when someone greeted them. They hated the world and people in it. And even when they were offered generosity or assistance, they were unappreciative.

As an illness of thoughts, emotions, and memories that encompasses a diverse range of symptoms, depression is shaped by a person's cultural traditions and language. The symptom or feeling that becomes definitive of the condition – low mood, tension, fatigue – depends on how someone expresses themselves, communicates, and connects their inner world to the environment that surrounds them. 'The experience of this condition is so deeply embedded in one's social world,' says Vikram Patel. In China, depression was more commonly referred to as neurasthenia, a term referring to nerve weakness that was popularised in the nineteenth century. Under the dictatorship of Chairman Mao, it was more socially acceptable for Chinese citizens to suffer from such a physical illness akin to fatigue. A diagnosis of low mood or mental depression might have been taken as an insult to the socialist state, or even to Mao himself. Only in recent decades, as the country has become more Westernised, has the symptom of low mood become a definitive descriptor of mental illness in China. In India, meanwhile, depression is felt as 'tension'. The muscles seize up and everyday movements and walking feel like the air has turned into thick, gloopy syrup. 'We never use the word depression because no one understands it,' says Patel. 'The literal translation will become something like, "Are you sad?" And they'll say, "Of course I'm sad. My life is miserable."'

The most common descriptor of the Western diagnosis of depression, however, is 'thinking too much', a phrase used across swathes of Africa, southeastern Asia, and South America.

These subtle variants don't mean that depression is different depending on where someone was raised. The underlying biology and symptoms are far more similar than they are dissimilar. Still, unlike cancer or heart disease, depression can't be reduced down to a failing organ or an uncontrollably dividing cell. Without a universal marker for depression, its social context has to be taken into account before it can be identified and treated.

Given the cross-cultural differences between the United States and Uganda, interpersonal therapy couldn't simply be translated into Luganda, word for word. The manual had to be made culturally appropriate. Although the key concepts were the same, there were a few important adaptations that Verdeli and Clougherty had to adopt. Most obvious was the therapy format. Sessions weren't one-to-one discussions between a lay-counsellor and a patient. Instead, a group of five to eight people met together, all of the same sex. 'In these cultures,' Verdeli and her colleagues wrote, 'people tend to see themselves as part of a family or community unit before they see themselves as individuals.' Even marriages and funerals are attended by the whole community, regardless of relation. Using the standard format of interpersonal therapy was, therefore, thought to be unsuitable. Led by a trained community member, people with *yo'kwekyawa* or *okwekubazida* were given the opportunity to support and advise their neighbours during each session, offering solutions to life events that they themselves might have faced in the past.

There were more subtle adaptations. Speaking negatively of the deceased – even those who had been abusive or unfaithful – was strictly prohibited in Ugandan culture. 'The dead are living among us,' was a common phrase heard in the villages. To respectfully approach any turbulent relationships, lay-counsellors were taught to ask questions such as 'were there times in your life together when you felt disappointed by the dead?' As polygamy was common in these villages, a common life event for women was how to deal with their husband's new wife, a shift in their household that often changed the role they once had in the family. Most importantly, however, was the conflict arising from HIV: how can widowed women earn money for their children or find someone else to support them? Simply knowing that HIV wasn't a form of punishment but a common infection that could be treated with the right medication could help allay some of the guilt and self-pity characteristic of *yo'kwekyawa* and *okwekubazida*.

With these modifications, group interpersonal therapy was an effective means of reducing depressive symptoms, especially in women. Compared to a control group that was offered a more basic form of care, the reduction in symptoms was three times as great as judged by a standardised health questionnaire. Not only were the results highly significant but they were also stable. During a six-month follow-up, the prevalence of depression had barely increased. There was an unexpected explanation for these long-term effects. Many of the groups continued to meet up without their lay-counsellor, supporting each other through shared hardships. Group interpersonal therapy wasn't just a 16-week trial, in other words. It was a process that built long-lasting social connections. The one group that didn't meet up after the trial showed significantly higher rates of depression than the others.

This informal 'social support system', as Verdeli and her colleagues wrote, provided a vital component of any treatment used in low-resource settings. With no option for frequent or prolonged treatment, any beneficial effects need to stand the test of time. Published in *JAMA* in the summer of 2003, Verdeli and her colleagues had shown that laypersons – people with no former training in psychiatry or medicine – were a valuable resource in the treatment of depression. That same year, two randomised-controlled trials were published in *The Lancet* from similar projects in low-income regions in Santiago, Chile, and Goa, India. Although they trained nurses or social workers (and not laypersons), all three studies showed that a psychology degree isn't a prerequisite for an effective therapist.

Care by the Community

Dixon Chibanda spent more time with Erica than most of his other patients. It wasn't that her problems were more serious than others' – she was just one of thousands of women in their mid 20s with depression in Zimbabwe. It was because she had travelled over 160 miles to meet him.

Erica lived in a remote village nestled in the highlands of eastern Zimbabwe, next to the border with Mozambique. Her family's thatch-roofed hut was surrounded by mountains. They tended to staples such as maize and kept chickens, goats, and cattle, selling surplus milk and eggs at the local market. Erica had passed her exams at school but was unable to find a job. Her family, she thought, wanted her only to find a husband. To them, the role of a woman was to be a wife and a mother. She wondered what her bride price might be. A cow? A few goats? As it turned out, the man she hoped to marry chose another woman. Erica felt totally worthless. She started thinking too much about her problems. Over and over, thoughts swirled through her head and began to cloud the world around her. She couldn't see any positivity in the future.

Given the importance that Erica would hold in Chibanda's future, it could be said that their meeting was fated. In truth, it was just the product of extremely high odds. At the time, in 2004, there were only two psychiatrists working in public healthcare in the whole of Zimbabwe, a country of over 12.5 million people. Both were based in Harare, the capital city. Unlike his besuited colleagues at Harare Central Hospital,

Chibanda dressed casually in a T-shirt, jeans and running trainers. After completing his psychiatric training at the University of Zimbabwe, he had found work as a travelling consultant for the World Health Organisation. As he introduced new mental-health legislation across sub-Saharan Africa, he dreamt about settling down in Harare and opening a private practice – the goal, he says, for most Zimbabwean doctors when they specialise.

Erica and Chibanda met every month for a year or so, sitting opposite one another in a small office in the one-storey hospital building in central Harare. He prescribed Erica amitriptyline. Although it came with a suite of side effects – dry mouth, constipation, dizziness – they would, he hoped, fade over time. After a month or so, Erica might be better able to cope with the difficulties back home in the highlands.

Isolated and unable to afford the bus journey to Harare, Erica took her own life in 2005.

Over a decade after her death, Erica was still at the front of Chibanda's mind. 'I've lost quite a number of patients through suicide – it's normal,' he says. 'But with Erica, I felt like I didn't do everything that I could.' Soon after her death, Chibanda's plans were flipped on their head. Instead of opening his own private practice – a role that would, to an extent, limit his services to the wealthy and provide ample financial support for his growing family – he founded a project that aimed to provide mental healthcare to the most disadvantaged communities in Harare.

Chibanda's roots are in Mbare, a southern district of Harare. Its low concrete buildings, wooden shacks, and dusty roads buzzing with traffic fail to capture the importance of this place. Even though it is half an hour from the city centre by road,

A Cure for Darkness

Mbare is widely considered to be the heart of Harare. As one waiter working in a barbecue chicken joint puts it: 'If you come to Harare and don't visit Mbare, then you haven't been to Harare.' Mbare has long been a political stronghold for the Movement for Democratic Change (MDC), a party that has fought long and hard, sacrificing tears and lives, against the ruling ZANU-PF party that was led by Robert Mugabe following independence in 1980. Back then, when Zimbabwe was called Southern Rhodesia, Harare was called Salisbury. Mbare, the southern district, was called Harare. As the country would later take this name for its capital (replacing Salisbury in 1982), it was a prescient reminder of the influence this southern district has on its country's future.

Chibanda's grandmother lived here for many years, seeing first hand its passing from Harare into Mbare. Whatever name it has been given, it has attracted people from all over the country to buy or sell groceries, electricals, and retro, often counterfeit, clothing. The line of wooden shacks that make up the daily market is a lifeline for thousands, an opportunity in the face of inescapable adversity.

In May 2005, the ruling ZANU-PF party initiated Operation Murambatsvina, or 'Clear out the Rubbish'. It was a nationwide, military-enforced clamp down on the people whose livelihoods were deemed to be either illegal or informal. An estimated 700,000 people across the country, the majority already in disadvantaged situations, lost their jobs, their homes or both. Over 83,000 children under the age of four were directly affected. Those places where resistance might have emerged, such as the MDC's stronghold of Mbare, were hit the hardest. The destruction also took its toll on people's mental health. With unemployment, homelessness, and hunger taking hold, depression found a place to germinate, like weeds among the rubble. And with fewer resources to deal with the consequences of the destruction, people were wrapped up in a vicious cycle of poverty and mental illness.

Chibanda was among the first people to measure the psychological toll of Operation Murambatsvina. After surveying 12 health clinics in Harare, he found that over 40 per cent of people scored highly on psychiatric health questionnaires, a large majority of whom met the clinical threshold for depression. Chibanda presented these findings at a meeting with people from the Ministry of Health and Child Care and the University of Zimbabwe. 'It was then decided that something needed to be done,' Chibanda says. 'And everyone sort of agreed. But no one knew what we could do.' There was no money for mental-health services in Mbare. There was no option to bring therapists in from abroad. And the nurses already there were far too busy dealing with infectious diseases, including cholera, tuberculosis, and HIV. Whatever the solution – if one actually existed – it had to be founded on the scant resources the country already had.

Chibanda returned to the Mbare clinic. This time, it was to meet his new colleagues: a group of 14 elderly women. In their roles as community health workers, grandmothers have been working for health clinics across Zimbabwe since the 1980s. Their work is as diverse as the thousands of families they visit, and includes supporting people with infectious diseases, teaching people how to dig latrines, and providing community health education. 'They are the custodians of health,' says Nigel James, the health promotion officer at the Mbare clinic. 'These women are highly respected. So much so that if we try to do anything without them, it is bound to fail.'

In 2006, they were asked to add depression to their list of responsibilities. Could they provide basic psychological therapies for the people of Mbare? Chibanda was sceptical. 'Initially, I thought, how could this possibly work, with these grandmothers?' he says. 'They are not educated. I was thinking, in a very Western, biomedical kind of sense: you need psychologists, you need psychiatrists.' This view was, and still is, common. But Chibanda soon discovered what a resource the grandmothers were. Not only were they trusted members of the community, people who rarely left their local district of Harare, but they could also translate medical terms into everyday words that would resonate culturally. With the buildings of the clinic already full of patients with infectious diseases, Chibanda and the grandmothers decided that a wooden bench, built by local craftsmen, would provide a suitable platform for their new project. Placed under the dappled shade of a tree, the locals could sit and talk at any time of day.

At first, Chibanda called it the 'Mental Health Bench'. The grandmothers told him that this sounded overly medicalised and were worried that no one would want to sit on such a bench. They were right – no one did. Through their discussions, Chibanda and the grandmothers came up with another name: Chigaro Chekupanamazano, or, as it became known, the 'Friendship Bench'. Its beauty was in its simplicity. There was no need for a formal appointment. There were no doctors or medical prescriptions. But, like the surrounding district of Mbare, the Friendship Bench was greater than the sum of its parts. This group of grandmothers, their bench, and the words that they use to express and soothe distress would soon be at the forefront of a global revolution in how we treat depression, one that would reach out from southern Harare into the towering cityscapes of New York and London. It was the Western world learning from sub-Saharan Africa, a reversal of damaging colonialist practices.

This inversion of history had been foreseen. 'Scientific knowledge tends to travel more easily from the developed world to the developing world,' wrote Ricardo Araya, a psychiatrist from King's College London, while working in Santiago, Chile. 'However, it is possible that something could be learned from studies using simple interventions with intensively trained personnel.'

Late in 2009, Melanie Abas was working at King's College London when she received a call. 'You don't know me,' she remembers a man saying. He told her he'd been using her work in Mbare and that it seemed to be working. Dixon Chibanda summarised his project, his team of 14 grandmothers, and their use of the seven-step plan for depression at three health clinics. To identify people who might benefit from this project, Chibanda used the work of Vikram Patel, who, also working in Harare in the mid 1990s, adopted the local idioms of distress to create a screening tool for depression and other common mental disorders. He called it the Shona Symptom Questionnaire, or SSQ-14. It was a mixture of the local and the universal, of *kufungisisa* and depression. As with the PHQ-9 used in English-speaking countries, it was incredibly straightforward. With just a pen and paper, patients answer 14 questions and their health worker determines if they are in need of psychological treatment. In the last week, have they been thinking too much? Have they thought of killing themselves? If someone answered 'yes' to eight or more of the questions, they were considered to be in need of psychiatric help. Fewer than eight and they weren't.

Patel acknowledges that this is an arbitrary cut-off point. It makes the best of a bad situation. In a country with few health services, the SSQ-14 is a quick and cost-effective way to allocate scant resources. Once patients were identified, Chibanda and his grandmothers could then lead them through the seven-step plan that Abas had developed in the 1990s. With its strong focus on social relationships and enforcing support networks, it was well-suited to the local area, a place where disputes over money and domestic violence are found in abundance. As with inter-personal therapy, patients are guided towards their own solutions.

Although the results were promising – in 320 patients, there was a significant reduction in depressive symptoms after three or more sessions on the bench – Chibanda was still apprehensive about telling Abas. He thought his data wasn't good enough for publication. Each patient had only received six sessions on the bench and there was no follow-up. What if they just relapsed a month after the trial? And there was no control group, an essential counterbalance to rule out whether a patient was just benefitting from meeting with a trusted health worker and spending time away from their problems.

Abas hadn't visited Zimbabwe since 1999 but still felt a deep connection to the country where she had lived and worked for two and a half years. She was thrilled to hear that her work had continued after she left. Straight away, she decided to help.

Chibanda travelled to London to meet Abas in 2010. She introduced him to people working on the Improving Access to Psychological Therapies (IAPT) programme at the Maudsley Hospital, a nationwide project that had started a couple of years earlier. Abas, meanwhile, pored over the data Chibanda had sent her. Together with Ricardo Araya, a colleague at King's College London, she found it to be worthy of publication. In October 2011, the first study from the Friendship Bench was published. The next step was to fill in the gaps – adding a follow-up and including a control group. Together with his colleagues from the University of Zimbabwe, Chibanda applied for funding to conduct a randomised-controlled trial, one that would split patients across Harare into two groups. One would meet with the grandmothers and receive a form of therapy that would help patients develop their own solutions to whatever social problems they brought to the bench. This was called problem-solving therapy, a descendent of CBT that aims to reduce depressive symptoms by guiding patients through potential solutions to any difficulties in their life.

One of the major life events that can be tied to the onset of depression is domestic violence. 'We have an epidemic of that,' Chibanda says. 'A lot of these women are in abusive relationships because they have absolutely nothing. They depend on this man for everything – literally everything.' From the beginning, therefore, it made sense for the grandmothers to help their clients earn some money of their own. Some asked relatives for a small kickstarter to buy and sell their chosen wares. Others crocheted handbags, known as Zee Bags, from colourful strips of recycled plastic (originally an idea from Chibanda's actual grandmother). With greater independence, the grandmothers found that marital disputes and domestic violence decreased. As Juliet Kusikwenyu, one of the grandmothers in Mbare, says, 'Clients normally come back and report that, "Ah, I actually have some capital now. I've even been able to pay school fees for my child. No longer are we fighting about money."'

Other problems are harder to solve. Tanya, a 42-year-old woman living in eastern Harare with her husband and two children, was diagnosed as HIV-positive in 1994 at the height of the epidemic. At this time, antiretroviral drugs were in short supply. HIV was seen as a demonic curse rather than an infectious disease. But the most pressing problem for Tanya was that her husband was found to be free of HIV. After his blood tests came back negative, he was convinced that she had been unfaithful and had caught this sexually transmitted disease from another man. Tanya was thrown out of her house, separated from her children, and began to think that her HIV status made her guilty, promiscuous, unworthy of life.

Serodiscordant relationships – in which one partner is HIV-positive and the other isn't – are quite common. It can be a result of having sex with someone who has HIV. But that isn't the only explanation. Blood transfusions can transfer the virus from one person to another. Sharing needles to inject drugs is another common pathway. There is also the possibility that the infection was present before the relationship and lay dormant for a decade or more. In this scenario, the virus might not have passed on to the partner by chance, or because they have a natural resistance to that strain of the virus. Tanya swore that she was faithful to her husband, but nothing would change his mind. She was never allowed back into the home they once shared.

Tanya spent years on the streets begging for food and money, and thinking about what happened to her over and over again. She felt trapped by her own thoughts. How were her children? When would this virus kill her? How was she HIV-positive when her husband wasn't? When she wasn't sleeping rough, Tanya spent time in a mental institution. With beds and drugs in short supply, she was soon forced out, just as she had been evicted from her own home. The church was not an option, either. Being HIV-positive was seen as the mark of the Devil or a punishment from God. Was she being punished for a sin she didn't think she had committed? Tanya became delusional. She was convinced that she had to kill herself and her two children, saving them from this cruel world. Nothing made more sense.

One day she walked into her local health clinic, the place where she collected her HIV medication, and heard about a new project that was available for people who were thinking too much. It was a form of talking therapy that was outside of the clinic walls, completely confidential, and unrelated to the church. After years of toil and suicidal thoughts, she sat down next to an elderly woman wearing brown overalls and started to talk. She learnt that HIV was nothing to be ashamed of; that *kufungisisa* is normal, especially for people with an infectious disease. But it doesn't have to make you feel miserable. Over the coming weeks and months, Tanya got back in touch with some family members and was reunited with her children. Although her husband's views were unchanged, Tanya held her head up high. At a 'holding hands together' meeting in 2018 in Harare, her eyes shaded by a wide-brimmed hat with the logo 'Ending HIV' on the front, she told a small gathering of Friendship Bench patients that she was HIV-positive, had *kufungisisa*, and was alive.

In 2016, a decade after Operation Murambatsvina had cleared out much of Mbare, Chibanda, Abas, Araya, and their colleagues published the results from the multi-centre clinical trial, incorporating 521 people from across Harare. Roughly half of this sample sat on the Friendship Bench and spoke to the grandmothers. The other half met with doctors or health workers, receiving support but no problem-solving therapy. Although they averaged the same score of depression on Patel's SSQ-14 before treatment, only the group from the Friendship Bench showed a significant decrease in symptoms, falling well below the threshold of depression. When tested against the gold-standard of medical science (the randomised placebo-controlled clinical trial), Chibanda and his group of grandmothers had passed with flying colours. 'They didn't have an intervention for depression before, so this was completely new in primary healthcare,' says Tarisai Bere, a clinical psychologist who trained 150 grandmothers across ten clinics. 'I didn't think they would understand it the way they did. They surprised me in so many ways ... They are superstars.'

Rudo Chinhoyi, a grandmother with faded roses on her bandana, says that she carries her printed manual – the screening tools and the therapy – in her brown canvas bag everywhere she goes. Anyone might need her services, not just the people who visit local health clinics. 'The Friendship Bench has become imaginary,' she says.

'I Live and Breathe Peer'

When she was a student at the New York Institute of Technology, Helen Skipper discovered the extracurricular activities that took place beneath the glitzy skyscrapers of Manhattan. Skipper had an analytical mind and an obsessive appetite for new information, but she suffered from a crushing side effect of boredom. Nothing could satisfy her craving for long. Textbooks for an entire semester were read – and understood – in an evening. Playing the class clown soon got old. Comic books were repetitive. After her first toke on a crack pipe, however, she felt like she had found what she had always been looking for. Her boredom dissipated in an instant. College seemed so mundane, meaningless, in comparison. Pleasure, success, friends, and life itself: it could all be bought for a few dollars a day.

Skipper was quickly pulled into the 1980s crack-cocaine epidemic. While the wealthy sniffed expensive lines of cocaine in the tower blocks above, those people living in lower-income neighbourhoods, often African American or Hispanic, were more likely to be addicted to crack. The punishment for mere possession of the latter was severe, a political sleight of hand that allowed presidents such as Richard Nixon and Ronald Reagan to punish people of colour, lock them up in prison, and take away their housing, employment, and suffrage. The local devastation of this so-called 'Crack Era' would later be compared to the aftermath of war or an economic depression. 'The subcultural behaviors associated with crack use also led to much interpersonal violence,

287

duplicity in relationships, increased prostitution, child neglect and abuse, and family dissolution,' wrote Eloise Dunlap, a sociologist from the University of California, Berkeley, in 2006. 'Crack users placed a heavy burden on families ... extended kin, and community members who sought to support these persons. Crack users also greatly disappointed their offspring who might otherwise have depended upon them, thereby placing additional burdens on family, kin, and community.'

Skipper, who was raised in a middle-class African American household, was first arrested when she was 17 years old. She would spend the next 20 years trapped in a cycle of imprisonment, rehab, homelessness, and crack cocaine. It was the drug that offered her work, money, and friendship. It was the New York State judiciary system that failed to help her get off the streets.

Years passed her by. Her mother kicked her out of the family home, a refuge with three bedrooms upstairs and two cars on the drive. Skipper gave birth to two sons but barely saw them. She missed their lives as they unfolded without her. There were no first steps, no first words. Separated from her family, ousted from her home, there was no one in the world to talk to but herself.

Skipper inherited a deep mistrust of professionals. The police. Lawyers and judges. People with 'MD' after their name. 'We never wanted to see a doctor, much less a therapist, or a psychiatrist, or a psychologist, or anything like that,' Skipper says. 'It's multigenerational. You know, like Grandma never went for help, and Grandma was sitting in the attic talking to herself at the time, and then my dad, he used to go into the backyard and talk to himself ... Me, I'm in the closet talking to myself. We all do it, it's normal.' The compulsory stints in rehab facilities that followed her imprisonment only stopped her from taking drugs. It didn't do anything to ameliorate her craving for crack, her psychological need for satisfaction and pain relief.

When all else seemed lost, she still had her smarts. After her stints in prison, she would write a résumé and land a menial admin job at one of New York's many financial institutions. She worked at Chase Bank. She made it onto Wall Street. When she had earned enough money, it was a smooth slide back into old habits, like putting on some comfy slippers. She smoked, sold, and delivered crack cocaine up and down the Upper West Side. When she inevitably lost her job, she begged for money. 'If you're working that area, you know you don't say anything to the black people because they won't give you anything,' she says. White tourists with cash, their eyes trans-fixed by the bright lights and advertising boards, were her prime targets.

Over two decades, Skipper slept on rooftops, in homeless shelters, and in mental institutions. Diagnosed with schizoaf-fective disorder, a dizzying mix of schizophrenia and depression that she thought were 'just pretty words', she was given pills that made her passive and groggy, nothing like the crack she was used to. One day, she watched a fellow inpatient sit in the corner of the room with his tongue lolling out, a living picture of suppression and enforced passivity. It was then that she decided enough was enough. 'I didn't want that for me, and I don't care how much you say it helps me,' she says. 'You're not going to do me like that.'

In her 40s, she reached out to a therapist as part of a drug- and mental-health rehabilitation programme. She told the therapist that she didn't want to be on medication for the rest of her life. She didn't want to continually relapse back into addiction. She wanted a life free of drugs, both medical and recreational. 'As luck would have it, I had a good therapist,' Skipper says, 'someone who really talked to me like she really *got* me. By talking to her and doing what I'm supposed to be doing with the rest of my life – like addressing my drug addiction, repairing the damage I did to my family, building up myself, my psyche, my self-esteem – I was finally able to come off it.' For those sleepless nights, she took sleeping pills to ease her racing mind but, on the whole, she was free of chemical dependency. Off the streets, out of jail, with no threat of institutionalisation, she decided to help others as her therapist had helped her. Hired by the the New York City Department of Health and Mental Hygiene (DOHMH) in 2007, she became a 'peer', someone who can reach into underserved areas of the city and talk to people about their problems. Skipper had no medical degrees or psychiatric qualifications of any kind. She was as far removed from the health system as one can get. But what she had was 'lived experience'. 'I've been in every situation, so there's not a lot that I cannot talk about from personal experiences,' she says. Addiction, severe mental illness, homelessness, unemployment, dropping out of education, she has been there and done it all. 'Basically,' Skipper says, 'I live and breathe peer.'

In 2017, Skipper, in her early 50s with short tan-coloured dreadlocks, half-rim glasses and a voice that quavers with the ups and downs of the past, applied for a new programme as part of the DOHMH. It was called Friendship Benches, and they needed a peer supervisor, someone to advise and train other peers across New York in mental healthcare for the community. Her application was a textbook example of what other people might try and hide from potential employers.

A criminal record. Mental-health problems. Institutionalisation. Drug addiction. But, for this particular role, they were requirements for the job. A doctor requires years of education, exams, training, and rotation. A peer supervisor needs to have lived in the underbelly of New York City as if it were a second home.

Skipper got the job, becoming the only peer supervisor at the DOHMH. By this time, she had been clean for over a decade and hadn't taken any medication for seven years. Her eldest son had a child of his own. Although Skipper was still estranged from her family, she was, by definition, a grandmother. Like the community health workers in Harare, she was a respected elder of the community, someone who broke down the barriers between clinical psychiatry and the people who might benefit from its care the most. As with *kufungisisa* in Zimbabwe, the Friendship Benches of New York City had to be made culturally appropriate. The benches were made out of bright orange plastic and looked like giant Lego bricks. Peers were trained to advise people on opioids such as heroin or fentanyl, drugs that, like crack cocaine, were fuelling an epidemic of addiction and overdoses across the United States. Often with lived experience themselves, Skipper's peers often knew where the best rehab centres were and were walking examples of recovery.

Move a few miles away from the manicured gardens of Central Park, and the unmistakable calling cards of drugs like heroin and fentanyl blend in with the yellow cabs and traffic lights. Empty needles litter the floor. Fast-food joints have their own security guards on the doorstep. Huge billboards advertise naloxone, an injectable drug that can reverse the effects of opioids in the event of overdose. 'People come to New York and they don't see this; they see the flashy lights,' says Beth Rodriguez, the coordinator of New York's Friendship

Benches, as she drives from East Harlem up into the low-income neighbourhoods of the Bronx, a borough that has the highest rate of lethal overdoses in the country (34.1 per 100,000 residents). 'This is darkness.'

Helen Skipper's ups and downs aren't uncommon experiences for people across the United States. An estimated one in ten people with disorders such as schizophrenia, depression, or bipolar disorder encounter the police before a psychiatrist or therapist. Imprisonment has, in part, replaced institutionalisation. Care homes have become the latest mental hospitals for chronically ill elderly persons, those with depressions that were once called involutional melancholia. As the number of psychiatric beds in American mental hospitals declined from 558,922 in 1955 to 159,405 in 1977 (largely as a result of the mass rollout of prescription drugs), community health services were stretched to breaking point, leaving those who might require long-term care on the streets, forced into crime and at risk of imprisonment. A classic study from a Los Angeles County Jail in 1983 found that out of those inmates with psychiatric disorders 'only 14 per cent were receiving mental health treatment (primarily medications only) at the time of arrest, and only 25 per cent altogether had ever received any form of outpatient mental health treatment at any time in their lives'.

Peers are just one way of filling this gap. Skipper doesn't use a diagnosis or medical reports in her work. Depression is just one of the many problems that she sees every day, from drug abuse to unemployment. 'Our discussion might not have anything to do with mental health,' she says. 'But it could well be about something that, if left unchecked, will lead to poor mental health. We don't discriminate; we don't say, okay, come back and see us when you have a mental illness. We want to stop it before it gets hold of you.'

'If we've gotta sit on the curb and have a conversation with you, we'll do that,' she adds. 'Because of my history I'm not afraid to go into a shooting den or something like that to talk to someone. I'm not afraid of that. I've been there. I've done that.'

In January 2018, Dixon Chibanda travelled from the summer of Harare into a freezing East Coast winter. He met with his new colleagues and the First Lady of New York City, Chirlane McCray. He was blown away by the support from New York's mayor Bill de Blasio, the number of people the project had reached (over 40,000), and by Skipper and her team. But it wasn't to last. In 2019, Friendship Benches in New York hired a clinical director who tried to medicalise peer support. Skipper felt so disheartened that she nearly left her profession altogether. Instead, she saw this disappointment as an opportunity. She returned to college, studying for a degree in criminal justice with minors in psychology and sociology.

As was the case 40 years ago at school, her grades weren't an issue (Skipper achieved 3.9 out of 4 on her grade point average, or GPA). The major challenge was finding the time to pack in all her ideas and interests. After her freshman year, she applied for a new job at the Criminal Justice Agency (CJA) as peer coordinator. After nearly leaving peer support she decided to use her lived experience to add a third tier to peer training: criminal justice. Currently, there are only two certifications for peers in New York: mental health and substance abuse. 'My job is to take elements of both those certifications and apply them to criminal justice,' Skipper says. 'I had complete control of the program from hiring to formulating policy and procedure.' Six months after she started, Skipper was given a raise and a budget to hire 12 peers. 'I am now the Manager of Peer Services at CJA and I do this job with the lens of creating spaces for those of us with lived experiences in an agency that is reforming the criminal justice system in New York. Not only that—I am completely validated in my role. The agency fully understands and sees the importance of peer support.' With training in mental health, substance abuse, and criminal justice, Skipper is creating a community of care that, crucially, is becoming culturally relevant to New York City. Mental healthcare in the United States needs to be culturally relevant. It needs to encompass the epidemics of drug addiction from crack cocaine in the 1980s to opioids today. It must educate people who are affected by a legal system that targets black Americans and inner-city neighbourhoods and strips away basic rights such as suffrage, affordable housing and employment. It must, in other words, channel Helen Skipper, a former drug addict, prison inmate, inpatient, and homeless person who is beginning to reshape New York City from the ground up.

PART FOUR

The Universe Within

'Depression is emotional pain without context.'

Helen Mayberg

'Many forms of insanity are unquestionably the external manifestations of the effects upon the brain substance of poisons
fermented within the body...'

Johann Ludwig Wilhelm Thudichum (1884)

'...either LSD is the most phenomenal drug ever introduced
into treatment in psychiatry, or else the results were evaluated
by criteria imposed by enthusiastic, if not positively prejudiced
people.'

Louis Jolyon West

It Feels Like Spring

On 23 May 2003, Helen Mayberg watched as a thin wire was guided into the middle of her patient's brain. Pushed through a guide tube, it reminded her of a cooked piece of spaghetti. At its end was an electrode composed of four rounded contacts that looked like the metallic ends of a battery. Each just over a millimetre in diameter, they were arranged vertically, like traffic lights, with tiny spaces in between. It was delicate work, requiring steady hands and years of medical experience. Although the neurosurgeon, Andres Lozano, was highly skilled and had performed this procedure many times before on patients with various movement disorders such as Parkinson's, Mayberg, a neurologist raised in California and an unmistakable maverick of her profession, was nervous. What if something went wrong? Even with thousands of successful operations in the past, the surgeon's experience, and the knowledge that the wire could just as easily be taken out as put in, an accident was always possible.

Lozano wasn't blind during this operation. After studying the brains of people with depression since the 1980s, Mayberg told him exactly where to put the electrode. Unlike antidepressants that were discovered by chance in a sanatorium for people with tuberculosis, this was a test of a hypothesis, a trial that asked a specific question – does this part of the brain control depression? – and sought to answer whether critically ill patients got better or worse.

Once everything was in position, the lowest of the four contacts was switched on, creating a gentle buzz of five milliamps into the surrounding tissue. Nothing. It was switched off. What about the next one up, second from the bottom? Still nothing. After the third contact was switched on, however, the patient asked, 'What are you doing?'

'Why do you ask?' Mayberg said.

'I suddenly feel relaxed.' Trying to further describe the feeling, she struggled to come up with a suitable metaphor.

'It's like the difference between a laugh and a smile,' she said.

Okay ... What the hell does that mean? Mayberg thought to herself. She watched as her patient tried to explain emotions that she obviously hadn't felt in a long time. 'She's struggling, it's clearly profound,' Mayberg recalls. 'She's getting kind of pissed off. We aren't understanding what she is trying to describe.'

Then the patient had it. It's like looking out the window in winter and seeing a crocus poking out of the snow, she said. 'It feels like spring.'

With a signal to her colleagues, Mayberg switched the electrode off. As though a light had been turned off, the feeling of spring disappeared; the crocus died. Perhaps it was nothing.

This patient was one of six people with depression to receive deep brain stimulation (DBS) between 2003 and 2004. In case reports, they were all classed as 'treatment-resistant'. Their depression seemed intractable. A diversity of drugs – antidepressants, antipsychotics, tranquillisers, mood stabilisers – couldn't budge their mental anguish. Psychotherapy had been a disappointment. For five out of six patients, even ECT had failed. On social benefits, living between the home and the hospital, these were some of the sickest people seen by a psychiatrist. 'These people are morbidly ill,' Mayberg says, 'and the goal was to help them.'

Although she studies psychiatric patients, Mayberg isn't a psychiatrist. She trained in neurology, a medical specialty that focuses on diseases of the brain and spinal cord. 'Psychiatry is interesting to a neurologist, but their language is just ridiculous,' she says. 'Strict classifications like major depressive disorder work pragmatically but don't make much sense biologically.' Despite there being general agreement among researchers and clinicians that depression has a biological basis that involves the brain, there are no definitive biological markers to identify such a diagnosis. From a young age, Mayberg pined for acuity, precision, something to anchor a messy field of classification into its discrete parts. Growing up in California, her father was a physician and her uncle, who she greatly admired, was a biochemist and nuclear medicine physician. Mayberg would take elements from all of these disciplines – chemistry, nuclear science, medicine – to understand the biological diversity of depression. Instead of opening up the skull and slicing through the brain as a neurosurgeon, she turned to the burgeoning field of brain scanning. After training in neurology in New York, she moved to Johns Hopkins University in Baltimore to study positron emission tomography (PET) scanning, a method that used radioactive tracers to visualise molecules of interest as they moved and settled within the receptors of the brain. It was nuclear science (radioactive particles) meeting neurosurgery (seeing inside the brain), but without the explosive or bloody manifestations of either.

Parkinson's, Huntington's, stroke: Mayberg studied various neurological disorders in the late 1980s and 1990s as she moved from Baltimore in Maryland to south-central Texas. She found that these neurological diseases, interesting in their own right, often came with depression. She was hooked by the opportunity to understand this mental disorder as a facet of other, well-studied diseases. Movement disorders and stroke had been mapped to regions of the brain and understood in significant detail. There were regular patterns in activity and atrophy. By comparing those who had depression to those who hadn't, patients with these diseases were the perfect blueprint to understand how depression reshapes and distorts the brain. 'I like controlling as many variables as possible,' Mayberg says. By studying the brains of well-known neurological diseases, she adds, 'we can match patients who are alike in all aspects of their illness except for being depressed or not.' To her, stroke, Parkinson's, and Huntington's were anchors to which she could test her burgeoning theory of how depression takes control of the brain, regardless of the cause.

Depression is often associated with other diseases. When it tags along with something like cancer or cardiovascular disease, it is termed 'secondary depression', a mental consequence of an underlying (primary) disease. Take Huntington's disease. Roughly 40 per cent of patients with this degenerative disorder show the hallmarks of depression, which often precede the more typical symptoms of speech impediments, muscle twitching, and paralysis. Depression can be the first indicator of the disease's trajectory. This association has been noted for as long as Huntington's has had a name in medical science; in 1872, George Huntington, the discoverer of this disease, wrote, 'the tendency to insanity and sometimes to that form of insanity which leads to suicide is marked'.

Although secondary, these depressions still respond to antidepressants, ECT, and psychotherapy. They aren't inevitable ramifications of a body in decline. 'In the last 30 years or so, depression in its various forms has come to be recognised as not an acceptable or normal part of growing old,' says Charles Reynolds, a professor of geriatric psychiatry at the University of Pittsburgh.

From her early research into depression in patients with neurological diseases, Mayberg found a surprisingly regular pattern of brain activity. Wherever she looked, whether it was stroke, Huntington's, or Parkinson's disease, there was a biological blueprint that separated people who had depression from those who did not. Depression came with a significant reduction in activity of the frontal cortex (specifically the prelimbic frontal and temporal cortex), the part of the brain that folds around the more central regions like the fingers of a clenched fist. Mayberg's later move from PET scans to fMRI (from radioactive tracers to powerful magnets), found similar patterns in activity, each pixelated blob in the front of the brain visualised in a cool blue colour, a sign of decrease in blood flow. Then she looked at the brains of patients with primary depression, people who didn't suffer from neurological disorders, and found exactly the same thing. The same blue dots in the prelimbic frontal and temporal cortex appeared from her datasets. As Lozano, Mayberg's neurosurgeon colleague, would later say, these brain regions were literal markers of 'the blues'.

What was going on? Why were these parts of the frontal cortex – previously linked to rational thought, attention, and decision-making – showing up as blue in their scans? Why were they hypoactive (the opposite of hyperactive)? The answer, Mayberg proposed, was to be found in a region of high activity toward the centre of the brain, a blob of tissue that sat in the middle of the curled fingers of the frontal lobes. This was Brodmann's area 25, an nexus of the brain that modulates memory, mood, appetite and sleep, and the future target of her DBS trials. Showing up as red (for increased blood flow or glucose metabolism) in these early brain scans, area 25 was a scream of activity that, she thought, caused other regions of the brain to shut down. Just as a booming voice might dominate a debate, not allowing the quieter, and perhaps more rational, views to be heard, was this part of the brain leading the whole system to break down from within?

This idea closely matched the reports from the depressed patients in her brain scanning studies. They often complained of feeling trapped within themselves, unable to reach out to others, deprived of any feeling of connection with those people closest to them – even their own children.

In 1999, Mayberg published one of her most famous studies in the *American Journal of Psychiatry*. It was a short paper, only six and a half pages long and with two figures of blurry brain scans, providing a concise insight into area 25 and how everyone – not only those who are depressed – can experience its fury. When asked to think about an extremely sad experience from their past, area 25 lit up like a beacon in the centre of the healthy volunteers' brains while parts of the frontal cortex switched off. When they stopped thinking about his sad experience, the brain returned to its previous state. Area 25 quietened. The frontal cortex jumped back to the fore. In people with depression, however, this same pattern was only achieved with antidepressant treatment. Perhaps, Mayberg reasoned, people who were depressed were stuck, they couldn't switch off this 'sadness centre'. It just kept firing, and firing, and firing. With such a constant barrage of painful signals, the circuitry within the brain starts to take on a different shape. Pieces start to malfunction. Parts of the cortex are silenced and pushed out of practice. Even after slight disappointments, full-blown depression becomes the norm. The brain settles into a disordered state that medication can often help disentangle.

This was the idea anyway, a theory that went beyond the influence of monoamines such as serotonin. Depression was a dysfunction in the circuitry of the brain, the neurological highways that carry the traffic of signals from one region of the brain to another. Mayberg was particularly interested in the limbic system – of which area 25 was a key component – that connects regions of the frontal cortex involved in motivation, drive, and rational thought with those more central parts of the brain that are crucial to memory and emotional regulation. Through the 'sadness centre', could this circuitry be recalibrated or rewired?

With a bob of brown hair and thick-framed glasses, Mayberg is unapologetically straight-talking. She speaks rapidly and often jumps from one topic to another as if her words are chasing thoughts through her brain's networks. 'I talk too much,' she admits. 'I like action.' In the same breath she adds how she tried her hand at neurosurgery as a student but found herself unsuited to its demands. 'I probably had the hands. I didn't have the patience.' When discussing her career in neurology and nuclear imaging, fields dominated by men, she says that she didn't feel any issue or discrimination over her sex. 'When people got blocked or undermined, I always considered it the competition of science. It's not a gentlemanly sport,' she says. 'Even when only men are involved. It's high stakes and low money. All you have is ego and data. And good ideas are not common. I was brought up to stay out of trouble, be sincere, and fight for what's yours, but work twice as hard as everybody else and take half the credit if it gets you where you want. I'm accustomed to unfairness. As Dad always told me: what made you think that life was fair?'

After studying in Baltimore and Texas, Mayberg packed up her things in 1999 and moved to Toronto in Canada, a bustling city with, at the time, the tallest building in the world – the CN Tower – at its centre. Here, she would eventually meet the treatment-resistant patients for the first DBS trial. She was also introduced to patients who contradicted all her previous work. Similarly depressed and in need of treatment, their brain scans revealed the reverse of what she had thought to be the common blueprint of depression. Parts of their frontal cortex were overactive, seething with red blobs where, she thought, there should only be blue. Their area 25 was quiet – hypoactive and not hyperactive. It was as if the brain scans she was accustomed to had been reversed by image-editing software. This was Mayberg's first hint of an exciting project that would run parallel to her trials in DBS: are there distinct forms of depression? If so, might this explain why some people respond to certain treatments while others don't? Might biological markers from brain scans be used to guide treatment?

For as long as there have been antidepressants and evidence-based psychotherapies, they have largely been handed out through trial and error. Often, the only metric used to evaluate whether a patient was prescribed an antidepressant was the number of 'endogenous' or 'atypical' features that they showed. Would they benefit from imipramine or a MAO inhibitor? But Mayberg's patients in Toronto provided another window into the diversity of depression. Although their brains were showing different blueprints of activity, their symptom profiles were of similar severity to those she had seen in Texas. They were no less depressed. But, as shown in trials that began in Toronto and continued in 2005 when she moved to Emory University in Atlanta, they responded to CBT far better than they did to antidepressants. With therapy, their overactive frontal cortex quietened – the reverse of medication. This, Mayberg, along with Boadie Dunlop, Edward Craighead, and her PhD student Callie McGrath, wrote in 2014, was a 'psychotherapy-responsive' form of depression.

The other kind of depression – the one with reduced activity in the frontal cortex, area 25 screaming in a flash of red pixels – is a little less straightforward to define. While some patients in this group responded well to antidepressants, there were some who didn't. They weren't the embodiment of an 'antidepressant-responsive' depression. Mayberg and her colleagues had seen this pattern before, however. It was the same brain type of those patients with treatment-resistant depression who were put forward for DBS. This begged the question of whether it was a more stubborn form of depression, one that required a more aggressive approach to treatment. In such medication and psychotherapy-resistant patients, one of the oldest treatments for depression can be used with remarkable effects. For severe depression that often comes with delusions, ECT is still the most effective treatment available. Over 80 years since it was invented in Rome, it is also now one of the safest procedures in all of medicine.

Rebirth

In a brightly lit operating suite in Brooklyn, New York, Alice lies on a padded gurney, feeling very anxious. As requested, the computer monitors that display her blood pressure, heart rate, and oxygen levels have been silenced. If they weren't, the incessant beeping that they make – and her body's rhythms that they monitor – would only add to her nervousness. The silence in the room is broken only by the chit-chat with the lead nurse and a routine set of questions that Alice answers quietly and without hesitation. What's your name? Date of birth? And what procedure are you having today? 'ECT,' Alice says.

She is then told that she will feel a cool sensation, as if her circulatory system is being fed by icy glacial streams, due to the anaesthetic that is administered through a cannula in her right arm. Alice falls into a deep sleep within seconds. She doesn't respond to any more questions. Since she recently had hip surgery, the anaesthesiologist increases Alice's dose of sux, the muscle relaxant that is kept cool in a small fridge in the corner of the room. Her eyebrows and facial muscles twitch as the drug starts to take effect. The anaesthesiologist switches her monitor's sound back on.

As the regular beeping returns to the room, the most important number on the anaesthesiologist's screen is the concentration of oxygen in Alice's blood. Recorded by a peg-like instrument attached to her index finger and displayed in bright blue numbers, it hovers around 98 per cent and is kept near to 100% throughout the procedure. Early practitioners of electroshock therapy didn't always use artificial respiration and cellular damage could occur as the brain was deprived of oxygen. In 2018, however, the year that ECT turned 80 years old, Alice doesn't have to worry about this. Her anaesthesiologist is equipped with an artificial respirator (a plastic rugby-ball-shaped instrument that connects to an oxygen mask) that she squeezes and expands throughout the session. 'It's my job to keep the patient breathing,' she says. Since all muscle relaxants stop the diaphragm from moving, artificial respiration is a necessity in modern ECT.

When all is ready and the numbers are looking stable, Tricia Papperone, a 30-year-old psychiatric resident, pushes the red button on the front of the ECT machine with her thumb. The word 'TREAT' flashes on the red LED display. It beeps for a few seconds then the room is still and silent but for Alice's regular heart rate. She hardly moves a muscle. But inside her brain, an electrical storm is circulating. Invisible and roughly recorded by scribbles on an EEG, her brain swirls with activity. Her synapses are flooded with neurotransmitters and growth-inducing molecules that, together, trigger cascade after cascade of signals that will continue long after Alice wakes from her sleep and returns to her flat in the Upper West Side of Manhattan. The convulsion is over in less than a minute but has long-lasting effects. Although it is still an active area of research, it is this burst of activity – and perhaps the regrowth of connections in the brain – that is thought to be at the core of ECT's efficacy in depression. Prolonged stress and severe depression are known to prune the brain's delicate wiring. Parts of the brain start to noticeably shrink. ECT is thought to undo this damage. Rather than damaging the brain, as many psychiatrists and activists have argued over the years, modern ECT is more akin to a fertiliser of new connections, a regenerative procedure that can reverse the destructive combination of stress, depression, and time. An alternative theory is that ECT acts as a reset button on regions that are hyperactive in depression, including Mayberg's area 25.

Whatever the true mechanism, Alice is simply happy that she has been given access to this life-saving treatment. (She was shocked to find how vehemently some people stigmatise this treatment and writes a blog to explain how boring and everyday ECT actually is.) Her own depression first arose in her mid teens and resulted in her admission to a mental hospital, an ever-changing pick and mix of pills, and ten years of recurrent depression. Nothing worked. 'I've always been a bit of a difficult case because people could not understand why I wasn't responding to medication,' she says. Alice lost count of how many psychiatrists she saw, how many drugs she has been given. In 2014, just before she turned 35 years old, her latest psychiatrist finally admitted that this 'shotgun' approach wasn't working. She needed a different type of treatment. She needed to meet Dr Kellner.

As of 2018, Charlie Kellner had performed 35,000 sessions of ECT and literally wrote the book on how it should be given and to whom. His first session was in 1978, the year he became a certified doctor in the United States. It was an unpopular and precarious career choice. After the 1960s, ECT had fallen into disrepute. Reports from across the pond were deeply concerning for psychiatrists around the world, and their patients. In the UK, the procedure was performed by untrained medical students in open wards where privacy was impossible. The machines themselves were often outdated and didn't conform to the latest medical safety regulations (some didn't have an automated pulse of electricity and the duration of the shock was dependent on the practitioner's finger). 'If ECT is ever legislated against or falls into disuse it will not be because it is an ineffective or dangerous treatment; it will be because psychiatrists have failed to supervise and monitor its use adequately,' an anonymous letter published in *The Lancet* in 1981 stated. 'It is not ECT which has brought psychiatry into disrepute. Psychiatry has done just that for ECT.' Most worryingly, perhaps, was that ECT was given to people who would never benefit from its effects while suffering from its very real side effects. Short-term memory loss, headaches, and confusion are common risks with this procedure, even today.

A change was badly needed. Like the patients it treated, ECT required a transformation of its own.

From his base at Mount Sinai Hospital in Manhattan, Charlie Kellner has spent his career teaching the next generation of psychiatrists – such as Tricia Papperone – how to do ECT properly. It starts with selecting the right patient. 'For the right kind of illness, [ECT] is almost as specific as penicillin [in the treatment of] Pneumococcal pneumonia,' Kellner says. People with psychosis, mania, catatonia, and even a form of self-harming autism have all been shown to respond to ECT. But severe depression is still the primary indication. Endogenous, delusional, and psychotic are terms still used today but, for Kellner, this disease doesn't require a name. He knows it when he sees it. These people are often suicidal, wake early in the morning, and suffer from a sluggishness that is more often associated with Parkinson's or Huntington's diseases. Their symptoms improve as the day progresses, but the next morning, when they wake at 3am they will be back in the same dangerous position. Their minds are fixated on a single delusion: their bodies are empty; their tissues are rotten; they are dying from a cancer that no doctor can detect.

Psychotic depression might be unfamiliar, even alien, to the general public, but it isn't rare. In 2002, a large survey of 18,980 people living in Europe found that nearly a fifth of people who fit the diagnosis of major depression also fulfilled the criteria for psychotic features. For people over 60 years of age who have been hospitalised with depression, delusions are found in up to a half of all cases. At high risk of suicide, such patients have often failed to respond to lists of medications – both antidepressants and antipsychotics – and feel like they are falling through the gaps, like grains of sand through an upturned hourglass.

Alice responded after the first session, a rare but not unheard-of occurrence. As she woke up from the general anaesthetic, she was met with two familiar faces: Dr Kellner on her left and her mum on her right. Both have been supportive throughout her recovery, remissions, and recurrences of depression. Almost immediately, Alice says, 'I felt like I had some sort of life, and some sort of chance.'

As with any medical treatment, the side effects are sometimes painful and disorientating. Headaches are the most common problem after receiving ECT. Painkillers and coffee are known to help soothe the pain and both are provided in the waiting area of Kellner's clinic. Then there are the memory disturbances. '[They] are very real,' says Alice. 'Anyone would admit that. There are memory problems. What I would say to that is that they do come back.' To help coax them back into her consciousness, Alice has started taking photos of her activities in the days and weeks preceding her appointments. 'I can look at the picture and be like, "Oh yeah! I remember doing that."' Although some people do lose personal moments for ever, Alice's main concern is how long it takes her to remember them.

Once a treatment for anyone and everyone, ECT is now mostly limited to the wealthy and the insured. It costs a lot of money just for an anaesthesiologist. Then there are the nurses, the trained psychiatrist, and the receptionists who organise the busy schedules and follow-up appointments. And then there are the modern machines, sedatives, and sux, which needs to be refrigerated during both transportation and storage. Added up, the price of just one session of ECT varies from $300 to $1,000. But the potential cost of not using ECT is far higher. As it can start to work after the very first treatment, ECT is one of the safest and most effective methods to prevent suicides. It can literally be a life-saver. But it is rarely used as such. People who have not responded to several types of antidepressants, such as Alice, might never be told about ECT. Psychiatrists are still hesitant to offer it, perhaps because they don't know much about it or they can't perform it themselves. 'People are allowed to remain sick for years,' Kellner says, 'and, after 15 to 20 medications, finally they get ECT and they end up saying, "Why didn't anybody tell me about this!"'

The moral argument of using ECT is its ability to make critically ill people better. But there is an economic argument here too. Even with its high up-front cost, the fact that it works, and works quickly, can help people return to their jobs and be more productive when they do. Plus, all those failed medications add up. Why not use something that works in a few weeks rather than throwing different varieties of pills and hoping one sticks? Plus, longitudinal studies show that depression is harder to treat with each successive episode. This makes it even more important to find a treatment that works early in its course.

For people with delusions, ECT should be a first-line treatment, Kellner says. While only 34 per cent of such patients respond to antidepressants, 82 per cent respond to ECT. Even when antidepressants and antipsychotics are combined – along with side effects such as weight gain and Parkinson's-like symptoms such as tremors, muscle stiffness, and sluggish speech and movement – they still don't reach the same efficacy as ECT on its own.

A study from 2018 put clinical outcomes to one side and focused on the economic argument for ECT. Daniel Maixner, Eric Ross, and Kara Zivin at the the University of Michigan in Ann Arbor found that ECT became cost-effective after two failed medications for severe depression. 'Two failed medication trials, not 22,' Kellner says. 'We should get away from this "last resort" business.'

Morally, economically, and scientifically, ECT shouldn't be pushed into the fringes of psychiatry. It should be offered to those people who need it. It should be used as part of a standardised regimen of treatment, one that includes regular psychotherapy and antidepressants. Doing otherwise, Kellner says, is tantamount to medical malpractice. Lothar Kalinowsky said exactly the same thing half a century ago. The effectiveness of ECT is the same no matter where in the world it is performed. For psychotic depressions, recoveries in 70 to 95 per cent of patients can be expected. It is one of the most effective treatments in the whole of medicine. And it is also one of the safest. The mortality rate is estimated to be 0.2 to 0.4 per 10,000 patients, a risk no higher than that of the general anaesthetic itself.

Away from sensational Hollywood movies and the misplaced opprobrium of the Church of Scientology, ECT has always had a few vocal advocates of its benefits. In her 1994 memoir *Undercurrents*, the psychiatrist Martha Manning writes that people are so shocked to hear that she received ECT for her depression that they think she must have been abused. 'People say, "You let them do that to you?!" I didn't let them,' she writes, 'I asked them to do it.' In *Shock: The Healing Power of Electroconvulsive Therapy*, Kitty Dukakis wrote, 'Feeling this good is truly amazing given where I am coming from, which is a very dark place that has lasted a very long time. It is not an exaggeration to say that electroconvulsive therapy has opened a new reality for me.' Even in Sylvia Plath's *The Bell Jar*, while the protagonist's first experience with unmodified electro-shock therapy is a horrific one – 'a great jolt drubbed me till I thought my bones would break and the sap fly out of me like a split plant' – the second was given with the correct safety precautions and was effective in treating her depression. 'All the heat and fear purged itself,' the narrator explains, mirroring Plath's experience with ECT in her own life. 'I felt surprisingly at peace.'

Alice, a concert violinist, didn't have the platform of a famous poet or a psychiatrist. She couldn't express her views through a protagonist or count on the support of a publisher. But, in a world where anyone can create a website for free, she did have her blog. Over four years, she wrote about her experience with ECT, how it saved her life, how to manage the side effects, and what she has to say to anyone who wants to ban its use. 'If you consider yourself a "victim",' she wrote in 2018, 'what gives you the right to want it to be BANNED for the many, many people who have benefitted? Are OUR lives less important? That's like the equivalent of wanting open heart surgery banned because your husband happened to die on the table.'

Alice wrote her blog anonymously. Her name and identify-ing details have been changed for this story. One day, however,

she hopes to be able to use her real name. She wants to celebrate her recovery and, she hopes, give other people the
confidence to speak up about their own treatment. It isn't an
experience limited to people who write memoirs or novels.
ECT should be a part of public discourse, like chemotherapy
or surgery. 'Amazingly, the people who claim to have been
harmed are OK with giving THEIR names,' Alice wrote in
November 2018, 'because they are supported by the general
[view] of the public. So WHEN can we give ours?'

Italy, the birthplace of ECT, has nearly banned its use entirely.
It is only employed by a select few psychiatrists and only in the
most life-threatening situations. This decline in popularity has
an explanation outside of medicine. Ugo Cerletti and Lucio
Bini created electroshock therapy at a time when fascism was at
its height in Europe. As with most academics living in Italy and
Germany at the time, neither Cerletti nor Bini spoke out against
the despot that ruled their country. Whether they actively supported Mussolini or not isn't clear, but their creation was still
tainted by the political environment in which it was invented.
Six years later, in 1944, its reputation took an insurmountable
hit when Emil Gelny modified an electroshock machine and
killed at least 149 patients. '[T]he unconscionable misuse of
those treatments in former mental institutions,' a group of
Italian doctors from the University of Naples wrote in 2016,
'still profoundly overshadows the very true nature of today's
psychiatric practice.' Even now, ECT is widely thought to be a
fascist treatment, a barbaric throwback to a time when millions
of people were imprisoned and murdered for their race, religion, gender, or disability. In truth, electroshock therapy was
rarely used in Nazi Germany; eugenics and the prevention of

hereditary diseases – through sterilisation or euthanasia – were more important than treatment. While an electroshock machine was built at Auschwitz in 1944, it was used to 'make emotionally disturbed people fit for work again', and not as a form of punishment. Elsewhere in the country, the public believed that 'psychiatry [was] becoming more and more superfluous since mentally ill people would soon become extinct due to racial hygiene laws,' wrote Ernst Rüdin, Emil Kraepelin's colleague in Munich. Despite the rapid decline in the popularity of eugenics in the twentieth century, electroshock still didn't become a regular form of psychiatric treatment. For decades, it was rarely performed in Germany. And yet neighbouring countries that are similar socially, politically, and culturally became global leaders in ECT research and its clinical practice. The progressive Scandinavian countries have some of the highest utilisation rates of ECT in the world. 'Tiny little Denmark has been a world leader for decades,' Kellner says. The division between one country and another is clear: history and politics – not science – dictates whether this treatment is available for people with depression and other mental disorders. Evidence is weighed down by the baggage of the past.

One of the most common arguments against the use of ECT is that we don't know its long-term impacts. In response to this question, Martin Jørgensen, a psychiatrist from the University of Copenhagen says, 'Well, that's bullshit.' In fact, ECT has some of the best longitudinal studies in psychiatry. Making use of the Danish cohort study, for example, Jørgensen and his colleagues assessed whether there were any differences between people with severe depression who had received ECT and those who hadn't. Over a 20-year period, did they show any notable differences in their health? They did. For patients over 70 years of age, there was a significant decrease in dementia for those who had received ECT compared with those who hadn't. One explanation for this pattern might be that the most severely ill people might also suffer from physical diseases that could make them unsuitable for ECT. But Jørgensen argues that it is exactly these patients that ECT is suitable for. Elderly patients with age-related diseases often can't take antidepressants because they simply don't work, or they interact with their list of other medications. For them, ECT is the safest option.

The most likely explanation to this pattern – better long-term health outcomes in patients who receive ECT – is that the treatment reduces the risk of dementia by successfully ameliorating the depression, a known risk factor for other age-related diseases. '[We know] there is an increased risk of dementia in people with depression,' says Poul Videbech, a psychiatrist-turned-neuroscientist who leads the Center for Neuropsychiatric Depression Research in Glostrup, a town a few miles west of Copenhagen. By removing one disease, another is also halted or significantly delayed. When taken over decades, in other words, ECT actually reduces the chances of significant memory loss.

A tall, stubbled, stylish man in a black roll-neck, Videbech likes to tell the story of another neuroscientist, Gabriele Ende, who investigated whether ECT led to permanent brain damage. As a student at University of California at San Francisco, Ende studied the hippocampus – the brain region devoted to memory – of epileptic patients and found the classic markers of brain damage. A physicist and not a physician, she had never heard of ECT until she moved to the Central Institute of Mental Health in Mannheim, Germany. There, she learnt of its remarkable efficacy in depressions but, given her previous research, hypothesised that it damaged the hippocampus in these patients. 'She did all these very good studies and she had to admit that she couldn't show any signs of damage,' Videbech says. Quite the opposite, in fact: she found very early signs of neural regeneration, possibly neurogenesis – that is, the growth of new connections in the brain. Since her first paper on this topic was published in 2000, Ende's research has been replicated by many others.

In 2019, Videbech and his student Krzysztof Gbyl provided the latest study to investigate the rejuvenating potential of ECT. While other studies had found that the hippocampus – the memory centre of the brain that is often shrunken in people with depression – increased shortly after the ECT treatment, this study found that a similar effect occurred in the frontal cortex, the part of the brain that sits behind the forehead and is associated with the higher functions of emotion, intelligence, and memory retrieval. Importantly, this neural growth was only found in patients who responded to the treatment. Out of 18 patients with endogenous or psychotic depression, 14 responded to ECT treatment. The brain regrowth was not found in the four who didn't respond.

Such studies are small in size and need to be replicated by other research groups. But the story so far is not one of damage. ECT, whether assessed through a brain scanner, animal studies, or blood tests, is a catalyst of regeneration.

Outside of Videbech's office in Glostrup is a scientific poster of their latest research. It shows a scan of Gbyl's own hippocampus from when he volunteered as a healthy, non-depressed model. Gbyl, a clinical psychiatrist who is studying for a PhD in neuroscience, shows it to visitors like a proud father flicking through photos of his children. 'Do you want to see my hippocampus?' he asks. Videbech, in his cool and measured voice, likes to make the joke that, with this brain scan, 'at least we know he has a brain'.

With such evidence for safety as well as efficacy, the rates of ECT are starting to increase in countries such as the United Kingdom, the United States, and even Germany. But there is a long way to go. The stigma surrounding the treatment can make some psychiatrists refuse to prescribe the treatment, even to those who might be most likely to respond. 'Psychiatry has to come back into the medical fold, and ECT has to become a part of the treatment of severe psychiatric illnesses,' Kellner says. 'It's not on the fringe. It's not a religion. I don't believe or not believe in it. It is what it is: demonstrably the most effective treatment for the most severely ill people.'

Even the effects of the best treatments for depression don't last for ever. In the majority of cases, patients require regular check-ups, fine tuning, and repeat prescriptions. It is rare for depression to be a one-off event. It requires constant vigilance and combinations of approaches. Alongside her ECT sessions, Alice continues to take antidepressants and regularly visits her therapist for CBT-based psychotherapy. They aren't in competition with each other. Psychotherapy, drugs, ECT: they are collaborators.

In late 2018, Alice performed at a large concert theatre in midtown Manhattan. Along with the strings, wind, and percussion, Alice's violin is just one sound among many, a soundwave that harmonises the orchestra just as a pulse of electricity helps recalibrate her brainwaves. She has played this gig many times before. But, for Alice, this one was particularly special. Although she couldn't see him among the bright sea of faces, she knew that Dr Kellner was somewhere in the audience. 'For someone who I really consider has saved my life to be there, with his wife, watching me do something that I can do, in part, because of him ... it was just so significant for me,' she says. '[Plus,] there's pretty much nothing cooler than standing on the stage, playing Handel's *Messiah* to a full house.' In three parts, the symphony progresses through the birth, sacrifice, and resurrection of Jesus Christ, a powerful celebration of a miraculous return to life.

The Epitome of Hopelessness

In her lectures, Helen Mayberg uses a quote from the author William Styron to describe what treatment-resistant depression feels like. 'In depression,' Styron wrote in his 1990 memoir *Darkness Visible*, 'faith in deliverance, in ultimate restoration, is absent. The pain is unrelenting, and what makes the condition intolerable is the foreknowledge that no remedy will come – not in a day, an hour, a month, or a minute.' Mayberg reminds her audiences around the world that Styron responded to standard antidepressant therapy, that his own restoration from depression was relatively routine. But imagine if this wasn't the case. Imagine that you've tried over a dozen different forms of antidepressants, suffered years of side effects, and seen countless psychiatrists and therapists, and still this unrelenting, intolerable pain finds no balm. This, Mayberg says, is the epitome of hopelessness, the extreme of depression that can't be captured by lists of symptoms but is the excruciating feeling that there is no help out there no matter where you look.

Although replicated by other laboratories using different methods, Mayberg's brain-based view of depression is still a work in progress. Even though the technology has come on leaps and bounds since she began her research in the 1980s, an MRI scan is still not a direct insight into how the brain works. It uses blood flow as a surrogate for activity rather than measuring the actual firing of neurons, the flow of a complex mix of brain chemicals, which would require a level of technological acuity that no scanner yet possesses. All that said, there is no doubt that her research has brought some much-needed clarity to the treatment of depression. As was the hope for neuroanatomists of the nineteenth century, Mayberg has shown that there are biological markers of depression in the brain. They're not faulty neurons or lesions that can be seen under the microscope. Rather, depression is a disease of brain circuitry, a dysfunction in how interconnected regions communicate with one another and how this dysfunction becomes normalised.

An accurate diagnosis doesn't always require a brain scan, a luxury that few health services or insurance companies would provide for everyone showing signs of depression. In clinical practice, Mayberg sees her work as being implemented after a few basic decisions. If someone is placed on CBT and can be guided into remission, then perhaps that was the correct decision. If they are still depressed, doctors or psychiatrists shouldn't try and push more psychotherapy into their heads in the hope that more equals better. It might be an expensive waste of time. Instead, they should have the option to switch to an antidepressant. The same can be said for a patient that first seeks treatment with medication but after three months doesn't recover. Instead of the usual switch to another antidepressant, the patient might first try a course of CBT. Although depression isn't always a binary set of outcomes, this strategy will increase the number of patients who, within six months of first meeting with a medical professional, will receive the treatment most suited to their illness, their brain type. For those who still show no sign of significant improvement after both classes of treatment, additional medications or other biological treatments might be considered, such as ECT, the newer approaches of transcranial magnetic stimulation and ketamine infusions, or an experimental treatment such as DBS. These are aggressive treatments with established risks that shouldn't be handed out indiscriminately. But for people whose symptoms are both severe and relentless, they can be worth the risk.

In 2019, in a paper from Mayberg's DBS team at Emory University, Andrea Crowell and her colleagues published the long-term outcomes of DBS for treatment-resistant patients. Like the first patient to receive DBS, 28 people with intractable depression had an electrode implanted in their brain, just next to area 25, that was controlled by a pacemaker in the chest. In total, they documented more than eight years of continuous stimulation. While there were untoward (but treatable) incidents – suicide attempts, infections, one non-lethal brain haemorrhage, and a seizure after surgery – there was also a staggering level of sustained improvement and recovery in such a hard-to-treat population. In the first year, there was a 50 per cent improvement in their stubborn symptoms. By the second year, 30 per cent of their patients were in full remission from their previously intractable depression. Although there was no control group and therefore no way of determining whether some recoveries were spontaneous, there was clear evidence that the ongoing stimulation in area 25 had a sustained antidepressant effect. When the electrode was switched off, the depression returned. When one patient relapsed, they found that the pacemaker that controlled the electrode had broken. And when the non-rechargeable batteries of these devices started to lose charge, the depressive symptoms started to return in tandem. Battery replacement or device repair restored the previous antidepressant effects. Importantly, there have been no relapses while sufficient stimulation has been provided, a remarkable milestone given that relapse is a common occurrence in depressed patients with multiple levels of treatment resistance.

Mayberg's first patient, the woman who described a feeling of spring in 2003, died six years after her first surgical operation. She was healthy for much of that time, walking around with the electrode in her brain and the pacemaker in her chest, but she had other issues in her life beyond the depression. Her death is a reminder that DBS isn't a cure. It is an experimental treatment guided by decades of research that can help break a relentless cycle of mental anguish. Oftentimes, it isn't enough. Full recovery requires a programme of social rehabilitation as well as surgical precision. To paraphrase one of Mayberg's patients: deep brain stimulation isn't perfect, it just makes life possible. When trying to help critically ill people, Mayberg has to accept that the road isn't going to be a straight line to success. 'It's a journey where the final destination is a more complete understanding of depression,' she says. 'Only then can we truly work towards a cure.'

Mind on Fire

Brian Leonard spends much of his time reading and writing in an old barn converted into an office. With thick stone walls, a slate roof, and double-glazed windows, it is a cosy refuge from the bitingly cold winds and pouring rains that sweep in – often unannounced – from the Atlantic Ocean, just a short walk back to the bungalow he shares with his wife and their elderly dogs. In 1999, Leonard retired from his position as professor of pharmacology at the National University of Ireland, Galway, a small campus of buildings that surround a Gothic quadrangle that first opened its doors to students in 1849. In his 80s, and frustrated with the sluggishness that comes with ageing, Leonard wishes that he could return to the laboratory and continue the research he started 40 years ago – now suddenly in vogue. In the 1980s, Leonard was a prominent voice within a fringe theory in psychiatry: depression was a product of the immune system. To him, it was akin to rheumatoid arthritis, a disease stemming from low-grade, chronic inflammation.

Our immune system evolved to protect us from harm, but it can also lead to some of the most painful and destructive diseases. They are embodiments of a paradox, afflictions that haunt millions of people every year. In 2004, *Time* magazine called inflammation the 'The Silent Killer' and the cause of many of the twenty-first century's most problematic diseases, such as diabetes, cardiovascular disease, inflammatory bowel disease, and cancer. In recent years, research into the immune system has shifted from physical diseases of the body to the disorders of the mind. Depression provides some of the most compelling evidence that mental illness is intimately tied with our immune system. Patients who don't respond to conventional antidepressants commonly show high levels of inflammation in their blood, suggesting that so-called treatment resistance might be tackled with anti-inflammatories. In 2013, a randomised-controlled trial found that the drug infliximab, an anti-inflammatory used to treat rheumatoid arthritis, had a similar level of efficacy as antidepressants in its reduction of depressive symptoms. Most persuasive, perhaps, is a longitudinal study that tracked the health of over 3,000 individuals from children to adults and found that elevated levels of inflammation at nine years old predicted the onset of depressive symptoms 12 years later.

In 2018, Edward Bullmore, a professor of psychiatry at the University of Cambridge, wrote *The Inflamed Mind: A Radical New Approach to Depression*, a popular-science book that pushed the link between inflammation and mental illness into the mainstream. The topic has become so normalised, so commonplace, that it is easy to forget where it came from and that it was initially seen as a fringe science. 'Now everybody believes it, and always did believe it,' said Michael Berk a professor at Deakin University in Geelong, southeast Australia. 'But history wasn't always so.'

From the pharmacology department in western Ireland, a single-storey building on the edge of campus that he still lovingly refers to as 'the hut', Leonard supervised 40 PhD students and mentored many more scientists who are now leading this field (Berk included). Working on the capricious Irish coastline, it often felt like he was isolated and exposed. Slowly, however, the four scientific institutions of Ireland – Queen's University Belfast, Trinity College Dublin, University College Dublin, and the National University of Ireland, Galway – started to meet twice a year, sharing their ideas and allowing their students to present their latest work. Leonard's students seemed to speak in a different language to their peers, however. While other labs were working on brain chemistry and neurons, the scientists in Leonard's 'hut' were increasingly focused on markers of the immune system in the blood. They spoke of macrophages and lymphocytes, the Pac-Man-esque cells of the immune system that gobble up unwanted intruders such as bacteria. They discussed cytokines, a mysterious family of molecules that seemed to control a person's immune response like temperature gauges control a central-heating system. They used terms like proinflammatory and anti-inflammatory. Secretly, they thought that serotonin might be a secondary consequence of a more central cause of depression, a subplot to an epic story that reached out of the synapse and encompassed the entire body.

Leonard and his students weren't the only ones to hold such radical views. 'The lack of scientific insight into mental disorders can be conveniently attributed to the enormous complexity and inaccessibility of the human brain,' one author working in San Jose, California, wrote in 1991. 'On the other hand, over 100 years of unsuccessful research on the [potential causes] of mental illness could be telling us that there is something wrong with our research.'

Until the 1980s, the study of the immune system, known as 'immunology', had largely taken place in test tubes and on sterile laboratory table tops. Macrophages, lymphocytes, and neutrophils – all types of white blood cell – were understood in closed and tightly controlled settings. But a human is nothing like a test tube. Our bodies are huge bioreactors of molecules, cells, and organ systems that are in constant communication and flux. 'It's time to put the immune system back in the body where it belongs,' said Karen Bullock, an immunologist from the State University of New York, Stony Brook, in 1985. The role of the immune system doesn't stop at infectious microbes but reaches into almost every aspect of our lives, from our guts to our brains. 'We're at a stage where it is difficult to say definitively what is happening,' said Nicholas Hall from George Washington University in Washington DC, referring to the broad topic of the immune system's connection to the brain. 'We're putting together two kinds of black boxes and trying to make sense of what happens.'

A few glimmers of light came from studying people with depression. In the late 1980s, several labs based in the United States and the Netherlands found in their blood the molecular markers of inflammation. Those molecules that cool the immune response, known as anti-inflammatories, were lacking. It was as if the temperature gauge of the immune system was kept slightly above normal. In his ramshackle pharmacology laboratory in Galway, one of Leonard's most productive and tireless students, Cai Song, had found similar patterns. After defrosting blood samples of depressed patients from a local psychiatric unit, she found that pro-inflammatory signals were consistently increased. Anti-inflammatory signals were decreased. A core group of inflammatory markers – C-reactive protein (CRP), interleukin-6 (IL-6), and tumour necrosis factor (TNF-α) – proved to be significant. Using different patients, blood samples, and equipment, the same findings emerged from a number of laboratories in the 1990s. In particular, a research group led by Michael Maes in Maastricht in the Netherlands was pivotal in illuminating the consistent patterns of inflammation in depressed patients.

There was an imbalance. Rather than suggesting that people with depression were deficient in one or two brain chemicals, a whole suite of immune signals pointed in the same direction: low-grade, chronic inflammation.

Inflammation is a bodily reaction often felt as heat and seen as swelling. It isn't always a bad thing. In fact, it is vital to our survival. When a threat to the body is detected – whether it is bacteria, a virus, or an injury – the immune system responds by sending a swarm of specific white blood cells to the necessary site. These cells then produce a cocktail of proteins that sterilise the area. The bacteria and viruses are, hopefully, vanquished. Dead or damaged cells are digested and cleared away. The body can then start the process of recovery and repair. This is acute inflammation. It is as explosive as it is necessary. 'That's not what we're talking about,' Leonard says. 'We're talking about chronic, low-grade inflammation ... It is absolutely different.' In such cases, there is no immediate threat to be killed and no injury to sterilise. With nothing else to do, the white blood cells start to attack the very cells they were supposed to protect – the body's, yours. Diabetes, rheumatoid arthritis, and Crohn's disease are all rooted in chronic, low-grade inflammation. Even a clogged artery, once believed to be caused by a build-up of sticky cholesterol, is more commonly the result of a localised swelling caused by a slight elevation of inflammation within a blood vessel.

As with Nathan Kline's hopes for an emotional pendulum in depression, this led to an obvious possibility in terms of treatment. Could anti-inflammatories be used to reduce the inflammation associated with depression and, in doing so, treat the depressive symptoms as well? Although this remained untested, there was evidence from the contrary: pro-inflammatory drugs seemed to *induce* a state of depression.

*

Alpha-interferon is a drug used to fight particularly stubborn forms of cancer. It works by increasing the activity of the immune system, turning its temperature up in order to help the body burn out those cells that are dividing out of control. In the 1980s, however, two research groups recorded that symptoms of anxiety and depression often emerged as side effects of this drug. 'Patients ignored their eating and other regular daily activities. [They] lost their appetite, and two refused to eat and drink anything and therefore needed intravenous fluid infusions,' researchers from the University of Helsinki wrote in 1988. 'Patients had slowed thinking, and they ceased to speak.' Their memory was affected, and they felt agitated and struggled to sleep. Although there wasn't a one-to-one relationship between pro-inflammation and depressive symptoms (one patient developed a phobia to pigeons), a large percentage of patients exhibited seven out of the nine symptoms listed in the *DSM-III* criteria for a major depressive episode. 'A patient only needs to exhibit five of the symptoms to be diagnosed with major depression,' one author noted.

When Andrew Miller saw his first patient on alpha-interferon in 1997 he was stunned. He had been called to the oncology department of Emory University, Atlanta, the institution where he worked as a psychiatrist, and found a woman sitting down, listless, and suicidal. Although she had come to terms with her cancer long ago, she suddenly felt like she might not be able to continue, that she had lost the love and affection she once felt toward her family. Every day was a battle. She couldn't sleep. Worst of all, she had no idea why she felt this way. 'This was a patient that was really describing a syndrome that, for me, was a carbon copy of what I see in my clinic in patients presenting with depression,' Miller says. The only difference was that this depression didn't follow some change in life like losing a job, divorce, or losing a family member. After a lengthy discussion, Miller was certain that it wasn't related to the stress of cancer and its window into mortality. 'There was no psychological context,' Miller says. 'It was occurring in a vacuum. We saw this happen over and over again. It's a very eerie thing for a psychiatrist to see a patient with a syndrome like depression without a psychological context.' This was a purely biological disorder. Once the alpha-interferon drug was discontinued, the depressive symptoms disappeared within two weeks.

What did this mean for our understanding of depression? Was this a previously unknown form of the illness? Was there a specific 'inflammation syndrome', associated more with fatigue, sleeplessness, and low mood? A few scientists proposed that there was indeed an overlap between so-called 'sickness behaviour' associated with other infections such as the common cold: social withdrawal, fatigue, a lack of motivation and drive. That was one possibility. The other was much grander in scope. Was inflammation the underpinnings of depression, full-stop? Rather than a brain disease, hatred turned inwards, or an imbalance of serotonin, was depression actually an immune disorder?

After Cai Song submitted her chunky thesis, finished her PhD, and left the Gothic scenes of Galway, Brian Leonard felt like there was a hole in his pharmacology department. Her tireless work ethic – Leonard sometimes had to kick her out of the laboratory in the evenings – made her departure feel even more obvious. In 1995, John Cryan, a cherubic young Irishman, had just finished his degree in biochemistry at the National University of Ireland, Galway, and, like Song, was more than happy to test novel approaches to treating depression. His interest wasn't as controversial as the immune system, however. It involved serotonin, the latest SSRI drugs, and research into the so-called 'lag phase' that had still failed to find a solution or an explanation. The few weeks before antidepressants fully take effect is more than just an academic puzzle. It is a dangerous window for depressed patients to take their own lives. 'The annual rate of suicide in depressed patients is three to four times that of other psychiatric diagnostic groups and 20 to 30 times higher than that of the general population,' Leonard wrote in 1994. 'This delay in onset [of antidepressants] exposes the patient to an increased period of suicide risk, may extend hospitalisation and certainly does little to alleviate the emotional distress of the condition.'

Working in the Experimental Medicine Building that adjoined Leonard's pharmacology hut, Cryan hoped to fill this gap. Was there some way to accelerate the antidepressants already available? Just as a catalyst speeds up a chemical reaction, could another substance boost the effects of these drugs? He was part of a global research effort in the late 1990s. As the number of new SSRIs being produced started to plateau, there was a desperate need for something new, even if it was just a chemical tweak of their effects, reducing their lag time from a few weeks to a few days. There were some persuasive findings. Beta-blockers and anti-cortisol (a stress hormone) drugs both showed early promise. But this line of research led to no breakthroughs. When taken outside of the lab and into human trials, they failed. The lag period remained, a gaping hole in the serotonin theory of depression and a dangerous reality for patients around the world.

At the suggestion of Leonard, Cryan finished his PhD and accepted a research position at a pharmaceutical firm. 'I sold my soul for a while,' he says. Working for Novartis in Basel, Switzerland, he watched as the psychiatry units were drained of money and closed down. By this time, in the early 2000s, there were plenty of antidepressants, all with similar effectiveness in clinical trials, and very little interest in producing any more. It costs around $985 million to take a drug from tests in mice into clinical trials in humans. Most of them fail. For the first time since their invention, drugs like Prozac were considered financially unviable. The only success came from Connie Sánchez, a pharmacologist who developed escitalopram (brand name Lexapro) while working at the pharmaceutical firm Lundbeck in Copenhagen, Denmark.

Feeling like his research in industry was a dead end, Cryan returned to Ireland in 2005 and accepted a position at the University College Cork, a university at the heart of a multicultural city in the southeast of the island. It was here that his career took an unexpected turn. From studying drugs and how they might work in the brain, he began focusing his attention at the opposite end of the body: the gut. Cryan became interested in how the millions of bacteria inside the coiling mass of intestines that connect the stomach to the colon might influence mood. Still a field in its infancy, scientists saw the microbiome – that ecosystem of bacteria and other microbes that live on and inside our bodies – as a regulator of health and disease. An institution that was strong in microbiology, University College Cork had set up a microbiome unit that was attracting students and scientists from around the world. They could raise their own germ-free mice in order to study how the microbiome, and even specific bacteria, influence the growth, development, and behaviour of mammals. Mainly studying rodents in the laboratory, Cryan paired up with Ted Dinan, a psychiatrist and pharmacologist who met face to face with patients, prescribed drugs (including MAO inhibitors), and could link the research from the laboratory in Cork to the clinic. It was an unusual situation: two pharmacologists with no experience in microbiology studying the little understood microbial ecosystem within the human body. Both fluent in neuroscience and drug therapy, Cryan and Dinan would soon be talking about probiotics, bacteria, and faecal transplants.

Leonard, still publishing his own theories on inflammation and depression, thought they were both crazy. Only later did he realise that their work might be the only safe and sustainable route to reducing low-grade inflammation in the body.

After Leonard retired from the National University of Ireland, Galway in 1999, he left Ireland to work with a leading figure in the inflammation theory of depression, Michael Maes, who had his own laboratory in Maastricht. Soon after his arrival, Leonard met Aye Mu Myint, a medical doctor and surgeon from Myanmar who had moved to Maastricht in her mid 40s to start a PhD in immunology. When they met, Leonard and Myint found that they had been thinking along the same lines for years. Specifically, they had been obsessing over the same molecular pathway inside the human body and how it might link depression to the immune system.

It starts with tryptophan, an essential amino acid found in most protein-rich foods, from chocolate to poultry, sesame seeds to tofu. Tryptophan has long been known to be an essential amino acid because it is the precursor to serotonin, the monoamine that, even if it isn't the cause of depression, is pivotal in the functioning human brain and, more significantly, the gut. But this is only a tiny glimpse into tryptophan's potential life cycle. In recent decades, another chemical pathway has been revealed and is taking the limelight at international conferences and in the psychiatric literature. It has Leonard hooked.

It is called the kynurenine (pronounced 'Ky-Nur-a-Neen') pathway, a family of chemicals that are produced from tryptophan and have wide-ranging effects on the body. Most commonly, tryptophan is broken down via the kynurenine pathway into a form of fuel used for energy production in our body's cells, literally allowing our muscles to move and our brains to flash with thought. This process takes place through enzymes in the liver, in the blood, and in muscle tissue. It accounts for 95 per cent of tryptophan usage in our body. But there is a Jekyll and Hyde moment in this pathway, a switch that, crucially for this story, takes place when inflammation is elevated in the body. When this happens, fuel production is stalled and kynurenine is broken down into quinolinic acid, a molecule that flows through the blood and reaches the neurons of the brain. There, it lives up to its acidic name. It breaks down neurons in the brain like hydrochloric acid in the gut kills bacteria. It is, in the parlance of immunology, neurotoxic.

In 2003, Myint and Y.K. Kim from Korea University's College of Medicine published a 'neurodegeneration hypothesis of depression'. With the kynurenine pathway at its core, they argued that depression was rooted in the death of neurons in the brain; a disease akin – and potentially a precursor – to dementia. 'It's very complicated and I wouldn't say that we have the answers,' Leonard admits as he looms over a figure of the kynurenine pathway in one of his textbooks. 'But it's trying to look in a ... well, what *I* consider to be a more creative way.'

First studied in detail by the Russian scientist Slava Lapin in the 1970s, kynurenine is currently a hot topic in the field of neuroimmunology. 'Everyone's talking about the kynurenine pathway, and really very seldom in the US or Europe [do scientists] give him credit,' says Leonard. 'He was the one who pinpointed this.' Before the Berlin Wall was torn down and the

Soviet Union disintegrated, Leonard managed to arrange a travel visa for Lapin, allowing him to present his work at a British Association for Psychopharmacology conference in Ireland. Leonard enjoyed his company like that of an old friend. 'He was one of the old-style nineteenth-century Russian intellectuals,' he says. Lapin spoke French fluently, played piano to a grade suited to grand concert halls, and rubbed shoulders with Russian intelligentsia such as Aleksandr Solzhenitsyn, the novelist who won a Nobel Prize for his writings on the gulags of the Soviet Union. But what Leonard most admired about Lapin was his approach to science: a holistic view that makes interconnections between once disparate theories.

Today, Leonard is still mobile, both on foot and in his small car, and has the same booming voice that once 'enlivened conferences too numerous to count'. But he is slower, more forgetful, and becoming increasingly disappointed with where science is heading. People become so specialised he says, so parochial, that they forget that the brain is a part of the body. 'The body doesn't work in bits,' he says. He reminisces over the days when he studied pharmacology at the University of Birmingham and saw the chemistry of the body as a huge puzzle that couldn't be understood without all the different parts. Whether the answer lies with the immune system or the microbiome, kynurenine or TNF-α, he is aghast at how psychiatry became so fixated on serotonin.

'For Life'

Although the term 'microbiome' was made famous by Nobel laureate Joshua Lederberg in 2001, its history reaches back to the late nineteenth century, a time when Sigmund Freud and Emil Kraepelin were paving the future of psychiatry. While working in Paris, the microbiologist and Nobel laureate Elie Metchnikoff put forward the idea that the microbes in our gut needn't be avoided (as the 'germ theory' of disease dictated). They could be beneficial and nurtured by certain foodstuffs. In particular, he wrote, fermented foods that contain lactic-acid-producing bacteria, such as *Lactobacillus bulgaricus*, could have far-reaching benefits for the mind and body. People who regularly drank fermented milk in Bulgaria lived longer and healthier lives, Metchnikoff noticed. He wanted the whole world to know their secret. '[T]here is hope that we shall in time be able to transform the entire intestinal flora from a harmful to an innocuous one,' Metchnikoff wrote in an article entitled 'Why Not Live Forever?' for *Cosmopolitan* in 1912. 'The beneficent effect of this transformation must be enormous.'

Metchnikoff was an internationally recognised scientist, a cantankerous but fatherly figure of immunology. He discovered the most fundamental part of the immune response: macrophages, those cells that flow through our blood and gobble up microbial invaders. Growing up in rural Russia, Metchnikoff had a precocious talent for science and medicine. He finished a four-year degree in just two. When he became a lecturer at the age of 22, many of his students were older than he was. In his later years, as his hair grew shaggier and his beard was so unkempt that it was once likened to 'fields of wheat after a thunderstorm', Metchnikoff's brilliance was used to boost the sales of unproven probiotics. 'Metchnikoff's great discoveries are now procurable in tablet form,' a full-page newspaper advert from the Berlin Labs in New York stated. Intesti-Fermin (a brand name of probiotic pills), they claimed, 'promotes physical and mental health and provides a truly scientific aid to high efficiency in everyday life'. What they didn't mention was that there was no evidence that these bacteria actually enter and colonise our guts. Passing through the strong digestive acid of our stomachs is just the first step. They have to find conditions within our intestines that are suitable to their needs. Is the pH okay? Are there nutrients tailored to the microbe's needs? And, importantly, are the other species already living there going to outcompete any newcomers, like reef fish quarrelling over a piece of coral? For bacteria in our intestines, the zones of habitability are clearly defined, and each is a battleground of millions.

As it turned out, *L. bulgaricus* didn't survive and multiply in our digestive system. But one of the benefits of bacteria is that there are many more options available. In our guts, for instance, there are an estimated 1,000 different species. In the 1920s, manufacturers replaced *L. bulgaricus* with *L. acidophilus*, a closely related species of bacteria that naturally inhabits our guts and was heralded as the latest probiotic fad for a healthy mind. 'The results, as thousands of physicians and users testify, are nothing short of amazing,' an advert in the *New York Times* stated. 'Not only a banishing of mental and physical depression, but a flooding of new vitality throughout the system.'

Such sensational adverts reach into the twenty-first century. 'There's "Metchnikoff's life", a fermented milk drink made by

South Korea's Hankuk Yakult that proudly displays Metchnikoff's patriarchal portrait on the cup,' writes Luba Vikhanski, a science journalist and writer, in her book *Immunity: How Elie Metchnikoff Changed the Course of Modern Medicine*. 'A recent Russian-language commercial for Danone yogurt featured a radiant Metchnikoff, played by a bearded actor. And since 2007 the Brussels-based International Dairy Federation, or IDF, has been awarding an IDF Elie Metchnikoff Prize to promote research "in the fields of microbiology, biotechnology, nutrition, and health with regard to fermented milks".'

In 2013, over a century after Metchnikoff's article in *Cosmopolitan*, Kirsten Tillisch and her colleagues at the University of California in Los Angeles provided the first evidence that bacteria can influence our brains. *Lactobacillus rhamnosus* is a species of lactic-acid-producing bacteria commonly found in fermented foods and drink. After eating two small pots of fermented yogurt a day for four weeks, the brains of a group of healthy women showed a decreased activity in those brain regions associated with interoception (the inner sense of the self) and emotional reactivity. 'These changes were not observed in a non-fermented milk product of identical taste,' Tillisch and her colleagues wrote in the journal *Gastroenterology*. '[T]he findings appear to be related to the ingested bacteria strains and their effect on the host.' By dampening the emotional response to the environment, could these probiotics be used as a treatment in mental disorders?

The term probiotic means 'for life'. They are health-promoting microbes. They are traditionally defined as 'living micro-organisms that contribute to intestinal microbial balance and have the potential to improve the health of their human host'. The same year that Tillisch published her landmark paper, Ted Dinan coined the term 'psychobiotics', a necessary break from the past fad of probiotics – such as Intesti-Fermin – and towards a future of bacteria specifically used to influence our mental health. He defines a psychobiotic as 'a live organism that, when ingested in adequate amounts, produces a health benefit in patients suffering from psychiatric illness'.

To study a new treatment for psychiatric illness, and to compare it to old pharmacological options, Dinan turned to Cryan for help. He had honed the so-called forced-swim test in mice into a fine art. First developed in the late 1970s, the forced-swim test involved giving mice an experimental drug, placing them in a jug of tepid water, and timing how long they swam for. Longer times were seen as a good sign of increased drive and motivation in the face of a stressful environment. Although there is no such thing as a depressed mouse (guilt and remorse are particularly difficult to replicate in a rodent), this was often the first test that modern antidepressants had to pass. Well before they were put into prescription, many SSRIs were first given to mice (or rats) and found to increase the amount of time they would swim before giving up.

One of the first bacterial strains to undergo the forced-swim test – inside the body of a rat – was *Bifidobacterium infantis*. In babies, *B. infantis* comprises 90 per cent of the microbes in the large intestine. As adults, that figure settles down to 3 or 5 per cent, still a sizeable chunk of the microbial ecosystem. When Lieve Desbonnet, a PhD student supervised by Dinan, gave *B. infantis* to rats as a probiotic solution she found that there was no change in how long they swam for. One of the first probiotics tested for its effects on the mind had just sunk along with the rodent that it was given to.

Lactobacillus rhamnosus, the species of bacteria that Kirsten Tillisch studied in yogurt, passed the forced-swim test. Mice swam for significantly longer after being fed this probiotic for two weeks, and it also showed anti-inflammatory properties. 'It looked like it was antidepressant, anxiolytic, and every flippin' thing under the sun,' says Dinan. These overwhelmingly positive findings in animal models gave Dinan and Cryan the confidence, and the funding, to start human trials. Rather than forcing the patients to swim, they could test them on standardised health questionnaires for depression and anxiety. They would pore through their blood samples for markers of inflammation, and their brain chemicals for changes in serotonin and glutamate (the most common neurotransmitter in the human brain and the molecular target of ketamine). It was an important step away from rodent models and into the first stages of using bacteria as potential anti-inflammatories and antidepressants.

'It was the most unbelievable result,' Dinan says. 'It did nothing. I mean, you've never seen such a tight relationship between probiotic and placebo in your life. We looked at immunology, endocrinology, behaviour, loads of things. It did nothing in humans.' As Cryan laconically summed up the results to a BBC reporter, 'you couldn't fit more negative data into that paper'. Published in late 2016, they called their study 'Lost in Translation'. After years of study and millions of pounds of research funding, this was a stark reminder that what works in mice doesn't guarantee clinical success in humans.

The process of peer-reviewed science is founded on, and fuelled by, positive results. The big journals such as *Science* and *Nature* want to publish new exciting discoveries. Scientists want a track record in big journals. Negative results are pushed to one side and left to collect dust on a bookshelf or slowly erode inside a computer's hard drive. 'The reality is that we've had loads of negative studies over the years,' Dinan says. But he thought that this particular non-finding was too important to ignore. 'This was the most positive [project] we've had in rodents, and it's the least positive we've ever done in humans.'

Large studies into the microbiome and mental health are few and far between. As Cryan joked at Mind, Mood & Microbes, an international conference held in Amsterdam in January 2019, there are more reviews of the scientific literature than there are original studies. On the second day of the conference, Kurosh Djafarian, a mild-mannered man with jet-black hair and neat stubble, presented the first randomised-controlled trial into probiotics and depression. A professor of clinical nutrition at Tehran University of Medical Sciences, Iran, Djafarian and his colleagues found that *Lactobacillus helveticus* and *Bifidobacterium longum* significantly reduced depressive symptoms over eight weeks of treatment. With 28 people in the probiotic group and 27 controls (people were given a sachet of powder that was the same flavour and colour as the probiotic mix), it wasn't a huge trial, but it was still one of the most persuasive at the time. In addition to reviews that show probiotics to have significant benefits for people with mild to moderate levels of depression, this work was a highlight of the conference for many people, a sign that 'good bacteria' could be used in the treatment of depression.

Listening to Djafarian in the audience was Scot Bay, a doctor from the United States wearing a brown woollen suit and tie. He had been excited to hear this talk since he first arrived in Amsterdam a few days prior. In his suburban private practice on the outskirts of Atlanta, he often meets with depressed people who haven't responded to multiple rounds of antidepressants and talking therapy. Interestingly, the majority also had comorbid digestive complaints such as irritable bowel syndrome. In 2015, he had listened to a podcast and heard Laura Steenbergen, an assistant professor at Leiden University, discuss her research into probiotics and their ability to reduce the body's stress response. She had given her patients Ecologic Barrier, a probiotic mixture that strengthens the internal wall of the intestines and helps to dampen any inflammation or infection. Bay ordered a box for eight of his treatment-resistant patients. 'They got better,' he says, excitement and surprise making the words pop from his mouth. 'They all got better.'

At the conference, Cryan reminded his audience that the field of the microbiome can easily slide from scientific research into pseudoscience, as it did in Metchnikoff's days in the twentieth century. Acknowledging the promise of a positive randomised-controlled trial, he added a necessary coolant to proceedings. 'Are we there yet?' he asked, referring to the microbiome's maturity as a clinical science. 'No, we're only a little up the road.'

One of the most persuasive studies in this field was published shortly after Mind, Mood & Microbes had finished and the scientists had returned to their far-flung institutions. Studying kindly donated stool samples from over 1,000 people living in Belgium, Mireia Valles-Colomer, Sara Vieira-Silva, and their colleagues from KU Leuven-University in Belgium found that people with depression had their own microbial 'fingerprint'. Although it didn't apply to all depressed people in their study, over a quarter of their volunteers were deficient in diversity, as if their gut ecosystem had suffered from a serious catastrophe that wiped out many of the species that usually lived there. In particular, the bacterial groups *Dialister* and *Coprococcus* were depleted compared to people without depression. This same pattern, interestingly, had been observed in Crohn's disease, a disorder of chronic, low-grade inflammation in the intestines.

Although this study was based on general practitioners' reports of depression (rather than psychiatrist-derived diagnoses), Valles-Colomer and her colleagues' findings were bolstered by large sample sizes. In total, they compared 151 patients against 933 controls (people without depression), a huge number for a field characterised by studies of a dozen or so patients. Did this mean that the lack of diversity caused the depression? Or did the depression result in the deficient microbiome as a consequence? 'Most people think that it's kind of a loop, that you tend to have a trigger of inflammation, whether it's having a bad diet for a long time or taking some medications or having very bad sleeping patterns – all can contribute to low-grade inflammation,' says Vieira-Silva. 'This will then benefit "bad" bacteria in your gut, and then bad bacteria benefits by triggering even more inflammation.'

The obvious corollary to this work is finding out whether this loop can be broken. How can low-grade inflammation, and the microbiome 'fingerprint' that it thrives upon, be persuaded into a more balanced state? 'Our personal experience is that we tend to see more effects from prebiotics than probiotics,' says Valles-Colomer, adding that fibre from fruit and vegetables is the most essential prebiotic anyone can add to their diet. 'But if you have a very disturbed microbiota then you might have lost key components of the microbiota, so then I would do a combined pre- and probiotic.' Together, that would introduce bacterial strains that might have been lost while also nurturing the low numbers of beneficial bacteria that are already present.

One of the most effective means of increasing the diversity of our microbial residents is through what we eat. What sustains us sustains them too, like feeding trillions of micro-scopic nest mates. Changing a few meals won't budge the already stable populations. It requires long-term dietary changes. But the benefits can be dramatic.

In 2017, Felice Jacka, professor at the Food and Mood Centre at Deakin University in southeast Australia, and her colleagues found that, over a three month period, depressed patients who ate more vegetables, fruits, wholegrains, legumes, fish, lean red meats, olive oil, and nuts, while cutting out 'extras' such as sweets, refined cereals, fried food, fast food, processed meats, and sugary drinks, saw a significant drop in their depressive symptoms compared to patients who had regular meetings with their counsellors but had no change in diet. In short, a Mediterranean-style diet can act as an antidepressant. Although this undoubtedly altered the patients' microbiomes, it is still unclear whether the diet was the reason for the effect. Though inflammation may have been reduced, it was not assessed in the study. However, as of 2019, Jacka's trial has been replicated by independent research groups using different methods and patient groups but, importantly, finding the same result. What-ever the mechanism, a varied diet, rich in fruit, vegetables, and a little bit of meat or fish, is a recipe for both physical and men-tal health.

After reading such studies, I changed my daily routine in 2018, around the time I was moving from citalopram to sertraline. After years of vegetarianism, I started to eat fish. River cichlid in Zimbabwe. Cod on the blustery coast of Suffolk, east Eng-land. The occasional salt morsel of anchovies in a Caesar salad. Not only was each bite a small assault on my environmental morals, I've never really had an appetite for seafood. I didn't eat much of it as a child, even less as an adult. But, like reaching out for psychotherapy or antidepressants, there's no greater motivator than finding something that works. I realised that my change in diet was built on thousands of years of writings on depression, from Galen to Felice Jacka. What we eat can influence our mood.

Did this balanced diet reduce inflammation levels in my blood? Was it protecting my brain from some of the neuro-toxic by-products of kynurenine? Was my microbiota changing into a less-depressed footprint? I would never know. But eating a healthy diet is an approach that I could control and implement almost immediately. I stopped eating share bags of crisps to myself. As alcohol is a known pro-inflammatory, I stopped drinking for two years and only rarely drink today. And after realising that omega-3 oils are actually produced by oceanic algae (which fish, in turn, eat), I returned to my vegetarian diet with vegan-friendly fish oils. Led by science, I was eating a Mediterranean-style diet without the fish.

Not everyone has access to cheap fresh groceries and omega-3 capsules made from algae. For me, a change in diet could happen almost immediately, a new treatment for depression after a walk to my local greengrocers. But for a growing number of people on shoe-string budgets or living in poverty, a change in diet can be an insurmountable task without external support. This isn't limited to low-income countries. It is a global problem. According to the Australian Health Survey of 2014–2015, for example, only 5.6 per cent of the population have a healthy proportion of fruits and vegetables in their diet. In the United Kingdom, 19 per cent of children live in households that frequently can't afford to buy the ingredients needed for a healthy diet. Cheap, processed, fatty foods that are full of salt and sugar are a common substitute, providing the sustenance that can be consumed in large quantities without satiation.

High in fat and low in protein and fibre, this quick-fix Western diet is a growing health concern. For both the rich and poor, it has led to a frightening increase in obesity. Around the world, an estimated 13 per cent of adults and 18 per cent of children are obese. In the United States, levels of adult obesity have risen from 10 per cent in the 1960s to over 40 per cent in 2018.

Defining obesity is an inexact science. It is based on a rough estimate of a person's volume (height squared) divided by their weight. And yet, this body-mass index (BMI) is a reliable indicator of a person's health. An overweight person ranges from a BMI of 25 to 29. Obesity begins at a BMI of 30 and is known to increase the risk of some of the most prevalent diseases of the twenty-first century. Heart disease, cancer, hypertension, type 2 diabetes: every increase in kilogram per square metre pushes the body towards a state of disease. Someone with a BMI of 30, for example, is 28 times more likely to develop diabetes compared to someone with a BMI of under 21. If BMI increases to 35 or more – a state known as 'morbidly obese' – the risk triples to 93 times.

These figures were listed in an oft-cited review in the journal *Nature*. Published in 2000, 'Obesity As a Medical Problem' welcomed the new millennium with a warning. 'Obesity should no longer be regarded as a cosmetic problem affecting certain individuals, but an epidemic that threatens global well-being,' wrote Peter Kopelman, a doctor then working at the Royal London School of Medicine. Although genetic susceptibility to obesity was a target for future studies (over 50 genes are thought to underlie this condition), the smoking gun behind this epidemic was rapid changes in diet and sedentary lifestyles. Wherever this Western lifestyle was introduced, obesity soon followed. Nowhere was this more evident than in the Pacific Islands, the 12,000 or so pockets of paradise that freckle the waters of the western Pacific. After the Second World War, a shift from subsistence farming to urban living and the import of cheap, processed foods led to some of the highest rates of obesity in the world. 'Traditional foods such as fish, taro, yams, and indigenous fruits and vegetables have been supplanted by imported rice, sugar, canned foods, soft drinks, and calorie-dense snack foods,' wrote epidemiologists Nicola Hawley and Stephen McGarvey in 2015. 'These imported foods are often of poor quality (fatty cuts of meat like turkey tails and lamb flaps which are often considered waste in their countries of origin, instant noodles, highly processed, high-sugar snack foods) but have come to represent prestige and cultural capital.' With a genetic predisposition to weight gain shared by many Pacific Islanders, these sandy microcosms represent a warning to the rest of the world. In American Samoa, over 70 per cent of the population are obese. In Tonga, Naaru, and Samoa, these fig-ures are still above 50 per cent. Diabetes, stroke, and cardiovascular disease are on the rise while life expectancy shrinks. People who would once live into their late 70s are now dying in their 60s.

In Peter Kopelman's review in 2000, physical diseases took centre stage. There was no mention of mental health. But in the two decades since it was published, depression has become intimate with obesity. It is now known as just another 'obesity-related disease'. 'With few exceptions,' Michael Berk and his colleagues wrote in 2013, 'studies have consistently shown a relationship between obesity and depression regardless of methodological variability.' Being obese increases the risk of depression by over 50 per cent, a rate that is mirrored by the risk of obesity for those who are depressed. It's another vicious cycle; like poverty, obesity is both a cause and a consequence of depression.

While the classical definitions of depression – melancholia, for example – are associated with a lack of appetite and weight loss, obesity is associated with a more 'atypical' symptom profile. Overeating, anxiety, fatigue, and oversleeping: it is a resurgence of a diagnosis that first gained popularity in the 1950s. Once prescribed MAO inhibitors, atypical depression remains a particularly stubborn ailment to treat, especially when a patient is obese. Although there are myriad explanations for this (both social and physiological), one of the central areas of research in recent years is inflammation. Fatty tissue – especially the kind that surrounds the abdomen – releases inflammatory molecules into the blood. Not only has this been associated with depression, but such chronic, low-grade inflammation is known to make standard antidepressants less effective.

Full disclosure: I'm slim, some might say skinny. I'm 178 centimetres tall (just over five feet and ten inches) and weigh 65 kilograms (ten and a half stone). My BMI hovers around 21, in the 'healthy' range that extends from 19 to 25. But I was an overweight child. I remember standing on the scales at primary school and feeling a sense of shame. I hid my rolls of fat and always wore baggy jumpers. A T-shirt and a breezy day would reveal the contours of my body and make me feel like the whole world was watching, laughing. My parents tried to reassure me that it was just 'puppy fat', an energy reserve to help me grow tall in my teens. But there were other explanations. In the late 1990s and early 2000s, desktop computers were becoming a common feature of the household. I sat and played video games – first with floppy discs and then CDs – and would watch television in the evenings. I played sport only on the weekends: badminton, cricket, and football. But there was a lot of idleness and overeating. At school, I could eat pizza, hamburgers, chips, and, for dessert, a crunchy chunk of corn-flakes baked with chocolate, syrup, and margarine that was aptly called tarmac. I would save up any loose change for the vending machine that sat in the musty-smelling corridor below the sports hall, a cheap dispenser of sugary drinks. Even in cooking lessons, we were taught how to cook pizza instead of healthier alternatives.

From 2005 onwards, Jamie Oliver, a then baby-faced and exuberant chef who had moved from the sweaty confines of restaurant kitchens to national TV in the late 1990s, helped to change how a nation fed its school children. I was nearing the end of my school years when the recommendations from *Jamie's School Dinners* were introduced. I saw the transformation take place in the cafeteria. Pasta replaced pizza. Hearty meals with vegetables sizzled where hamburgers were once stacked. The infamous Turkey Twizzlers disappeared alto-gether and only lived on through nostalgia, a ghost of a more processed past. A study in 2009 found that this healthier diet – although not accepted by everyone – had an immediate impact on school attendance and the number of children achieving top grades. Jamie Oliver didn't mention depression in his 'Feed Me Better' petition to the government in 2005. But some argue that his work had – and is still having – a significant impact on mental health. 'I think he's very important,' says Berk, the for-mer mentee of Brian Leonard and a colleague of Felice Jacka at Deakin University. 'His work will play a role in preventing depression. Although the magnitude of the effect might be really small, it will have a big community impact because the entire population is involved.'

Eating a diet full of fibre – particularly from fruit and vegeta-bles – is just one way to reduce obesity, inflammation, and the vicious cycle that encompasses diabetes, heart disease, and depression. The other is exercise. Since the 1980s, dozens of clinical trials have found exercise to have an antidepressant effect. In a study published in 2005, Andrea Dunn from the Cooper Institute in Colorado and her colleagues found that three days of moderate exercise per week – as gauged by time spent on a treadmill or stationary bicycle – had the same efficacy in treating depression as first-line treatments such as SSRIs and CBT. Then, in 2013, a study from Madhukar Trivedi, professor of psychiatry at the University of Texas Southwestern Medical Center, and his colleagues found that the antidepressant effects of moderate exercise are most pronounced in people who have high levels of inflammatory markers in their blood, whether obese or not.

This presents an opportunity for precision medicine. Since current antidepressants are least effective in people who have high levels of inflammatory markers, exercise could be used both as a standalone treatment and a boost to subsequent drug therapy. If the depression is unmoved by physical activity, levels of inflammation in a person's body may have been reduced to a level at which antidepressants are more likely to work. There's even a choice between antidepressants, some being more suitable for people with inflammatory markers in their blood. A large clinical trial from 2014, for example, found that nortriptyline (a tricyclic antidepressant) was more effective than escitalopram (an SSRI) at treating depression in people with elevated levels of C-reactive protein, a marker of inflammation that can be assessed with a quick blood test. Three years later, a similar study found that another marker, interleukin-17 (IL-17), predicted a better response to a combination of an SSRI and bupropion – a dopamine-based drug that's also an anti-inflammatory – compared to an SSRI on its own. Whether it's exercise or a certain type of antidepressant, chronic, low-grade inflammation can be used as a window into a more effective future.

It is easier to administer drugs than it is to prescribe exercise. Insurance companies and national health services often don't cover personal trainers or gym memberships in the same way that they subsidise drugs or therapists. Running shoes, yoga courses, and court fees can be costly. And finding the time for regular exercise is difficult even for people who are mentally healthy, never mind for those who might be suffering from a crippling lack of motivation, drive, and self-esteem. But, for me, the alternative is much worse. Depression is a huge motivator, one of the most powerful forces that gets me up in the morning and out for a run.

When I was withdrawing from sertraline in early 2020, I thought that the more I ran the better I would feel. As my dose tapered toward zero, I slowly increased the number of kilometres I was covering per week. After a few months, I was running the equivalent of a half-marathon once or twice a week. It was too much. I often felt fatigued and low in the days after exercise. And this was frustrating. Why don't I feel over the moon after such a weekly achievement? Am I destined to be depressed no matter how hard I work against it? Then I read a study that offered an explanation, and it again related to the new buzz-word of psychiatry: kynurenine. In 2015, a group of Austrian researchers found that intense exercise – even in athletes – can activate the kynurenine pathway and shunt tryptophan away from serotonin, reducing the amount of this neurotransmitter available for brain function; that is, a reversal of an antidepressant effect. 'One may conclude that sport performed occasionally with two or three days interval exerts a beneficial effect on general well-being, as it is the case when it is performed as a recreational activity,' Barbara Prüller Strasser from Medical

University Innsbruck and her colleagues wrote, 'whereas intense training will more and more achieve adverse effects on both mood and the immune system.'

Reading this, I tried running for shorter distances three times a week. Five or 10 kilometres: it felt like a healthier routine and didn't leave me exhausted. Afterwards, our dog Bernie is still panting, his tongue lolling out of his mouth as he waits patiently for breakfast. As I stretch my muscles and warm down, I contemplate what is happening inside my body. Is my brain being flooded with neurotransmitters and endorphins? Are its synapses making new connections, reversing the effects of stress and depression? Are the trillions of bacteria inside my gut sending a cacophony of healthy signals to my brain through the vagus nerve? Are levels of inflammation running on a cool norm? Even if it's a temporary high, I feel empowered by those treatments I can tweak and modify from one day to the next. The food I eat and the amount I exercise are antidepressants that I prescribe. They are as much a part of my treatment as drugs and psychotherapy, and they come with fewer side effects.

The Beginning

There is a chicken-or-egg question in the study of inflammation and depression. Which came first? Did the inflammation trigger the depression? Or was it the depression that caused the body to become inflamed? 'We know that psychological stress activates our immune response,' says Golam Khandaker, an epidemiologist at the University of Cambridge. 'People who are stressed have higher levels of immune activity. So it's possible that the increased inflammatory proteins in depressed patients is just a manifestation of these people being psychologically stressed, because we know depression is a very stressful condition.'

But there are multiple lines of research that show inflammation to be the cause – and not the consequence – of depression. First, longitudinal studies that have tracked the health of over 100,000 people in the United Kingdom, the Netherlands, Denmark, and the United States, show that people with slightly elevated markers of inflammation in the blood are significantly more likely to develop depression later in life. Interestingly, people who have a genetic predisposition for lower levels of inflammation in life have been found to be at a lower risk of becoming depressed. Further, not only do pro-inflammatory drugs such as alpha-interferon often lead to depression, but patients given anti-inflammatories for immune-related diseases such as psoriasis, Crohn's disease, or rheumatoid arthritis show a marked decrease in their depressive symptoms. Importantly, these reductions didn't correlate with whether their immune-related disease was improving. Even if their joints were stiff, their intestines were inflamed, or their skin covered in itchy rashes, their mental health showed remarkable transformations.

These studies have now paved the way for more direct clinical trials. 'What's exciting about this field now is that on the back of a lot research based on healthy volunteers, patients, genes, population studies, we have now reached the stage of clinical trials in patients with depression,' says Khandaker who, along with his colleagues at the University of Cambridge, is conducting one such clinical trial. 'The Insight Study' begins with one of the most important facts about this field: not everyone with depression is inflamed. The latest estimates suggest that one quarter to a third of people with depression show increased levels of CRP and IL-6, two inflammatory markers that are easily tested in the blood and that, importantly, don't change with the time of day or fluctuate after meals. Once such patients have been identified – through two blood tests and the identification of inflammation-related symptoms such as fatigue, sleep disturbances, and concentration problems – Khandaker and his colleagues will then either provide an infusion of a placebo or an anti-inflammatory. Such a rigorous selection process is paramount when it comes to patient safety. As they dampen the immune response, anti-inflammatories can lead to infections, disrupt brain function, and should only be given to people who show the hallmark signs of inflammation. If given to depressed patients without any signs of inflammation, these drugs can be harmful rather than helpful.

Even with the bulk of evidence that this field has accrued over the last two decades, Khandaker still takes the ruthlessly sceptical worldview that only scientists can muster. 'I am not drawing any firm conclusions based on what we know. And I think it would be foolish to draw any firm conclusions regarding whether anti-inflammatory drugs have a role in mental health or not,' he says. 'This is just the beginning.'

From his converted barn in Galway, Brian Leonard watches as the field he helped create takes its first steps into the real world. In his textbooks and reviews, Leonard frequently quotes Arthur Schopenhauer, the wild-haired German philosopher from the nineteenth century. 'All truth passes through three stages,' Schopenhauer wrote. 'First it is ridiculed. Second it is violently opposed. Third it is accepted as being self-evident.' Twenty years ago, Leonard believed that the field of neuroimmunology was somewhere between one and two, still being ridiculed and beginning to experience serious criticism. By 2013, he thought it was at stage three: self-evident. 'Unlike false hopes raised by earlier theories of mental illness,' Leonard and Angelos Halaris from the University of Chicago wrote, 'we are confident that this relatively young subspecialty will have staying power.'

Surfing in the Brain Scanner

On the 'Day of the Dead', 2 November 2005, Draulio Barros de Araujo, a neuroscientist from the University of São Paulo in Brazil, experienced his first psychedelic trip on ayahuasca, a traditional tea made from two or more plants found in the Amazon Basin. One of his PhD students was a member of the local Santo Daime Church, a religious institution that has been drinking ayahuasca as a part of their ceremonies since the 1930s, and thought that Araujo would be interested in the experience. After all, he had spent his career using brain-imaging technologies and developing mathematical models to 'see' how the mind works. How might his scientific expertise be reshaped by a drug that can produce vivid images of nature, a tea that can summon gods down from the heavens to provide counsel to mortals? Science called these visions hallucinations. But members of the Santo Daime Church call them *mirações*: seeings. These images are as real as any wavelength of light that tickles a retina.

Araujo felt honoured at the invite. Ayahuasca ceremonies weren't just a central pillar of his student's spiritual world but a rich part of Brazilian culture that reached back centuries, into the very heart of the Amazon rainforest and its people. A neuroscientist and former physicist with his feet firmly rooted in peer-reviewed journals and statistical significance, Araujo replaced his scientific cap for the wide-brimmed hat of an explorer.

The active ingredient of ayahuasca, the molecule that is responsible for these *mirações*, is called N,N-Dimethyltryptamine

(DMT). It is naturally found in the bush *Psychotria viridis* and, when digested and shuttled into the brain's synapses, interacts with a specific type of serotonin receptor to produce psychedelic experiences. (Another form of DMT called 5-MeO-DMT is extracted from the venom of the Sonoran Desert toad, *Bufo alvarius*.) The same basic mechanism underlies the effects of psilocybin, the active ingredient of magic mushrooms, and the laboratory-made LSD. But ayahuasca isn't just rooted in *P. viridis* and the DMT it contains. There is a second ingredient that is vital to its effects. Extracted from the climbing vine *Banisteriopsis caapi*, harmine is a naturally occurring MAO inhibitor, a chemical akin to iproniazid and tranylcypromine. By blocking the enzymes within the synapse, harmine prevents DMT from being broken down and flushed away in urine. In other words, MAO inhibitors weren't 'discovered' with the first antidepressants in the 1950s. They had been a part of indigenous traditions for hundreds of years.

Ayahuasca is a potent brew. Half a cup of this tea often leads to severe nausea, stomach cramps, and diarrhoea before inducing a dreamlike state that can last for four or more hours. The images people see are often surreal, majestic, and awesome. But they can also be frightening and unbearable. In the Santo Daime Church, it is likened to manual work, a process of heavy lifting. Shamanic rituals refer to an ayahuasca trip as 'labour'.

Araujo's first experience was a confusing constellation of geometric images, animals, and plant life. It didn't make much sense. It was only after the experience that he realised how significant his trip had been. Although it felt like he was dreaming, these images were just as real as his everyday conscious thoughts. 'The difference with ayahuasca is that when I woke up from the bizarre dream I was having, that sometimes resembled nightmares, it was not just a dream,' Araujo says. 'It was real. For someone who was interested in the human mind, that was just astonishing.'

Living in one of the most psychedelic countries in the world, one in which ayahuasca has been legal in religious ceremonies since the late 1980s, Araujo found himself in the perfect place to learn more about this experience. He turned to his local experts, churchgoers who had been using ayahuasca every two weeks for years and, in some cases, decades. 'This is the level of experience that a lot of people in the church have,' he says. Their familiarity with the psychedelic experience, he thought, was the perfect base on which to design an experiment. Not only would they be able to cope with the experience while lying down in the unfamiliar setting of a brain scanner, they might also be able to perform basic psychological tasks while doing so. 'It's similar to having someone do a task while surfing,' Araujo says. 'If you don't know how to surf, then it's going to be really hard to do a task on top of surfing.'

Araujo, a smiley and slim man with short grey hair, found ten volunteers who had surfed the psychedelic waves of ayahuasca for decades and were willing to be a part of his study. One man couldn't keep his head still during the scan, however, leaving nine in total (four men and five women). Inside the doughnut-shaped scanner, their brains showed wondrous things. In particular, when told to imagine a photograph they had just been shown, the parts of the brain involved in memory and vision were alight in activity, sometimes resembling the patterns seen in lucid dreaming. But the person was wide awake. From Araujo's point of view, it seemed as if they were actually seeing those images right in front of them, as if the trees, animals, or people they had previously been shown were actually in the brain scanner. 'By boosting the intensity of recalled images to the same level of [a] natural image,' Araujo and his colleagues wrote, 'ayahuasca lends a status of reality to inner experiences.' The title of their paper was 'Seeing with the Eyes Shut'.

Outside of the scanner and back in the Santo Daime ceremonies, it was obvious that the visions had benefits that far outlasted the ayahuasca trip. People with alcohol dependency or depression felt that they had worked through their problems. Again, this had been known since time immemorial. Although the psychedelic experiences on LSD and, more recently, psilocybin in Europe and the United States often focus on transcendental visions of God or an insight into an ultimate truth of the cosmos, the centuries-old use of ayahuasca has a slightly different modality: making sick people better. The visions of divine figures have, historically, been seen as real spirits or demons that have to be vanquished from the body through shamanic ritual. But these weren't seen as mystical experiences. They were purely medicinal, like removing a splinter from under the skin or an inflamed appendix. Araujo hoped to tap into this history of healing and see whether it could purge depression from people who hadn't responded to rounds of psychotherapy, antidepressants, and ECT.

'Turn On, Tune In, and Drop Out'

Extracted from climbing vines, leafy bushes, prickly cacti, or pimple-headed mushrooms, chemicals that can twist our sense of reality have been used by indigenous cultures for thousands of years, from Siberia to the Sahara and down into Mesoamerica. The word 'psychedelic', meaning 'mind manifesting', meanwhile, is a recent invention. It was coined in the 1950s by a doctor working in Canada, Humphry Osmond, as an alternative to hallucinogenic, a term that seemed overly negative for drugs that were hailed as direct lines to God and catalysts of love and peace. Writing to Aldous Huxley, the author of *Brave New World* and *The Doors of Perception*, Osmond summarised his choice in a poem:

> To fathom Hell or soar angelic,
> Just take a pinch of psychedelic.

As with cocaine in the nineteenth century, LSD – or Lysergic acid diethylamide – was the chemical encapsulation of hundreds of years of herbalism. First synthesised in 1938, it was seen as much a part of psychiatric treatment as the emerging antidepressants such as MAO inhibitors and imipramine. At a time when psychoanalysis was still at its height, LSD was seen as a catalyst to psychotherapy, a key that could unlock the cargo of the unconscious.

Betty Eisner, a therapist living in Los Angeles in the 1950s, was amazed at how this hallucinogenic drug could uncover, layer by layer, repressed memories and traumatic experiences as if it were a knife slicing through the onion of the unconscious. 'LSD makes available, from the very first session, other levels of consciousness which might require months or years of conventional therapy to effect,' she wrote. After her own experiments with the drug (the second ending with a deep depression that felt like the 'universe had collapsed' on her), she estimated that six hours of an LSD trip was equivalent to four years of psychoanalysis. This drug was so powerful that it could make the most seasoned analyst sit back and try not to get in the way of its progress. 'I think the function of the therapist is to optimise conditions for the LSD to work,' Eisner wrote.

In a standard hospital room in Los Angeles, Eisner's therapy sessions were simple but otherworldly. She provided her patients with a large hand-held mirror, advised them to bring a few family photographs from their childhood, and then gave them a small dose of LSD. During the eight hours of an LSD trip, patients could reframe old memories and see themselves from a different – and hopefully more positive – angle. All the while, the phonograph in the room spun through scores of classical music that seemed to harmonise the whole experience, guiding patients through the ups and downs of their past as if they were strung along a wave of sound. 'Concertos seemed to express and enhance the relationship of the individual to the environment as expressed by the interaction of the soloist with the orchestra,' Eisner wrote. 'I've found a Mantovani record of classical selections is good to start – and then Chopin's first piano concerto is better than anything.'

Throughout the 1950s and into the early 1960s, LSD was employed as an aid to psychotherapy for a range of mental illnesses, from anxiety to alcoholism and impotence to homosexuality (which was listed in the psychoanalysis-driven *DSM-I* as a 'sociopathic personality disturbance'). Its usefulness in depressions was first tested in 1952, four years before imipramine and iproniazid were first given to depressed patients in New York and Münsterlingen. Working in New York, Charles Savage gave LSD to 15 patients with depression – both endogenous and reactive – and found that three people recovered and four improved. But a comparable group of patients, matched for age, sex, and type of depression, showed similar rates of recovery with psychotherapy on its own. LSD's effects, in other words, seemed to offer no more than standard treatment. Further, while brief moments of euphoria were commonly observed, severe anxiety frequently surfaced and 'encouraged reticence rather than confidence,' Savage wrote. Rather than opening up the minds of depressed patients, LSD could just as easily close them shut. 'However,' Savage concluded, 'LSD affords therapeutically valuable insights into the unconscious processes by the medium of the hallucinations it produces.' To him, LSD was a tool for understanding, not for recovery.

Although Betty Eisner didn't specialise in depressed patients, she furnished psychedelic therapy with its future surroundings. She realised that the setting of these experiences was just as important as the drug that induced them. LSD didn't just create random visions of colour or the cosmos but seemed to blur the human sensorium with past memories and thoughts, painting them onto an ever-changing tapestry. With music, photographs, and the occasional piece of advice, Eisner became a conductor within her little hospital room, working to channel her patients' experiences towards a therapeutic crescendo. She was good at it. Sometimes it felt as if she had a natural gift for making people feel better. Although she could speak fluently in psychological and pharmacological terminology, she never forgot that the patient before her was a human in need of support. 'The one thing I have noticed is that the subject who takes LSD should be the whole centre of attention for as long as he or she needs it.'

Almost every trip on LSD led to moments of suffering and the potential for pain. After all, uncovering traumatic experiences is never easy. What might emerge? A dormant monster of their past? A memory that they thought was best left alone? After taking an inventory of her patients' lives as a barometer for what might emerge during the LSD session, Eisner told them to confront whatever fears they faced. '[T]he main technique which was found effective for basic problems which presented themselves in symbolic terms – such as raging fires, the void, dragons, a vortex – was to instruct the individual to move toward whatever appeared,' Eisner wrote. Although they didn't walk about in the room and could even lay completely still, in their minds they were taking some of the most difficult steps of their life. '[As] the individual under LSD "walked" toward the fire in order to be consumed, the flames which appeared to be of hellish intensity, suddenly changed in the moment of impact, of stepping into their midst, and were transformed, as though miraculously, into a situation capable of resolution.'

During a trip to Europe in 1958, Eisner met with many like-minded LSD researchers. In England, Germany, Czechoslovakia (a communist state that would split into the Czech Republic and Slovakia in 1993) and Italy, researchers were trying to grapple with the secrets that this drug seemed to uncover. As psychedelic trips often involved journeys through the stars and planets, were they an insight into our innate connection with the cosmos? Were the images projections of the internal workings of the mind? Or, as Eisner believed, was LSD a bridge from human to human, and, ultimately, from human to God? Whatever theories her peers held, Eisner found that her methods were unique. At Powick Hospital in Worcester, England, for instance, she found that patients were often left without a therapist – a guide – for long hours of their psychedelic trip. There was no music. No photographs or mirrors. And although art equipment was provided, it seemed as if their technique lacked the necessary element of individuality that she was accustomed to back in Los Angeles.

In September of that year, Eisner attended the first meeting of the International Congress of Neuro-Pharmacology, an academic summit that brought the leading figures of biological psychiatry to Rome. The three-day event, held in a building complex built under Mussolini, was dominated by the recent introduction of antidepressants and antipsychotics and what they might tell us about the chemical workings of the mind. But Eisner found enough researchers working on LSD for a lifetime of discussion. 'It was not only hearing what each one of us who was working with LSD had done, it was hearing what effect it had and why, what might have been a different and better way to use the drug, what each of us thought was the optimal method of dealing with different kinds of patients and situations, and basically and continually, the consideration of psychedelics in all their ramifications,' Eisner wrote.

On the final day of the conference, Eisner presented her work into LSD and psychotherapy to a small audience. Still, she felt honoured to be there. 'I felt like a true pioneer, reporting the results of my explorations to far and unknown lands,' she wrote. That evening, while walking through the mist and blurred lights along the River Tiber, Eisner spoke with Albert Hofmann, the chemist who had first synthesised LSD in 1938 and, two decades later, isolated psilocybin, the active molecule of magic mushrooms, and felt as if she were dreaming. '[It was] a fitting end to a magical trip,' she wrote. 'But one must always come back to Earth.'

While her early years of LSD research were defined by excitement and the hope of a new form of psychotherapy, Eisner soon found herself alone in an increasingly hostile world. While she tried to distance herself from Timothy Leary – the Harvard psychologist whose evangelical views on psilocybin led to his dismissal and exacerbated a general feeling of antagonism towards such psychoactive drugs – she nevertheless felt as if resistance to her own work was bubbling up. Sometimes, it felt like it wasn't about the drug at all. Many of her peers criticised her for giving LSD to patients when she 'only' had a PhD in psychology from UCLA, and therefore wasn't a trained psychiatrist, an MD. 'It does get discouraging to run into the prejudice which judges more from the initials after one's name (or one's sex, because I'm afraid this had some bearing, too) than by what the individual is and can do,' she wrote to Humphry Osmond in 1961. 'I get tired of carrying the torch and fighting the battle.' Her former supervisor at UCLA, Sidney Cohen, a bright and prematurely greying pharmacologist, split from Eisner for other reasons. He couldn't accept her theories of LSD that merged science with spirituality. While images of Ancient Greece, Egypt, or India were just hallucinations to Cohen, Eisner saw them as evidence for a collective consciousness of the human species. To her, these visions weren't illusions. They were memories.

Cohen was a level-headed pharmacologist, a scientist of chemical pathways and drug dynamics, and he worried that LSD was dangerous. As excitement over LSD-led psychotherapy was reaching its acme, he reached out to his peers from around the country and asked whether they'd had any problems during their LSD sessions. In total, 44 replied. From a collective sample of 5,000 individuals, Cohen felt reassured that there were no reported deaths from overdose, and while enduring psychotic episodes were a known risk, they were rare and often treatable with antipsychotics. Suicide was even rarer. Cohen only found two confirmed cases of users killing themselves 'directly due to LSD'. In 1960, he concluded that it was a relatively safe drug.

By 1962, he had changed his tune. 'Recently, we have encountered an increasing number of untoward events in connection with LSD-25 administration,' he wrote with his colleague in California, Keith Ditman. As LSD became more popular in the counterculture of California, and more suicides were found to have occurred during or shortly after an LSD trip, Cohen wrote several rebuttals to his initial publication and tried to warn fellow researchers and the general public of the potential dangers of this psychedelic drug. He wasn't alone in his caution; the scientific literature was replete with similar warnings. 'That it is a dangerous, toxic substance and not an innocent aid like milk, wheaties and orange juice ... has been pointed out on different occasions,' an editorial in *The New England Journal of Medicine* stated. 'Among the ominous effects of LSD are chronic hallucinosis, panic, severe paranoid reactions, suicide, various other psychotic development and reappearance of LSD symptoms a month to over a year after the original use, without reingestion.' Such 'flashbacks' seemed to follow no pattern, and no one could explain when or why they might occur. 'At present,' the editorial concluded, 'further work with these drugs certainly should be undertaken only in controlled settings by scientists capable of impartial, critical judgement.'

That already seemed an impossibility. Between 1959 and 1961, the Hollywood actor Cary Grant – one of the most famous people in the world at the time – had over 60 sessions of LSD therapy for his depression and, through an article published in *Good Housekeeping* in September 1960, helped push its use into the mainstream. Meanwhile, up and down the west coast of California, LSD parties were being held in psychologists' homes and on university campuses. Psychedelic bootleggers managed to create their own homemade stash of LSD and push the cultural swing from the black jumpers of the beatniks to the tie-dye T-shirts of hippies. Ken Kesey, the author of *One Flew Over the Cuckoo's Nest*, held so-called 'acid tests' across California in which live music – provided by bands such as the Grateful Dead – and LSD were mixed into powerful, mind-altering cocktails. Passing this test was like climbing a mountain: often strenuous with sheer drops at one side, but the view from the top was said to be spectacular. The whole scene was encapsulated by Timothy Leary: 'Turn on, tune in, and drop out.'

At an LSD party in Hollywood, Sidney Cohen met someone who soaked sugar cubes in doses of LSD that were ten times stronger than the average dose. After a ten-year-old boy accidentally ate one of these sugar cubes and had psychotic reactions for months afterwards, the FDA heeded the warnings from medical professionals such as Cohen and tried to take control of the drug. Sandoz, the pharmaceutical company that produced LSD, restricted supply of its product to psychiatrists funded by the National Institute of Mental Health, cutting its customers from 200 to 70 in one go. Charles Savage, the psychiatrist who first gave LSD to depressed patients, argued that the misuse in California shouldn't blight everyone's prospects of studying the drug. 'LSD therapy should not be seen from the narrow vantage point of Southern California where it has been vastly misused.' With her PhD in psychology, Betty Eisner was one of the researchers whose supply of LSD was cut, bringing her therapy sessions to an abrupt end.

In 1966, two US Senate meetings were held to discuss LSD. Timothy Leary, recently sacked from Harvard, used Sidney Cohen's 1960 paper to argue that LSD was 'remarkably safe'. Cohen, meanwhile, put forward his updated perspective. 'We have seen something which in a way is most alarming, more alarming than death in a way, and that is the loss of all cultural values, the loss of feeling of right and wrong, of good and bad,' he said. 'These people lead a valueless life, without motivation, without any ambition ... they are deculturated, lost to society, lost to themselves.' LSD was said to cause mental illness – turning a mild-mannered individual into a psychotic killer, for instance – and legislation against its use was destined for a signature. While not everyone was against Leary and LSD – Senator Robert Kennedy, whose wife had undergone LSD therapy, said, 'perhaps to some extent we have lost sight of the fact that it can be very, very helpful in our society if used properly' – LSD was made an illegal substance in the United States in October 1968. By 1970, it was banned in the UK and throughout much of Europe. Only in the Netherlands was it used into the 1980s as an aid to help concentration-camp survivors explore and come to terms with their traumatic past.

Building a New System

In his late 60s, David Nutt is a moustachioed grandfatherly figure of psychedelic therapy who wears knitted sweaters and swears a lot. A neuroscientist and pharmacologist by training, he has built his career on understanding drugs that politicians prefer to ignore: MDMA, ketamine, cannabis, and, most recently, psilocybin. He was once an adviser to the UK government but, in 2009, was expelled from the committee after he claimed that taking ecstasy was safer than riding a horse, a pastime that kills ten people per year in the UK and leads to thousands of permanent head injuries. (In the *Journal of Psychopharmacology*, Nutt sarcastically called this 'overlooked addiction' Equasy, or 'Equine Addiction Syndrome', and wrote, 'Making riding illegal would completely prevent all these harms and would be, in practice, very easy to do – it is hard to use a horse in a clandestine manner or in the privacy of one's own home!') In his office in west London, Nutt has a metallic plaque advertising LSD and a giant mushroom made from a yew tree, a type of wood historically selected for the manufacture of longbows to defend churches in Britain. Nutt beams with delight in the knowledge that every church in England had at least one yew tree growing inside its perimeter. Such topical digressions distract him from the nonsensical reality that consumes most of his energy.

'It's the worst censorship of research in the history of the world,' he says, referring to the existing legislation on psychoactive substances such as psychedelics and MDMA. Across

North America and Europe, psilocybin and other psychedelics are listed as Schedule 1 drugs (substances that have no accepted medicinal use and a high potential for abuse). Such a classification infuriates Nutt. 'Even if the war on drugs stopped people using drugs, which it doesn't, it still would not justify denying these drugs for treatment,' he says. 'And it doesn't even do that! As far as we can ascertain, [current drug legislation] doesn't affect use at all; other than making use more dangerous. It's outrageous, it's absurd. The whole thing is just a fucking farce.'

Despite its legal classification, Nutt and his colleagues at Imperial College London were given access to psilocybin for their first study in 2011. As with Draulio Barros de Araujo in Brazil, they initially gave the drug to healthy volunteers and scanned their brains during their psychedelic trips. It was then that they saw the antidepressant potential of this drug shining through their datasets. Part of the limbic system that was often found to be overactive in depressed people was shut down. Nutt calls this the 'Mayberg centre' after Helen Mayberg and her research into area 25. After being silenced or quietened, other parts of the brain began to communicate with each other, creating a rich harmony of brain signals that reintroduced regions that had previously been rigidly isolated. It was from this finding that, Nutt says, depression seemed like a worthy target for psychedelic therapy. 'Depression is classically a disorder where people are over engaged in internal thought. They feel guilty, they think about themselves, about what they've done wrong, they can't disengage from that inner thought process, which is usually negative,' he says. 'And psychedelics usually disrupt that.'

The first trial, published in 2015, was in a familiar setting, one that transported the work of Betty Eisner into the twenty-first century. The hospital room at Imperial College London was furnished with fake candles, essential oils, flowers, and a twirling model of the solar system floating above a padded gurney. A specially selected playlist filled the room with a suitable auditory landscape. The psilocybin was made in a laboratory. The experience was largely artificial – that is, a construct made from predetermined settings, sensations, and quality-controlled doses. But the experience was nonetheless magical. 'I cried a lot during the experience, but I also laughed a lot,' one patient, a 36-year-old man who had been abused as a child and gripped by depression ever since, says. 'I learnt so much in such a short period of time. Certain things I've thought before, but they weren't thoughts any more. They were truth.' When his depression returned six months after the trial, this patient contacted Amanda Feilding, the creator of the Beckley Foundation that partly funded the work at Imperial College, and asked for another dose. But she couldn't help him. This was a research project that cost millions of dollars and took years of planning. Psilocybin wasn't a legal prescription. It was still Schedule 1, a drug judged to have no medicinal value. As someone who remembered the days when LSD was legal in the 1960s, Feilding was furious. 'It seems to be absolutely insane, and also criminal, that there's no way, under present regulation, where one can offer a booster for someone who has had a successful treatment,' she says. 'We must open this treatment up to suffering patients.'

Not everyone is as eager to push psychedelics into mainstream medicine. 'We have to establish whether it's a treatment,' says James Rucker who, in 2016, moved from the group at Imperial College to start his own research project at King's College London. 'There's this thing called the winner's curse in research,' he explains. 'A research team has an idea: they think psilocybin is going to be a treatment for depression. Part of the

reason why they have that idea is because they have a precon-
ception in their head about the fact that the treatment's going
to work.' The scientists carrying out the work expect positive
results and this expectation influences how patients respond to
the new treatment. In a way, the winner's curse is the first step
toward a placebo effect. 'This is what happens for a lot of treatments for depression,' Rucker adds. 'The first trials with Prozac
were quite similar. People who hadn't responded to anything
else miraculously got better on this new and novel drug that
was thought to be the next miracle cure.' Today, Prozac is
known to have no greater effects than any other antidepressant,
and, according to a large meta-analysis on 21 different antidepressants published in *The Lancet* in 2018, is significantly less
effective than escitalopram, another SSRI. Rucker, a quiet per-
fectionist born in 1978, a time when the first personal computers
were beginning to hit the market, exudes a youthful manner
that belies his clinical experience. He first became interested in
the brain as a child, comparing its trillions of neurons to the
electrical wiring in his computer's hardware. Now in his mid
40s, he has been a psychiatrist for over 15 years and has struggled with his own mental health for much longer. 'Depression
runs through my family like a knife,' he says. After trying several SSRIs, he was eventually given the same drug his father
was once prescribed: imipramine. 'It actually worked brilliantly
for me. I stayed on it for about 10 years.' He felt no real side
effects other than slight constipation, but that was a small price
to pay compared to the libido-sapping effects of some SSRIs.

Today, Rucker is part of an international collaboration that
aims to assess whether psychedelics might add to the pharmacological and psychological approaches to depression, or
whether they are a colourful flavour of the winner's curse.
Funded by COMPASS Pathways, a research initiative set up by

99

0

0280

George Goldsmith and Ekaterina Malievskaia in 2016 after their son didn't respond to conventional antidepressant therapy, this multi-centre trial includes 216 patients from 11 cities dotted across northern Europe and the eastern United States and Canada. 'We came at this not from a position of favouring the legalisation of psychedelics,' Malievskaia told a reporter at *International Business Times* in 2017. 'We came from a perspective of creating another option for patients who have exhausted all the others.'

'They've done what no one else has done,' Rucker says, referring to Goldsmith and Malievskaia. 'There are very strict rules about how pure you have to manufacture a compound in order to use it as a medicine in humans. It's difficult. And it's particularly difficult for a drug that is Schedule 1. And they've done it.' Although COMPASS Pathways provides the drug free of charge to psychiatrists like Rucker, it is still the most expensive component of the clinical trial. The strict legislation that surrounds the drug means that its transportation – from manufacturers in the UK to King's College London, for example – requires a series of high-security stop-off points. The capsules are delivered by a special courier under constant surveillance, have to be triple signed during any handover, and are kept in safes bolted into a concrete floor. 'All of that has a cost implication,' says Rucker, 'and we have to pay for that.' At New York University, scientists have to weigh their supply of psilocybin twice a day, just in case someone decided to steal some. Psilocybin is a chemical found in a smorgasbord of mushrooms around the world and has been used in spiritual ceremonies for millennia. In academic research, however, it is being treated as if it is a nuclear weapon.

Unlike many other researchers in this field of psychedelic medicine, Rucker is grateful that it is so strictly monitored.

Schedule 1 doesn't reflect its potential therapeutic qualities, but it reduces the chance of history repeating itself, he says. In the 1960s, LSD filtered into the counterculture and its promiscuous use led to a widespread ban. Today, with strict laws prohibiting the use of psychedelics in the public, Rucker thinks that this will help keep the drug within psychiatric facilities, a restriction that keeps its use open to people who might benefit from the drug. 'Of course, recreational use still happens,' he says. 'It happens anyway,' regardless of what schedules or laws are placed on a substance that can be harvested in a local park or from a cowpat in an open meadow.

In late 2017, I had recently turned 27 years old and was more desperate than ever. Still on the highest dose of citalopram, I felt nauseous and fed up, and I was on the lookout for alternatives. I had started researching depression treatment, and I felt like the medical literature had more to offer than my doctor could provide. I quickly realised that one class of drugs that was soaking up a lot of media attention – in brain-imaging studies and on the front cover of magazines like *New Scientist*, psychedelic therapy was the next big thing in treatment. Early trials with psilocybin in people with cancer and depression suggested that this was *the* treatment for people who had failed to respond to other treatments. In a less rational, more desperate mood, I was willing to try anything to feel better. I decided to harvest some mushrooms of my own.

It wouldn't be my first experience with psychedelics, but it was the first time I was hoping for more than just some trippy images with friends. In what's called a washout period, I reduced the dose of citalopram gradually over a few weeks, hoping this would be the last time I would ever have to request a prescription from my doctor.

The mushrooms tasted earthy and, although there was a slightly bitter aftertaste, weren't wholly unappetising. Their stems were white with bright blue bruises, the hallmark sign of psilocybin. Though they were listed as Schedule 1, illegal to buy, grow, or consume, I didn't care. If the studies were correct, this might actually be an antidepressant that worked. I prepared music that I enjoyed and thought would be soothing under the influence of the drug.

I kept a notebook of my experience, noting down anything that I felt, thought and saw. With a hologram of stormtroopers from *Star Wars* on its front cover, I wrote down what might emerge during my trip: my childhood anxieties, the conflicts and separation in my family, my former loves and my future hopes, suicide. Then the psilocybin started to take effect.

'I don't want to throw up,' I wrote. 'A warmth inside my body. A glow like a heating filament. Tiny glowing lights behind closed eyelids – purple and green. Illuminating and then fading.'

At one point, I appreciated a cup of tea not only for its taste but also for how it seemed to move. 'The tea is breathing,' I wrote. 'As the steam comes out of the top, the tea level seems to move, tidally.'

I then had an interaction with a squirrel I saw out of the window. 'Beauty,' I wrote. 'Soft skips from one moment to the next. Cleaning of the face and tail, all otherworldly cuteness. The neighbour walks down his garden, his formal shoes clapping on the stone flags. The squirrel freezes. Two front legs braced like furniture. I feel it. Everyone gets anxious.' Then: 'I'm going to close the curtain, to take the sharpness out of the sun.'

After further ramblings on the dustiness of our flat, how my pen is a tool for ink, and the stressful, irritating and then beautiful moments of Peter Green's Fleetwood Mac, I drew a line under my notes. They stopped for a few hours. At three o'clock in the afternoon, I summarised what had just happened. 'A tremendous force was pushing down on me, reducing me to insignificance. My mouth was relaxed, open. Only air coming in, air coming out.' But it wasn't me breathing – I was a mere apparatus for air, like a wind instrument, that someone else was playing through the rhythms of life. 'I feel small, fragile, something to be preserved and taken care of. My shoulders are only so wide and I can feel my bones through a thin layer of skin.'

As I wrote during this trip, I thought this was the end of my citalopram prescription. What if I could take smaller doses of magic mushrooms in order to adjust my perspective on life, to see beauty rather than blight?

After six or so hours, I moved into the kitchen, sat on a footstool, and ate some vegetable soup.

It was soon clear that this day had little effect on my well-being. There were moments of peace and periods of darkness, but there were few long-lasting benefits or nuggets of understanding that I could employ in my everyday life. But I was missing a crucial part of psychedelic therapy. The drug is only useful in the right setting. I had no guidance from a trained therapist, and the music I chose was sometimes terrifying. Despite my intentions, it was a recreational experience and not medicinal.

Wanting to know more about psychedelic therapy, I reached out to Ros Watts, a silver-haired clinical psychologist at Imperial College London who guides people with depression through psilocybin trips. The guidance begins long before any pill of psilocybin is taken. Watts instils a few important maxims into her patients during their first check-ups. 'Trust, let go, be open,' for example. '"In and Through", which is a very good one,' Watts says. 'If you see a monster, don't run away from it, don't try and hide, look it in the eye and try to go through it.'

Formerly a NHS psychotherapist, Watts became tired and deflated by the quality of the services provided and the long waiting lists to receive them. She thought that the standard five or six sessions of CBT weren't sufficient for many of her patients. 'Therapy takes a really long time,' Watts says. 'But if you've got five sessions with someone and you've got a complex history of trauma, then it's really hard – it's just not enough.' Plus, with patients far outnumbering the number of therapists, the waiting time for therapy was eight months to a year. Who knows what could happen in that stretch of time? Inspired by one of her friends who found relief from her own depression after visiting an ayahuasca retreat, Watts moved to Imperial College London in 2015 and became the latest member of a psychedelic revolution. 'Either you stay within a system that isn't working,' Watts says, 'or build a new one that does work.'

Seeing with Eyes Shut

In 2018, Draulio Barros de Araujo, his PhD student Fernanda Palhano-Fontes, and their colleagues in Brazil published the first randomised placebo-controlled trial into psychedelic therapy for depression. Although legal to use in religious ceremonies, it is still difficult to obtain ethical licences to test ayahuasca on critically ill people. It took Araujo years to obtain approval for a trial encompassing just 29 patients.

But the results were worth the wait. Just one week after their ayahuasca experience, around 57 per cent of the participants showed a significant drop – more than a 50 per cent cut in their scores on standardised health questionnaires – in their depressive symptoms, a rapidity that far exceeds the three to four weeks of standard antidepressants. Although it is impossible to create a placebo of a drug that leads to visions and distortions of space, Araujo used an 'active placebo' that led to the familiar gastrointestinal distress of ayahuasca. A mixture of water, yeast, citric acid, zinc sulphate, and caramel food colouring, this drink had no psychedelic effects whatsoever but could be mistaken for the real thing by people who had never tried ayahuasca before, which was true for all of the people in the trial. Using this clever trick, Araujo found that only 20 per cent of patients given this active placebo showed significant improvement, less than half the rate of those who were given ayahuasca. Importantly, the only people who became substantially more depressed during this time were four people who were given the placebo.

Based at the Brain Research Institute in Natal – a three-storey, white-washed building set upon a hillside in one of the least developed regions of north east Brazil – it was certainly a change in scenery from the metropolis of São Paulo where Araujo had worked until 2009. His patients, meanwhile, had never seen anything like the state-of-the-art institute and the Onofre Lopes University Hospital nearby. 'A lot of our patients come from very difficult realities,' Araujo says. 'We are talking about one of the poorest parts of Brazil. [And] Brazil is already a poor country.' One of the most common social problems was losing sons, brothers, or fathers to drug trafficking. Either they were imprisoned, disappeared, or dead. Although they were only meant to stay from Tuesday to Friday, several patients asked if they could stay for a few more nights over the weekend.

Araujo will never forget the 63-year-old man with intractable depression and a stomach as rigid as wood. He told Araujo that he had been a fisherman all his life but, over the last ten years, he had rarely left his home. He hadn't seen the ocean in years. After the ayahuasca trial, he had a dream that brought these two aspects of his life into perspective. What if, after spending all of his working life at sea, the ocean had become the only place he felt comfortable, content, at peace? Could this explain his depression? Could the sights and smells of the ocean be curative? 'You know what, Doctor?' the patient told Araujo. 'Your tea of the Indians [ayahuasca] just relieved me from something that I had for years. I woke up thinking that I want to go to the ocean.' After leaving Araujo's lab, he went straight to shore and peered over the endless blue towards the horizon.

The old fisherman had never taken ayahuasca before and didn't know where the experience would lead him.

Unbeknownst to him, he still hadn't taken ayahuasca, even after the trial had finished. He had been given a placebo. 'For me, it was the most beautiful moment I've had in the trial,' says Araujo, chuckling at the thought of it coming from a fake ayahuasca drink.

'Psychiatrists treat the placebo effect as something that's bad,' Araujo says. 'After the experience we had in our trials, the placebo effect is one of the most beautiful things I've ever seen.' Some patients had been depressed for decades, had lists of medications that were two-pages long, and had been given several sessions of ECT. Easily making the cut for a diagnosis of treatment-resistant depression, some of them, like the retired fisherman, responded beautifully to a drink that was little more than lemon juice turned brown.

A week after his fake ayahuasca drink, the retired fisherman returned to Onofre Lopes University Hospital in Natal. At a meeting with a psychiatrist, he lifted up his shirt and revealed his belly. It was no longer stiff as it had been when he was depressed. Though he had never met this psychiatrist before, he was delighted to show her, rolling his belly in and out like the undulating waves of the open ocean.

Whether they are swallowed as a pill, eaten as mushrooms, or drunk as a tea, psychedelics force us to rethink the placebo effect. 'The placebo effect is all about the expectations we bring to a treatment, and that is all cognitively mediated – in our brains,' says James Rucker, the youthful psychiatrist from King's College London. 'And it's precisely that mechanism that psychedelics seem to effect – they dissolve our opinion structure and expectation-driven models of reality.' Whether it is ayahuasca, psilocybin, mescaline, DMT, or LSD, psychedelics are catalysts of expectation. The thoughts that someone brings into a psychedelic session can be manufactured into a sense of reality, with an added flash of colour. If someone has heard that they could see a glimpse of the cosmos, they might end up flying at hyper-speed toward the stars, floating among the Milky Way, or getting sucked into a black hole. If someone thinks that these drugs can bring them into greater harmony with the trauma of their past, they might meet a former abuser or see a vision of themselves happy and at peace. As Jules Evans, policy director at the Centre for the History of the Emotions at the University of London, wrote in *Aeon* magazine, 'Ayahuasca reflected my beliefs back to me, in glorious technicolour, and made them feel transcendentally true.' If someone *wants* to recover from depression, in other words, maybe these drugs can make that into a reality.

If the early trials into psychedelics are repeated and confirmed, what can explain their antidepressant effect? Although the details are somewhat nebulous, there are two leading explanations. The first, frequently promoted by European and American research groups working on psilocybin, is that they decrease the amount of 'mind-wandering'. When not engaged in a task such as conversation or manual labour, the brain shows a typical pattern of activity called the default mode network (DMN), a neuronal highway that connects disparate parts of the brain involved in intention, memory, and vision. When the body is not doing anything, the mind is active, thinking about the future, musing over ourselves and how we feel, and dwelling on the past. As Fernanda Palhano-Fontes and her colleagues wrote in 2015, it is 'a private, continuous and often unnoticed phenomenon'. But, over the last decade or so, brain-imaging techniques have allowed scientists to take note of this phenomenon. A famous study from 2012, for example, found that experienced meditators who were trained in either concentration, loving-kindness, or choiceless-awareness practices could shut down the DMN by reducing the amount of mind wandering that takes place when focusing on their breath and allowing thoughts to flow through their mind without friction.

Similar effects have been found for all the psychedelics so far tested. The activity of the default mode network is reduced. In 2015, for example, Araujo and his colleagues found that eight brain regions that comprise the DMN showed significant drops in activity after ayahuasca intake. But he is hesitant to jump to conclusions about what this might mean in terms of how psychedelics work. 'I have a lot of issues with the hype around the default mode network,' he says. Many studies don't actually show that the network is downregulated, even the study into meditation from 2012. Instead, they focus on one or two parts of the brain that are associated with the network. But a network, by definition, is an interconnected series of parts that can't be seen in isolation. 'If you look at [the psilocybin] data, if you look at the meditation data, you will see that whatever is being called the "default mode network" is actually one single area, which is the posterior cingulate cortex,' Araujo says.

Then there's the simplest explanation, the Occam's razor of psychedelic therapy. Since ayahuasca trips have long been referred to as 'labour', perhaps any reduction in the DMN is not because people are reducing their mind wandering but because they are hard at work. The heavy lifting might naturally switch off the DMN, as any form of activity does in normal consciousness. People are so focused on their trip, so dedicated to the labour that it entails, that their brains aren't in default mode.

After spending two years on sabbatical in Santa Barbara on the west coast of California, Araujo has sifted through his datasets from Natal and has found a more illuminating theory that doesn't involve the DMN. Suitably, it relates to the original descriptor of the hallucinations that this tea creates: *mirações*, seeings. While under the influence of ayahuasca, the visual cortex of Araujo's original volunteers, his psychedelic 'surfers', showed the same patterns of activity as when someone is awake with their eyes open. Even when their eyes were closed, these same patterns, known as alpha waves, remained stable. (The same result was found by researchers in London using DMT.) Whatever visions ayahuasca generates, the brain interprets them as reality, not as dream-like hallucinations. 'The interpretation is that when you are under the influence of psychedelics, you lose the mechanism that [occurs] when you have your eyes closed,' Araujo says. 'In other words, you gain the ability to "see" while you have your eyes closed. And what is it that you see? In our hypothesis, what you see is your thoughts.'

We usually experience our thoughts. We don't see them. 'So what we think is that what these [psychedelic] substances do is to increase your awareness to this process of spontaneous thinking,' Araujo adds. And as humans we believe what we see. This might even explain why these substances can be so effective in the treatment of depression.

If the old fisherman's insights from the active placebo were beautiful, the patients who actually received ayahuasca brought a harrowing insight on this 'seeing with the eyes shut' theory. One patient was walking over a meadow of wild flowers and luscious green grass on a sunny day. It was a peaceful paradise. Then she saw her dead sister standing in front of her. As real as any conversation she has ever had, her sister then told her that she was fine, that she should look after herself rather than worrying about those who had passed away. It was as if she had been resurrected to give her this message. When she returned from her trip, this didn't feel like a dream at all. It felt like aya-huasca had summoned her sister from the heavens to show her that she was okay. 'That's gotta be powerful,' Araujo says. Another patient was a woman who had tried to kill herself. During her ayahuasca trip, she was lying in a coffin as her mother cried inconsolably outside. But in this vision she was conscious and was trying to tell her mum that she was okay. But she couldn't. When the trip subsided, this image provided an alternative perspective on her potential absence and made her realise just how missed she would be.

Whether it is down to the DMN, the catalysis of the placebo effect, or the photographic realism of dreams, the exact mech-anism of how psychedelics work remains a mystery. But this is true for a range of standard prescriptions, from aspirin to anti-depressants. What brings the nascent field of psychedelics a little closer to a clinical reality is that there is already a psyche-delic drug that has been approved by the European Commission and the FDA in the United States.

In the late 1990s, as John Cryan was searching for novel ways to reduce the lag time in serotonin-based antidepressants, a very different drug emerged onto the scene. It took effect within hours rather than weeks. It didn't work through serotonin, instead blocking the receptor of glutamate, the most common neurotransmitter in the human brain. And it had been on the World Health Organisation's Essential Medicines List since 1985, a drug that was well stocked in medical cabinets around the world. This latest breakthrough was with the anaesthetic known as ketamine. After finding promising results in animal studies, researchers from a small health centre in Connecticut, New Haven, found that in just four hours seven people with depressions that hadn't responded to typical antidepressants

started to improve on this drug. With a single injection of ketamine solution, their improvements lasted for up to three
weeks. 'These findings represent one of the most significant
advances in the field of depression over the past 50 years,' two
psychiatrists later wrote, 'a novel, rapid-acting, efficacious antidepressant agent with a mechanism that is completely different
from currently available medications.'

Although this clinical trial – the first with ketamine and
depressed patients – was published in 2000, the drug wasn't
unknown to the field of psychedelic therapy. In 1973, Betty Eisner read that ketamine held some of the key features that she
found so useful in LSD. '[Ketamine] led to a loss of time sense
and detachment from the environment,' two doctors working
in Shiraz, Iran, wrote that year. 'It activated the unconscious
and repressed memories, while it temporarily transported the
patient back into childhood with frightening reality, reviving
traumatic events with intense emotional reaction. Some had
recall of events leading to their illness.' One patient reported
that, after a dose of ketamine, a 'heavy burden of sin is now
gone'. Another felt 'carefree with no worries'.

Ketamine is a controversial drug. Nicknamed 'Special K' or
simply 'ket', it has been a popular drug of choice at rave parties
since the 1990s. Prolonged daily use can lead to irreversible
damage to the bladder and kidney, as well as intense stomach
cramps colloquially known as 'K-cramps'. And although it
undoubtedly has some remarkable effects on depressed patients
in the short term, its suitability for long-term treatment is still
a matter of concern. 'Currently, there is limited evidence to
recommend ketamine as a viable treatment option for treatment-resistant depression,' a report from the Royal College of
Psychiatrists stated in February 2017. 'Short-term efficacy has
been demonstrated after a single treatment, but benefits are

not lasting for most patients, and mood can rapidly decline after initial improvement, potentially increasing suicide risk.' In the US, the FDA approved esketamine (a drug that is the molecular mirror image of ketamine and has very similar effects) for treatment-resistant depression in March 2019. 'There has been a long-standing need for additional effective treatments for treatment-resistant depression, a serious and life-threatening condition,' said Tiffany Farchione, acting director of the Division of Psychiatry in the FDA's Centre for Drug Evaluation and Research, in a press release. 'Because of safety concerns, the drug will only be available through a restricted distribution system and it must be administered in a certified medical office where the health care provider can monitor the patient.' For people who have received at least two antidepressants at an adequate dose and duration and didn't respond to either, esketamine provides a sense of hope, a shift from serotonin. For some patients, it can be a long-awaited lifeline.

Manufactured in 1962, used to treat nerve pain in American soldiers during the Vietnam War, and given to farm animals as a sedative before surgical operations, ketamine also has none of the historical and cultural foundations that other psychedelics have accrued over centuries. Nonetheless, Araujo sees an opportunity in its example. By using a fast-acting psychedelic with a short duration of action – such as DMT, one of the core ingredients of ayahuasca – could intensive therapy sessions be provided in a clinic setting on an outpatient basis? Instead of spending an entire night at a religious retreat, psychedelic therapy could be provided within one hour. 'One thing I have to do as a scientist, and believing that these substances might be helpful for a lot of people, is to incentivise the opening of places that different types of people could have access to,' Araujo says. 'So we already have the [Santo Daime] church.

Now, I think we need therapeutic centres for people that might find other [non-religious] settings more helpful.'

As with moral treatment in the eighteenth century, the secrets and traditions of religious practices are still offering new avenues for therapy. Although translated into the jargon of science and brain imaging, this rich history shouldn't be ignored as psychedelic therapy grows in popularity. Araujo never loses sight of the cultural roots of his research. 'It bothers me that part of my science will be interpreted as "new knowledge",' he says, 'when I know from the bottom of my heart that we didn't do anything. We're just playing. We're hardly scratching the surface.'

As scientists around the world delve deeper into the potential for psychedelic therapy in the treatment of depression, they push the two fields of psychiatry into closer union. Whether it's a cup of ayahuasca tea or a pill of psilocybin, each trip crashes psychological and biological treatments together in a flash of colour. There's the use of a drug with antidepressant qualities, a welcome addition to the chemicals that first amazed Nathan Kline and Roland Kuhn in the late 1950s. Crucially, there's the psychotherapy that combines the work of Sigmund Freud, Myrna Weissman, and Aaron Beck, guiding patients through repressed thoughts, problematic relationships, and traumatic memories that surface during the session. The legacy of Freud is also seen in the comfortable and confidential room, the couch-like hospital bed. On top of this basic setting, the specifically chosen music, fragrances, and ornaments are a reminder of the little-known work of Betty Eisner. And then there are the scientific methods – brain scans, blood tests, health questionnaires – that call to mind the laboratories of Emil Kraepelin's clinic in Munich. Within a few hours, a century of psychiatry unfolds.

Epilogue – New Life

In March 2020, a few days after I had weaned myself off sertraline, I discovered that a new phase of my life had already begun. Lucy was pregnant. The two lines on the pregnancy tests were clear. In just under nine months, all going well, we would be expecting our first child. As the embryo grew, the pregnancy app we had downloaded suggested some strange developmental comparisons. One week it was the size of a ladybird, the next a raspberry. At the 12-week scan, the very real baby appeared instantaneously on the screen in front of us. I was silent, stunned at how obviously human this image was. Here was our future. My glasses were steamed up from wearing a face mask – fashioned from material with dog prints on it – that I hoped would help reduce the spread of Covid-19. My tears flowed down my cheeks and soaked into the fabric. At the 20-week scan, with the peak of the pandemic just a few months behind us, I wasn't allowed into the hospital. I sat on a wall outside and waited for any news.

After half an hour or so, Lucy texted me to say that 'everything is perfect,' adding that she thought the baby looked like me. As a concession for Covid-19 restrictions, the hospital was handing out envelopes to those couples who wanted to know the sex of their baby. During a time of crippling uncertainty we opted in to this small insight into our future. We opened ours at a wildflower garden at the university campus nearby. We were having a girl.

Depression often coincides with new life. Magical, mesmerising, and crazy to even contemplate, the growth of a single cell into a human baby can be a time of darkness for many soon-to-be mothers. (Depression runs through Lucy's family as well as mine, and she has a close network of relatives that can offer support and share their own lived experiences.) For an estimated one in every ten pregnant women, antenatal depression is a burden that can far outweigh that of the expanding bump. Once the baby is born, the risks are increased further. By some estimates, postnatal depression affects two out of every ten women. In some countries around the world, that figure can rise to one in two – half of all new mothers. 'It's called postpartum depression, but actually a lot of cases actually started in pregnancy,' says Louise Howard, professor of women's mental health at King's College London. 'So the perinatal period is a time when interventions do need to be tailored to the woman.'

I have also worried how a child might affect my own mental health. In my most desperate moment, I told Lucy that I never wanted to have children, not only to prevent my depression being passed on to future generations but also to reduce my risk of relapse. I worried that the sleepless nights and the stress of caring for a child might exacerbate my anguish. In the worst-case scenario, I saw the stress building to such a degree that suicide left a permanent hole in the family, inevitably causing my child to suffer. Nature and nurture combine, the cycle is renewed. Depression takes root.

I regretted my comment to Lucy, both for how much pain it caused, and also for how inaccurate it was. Some people are at higher risk than others, but depression isn't solely determined by the genome. While parenting is stressful, it also can be life-affirming. And my worries over how I might deal with the life transition of becoming a father were overly pessimistic. There is every chance that I'll be a great parent. After all, I have loved watching my baby nephew grow from a gurgling blob into a child who can smile, finish 20-piece jigsaw puzzles in seconds, and talk. When it's my own child developing, surely the joy of such achievements will be even greater. Reality testing, overturning negative thought patterns: this is no longer cognitive therapy but a part of my everyday life.

Despite our best efforts, the risk of depression can only be reduced; it can't be removed entirely. To remove depression from society would require the removal of all of its triggers – both social and biological, known and unknown. We can't kill depression. But, with treatment, we can stop it from killing us.

In April 2020, a month after my last dose of sertraline, my motivation started to wane. Thoughts of suicide became more appealing, seductive. Ideas of failure became all-encompassing. The pain inside my skull was often unbearable. Was this a temporary dip caused by the unforeseen stress of life in lockdown? Or, despite my best efforts, was I still not ready to live life without the support of antidepressants? Each day I wondered whether sertraline was key to my contentment in life, my ability to function. Was I only interested in life when I was on drugs? I tried to rationalise this latter question: being on antidepressants isn't a sign of weakness or failure, I told myself. I am not a machine with broken parts. I am someone who has a family history of mental disorder, has experienced life events that are known to trigger depression, and is currently living through a global health crisis and the second recession in my adult life.

In early June 2020, three months after my last dose, I returned to sertraline. My condition had been worsening for weeks, I was crippled by a lack of motivation, and my suicidal thoughts were becoming more threatening. I started to believe that our unborn child would be better off without me. I told Lucy all this, not to upset her but so we could discuss our options. We agreed that antidepressants were still a necessary part of my life. I applied for a course of high-intensity CBT and, as the waiting list was at least four months, swallowed my sertraline before bed.

I had forgotten how sick these drugs make me feel. The nausea, at least for the first couple of weeks, made the sides of my tongue tickle and the pit of my stomach swirl. I yawned a lot. Diarrhoea was as unwelcome as it was frequent. A headache sat right behind my forehead and wouldn't budge. And yet, even those first few days were a relief. The initial dizziness and drowsiness of these drugs had a calming effect on my mind. Although I wasn't feeling good, it was still a refreshing way of feeling bad. Once the nausea and confusion subsided, I slowly noticed myself changing, just as I had when I first took sertraline in early 2018. I felt calmer, less anxious. I enjoyed sleep. I could read and write – two important pastimes for an author – and not feel like I was a failure. I came to the conclusion that antidepressants are effective treatments for my depression and feel overwhelmed with relief that they exist.

I wonder what treatments will be available for our child if she ever needs support. Depression is more common in women than in men, and we know that mental disorders run in families. I hope that unlike when I was growing up in the 1990s, talking therapy will be seen as a natural part of the healthcare system, like going to the dentist or seeing your doctor for vaccinations. Perhaps it won't be viewed as something negative, as the word 'treatment' suggests, but as a restorative activity that can tease apart the stresses that everyone faces. Whether it is in schools or at doctors' practices, might we call it health promotion rather than psychological therapy? Will treatments be tailored to the symptoms that are most intrusive on a person's mental health? Will there be blood tests for levels of inflammation? Will specific diet and exercise regimens be prescribed for their antidepressant qualities? Will brain scans – or the symptom profiles to which they are associated – be used to predict who might respond to biological treatments or talking therapies from day one?

Will we even use the word depression? Over the last decade, there has been a trend in psychiatry to do away with diagnoses all together. There is an emerging argument that all mental illnesses are interconnected, like the branches of a tree growing from the same trunk. Whether it's bipolar and schizophrenia, anxiety and depression, or autism and ADHD, there is a high level of overlap between one mental disorder and another. Symptoms are shared. Patterns in brain activity overlap. And the genetic risk factors for each disorder – while diverse and small in effect – can be the same whether someone is diagnosed with major depression or generalised anxiety disorder. These common threads extend into treatments as well. People with anxiety disorders respond to antidepressants. People with severe depression respond to antipsychotics. CBT can help people manage pretty much any mental concern, from insomnia to psychosis.

One common thread that might connect mental disorders such as depression and anxiety is called neuroticism, a gauge of a person's reactivity to stress. Not only does this personality trait have a high genetic component, there is evidence that it is also a precursor to depression in adolescents. Childhood influences, personality traits, and an absence of strict diagnoses: psychiatry might be moving away from the legacy of Emil Kraepelin and towards that of Sigmund Freud. Although this idea of an interconnected tree of psychiatric possibility is in its infancy, it might be another turning point in the history of mental healthcare.

Whatever paradigm shifts lie in the future, there are likely to be revolutions in unlikely places. As history teaches us, treatments can emerge from sanatoriums in New York, slaughterhouses in Rome, and grandmothers in Zimbabwe. The treatment of depression is a story that connects us all, no matter our sex, age, or where we live.

Six months after his trip to the United States, Dixon Chibanda walked into a glitzy hotel in central London wearing trainers, smart trousers, a shirt, and his favourite leather jacket. Along with 11 other leaders in the field of global mental health, he was introducing his work in Zimbabwe to the general secretary of the United Nations, António Guterres. Vikram Patel, an elder of the field of global mental health, was presenting his case for scaling up mental healthcare systems that are culturally relevant. In Zimbabwe, there are grandmothers. In India, there are social workers. And in the United States, there are peers like Helen Skipper. Waiting in the gold-trimmed hotel lobby, besuited staff buzzing around the floor as they carried the bags and coats of arriving guests, both Chibanda and Patel thought that this might be a turning point in their field. Unlike a meeting with a member of the World Health Organization, Patel says, the UN doesn't just advocate around health issues but also political and social crises. If such an intergovernmental organisation is on board and funding global mental-health projects, he adds, they will have gained a much-needed champion. Without this, global

mental health might remain a series of isolated, small projects that can't be scaled up.

Chibanda was more optimistic than ever before. 'The whole
global mental health community is really pushing in the same
direction, together. It's taken years [and] a lot of work from
quite a number of different people,' he says. 'I would say that
we now have a critical mass to really bring about change, and
at a global level. I really feel that we're onto something big.
The last five years or so, for me, have been quite the turning
point. Observing my own work [on the Friendship Bench], and
others, that's when I started to realise that this was going viral,
so to speak.'

Although it might take years for the UN and other organisations to make a decision on how to support projects like
Chibanda's Friendship Bench and Patel's Healthy Activity Program in Goa, India, the current state of global mental health
continues to be pretty desperate. In many low-income countries, nine out of ten people with mental illness still don't have
access to any form of psychiatric care, whether it be in the
community or otherwise. 'It's really pretty grim,' Patel says.
'The situation right now is probably grimmer than any other
area of health – not probably, it is grimmer.'

Without significant investment, this gloomy situation is
likely to become much worse following the Covid-19 outbreak.
While loneliness, distress, and grief are normal reactions to a
global health crisis, they are also the fertile soil on which long-
term mental disorders can take root and grow. Mental health
services – whether it's phone-based therapy, community health
workers, or improving access to medication – require international attention before these roots grow too deep, before
mental disorders become the next invisible diseases to bring
the world to a standstill.

Long-term epidemiological studies will soon reveal the people at highest risk of depression in the wake of this crisis, and what can be done to protect them. As Myrna Weissman's transgenerational cohort entered its 40th year during the pandemic, she saw an opportunity to understand how Covid-19 impacts mental health. It will take years before any robust conclusions can be drawn. 'The final story will never really be the final story, except for the overall message: Covid-19 is going to have a big impact on people's mental health,' Weissman says. 'I mean, how couldn't it? Losing your job, not being able to take care of your children, uncertainty, social isolation … I mean, that's like every known risk factor for depression and anxiety disorder.'

And yet, there is hope in every crisis. Since the start of the pandemic, science has come to fore in the search for a vaccine. Epidemiologists and science writers have skipped into the spotlight to offer rational, evidence-based guidance for an unpredictable future. Regular exercise became a mainstay of life in lockdown. And, whether they occur in person, over the phone, or through a screen, discussions on mental health have become everyday, normalised. Psychiatrists and psychologists from around the world are hoping that Covid-19 provides the wake-up call that governments needed, a death knell for inaction. 'Despite the evidence, known for decades, that depression is a leading and growing cause of avoidable suffering in the world, it has attracted relatively little attention from policy makers,' the Lancet Commission for Depression 2021 states. 'It has generated a "perfect storm" that requires responses at multiple levels. It underscores the need to make the prevention, recognition, and treatment of depression an immediate global priority. This is a historic opportunity to transform not just the ailing health care systems of the world, but society itself.'

If there is a future in global mental health, then it is embodied by Dixon Chibanda and the grandmothers who helped make his project a success. Since the clinical trial in 2016, he has established benches on the island of Zanzibar off the eastern coast of Tanzania, in Malawi, and in the Caribbean. He now plans to train community health workers and set up benches in the United Kingdom and across the United States. He has graced international conferences and rubbed shoulders with world leaders. At the World Economic Forum, he sat next to Jacinda Ardern, the prime minister of New Zealand. At the inaugural Global Ministerial Mental Health Summit in London in 2018, Prince William and the Duchess of Cambridge sat on a friendship bench that was assembled for the occasion. At Davos, Chibanda took a seat along with Elisha London, CEO of United for Global Mental Health. Casually dressed in jeans, a padded gilet, and a jangle of copper wristbands, he smiled as he delicately held up a banner that read 'Everyone, everywhere should have someone to turn to in support of their mental health'.

Acknowledgements

First and foremost, I would like the thank the people who spoke to me about their experiences with depression and its treatment. Most have been anonymised and their identifying details blurred but their stories are no less real. Each of their experiences is a testament to the struggles faced by people with depression around the world, and how recovery is still possible even in the most hopeless scenarios. This book couldn't have been written without their generosity, kindness, and courage.

I have spoken many researchers – scientists, psychiatrists, psychologists – and their research and knowledge provides the backbone to this book. Myrna Weissman, Helen Mayberg, Arthur Kleinman, Dixon Chibanda, Vikram Patel, Ted Dinan, John Cryan, Melanie Abas, and Draulio Barros de Araujo are just a few names that have been indispensable throughout this process. (Many researchers have also read this book in various forms of completion; thanks to Brian Leonard, James Rucker, Charles Reynolds, Charlie Kellner, Eric Engstrom, Michael Berk, Carmine Pariante, Chrissie Giles, Siri Carpenter, and Chris Dowrick for their time, comments, and support.) I have also been guided by some welcoming archivists and historians who have given me access to often precious documents and books that were bound before Sigmund Freud was born. I would like to thank Colin Gale from Museum of the Mind, Daniela Finzi at the Freud Museum in Vienna, Ralf Gebhardt and Gerhard Dammann at the psychiatric institute in Münsterlingen, Bill Roberts at the Berkeley Historical Society, and Stuart Moss at the Nathan Kline Institute in New York. A special thanks to the kind woman from Hartheim Castle who drove me back to Linz at a time when all buses had stopped running, then gave me herbal tea and dried apple slices from her parents' orchard.

I wouldn't have been able to make the transition from academia to science writing without the help of some very patient editors.

Lina Zeldovich, Ed Lake, Tim De Chant, Michael Marshall, Adrienne Mason, Sally Davies, Richard Fisher, Catherine Brahic, Chrissie Giles, and David Robson are just a few names who deserve recognition for their teachings. A special mention is required for Siri Carpenter, editor in chief of *The Open Notebook*, who gave me the confidence, freedom, and support to write openly about my experience with depression and suicide as a freelance writer. After he read this article, Steve Silberman has been a vital source of confidence and a champion of this book from the beginning.

A huge thank you to my editors Sally Howe at Scribner and Robyn Drury at Ebury who read through every draft, answered every email, and offered indispensable suggestions that made this book a much smoother read from start to finish. I would also like to mention Daniel Loedel, former commissioning editor at Scribner, who first saw the potential in my proposal and helped to broaden its scope without losing its central story. I reserve my warmest appreciation and thanks to my agent, Carrie Plitt, an indefatigable ally who helped transform a nebulous set of ideas into a 100-page proposal fit for publishers. As well as being my agent, she has also been a friend who I can turn to for guidance and counsel.

Support also came from old friends and family over the last few years. Thanks to my brother Rupert for his continued interest and excitement in my work; to my Dad who has read every article I have ever written at least twice (mainly because he was never taught science at school); to my Mum for her openness when discussing her past; and to my friends Angus and Will who frequently let me sleep on their sofa after I had spent long hours staring at books at the British Library in London. Ben, Jim, Ketki, Conal, Cat, and Steve: you have provided refuges for me over the years, both when I was stable and also when I was not. Finally, to Barbara Mary Boyd (Granny B.) who single-handedly created a welcoming home for so many generations before she passed in 2020.

There is one person I would like to thank most of all: Lucy. She has seen every twist and turn of this book, a personal drama played out in the flats and houses we've called home over the last few years. I depended on her support. She was constant comfort and saw a brighter future even when I couldn't even imagine one. For her love, strength, compassion, and kindness, this book is dedicated to her.

Endnotes

Introduction

xiv *the social triggers for depression*: Paykel, E.S., et al. (1969) *Arch. Gen. Psychiatry*, 21: 753–60. And: Brown, G.W. & Harris, T. (1978) *Social Origins of Depression*. Tavistock Publications.

xv *recalibrate the immune system*: Black, D.S. & Slavich, G.M. (2016) '*Ann. N. Y. Acad. Sci.*, 1373: 13–24.

xv *running ... as effective ... as first-line treatments*: Dunn, A.L., et al. (2005) *Am. J. Prev. Med.*, 28(1): 1–8.

xvi *share nutrients with their neighbours*: Klein, T., Siegwolf, R.T.W. & Körner, C. (2016) *Science*, 352(6283): 342–344.

xix *risk of depression in children threefold*: Weissman, M.M., et al. (2016) *JAMA Psychiatry*, 73(9): 970–7.

Part One – Cutting Steps into the Mountain

1 '*The day will come*': Freud, S. (1968) *Introductory Lectures on Psycho-analysis*. George Allen & Unwin Ltd.

1 '*If a fright or despondency*': Hippocrates, Aphorisms. Section 6, no. 23.

1 '*The time has gone by*': Dix, D. (1848) 'Memorial Soliciting a State Hospital for the Protection and Cure of the Insane', submitted to the General Assembly of North Carolina. House of Commons Document, No. 2.

The Anatomists

3 *elegant English dresses ... 'seconds from the seashore'*: Gandolfi, L. (2010) *Psychoanal. Hist.*, 12(2): 129–51. p. 135.

3 '*lobed organs*' ... '*Recently a Trieste zoologist*': Weiser, M. (2013) *J. Hist. Behav. Sci.*, 49(3): 1–22.

4 *400 dead eels*: Triarhou, L.C. & del Cerro, M. (1985) *JAMA Neurol.*, 42: 282–7.

4 '*white and red blood*': Schroter, L. (2009) *The Little Book of the Sea*. Granta Books. p. 165.

5 *excelled at school*: Jones, E. (1967) *The Life and Work of Sigmund Freud*. Penguin Books. p. 72.

5 *top of his class*: Ibid., p. 48.

5 *seven languages ... read Shakespeare*: Ibid., p. 49.

5   *'kymographs, a myograph'*: Lesky, E. (1976) *The Vienna Medical School of the 19th Century*. The Johns Hopkins University Press. p. 237.

5   *sewage flowed uncovered . . . 'In the streets, in the squares'*: Ibid., p. 248.

5   *cast a dark shadow*: Koller, B. (1974) 'Carl Koller' In Freud, S. *Cocaine Papers*. N.Y. Stonehill Pub.

6   *zero tolerance*: Jones, E. (1967) *The Life and Work of Sigmund Freud*. Penguin Books. 'sensitive to the slightest hint of anti-Semitism'.

6   *dreamt of England*: Ibid., p. 50. 'land of his dreams'.

6   *hat flung into the* gutter: Gay, P. (1995) *Freud: A Life for Our Time*. Papermac. p. 11.

6   *'primary tool of observation'*: Jones, E. (1967). *The Life and Work of Sigmund Freud*. Penguin Books. p. 70.

6   *Crafted from brass and steel*: http://www.microscopy-uk.org.uk/mag/artoct06/mc-freud.html

6   *Edmund Hartnack*: Triarhou, L.C. (2009) *Hell. J. Psychol.*, 6: 1–13.

7   *up to 300 or 500 times*: http://www.microscopy-uk.org.uk/mag/artoct06/mc-freud.html

7   *rifle factory . . . a stable*: Lesky, E. (1976) *The Vienna Medical School of the 19th Century*. The Johns Hopkins University Press. p. 231.

7   *'spinal ganglion cells'*: Jones, E. (1967) *The Life and Work of Sigmund Freud*. Penguin Books. p. 66.

7   *'alien eyeballs bobbing in space'*: 'Analyse These'. *New York Times*, 25 April 2006.

8   *'[B]y this method'*: Freud, S. (1884) *Brain*, 7: 86–8.

8   *'I see your methods alone'*: Freud, E. (1992) *The Letters of Sigmund Freud*. Dover. p. 73: Letter 27.

8   *Silver-based stain*: Solms, M. (2002) 'An introduction to the neuroscientific works of Sigmund Freud'. In van de Vijver, G. & Geerardyn, F. eds. *The Pre-psychoanalytic Writings of Sigmund Freud*. Karnac.

8   *he came excruciatingly close*: Triarhou, L.C. & del Cerro, M. (1985) *JAMA Neurol.*, 42: 282–7.

9   *Cajal cited Freud's work*: Triarhou, L.C. (2009) *Hell. J. Psychol.*, 6: 1–13.

9   *hungry from one day to the next*: Teusch, R.K. (2017) *J. Am. Psychoanal. Assoc.* 65(1): 111–25.

9   *'It increases my self-respect'*: Jones, E. (1967) *The Life and Work of Sigmund Freud*. Penguin Books. p. 156.

9   *stain on young Freud's suit*: Freud, E. (1992) *The Letters of Sigmund Freud*. Dover. p. 122: Letter 50.

9   *beef, cheese, and bread*: Jones, E. (1967) *The Life and Work of Sigmund Freud*. Penguin Books. p. 154.

10 *scraps of paper*: Freud, E. (1992) *The Letters of Sigmund Freud*. Dover. p. 126: Letter 54.

10 *'I will love you very much'*: Ibid., p. 94: Letter 36.

10 *'I have been so caught up in myself'*: Ibid., p. 89: Letter 33.

10 *'happy nowadays only in your presence'*: Ibid., p. 123: Letter 51.

11 *a single delusion*: Lewis, A. (1934) *J. Ment. Sci.*, 80: 1–42.

11 *world was about to fall*: Jackson, S.W. (1978) *J. Hist. Med.*, 33(3): 367–76.

11 *gifted in the arts*: Radden, J. (2000) *The Nature of Melancholy*. Oxford University Press. p. 87.

11 *'The word melancholia' ... 'tristimania'*: Berrios, G. (1996) *The History of Mental Symptoms*. Cambridge University Press.

12 *'nerves' was sweeping through*: Shorter, E. (1997) *A History of Psychiatry*. Wiley.

12 *caring for sick relatives*: Bassuk, E.L. (1985) *Poetics Today*, 6: 245–57.

12 *it made a visit to mental asylums ... unlikely*: Shorter, E. (1997) *A History of Psychiatry*. Wiley. p. 113.

13 *'Institution for Brain and Nervous Disease'*: Ibid., p. 118.

13 *'I do not permit the patient'*: Poirier, S. (1983) *Women's Stud.*, 10: 15–40. p. 20.

13 *their mail was carefully checked*: Bassuk, E.L. (1985) *Poetics Today*, 6: 245–57.

13 *lashings were used*: branchcollective.org/?ps_articles=anne-stiles-the-rest-cure-1873–1925

13 *dozens of eggs*: Martin, D. (2007) *Am. J. Psychiatry*, 164(5): 737–8.

14 *electric current was applied*: Weisenberg, T.H. (1925) *Arch. Clin. Neuropsychol.*, 14(3): 384–9.

14 *Regular massages*: Vertinsky, P. (1989) *J. Sport. Hist.*, 16: 5–26. p. 14.

14 *'wretched eight months in my life'*: Woolf, V. (2017) *The Complete Collection*. Century Book. Letter 186.

14 *'the slightest idea of the nature'*: branchcollective.org/?ps_articles=anne-stiles-the-rest-cure-1873–1925

15 *'means of humanitarian action'*: Poirier, S. (1983) *Women's Stud.*, 10: 15–40.

15 *the 'west cure'*: Stiles, A. (2012) 'Go rest Young Man'. *APA*, 43: 32.

15 *'the only entrance'*: Kraepelin, E. (1987) *Memoirs*. Springer-Verlag Berlin Heidelberg.

16 *'an entire rabbit brain'*: Danek, A., et al. (1989) *Hist. Neurol.*, 46: 1349–53.

16 *brains of reptiles*: Hippius, H., et al. (2008) *The University Department of Psychiatry in Munich*. Springer.

16 *'With the means available'*: Kraepelin, E. (1987) *Memoirs*. Springer-Verlag Berlin Heidelberg. p. 27.

17 *'In spite of the Spartan simplicity'*: Ibid.

17 *a yellowish complexion*: Engstrom, E. (1991) *Hist. Psychiatry*, ii: 111–32.

17 *raspberry syrup*: Muller, U., et al. (2006) *Psychopharmacol.*, 184: 131–8. p. 135.

17 *higher doses caused an earlier onset*: Ibid., p. 133.

18 *carbonated water as a control ... 'danger of developing morphinism'*: Ibid., p. 135.

19 *'we were trailblazers'*: Kraepelin, E. (1920) *Z. Gesamte Neurol. Psychiatr.*, 61: 351–62.

19 *Wundt ... didn't even mention*: Muller, U., et al. (2006) *Psychopharmacol.*, 184: 131–8.

20 *Easter holidays*: Hippius, H., et al. (2008) *The University Department of Psychiatry in Munich*. Springer. Chapter 7.

20 *hesitant to write anything at first*: Kraepelin, E. (1987) *Memoirs*. Springer-Verlag Berlin Heidelberg.

20 *In its 300 pages*: Blashfield, R. (1984) *The Classification of Psychopathology*. Springer US.

20 *lack of effective treatments ... 'confusing mass'*: Hippius, H., et al. (2008) *The University Department of Psychiatry in Munich*. Springer. Chapter 7.

20 *Litres of alcohol were used*: Kraepelin, E. (1987) *Memoirs*. Springer-Verlag Berlin Heidelberg. p. 11.

20 *grow in size and popularity*: Shorter, E. (1997) *A History of Psychiatry*. Wiley. p. 103.

Über Coca

21 *'A German has tested this stuff'*: Freud, S. (1974) *Cocaine Papers*. N.Y. Stonehill Pub. Chapter 11.

21 *'capable of endurance'*: Freud, E. (1992) *The Letters of Sigmund Freud*. Dover. p. 107: Letter 43.

21 *'Perhaps others are working at it'*: Jones, E. (1967) *The Life and Work of Sigmund Freud*. Penguin Books. p. 90.

22 *similar to caffeine in tea*: Freud, S. (1974) *Cocaine Papers*. N.Y. Stonehill Pub. p. 58.

22 *German pharmaceutical company Merck*: Jones, E. (1967) *The Life and Work of Sigmund Freud*. Penguin Books. p. 90.

22 *one part cocaine ... not at all unpleasant*: Freud, S. (1974) *Cocaine Papers*. N.Y. Stonehill Pub. p. 58.

22 *heat spread through his skull*: Ibid., p. 59.

22 *'In my last severe depression'*: Ibid., p. 10.

22 *'a song of praise' ... well-stocked library*: Jones, E. (1967) *The Life and Work of Sigmund Freud*. Penguin Books. p. 95.

22 *rain was pouring*: Freud, E. (1992) *The Letters of Sigmund Freud*. Dover. p. 119. 1 July 1884.

23 *'It was inevitable that a plant'*: Freud, S. (1974) *Cocaine Papers*. N.Y. Stonehill Pub. p. 63.

23 *In 1860, a young graduate student*: Albert Niemann.

23 *'almost all the maladies'*: Freud, S. (1974) *Cocaine Papers*. N.Y. Stonehill Pub. p. 128.

23 *'the morose, silent, taciturn'*: Spillane, J. (2002) *Cocaine*. The Johns Hopkins University Press.

23 *'as if by magic' ... beard trimmed*: Freud, S. (1974) *Cocaine Papers*. N.Y. Stonehill Pub. p. 145.

24 *'Psychiatry is rich in drugs'*: Ibid. Chapter 8.

24 *the first antidepressant*: Ibid. 1970 symposium on psychomimetic agents, Dr Larry Stein: 'Cocaine is almost the perfect tricyclic antidepressant ... but we heard that from Freud 80 years ago.'

24 *oft-used portrait*: Halberstatt, M. (1932) *Sigmund Freud*. Freud Museum London.

25 *first article on psychoanalysis*: Freud, S. (1896) *Rev. neurol. (Paris)*, 4: 161–9.

25 *widely known for his work*: Makari, G. (2008) *Revolution in Mind*. Harper. p. 299.

25 *Drinking cocaine to calm*: Ibid., p. 71.

26 *'new perception of perfection'*: Gay, P. (1995) *Freud: A Life for Our Time*. Papermac. p. 49.

26 *a disorder of women*: Makari, G. (2008) *Revolution in Mind*. Harper. p. 15.

26 *study cerebral paralysis and aphasia*: Gay, P. (1995) *Freud: A Life for Our Time*. Papermac. p. 48.

27 *'wake' up and make this into a reality*: Makari, G. (2008) *Revolution in Mind*. Harper. p. 18.

27 *'the profoundest impression'*: Freud, S. (1925) *An Autobiographical Study*. The Hogarth Press.

27 *'artificial form of alienation'*: Jones, E. (1967) *The Life and Work of Sigmund Freud*. Penguin Books.

27 *'finds, its scientific basis'*: Shorter, E. (1997) *A History of Psychiatry*. Wiley. p. 77.

28 *These unfortunate beings*: Lewin, L. (1998) *Phantastica*. Inner Traditions Bear and Company.

28 *'third scourge of humanity'*: Bernfeld, S. (1954) *J. Am. Psychoanal. Assoc.*, 35: 581–613. p. 603.

29 *saw white snakes*: Freud, S. (1974) *Cocaine Papers*. N.Y. Stonehill Pub. p. 158.

29 *'a thoroughly excellent person'*: Ibid., p. 158.

29 *He decried Albrecht Erlenmyer's statement*: Bernfeld, S. (1954) *J. Am. Psychoanal. Assoc.*, 35: 581–613.

29 *'an aversion to the drug'* . . . *'It made no impression'*: Ibid., p. 604.

30 *'Haven of happiness'*: Jones, E. (1967) *The Life and Work of Sigmund Freud*. Penguin Books. 'Chapter 8. Marriage'.

30 *Rembrandt's* Anatomy Lesson: Johnstone, W. (1983) *The Austrian Mind*. University of California Press. p. 240.

31 *'removed chemically'*: Bernfeld, S. (1954) *J. Am. Psychoanal. Assoc.*, 35: 581–613 p. 601.

'Psychiatry's Linnaeus'

32 *over the river Embach*: Steinberg, H. & Angermeyer, M.C. (2001) *Hist. Psychiatry*. 12: 297–327.

32 *'kind of exile'*: Kraepelin, E. (1987) *Memoirs*. Springer-Verlag Berlin Heidelberg. p. 57.

32 *'trains came so rarely'*: Ibid., p. 47.

32 *son, died of sepsis*: Hippius, H., et al. (2008) *The University Department of Psychiatry in Munich*. Springer. Chapter 7.

32 *'little book'*: Kraepelin, E. (1987) *Memoirs*. Springer-Verlag Berlin Heidelberg.

32 *3,000-page, four-volume tome by 1915*: Blashfield, R. (1984) *The Classification of Psychopathology*. Springer US.

33 *'My wife and I are fine'*: Steinberg, H. & Angermeyer, M.C. (2001) *Hist. Psychiatry*. 12: 297–327.

33 *'into the fresh air'*: Hippius, H., et al. (2008) *The University Department of Psychiatry in Munich*. Springer. Chapter 7.

33 *ruby-tailed wasps*: Research trip to Heidelberg by author, October 2018.

33 *'Psychiatry's Linnaeus'*: Engstrom, E.J. & Kendler, K. (2015) *Hist. Psychiatry*. 172(12): 1190–6.

34 *'place in the country'*: Kahn, E. (1956) *The Emil Kraepelin Memorial Lecture*. New York Meeting.

35 *Lake Maggiore*: Hippius, H., et al. (2008) *The University Department of Psychiatry in Munich*. Springer. Fig. 7.8.

35 *'[he] worked through thousands'*: Weber, M.M. & Engstrom, E.J. (1997) *Hist. Psych.*, 8: 375–85.

35   *in young adulthood*: Kraepelin, E. (1921) *Manic Depressive Insanity and Paranoia*. E. & S. Livingstone.

36   *bipolar ... 1957*: Mendelson, M. (1974) *Psychoanalytic Concepts of Depression*. Spectrum. p. 25:

36   *'one disease process'*: Kahn, E. (1956) *The Emil Kraepelin Memorial Lecture*. New York Meeting.

36   *'defective heredity'*: Kraepelin, E. (1921) *Manic Depressive Insanity and Paranoia*. E. & S. Livingstone.

36   *'[S]o-called psychic causes'*: Shepherd, M. (1995) 'Two Faces of Emil Kraepelin'. *Br. J. Psychiatry*, 167: 174–83.

36   *'sources of emotional disturbance'*: Kraepelin, E. (1921) *Manic Depressive Insanity and Paranoia*. E. & S. Livingstone.

37   *'begins with Kraepelin'*: Slater, E. & Roth, M. (1969) *Clinical Psychiatry*. Tindall & Cassell. p. 10.

37   *'an icon who helped guide us'*: Engstrom, E.J. & Kendler, K. (2015) *Hist. Psychiatry*. 172(12): 1190–6.

37   *'cutting steps into the mountain'*: Hansson, N., et al. (2016) *TRAMES*, 20: 393–401. p. 398.

A Melancholic Humour

38   *'in strength and quantity'*: Lloyd, G.E.R., ed. (1983) *Hippocratic Writings*. Penguin Classics. p. 262.

39   *physician to gladiators ... died in AD 200*: Galen, C. (165 CE) 'On the Affected Parts'. In Radden, J. ed. (2000) *The Nature of Melancholy*. Oxford University Press. p. 61.

40   *'gassy disease' ... 'atrabilious blood is generated by' ... 'If the outflowing blood'*: Galen, C. (165 CE) 'On the Affected Parts'. In Radden, J. ed. (2000) *The Nature of Melancholy*. Oxford University Press. p. 66.

42   *Abu Zayd al-Balkhi*: Badri, M. (2014) *Abu Zayd al-Balkhi's* Sustenance of the Soul. IIIT.

43   *two missionaries*: Radden, J. ed. (2000) *The Nature of Melancholy*. Oxford University Press. p. 75.

44   *'out of Adam's semen'*: Hildegard of Bingen (1151–1158 CE) *Book of Holistic Healing*. In Radden, J. ed. (2000) *The Nature of Melancholy*. Oxford University Press. p. 81.

44   *'the most subtle vapour'*: Burton, R. (2001) *The Anatomy of Melancholy*. NYRB. p. 146.

45   *'arise from a Melancholick humour'*: Jackson, S. (1978) *J. Hist. Med.*, 33(3): 367–76.

45   *circulation of blood*: Ribatti, D. (2009) *J. Angiogenes. Res.*, 1:3.

45   *microscopic cells*: Schwann, T. (1839) *Mikroskopische Untersuchungen über die Übereinstimmung in der Struktur und dem Wachsthum der Thiere und Pflanzen*. Sander.

Instruments of Cure

46   *10.5 million to 21 million*: Jefferies, J. (2005) *Focus on People and Migration*. p. 3

46   *Mania and melancholia*: Haslam, J. (1809) *Observations on Madness and Melancholy*. J. Callow. p. 19.

47 *'practice invariably for years'*: Glover, M. (1984) *The Retreat, York.* William Sessions.

47 *'beasts of the field'*: Connolly, J. (1856) *Treatment of the Insane Without Mechanical Restraints.* Dawsons of Pall Mall.

48 *'low and melancholy'* ... *'brink of destruction'*: Glover, M. (1984) *The Retreat, York.* William Sessions. p. 36

49 *100 per cent to 12 per cent:* Ibid.

50 *'What tenderness with strength combined'*: Ibid.

50 *'Darkness and bonds'*: Conolly, J. (1856) *Treatment of the Insane Without Mechanical Restraints.* Dawsons of Pall Mall. p. 166.

51 *'The old prison-air'*: Ibid., p. 82.

51 *'Not only to the maniacal'*: Ibid., p. 60.

51 *'Recreation ... is so necessary'*: Ashworth, A.L. (1975) *Stanley Royd Hospital, Wakefield.* Stanley Royd Hospital. p. 51.

51 *there was cricket:* Rutherford, S. (2008) *The Victorian Asylum.* Shire.

51 *'wear an expression'*: Conolly, J. (1856) *Treatment of the Insane Without Mechanical Restraints.* Dawsons of Pall Mall. p. 87.

52 *beef tea and arrowroot:* Digby, A. (1985) 'Moral Treatment at the Retreat 1796–1846'. In Porter, R., Bynum, W.F. & Shepherd, M. eds. *The Anatomy of Madness, vol. II.* Tavistock. p. 66.

52 *brewed its own beer on-site:* Ashworth, A.L. (1975) *Stanley Royd Hospital, Wakefield.* Stanley Royd Hospital.

52 *rhubarb ... a natural laxative:* Rutherford, S. (2008) *The Victorian Asylum.* Shire.

52 *'mournful prophet'*: Ikuigu, M.N. & Ciaravino, E.A. (2007) *Psychosocial Conceptual Practice Models in Occupational Therapy.* Elsevier Health Sciences.

52 *Dorothea Dix helped:* https://socialwelfare.library.vcu.edu/issues/moral-treatment-insane/

52 *nervous breakdown in 1836:* Ikuigu, M.N. & Ciaravino, E.A. (2007) *Psychosocial Conceptual Practice Models in Occupational Therapy.* Elsevier Health Sciences.

53 *spontaneously recover:* Haslam, J. (1809) *Observations on Madness and Melancholy.* J. Callow. p. 257.

53 *10 to 15 per cent:* Gonda, X., et al. (2007) *Ann. Gen. Psychiatry.* 6: 23.

53 *Chronic depression:* See: Ten Have, M., et al. (2018) *Acta Psychiatr. Scand.,* 137(6): 503–15.

54 *'efficacy'*: Gielen, U.P., et al. eds. (2004) *Handbook of Culture, Therapy, and Healing.* Lawrence Erlbaum Associates Publishers.

54 *'sleeping without beds'*: Shorter, E. (1997) *A History of Psychiatry.* Wiley. p. 47.

54 *150,000 people:* Ibid., p. 34.

54 *'The treatment is humane'*: Jones, K. (1993) *Asylums and After. A Revised History of the Mental Health Services.* Continuum International Publishing Group Ltd.

54 *'being in a show'*: Digby, A. (1985) 'Moral Treatment at the Retreat 1796–1846'. In Porter, R., Bynum, W.F. & Shepherd, M. eds. *The Anatomy of Madness, vol. II.* Tavistock.

55 *half a kilometre long ... a jangle of keys:* Jones, K. (1993) *Asylums and After. A Revised History of the Mental Health Services.* Continuum International Publishing Group Ltd.

55 'illnesses of the nerves': Shorter, E. (1997) *A History of Psychiatry*. Wiley.
55 'the most terrible maladies': Davis, G. (2012) *J. R. Coll. Physicians Edinb.*, 42: 266–73.
56 'groping in the dark': Savage, G.H. (1884) *Insanity and Allied Neuroses*. Cassell.

The Talking Cure

57 'Sigmund Freud did not': Makari, G. (2008) *Revolution in Mind*. Harper. p. 5.
58 'agrammatical jargon': Ellenberger, H.F. (1972) *J. Hist. Behav. Sci.*, 8: 267–79.
58 'real one and an evil one': Makari, G. (2008) *Revolution in Mind*. Harper. p. 39.
59 *Newfoundland dog* ... 'talking cure': Ellenberger, H.F. (1972) *J. Hist. Behav. Sci.*, 8: 267–79. p. 269.
61 *next few years institutionalised*: Makari, G. (2008) *Revolution in Mind*. Harper. p. 39.
61 'the symptoms vanished': Freud, S. (1968) *Introductory Lectures on Psycho-analysis*. George Allen & Unwin Ltd. p. 236.
62 'Insight such as this': Freud, S. (1976) *The Interpretation of Dreams*. Pelican Books. 'Preface'.
62 *favourite book*: Börne, L. (1823) *Harvard Review*, 31: 71–76.
63 'meaning of a symptom': Freud, S. (1968) *Introductory Lectures on Psycho-analysis*. George Allen & Unwin Ltd. p. 230.
63 *few, if any, depressed*: Wallenstein, R. (1995) *The Talking Cures*. Yale University Press.
63 'who interacts sparsely with others': Shorter, E. (2013) *How Everyone Became Depressed*. Oxford University Press.
64 *too much masturbating*: Zucker, K.J (1979) *J. AAPDP*, 7(1): 15–32.
64 *351 copies*: Freud, S. (1976) *The Interpretation of Dreams*. Pelican Books. p. 43.
64 'attitude adopted by reviewers': Ibid., p. 46.

Love and Hate

70 *theory of depression*: May-Tolzmann, U. (1997) *Luzif Amor*, 10(20): 98–131.
70 *protégé, Carl Jung, closer*: Makari, G. (2008) *Revolution in Mind*. Harper. p. 374.
70 'not found similar consideration': Shorter, E. (2013) *How Everyone Became Depressed*. Oxford University Press. p. 114.
71 *his mother died*: May, U. (2001) *In. J. Psychoanal.* 82: 283–305. p. 289.
71 'ambivalence': Makari, G. (2008) *Revolution in Mind*. Harper. p. 209.
71 'I cannot love people': Abraham, K. (1911) 'Notes on the psycho-analytical investigation and treatment of manic-depressive insanity and allied conditions'. In Abraham, K. & Jones, E. (1927) *Selected Papers on Psychoanalysis*. Hogarth Press.
71 *masochistic desires*: Freud, E. (1992) *The Letters of Sigmund Freud*. Dover. Letter 273A.
71 'A recurring theme' ... 'physically present': Bentinck van Schoonheten, A. (2015) *Karl Abraham*. Routledge. p. 7.
72 *Segantini had died*: May, U. (2001) *In. J. Psychoanal.* 82: 283–305. p. 289.
73 'his silence was justified': Bentinck van Schoonheten, A. (2015) *Karl Abraham*. Routledge. 'Chapter 13'.
73 *their first meeting*: Ibid. 'Chapter 5'.

73 *'in Berlin for 24 hours'*: Abraham, H. & Freud, E. eds (1965) *A Psycho-Analytical Dialogue*. Hogarth Press. 49F.

73 *'I must beg you'*: Ibid., 50A.

74 *'what interests me particularly'*: Ibid., 68A.

74 *'gave me most pleasure'*: Ibid., 70A.

74 *'paid rich scientific dividends'*: Ibid. 'Foreword'.

74 *fire station with a sand pit*: Bentinck van Schoonheten, A. (2015) *Karl Abraham*. Routledge. Chapter 9.

75 *'never happened before' 'happier and more care-free'* ... *'as regards a cure'*: Abraham, K. (1911) 'Notes on the psycho-analytical investigation and treatment of manic-depressive insanity and allied conditions'. In Abraham, K., & Jones, E. (1927) *Selected Papers on Psychoanalysis*. Hogarth Press.

76 *'difficult but important soil'*: Abraham, H. & Freud, E. eds (1965) *A Psycho-Analytical Dialogue*. Hogarth Press. 47F.

77 *'the Freudian trend'*: Decker, H. (2013) *The Making of DSM-III*. Oxford University Press.

77 *'blackest clique'*: Hippius, H., et al. (2008) *The University Department of Psychiatry in Munich*. Springer. Chapter 7.

77 *'to various compulsions'*: Freud, S. (1968) *Introductory Lectures on Psycho-analysis*. George Allen & Unwin Ltd. p. 221.

77 *'content himself with a diagnosis'*: Ibid., p. 213.

77 *'condemnation instead of an explanation'*: Ibid., p. 221.

78 *Jacobson, a German émigré*: Kronold, E. (1980) *Psychiatr. Q.*, 49: 505–7.

78 *'the deep blue sea'*: Jacobson, E. (1954) *J. Am. Psychoanal. Assoc.*, 2(4): 595–606.

78 *'Words and magic'*: Freud, S. (1968) *Introductory Lectures on Psycho-analysis*. George Allen & Unwin Ltd. p. 13.

A First Sketch

79 *horseshoe-shaped*: Hippius, H., et al. (2008) *The University Department of Psychiatry in Munich*. Springer. Fig 6.4.

79 *experimental psychology,* ... *genealogy*: Blashfield, R. (1984) *The Classification of Psychopathology*. Springer US.

79 *all of his Zählkarte*: Hippius, H., et al. (2008) *The University Department of Psychiatry in Munich*. Springer. Chapter 7..

79 *'Alzheimer's disease'*: Ibid.

79 *blood sugar, measures of metabolism*: Mapother, E., et al. (1926) *Brit. Med. J.*, 2: 872–9.

80 *'Whoever has listened'*: Passione, R. (2004) *Hist. Psychiatry.*, 15: 83–104.

80 *'thought compulsion'*: Lewis, A. (1934) *J. Ment. Sci.*, 80: 1–42. p. 24.

81 *'only a first sketch'*: Blashfield, R. (1984) *The Classification of Psychopathology*. Springer US.

81 *'ever more blurred'*: Engstrom, E.J. & Kendler, K. (2015) *Hist. Psychiatry.* 172(12): 1190–6. p. 1194.

81 *'"turning of the page"'*: Shorter, E. (2015) *Dialogues Clin. Neurosci.*, 17(1): 59–67. p. 59.

82 *a bucolic setting*: Abraham, H. & Freud, E. eds (1965) *A Psycho-Analytical Dialogue*. Hogarth Press. 274A.

82 *'the solution of melancholia'*: Ibid., 272F.

82 *'the genius'*: Abraham, K. (1924) 'A short study of the development of the libido, viewed in light of mental disorders (Abridged)'. In Frankiel, R.V. ed. (1994) *Essential Papers on Object Loss*. New York University Press.

82 *found something that he had not*: Ibid., p. 81.

82 *'retroflected hostility'*: 'The Doctor Is In'. *The American Scholar*, 1 September 2009.

83 *'incapable of any achievement'*: Freud, S. (1917) *Mourning and Melancholia*, Vintage.

83 *he waited a month to reply*: Abraham, H. & Freud, E. eds (1965) *A Psycho-Analytical Dialogue*. Hogarth Press. 272F (from Freud), 18 February 1915. 273A (from Abraham). 31 March 1915.

83 *'like to remind you'*: Ibid., 273A.

84 *'we owe the most important'*: Bentinck van Schoonheten, A. (2015) *Karl Abraham*. Routledge. Chapter 14.

85 *'earliest sense of satisfaction'* ... *'Abraham's [ideas] about a pre-oedipal'*: Ibid., Chapter 8.

86 *'Melanie Klein who first elaborated'*: Mendelson, M. (1974) *Psychoanalytic Concepts of Depression*. Spectrum.

86 *hair grey and his body thin*: Bentinck van Schoonheten, A. (2015) *Karl Abraham*. Routledge. Chapter 16.

86 *Grecian stone*: Ibid., Chapter 11.

87 *'in future be recognised'*: Abraham, H. & Freud, E. eds (1965) *A Psycho-Analytical Dialogue*. Hogarth Press. 'Foreword'.

87 *'fish bone lodged in his throat'*: Ibid. Letter 482A.

87 *deck chair at the Hotel Victoria*: Ibid., Letter 488A.

87 *read his favourite philosopher*: Ibid., Letter 490A.

87 *'a man continually and unfailingly at work'*: Ibid., Letter 484F.

88 *'I have no substitute for him'*: Ibid., Letter 501F.

88 *'The loss is quite irreplaceable'*: Bentinck van Schoonheten, A. (2015) *Karl Abraham*. Routledge. Chapter 16.

88 *'Dein Name mag vergehen'*: Research trip to Bergfriedhof Heidelberg by author, October 2018.

Part Two – 'The Biological Approach Seems to Be Working'

Fighting Fire with Fire

91 *£30,000*: Aldridge, P. (1991) 'The foundation of the Maudsley Hospital'. In Berrios, G. & Freeman, H. eds. *150 Years of British Psychiatry, 1841–1991*. Gaskell. p. 87.

91 *from German to English*: Hayward, R. (2010) 'International Relations in Psychiatry'. In Roelcke, V., Weindling, P.J., & Westwood, L. eds (2010) *International Relations in Psychiatry*. Boydell & Brewer.

91 *Portland stone and red bricks*: Aldridge, P. (1991) 'The foundation of the Maudsley Hospital'. In Berrios, G. & Freeman, H. eds. *150 Years of British Psychiatry, 1841–1991*. Gaskell. p. 87.

92 *Battle of Loos*: Jones, E. (2003) *Med. Hist. Suppl.*, 22: 3–38.

92 *the complete opposite conditions*: Shorter, E. (2013) *How Everyone Became Depressed*. Oxford University Press.

93 *'could not feel it.'* ... *'infinitely in degree'*: Mapother, E. (1926) *Br. Med. J.*, 2: 872–9. p. 878.

93 *'nor susceptibility to psychotherapy'*: Ibid., p. 872.

93 *'massage is a useful substitute'* ... *'analysis of any kind,'*: Ibid., p. 876.

94 *'faced with a depressed patient'*: Lehman, H.E. & Kline, N. (1983) 'Chapter 5. Antidepressants'. In Ayd, F.J. & Blackwell, B. eds *Discoveries in Pharmacology*. Elsevier.

94 *A range of treatments*: Lehman, H.E. & Kline, N. (1983) 'Chapter 5. Antidepressants'. In Ayd, F.J. & Blackwell, B. eds *Discoveries in Pharmacology*. Elsevier.

94 *opium*: Kalinowsky, L. (1970) 'Biological Treatments Preceding Pharmacotherapy'. In Ayd, F.J. & Blackwell, B. eds *Discoveries in Biological Psychiatry*. J.B. Lippincott Company.

94 *the removal of teeth*: Bested, A.C., Logan, A.C., & Selhub, E.M. (2013) *Gut Pathog.*, 5:5.

94 *neurotic types*: Shorter, E. (2013) *How Everyone Became Depressed*. Oxford University Press. Chapter 6.

94 *'a large preponderance of women'*: Buzzard, E.F., et al. (1930) *Proc. R. Soc. Med.* 23(6): 881–895.

95 *'any relief for his suffering'*: Jones, E. & Rahman, S. (2008) *Soc. Hist. Med.*, 21: 1–18.

95 *familiar stages*: Davis, G. (2012) *J. R. Coll. Physicians Edinb.* 42: 266–73.

95 *'case is without hope'*: Brown, E. M. (2000) *Hist. Psychiatry*, 11: 371–82. p. 373.

95 *60 per cent*: Ibid, p. 379.

95 *over 72 per cent*: Solomon, H.C. (1923) *Bost. Med. & Surg. J.*, 188(17): 635–9.

96 *'tertiary malaria'*: Wagner-Jauregg, J. (1946) *Am. J. Psychiatry*, 151: 231–5.

96 *Wagner-Jauregg's legacy*: Endler, N. & Persad, E. (1988) *Electroconvulsive Therapy*. Hans Huber Publishers.

96 *'minimum of highly trained staff'*: Valenstein, E. (1986) *Great and Desperate Cures*. Basic Books, Inc. p. 34.

96 *'preferable to confessing helplessness'*: Ibid. p. 44.

Unfixing Thoughts

97 *throw her own faeces*: Freeman, F. & Watts, J.W. (1947) *Arch. Neurol. & Psychiatry*, 58(4): 417–25.

97 *completely different chimp*: Jacobsen, C.F. (1936) *Studies of Cerebral Function in Primates*. Williams and Wilkins. Vol 13: 1–60.

97 *remain unfazed*: Freeman, W. & Watts, J.W. (1950) *Psychosurgery*. Blackwell Scientific Publications.

97 *'happiness cult'*: Fulton, J.F. (1947) *Acta Medica Scandinavica*, 128: 617–25. p. 621.

98 *bits of brain and blood*: Harlow, J.M. (1993) *Hist. Psychiatry*, 4: 274–81.

98 *'it conflicts with his desires'*: O'Driscoll, K. & Leach, J.P. (1998) *Br. Med. J.*, 317: 1673–4.

98 *they refused to offer him another job*: Harlow, J.M. (1993). *Hist. Psychiatry*, 4: 274–81.

98 *'Patient A.'*: Brickner, R. (1939) *AMA Arch. Neurol. Psychiatry* 41(3): 580–5.

99 *a 60-year-old neurologist*: El-Hai, J. (2005) *The Lobotomist*. Wiley. p. 95.

99 *shiny toupee*: Valenstein, E. (1986) *Great and Desperate Cures*. Basic Books, Inc. p. 73. Figure 4.4.

99 *Moniz asked Jacobsen*: Kucharski, A. (1984) *Neurosurg.*, 14(6): 765–72.

99 *500 years in Avanca*: Tierney, A.J. (2000) *J. Hist. Neurosci.*, 9: 22–36.

100 *he met ... Ramon y Cajal*: Valenstein, E. (1986) *Great and Desperate Cures*. Basic Books, Inc. p. 67.

100 *the first Portuguese scientist*: Ibid., p. 63.

100 *first photos of cerebral angiography ... over one hundred articles*: Tierney, A.J. (2000). *J. Hist. Neurosci.*, 9: 22–36.

100 *over an entire wall*: Valenstein, E. (1986) *Great and Desperate Cures*. Basic Books, Inc. p. 77.

101 *'a therapeutic procedure'*: Pressman, J. (1998) *Last Resort*. Cambridge University Press. 'Chapter 2. Sufficient Promise'.

101 *severe depression and paranoia*: Valenstein, E. (1986) *Great and Desperate Cures*. Basic Books, Inc. p. 103.

101 *gout that had painfully erupted*: Ibid., p. 65.

101 *'frontal barrier'*: Kotowicz, Z. (2005) *Gesnerus*, 62: 77–101. p. 81.

101 *'clinical cure'*: Valenstein, E. (1986) *Great and Desperate Cures*. Basic Books, Inc. p. 104.

102 *Nine of the patients*: Berrios, G. (1997) *Hist. Psychiatry*, 8: 61–81. p. 75, Table 2.

102 *After the seventh patient*: Valenstein, E. (1986) *Great and Desperate Cures*. Basic Books, Inc. p. 107.

102 *'core operation'*: Ibid., p. 106.

102 *'made with an organic orientation'*: Ibid., p. 81.

102 *'fixed connections'*: Berrios, G. & Freeman, H. eds. (1991) *150 Years of British Psychiatry, 1841–1991*. Gaskell. p. 188.

103 *'keeping it in constant activity'*: Berrios, G. (1997) *Hist. Psychiatry*, 8: 61–81. p. 74.

103 *poo-flinging alter-ego*: Jacobsen, C.F. (1936) *Studies of Cerebral Function in Primates*. Williams and Wilkins. Vol 13: 1–60.

103 *'ignored the rest'*: Valenstein, E. (1986) *Great and Desperate Cures*. Basic Books, Inc. p. 91

104 *'pure cerebral mythology'*: Ibid., p. 99.

'The Brain Has Ceased to Be Sacred'

105 *substituted for entertainment*: El-Hai, J. (2005) *The Lobotomist*. Wiley. p. 92.

105 *with both hands*: Valenstein, E. (1986) *Great and Desperate Cures*. Basic Books, Inc. p. 132.

105 *became a secretary*: Ibid., p. 135.

106 *vaulted over a few rows*: El-Hai, J. (2005) *The Lobotomist*. Wiley. p. 90.

106 *'beautiful pair of hands'*: Pressman, J. (1998) *Last Resort*. Cambridge University Press. 'Chapter 2. Sufficient Promise'.

106 *the same French supplier*: El-Hai, J. (2005) *The Lobotomist*. Wiley. p. 106.

106 *Following her first pregnancy*: Ibid., p. 9.

107 *'no longer cared'*: Valenstein, E. (1986) *Great and Desperate Cures*. Basic Books, Inc. p. 142.

107 *'are relieved'*: Ibid. p. 143.

107 *'the involutional melancholic'*: Shorter, E. (2013) *How Everyone Became Depressed*. Oxford University Press. Chapter 6.

108 *a strict routine*: Freeman, W., et al. (1942) *Psychosurgery*. Charles C. Thomas. 'Chapter XIX: Affective Reaction Types'.

108 *'rigid ethical code'*: Henderson, D. & Gillespie, R.D. (1956) *A Text-Book of Psychiatry*. Oxford University Press. p. 279.

108 *'the "might-have-beens",'*: Ibid., p. 278.

108 *'perfectly wretched about it'*: Kraepelin, E. (1904) *Clinical Psychiatry*. Macmillan. 'Chapter: Involutional Psychoses'.

108 *'All wickedness is due to them'*: Ibid.

109 *the treatment of choice*: Wohlfahrt, S. (1947) *Acta Psych. Scandin.*, 22: 348–67.

109 *'They all responded remarkably'*: Myerson, A. & Myerson, P.G. (1947) *N. Engl. J. Med.*, 237(14): 511–12.

109 *'become more placid'*: Valenstein, E. (1986) *Great and Desperate Cures*. Basic Books, Inc. p. 143.

109 *'some flavour of the personality'*: Freeman, W. & Watts, J. (1937) *South. Med. J.*, 30: 23–31.

110 *'little capacity for any emotional experiences'*: Hoffman, J.L. (1949) *N. Engl. J. Med.*, 241(6): 233–6. p. 234

110 *'he is not the same'*: Furtado, D., et al. (1949) *Psychiatrie und Neurologie*, 117(2): 65–76. p. 67.

110 *'in some way lost'*: Swayze, V. W. (1995) *Am. J. Psychiatry*, 152(4): 505–15.

110 *'precision method'*: Freeman, W., et al. (1942) *Psychosurgery*. Charles C. Thomas.

111 *engraved both their names*: El-Hai, J. (2005) *The Lobotomist*. Wiley. p. 144.

111 *a series of landmarks*: Freeman, W., et al. (1942) *Psychosurgery*. Charles C. Thomas.

111 *disconnected the frontal lobes*: Freeman, F. & Watts, J.W. (1947) *Psychosurgery*. Charles C. Thomas.

111 *the less emotional oomph*: Myerson, A. & Myerson, P.G. (1947) *N. Engl. J. Med.* 237(14): 511–12. p. 511.

111 *'minimal' or 'standard'*: Freeman, W. & Watts, J.W. (1946) *Am. J. Med. Sci.*, 211: 1–8.

111 *'as if by magic'*: Rylander, C. (1948) *Assoc. Res. Nerv. Ment. Dis.*, 27(1): 691–705.

112 *'this is a mutilation'*: Valenstein, E. (1986) *Great and Desperate Cures*. Basic Books, Inc. p. 146.

112 *'consciousness of the self'*: Freeman, W., et al. (1941) *JAMA*, 117(7): 517–27. p. 517

112 *'telescoped for them'*: Freeman, W. & Watts, J.W. (1950) *Psychosurgery*. Blackwell Scientific Publications. 'Chapter XXV'.

112 *'became happy, cheerful' . . . 'contentment with existence'*: Freeman, W., et al. (1941) *JAMA*, 117(7): 517–27. p. 519.

113 *$351,000 every year*: Ibid., p. 520.

114 *10 or even 20 per cent*: Swayze, V. W. (1995) *Am. J. Psychiatry*, 152(4): 505–15.

114 *'not seen a single case'*: Freeman, W., et al. (1941) *JAMA*, 117(7): 517–27. p. 520.

115 *'there is no return'*: Ibid., p. 525.

115 *journalists were largely positive*: Diefenbach, G.J., et al. (1999) *J. Hist. Neurosci.*, 8(1): 60–9.

115 *'ceased to be sacred'*: 'Turning the Mind Inside Out'. *Saturday Evening Post*, 24 May 1941.

115 *'a valid operation'*: Freeman, W., et al. (1942) *Psychosurgery*. Charles C. Thomas.

115 *shot four times*: Ibid. 'Introduction'.

116 *'enormous depression'*: Ibid. 'Chapter XIX: Affective Reaction Types'.

117 *'excellent condition' ... 'I look ten years younger'*: Ibid.

119 *'disturbance ... overtaken her' ... a Boston-based doctor*: Clifford Larson, K. (2016) *Rosemary*. Mariner Books. p. 157.

119 *not far from Rosemary's school*: El-Hai, J. (2005) *The Lobotomist*. Wiley. p. 173.

119 *'agitated depression'*: Clifford Larson, K. (2016). *Rosemary*. Mariner Books. p. 162.

119 *a local anaesthetic, for comfort*: El-Hai, J. (2005) *The Lobotomist*. Wiley. p. 145.

119 *'a grinding sound'*: Ibid., p. 146.

119 *'We made an estimate'*: Kessler, R (1996) *The Sins of the Father*. Warner Books. p. 243.

119 *'Kennedy Cottage'*: Leamer, L. (1994) *The Kennedy Women*. Villard Books. p. 412.

120 *'she left nursing altogether'*: Clifford Larson, K. (2016) *Rosemary*. Mariner Books. p. 170.

120 *'does not know what he sees'*: El-Hai, J. (2005) *The Lobotomist*. Wiley. p. 217.

120 *'ours was the best'*: Ibid., p. 219.

120 *3,000 operations during his career*: McKissock, W. (1959) *Proc. R. Soc. Med.*, 52: 203–10.

120 *'not a time-consuming operation'*: McKissock, W. (1951) *Lancet*, 2(6673): 91–4.

121 *'the ideal operation'*: Kucharski, A. (1984) *Neurosurg.*, 14(6): 765–72.

121 *driving over 11,000 miles*: Valenstein, E. (1986) *Great and Desperate Cures*. Basic Books, Inc. p. 229.

121 *'"black eyes"'*: Freeman, W. & Watts, J.W. (1950). *Psychosurgery*. Blackwell Scientific Publications. 'Chapter III'.

121 *'cat who walks by himself'*: Pressman, J. (1998) *Last Resort*. Cambridge University Press. 'Chapter 2. Sufficient Promise'.

121 *'Why not use a shotgun?'*: Valenstein, E. (1986) *Great and Desperate Cures*. Basic Books, Inc. p. 205.

121 *first use in 1946*: El-Hai, J. (2005) *The Lobotomist*. Wiley. p. 187.

122 *'major surgical operation'*: Freeman, W. & Watts, J.W. (1950) *Psychosurgery*. Blackwell Scientific Publications. Chapter III.

122 *'it is a minor operation'*: El-Hai, J. (2005) *The Lobotomist*. Wiley. p. 192.

122 *'yield much of value'*: Wohlfahrt, S. (1947) *Acta Psych. Scandin.*, 22: 348–67. p. 358.

122 *'sensational'*: Ibid., p. 355.

123 *taking the 'sting' out*: Freeman, W., et al. (1942) *Psychosurgery*. Charles C. Thomas. 'Preface'.

123 *'families gratified'*: Greenblatt M. & Solomon, H.C. (1953) *Frontal Lobes and Schizophrenia*. Springer. p. 29.

124 *'violates the principles of humanity'*: Diefenbach, G.J., et al. (1999) *J. Hist. Neurosci.*, 8(1): 60–9.

124 *a few hundred operations*: Zajicek, B. (2017) *Bull, Hist. Med.*, 91(1): 22–61.

124 *signed a decree*: Ibid., p. 59.

124 *'considerable concern'*: Diefenbach, G.J., et al. (1999) *J. Hist. Neurosci.*, 8(1): 60–9. p. 65.

The Most Powerful Reaction

125 *'Electrical slaughtering'* ... *the humane part* ... *'It occurred to me'*: Cerletti, U. (1956) 'Electroshock therapy'. In Sackler, A.M. ed. *The Great Physiodynamic Therapies in Psychiatry*. Hoeber.

126 *electricity running for over a minute*: Shorter, E. & Healy, D. (2007) *Shock Therapy*. Rutgers University Press. p. 36.

126 *'a complete convulsive seizure'*: Ibid.

126 *ochre-coloured* ... *building*: Palmer, R.L. ed. (1981) *Electroconvulsive Therapy*. Oxford University Press. p. 7.

126 *municipal dog catcher*: Endler, N. (1988) *Convulsive Therapy*, 4(1): 5–23.

126 *'like a falcon'*: Accornero, F. (1988) *Convulsive Therapy*, 4(1): 40–9.

126 *Cerletti nor Bini saw anything*: Cerletti, U. & Bini, L. (1940) *Rivista Sperimentale di Freniatria* 64: 311.

126 *'most powerful reaction'*: Cerletti, U. (1956) 'Electroshock therapy'. In Sackler, A.M. ed. *The Great Physiodynamic Therapies in Psychiatry*. Hoeber. p. 95.

127 *'one species of spasm'*: Fink, M. (1979) *Convulsive Therapy: Theory and Practice*. Raven Press. p. 5.

127 *'complete cure followed'*: Sackler, A.M. ed. (1956) *The Great Physiodynamic Therapies in Psychiatry*. Hoeber.

127 *'his reason will return'*: Palmer, R.L. ed. (1981) *Electroconvulsive Therapy*. Oxford University Press.

128 *'opposite, a paralysing, effect'*: Meduna, L.M. (1956) 'The Convulsive Treatment'. In Sackler, A.M. ed. *The Great Physiodynamic Therapies in Psychiatry*. Hoeber.

128 *'biological antagonism'*: Fink, M. (1979) *Convulsive Therapy: Theory and Practice*. Raven Press. Chapter 2.

128 *could one disease treat another?*: Meduna, L.M. (1956) 'The Convulsive Treatment'. In Sackler, A.M. ed. *The Great Physiodynamic Therapies in Psychiatry*. Hoeber.

128 *Strychnine, thebaine* ...: Fink, M. (1984) *Am. J. Psychiatry*, 141: 1034–41. p. 1035.

128 *'impending doom'*: Dunne, R.A. & McLoughlin, D. M. (2012) *Core Psychiatry*, 617–27.

128 *familiar stages*: Fleming, G.W.T.H. & Golla, F.L. (1939) *Lancet*, 234: 1353–55.

128 *urine, faeces, and, for men, semen*: Cerletti, U. (1956) 'Electroshock therapy'. In Sackler, A.M. ed. *The Great Physiodynamic Therapies in Psychiatry*. Hoeber.

129 *Frothing at the mouth*: Shepley, H. & McGregor, J.S. (1939) *Br. Med. J.*, 2: 1269–71.

129 *rid of the hallucinations*: Fink, M. (1979) *Convulsive Therapy: Theory and Practice*. Raven Press. Chapter 2.

129 *'a new art'*: Fink, M. (1984) *Am. J. Psychiatry*, 141: 1034–41. p. 1035.

129 *training course in convulsive therapy*: Palmer, R.L. ed (1981) *Electroconvulsive Therapy*. Oxford University Press. p. 21

129 *'any practical application'*: Cerletti, U. (1956) 'Electroshock therapy'. In Sackler, A.M. ed. *The Great Physiodynamic Therapies in Psychiatry*. Hoeber.

130 *'does not give fruit'*: Accornero, F. (1988) *Convulsive Therapy*, 4(1): 40–9. p. 44.

130 *Used only by a laboratory technician*: Endler, N. (1988) *Convulsive Therapy*, 4(1): 5–23.

130 *poke his head out*: Accornero, F. (1988) *Convulsive Therapy*, 4(1): 40–9. p. 45.

130 *former student of Emil Kraepelin*: Passione, R. (2004) *Hist. Psychiatry* 15: 83–104.

130 *'the Maestro'*: Accornero, F. (1988) *Convulsive Therapy*, 4(1): 40–9. p. 42.

130 *'Cerletti atmosphere' ... 'youthful enthusiasm' of Bini*: Endler, N. (1988) *Convulsive Therapy*, 4(1): 5–23.

131 *counting ... beaded with sweat ... 'glanced at each other'*: Accornero, F. (1988) *Convulsive Therapy*, 4(1): 40–9. p. 47.

132 *The details of the first session*: Aruta, A. (2011) *Med. Hist.* 55: 407–12.

132 *'usual loose way'*: Bini, L. (1995) *Convulsive Therapy*, 11: 260–1.

132 *11 sessions*: Endler, N. (1988) *Convulsive Therapy*, 4(1): 5–23.

132 *discharged ... 17 June 1938*: Cerletti, U. (1956) 'Electroshock therapy'. In Sackler, A.M. ed. *The Great Physiodynamic Therapies in Psychiatry*. Hoeber.

132 *Electroshock didn't come with these drawbacks*: Berrios, G. (1997) *Hist. Psychiatry*, viii: 105–19.

132 *'Loss of consciousness'*: Metastasio, A. & Dodwell, D. (2013) *Eur. J. Psychiatry*, 27: 231–9. p. 236.

133 *'do not remember anything'*: Ibid., p. 237.

133 *out-of-tune trumpet*: Endler, N. (1988) *Convulsive Therapy*, 4(1): 5–23.

134 *'reluctant to earmark the new treatment'*: 'Insanity Treated By Electric Shock'. *NY Times*, 6 July 1940.

134 *'particularly in depressive episodes'*: Cerletti, U. (1940) *Rivista Sperimentale di Freniatri*, 64.

134 *only four sessions*: Fink, M. (1979) *Convulsive Therapy: Theory and Practice*. Raven Press. Chapter 2.

134 *'A series of complete remissions'*: Cerletti, U. (1940) *Rivista Sperimentale di Freniatri*, 64.

135 *'white as a sheet'*: Tondo, L. (1990) *Clin. Neuropsychiatry*, 8: 303–18. p. 305.

135 *high-pitched yelp*: Shorter, E. & Healy, D. (2007) *Shock Therapy*. Rutgers University Press. p. 127.

135 *1,000 sessions*: Kalinowsky, L. & Barrera, S.E. (1940) *Psychiatr. Q.*, 14: 719–30. p. 727.

135 *'depressions of various depths'*: Kalinowsky, L.B. (1949) *Bull. N.Y. Acad. Med.*, 25: 541–53.

135 *leaving behind their home*: Abrams, R. (1988) *Convulsive Therapy*, 4: 25–39. p. 31.

136 *blueprint of Bini's electroshock machine*: Tondo, L. (1990) *Clin. Neuropsychiatry*, 8: 303–18. p. 305.

136 *showed Bini's designs to directors*: Endler, N. (1988) *Convulsive Therapy*, 4(1): 5–23.

136 *Aubrey Lewis ... stern indifference*: Rzesnitzek, L. (2015) *Hist. Psychiatry*, 26(4): 433–51. p. 439

136 *attracted psychiatrists from all over*: Shorter, E. & Healy, D. (2007) *Shock Therapy*. Rutgers University Press. p. 79.

136 *'"Johnny Appleseed"'*: Shorter, E. (1997) *A History of Psychiatry*. Wiley, Inc. p. 221.

137 *A small fraction*: Kalinowsky, L., et al. (1941) *Psychiatr. Q.*, 15: 450–9. p. 451.

137 *'typical American enthusiasm'*: Endler, N. (1988) *Convulsive Therapy*, 4(1): 5–23.

137 *near to 100 per cent*: Bennett, A.E. (1945) *Psychiatr. Q.*, 19: 465–77.

137 *'terminates depressive psychoses'*: Ibid., p. 470.

137 *'came back to life'*: Shorter, E. & Healy, D. (2007) *Shock Therapy*. Rutgers University Press. p. 79.

138 *rarely as effective*: Consensus Conference (1985) *JAMA*, 254: 2103–8.

138 *great debate*: See: Mendelson, M. (1974) *Psychoanalytic Concepts of Depression*. Spectrum.

139 *'the better the treatment'*: Kalinowsky, L. (1944) *Bull. N.Y. Acad. Med.*, 20(9): 485–94. p. 488.

139 *'Psychoanalysts were never in doubt'*: Mendelson, M. (1974) *Psychoanalytic Concepts of Depression*. Spectrum.

139 *'trials of psychotherapy were exhausted'*: Shorter, E. & Healy, D. (2007) *Shock Therapy*. Rutgers University Press. p. 92.

139 *'when their mothers get depressed'*: Ibid., p. 85.

Legacy

140 *'they are content with burning my books'*: Hergenhahn, B.R. (1980) *An Introduction to the History of Psychology*. Engage Learning. p. 509

140 *family at Victoria Station*: Jones, E. (1967) *The Life and Work of Sigmund Freud*. Penguin Books. p. 643.

140 *admired England from afar*: Ibid., p. 50.

140 *he hoped that he wouldn't live to see*: Ibid., p. 633.

141 *'a little island of pain'*: Ibid., p. 653.

141 *three centigrams of morphine*: Gay, P. (1995) *Freud: A Life for Our Time*. Parpermac. p. 651.

141 *four of his five sisters*: Freud, E. (1992) *The Letters of Sigmund Freud*. Dover. p. 455.

141 *'no gross distortion'*: American Psychiatric Association (1952) *Diagnostic and Statistical Manual of Mental Disorders*. Washington, DC.

142 *relatives have often suffered*: Kraepelin, E. (1921) *Manic Depressive Insanity and Paranoia*. E. & S. Livingstone.

142 *'empirical heredity prognosis'*: Kösters, G., et al. (2017) *PLoS Genetics*, 11(11): 1–14.

143 *'[Rüdin's] demands for negative eugenic measures'*: Ibid., p. 8.

143 *'only the healthy beget children'*: Lifton, R.J. (2000) *Nazi Doctors*. Basic Books. p. 22.

144 *'nothing but applied biology'*: Ibid., p. 31.

144 *410,000 people ... surgically sterilised*: Ibid., p. 25.

144 *buried in mass graves*: Ibid., p. 78.

144 *70,000 people were murdered*: Gazdag, G., et al. (2017) *Hist. Psychiatry*, 28(4): 482–8.

144 *'most significant Renaissance castles'*: Loistl, S., & Schwanninger, F. (2017) *Int. J. Hist. Achaeol.*, 22(3): 614–38. p. 614.

144 *18,000 people were killed*: Ibid., p. 616.

144 *an ecumenical ceremony*: Research trip to Hartheim Castle by the author in October 2018.

145 *'life unworthy of life'*: Lifton, R.J. (2000) *Nazi Doctors*. Basic Books. p. 46.

145 *'wild euthanasia'*: Czech, H. (2016) *Documentation Centre of Austrian Resistance (DÖW)*. p. 18.

145 *killed 300 mentally ill patients*: Rzesnitzek, L. & Lang, S. (2017) *Med. Hist.*, 61: 66–88. p. 86.

145 *wrists and ankles ... dead in less than ten minutes*: Gazdag, G., et al. (2017) *Hist. Psychiatry*, 28(4): 482–8.

146 *a means of punishing ... 'he is bedridden'*: Jacoby, M.G. (1958) *Br. Med. J.*, 1: 282.

146 *'The recovery of the severe'*: Smith, L.H., et al. (1942) *Am. J. Psychiatry* 98(4): 558–61.

146 *80 and 90 per cent*: Bennett, A.E. (1945) *Psychiatr. Q*, 19: 465–477. Also: Smith, L.H., et al. (1942) *Am. J. Psychiatry* 98(4): 558–61.

146 *'I would not have lasted'*: Post, F. (1978) *Br. J. Psychiatry*, 133: 83–6.

147 *10,000 sessions ... 'relatively harmless'*: Kalinowsky, L. & Barrera, S.E. (1940) *Psychiatr. Q.*, 14: 719–30. p. 727.

147 *'a mild approach'*: Myerson, A. (1942) *N. Engl. J. Med.*, 227(11): 403–7.

Cerletti's Monster

148 *'some neurotics may be harmed'*: Kalinowsky, L.B. (1949) *Bull. N.Y. Acad. Med.*, 25: 541–53. p. 552.

148 *rapid and drastic treatment*: Mettler, F.A. ed. (1949) *Selective Partial Ablation of the Frontal Cortex*. Paul B. Hoeber.

148 *willing to try anything*: Valenstein, E. (1986) *Great and Desperate Cures*. Basic Books, Inc. p. 229.

149 *a 'last resort'*: Ibid., p. 198.

149 *'unnecessary damage eliminated?'*: Mettler, F.A. ed. (1949) *Selective Partial Ablation of the Frontal Cortex*. Paul B. Hoeber.

149 *survey from 44 neurosurgical centres*: Baraclough, B.M. & Mitchell-Heggs, N.A. (1978) *Br. Med. J.*, 2: 1591–3.

150 *'the new psychosurgery'*: El-Hai, J. (2005) *The Lobotomist*. Wiley. p. 311.

150 *Fractures in ... 23 per cent*: Lingley, J.R. & Robbins, L.L. (1947) *Radiology*, 48: 124–8.

150 *43 per cent*: Shorter, E. & Healy, D. (2007) *Shock Therapy*. Rutgers University Press. p. 65.

150 *'If shock treatment is to survive'*: Bennett, A.E. (1940) *JAMA*, 114(4): 322–4. p. 322.

150 *rather than suffer*: Katzenelbogen, S., et al. (1944) *AMA Arch. Neurol. Psychiatry*, 52(4): 323–6.

151 *no evidence of damage*: Kalinowsky, L., et al. (1941) *Psychiatric Quarterly* 15: 450–9.

151 *military service could be forgotten*: Interview with Poul Videbech in Glostrup by author, 24 January 2019.

151 *forgot that they were ill*: Smith, L.H., et al. (1942) *Am. J. Psychiatry*, 98(4): 558–61.

151 *'negligible'*: Maclay, W.S. (1952) *Proc. R. Soc. Med.*, 46: 13–20.

151 *heart failure*: Pacella (1944) *Bull. N.Y. Acad. Med.*, 20(11): 575–87.

151 *'other than the electrical treatment' ... 'responsibility to bear'*: Maclay, W.S. (1952) *Proc. R. Soc. Med.*, 46: 13–20.

152 *a staple of psychiatry*: Shorter, E. & Healy, D. (2007) *Shock Therapy*. Rutgers University Press. p. 51.

152 *'Our evidence, however'*: Tillotson, K.J. & Sulzbach, W. (1945) *Am. J. Psychiatry*, 101(4): 455–9.

153 *'progress cannot be made'*: Passione, R. (2004) *Hist. Psychiatry*, 15: 83–104.

153 *'away from the use of electroshock'*: Cerletti, U. (1956) 'Electroshock therapy'. In Sackler, A.M. ed. *The Great Physiodynamic Therapies in Psychiatry*. Hoeber. p. 106.

154 *'domain of biochemists'*: Ibid., p.115.

154 *Cerletti had failed chemistry*: Passione, R. (2004) *Hist. Psychiatry* 15: 83–104.

154 *'acroaganines' ... 'highly vitalising substances'*: Cerletti, U. (1956) 'Electroshock therapy'. In Sackler, A.M. ed. *The Great Physiodynamic Therapies in Psychiatry*. Hoeber.

154 *gloopy and sickly yellow*: Trip to Museum of History of Medicine in Rome by author, October 2018.

155 *'Fear of imminent death'*: Miller, E. (1967) *Br. J. Psychiatry*, 113: 301–11.

155 *'through the patient's autism'*: Weigert, E.V. (1940) *Psychiatry*, 3(2): 189–209.

155 *'[W]hatever doubt may exist'*: Selenski, H. (1943) *Bull N.Y. Acad Med.*, 19: 245–52.

155 *'no adequate theory'*: Kalinowsky, L.B. (1949) *Bull. N.Y. Acad. Med.*, 25: 541–53.

156 *'Risks ... justified'*: Kalinowsky, L.B. & Hoch, P. (1961) *Somatic Treatments in Psychiatry*. Grune & Stratton. p. 173.

156 *one tenth of a lethal dose*: Bennett, A.E. (1940) *JAMA*, 114(4): 322–4. p. 322.

156 *15 to 20 minutes*: Bennett, A.E. (1940) *Convulsive Therapy*, 13(2): 93–107.

157 *'first and only fatality'*: Abrams, R. (1988) *Convulsive Therapy*, 4: 25–39. p. 36.

157 *'dangerous than the complications'*: Kalinowsky, L.B. (1949) *Bull. N.Y. Acad. Med.*, 25: 541–53.

157 *cancer more likely*: Batty, G.D., et al. (2017) *Br. Med. J.*, 356: 1–11.

157 *diabetes*: Zhang, X., et al. (2005) *Am. J. Epidemiol.*, 161(7): 652–60.

157 *die from heart complications*: Barth, J. (2004) *Psychosom. Med.*, 66: 802–13.

158 *just a stone's throw ... 'curare of short action'*: Cozanitis, D.A. (2016) *Wien. Med. Wochenschr. Suppl.*, 166: 487–99.

158 *'electroplexy'*: Smith, S. (1956) *J. Ment. Sci.* 102: 796–800.

158 *'CSPR'*: Spiro, H. (1992) 'Chapter 17. The Stigma of Electroconvulsive Therapy: A Workshop'. In Fink, P.J. & Tansman, A. eds. *Stigma and Mental Illness*. American Psychiatric Press, Inc.

158 *'had been somehow erased'*: Shorter, E. & Healy, D. (2007) *Shock Therapy*. Rutgers University Press. p. 161.

The Psychic Energisers

159 *buzz with energy*: Chessin, M., et al. (1956) *J. Pharmacol. Exp. Ther.*, 119: 453–60.

159 *'twinkle in his eye'*: Ayd, F. (1996) *Discovery of Antidepressants*. In Healy, D. *The Psychopharmacologists*. Chapman & Hall.

159 *laboratories of Charles Scott*: Kline, N.S. (1970) 'MAOIs: An Unfinished Picaresque Tale'. In Ayd, F.J. & Blackwell, B. eds *Discoveries in Biological Psychiatry*. J.B. Lippincott Company.

159 *sarpagandha ... used for a variety of ills*: Monachino, J. (1954) *Econ Bot.*, 8: 349–65.

159 *'attain states of introspection'*: Meyers, M. (2007) *Happy Accidents*. Arcade Publishing Inc. p. 274.

160 *the hospital's glazier*: Healy, D. (1997) *The Antidepressant Era*. Harvard University Press. p. 55.

160 *lethargic side effects*: Kline, N. (1954) Ann. N.Y. Acad. Sci., 59(1): 107–32.

160 *'I could sleep'*: Interview with Thomas Ban by author, 20 March 2018.

160 *'most exciting periods'*: Platt, M. (2012) *Storming the Gates of Bedlam*. Depew Publishing. p. 31.

161 *stocky, balding*: Ayd, F. (1996) 'Discovery of Antidepressants'. In Healy, D. *The Psychopharmacologists*. Chapman & Hall.

161 *'swing it up'*: Lehmann, H.E. & Kline, N.S. (1980) 'Clinical discoveries with anti-depressant drugs'. In Parnham, M.J. & Bruinvels, J. eds *Discoveries in Pharmacology, Vol 1*. 209–21

162 *bought these redundant reserves*: Sandler, M. (1990) *J. Psychopharmacol.*, 4(3): 136–9. p. 136.

162 *In 1951 … isoniazid*: Aronson, J.D., et al. (1952) *Proc. Soc. Exp. Biol. Med.* 80(2): 259–62.

162 *It killed Mycobacterium*: Fox, H. (1952) *Science*, 116: 129–34.

162 WONDER DRUG FIGHTS TB: Cited in 'Medicine: TB – and Hope'. *Time* magazine, 3 March 1952.

162 *15-minute radio broadcast*: Ryan, F. (1992) *Tuberculosis*. Swift Publishers. p. 360.

163 *a $4 million complex … 'largest and finest hospital'*: Norman, G.A., et al. (1985) Designation Report. p. 18.

163 *'coughing up their lives'*: López-Muñoz, F. & Alamo, C. (2009) *Curr. Pharm. Des.* 15: 1563–86. p. 1566.

163 *'dancing in the halls'*: Bullmore, E. (2018) *The Inflamed Mind*. Short Books. p. 93. Figure 7.

163 *'No bed cases remain'*: Crane, G. (1956) *Am. J. Psychiatry* 112: 494–501. p. 494.

163 *reserpine reduced the levels*: Shore, P.A, et al. (1957) *Ann. N.Y. Acad. Sci.*, 66(3): 609–15.

163 *iproniazid increased them*: Shore, P.A., et al. (1957) *Science*, 126: 1063–4.

163 *Betty Twarog … first found evidence*: Twarog, B.M. & Page, I.H. (1953) *Am. J. Phsyiol.*, 175: 157–61.

163 *and the gut*: Whitaker-Azmitia, P.M. (1999) *Neuropsychopharmacology*, 21(5): 2S–8S.

163 *90 per cent of serotonin*: Hata, T., et al. (2017) *PLoS ONE*. 12(7): e0180745.

163 *studied in the blood serum*: Page, I.H. (1976) *Perspect. Biol. Med.*, 20: 1–8.

164 *'quiet, withdrawn' … 70 per cent*: Loomer, et al. (1957) *Psychiatr. Res. Rep.*, 8: 129–41. p. 136.

164 *black Thunderbird soft-top*: Platt, M. (2012) *Storming the Gates of Bedlam*. Depew Publishing. p. 93.

165 *'metastasis from the Museum of Modern Art'*: Research trip to Nathan Kline Institute by author, November 2018.

165 *five nurses and three psychiatrists*: Ibid.

165 *Over two thirds of his patients … 'Suffer is often too mild'*: Kline, N.S. (1969) *Depression*. S Karger.

165 *'You see, doctor'*: Kline, N.S., et al. (1957) 'Iproniazid in Depressed and Regressed Patients'. In Rinkel, M. & Denber, C.B. eds. *Proceedings of the Symposium on Chemical Concepts of Psychosis, 1957*. Peter Owen.

165 *30 'responded with complete remission'*: Ibid.

165 *'There is a revolution in psychiatry'*: Platt, M. (2012) *Storming the Gates of Bedlam.* Depew Publishing. p. 37.

168 *'One supposed mode'*: Kline, N.S. (1974) *From Sad to Glad.* Ballantine Books. p. 50.

168 *'I was making a fool of myself'*: Kline, N.S. (1974). *From Sad to Glad.* Ballantine Books. p. 67.

169 *'No one in their right mind'*: 'Drug for Treating Schizophrenia Identified'. *PBS,* 1998. Heinz Lehmann.

169 *'had flair, flamboyance'*: 'Boss "Nucky" Johnson is dead at 85 – Unconscious 25 Hours Before "Time Took Him"'. *Atlantic City Press,* 10 December 1968.

169 *'whisky, wine, women'*: 'Prohibition-Era Ruler of Atlantic City, 85, Dies'. *NY Times,* 10 December 1968.

169 *'thought everyone lived that way'*: Platt, M. (2012) *Storming the Gates of Bedlam.* Depew Publishing. p. 59.

170 *president to lunch*: López-Muñoz, F. & Alamo, C. (2009). *Curr. Pharm. Des.,* 15: 1563–86.

170 *known for his womanising*: Platt, M. (2012) *Storming the Gates of Bedlam.* Depew Publishing. p. 129.

170 *antagonised his peers*: Ayd, F. (1996) 'Discovery of Antidepressants'. In Healy, D. *The Psychopharmacologists.* Chapman & Hall.

The Shoes that Prozac Would Fill

171 *a potential decongestant*: Rasmussen, N. (2006) *J. Hist. Med. Allied Sci.,* 61(3): 288–323.

171 *'increased tendency to talk'* ... *'exulted being'*: Peoples, S.A. & Guttmann, E. (1936) *Lancet,* 227: 1107–9. p. 1109.

171 *'energy and self-confidence'*: Guttmann, G. (1936) *J. Ment. States,* 82(340): 618–25.

171 *'As soon as I started'*: Wilbur, D.W., MacClean, A.R., & Allen, E.V. (1937) *JAMA,* 109(8): 549–54. p. 552.

172 *'Benzedrine is a stimulant'*: Davies, I.J. et al. (1938) *Proc. R. Soc. Med.,* 32: 385–98. p. 391.

172 *the Nazis preferred Pervitin*: Rasmussen, N. (2008) *Am J. Public Health,* 98(6) 974–85.

172 *students fainting and dying*: 'Pep-Pill Poisoning'. *Time* magazine, 10 May 1937.

173 *'a therapeutic weapon'*: Rasmussen, N. (2008) *Am J. Public Health,* 98(6) 974–85. p. 975.

173 *not in any sense curative*: Myerson, A. (1936) *Arch. Neuropsych.,* 36(4): 816–22. p. 822.

173 *'mutually corrective'*: Legge, D. & Steinberg, H. (1962) *Br. J. Pharmacol.,* 18: 490–500.

173 *800 metric tons*: Rasmussen, N. (2008) *Am J. Public Health,* 98(6) 974–85. p. 977.

174 *'the shoes that Prozac'*: Rasmussen, N. (2006) *J. Hist. Med. Allied Sci.,* 61(3): 288–323.

176 *'fatalities may occur'*: Kraai, E.P. & Seifert, S.A. (2014) *J. Med. Toxicol.* 11: 232–6.

177 *7.2 per cent ... US population*: Luo, Y., et al. (2020) *Front. Psychiatry,* 11(35).

177 *16.6 per cent of the UK*: Marsden J., et al. (2019) *Lancet Psychiat.,* 6(11): 935–50.

177 *In Australia ... 15 per cent*: OECD (2017) 'Antidepressant drugs consumption, 2000 and 2015 (or nearest year)'. OECD Publishing.

177 *if they are severely depressed*: Arrol, B., et al. (2009) *Cochrane Database of Systematic Review, Issue 3,* No. CD007954. And: Fournier, J.C., et al. (2010) *JAMA,* 303(1): 47–53.

177 *contradictory reviews*: Jakobsen, J.C., et al. (2019) *BMJ Evid. Based Med.,* Epub: doi:10.1136/bmjebm-2019-111238.

178 *21 different antidepressants*: Cipriani, A., et al. (2018) *Lancet*, 391: 1357–66.
179 *'more readily generalisable'*: Lewis, G., et al. (2019) *Lancet Psychiat.*, 6: 903–14.

G22355

180 *developed into a small cyclone*: Rinkel, M. & Denber, C.B. eds (1960) *Proceedings of the Symposium on Chemical Concepts of Psychosis, 1957*. Peter Owen.
180 *test his latest quip*: Platt, M. (2012) *Storming the Gates of Bedlam*. Depew Publishing. p. 42.
180 *the crafty Schizococcus! ... 'It is almost a truism'*: Rinkel, M. & Denber, C.B. eds (1960) *Proceedings of the Symposium on Chemical Concepts of Psychosis, 1957*. Peter Owen.
181 *whisper-soft voice*: Shorter, E. (2009) *Before Prozac*. Oxford University Press. p. 60.
182 *Kline didn't even know who Kuhn was*: Kline, N.S. (1974) *From Sad to Glad*. Ballantine Books. p. 107.
182 *fog blankets the streets*: Research trip to Münsterlingen by author, September 2018.
182 *trio of tall buildings*: Ammann, J. (1990) *150 Jahre Münsterlingen*. p. 115.
182 *an atom of sulphur*: Lehmann, H.E., et al. (1958) *Can. J. Psych.* 3(4): 155–64. p. 156.
183 *'undergone a transformation'*: 'The First Patient Treated with Imipramine'. Photocopy from medical history #21502 of the 'Kantonal Treatment and Care Clinic in Munsterlingen' concerning female patient Paula F.J., born 30 April 1907.
183 *elevate mood in 40*: Brown, W.A. & Rosdolsky, M. (2015) *Am. J. Psychiatry*, 172: 426–9.
183 *'depression ... gave way to friendly'*: López-Muñoz, F. & Alamo, C. (2009). *Curr. Pharm. Des.*, 15: 1563–86. p. 1569.
184 *the room remained quiet*: Healy, D. (1997). *The Antidepressant Era*. Harvard University Press. p. 52.
184 *The dozen or so*: López-Muñoz, F. & Alamo, C. (2009). *Curr. Pharm. Des.*, 15: 1563–86. p. 1569.
184 *didn't make it to Kuhn's talk*: Ban, T. (1999) 'Heinz Lehmann and Psychopharmacology'. INHN.
184 *aware of the Swiss psychiatrist's work*: Lehmann, H.E. & Kline, N.S. (1980). 'Clinical discoveries with antidepressant drugs'. In Parnham, M.J. & Bruinvels, J. eds *Discoveries in Pharmacology, Volume 1*. 209–21
184 *skiing holiday*: Paris, J. (1999) *Can. J. Psychiatry*, 44: 441–2.
185 *60 per cent ... fully recovered*: Lehmann, H.E., et al. (1958). *Can. J. Psych.* 3(4): 155–64. p. 163.
185 *'The effect is striking'*: Kuhn, R. (1958) *Am. J. Psychiatry* 115(5): 459–64.
186 *'imipramine is of special significance'*: Freyhan, F. (1960) *Am. J. Psychiatry*, 116: 1057–64. p. 1061.
187 *'less spectacular than'*: Lehmann, H.E., et al. (1958) *Can. J. Psych.* 3(4): 155–64. p. 161.
187 *'most effective treatment'*: McDonald, I.M., et al. (1966) *Am. J. Psychiatry* 122(12): 1427–31.
187 *two large scale studies*: Greenblatt, M., et al. (1964) *Am. J. Psychiatry* 120(10): 935–43. And: The Northwick Park ECT Trial (1965) *Br. Med. J.*, 1: 881–6.

187 *higher rate of suicide*: Gournellis, R., et al. (2018) *Ann. Gen. Psychiatry* 17: 39.

187 *'22 patients with delusions'*: Clinical Research Centre (1984) *Br. J. Psychiatry* 144: 227–37. p. 235.

188 *'for ECT over medication'*: Payne, N.A. & Prudic, J. (2009) *J. Psychiatr. Pract.* 15(5): 346–68.

188 *first reported case*: Lancaster, N.P. & Foster, A.R. (1959) Br. *Med. J.*, 2(5164): 1458.

189 *low as 25 per cent*: West, E.D. & Dally, P.J. (1959) *Br. Med. J.*, 1(5136): 1491–4.

190 *1959, bipolar disorder*: Mendelson, M. (1974). *Psychoanalytic Concepts of Depression.* Spectrum. p. 25.

191 *'difficult to treat by any method'*: Sargant, W. (1960) *Psychosomatics*, 1: 14–17. p. 16.

191 *within five to eight days*: Davidson, J.T., et al. (1982) *Arch. Gen. Psychiatry*, 39: 527–34. p. 532.

191 *defining feature of MAO inhibitors*: Sargant, W. (1960). *Psychosomatics*, 1: 14–17. p. 16.

191 *four or more weeks*: Davidson, J.T., et al. (1982) *Arch. Gen. Psychiatry*, 39: 527–34. p. 532.

191 *ECT ... avoided for such patients*: Ibid., p. 533.

191 *'of greatest importance'*: West, E.D. & Dally, P.J. (1959). *Br. Med. J.*, 1(5136): 1491–4.

192 *one patient in every 500*: Sargant, W. (1960). *Psychosomatics*, 1: 14–17. p. 15.

192 *'some who had ski accidents'*: Kline, N.S. (1974) *From Sad to Glad*. Ballantine Books. p. 103.

192 *iproniazid was withdrawn*: López-Muñoz, F. & Alamo, C. (2009). *Curr. Pharm. Des.*, 15: 1563–86. p. 1572.

192 *'"acres of diamonds" affairs'*: Lehmann, H.E. & Kline, N.S. (1980). 'Clinical discoveries with antidepressant drugs'. In Parnham, M.J. & Bruinvels, J. eds *Discoveries in Pharmacology, Volume 1*. 209–21

193 *considered the safest*: Atkinson, R.M. & Ditman, K.S. (1965) *Clin. Pharmacol. Ther.*, 6: 631–55. p. 632.

The Mysterious Case of the Lethal Headaches

194 *27-year-old man*: McClure, J.L (1962) *Lancet*, i, 1351.

194 *'devastating headache'*: Blackwell, B. (1963) *Lancet*, 282: 849–51.

194 *quickly lost interest ... playing rugby*: Blackwell, B. (2012) *Bits and Pieces of a Psychiatrist's Life.* XLIBRIS.

195 *'I was transformed by contact with patients'*: Ibid.

195 *rows of pendant lights ... smell of coffee*: Research trip to Bethlem Museum of the Mind by author, December 2017.

195 *'Was she taking tranylcypromine?'*: Blackwell, B. (2012). *Bits and Pieces of a Psychiatrist's Life.* XLIBRIS.

196 *a short letter*: Blackwell, B. (1963) *Lancet*, 281(7273): 167–8.

197 *pharmacist working in Nottingham*: Blackwell, B. (1970) 'The Process of Discovery'. In Ayd, F.J. & Blackwell, B. eds *Discoveries in Biological Psychiatry*. J.B. Lippincott Company.

197 *'No effects are caused by butter'*: 'Adumbration: A History Lesson'. *INHN*, 18 December 2014.

197 *knew she was vegetarian ... breakfast of cheese*: Blackwell, B. (1970). 'The Process of Discovery'. In Ayd, F.J. & Blackwell, B. eds *Discoveries in Biological Psychiatry*. J.B. Lippincott Company.

198 *depressive-like condition*: Achor, R.W.P., Hanson, N.O., & Gifford, R.W. (1955) *JAMA*, 159: 841–5.

198 *'a reductionist oversimplification'*: Schildkraut, J.J. (1965) *Am. J. Psychiatry*, 122(5): 509–22. p. 517.

199 *studies in rat brains in 1978*: Carlsson, A. & Lindqvist, M. (1978) *J. Neural. Transm.* 43: 73–91.

199 *eventual ban in 1983*: Fagius, J., et al. (1985) *J. Neurol. Neurosurg. Psychiatry*, 48: 65–9.

199 *15 years for this drug to be released*: López-Muñoz, F. & Alamo, C. (2009) *Curr. Pharm. Des.*, 15: 1563–86. p. 1576.

199 *Although they offered no improvement in efficacy*: Ban, T.A. (2001) *J. Neural Trans.*, 108: 707–16.

202 *lead them into complete remission*: Rush, A.J., et al. (2006) *N. Engl. J. Med.*, 354(12): 1231–42.

204 *moonlighting as a medical officer*: Blackwell, B. (2012). *Bits and Pieces of a Psychiatrist's Life*. XLIBRIS.

205 *painful headache ... rushed through the corridor*: Blackwell, B. (1970) 'The Process of Discovery'. In Ayd, F.J. & Blackwell, B. eds *Discoveries in Biological Psychiatry*. J.B. Lippincott Company.

205 *Eight had definitely eaten cheese*: Blackwell, B. (1963) *Lancet*, 282: 849–51.

205 *'the idea that a common dietary substance'*: Blackwell, B. (1970) 'The Process of Discovery'. In Ayd, F.J. & Blackwell, B. eds *Discoveries in Biological Psychiatry*. J.B. Lippincott Company.

205 *'unscientific and premature'*: Blackwell, B. (2012) *Bits and Pieces of a Psychiatrist's Life*. XLIBRIS.

206 *Kline read the worrying reports*: Research trip to Nathan Kline Institute, Orangeburg, by author in October 2018.

206 *Forty peopled died*: Atkinson, R.M. & Ditman, K.S. (1965) *Clin. Pharmacol. Ther.*, 6: 631–55. p. 640.

206 *list of restricted substances*: Marley, E. & Blackwell, B. (1971) *Adv. Pharmacol.*, 8: 185–239.

207 *The people who really benefit*: Interview with Ted Dinan in Cork, Ireland, by author. November 2018.

207 *Several clinical trials*: Quitkin, F.M., et al. (1988) *Am. J. Psychiatry*, 145: 306–11. Review: Thase, M.E., Trivedi, M.H., & Rush, A.J. (1995) *Neuropsychopharmacology*, 12(3): 185–219.

207 *'like magic'*: Interview with Ted Dinan in Cork, Ireland, by author. November 2018.

208 *'no drug in history was so widely used'*: Kline, N.S. (1970) 'MAOIs: An Unfinished Picaresque Tale'. In Ayd, F.J. & Blackwell, B. eds *Discoveries in Biological Psychiatry*. J.B. Lippincott Company.

208 *400,000 people in the US*: López-Muñoz, F. & Alamo, C. (2009) *Curr. Pharm. Des.*, 15: 1563–86. p. 1567.

208 *trials started in January 1956*: Kuhn, R. (1970) 'The Imipramine Story'. In Ayd, F.J. & Blackwell, B. eds *Discoveries in Biological Psychiatry*. J.B. Lippincott Company.

208 *front cover of* Fortune *magazine*: Healy, D. (1997). *The Antidepressant Era*. Harvard University Press. p. 68.

208 *'The amount involved . . . was vast'*: Ibid., p. 66.

209 Oxford English Dictionary: Blackwell, B. (2018) 'Pioneers and Controversies in Psychopharmacology'. 'Chapter 8: Nathan (Nate) Kline and the Monoamine Oxidase Inhibitors'. *INHN*, eBook.

209 *'a wheeler-dealer's arrogance'* . . . *'courageous'*:: Goldberg, J. (1989) *Anatomy of a Scientific Discovery*. Bantam.

210 *thanks largely to . . . Frances Kelsey*: 'The Thalidomide Tragedy'. *Helix*, 28 July 2009.

210 *'liked the limelight too much'*: Goldberg, J. (1989) *Anatomy of A Scientific Discovery*. Bantam. p. 137

211 *'resemblance to Charlton Heston's Moses'*: Ibid., p. 121.

211 *'a nonsense study'*: Ibid., p. 137.

211 *'slow agony'*: Ibid., p. 202.

211 *'any investigational new drug'*, 'Psychiatrist Barred from Administering Experimental Drug'. *NY Times*, 25 May 1982.

211 *retired from a 30-year career*: 'Nathan Kline, Developer of Antidepressants, Dies.' *NY Times*, 14 February 1983.

211 *'unfortunate matter behind me'*: 'Psychiatrist Barred from Administering Experimental Drug'. *NY Times*, 25 May 1982.

212 *boxed away in a disused room*: Research trip to Nathan Kline Institute in Orangeburg by author, November 2018.

Part Three – Getting Therapy

213 *'mobile societies'*: Klerman, G.L., et al. (1984) *Interpersonal Psychotherapy of Depression*. Basic Books. p. 50.

213 *'psychotherapy cannot be expected'*: Neki, J.S. (1975) *Am. J. Psychother.*, 29(1): 92–100.

213 *'encourage the old'*: Kline, N.S. (1974) *From Sad to Glad*. Ballantine Books.

In Your Dreams, Freud

215 *'He will not die!'* . . . *90 per cent mortality*: Weishaar, M.E. (1993) *Aaron T. Beck*. Sage Publications. p. 9.

215 *'if I got into a hole, I could dig myself out'*: Ibid., p. 10.

215 *He was told that a Jewish boy*: Ibid., p. 12.

216 *'deep, dark invisible forces'* . . . *'had answers for everything'*: Ibid., p. 15.

217 *quite banal*: 'The Doctor Is In'. *The American Scholar*, 1 September 2009.

217 *a rigged card game*: 'A Psychiatrist Who Wouldn't Take No for an Answer'. *NY Times*, 11 August 1981.

218 *'A brilliant academician'* . . . *'magnify any failures'*: Beck, A.T. (1963) *Arch. Gen Psychiatry*, 9: 324–33. p. 326.

218 *'Intrinsic to this type of thinking'*: Ibid., p. 328.

219 *pigeon's pecking at levers*: Dember, W.N. (1974) *Am. Psychol.*, 29(3): 161–8.

220 *Medium-sized 'mongrel dogs'*: Seligman, M.E.P. & Maier, S.F. (1967) *J. Exp. Psychol.*, 74(1): 1–9.

220 *'severe, pulsating' … 50 seconds*: Seligman, M.E.P (1972) *Annu. Rev. Med.*, 23: 407–12. p. 408.

220 *'"getting going"'*: Ibid., p. 410.

220 *lower levels of noradrenaline*: Ibid., p. 408.

221 *'positively reinforced behaviours that are missing'*: Ferster, C.B. (1973) *Am. Psychol.*, 28(10): 857–70.

221 *80 per cent*: Wolpe, J. (1981) *Am. Psychol.*, 36: 159–64. p. 161.

221 *'reject the conditioning theory'*: Wolpe, J. (1989) *J. Behav. Ther. Exp. Psychiatry* 20(1): 3–15.

221 *'subclass of behaviour therapy'*: Wolpe, J. (1976) *J. Behav. Ther. Exp. Psychiatry* 7: 109–16. p. 114.

222 *'change the "minds and hearts"'*: Skinner, B.F. (1977) *Behaviourism*, 5(2): 1–10.

222 *'very much on our own'*: Weishaar, M.E. (1993) *Aaron T. Beck*. Sage Publications. p. 23.

223 *'excitement of being the underdog'*: Ibid., p. 27.

223 *'promote cognitive change'*: Ibid., p. 90.

223 *cured his mother's depression*: Ibid., p. 9.

224 *'Beck Depression Inventory'*: Beck, A.T., et al. (1961) *Arch. Gen. Psychiatry*, 4: 53–63.

225 *highlight his own cognitive distortions*: 'The Doctor Is In'. *The American Scholar*, 1 September 2009.

225 *tennis, napping, … cinema*: Rosner, R. (2014) *Isis*, 105(4): 734–58. p. 751.

225 *'spiral-bound notebooks'*: Ibid., p. 755.

225 *'She was my reality tester'*: 'Scientist at Work: Aaron T. Beck'. *NY Times*, 11 January 2000.

226 *red one for special occasions*: Rosner, R. (2014) *Isis*, 105(4): 734–58. p. 751.

226 *pale blue eyes*: 'Scientist at Work: Aaron T. Beck'. *NY Times*, 11 January 2000.

226 *rundown offices*: 'The Doctor Is In'. *The American Scholar*, 1 September 2009.

226 *'more effective'*: 'A Psychiatrist Who Wouldn't Take No for an Answer'. *NY Times*, 11 August 1981.

More Than One Psychotherapy

227 *an expert on tricyclic*: Klerman, G.L. & Cole, J.O. (1965) *Pharmacol. Rev.*, 17(2): 101–41.

227 *'inverse correlation'*: Eysenck, H.J. (1952) *J. Consult. Clin. Psychol.*, 16: 319–24.

228 *framed photograph … 'We were friends' … he was God*: Interview with Myrna Weissman at NYS Psychiatric Institute by author, November 2018.

229 *'hallmark of the [human] species'*: Bowlby, J. (1958) *Int. J Psychoanal.*, 39: 350–73.

229 *'departures from the social field'*: Paykel, E.S., et al. (1969) *Arch. Gen. Psychiatry*, 21: 753–60.

230 *'loss and disappointment'*: Brown, G.W. & Harris, T. (1978) *Social Origins of Depression*. Tavistock Publications. p. 105.

231 *'find out what is going on'*: Interview with Myrna Weissman at NYS Psychiatric Institute by author, November 2018.

231 *'sick-role'*: Weissman, M.M. & Markowitz, J.C. (1994) *Arch. Gen. Psychiatry*, 51: 599–606.

232 *79 per cent*: Rush, A.J., et al. (1977) *Cognit. Ther. Res.*, 1: 17–37.

232 *'sense of mastery'*: 'New Theories of Depression Hold Promise of Simpler Remedy'. *NY Times*, 2 June 1981.

233 *Beck complained that this wasn't sufficient*: Weishaar, M.E. (1993) *Aaron T. Beck*. Sage Publications. p. 38.

233 *'lost in translation'*: Ibid., p. 39.

233 *compared the therapists … to junior doctors*: Ibid., p. 38.

233 *'The immediate goal'*: Elkin, I., et al. (1985) *Arch. Gen. Psychiatry*, 42: 305–16. p. 308.

234 *'"this won't [turn] out",'*: Weishaar, M.E. (1993) *Aaron T. Beck*. Sage Publications. p. 39.

234 *'the most intensive training'*: Elkin, I., et al. (1985) *Arch. Gen. Psychiatry*, 42: 305–16. p. 309.

234 *lowest for … cognitive therapy*: Shea, M.T., et al. (1992) *Psychiatry*, 49: 782–7. p. 786:

235 *'major contribution'*: Weishaar, M.E. (1993) *Aaron T. Beck*. Sage Publications. p. 41.

235 *'strongest evidence is for CBT'*: Interview with Helen Christensen by author, August 2018.

237 *a study of 400 people*: Ali, S., et al. (2017) *Behav. Res. Ther.*, 94: 1–8.

238 *benefits of 12 to 18 sessions*: Wiles, N.J. (2016) *Lancet Psychiatry*, 3: 137–44.

240 *'so little on improving its quality'*: Layard, R. & Clark, D.M. (2014) *Thrive*. Allen Lane. p. 89.

'If Mom Ain't Happy Ain't Nobody Happy'

241 *'shouldn't be one psychotherapy'*: Interview with Myrna Weissman at NYS Psychiatric Institute by author, November 2018.

241 *'historical picture of a Yalie'*: Weissman, M.M. (2009) *Ann. Epidemiol.*, 19(4): 264–7.

243 *In her first survey*: Weissman, M.M. & Myers, J.K. (1978) *Arch. Gen. Psychiatry*, 35: 1304–11.

243 *a disorder of menopausal women … handwritten drafts*: Weissman, M.M. (2009) *Ann. Epidemiol.*, 19(4): 264–7. p. 265.

244 *(ECA) programme*: Reiger, D.A., et al. (1984) *Arch. Gen. Psychiatry*, 41: 934–41.

244 *5 per cent of American people*: Weissman, M.M., et al. (1988) *Psychol. Med.*, 18: 141–53.

244 *lower than New Zealand and France*: Weissman, M.M., et al. (1996) *JAMA*, 276(4): 293–4.

245 *two to four times higher … divorced*: Ibid.

245 *'astronomical in terms of lost productivity alone'*: Glass, R.M. & Freedman, D.X. (1985) *JAMA*, 254(16): 2280–3. p. 2282.

245 *interpersonal therapy provided a boost*: DiMascio, A., et al. (1979) *Arch. Gen. Psychiatry*, 36: 1450–6.

246 *'an additive effect'*: 'Yale Researchers'. *NY Times*, 6 August 1978.

246 *roughly half of patients*: Elkin, I., et al. (1989) *Arch. Gen. Psychiatry*, 46: 971–83. p. 977. Figure 2. Also: Cuijpers, P., et al. (2011) *Am. J. Psychiatry*, 168(6): 581–92. p. 8.

246 *depression in mothers*: Swartz, H.A., et al. (2008) *Am. J. Psychiatry*, 165(9): 1155–62.

246 *'medicine has lost'* ... *'cleansing clarity'*: Keller, M.B. (1992) *J. Clin. Psychopharmacol.*, 12(6): 379–81.

247 *'[interpersonal therapy] aside'*: Interview with Myrna Weissman at NYS Psychiatric Institute by author, November 2018.

248 *'abnormal grief reactions'*: Klerman, G.L., et al. (1984) *Interpersonal Psychotherapy of Depression*. Basic Books. p. 96.

248 *'That's not rocket science'*: Interview with Myrna Weissman at NYS Psychiatric Institute by author, November 2018.

248 *ten-year mark*: Weissman, M.M., et al. (1997) *Arch. Gen. Psychiatry*, 54: 932–40.

248 *'three times as high'*: Weissman, M.M., et al. (2016) *JAMA Psychiatry*, 73(9): 970–7.

249 *'you can modify that'*: Interview with Myrna Weissman at NYS Psychiatric Institute by author, November 2018.

249 *crucial element was remission*: Weissman, M.M., et al. (2006) *JAMA*, 295(12): 1389–1398.

249 *'If mom ain't happy'*: Interview with Myrna Weissman at NYS Psychiatric Institute by author, November 2018.

250 *'we did another study'*: Interview with Myrna Weissman at NYS Psychiatric Institute by author, November 2018.

250 *Published ... in 2015*: Weismann, M.M., et al. (2015) *Am. J. Psychiatry*, 172(5): 450–9.

250 *'the kids got better'*: Interview with Myrna Weissman at NYS Psychiatric Institute by author, November 2018.

251 *replicated Weissman's STAR*D results*: Swartz, H.A., et al. (2008) *Am. J. Psychiatry* 165(9): 1155–62.

251 *'who's going to get depressed'*: Interview with Helen Christensen by author, August 2018.

251 *trials in Chile*: Araya, R., et al. (2013) *JAMA Pediatr.*, 167(11): 1004–10.

251 *the UK*: Stallard, P., et al. (2012) *Br. Med. J.*, 345: e6058.

251 *'prevention remains a challenge'*: Whittaker, R., et al. (2017) *J. Child Psychol. Psychiatry*, 58(9): 1014–22.

252 *Judy Garber and her colleagues*: Garber, J., et al. (2009) *JAMA*, 301(21): 2215–24.

252 *'a moderator effect'*: Interview with Judy Garber by author, September 2019.

'Happier Than We Europeans'

253 *'hardly eating, hardly moving'* ... *'early confidence'*: Interview with Melanie Abas by author, February 2018.

254 *20,000 Ndebele citizens*: Mashingaidze, T.M. (2005) 'The 1987 Zimbabwe National Unity Accord and its Aftermath'. In Hendricks, C. & Lushaba, L. eds. *From National Liberation to Democratic Renaissance in Southern Africa*. Codesria. p. 82–92.

254 *'washes away the chaff'*: 'British policy towards Zimbabwe during Matabeleland massacre: licence to kill'. *The Conversation*, 17 September 2017.

254 *'worst drought in living memory'*: Maphosa, B. (1994) *Nord. J. Afr. Stud.*, 3(1): 53–8.

254 *87 children*: https://data.unicef.org/country/zwe/ (86.6 per 1,000 live births.)

254 *11 times higher*: https://data.unicef.org/country/gbr/ (7.4 per 1,000 live births.)

254 *HIV ... infect a quarter*: Mugurungi, O., et al. (2007) 'HIV in Zimbabwe 1985–2003'. In Caraël, M., Glynn, J.R. eds. *HIV, Resurgent Infections and Population Change in Africa*. International Studies in Population, Vol 6. Springer.

255 *1 in every 4,000 patients ... 'In rural clinics'*: Broadhead, J. & Abas, M. (1994) *Trop. Doct.*, 24: 27–30. p. 27.

255 *9 per cent of women*: Abas, M. & Broadhead, J. (1997) *Psychol. Med.*, 27: 59–71.

255 *'[N]othing is so gentle'*: Rousseau, J-J. (1987) 'Discourse on the Origin of Inequality.' In D.A. Cress (ed., trans.), *Basic Political Writings*. Hackett Publishing, 25–82.

256 *'happier than we Europeans'*: '"They are all dead": for indigenous people, Cook's voyage of "discovery" was a ghostly visitation'. *The Conversation*, 28 April 2020.

256 *'decay of the species'*: Rousseau, J-J. (1987) 'Discourse on the Origin of Inequality.' In D.A. Cress (ed., trans.), *Basic Political Writings*. Hackett Publishing, 25–82.

256 *'scramble for Africa'*: Pakenham, T. (2015) *The Scramble for Africa*. Abacus.

257 *'entire villages were stolen'*: 'Human zoos: When real people were exhibits'. BBC News, 27 December 2011.

257 *'classical depressive syndromes are seldom seen'*: Carothers, J. (1953) *The African Mind in Health and Disease*. WHO Monograph Series, no. 17.

258 *'"life would be wonderful"'*: Ben-Tovim, D. (1987) 'Mental Health and Primary Health Care in Botswana'. In Rutter, M. ed. *Development Psychiatry*. American Psychiatric Press.

258 *Portuguese explorers*: Hall, M. & Stefoff, R. (2006) *Great Zimbabwe*. Oxford University Press. p. 10.

258 *trade networks*: Pwiti, G. (1991) *Zambezia*, 18(2): 119–29.

258 *between 10,000 and 18,000*: Chirikure, S., et al. (2017) *PLoS ONE*, 12(6): e0178335.

259 *mythical Queen of Sheba*: Randall-MacIver, D. (1906) *Geogr. J.*, 27(4): 325–36.

259 *'Erythean' people*: Carroll, S.T. (1988) *Int. J. Afr. Hist. Stud.*, 21(2): 233–47.

259 *Arabs from the Middle East*: Mullan, J.E. (1969) *The Arab Builders of Zimbabwe*. Salisbury.

259 *'Censorship of guidebooks'*: Garlake, P. (1974) *The Ruins of Zimbabwe*. The Historical Association of Zambia.

259 *'has but few gifts for work' ... 'relatively rare'*: Carothers, J. (1953) *The African Mind in Health and Disease*. World Health Organisation Monograph Series, no. 17.

260 *'glorified pseudo-scientific novels'*: Prince, R.H. (1996) *Transcult. Psychiatric Res. Rev.*, 33: 226–40. p. 231.

260 *'radiated power and presence'*: 'Remembering Thomas Adeoye Lambo and the Mysteries of the African Mind'. *The News Nigeria*, 9 January 2018.

260 *'that they can no longer be seriously presented'*: Prince, R.H. (1996) *Transcult. Psychiatric Res. Rev.*, 33: 226–40. p. 231.

261 *rates of depression soared*: Price, R.H. (1967) *Can. J. Afr. Stud.*, 1(2): 177–92.

261 *two Ugandan villages*: Orley, J. & Wing, J. (1979) *Arch. Gen. Psychiatry*, 36: 513–20.

261 *Among the Yoruba*: Leighton, A.H., et al. (1963) *Psychiatric Disorder Among the Yoruba*. Cornell University Press.

261 *'trained in one's own culture'*: Rao, V. (1984) *Indian J. Psychiatry*, 26(4): 301–11.

Kufungisisa

262 *200 households*: Abas, M. & Broadhead, J. (1997) *Psychol. Med.*, 27: 59–71.

262 *'thinking too much'*: Abas, M., et al. (1994) *Psychiatry*, 164: 293–6.

262 *'pretty classical depression'*: Interview with Melanie Abas by author, February 2018.

263 *'one in every five people'*: Abas, M. & Broadhead, J. (1997) *Psychol. Med.* 27: 59–71.

263 *methods of George Brown*: Brown, G.W. & Harris, T. (1978) *Social Origins of Depression*. Tavistock Publications.

263 *a strong pattern emerge*: Broadhead, J.C. & Abas, M. (1998) *Psychol. Med.*, 28: 29–38.

263 *'in Zimbabwe, there were a lot more of these events'*: Interview with Melanie Abas by author, February 2018.

263 *twice as likely to be depressed*: Chibanda, D., et al. (2016) *Journal Affect. Disord.*, 198: 50–5.

263 *both a trigger*: Lund, C. (2011) *Lancet*, 378: 1502–14.

263 *in the 1990s, over 100 million people*: Liu, Q., et al. (2020) *J Psychiatric Res.* 126: 134–40.

264 *90 per cent*: Chisholm, D., et al. (2016) *Lancet Psychiatry*, 3: 415–24. Table 1.

264 *'all developing countries'*: Mohammadi, D. (2017) *Lancet Psychiatry* 4(5): 359.

264 *'share their sadness'*: Abas, M., et al. (1994) Br. J. *Psychiatry* 164: 293–6. p. 294.

265 *ten psychiatrists*: Ibid., p. 296.

265 *'Thinking too much makes people ill'*: Ibid., p. 295.

266 *just one or two*: Interview with Dixon Chibanda in Harare by author, April 2018. (Himself and Dr Nhiwatiwa.)

267 *'Disability-Adjusted Life Year'*: 'World Development Report: Investing in Health'. *The World Bank*, 1993.

267 *'one lost year of "healthy" life'*: 'Metrics: Disability-Adjusted Life Year (DALY)'. *World Health Organisation*.

267 *8 per cent 'despite the importance'*: Desjarlais, R., et al. (1995) *World Mental Health*. Oxford University Press. p. 4.

267 *'knocked off the agenda'*: Interview with Arthur Kleinman by author at Harvard University, May 2018.

268 *'That's the only way to go'*: Presentation by Vikram Patel at the Harvard Center for Global Health Delivery in Dubai.

269 *'in the twenty-first century?'*: Interview with Arthur Kleinman by author at Harvard University, May 2018.

269 *they asked their relatives*: Interview with Helen Verdeli by author.

270 *'outcomes that paraprofessionals achieve'*: Durlak, J.A. (1979) *Psychol. Bull.*, 86(1): 80–92.

271 *quarter of people ... infected*: Bolton, P., et al. (2003) *JAMA*, 289(23): 3117–24.

271 *21 per cent of people ... previous study*: Verdeli, H., et al. (2003) *World Psychiatry*, 2(2): 114–20. p. 114.

271 *inability to help*: Ibid., p. 115.

271 *Yo'kwekyawa and okwekubazida*: Bolton, P., et al. (2003) *JAMA*, 289(23): 3117–24. p. 3119.

271 *nuances of their own*: Verdeli, H., et al. (2003) *World Psychiatry*, 2(2): 114–20. p. 115.

272 *'embedded in one's social world' ... 'never use the word'*: Interview with Vikram Patel by author, March 2018.

272 *In China ... neurasthenia*: Kleinman, A. (1977) *Soc. Sci. Med.*, 11: 3–10.

272 *socially acceptable*: Lee, S. (1999) *Cult. Med. Psychiatry*, 23: 349–80.

272 *'tension'*: Roberts, T., et al. (2020) *Soc. Sci. Med.*, 246: ePub: 112741.

272 *The most common descriptor*: Kidia, et al. (2015) *Trop. Med. Int. Health* 20(7): 903–13.

273 *'part of a family'*: Verdeli, H., et al. (2003) *World Psychiatry*, 2(2): 114–120. p. 115.

273 *'dead are living among us'*: Ibid., p. 117.

274 *three times as great*: Bolton, P., et al. (2003) *JAMA*, 289(23): 3117–24.

275 *projects in . . . Santiago, Chile*: Araya, R., et al. (2003) *Lancet*, 361: 995–1000.

275 *and Goa, India*: Patel, V., et al. (2003) *Lancet*, 361: 33–9.

Care by the Community

277 *'lost quite a number'*: Interview with Dixon Chibanda in Harare by author, April 2018.

278 *'If you come to Harare'*: Chat with waiter at Alechi Portuguese Grill by author, April 2018.

278 *'Clear out the Rubbish' . . . 700,000 people*: Tibaijuka, A. (2005) 'Report of the Fact-Finding Mission to Zimbabwe to Assess the Scope and Impact of Operation Murambatsvina by the UN Special Envoy on Human Settlements Issues in Zimbabwe'.

279 *a large majority . . . met the clinical threshold*: Interview with Dixon Chibanda by author in Harare, April 2018.

279 *'no one knew what we could do'*: Ibid.

279 *14 elderly women*: 'Dixon Chibanda: Grandmothers Help to Scale up Mental Health Care'. *Bulletin of the World Health Organisation*, June 2018.

279 *'custodians of health'*: Interview with Nigel James at Mbare clinic by author, April 2018.

280 *'how could this possibly work'*: Interview with Dixon Chibanda in Harare by author, April 2018.

280 *translate medical terms*: Abas, M., et al. (2016) *Int. J. Ment. Health Syst.*, 10: 39.

280 *built by local craftsmen*: Chibanda, D., et al. (2011) *BMC Public Health*, 11: 828. p. 4.

280 *Chigaro Chekupanamazano*: Abas, M., et al. (2016) *Int. J. Ment. Health Syst.*, 10: 39.

281 *'knowledge tends to travel'*: Araya, R., et al. (2006) *Am. J. Psychiatry* 163: 1379–87. p. 1385.

281 *'You don't know me'*: Interview with Melanie Abas by author, February 2018.

281 *SSQ-14*: Patel, V., et al. (1997) *Acta Psychiatr. Scand.*, 95: 469–75.

282 *a significant reduction*: Chibanda, D., et al. (2011) *BMC Public Health*, 11: 828. p. 6. Figure 2.

283 *'We have an epidemic of that'*: Interview with Dixon Chibanda by author in Harare, April 2018.

283 *'No longer are we fighting'*: Interview with the grandmothers at Mbare clinic by author, April 2018. Interpreter: Nigel James.

284 *Serodiscordant*: Eyawo O., et al. (2010) *Lancet Infect. Dis.*, 2010, 10(11): 770–7.

284 *had to kill herself*: Tanya speaking at a Circle Kubatana Tose meeting in Harare, 2018. Interpreter: Ropalloyd Dzapasi.

285 *the multi-centre clinical trial*: Chibanda, D., et al. (2016) *JAMA*, 316(24): 2618–26.

286 *'They are superstars'*: Interview with Tarisai Bere in Harare by author, April 2018.

286 *'The Friendship Bench has become imaginary'*: Interview with four grandmothers at Mbare clinic by author, April 2018. Interpreter: Nigel James.

'I Live and Breathe Peer'

287 *extracurricular activities*: Interview with Helen Skipper in East Harlem by author, April 2018.

287 *likely to be addicted to crack*: Palomar, J.J., et al. (2015) *Drug Alcohol Depend.*, 149: 108–16.

287 *'The subcultural behaviors'*: Dunlap, E., et al. (2006) *J. Sociol. Soc. Welf.*, 33(1): 115–39. p. 121.

288 *'never wanted to see a doctor'* ... *'If you're working that area'* ... *'not going to do me like that'* ... *'I had a good therapist'* ... *'I've been in every situation'*: Interview with Helen Skipper in East Harlem by author, April 2018.

291 *giant Lego bricks*: Reporting trip to New York by author, April 2018.

292 *highest rate of lethal overdoses*: 'The Bronx Continues to See Highest Number of Opioid Overdose Deaths'. Spectrum News NY1, 23 November 2019.

292 *'This is darkness'*: Interview with Bethsaida George-Rodriguez in New York by author, April 2018.

292 *one in ten people*: Livingstone, J.D. (2016) *Psychiatr. Serv.*, 67: 850–7. p. 852.

292 *from 558,922 in 1955*: Pepper, B., et al. (1981) *Hosp. Comm. Psychiatry*, 32: 463–9. p. 463.

292 *'only 14 per cent'*: Lamb, H.R. & Grant, R. (1983) *Arch. Gen. Psychiatry*, 40: 363–8.

292 *'before it gets hold of you'*: Interview with Helen Skipper in East Harlem by author, April 2018.

293 *project had reached (over 40,000)*: 'Friendship Benches. Program Overview: July – December'. Printed document.

293 *'Manager of Peer Services'*: Email correspondence between Helen Skipper and author, September 2020.

Part Four – The Universe Within

295 *'emotional pain without context'*: 'Post-Prozac Nation' *NY Times*, 19 April, 2012.

295 *'poisons fermented within the body'*: Leonard, B.E. (1975) *Int. Rev. Neurobiol*, 18: 357–387.

295 *'either LSD is the most phenomenal'*: Novak, S.J. (1997) *Isis*, 88: 87–110.

It Feels Like Spring

297 *a cooked piece of spaghetti*: Interview with Helen Mayberg in New York by author, October 2018.

297 *thousands of successful operations*: Hamani, C., Neimat, J., & Lozano, A.M. (2006) 'Deep Brain Stimulation for the Treatment of Parkinson's Disease'. In Riederer, P., et al. eds. *Parkinson's Disease and Related Disorders*. Springer.

298 *buzz of five milliamps*: Mayberg, H.S., et al. (2005) *Neuron*, 45: 651–60.

298 *'What are you doing?'*: Interview with Helen Mayberg in New York by author, October 2018.

298 *even ECT had failed*: Mayberg, H.S., et al. (2005) *Neuron*, 45: 651–60. p. 653. Table 1.

299 *'These people are morbidly ill'* ... *'just ridiculous'*: Interview with Helen Mayberg by author, February 2018.

299 *Parkinson's, Huntington's, stroke*: Mayberg, H.S. (1994) *J. Neuropsychiatry Clin. Neurosci.*, 6: 428–42.

300 *'as many variables as possible'*: Interview with Helen Mayberg in New York by author, October 2018.

300 *40 per cent* ... *'the tendency to insanity'*: Mayberg, H.S. (1994) *J. Neuropsychiatry Clin. Neurosci.*, 6: 428–42.

301 *'normal part of growing old'*: Interview with Charles Reynolds by author, August 2018.

301 *prelimbic frontal and temporal cortex*: Mayberg, H.S. (1994) *J. Neuropsychiatry Clin. Neurosci.*, 6: 428–42.

301 *brains of patients with primary depression*: Ibid.

301 *markers of 'the blues'*: 'Parkinson's, depression and the switch that might turn them off'. *TEDx Caltech, January 2013*.

302 *most famous studies*: Mayberg, H.S., et al. (1999) *Am. J. Psychiatry*, 156(5): 675–82.

303 *'I talk too much'*: Interview with Helen Mayberg in New York by author, October 2018.

304 *area 25 was quiet – hypoactive*: Mayberg, H.S., et al. (1999) *Am. J. Psychiatry*, 156(5): 675–82. p. 678. Figure 1.

305 *'psychotherapy-responsive'*: Dunlop, B.W. & Mayberg, H.S. (2014) *Dialogues Clin. Neurosci.*, 16: 479–90.

305 *one of the safest procedures*: Fink, M. (1979) *Convulsive Therapy*. Raven Press. Chapter 4: 0.03 per cent death rate.

Rebirth

306 *'ECT,' Alice says*: Visit to ECT clinic in New York by author, October 2018.

307 *cellular damage could occur*: Holmberg, G. (1953) *Am. J. Psychiatry*, 110(2): 115–18.

307 *'keep the patient breathing'*: Discussion with anaesthesiologist by author, October 2018.

307 *growth-inducing molecules*: Jorgensen, A., et al. (2016) *Acta Psychiatr. Scand.*, 133: 154–64.

307 *prune the brain's delicate wiring*: Warner-Schmidt, J.L. & Duman, R.S. (2006) *Hippocampus*, 16: 239–49.

307 *start to noticeably shrink*: Videbech, P. & Ravnkilde, B. (2004) *Am. J. Psychiatry*, 161: 1957–66.

308 *'bit of a difficult case'*: Patient interview with author, January 2019.

308 *performed 35,000 sessions*: Interview with Charlie Kellner in Brooklyn by author, October 2018.

308 *literally wrote the book*: Kellner, C.H. (2018) *Handbook of ECT: A Guide to Electroconvulsive Therapy for Practitioners*. Cambridge University Press.

308 *first session was in 1978*: Interview with Charlie Kellner in the Upper East Side, New York, by author, October 2018.

309 *didn't have an automated pulse*: 'ECT in Britain: A Shameful State of Affairs'. *Lancet*, 28 November 1981.

309 *'If ECT is ever legislated against'*: Ibid.

309 *'For the right kind of illness'*: Interview with Charlie Kellner in the Upper East Side, New York, by author, October 2018.

310 *nearly a fifth*: Ohayon, M.M. & Schatzberg, A.F. (2002) *Am. J. Psychiatry.* 159: 1855–61.

310 *half of all patients*: Gournellis, R., & Lykouras, L. (2006) *Curr. Psychiatry Rev.* 2: 235–44.

310 *'I felt like I had some sort of life'* ... *'[They] are very real'*: Patient interview with author, January 2019.

311 *varies from $300 to $1,000*: Ross, E.L. Zivin, K., & Maixner, D.F. (2018) *JAMA Psychiatry*, 75(7): 713–22.

311 *prevent suicides*: Avery, D. & Winokur, G. (1978) Arch. Gen. *Psychiatry* 35(6): 749–53. And: Prudic, J. & Sackheim, H.A. (1999) J. *Clin. Psychiatry*, 60(2): 104–10.

311 *'remain sick for years'*: Interview with Charlie Kellner in the Upper East Side, New York, by author, October 2018.

311 *harder to treat*: Monroe, S.M. & Harkness, K.L (2011) *Psychol. Rev.* 118(4): 655–74.

312 *82 per cent respond to ECT*: Kroessler D. (1985) *Convulsive Therapy*, 1(3): 173–82. And: Parker, G., et al. (1992) *J. Affect. Disord.*, 24: 17–24.

312 *after two failed medications*: Ross, E.L. Zivin, K., & Maixner, D.F. (2018) *JAMA Psychiatry*, 75(7): 713–22.

312 *'not 22'*: Interview with Charlie Kellner in the Upper East Side, New York, by author, October 2018.

312 *70 to 95 per cent of patients*: Flint, A.J. & Gagnon, N. (2002) *Can. J. Psychiatry*, 47: 734–41.

312 *effective treatments in the whole of medicine*: Bolwig, T. (2014) *Acta Psychiatr. Scand.*, 129: 415–16.

312 *0.2 to 0.4 per 10,000 patients*: Ibid. Also: Fink, M. (1981) *Ann. Rev. Med.*, 32: 405–12.

313 *'I asked them to do it'*: Manning, M. (1995) *Undercurrents*. Harper San Francisco.

313 *'Feeling this good'*: Dukakis, K. & Tye, L. *Shock*. Avery. p. 120

313 *'fear purged itself'*: Keller, C.H. (2013) *Prog. Brain Res,*, Volume 206. p. 225.

313 *'a "victim",'* ... *'WHEN can we give ours?'*: 'ECT and Me'. *Upside Down and Inside Out*, 14 November 2018.

314 *nearly banned its use entirely*: Buccelli, C., et al. (2016) J. *ECT*, 32: 207–11.

314 *neither Cerletti nor Bini spoke out* ... *'[T]he unconscionable misuse'*: Ibid., p. 207.

314 *rarely used in Nazi Germany*: Rzesnitzek, L. & Lang, S. (2017) *Med. Hist.*, 61: 66–88. p. 81.

315 *'fit for work again'*: Ibid., p. 85.

315 *'more and more superfluous'*: Ibid., p. 78

315 *rarely performed in Germany*: Loh, N., et al. (2013) *World J. Biol. Psychiatry*, 14(6): 432–40.

315 *highest utilisation rates of ECT*: Bjørnshauge, D., et al. (2019) J. *ECT*, 35(4): 258–63.

315 *'Tiny little Denmark'*: Interview with Charlie Kellner in the Upper East Side, New York, by author, October 2018.

315 *'that's bullshit'*: Interview with Martin Jørgensen in Copenhagen by author, January 2019.

316 *decrease in dementia*: Osler, M., et al. (2018) *Lancet Psychiatry* 5(4): 348–56.

316 *increased risk of dementia'*: Interview with Poul Videbech in Glostrup by author, January 2019.

317 *'early signs of neurogenesis'*: Ende G., et al. (2000)Arch. Gen. *Psychiatry*, 57(10): 937–43.

317 *in the frontal cortex*: Gbyl, K., et al. (2019) *Acta Psychiatric. Scand.*, 140(3): 205–16.

317 *brain scanner, animal studies, or blood tests*: Interview with Poul Videbech in Glostrup by author, January 2019.

318 *'at least we know he has a brain'*: Interview with Poul Videbech in Glostrup by author, January 2019.

318 *rates of ECT*: 'Electroconvulsive therapy on the rise again in England'. *The Guardian*, 16 April 2017.

318 *'into the medical fold'*: Interview with Charlie Kellner in the Upper East Side, New York, by author, October 2018.

319 *'so significant for me'*: Patient interview with author, January 2019.

The Epitome of Hopelessness

320 *In her lectures*: 'Tuning Depressions Circuits Using DBS'. Stockholm Psychiatry Lecture, 19 April 2012.

320 *'In depression'*: Styron, W. (1991) *Darkness Visible*. Random House Inc.

320 *'other laboratories'*: Holtzheimer, P.E., et al. (2012) *Arch. Gen. Psychiatry*, 69(2): 150–8. And: Puigdemont, D., et al. (2012) *Int. J Neuropsychopharmacol.*, 15(1): 121–33. And: Pizzagalli, D.A., et al. (2018) *JAMA Psychiatr.*, 75(6): 547–54.

321 *a few basic decisions*: Interview with Helen Mayberg in New York by author, October 2018.

321 *outcomes of DBS*: Crowell, A.L., et al. (2019) *Am. J. Psychiatry*, 176(11): 949–56.

323 *makes life possible*: 'Tuning Depressions Circuits Using DBS'. Stockholm Psychiatry Lecture, 19 April 2012.

323 *'It's a journey'*: Interview with Helen Mayberg in New York by author, October 2018.

Mind on Fire

324 *an old barn*: Visit to Leonard's home by author, February 2019.

324 *In 1999, Leonard retired*: 'Lifetime Achievement Award 2008: Professor Brian Leonard'. *Br. Assoc. Psychopharmacol.*

324 *opened its doors ... in 1849*: 'Our History and Heritage'. https://www.nuigalway.ie/about-us/

324 *Leonard was a prominent voice*: Interview with Michael Berk by author, June 2018.

325 *Patients who don't respond*: Eller, T., et al. (2008) *Prog. Neuro-Psychopharmacol. Biol. Psychiatry*, 32: 445–50. And: Lanquillon, S., et al. (2000) *Neuropsychopharmacol.*, 22: 370–9.

325 *a randomised-controlled trial*: Raison, C.L., et al. (2013) *JAMA Psychiatry*, 70(1): 31–41.

325 *predicted the onset of depressive symptoms*: Gimeno, D., et al. (2009) *Psychologic. Med.*, 39: 413–23.

325 *'Now everybody believes it'*: Interview with Michael Berk by author, June 2018.

325 *'the hut'*: Interview with Brian Leonard in Galway by author, February 2019.

40 *PhD students*: 'Lifetime Achievement Award 2008: Professor Brian Leonard'. *Br. Assoc. Psychopharmacol.*

326 *'lack of scientific insight'*: Smith, R.S. (1991) *Med. Hypotheses*, 35: 298–306.

327 *'back in the body' . . . 'it is difficult to say'*: Marx, J.L. (1985) *Science*, 227: 1190–2.

327 *several labs*: Kronfol, Z. & House, J.D. (1989) *Acta Psychiatric. Scand.*, 80: 142–7.

327 *Song, had found similar patterns*: Song, C., et al. (1994) *J. Affect. Disord.*, 30: 283–8.

327 *core group of inflammatory markers*: Capuron, L. & Miller, A.H. (2011) *Pharmacol. & Ther.*, 130(2): 226–38.

328 *'That's not what we're talking about'*: Interview with Brian Leonard in Galway by author, February 2019.

328 *a clogged artery*: Malhotra, A., et al. (2017) *Br. J. Sports Med.*, 51: 1111–12.

329 *'ignored their eating'*: Niiranen, A., et al. (1988) *Acta Psychiatric. Scand.*, 78: 622–6.

329 *'only needs to exhibit five'*: Smith, R.S. (1991) *Med. Hypotheses*, 35: 298–306. p. 300.

330 *'no psychological context'*: Interview with Andrew Miller by author, March 2020.

330 *disappeared within two weeks*: Niiranen, A., et al. (1988) *Acta Psychiatric. Scand.*, 78: 622–6. p. 624.

330 *'sickness behaviour'*: Hart, B.L. (1988) *Neurosci & Biobehav. Rev.*, 12: 123–37.

331 *'annual rate of suicide'*: Norman, T.R. & Leonard, B.E. (1994) *CNS Drugs*, 2(2): 120–31.

331 *Beta-blockers and anti-cortisol*: Cryan, J.F., et al. (1998) *Eur. J. Pharmacol.*, 352 (1): 23–8

331 *no breakthroughs . . . 'sold my soul'*: Interview with John Cryan by author, September 2017.

332 *$985 million to take a drug*: Wouters, O.J., et al. (2020) *JAMA*, 323(9): 844–53.

332 *Sánchez . . . developed escitalopram*: Sánchez, C., et al. (2003) *Psychopharmacol.*, 167: 353–62.

332 *a microbiome unit*: APC Microbiome Ireland: https://apc.ucc.ie/about-2/introduction/

323 *own germ-free mice*: Yi, P. & Li, L.-J., (2012) *Vet. Microbiol.*, 157: 1–7.

333 *the gut*: Mahony, O., et al. (2008) *Biol. Psychiatry*, 65(3): 263–7.

334 *95 per cent of tryptophan . . . quinolinic acid . . . neurotoxic*: Cervenka, I., et al. (2017) *Science*, 357: eaaf9794. p. 2.

334 *'neurodegeneration hypothesis'*: Myint, A.M. & Kim, Y.K. (2003) *Med. Hypotheses*, 61: 519–25.

334 *'It's very complicated'*: Interview with Brian Leonard in Galway by author, February 2019.

334 *'who pinpointed this'*: Lapin, I.P. (1972) *Psychopharmacol.*, 26: 237–47.

335 *pianist . . . Russian intelligentsia*: Oxenkrug, G. & Riederer, P. (2012) *J. Neur. Trans.*, 119: 1465–6.

335 *'enlivened conferences'*: 'Lifetime Achievement Award 2008: Professor Brian Leonard'. *Br. Assoc. Psychopharmacol.*

335 *'body doesn't work in bits'*: Interview with Brian Leonard in Galway by author, February 2019.

'For Life'

336 *made famous by . . . Lederberg*: "Ome Sweet 'Omics'. *The Scientist Magazine*, 2 April 2001.

336 *'an innocuous one'*: Metchnikoff, E. & Williams, H.S. (1912) 'Why Not Live Forever?' *Cosmopolitan* 53: 436–46.

336 *degree in just two*: Vikhanski, L. (2016) *Immunity*. Chicago Review Press. p. 24.

337 *'wheat after a thunderstorm'*: Ibid., p. 143.

337 *'Metchnikoff's great discoveries'* ... *'promotes physical and mental'*: Bested, A.C., et al. (2013) *Gut Pathog.*, 5: 5.

337 *L. bulgaricus with L. acidophilus* ... *'The results ... are nothing short of amazing'*: Ibid.

338 *Kirsten Tillisch and her colleagues*: Tillisch, K., et al. (2013) *Gastroenterology*, 144: 1394–1401.

338 *'for life'*: Desbonnet, L., et al. (2008) *J. Psychiatr. Res.*, 43: 164–74. p. 165.

338 *'health of their human host'*: Ibid., p. 164.

338 *'psychobiotics'*: Dinan, T.G., et al. (2013) *Biol. Psychiatry*, 74: 720–6.

339 *developed in the late 1970s*: Porsolt, R.D, et al. (1977) *Nature*, 266: 730–2.

339 *first given to mice*: 'Depression Researchers Rethink Popular Mouse Swim Tests'. *Nature News*, 18 July 2019.

339 *B. infantis* ... *90 per cent* ... *no change in how long*: Desbonnet, L., et al. (2008) *J. Psychiatr. Res.*, 43: 164–74.

339 *Lactobacillus rhamnosus* ... *passed*: Bravo, J.A., et al. (2011) *PNAS*, 108: 16050–5.

340 *'every flippin' thing'*: Interview with Ted Dinan in Cork, Ireland, by author. November 2018.

340 *'couldn't fit more negative'*: *The Second Genome*. BBC Radio 4, 24 April 2018.

340 *'Lost in Translation'*: Kelly, J.R., et al. (2017) *Brain Behav. Immun.*, 61: 50–9.

340 *'loads of negative studies'*: Interview with Ted Dinan in Cork, Ireland, by author. November 2018.

341 *first randomised-controlled trial*: Kazemi, A., et al. (2019) *J. Funct. Foods*, 52: 596–602.

341 *'people with mild'*: Xiang, Q., et al. (2017) *J. Affect. Disord.*, 228: 13–19.

342 *listened to a podcast* ... *'They got better'*: Interview with Scot Bay at Mind Mood Microbes by author, January 2019.

342 *'Are we there yet?'*: Closing Remarks by John Cryan at Mind Mood Microbes, January 2019.

342 *microbial 'fingerprint'*: Valles-Colomer, M., et al. (2019) *Nat. Microbiol.*, 4: 623–32.

343 *'it's kind of a loop'*: Interview with Mireia Valles-Colomer and Sara Vieira-Silva by author, June 2019.

343 *'more effects from prebiotics'*: Ibid.

344 *It requires long-term dietary changes*: Voreades, N., et al. (2014) *Front. Microbiol.*, 5: 494. p. 4.

344 *Mediterranean-style diet*: Jacka, F.N., et al. (2017) *BMC Med.*, 15: 23.

344 *replicated by independent research*: Parletta, N., et al. (2017) *Nutr. Neurosci.*, 22(7): 474–87.

345 *produced by oceanic algae*: Winwood, R.J. (2013) 'Algal Oil As a Source of Omega-3 Fatty Acids'. In Jacobsen, C., et al. eds. *Food Enrichment with Omega-3 Fatty Acids*. Woodhead Publishing.

345 *5.6 per cent*: Jacka, F.N., et al. (2017) *BMC Med.*, 15: 23. p. 12.

345 *19 per cent*: 'Food Poverty: Agony of Hunger the Norm for Many Children in the UK'. *The Conversation*, 30 April 2019.

346 *13 per cent of adults and 18 per cent of children*: 'Obesity and Overweight'. *World Health Organisation*, 1 April 2020.

346 *over 40 per cent in 2018*: Hales, C.M., et al. (2020) *NCHS Data Brief*, 360.

346 *28 times more likely to develop diabetes … 'an epidemic'*: Kopelman, P.G. (2000) *Nature*, 404: 635–43.

346 *over 50 genes*: Choquet, H. & Meyre, D. (2011) *Curr. Genomics*, 12(3): 169–79.

347 *'Traditional foods'*: Hawley, N.L. & McGarvey, S.T. (2015) *Curr. Diab. Rep.*, 15: 29.

347 *predisposition to weight gain*: Minster, R.L., et al. (2016) *Nat. Genet.*, 48(9): 1049–54.

347 *'With few exceptions' … over 50 per cent*: Berk, M., et al. (2013) *BMC Med.*, 11: 200.

348 *'atypical' symptom profile*: Milaneschi, Y., et al. (2019) *Mol. Psychiatry*, 24: 18–33.

349 *achieving the top grades*: 'Healthy School Meals and Educational Outcomes'. ISER, January 2009.

349 *'Feed Me Better' petition*: 'TV chef welcomes £280m meals plan'. BBC News, 30 March 2005.

349 *'he's very important'*: Interview with Michael Berk by author, June 2018.

350 *dozens of clinical trials*: Blumenthal, J.A., et al. (2007) *Psychosom. Med.*, 69(7): 587–96.

350 *same efficacy … as first-line treatments*: Dunn, A.L., et al. (2005) *Am. J. Prev. Med.*, 28(1): 1–8.

350 *In 2013, a study*: Rethortst, C.D., et al. (2013) *Mol. Psychiatry*, 18: 1119–24.

350 *clinical trial from 2014*: Uher, R., et al. (2014) *Am. J. Psychiatry*, 171: 1278–86.

350 *a similar study*: Jha, M.K., et al. (2017) *Brain Behav. Immun.*, 66: 103–10.

351 *activate the kynurenine pathway*: Strasser, B., et al. (2016) *PLoS ONE*, 11(4): e0153617.

The Beginning

353 *'activates our immune response'*: Interview with Golam Khandaker by author, March 2020.

353 *over 100,000 people*: Gimeno, D., et al. (2009) *Psychol. Med.*, 39: 413–23. And: Wium-Andersen, M.K., et al. (2013) *JAMA Psychiatry*, 70(2): 176–84. And: Khandaker, G., et al. (2014) *JAMA Psychiatry*, 71(10): 1121–8.

353 *genetic predisposition*: Khandaker, G.M., et al. (2018) *Brain, Behav., Immun.*, 69: 264–72.

353 *decrease in their depressive symptoms*: Kappelman, N., et al. (2018) *Mol. Psychiatry*, 23: 335–43.

354 *'What's exciting'*: Interview with Golam Khandaker by author, March 2020.

354 *'The Insight Study'*: Khandaker, G.M., et al. (2018) *BMJ Open*, 8(9): e025333.

354 *disrupt brain function*: Raison, C.L. & Miller, A.H. (2013) *Cerebrum*, August 2013.

355 *'just the beginning'*: Interview with Golam Khandaker by author, March 2020.

355 *'will have staying power'*: Halaris, A. & Leonard, B. eds (2013) *Inflammation and Psychiatry*. Karger. 'Preface'.

Surfing in the Brain Scanner

356 *ceremonies since the 1930s*: 'The History of a Doctrine'. https://santodaime.com/en/doctrine/history/

356 *mirações*: de Araujo, D.B., et al. (2011) *Hum. Brain Mapp.*, 33(11): 2550–60.

357 *DMT ... the bush* Psychotria viridis: Palhano-Fontes, F., et al. (2015) *PLoS ONE*, 10(2): e0118143. p. 2.

357 *serotonin receptor:* Nichols, D.E. (2004) *Pharmacol. Therap.*, 101: 131–81.

357 *Banisteriopsis caapi, harmine:* Palhano-Fontes, F., et al. (2015) *PLoS ONE*, 10(2): e0118143. p. 2.

357 *four or more hours:* de Araujo, D.B., et al. (2011) *Hum. Brain Mapp.*, 33(11): 2550–60.

357 *'labour':* Palhano-Fontes, F., et al. (2015) *PLoS ONE*, 10(2): e0118143. p. 8.

358 *'that was just astonishing':* Interview with Draulio Barros de Araujo by author, November 2017.

358 *'the level of experience':* Interview with Draulio Barros de Araujo by author, November 2017.

358 *ten volunteers ... 'a status of reality':* de Araujo, D.B., et al. (2011) *Hum. Brain Mapp.*, 33(11): 2550–60.

359 *'alcohol dependency or depression':* Interview with Draulio Barros de Araujo by author, November 2017.

'Turn On, Tune In, and Drop Out'

360 *used by indigenous cultures:* Miller, M.J., et al. (2019) *PNAS*, 116(23): 11207–12.

360 *Siberia to the Sahara:* Akers, B.P., et al. (2011) *Econ. Bot.*, 65(2): 121–8.

360 *'a pinch of psychedelic':* Tanne, J.H. (2004) *Br. Med. J.*, 20: 328.

360 *First synthesised in 1938:* Hofmann, A. (1970) 'The Discovery of LSD and Subsequent Investigations on Naturally Occurring Hallucinogens'. In Ayd, F.J. & Blackwell, B. eds. *Discoveries in Biological Psychiatry.* J.B. Lippincott Company.

361 *'LSD makes available':* Eisner, B. (2002) *Remembrances of LSD Therapy Past.* Unpublished memoir. p. 129.

361 *'universe had collapsed' on her:* Ibid., p. 16.

361 *equivalent to four years of analysis:* Ibid., p. 20.

361 *'the function of the therapist':* Ibid., p. 55.

361 *'Chopin's first piano concerto':* Ibid., p. 31.

361 *impotence to homosexuality:* Sandison, R.A. & Whitelaw, J.D.A. (1957) *J. Ment. Sci,,* 103(431): 332–43.

362 *'sociopathic personality disorder':* Drescher, J. (2015) *Behav. Sci.*, 5(4): 565–75.

362 *'reticence rather than confidence':* Savage, C. (1952). *Am. J. Psychiatry*, 108: 896–900. p. 900.

362 *gift for making people feel better:* Eisner, B. (2002) *Remembrances of LSD Therapy Past.* Unpublished memoir.

363 *'The one thing I have noticed':* Ibid., p. 24.

363 *'raging fires, the void, dragons, a vortex':* Ibid., p. 53.

364 *from human to God:* Ibid., p. 25.

364 *often left without a therapist:* Ibid., p. 83.

364 *psychedelics in all their ramifications:* Ibid., p. 84.

364 *small audience ... 'I felt like a true pioneer' ... 'fitting end to a magical trip':* Ibid., 89.

364 *Hofmann ... isolated psilocybin*: Hofmann, A. (1970) 'The Discovery of LSD and Subsequent Investigations on Naturally Occurring Hallucinogens'. In Ayd, F.J. & Blackwell, B. eds. *Discoveries in Biological Psychiatry*. J.B. Lippincott Company.

365 *'It does get discouraging'*: Ibid., p. 188.

366 *44 replied.. 'directly due to LSD'*: Novak, S.J. (1997) *Hist. Sci. Soc.*, 88: 87–110.

366 *'untoward events'*: Cohen, S. & Ditman, K. (1962) *JAMA*, 181(2): 161–82. p. 181.

366 *'not an innocent aid'*: 'LSD – A Dangerous Drug'. N. Engl. J. Med., 2 December 1965.

367 *published in* Good Housekeeping: 'Ageless Cary Grant'. *Good Housekeeping*, September 1960. p. 64.

367 *push its use into the mainstream*: Meyers, M. (2007) *Happy Accidents*. Arcade Publishing Inc.

367 *'turn on, tune in'*: Novak, S.J. (1997) *Hist. Sci. Soc.*, 88: 87–110.

367 *ten-year-old boy*: Cohen, S. & Ditman, K.S. (1962) *JAMA*, 181(2): 161–2.

367 *200 to 70*: Novak, S.J. (1997) *Hist. Sci. Soc.*, 88: 87–110. p. 108.

367 *'LSD therapy should not' ... 'remarkably safe'*: Ibid., p. 108.

368 *lost to society, lost to themselves*: 'When Bobby Kennedy Defended LSD'. *MAPS*, 11 July 2012.

368 *psychotic killer*: 'A Slaying Suspect Tells of LSD Spree'. *NY Times*, 12 April 1966.

368 *'very helpful in our society if used properly'*: 'When Bobby Kennedy Defended LSD'. *MAPS*, 11 July 2012.

368 *illegal substance ... in October 1968*: Public Law 90–639, 24 October 1968.

368 *help concentration camp survivors*: 'The LSD Therapy Career of Jan Bastiaans, M.D.'. *MAPS*, Spring 1998. pp. 18–20.

Building a New System

369 *safer than riding a horse*: Nutt, D.J. (2009 *J. Psychopharmacol.*, 23: 3.

369 *'worst censorship'*: Interview with David Nutt by author at Imperial College London, December 2017.

370 *first study in 2011*: Carhart-Harris, R.L., et al. (2011) *J. Psychopharmacol.*, 25(11): 1562–7.

370 *'Mayberg centre' ... 'disrupt that'*: Interview with David Nutt by author at Imperial College London, December 2017.

370 *The hospital room ... 'I cried a lot'*: Interview with patient by author, January 2018.

371 *'open this treatment up'*: Interview with Amanda Feilding by author, August 2017.

371 *'establish whether it's a treatment'*: Interview with James Rucker in London by author, November 2018.

372 *significantly less effective than escitalopram*: Cipriani, A., et al. (2018) *Lancet*, 391: 1357–66. Figure 4. Head-to-head comparison between 'Esci' and 'Fluo' = 1.34 (1.11–1.61), in favour of escitalopram.

372 *'runs through my family'*: Interview with James Rucker in London by author, November 2018.

373 *216 patients from 11 cities*: 'COMPASS Pathways Granted Patent Covering Use of its Psilocybin Formulation in Addressing Treatment-Resistant Depression'. *COMPASS News*, 15 January 2020.

373 *'not from a position'*: 'Two parents' fight to set up the largest ever magic mushroom trial for depression is nearly over'. *International Business Times*, 15 September 2017.

373 *'very strict rules'*: Interview with James Rucker in London by author, November 2018.

374 *cover of magazines like* New Scientist: 'Psychedelic Medicine'. *New Scientist*, 21 November 2017.

374 *Early trials with psilocybin*: Griffiths, R.R., et al. (2016) *J. Psychopharmacol.*, 30(12): 1181–97.

376 *'Trust, let go'* ... *'Therapy takes a really long time'*: Interview with Ros Watts by author, October 2017.

Seeing with Eyes Shut

378 *first randomised placebo-controlled trial*: Palhano-Fontes, F., et al. (2018) *Psychol. Med.*, 49: 655–63.

378 *water, yeast, citric acid*: Ibid., p. 656.

379 *a three-storey, white-washed building*: Photo by 'Kulinai'. Wikimedia Commons, 2 May 2019.

379 *'very difficult realities'*: Interview with Draulio Barros de Araujo by author, November 2017.

379 *'You know what doctor'*: Interview with Draulio Barros de Araujo by author, November 2017.

380 *several sessions of ECT*: Palhano-Fontes, F., et al. (2018) *Psychol. Med.*, 49: 655–63. p. 658.

380 *'The placebo effect'*: Interview with James Rucker in London by author, November 2018.

381 *'Ayahuasca reflected my beliefs'*: 'Caves All the Way Down'. *Aeon Magazine*, 17 July 2018.

381 *'mind-wandering'* ... *'often unnoticed'*: Palhano-Fontes, F., et al. (2015) *PLoS ONE*, 10(2): e0118143. p. 2.

381 *A famous study*: Brewer, J.A., et al. (2012) *PNAS*, 108(50): 20254–9.

382 *eight brain regions*: Palhano-Fontes, F., et al. (2015) *PLoS ONE*, 10(2): e0118143. Table 1.

382 *'a lot of issues'*: Interview with Draulio Barros de Araujo by author, December 2019.

383 *alpha waves, remained stable*: Tófoli, L.F. & de Araujo, D.B. (2016) *Int. Rev. Neurobiol.*, 129: 157–85.

383 *researchers in London*: Timmermann, C., et al. (2019) *Sci. Rep.*, 9: 2045–2322.

384 *'gotta be powerful'*: Interview with Draulio Barros de Araujo by author, December 2019.

384 *approved by the European Commission*: 'Esketamine Is Approved in Europe for Treating Resistant Major Depressive Disorder'. *Br. Med. J.*, 20 December 2019.

384 *and the FDA*: 'FDA approves new nasal spray medication for treatment-resistant depression'. *US FDA*, 5 March 2019.

384 *in just four hours*: Berman, R.M., et al. (2000) *Biol. Psychiatry*, 47: 351–4.

385 *'the most significant advances'*: Duman, R.S. & Li, N. (2012) *Phil. Trans. Royal Soc. B.*, 367: 2475–2484. p. 2478

385 *'[Ketamine] led to a loss of time'*: Khorramzadeh, E. & Lofty, A.O. (1973) *Psychosomatics*, 14: 344–6.

385 *rave parties since the 1990s*: Morgan, C.J.A. & Curran, H.V. (2011) *Addiction*, 107: 27–38. p. 28.

385 *bladder and kidney*: Ibid., p. 31.

385 *'there is limited evidence'*: 'Statement on Ketamine to Treat Depression'. RCPsych, February 2017.

386 *Manufactured in 1962*: 'Fact File on Ketamine'. *World Health Organisation*, March 2016.

386 *soldiers during the Vietnam War*: Morgan, C.J.A. & Curran, H.V. (2011) *Addiction*, 107: 27–38. p. 27.

386 *'One thing I have to do'*: Interview with Draulio Barros de Araujo by author, December 2019.

387 *'hardly scratching the surface'*: Interview with Draulio Barros de Araujo by author, November 2017.

Index